W9-COJ-752

Gruber

2015-16

SAT*

STRATEGIES, PRACTICE AND REVIEW

By Gary R. Gruber, PhD

*SAT® is a registered trademark of the College Entrance Examination Board.
The College Entrance Examination Board is not associated with and does not endorse this book.

Copyright 2015 by Gary R. Gruber

Cover and Internal Design Copyright 2015 by Dear Boy Publishing LLC

All rights reserved. No part of this book may be reproduced in any form or by any means without the written permission of the copyright owners.

All brand names and product names referenced in this book are trademarks, regis-tered trademarks, or trade names of their respective holders. Dear Boy Publishing LLC is not associated with any product or vendor in this book.

Published by Dear Boy Publishing LLC, a Delaware registered company.

All Inquiries should be addressed to:
Dear Boy Publishing LLC
5 E 19th St, 3rd Floor
New York
NY 10003
info@dearboy.co

ISBN Number: 978-0-578-16856-2

Recent and forthcoming study aids from Dr. Gary Gruber include

Gruber's Complete PSAT/NMSQT Guide 2016
Gruber's Complete ACT Guide 2016
Gruber's Complete GRE Guide 2016
Gruber's SAT 2400
Gruber's 500 Essential Math Questions by Topic and Difficulty
Gruber's 500 Essential Reading Comprehension Questions by Topic and Difficulty
Gruber's Essential AP US History by Topic and Difficulty
Gruber's Essential AP Biology by Topic and Difficulty
Gruber's Essential AP Macroeconomics by Topic and Difficulty
Gruber's Essential AP Calculus AB by Topic and Difficulty
Gruber's Essential AP Psychology by Topic and Difficulty
Gruber's New SAT 2016
Gruber's New SAT 1600

www.gruberprep.com

Want to see your score climb even higher with online, personalized and tutor-supported SAT preparation from as low as $14.99 per month?

Head to *www.gruberprep.com/sat-book-trial* to sign up for a FREE trial of our comprehensive Gruber SAT online course.

Our Gruber SAT online program gives you:

1. A flexible online platform with 3,000 Diagnostic Questions and 4 Full Practice Tests. You can begin and end on your own time.

2. Access to real tutors on-demand who can walk you through solutions at no extra cost.

3. Personalized learning paths based on your strengths and weaknesses with detailed progress reports.

As a Gruber book student, you are eligible for a FREE 5-day trial that includes:

1. 18 Question SAT Score, Strength & Weaknesses Diagnostic Test with Full Video Solutions, and a 10 Hour Personalized Study Plan Diagnostic Test

2. Vocabulary Diagnostic Test and Strategies to Solve Problems in less than 20 seconds

3. Math strategies such as Recognizing Math Patterns that are each worth up to 200 Points on the SAT

Visit www.gruberprep.com/sat-book-trial today
to watch testimonials from real students, chat on-demand with tutors,
and chart your course to a better SAT score.

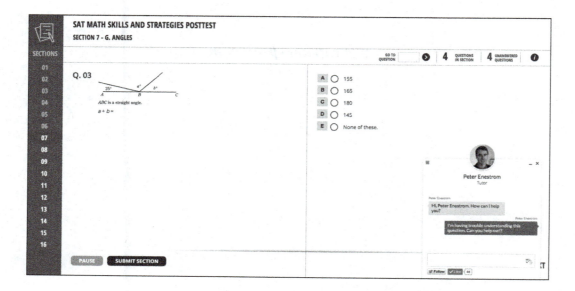

Contents

Important note about this book and its author

This book is the most up-to-date and complete book on the current SAT. EVERY EXAM is patterned after the SAT, and *all* the strategies and techniques deal with the SAT. The SAT incorporates all the Gruber Critical-Thinking Strategies.

This book was written by Dr. Gary Gruber, the leading authority on the SAT, who knows more than anyone else in the test-prep market exactly what is being tested on the SAT. In fact, the procedures to answer the SAT questions rely more heavily on the Gruber Critical-Thinking Strategies than ever before, and this is the only book that has the exact thinking strategies you need to use to maximize your SAT score. Gruber's SAT books are used by the nation's school districts more than any other books and are proven to get the highest documented school district SAT scores.

Dr. Gary Gruber has published more than 40 books with major publishers on test-taking and critical thinking methods, with more than 7 million copies sold. He has also authored more than 1,000 articles on his work in scholarly journals and nationally syndicated newspapers, has appeared on numerous television and radio shows, and has been interviewed in hundreds of magazines and newspapers. He has developed major programs for school districts and for city and state educational agencies for improving and restructuring curriculum, increasing learning ability and test scores, increasing motivation and developing a passion for learning and problem solving, and decreasing the student dropout rate. For example, PBS (Public Broadcasting System) chose Dr. Gruber to train the nation's teachers on how to prepare students for the SAT through a national satellite teleconference and video. His results have been lauded by people throughout the country from all walks of life.

Gruber's unique methods have been and are being used by the nation's learning centers, by international encyclopedias, by school districts throughout the country, by real people in homes and workplaces across the nation, and by a host of others looking to learn.

His goal and mission is to get people's potential realized and the nation impassioned with learning and problem solving, so that they don't merely try to get a fast, uncritical answer, but actually enjoy and look forward to solving the problem and learning. To learn more about Dr. Gruber, visit his website at *www.drgarygruber.com*

For more information on Gruber courses and additional Gruber products, visit *www.gruberprep.com*

Important: Many books do not reflect the current SAT questions. Don't practice with questions that misrepresent the actual questions on the SAT. For example, the math questions created by the test makers are oriented to allow someone to solve many problems without a calculator as fast as he or she could with one, and some can be solved faster without a calculator. This book reflects the SAT more accurately than any other commercial book, and the strategies contained in it are exactly those needed to be used on the SAT. It is said that only Dr. Gruber has the expertise and ability to reflect the exam far more closely than any competitor! Don't trust your future with less than the best material.

The author has something important to tell you about how to raise your SAT score

■ **What Are Critical-Thinking Skills?**

First of all, I believe that intelligence can be taught. Intelligence, simply defined, is the aptitude or ability to reason things out. I am convinced that *you can learn to think logically* and figure things out better and faster, *particularly in regard to SAT Math and Verbal problems.* But someone must give you the tools. Let us call these tools *strategies.* And that's what Critical Thinking-Skills are all about—*strategies.*

■ **Learn the Strategies to Get More Points**

The Critical-Thinking Skills will sharpen your reasoning ability so that you can increase your score dramatically on each part of the SAT.

These Critical-Thinking Skills—5 General Strategies, 19 Math Strategies, and 16 Verbal Strategies—course right through this book. The Explanatory Answers for the 5 Practice Tests in the book direct you to those strategies that may be used to answer specific types of SAT questions. The strategies in this book are usable for more than 90 percent of the questions that will appear on your SAT. Each additional correct answer gives you approximately 10 points. It is obvious, then, that your learning and using the 40 easy-to-understand strategies in this book will very likely raise your SAT score substantially.

■ **Are the Practice Tests in This Book Like an Actual SAT?**

If you compare any one of the 5 Practice Tests in this book with an actual SAT, you will find the book test very much like the *actual* test in regard to *format, question types,* and *level of difficulty.* Compare our book tests with one of the official tests published by the College Board!

■ **The Explanatory Answers to Questions Are Keyed to Specific Strategies and Basic Skills**

The Explanatory Answers in this book are far from skimpy—unlike those of other SAT books. Our detailed answers will direct you to the strategy that will help you to arrive at a correct answer quickly.

■ **Lift That SAT Score**

By using the material in this book—that is, by taking the tests, learning the specific strategies, and refreshing your basic skills, as described above—you should increase your SAT score substantially.

—GARY GRUBER

Important note

I am the only test prep book author whom the College Board has used to discuss what the New SAT should be like.

Although I will be coming out with a New SAT book for the New March 2016 SAT with complete Practice Tests, I wanted to let you know what will be asked on the New SAT.

This new test will rely more heavily on "process" thinking—that is how you are approaching a question, more than ever. You will need to get involved with the best "process" for the problem rather than just relying on getting a bottom-line answer. And of course this is what I have been advocating in all my books and you can certainly use all the strategies in this book for that New SAT.

If you are taking the SAT in March 2016 you may want to be aware of the changes described as follows.

Vocabulary words

Vocabulary words will test vocabulary that students can expect to use in life and be tested in the context of a passage. There will be no sentence completions on the new test which will of course eliminate testing of those esoteric and difficult words.

Reading

1. Passages will deal with "Evidence Based Reasoning" where you will be tested on your ability to comprehend and combine many sources of evidence to answer the questions.
2. There will be various forms of evidence which will be provided in passages and in graphics such as tables, charts, and graphs.
3. At lease one question in a passage will require you to choose a quotation in the passage that supports your answer to a previous question.
4. One of the passages will deal with the subject of the Founding Fathers (founding documents) or from a text from the global conversation.

Writing

These questions will include analysis to determine grammatical correctness from multiple paragraphs. Graphics will also be included in the form of tables, charts and graphs.

Essay

1. Essay will be optional, but may be required by some colleges
2. The essay prompt will be the same for many test dates and you will be able to see what the prompt is in advance of the test.
3. You will have to write your essay on a provided text, where you will have to draw evidence to support your argument.
4. The essay will focus on the analysis of multiple arguments.

Math

The Math Section will include questions on Problem Solving and Data Analysis including ratios, percentages, and proportions.

Creating and analyzing relationships using ratios, proportions, percentages, and units; Describing relationships shown graphically; summarizing qualitative and quantitative data

Heart of Algebra including use of linear equations to aid in the interpretation of more abstract concepts and problems.

Analyzing and solving equations; creating expressions, equations, and inequalities to represent relationships between quantities and to solve problems; rearranging and interpreting formulas.

Passport to Advanced Math where you will need to use and manipulate more complex equations.

Rewriting expressions using their structure; creating, analyzing, and solving quadratic and higher-order equations; manipulating polynomials to solve problems

Additional topics

Making area and volume calculations; analyzing lines, angles, triangles, and circles; knowing how to use trigonometric functions

Calculator use

The SAT calculator will be able to be used on one of the two math sections.

No penalties for wrong answers

You will no longer get a penalty for a wrong answer. Presently you get ¼ point deduction for a wrong answer, although I show you in this book that it doesn't make that much of a difference if you guess on the current SAT as far as a penalty is concerned.

Format

The Current SAT has three sections – Writing, Reading and Math -and an essay.

The New SAT will have two sections – Evidence Based Reading and Writing and Math – and an optional essay.

The current SAT is scored from 600-2400. The New SAT will be scored from 400- 1600.

Format of the new SAT

Reading

Time
65 minutes

Passage Word Count
3,250 words; 4 single passages; one double passage
500-750 words per passage or double passage

Questions Total
52

Words in Context
10 questions; 2 per double passage
(Reading, Writing)

Command of Evidence
10 questions; 2 per double passage
(Reading, Writing)

History/Social Studies
21 questions
(Math,Reading, and Writing)

Science
21 questions
(Math, Reading, and Writing)

Subjects of Passages

US and World Literature
10 questions; 1 passage

History/Social Studies
10-11 questions; 2 passages or 1 passage and 1 double passage

---

Science
10-11 questions; 2 passages or 1 passage and 1 double passage

---

Graphics

1-2 graphics in 1 History/Social Studies and 1 Science passage

Writing

Time
35 minutes

Passage Word Count
1700 words; 4 passages; 400-450 words per passage

Questions	Number
Total	*44*
Expression of Ideas	*24*
Standard English Conventions	*20*

Words in Context

8; 2 per double passage
(Reading, Writing)

Command of Evidence
8; 2 per double passage
(Reading, Writing)

History/Social Studies
6; all Expression of Ideas in history/social studies
(Math,Reading,Writing)

Science
6; all Expression of ideas in science
(Math,Reading and Writing)

Passage contents

Careers	11 questions; 1 passage
History/Social Studies	11 questions; 1 passage
Humanities	11 questions; 1 passage
Science	11 questions; 1 passage
Graphics	1 or more graphics in 1 or more sets of questions

Text Types

Argument	1-2 passages
Informative/Explanatory Text	1-2 passages
Non-fiction Narrative	1 passage

Math

Total Time	80 minutes
Calculator Section	55 minutes
Non-Calculator Section	25 minutes

Questions

Total	57 questions
Multiple-Choice (4 choices)	45 questions
Grid In	11 questions
Extended Thinking –Grid In	1 question

Categories

Heart of Algebra	21 questions
Problem Solving and Data Analysis	14 questions
Passport to Advanced Math	16 questions
Additional Topics *	6 questions

* These do not contribute to a subscore but do contribute to total score

INTRODUCTION

Important facts about the SAT

- ## What is on the SAT?

It will include a student-written essay and a multiple-choice writing section testing students' ability to identify sentence errors, improve sentences, and improve paragraphs. Although grammar and usage will be tested, students will not be asked to define or use grammatical terms, and spelling and capitalization will not be tested. The essay section will be the first part of the test. The Math section will include arithmetic, geometry, Algebra I, and some advanced math covering topics in Algebra II, statistics, probability, and data analysis. The test will measure reasoning ability and problem-solving skills. The other parts of the test will contain some long and shorter reading passages, long paired passages, short paired passages, and sentence completion questions.

- ## How will the test be scored?

There will be a range of three scores, each from 200 to 800, for the Writing, Math, and Critical Reading sections.

- ## How long will the test be?

The total time of the test will be 3 hours and 45 minutes.

- ## What verbal background must I have?

The reading and vocabulary level is at the 10th- to 12th-grade level, but strategies presented in this book will help you even if you are at a lower grade level.

- ## What math background must I have?

The Math part will test first- and second-year algebra (Algebra I and II) and geometry. However, if you use common sense, rely on just a handful of geometrical formulas, and learn the strategies and thinking skills presented in this book, you don't need to take a full course in geometry or memorize all the theorems. If you have not taken algebra, you should still be able to answer many of the math questions using the strategies presented in this book.

- ## SAT vs. ACT: How should students decide which test to take?

The correlation happens to be very high for both tests; if you score well on one, you will likely score about as well on the other. They cover a lot of the same material. Both exams test grammar, math, and critical reading skills. However, the ACT includes a whole section on scientific data interpretation (the SAT has a few similar questions in its Math section); fortunately, you don't have to have a scientific background to excel on the ACT.

The ACT is more *memory*-oriented, while the SAT is more *strategy*-oriented. If you memorize quickly and retain facts well under pressure, I recommend the ACT. If you are more prone to strategizing or you like puzzles, I would take the SAT. In any event, I would check with the schools that you are applying to and find out which test they prefer.

- ## Is guessing advisable?

Although there is a small penalty for wrong answers ($\frac{1}{4}$ point for 5-choice questions), in the long run, you *break even* if you guess *or* leave the answer blank. For a full explanation of why, see page 63, Strategy 3. So it really will not affect your score in the long run if you guess or leave answers out. And, if you can eliminate an incorrect choice, it is imperative that you do not leave the answer blank.

- ## Can I use a calculator on the math portion of the test?

Students can use a four-function, scientific, or graphing calculator. While it is possible to solve every question without the use of a calculator, it is recommended that you use a calculator if you don't immediately see a faster way to solve the problem without one.

- ## Should I take an administered actual SAT for practice?

Yes, but only if you will learn from your mistakes by recognizing the strategies you should have used on your exam. Taking the SAT merely for its own sake is a waste of time and may in fact reinforce bad methods and habits. Note that the SAT is released to students on the Question-and-Answer Service three times a year, usually in the January, May, and October administrations. It is wise to take exams on these dates if you wish to see your mistakes and correct them.

- ## Can I get back the SAT with my answers and the correct ones after I take it? How can I make use of this service?

The disclosed SAT is sent back to the student on request with an $18.00 payment. You can also order a copy of your answer sheet for an additional $25.00 fee. Very few people take advantage of this fact or use the disclosed SAT to see what mistakes they've made and what strategies they could have used on the questions.

Check in your SAT information bulletin or log on to www.collegeboard.com for the dates this Question-and-Answer Service is available.

- ## A table of what's on the SAT

Math

Time	70 minutes (Two 25-minute sections, one 20-minute section)
Content	Multiple-Choice Items Student-Produced Responses Measuring: Numbers and Operations Algebra I, II, and Functions Geometry, Statistics, Probability, and Data Analysis
Score	M 200–800

Critical Reading

Time	70 minutes (Two 25-minute sections, one 20-minute section)
Content	Sentence Completion Critical Reading: Short and Long Reading Passages with one Double Long Passage and one Double Short Passage
Score	CR 200–800

Writing

Time	60 minutes (25-minute essay, 35-minute multiple-choice exam in two sections)
Content	Multiple-Choice: Identifying Errors Improving Sentences and Paragraphs Student-Written Essay Effectively Communicating a Viewpoint, Defining and Supporting a Position
Score	W 200–800 Essay Subscore: 0–12 Multiple-Choice Subscore: 20–80

Note: There is an experimental section that does not count toward your SAT score. This section can contain any of the SAT item types (writing [multiple-choice], critical reading, or math) and can appear in any part of the test. Do not try to outguess the test maker by trying to figure out which of the sections is experimental on the actual test (believe me, you won't be able to)—treat every section as if it counts toward your SAT score.

- ## A table of what's on the 2015 PSAT

Math

Time	70 minutes total – 47 questions – 2 sections (1 calculator, 1 non-calculator)
Content	Multiple-Choice Items Student-Produced Responses Measuring: Numbers and Operations Algebra I and Functions Geometry and Measurement; Statistics, Probability, and Data Analysis, Trigonometry
Score	200–800

Reading

Time	47 questions – 60 minutes – 1 section
Content	Critical Reading: Short and Long Reading Passages, with one Double Passage Graphs included in some passages
Score will be combined with Writing & Language and shown as 200–800	

Writing & Language

Time	44 questions – 35 minutes – 1 section
Content	Identifying Errors Test will contain passages where corrections or additions need to be made Improving Sentences and Paragraphs Measuring: Grammar, Usage, Word Choice, Passage Construction
Score will be combined with Reading and shown as 200–800	

Note: Questions with choices will have 4 choices; with no penalty for incorrect answers.

- ## Should I use scrap paper to write on and to do calculations?

Always use your test booklet (not your answer sheet) to draw on. Many of my strategies expect you to label diagrams, draw and extend lines, circle important words and sentences, etc., so feel free to write anything in your booklet. The booklets aren't graded—just the answer sheets.

- ## Should I be familiar with the directions to the various items on the SAT before taking the SAT?

Make sure you are completely familiar with the directions to each of the item types on the SAT—the directions for answering the Sentence Completions, the Reading, the Writing, the Regular Math, and especially the Grid-Type.

- ## What should a student bring to the exam on the test date?

You should bring a few sharpened #2 pencils with erasers and also your ID.

Bring a calculator to the test, but be aware that every math question on the SAT can be solved without a calculator; in many questions, it's actually easier not to use one.

Acceptable calculators: Graphing calculators, scientific calculators, and four-function calculators (the last is not recommended) are all permitted during testing. If you have a calculator with characters that are one inch or higher, or if your calculator has a raised display that might be visible to other test takers, you will be seated at the discretion of the test supervisor.

Unacceptable calculators: Laptops or portable/handheld computers; calculators that have a QWERTY keyboard, make noise, use an electrical outlet, or have a paper tape; electronic writing pads or stylus-driven devices; pocket organizers; and cell phone calculators will not be allowed during the test.

- ## How much time should one spend on each question?

Calculate the time allowed for the particular section. For example, 25 minutes. Divide by the number of questions. For example, 20. That gives you an average of spending $1\frac{1}{4}$ minutes per question in this example. However, the first set of questions within an item type in a section is easier, so spend less than a minute on the first set of questions and perhaps more than a minute on the last set. With the reading passages you should give yourself only about 30 seconds a question and spend the extra time on the reading passages. Also, more difficult reading questions may take more time.

- ## How is the exam scored? Are some questions worth more points?

Each question is worth the same number of points. After getting a raw score—the number of questions right minus a penalty for wrong answers—this is equated to a "scaled" score from 200 to 800 in each of the Critical Reading, Math, and Writing sections. A scaled score of 500 in each part is considered average.

- ## What is the most challenging type of question on the exam and how does one attack it?

Many questions on the test, especially at the end of a section, can be challenging. You should always attack challenging questions by using a specific strategy or strategies and common sense.

- ## What should a student do to prepare on friday night? Cram? Watch TV? Relax?

On Friday night, I would just refresh my knowledge of the structure of the test, some strategies, and some basic skills (verbal or math). You want to do this to keep the thinking going so that it is continual right up to the exam. Don't overdo it; just do enough so that it's somewhat continuous—this will also relieve some anxiety, so that you won't feel you are forgetting things before the exam.

- ### The test is given in one booklet. Can a student skip between sections?

  No—you cannot skip between the sections. You have to work on the section until the time is called. If you get caught skipping sections or going back to earlier sections, then you risk being asked to leave the exam.

- ### Should a student answer all easy questions first and save difficult ones for last?

  The easy questions usually appear at the beginning of the section, the medium-difficulty ones in the middle, and the hard ones toward the end. So I would answer the questions as they are presented to you, and if you find you are spending more than 30 seconds on a question and not getting anywhere, go to the next question. You may, however, find that the more difficult questions toward the end are actually easy for you because you have learned the strategies in this book.

- ### What is the recommended course of study for those retaking the exam?

  Try to get a copy of the exam that you took if it was a disclosed one—the disclosed ones, which you have to send a payment for, are usually given in October, January, and May. Try to learn

  from your mistakes by seeing what strategies you could have used to get questions right. Certainly learn the specific strategies for taking your next exam.

- ### What are the most crucial strategies for students?

  All specific Verbal (Critical Reading) and Math Strategies are crucial, including the general test-taking strategies: guessing, writing and drawing in your test booklet, and being familiar with question-type directions. The key Reading Strategy is to know the four general types of questions that are asked in reading—main idea, inference, specific details, and tone or mood. In math, it's the translations strategy—words to numbers, drawing of lines, etc. Also make sure you know the basic math skills.

- ### I know there is an experimental section on the exam that is not scored. How do I know which section it is?

  The SAT people have now made it so difficult to tell which is the experimental section, I would not take a chance second-guessing them and leaving it out. It will look like any of the other sections. It is true that if there are, for example, two of the same sections, such as two sections that both deal with grid questions, one of them is experimental—but you won't know which one it is. Also, if there are two sections with a long double reading passage, one of those sections is experimental, but again you won't know which one it is.

- **Can I take the test more than once, and if so, how will the scores be reported to the schools of my choice? Will all scores be reported to the schools, and how will they be used?**

  Check with the schools to which you are applying to see how they use the reported scores, e.g., whether they average them or whether they take the highest. Ask the schools whether they see unreported scores; if they do, find out how the individual school deals with single and multiple unreported scores.

- **How do other exams compare with the SAT? Can I use the strategies and examples in this book for them?**

  Most other exams are modeled after the SAT, so the strategies used here are definitely useful when taking them. For example, the GRE (Graduate Record Examinations, for entrance into graduate school) has questions that use the identical strategies used on the SAT. The questions are just worded at a slightly higher level. The ACT (American College Testing Program), another college entrance exam, reflects more than ever strategies that are used on the SAT. For the ACT, you can get *Gruber's Complete ACT Guide 2016*. For the GRE, you can get *Gruber's Complete GRE Guide 2016*.

- **How does the Gruber preparation method differ from other programs and SAT books?**

  Many other SAT programs try to use "quick-fix" methods or subscribe to memorization. So-called quick-fix methods can be detrimental to effective preparation because the SAT people constantly change questions to prevent "gimmick" approaches. Rote memorization methods do not enable you to answer a variety of questions that appear in the SAT exam. In more than thirty years of experience writing preparation books for the SAT, Dr. Gruber has developed and honed the Critical-Thinking Skills and Strategies that are based on all standardized tests' construction. So, while his method immediately improves your performance on the SAT, it also provides you with the confidence to tackle problems in all areas of study for the rest of your life. He remarkably enables you to be able to look at a problem or question without panic, extract something curious or useful from the problem, and move on to the next step and finally to a solution, without rushing into a wrong answer or getting lured into a wrong choice. It has been said that test taking through his methodology becomes enjoyable rather than painful.

The inside track on how SAT questions are developed and how they vary from test to test

When an SAT question is developed, it is based on a set of criteria and guidelines. Knowing how these guidelines work should demystify the test-making process and convince you why the strategies in this book are so critical to getting a high score.

Inherent in the SAT questions are Critical-Thinking Skills, which present strategies that enable you to solve a question by the quickest method with the least amount of panic and brain-racking, and describe an elegance and excitement in problem solving. Adhering to and using the strategies (which the test makers use to develop the questions) will let you sail through the SAT. This is summed up in the following statement:

Show me the solution to a problem, and I'll solve that problem. Show me a Gruber strategy for solving the problem, and I'll solve hundreds of problems.

Here's a sample of a set of guidelines presented for making up an SAT-type question in the Math area:

The test maker is to make up a hard problem in the regular Math multiple-choice area, which involves

(A) algebra
(B) two or more equations
(C) two or more ways to solve: one way being standard substitution; the other, faster way using the *strategy* of merely *adding* or *subtracting* equations.

Previous examples given to the test maker for reference:

1. If $x + y = 3$, $y + z = 4$, and $z + x = 5$, find the value of $x + y + z$.

    (A) 4
    (B) 5
    (C) 6
    (D) 7
    (E) 8

Solution: *Add* equations and get $2x + 2y + 2z = 12$; divide both sides of the equation by 2 and we get $x + y + z = 6$. (Answer C)

2. If $2x + y = 8$ and $x + 2y = 4$, find the value of $x - y$.

    (A) 3
    (B) 4
    (C) 5
    (D) 6
    (E) 7

Solution: *Subtract* equations and get $x - y = 4$.

(Answer B)

Here's an example from a recent SAT.

If $y - x = 5$ and $2y + z = 11$, find the value of $x + y + z$.

(A) 3
(B) 6
(C) 8
(D) 16
(E) 55

Solution: *Subtract* equation $y - x = 5$ from $2y + z = 11$. We get $2y - y + z - (-x) = 11 - 5$.
So, $y + z + x = 6$. (Answer B)

What are critical-thinking skills?

Critical-Thinking Skills, a current buzz phrase, are generic skills for finding the most creative and effective way of solving a problem or evaluating a situation. The most effective way of solving a problem is to extract some piece of information or observe something curious from the problem and then use one or more of the specific strategies or Critical-Thinking Skills (together with basic skills or information you already know) to get to the next step in the problem. This next step will catapult you toward a solution with further use of the specific strategies or thinking skills.

> **1.** EXTRACT OR OBSERVE SOMETHING CURIOUS.
> **2.** USE SPECIFIC STRATEGIES TOGETHER WITH BASIC SKILLS.

These specific strategies will enable you to "process" think rather than just be concerned with the end result; the latter usually gets you into a fast, rushed, and wrong answer. The Gruber strategies have been shown to make test takers more comfortable with problem solving and to make the process enjoyable. The skills will last a lifetime, and you will develop a passion for problem solving. These Critical-Thinking Skills show that conventional "drill and practice" is a waste of time unless the practice is based on these generic thinking skills.

Here's a simple example of how these Critical-Thinking Skills can be used in a math problem:

> Which is greater, $7\frac{1}{7} \times 8\frac{1}{8} \times 6\frac{1}{6}$ or $8\frac{1}{8} \times 6\frac{1}{6} \times 7$?

Long and tedious way

Multiply $7\frac{1}{7} \times 8\frac{1}{8} \times 6\frac{1}{6}$ and compare it with $8\frac{1}{8} \times 6\frac{1}{6} \times 7$.

Error in doing the problem the "long way"

You don't have to *calculate;* you just have to *compare,* so you need a *strategy* for *comparing* two quantities.

Critical-Thinking way

1. *Observe:* Each expression contains $8\frac{1}{8}$ and $6\frac{1}{6}$.

2. *Use Strategy:* Since both $8\frac{1}{8}$ and $6\frac{1}{6}$ are just weighting factors, like the same quantities on both sides of a balance scale, just *cancel* them from both multiplied quantities above.

3. You are then left comparing $7\frac{1}{7}$ with 7, so the first quantity, $7\frac{1}{7}$, is greater. Thus $7\frac{1}{7} \times 8\frac{1}{8} \times 6\frac{1}{6}$ is greater than $8\frac{1}{8} \times 6\frac{1}{6} \times 7$.

Here's a simple example of how Critical-Thinking Skills can be used for a Verbal problem:

If you see a word such as DELUDE in a sentence or in a reading passage, you can assume that the word DELUDE is negative and probably means "taking away from something" or "distracting," since the prefix DE- means "away from" and thus has a negative connotation. Although you may not get the exact meaning of the word (in this case the meaning is to "deceive" or "mislead"), you can see how the word may be used in the context of the sentence it appears in, and thus get the flavor or feeling of the sentence, paragraph, or sentence completion.

Notice that the Critical-Thinking approach gives you a fail-safe and exact way to the solution without superficially trying to solve the problem or merely guessing at it. This book contains all the Critical-Thinking Strategies you need to know for the SAT test.

Dr. Gruber has researched hundreds of SAT tests (thousands of SAT questions) and documented 40 Critical-Thinking Strategies (all found in this book) common to every test. These strategies can be used for any Math, Verbal, or Logical Reasoning problem.

In short, you can learn how to solve a specific problem and thus find how to answer that specific problem, or you can learn a powerful strategy that will enable you to answer hundreds of problems.

Multilevel approaches to the solution of problems

How a student answers a question is more important than the answer given by the student. For example, the student may have randomly guessed, the student may have used a rote and unimaginative method for solution, or the student may have used a very creative method. It seems that one should judge the student by the way he or she answers the question and not just by the answer to the question.

Example:

> ### Question: Without using a calculator, which is greater:
>
> ### 355×356 or 354×357?

Case 1. **Rote Memory Approach** (a completely mechanical approach not realizing that there may be a faster method that takes into account patterns or connections of the numbers in the question): The student multiplies 355×356, gets 126,380, and then multiplies 354×357 and gets 126,378.

Case 2. **Observer's Rote Approach** (an approach that makes use of a mathematical strategy that can be memorized and tried for various problems): The student does the following:

He or she divides both quantities by 354.

He or she then gets $\dfrac{355 \times 356}{354}$ compared with $\dfrac{354 \times 357}{354}$.

He or she then divides these quantities by 356 and then gets $\dfrac{355}{354}$ compared with $\dfrac{357}{356}$.

Now he or she realizes that $\dfrac{355}{354} = 1\dfrac{1}{354}; \dfrac{357}{356} = 1\dfrac{1}{356}$.

He or she then reasons that since the left side, $1\dfrac{1}{354}$, is greater than the right side, $1\dfrac{1}{356}$, the left side of the original quantities, 355×356, is greater than the right side of the original quantities, 354×357.

Case 3. **The Pattern Seeker's Method** (the most mathematically creative method—an approach in which the student looks for a pattern or sequence in the numbers and then is astute enough to represent the pattern or sequence in more general algebraic language to see the pattern or sequence more clearly):

Look for a pattern. Represent 355×356 and 354×357 by symbols.

Let $x = 354$.

Then $355 = x + 1; 356 = x + 2; 357 = x + 3$.

So $355 \times 356 = (x + 1)(x + 2)$ and $354 \times 357 = x(x + 3)$.

Multiplying the factors, we get

$355 \times 356 = x^2 + 3x + 2$ and $354 \times 357 = x^2 + 3x$.

The difference is $355 \times 356 - 354 \times 357 = x^2 + 3x + 2 - x^2 - 3x$, which is just 2.

So 355×356 is greater than 354×357 by 2.

Note: You could have also represented 355 by x. Then $356 = x + 1$; $354 = x - 1$; $357 = x + 2$. We would then get $355 \times 356 = (x)(x + 1)$ and $354 \times 357 = (x - 1)(x + 2)$. Then we would use the method above to compare the quantities.

OR

You could have written 354 as a and 357 as b. Then $355 = a + 1$ and $356 = b - 1$. So 355×356 $= (a + 1)(b - 1)$ and $354 \times 357 = ab$. Let's see what $(355 \times 356) - (354 \times 357)$ is. This is the same as $(a + 1)(b - 1) - ab$, which is $(ab + b - a - 1) - ab$, which is in turn $b - a - 1$. Since $b - a - 1 = 357 - 354 - 1 = 2$, the quantity $355 \times 356 - 354 \times 357 = 2$, so 355×356 is greater than 354×357 by 2.

Case 4. **The Astute Observer's Approach** (the simplest approach—an approach that attempts to figure out a connection between the numbers and uses that connection to figure out the solution):

$355 \times 356 = (354 + 1) \times 356 = (354 \times 356) + 356$ and

$354 \times 357 = 354 \times (356 + 1) = (354 \times 356) + 354$

One can see that the difference is just 2.

Case 5. **The Observer's Common Relation Approach** (the approach that people use when they want to connect two items to a third to see how the two items are related):

355×356 is greater than 354×356 by 356.

354×357 is greater than 354×356 by 354.

So this means that 355×356 is greater than 354×357.

Case 6. **Scientific, Creative, and Observational Generalization Method** (a highly creative method and the most scientific method, as it spots a critical and curious aspect of the sums being equal and provides for a generalization to other problems of that nature):

Represent $354 = a$, $357 = b$, $355 = c$, and $356 = d$

We have now that (1) $a + b = c + d$

(2) $|b - a| > |d - c|$

We want to prove: $ab < dc$

Proof:

Square inequality (2): $(b - a)^2 > (d - c)^2$

Therefore: (3) $b^2 - 2ab + a^2 > d^2 - 2dc + c^2$

Multiply (3) by -1, and this reverses the inequality sign:
$-(b^2 - 2ab + a^2) < -(d^2 - 2dc + c^2)$

OR

(4) $-b^2 + 2ab - a^2 < -d^2 + 2dc - c^2$

Now square (1): $(a + b) = (c + d)$ and we get:

(5) $a^2 + 2ab + b^2 = c^2 + 2dc + d^2$

Add inequality (4) to equality (5) and we get:

$4ab < 4dc$

Divide by 4 and we get:

$ab < dc$

The generalization is that for any positive numbers a, b, c, d, when $|b - a| > |d - c|$ and $a + b = c + d$, then $ab < dc$.

This also generalizes in a geometrical setting where for two rectangles whose perimeters are the same $(2a + 2b = 2c + 2d)$, the rectangle whose absolute difference in sides $|d - c|$ is *least* has the *greatest* area.

Case 7.   **Geometric and Visual Approach**[*] (the approach used by visual people or people who have a curious geometric bent and possess "out-of-the-box" insights):

Where $a = 354$, $b = 357$, $c = 355$, and $d = 356$, we have two rectangles where the first one's length is d and width is c, and the second one's length is b (dotted line) and width is a.

Now the area of the first rectangle (dc) is equal to the area of the second (ab) minus the area of the rectangular slab, which is $(b - d)a$, plus the area of the rectangular slab $(c - a)d$. So we get: $cd = ab - (b - d)a + (c - a)d$. Since $b - d = c - a$, we get $cd = ab - (c - a)a + (c - a)d = ab + (d - a)(c - a)$.

Since $d > a$ and $c > a$, $cd > ab$. So $355 \times 356 > 354 \times 357$.

Note: Many people have thought that by multiplying units digits from one quantity and comparing that with the multiplication of the units digits from the other quantity that they'd get the answer. For example, they would multiply $5 \times 6 = 30$ from 355×356, then multiply $4 \times 7 = 28$ from 354×357, and then say that 355×356 is greater than 354×357 because $5 \times 6 > 4 \times 7$. They would be lucky. That works if the sum of units digits of the first quantity is the same as or greater than the sum of units digits of the second quantity. However, if we want to compare something like $354 \times 356 = 126,024$ with $352 \times 359 = 126,368$, that method would not work.

---

[*] This method of solution was developed by and sent to the author from Dr. Eric Cornell, a Nobel laureate in Physics.

Format of the SAT

Total time for "counted" (not experimental) CRITICAL READING: 70 minutes—67 questions

Total time for "counted" (not experimental) MATH: 70 minutes—54 questions

Total time for "counted" (not experimental) WRITING (Multiple-Choice): 35 minutes—49 questions

Total time for WRITING (Essay): 25 minutes—1 or 2 prompts

Total time for experimental, pre-test items: 25 minutes—number of questions varies

Note: The following represents a form of an SAT. The SAT has many different forms, so the order of the sections may vary, and the experimental section* may not be the third section as we have here. However, the first section will always be the Essay, and the last section will be a 10-minute Multiple-Choice Writing section.

10 Sections of the SAT*		Number of Questions	Number of Minutes
Section 1:	**WRITING (Essay)**	1	25
Section 2:	**MATH**	20	25
	Regular Math	20	
			5 minute break
Section 3:	**EXPERIMENTAL**	Varies	25
	Could be writing, critical reading or math		
Section 4:	**CRITICAL READING**	24	25
	Sentence Completion	8	
	1 short passage (60–125 wds)	2	
	1 short passage (60–125 wds)	2	
	1 passage (650–850 wds)	11–13	
	OR		
	Double reading passages (350–450 wds each)	11–13	
			1 minute break
Section 5:	**WRITING (Multiple Choice)**	35	25
	Improving Sentences	11	
	Identifying Errors	18	
	Improving Paragraphs	6	

10 Sections of the SAT*	Number of Questions	Number of Minutes
Section 6: **MATH**	18	25
Regular Math	8	
Student Produced ("grid type")	10	
5 minute break		
Section 7: **CRITICAL READING**	24	25
Sentence Completion	5	
1 paired short passage (about 130 wds each)	4	
1 passage (400–550 wds)	5–7	
1 passage (550–700 wds)	8–10	
Section 8: **MATH**	16	20
Regular Math	16	
Section 9: **CRITICAL READING**	19	20
Sentence Completion	6	
Double reading passage (350–450 wds)	13	
OR		
1 passage (650–850 wds)	13	
Section 10: **WRITING (Mutiple Choice)**	14	10
Improving Sentences	14	
	TOTAL MINUTES = 225 ($3\frac{3}{4}$ hours)	

---

* The order of the sections on the actual test varies, since the SAT has several different forms. There will be passages on Humanities, Social Sciences, Natural Sciences, and Narrative (fiction or nonfiction). The total number of counted reading questions will be 48.

Note: One of the sections is experimental. An experimental section does not count in your SAT score. You cannot tell which of the sections of the test is experimental.

STRATEGY SECTION

Using critical-thinking skills to score high on the SAT

5 General strategies

General strategies for taking the SAT examination

Before studying the 35 specific strategies for the Math and Critical Reading questions, you will find it useful to review the following 5 General Strategies for taking the SAT examination.

Strategy 1

DON'T RUSH INTO GETTING AN ANSWER WITHOUT THINKING. BE CAREFUL IF YOUR ANSWER COMES TOO EASILY, ESPECIALLY IF THE QUESTION IS TOWARD THE END OF THE SECTION.

Beware of Choice A If You Get the Answer Fast or Without Really Thinking

Everybody panics when they take an exam like the SAT. And what happens is that they rush into getting answers. That's OK, except that you have to think carefully. If a problem looks too easy, beware! And, especially beware of the Choice A answer. It's usually a "lure" choice for those who rush into getting an answer without critically thinking about it. Here's an example:

Below is a picture of a digital clock. The clock shows that the time is 6:06. Consider all the times on the clock where the hour is the same as the minute, like in the clock shown below. Another such "double" time would be 8:08 or 9:09. What is the smallest time period between any two such doubles?

(A) 61 minutes
(B) 60 minutes
(C) 58 minutes
(D) 50 minutes
(E) 49 minutes

6:06

Did you subtract 7:07 from 8:08 and get 1 hour and 1 minute (61 minutes)? If you did you probably chose Choice A: the *lure choice*. Think—do you really believe that the test maker would give you such an easy question? The fact that you figured it out so easily and saw that Choice A was your answer should make you think twice. The thing you have to realize is that there is another possibility: 12:12 to 1:01 gives 49 minutes, and so Choice E is correct.

So, in summary, if you get the answer fast and without doing much thinking, and it's a Choice A answer, think again. You may have fallen for the Choice A lure.

Note: Choice A is often a "lure choice" for those who quickly get an answer without doing any real thinking. However, you should certainly realize that Choice A answers can occur, especially if there is no "lure choice."

Strategy 2

KNOW AND LEARN THE DIRECTIONS TO THE QUESTION TYPES BEFORE YOU TAKE THE ACTUAL TEST.

Never Spend Time Reading Directions During the Test or Doing Sample Questions That Don't Count

All SATs are standardized. For example, all the Regular Math questions have the same directions from test to test, as do the Sentence Completions, etc. So it's a good idea to learn these sets of directions and familiarize yourself with the types of questions early in the game before you take your actual SAT.

Here's an example of a set of SAT directions, together with an accompanying example for the Sentence Completion type of questions.

For each question in this section, select the best answer from among the choices given and fill in the corresponding oval on the answer sheet.

Directions:

Each sentence below has one or two blanks, each blank indicating that something has been omitted. Beneath the sentence are five words or sets of words labeled A through E. Choose the word or set of words that, when inserted in the sentence, *best* fits the meaning of the sentence as a whole.

Example:

Hoping to _____ the dispute, negotiators proposed a compromise that they felt would be _____ to both labor and management.

(A) enforce…useful

(B) end…divisive

(C) overcome…unattractive

(D) extend…satisfactory

(E) resolve…acceptable

If on your actual test you spend time reading these directions and/or answering the sample question, you will waste valuable time.

As you go through this book, you will become familiar with all the question types so that you won't have to read their directions on the actual test.

Strategy 3

IT MAY BE WISER NOT TO LEAVE AN ANSWER BLANK.

The Penalty for Guessing Is Much Smaller Than You Might Expect

On the SAT you lose a percentage of points if you guess and get the wrong answers on the multiple-choice questions. Of course, you should always try to eliminate choices. After going through this book, you'll have a better chance of eliminating wrong answers. However, if you cannot eliminate any choice in a question and have no idea of how to arrive at an answer, you might want to pick any answer and go on to the next question.

There are two reasons for this:

1. You don't want to risk mismarking a future answer by leaving a previous answer blank.

2. Even though there is a penalty for guessing, the penalty is much smaller than you might expect, and this way you have at least a chance of getting the question right. Suppose, for example, that you have a five-choice question:

From a probabilistic point of view, it is very likely that you would get one question right and four wrong (you have a 1 in 5 chance of getting a five-choice question right) if you randomly guess at the answers. Since $1 \underline{} 4$ point is taken off for each wrong five-choice question, you've gotten $1 - 1 \underline{} 4 \times 4 = 0$ points, because you've gotten 1 question right and 4 wrong. Thus you break even. So the moral is whether you randomly guess at questions you're not sure of at all or whether you leave those question answers blank, it doesn't make a difference in the long run!

Strategy 4

WRITE AS MUCH AS YOU WANT IN YOUR TEST BOOKLET.

Test Booklets Aren't Graded—So Use Them as You Would Scrap Paper

Many students are afraid to mark up their test booklets. But the booklets are not graded! Make any marks you want. In fact, some of the strategies demand that you extend or draw lines in geometry questions or label diagrams, circle incorrect answers, etc. That's why when I see computer programs that show only the questions on a screen and prevent the student from marking a diagram or circling an answer, I realize that such programs prevent the student from using many powerful strategies. *So write all you want in your test booklet—use your test paper as you would scrap paper.*

Strategy 5

USE YOUR OWN CODING SYSTEM TO TELL YOU WHICH QUESTIONS TO RETURN TO.

If You Have Extra Time after Completing a Test Section, You'll Know Exactly Which Questions Need More Attention

When you are sure that you have answered a question correctly, mark your question paper with ⏲. For questions you are not sure of but for which you have eliminated some of the choices, use **?**. For questions that you're not sure of at all or for which you have not been able to eliminate any choices, use **??**. This will give you a bird's-eye view of what questions you should return to if you have time left after completing a particular test section.

35 Easy-to-learn strategies

19 math strategies + 16 verbal (critical reading) strategies

Critical thinking is the ability to think clearly in order to solve problems and answer questions of all types—SAT questions, for example, both Math and Verbal!

Educators who are deeply involved in research on Critical-Thinking Skills tell us that such skills are straightforward, practical, teachable, and learnable.

The 19 Math Strategies and 16 Verbal Strategies in this section are Critical-Thinking Skills. These strategies have the potential to raise your SAT scores dramatically. Since each correct SAT question gives you an additional 10 points on average, it is reasonable to assume that if you can learn and then use these valuable SAT strategies, you can boost your SAT scores phenomenally!

BE SURE TO LEARN AND USE THE STRATEGIES THAT FOLLOW!

How to learn the strategies

1. For each strategy, look at the heading describing the strategy.

2. Try to answer the first example without looking at the EXPLANATORY ANSWER.

3. Then look at the EXPLANATORY ANSWER and, if you got the right answer, see if the method described will enable you to solve the question in a better way with a faster approach.

4. Then try each of the next EXAMPLES without looking at the EXPLANATORY ANSWERS.

5. Use the same procedure as in (3) for each of the EXAMPLES.

Before you start the Math Strategies, it would be wise for you to look at the *Important Note on the Allowed Use of Calculators on the SAT*, following; the *Important Note on Math Questions on the SAT*, *The Grid-Type Math Question*, and *Use of a Calculator in the Grid-Type Question*.

Important note on the allowed use of calculators on the SAT

Although the use of calculators on the SAT will be allowed, using a calculator may be sometimes more tedious, when in fact you can use another problem-solving method or shortcut. So you must be selective on when and when not to use a calculator on the test.

Here's an example of when a calculator should *not* be used:

$$\frac{2}{5} \times \frac{5}{6} \times \frac{6}{7} \times \frac{7}{8} \times \frac{8}{9} \times \frac{9}{10} \times \frac{10}{11} =$$

(A) $\frac{9}{11}$

(B) $\frac{2}{11}$

(C) $\frac{11}{36}$

(D) $\frac{10}{21}$

(E) $\frac{244}{360}$

Here the use of a calculator may take some time. However, if you use the strategy of canceling numerators and denominators (Math Strategy 1, Example 3) as shown,

Cancel numerators/denominators:

$$\frac{2}{\cancel{5}} \times \frac{\cancel{5}}{\cancel{6}} \times \frac{\cancel{6}}{7} \times \frac{7}{\cancel{8}} \times \frac{\cancel{8}}{\cancel{9}} \times \frac{\cancel{9}}{\cancel{10}} \times \frac{\cancel{10}}{11} = \frac{2}{11}$$

you can see that the answer comes easily as $\frac{2}{11}$.

Later I will show you an example in the *grid-type* question where the use of a calculator will also take you a longer time to solve a problem than without the calculator. Here's an example where using a calculator may get you the solution *as fast as* using a strategy without the calculator:

25 percent of 16 is equivalent to $\frac{1}{2}$ of what number?

(A) 2
(B) 4
(C) 8
(D) 16
(E) 32

Using a calculator, you'd use Math Strategy 2 (translating *of* to *times* and *is* to *equals*), first calculating 25 percent of 16 to get 4. Then you'd say 4 = half of what number and you'd find that number to be 8.

Without using a calculator, you'd still use Math Strategy 2 (the translation strategy), but you could write 25 percent as $\frac{1}{4}$, so you'd figure out that $\frac{1}{4} \times 16$ is 4. Then you'd call the number you want to find x, and say $4 = \frac{1}{2}(x)$. You'd find $x = 8$.

Note that both methods, with and without a calculator, are about equally efficient; however, the technique in the second method can be used for many more problems and hones more thinking skills.

Important note on math questions on the SAT

There are two types of math questions on the SAT.

1. The Regular Math (total of 44 counted questions), which has five choices.

2. The Grid-Type Math Question (total of 10 counted questions) is described below.

> **Note:** The grid-type questions can be solved using the Regular Math Strategies.

The grid-type math question

There will be 10 questions on the SAT where you will have to grid in your answer rather than choose from a set of five choices. Here are the directions to the grid-type question. Make sure that you understand these directions completely before you answer any of the grid-type questions.

Directions: For Student-Produced Response questions 1–15, use the grids on the following page.

Each of the remaining questions requires you to solve the problem and enter your answer by marking the circles in the special grid, as shown in the examples below. You may use any available space for scratchwork.

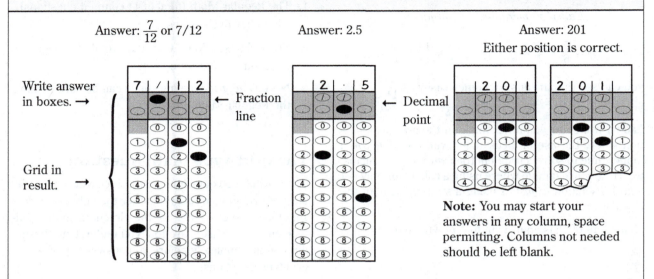

Answer: $\frac{7}{12}$ or 7/12   Answer: 2.5   Answer: 201
Either position is correct.

Write answer in boxes. → ← Fraction line

← Decimal point

Grid in result. →

Note: You may start your answers in any column, space permitting. Columns not needed should be left blank.

- Mark no more than one oval in any column.

- Because the answer sheet will be machine-scored, **you will receive credit only if the ovals are filled in correctly.**

- Although not required, it is suggested that you write your answer in the boxes at the top of the columns to help you fill in the ovals accurately.

- Some problems may have more than one correct answer. In such cases, grid only one answer.

- No question has a negative answer.

- **Mixed numbers** such as $2\frac{1}{2}$ must be gridded as 2.5 or 5/2. (If $2\frac{1}{2}$ is gridded, it will be interpreted as $\frac{21}{2}$, not $2\frac{1}{2}$.)

- **Decimal Accuracy:** If you obtain a decimal answer, **enter the most accurate value the grid will accommodate.** For example, if you obtain an answer such as 0.6666..., you should record the result as .666 or .667. **Less accurate values such as .66 or .67 are not acceptable.**

Acceptable ways to grid $\frac{2}{3}$ = .6666...:

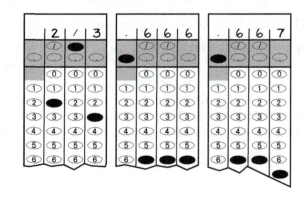

Practice with grids

According to the directions on the previous page, grid the following values in the grids 1−15:

317	4.2	.5	$\dfrac{1}{12}$	2,474

1 **2** **3** **4** **5**

$3\dfrac{1}{2}$	$\dfrac{57}{3}$	0	.346	$4\dfrac{3}{4}$

6 **7** **8** **9** **10**

39	1	$\dfrac{3}{8}$	45.3	$8\dfrac{1}{7}$

11 **12** **13** **14** **15**

Answers

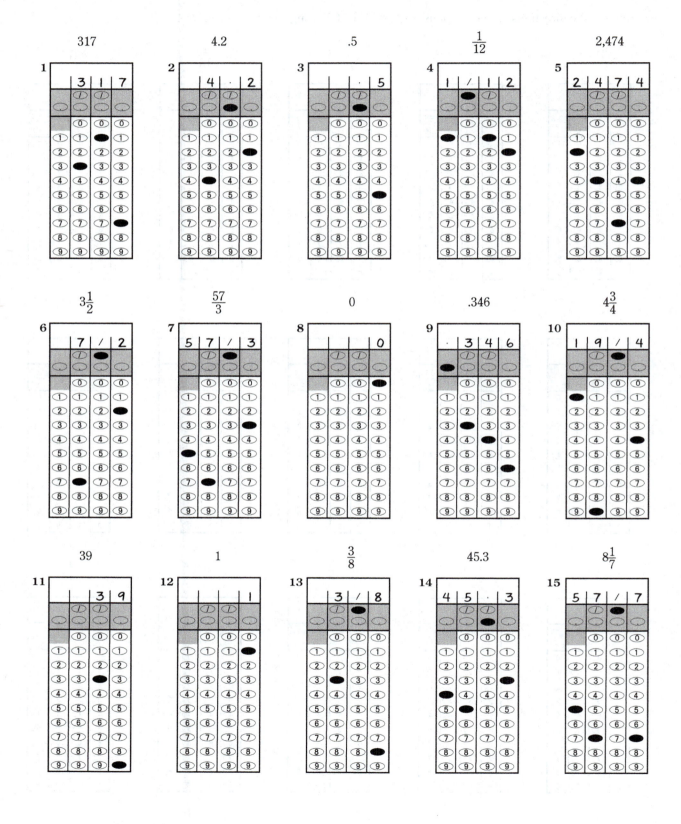

Use of a calculator in the grid-type question

In the following example, you can either use a calculator or not. However, the use of a calculator will require a different gridding.

Example

If $\frac{2}{7} < x < \frac{3}{7}$ find one value of x.

SOLUTION WITHOUT A CALCULATOR

Get some value between $\frac{2}{7}$ and $\frac{3}{7}$. Write $\frac{2}{7} = \frac{4}{14}$ and $\frac{3}{7} = \frac{6}{14}$.

So we have $\frac{4}{14} < x < \frac{6}{14}$ and x can be $\frac{5}{14}$.

The grid will look like this:

SOLUTION WITH A CALCULATOR

Calculate on a calculator:

$\frac{3}{7} = .4285714\ldots$

$\frac{2}{7} = .2857142\ldots$

So $.2857142 < x < .4285714$.

You could have the grid as follows:

all the way to

19 MATH STRATEGIES

Using Critical-Thinking Skills in Math Questions

MATH STRATEGY 1

Cancel quantities to make the problem simpler

> Cancel numbers or expressions that appear on both sides of an equation; cancel same numerators and denominators. But make sure that you don't divide by 0 in what you're doing! You will save precious time by using this strategy. You won't have to make any long calculations.

Example 1

If $P \times \frac{11}{14} = \frac{11}{14} \times \frac{8}{9}$, then $P =$

(A) $\frac{8}{9}$

(B) $\frac{9}{8}$

(C) 8

(D) 11

(E) 14

Choice A is correct. Do not multiply $\frac{11}{14} \times \frac{8}{9}$!

Cancel the common $\frac{11}{14}$:

$$P \times \frac{\cancel{11}}{\cancel{14}} = \frac{\cancel{11}}{\cancel{14}} \times \frac{8}{9}$$

$P = \frac{8}{9}$ (*Answer*)

Note: You can cancel the $\frac{11}{14}$ because you are *dividing* both sides by the same nonzero number. Suppose you had a problem like the following:

If $R \times a = a \times \frac{4}{5}$, then $R =$

(A) $\frac{2}{3}$

(B) $\frac{4}{5}$

(C) 1

(D) $\frac{5}{4}$

(E) Cannot be determined.

What do you think the answer is? It's not Choice B! It is Choice E, because you cannot cancel the a, because a may be 0 and you cannot divide by 0. So if $a = 0$, R can be *any* number.

Example 2

If $y + \frac{7}{13} + \frac{6}{19} = \frac{3}{5} + \frac{7}{13} + \frac{6}{19}$, then $y =$

(A) $\frac{6}{19}$

(B) $\frac{13}{32}$

(C) $\frac{7}{13}$

(D) $\frac{3}{5}$

(E) $\frac{211}{247}$

Choice D is correct. *Do not add the fractions!*

Don't add $\frac{3}{5} + \frac{7}{13} + \frac{6}{19}$! You waste a lot of time!
There is a much shorter way to do the problem.
Cancel $\frac{7}{13} + \frac{6}{19}$ from both sides of the equation. Thus,

$$y + \frac{\cancel{7}}{\cancel{13}} + \frac{\cancel{6}}{\cancel{19}} = \frac{3}{5} + \frac{\cancel{7}}{\cancel{13}} + \frac{\cancel{6}}{\cancel{19}}$$

$y = \frac{3}{5}$ (*Answer*)

Example 3

$$\frac{2}{5} \times \frac{5}{6} \times \frac{6}{7} \times \frac{7}{8} \times \frac{8}{9} \times \frac{9}{10} \times \frac{10}{11} =$$

(A) $\frac{9}{11}$

(B) $\frac{2}{11}$

(C) $\frac{11}{36}$

(D) $\frac{10}{21}$

(E) $\frac{244}{360}$

Choice B is correct.

Cancel numerators/denominators:

$$\frac{2}{\cancel{5}} \times \frac{\cancel{5}}{\cancel{6}} \times \frac{\cancel{6}}{\cancel{7}} \times \frac{\cancel{7}}{\cancel{8}} \times \frac{\cancel{8}}{\cancel{9}} \times \frac{\cancel{9}}{\cancel{10}} \times \frac{\cancel{10}}{11} = \frac{2}{11}$$

Example 4

If $a + b > a - b$, which must follow?

(A) $a < 0$

(B) $b < 0$

(C) $a > b$

(D) $b > a$

(E) $b > 0$

Choice E is correct.

$a + b > a - b$

Cancel common a's:

$$\cancel{a} + b > \cancel{a} - b$$
$$b > -b$$
Add b: $\quad b + b > b - b$
$$2b > 0$$
$$b > 0$$

Example 5

If $7\frac{2}{9} = 6 + \frac{y}{27}$, $y =$

(A) 8

(B) 30

(C) 35

(D) 37

(E) 33

Choice E is correct.

Subtract 6 from both sides:

$$7\frac{2}{9} - 6 = 6 + \frac{y}{27} - 6$$

$$1\frac{2}{9} = \frac{y}{27}$$

$$\frac{11}{9} = \frac{y}{27}$$

$$\frac{33}{27} = \frac{y}{27}$$

$$y = 33$$

MATH STRATEGY 2

Translate English words into mathematical expressions

Many of the SAT problems are word problems. Being able to translate word problems from English into mathematical expressions or equations will help you to score high on the test. The following table translates some commonly used words into their mathematical equivalents:

TRANSLATION TABLE

Words	Math Way to Say It
is, was, has, cost	= (equals)
of	$\times$ (times)
percent	$\overline{}{100}$ (the percent number over 100)
x percent	$\dfrac{x}{100}$
which, what	x (or any other variable)
x and y	$x + y$
the sum of x and y	$x + y$
the difference between x and y	$x - y$
x more than y	$x + y$
x less than y	$y - x$
the product of x and y	xy
the square of x	x^2
x is greater than y	$x > y$ (or $y < x$)
x is less than y	$x < y$ (or $y > x$)
y years ago	$- y$
y years from now	$+ y$
c times as old as John	$c \times$ (John's age)
x older than y	$x + y$
x younger than y	$y - x$
the increase from x to y	$y - x$
the decrease from x to y	$x - y$
the percent increase from x to y $(y > x)$	$\left(\dfrac{y-x}{x}\right)100$
the percent decrease from x to y $(y < x)$	$\left(\dfrac{x-y}{x}\right)100$
the percent of increase	$\left(\dfrac{\text{amount of increase}}{\text{original amount}}\right) \times 100$
the percent of decrease	$\left(\dfrac{\text{amount of decrease}}{\text{original amount}}\right) \times 100$
n percent greater than x	$x + \left(\dfrac{n}{100}\right)x$
n percent less than x	$x - \left(\dfrac{n}{100}\right)x$

By knowing this table, you will find word problems much easier to do.

OPTIONAL QUIZ ON TRANSLATION TABLE

Take this quiz to see if you understand the translation table before attempting the problems in Strategy #2 that follow.

1. **Mila is five years older than Juan** translates to:

    (A) $J = 5 + M$

    (B) $M + J = 5$

    (C) $M > 5 + J$

    (D) $M = 5 + J$

    (E) None of these.

    (D) Translate: **Mila** to M; **Juan** to J; **is** to =; **older than** to +

    So **Mila is five years older than Juan** becomes:

    $$\downarrow \quad \downarrow \ \downarrow \qquad\quad \downarrow \qquad\qquad \downarrow$$
    $$M \ = \ 5 \qquad\quad + \qquad\qquad J$$

2. **3 percent of 5** translates to:

    (A) $\dfrac{3}{5}$

    (B) $\dfrac{3}{100} \div 5$

    (C) $\left(\dfrac{3}{100}\right) \times 5$

    (D) $3 \times 100 \times 5$

    (E) None of these.

    (C) percent or % = $\dfrac{}{100}$; of = ×; so

    3% of 5 translates to:

    $$\downarrow \quad \downarrow \ \downarrow$$
    $$\dfrac{3}{100} \times \ 5$$

3. **What percent of 3** translates to:

    (A) $x(100) \times 3$

    (B) $\left(\dfrac{x}{100}\right) \times 3$

    (C) $\left(\dfrac{x}{100}\right) \div 3$

    (D) $\left(\dfrac{3}{100}\right)x$

    (E) None of these.

    (B) Translate: **what** to x; **percent** to $\dfrac{}{100}$. Thus

What percent of 3 becomes:

$$\downarrow \qquad \downarrow \qquad \downarrow \qquad \downarrow$$
$$x \qquad \dfrac{}{100} \qquad \times \qquad 3$$

4. **Six years ago, Sophia was 4 times as old as Jacob was then** translates to:

    (A) $S - 6 = 4J$

    (B) $6 - S = 4J$

    (C) $6 - S = 4(J - 6)$

    (D) $S - 6 = 4(J - 6)$

    (E) None of these.

    (D) **Six years ago, Sophia was** translates to $S - 6$. **4 times as old as Jacob is** would be $4J$. However, **4 times as old as Jacob was then** translates to $4(J - 6)$. Thus **six years ago, Sophia was 4 times as old as Jacob was then** translates to:

    $$S - 6 = 4 \times (J - 6)$$

5. **The percent increase from 5 to 10** is

    (A) $\left[\dfrac{(10 - 5)}{5}\right] \times 100$

    (B) $\left[\dfrac{(5 - 10)}{5}\right] \times 100$

    (C) $\left[\dfrac{(10 - 5)}{10}\right] \times 100$

    (D) $\left[\dfrac{(5 - 10)}{10}\right] \times 100$

    (E) None of these.

    (A) Percent increase from a to b is $\left[\dfrac{(b - a)}{a}\right] \times$ 100. So **the percent increase from 5 to 10** would be $\left[\dfrac{(10 - 5)}{5}\right] \times$ 100.

6. **Hudson is older than John and John is older than Madison** translates to:

    (A) $H > J > M$

    (B) $H > J < M$

    (C) $H > M > J$

    (D) $M > H > J$

    (E) None of these.

(A) **Hudson is older than John** translates to: $H > J$. **John is older than Madison** translates to $J > M$. So we have $H > J$ and $J > M$, which, consolidated, becomes $H > J > M$.

7. **Even after Phil gives Sam 6 DVDs, he still has 16 more DVDs than Sam has** translates to:

    (A) $P - 6 = 16 + S$

    (B) $P - 6 = 16 + S + 6$

    (C) $P + 6 = 16 + S + 6$

    (D) $P + 6 + 16 + S$

    (E) None of these.

    (B) **Even after Phil gives Sam 6 DVDs** translates to:

    $P - 6$ $\boxed{1}$

    He still has 16 more DVDs than Sam has translates to:

    $= 16 + S + 6$ $\boxed{2}$

    since Sam has gotten 6 additional DVDs. Thus, combining $\boxed{1}$ and $\boxed{2}$, we get: $P - 6 = 16 + S + 6$.

8. **q is 10% greater than p** translates to:

    (A) $q = \left(\dfrac{10}{100}\right)q + p$

    (B) $q > \left(\dfrac{10}{100}\right)p$

    (C) $q = \left(\dfrac{10}{100}\right)p + p$

    (D) $q = \left(\dfrac{10}{100}\right) + p$

    (E) None of these.

    (C) **q is** translates to $q =$ $\boxed{1}$

    10% greater than p translates to $\boxed{2}$

    $\left(\dfrac{10}{100}\right)p + p$ so

$$\text{translates to:} \quad \overset{\textstyle q}{\downarrow} \; \overset{\textstyle \text{is}}{\downarrow} \; \overbrace{\textbf{10\% greater than } p}$$

$$q = \left(\frac{10}{100}\right)p + p$$

9. **200 is what percent of 20** translates to:

    (A) $200 = x \times 100 \times 20$

    (B) $200 = \left(\dfrac{x}{100}\right) \div 20$

    (C) $200 = \left(\dfrac{x}{100}\right) \times 20$

    (D) $200 = x \times 20$

    (E) None of these.

    (C) Translate **is** to $=$; **what** to x; **percent** to $\frac{}{100}$; **of** to $\times$ so we get that:

    200 is what percent of 20 translates to:

$$\overset{\textstyle 200}{\downarrow} \; \overset{\textstyle =}{\downarrow} \; \overset{\textstyle x}{\downarrow} \quad \overset{\textstyle \frac{}{100}}{\downarrow} \; \overset{\textstyle \times}{\downarrow} \; \overset{\textstyle 20}{\downarrow}$$

10. **The product of the sums of x and y and y and z is 5** translates to:

    (A) $xy + yz = 5$

    (B) $x + y + y + z = 5$

    (C) $(x + y)(yz) = 5$

    (D) $(x + y)(y + z) = 5$

    (E) None of these.

    (D) **The sum of x and y is** $x + y$. **The sum of y and z is** $y + z$. So the **product of those sums** is $(x + y)(y + z)$.

    Thus **The product of the sums of x and y and y and z is 5** translates to:
    $(x + y)(y + z) = 5$

Strategy 2, Example 1

Sarah is twice as old as John. Six years ago, Sarah was 4 times as old as John was then. How old is John now?

(A) 3
(B) 9
(C) 18
(D) 20
(E) impossible to determine

Choice B is correct. Translate:

Sarah is twice as old as John.
$$\downarrow \quad \downarrow \quad \downarrow \quad \downarrow \qquad \downarrow$$
$$S \;=\; 2 \;\times\; J$$
$$S = 2J \qquad \boxed{1}$$

Six years ago Sarah was 4 times as old as John was then
$$\downarrow \qquad\qquad \downarrow \quad \downarrow\downarrow \quad \downarrow \qquad\qquad \downarrow$$
$$-6 \qquad\qquad S \;=\; 4 \;\times\; (J-6)$$

This becomes $S - 6 = 4(J - 6)$ $\boxed{2}$

Substituting $\boxed{1}$ into $\boxed{2}$:

$2J - 6 = 4(J - 6)$
$2J - 6 = 4J - 24$
$\quad\; 18 = 2J$
$\qquad 9 = J \qquad$ (*Answer*)

Example 2

200 is what percent of 20?

(A) $\frac{1}{10}$
(B) 10
(C) 100
(D) 1,000
(E) 10,000

Choice D is correct. Translate:

200 is what percent of 20
$$\downarrow \quad \downarrow \quad \downarrow \qquad \downarrow \qquad \downarrow \quad \downarrow$$
$$200 \;=\; x \quad \overline{100} \;\times\; 20$$

$200 = \frac{x}{100}(20)$

Divide by 20: $10 = \frac{x}{100}$

Multiply by 100: $1,000 = x$ (*Answer*)

Example 3

If A is 250 percent of B, what percent of A is B?

(A) 125%
(B) $\frac{1}{250}$%
(C) 50%
(D) 40%
(E) 400%

Choice D is correct.

If A is 250 percent of B becomes
$$\downarrow\downarrow\;\downarrow \qquad \downarrow \qquad \downarrow\downarrow$$
$$A = 250 \quad \overline{100} \;\times B$$

What percent of A is B? becomes
$$\downarrow \qquad\quad \downarrow \quad \downarrow\downarrow\downarrow$$
$$x \qquad \overline{100} \;\times A = B$$

Set up the equations:
$$A = \frac{250}{100}B \qquad\qquad \boxed{1}$$
$$\frac{x}{100}A = B \qquad\qquad \boxed{2}$$

Divide equation $\boxed{1}$ by equation $\boxed{2}$:

We get:
$$\frac{A}{\frac{x}{100}A} = \frac{\frac{250}{100}B}{B}$$

$$\frac{1}{\frac{x}{100}} = \frac{250}{100}$$

Inverting, we get:

$\frac{x}{100} = \frac{100}{250}$

$x = \frac{10,000}{250}$

To simplify, multiply both numerator and denominator by 4:
$$x = \frac{10,000 \times 4}{250 \times 4} = 40$$

$$x = \frac{40,000}{1,000} = 40$$

Alternate way:

Let $B = 100$ (choose any number for B).
We get (after translation)

$$A = \left(\frac{250}{100}\right)100 \qquad \boxed{1}$$

$$\left(\frac{x}{100}\right)A = 100 \qquad \boxed{2}$$

From $\boxed{1}$,

$A = 250$ $\qquad\qquad \boxed{3}$

Substituting $\boxed{3}$ into $\boxed{2}$, we get

$$\left(\frac{x}{100}\right)250 = 100 \qquad \boxed{4}$$

Multiplying both sides of $\boxed{4}$ by 100,

$$(x)(250) = (100)(100)$$

Dividing by 250:

$$x = \frac{100 \times 100}{250}$$

Simplify by multiplying numerator and denominator by 4:

$$x = \frac{100 \times 100 \times 4}{250 \times 4} = \frac{40,000}{1,000}$$
$$= 40$$

Example 4

John is now m years old and Sally is 4 years older than John. Which represents Sally's age 6 years ago?

(A) $m + 10$

(B) $m - 10$

(C) $m - 2$

(D) $m - 4$

(E) $4m - 6$

Choice C is correct.

Translate:

John is now m years old
  ↓ ↓   ↓
  J = m

Sally is 4 years older than John
  ↓ ↓↓   ↓   ↓
  S = 4   + J

Sally's age 6 years ago
  ↓   ↓
  S −   6

So we get: $\quad J = m$
$\qquad\qquad\quad S = 4 + J$

and find: $\quad S - 6 = 4 + J - 6$
$\qquad\qquad\quad S - 6 = J - 2$
$\qquad\qquad\quad S - 6 = m - 2$ (substituting m for J)

See Math Strategy 7, Example 2 for an alternate approach to solving this problem, using a different strategy: **Use Specific Numerical Examples to Prove or Disprove Your Guess**.

Example 5

Phil has three times as many DVDs as Sam has. Even after Phil gives Sam 6 DVDs, he still has 16 more DVDs than Sam has. What was the original number of DVDs that Phil had?

(A) 20

(B) 24

(C) 28

(D) 33

(E) 42

Choice E is correct.

Translate:

Phil has three times as many DVDs as Sam has
  ↓ ↓   ↓   ↓   ↓
  P = 3   × S

Even after Phil gives Sam 6 DVDs, he still has 16
            ↓   ‾‾‾↓‾‾‾ ↓   ↓ ↓
            P −   6   = 16

more DVDs than Sam has
  ↓   ‾↓‾
  + $S + 6$

Sam now has $S + 6$ DVDs because Phil gave Sam 6 DVDs. So we end up with the equations:

$P = 3S$

$P - 6 = 16 + S + 6$

Find P; get rid of S:

$$P = 3S; \qquad \frac{P}{3} = S$$

$$P - 6 = 16 + \frac{P}{3} + 6$$

$$P - 6 = \frac{48 + P + 18}{3}$$

$$3P - 18 = 48 + P + 18$$

$$2P = 84$$

$$P = 42$$

Example 6

If q is 10% greater than p and r is 10% greater than y, qr is what percent greater than py?

(A) 1%

(B) 20%

(C) 21%

(D) 30%

(E) 100%

Choice C is correct.

Translate:

If q is <u>10% greater than p</u>
$\downarrow \downarrow \qquad\qquad \downarrow$
$q = \qquad \frac{10}{100}p + p$

and r is <u>10% greater than y</u>
$\downarrow \downarrow \qquad\qquad \downarrow$
$r = \qquad \frac{10}{100}y + y$

qr is <u>what percent greater than py?</u>
$\downarrow \downarrow \qquad\qquad \downarrow$
$qr = \qquad \frac{x}{100}py + py$

So we have three equations:

$$q = \frac{10}{100}p + p = \left(\frac{10}{100} + 1\right)p \qquad \boxed{1}$$

$$r = \frac{10}{100}y + y = \left(\frac{10}{100} + 1\right)y \qquad \boxed{2}$$

$$qr = \frac{x}{100}py + py = \left(\frac{x}{100} + 1\right)py \qquad \boxed{3}$$

Multiply $\boxed{1}$ and $\boxed{2}$:

$$qr = \left(\frac{10}{100} + 1\right)^2 py \qquad\qquad \boxed{4}$$

Now equate $\boxed{4}$ with $\boxed{3}$:

$$qr = \left(\frac{x}{100} + 1\right)py = \left(\frac{10}{100} + 1\right)^2 py$$

You can see that $\left(\frac{10}{100} + 1\right)^2 = \frac{x}{100} + 1$, canceling py.

So, $\left(\frac{10}{100} + 1\right)^2 = \frac{100}{10,000} + 2\left(\frac{10}{100}\right) + 1 = \frac{x}{100} + 1$

$$\frac{100}{10,000} + \frac{20}{100} = \frac{21}{100} = \frac{x}{100}$$

$$21 = x$$

The answer is $x = 21$.

Alternate approach: Choose numbers for p and for y:

Let $p = 10$ and $y = 20$

Then, since q is 10% greater than p:

$q = 10\%$ greater than 10

$$q = \left(\frac{10}{100}\right)10 + 10 = 11$$

Next, r is 10% greater than y:

$r = 10\%$ greater than 20

Or, $r = q\ 5\ (\ 10\ \underline{\quad}\ 100\ )10 + 10\ 5\ 1120 + 20 = 22$

Then:

$$qr = 11 \times 22$$

and $py = 20 \times 10$

So, to find what percent qr is greater than py, you would need to find:

$$\frac{qr - py}{py} \times 100 \text{ or}$$

$$\frac{11 \times 22 - 20 \times 10}{20 \times 10} \times 100$$

This is:

$$\frac{42}{200} \times 100 = 21$$

Example 7

Sales of Item X
Jan–Jun 2004

Month	Sales ($)
Jan	800
Feb	1,000
Mar	1,200
Apr	1,300
May	1,600
Jun	1,800

According to the above table, the percent increase in sales was greatest for which of the following periods?

(A) Jan–Feb

(B) Feb–Mar

(C) Mar–Apr

(D) Apr–May

(E) May–Jun

Choice A is correct.

The percent increase from Month A to Month B =

$$\frac{\text{sales (month B)} - \text{sales (month A)}}{\text{sales (month A)}} \times 100$$

Month	Sales ($)	Periods	% Increase in Sales
Jan	800	Jan–Feb	$\frac{1,000 - 800}{800} \times 100 = \frac{200}{800} \times 100$
Feb	1,000	Feb–Mar	$\frac{1,200 - 1,000}{1,000} \times 100 = \frac{200}{1,000} \times 100$
Mar	1,200	Mar–Apr	$\frac{1,300 - 1,200}{1,200} \times 100 = \frac{100}{1,200} \times 100$
Apr	1,300	Apr–May	$\frac{1,600 - 1,300}{1,300} \times 100 = \frac{300}{1,300} \times 100$
May	1,600	May–Jun	$\frac{1,800 - 1,600}{1,600} \times 100 = \frac{200}{1,600} \times 100$
Jun	1,800		

You can see that $\frac{200}{800} \times 100$ (Jan–Feb) is the greatest.

MATH STRATEGY 3

Know how to find unknown quantities (areas, lengths, arc and angle measurements) from known quantities (the whole equals the sum of its parts)

When asked to find a particular area or length, instead of trying to calculate it directly, find it by subtracting two other areas or lengths—a method based on the fact that the whole minus a part equals the remaining part.

This strategy is very helpful in many types of geometry problems. A very important equation to remember is

The whole = the sum of its parts $\boxed{1}$

Equation $\boxed{1}$ is often disguised in many forms, as seen in the following examples:

Example 1

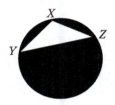

In the diagram above, $\triangle XYZ$ has been inscribed in a circle. If the circle encloses an area of 64, and the area of $\triangle XYZ$ is 15, then what is the area of the shaded region?

(A) 25

(B) 36

(C) 49

(D) 79

(E) It cannot be determined from the information given.

Choice C is correct. Use equation $\boxed{1}$. Here, the whole refers to the area within the circle, and the parts refer to the areas of the shaded region and the triangle. Thus,

Area within circle =

Area of shaded region +

Area of $\triangle XYZ$

64 = Area of shaded region + 15

or Area of shaded region = 64 − 15 = 49 (*Answer*)

Example 2

In the diagram below, $\overline{AE}$ is a straight line, and F is a point on $\overline{AE}$. Find an expression for $m \angle DFE$.

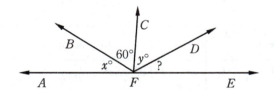

(A) $x + y - 60$

(B) $x + y + 60$

(C) $90 - x - y$

(D) $120 - x - y$

(E) $180 - x - y$

Choice D is correct. Use equation $\boxed{1}$. Here, the whole refers to the straight angle, $\angle AFE$, and its parts refer to $\angle AFB$, $\angle BFC$, $\angle CFD$, and $\angle DFE$. Thus,

$$m \angle AFE = m \angle AFB + m \angle BFC + m \angle CFD + m \angle DFE$$
$$180 = x + 60 + y + m \angle DFE$$

or $m \angle DFE = 180 - x - 60 - y$
$m \angle DFE = 120 - x - y$ (*Answer*)

Example 3

In the diagram below, $AB = m$, $BC = n$, and $AD = 10$. Find an expression for CD.

(Note: Diagram represents a straight line.)

(A) $10 - mn$

(B) $10 - m - n$

(C) $m - n + 10$

(D) $m + n - 10$

(E) $m + n + 10$

Choice B is correct. Use equation $\boxed{1}$. Here, the whole refers to AD, and its parts refer to AB, BC, and CD. Thus,

$$AD = AB + BC + CD$$
$$10 = m + n + CD$$
or $\quad CD = 10 - m - n$ (*Answer*)

Example 4

The area of triangle $ACE = 64$. The sum of the areas of the shaded triangles ABF and FDE is 39. What is the side of square $BFDC$?

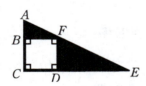

(A) 5

(B) 4

(C) $\sqrt{5}$

(D) $\sqrt{44}$

(E) Cannot be determined.

EXPLANATORY ANSWER

Choice A is correct.

Since we are dealing with areas, let's establish the area of the square $BFDC$, which will then enable us to get its side.

Now, the area of square $BFDC$ = area of triangle ACE − (area of triangles $ABF + FDE$)

Area of square $BFDC = 64 - 39$
$$= 25$$

Therefore, the side of square $BFDC = 5$.

Example 5

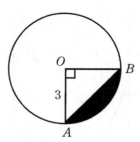

In the figure above, O is the center of the circle. Triangle AOB has side 3 and angle $AOB = 90°$. What is the area of the shaded region?

(A) $9\left(\dfrac{\pi}{4} - \dfrac{1}{2}\right)$

(B) $9\left(\dfrac{\pi}{2} - 1\right)$

(C) $9(\pi - 1)$

(D) $9\left(\dfrac{\pi}{4} - \dfrac{1}{4}\right)$

(E) Cannot be determined.

EXPLANATORY ANSWER

Choice A is correct.

Subtract knowns from knowns:

Area of shaded region = area of quarter circle AOB − area of triangle AOB

Area of quarter circle $AOB = \dfrac{\pi(3)^2}{4}$ (since $OA = 3$ and area of a quarter of a circle $= \dfrac{1}{4} \times \pi \times$ radius^2)

Area of triangle $AOB = \dfrac{3 \times 3}{2}$ (since $OB = 3$ and area of a triangle $= \dfrac{1}{2}$ base $\times$ height)

Thus, area of shaded region $= \dfrac{9\pi}{4} - \dfrac{9}{2} = 9\left(\dfrac{\pi}{4} - \dfrac{1}{2}\right)$.

Example 6

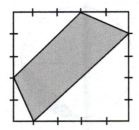

The sides in the square above are each divided into five equal segments. What is the value of

$$\frac{\text{area of square}}{\text{area of shaded region}}?$$

(A) $\frac{50}{29}$

(B) $\frac{50}{21}$

(C) $\frac{25}{4}$

(D) $\frac{29}{25}$

(E) None of these.

EXPLANATORY ANSWER

Choice B is correct.

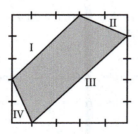

Subtract knowns from knowns:

Area of square = $5 \times 5 = 25$

Area of shaded region = area of square − area of I − area of II − area of III − area of IV

$$\text{Area of I} = \frac{3 \times 3}{2} = \frac{9}{2}$$

$$\text{Area of II} = \frac{2 \times 1}{2} = 1$$

$$\text{Area of III} = \frac{4 \times 4}{2} = 8$$

$$\text{Area of IV} = \frac{2 \times 1}{2} = 1$$

Area of shaded region $= 25 - \frac{9}{2} - 1 - 8 - 1 = \frac{21}{2}$

$$\frac{\text{area of square}}{\text{area of shaded region}} = \frac{25}{\frac{21}{2}} = 25 \times \frac{2}{21} = \frac{50}{21}$$

Example 7

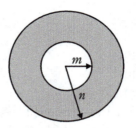

Two concentric circles are shown above with inner radius of m and outer radius of n. What is the area of the shaded region?

(A) $\pi(n - m)^2$

(B) $\pi(n^2 + m^2)$

(C) $\pi(n^2 - m^2)$

(D) $2\pi(n - m)$

(E) $2\pi(n + m)$

EXPLANATORY ANSWER

Choice C is correct.

Subtract knowns from knowns:

Area of shaded region = area of circle of radius n − area of circle of radius m

Area of circle of radius $n = \pi n^2$

Area of circle of radius $m = \pi m^2$

Area of shaded region $= \pi n^2 - \pi m^2$

$$= \pi(n^2 - m^2)$$

MATH STRATEGY 4

Remember classic expressions such as

$$x^2 - y^2, \; x^2 + 2xy + y^2, \; x^2 - 2xy + y^2, \; \frac{x+y}{xy}$$

Memorize the following factorizations and expressions:

$x^2 - y^2 = (x + y)(x - y)$ Equation 1

$x^2 + 2xy + y^2 = (x + y)(x + y) = (x + y)^2$ Equation 2

$x^2 - 2xy + y^2 = (x - y)(x - y) = (x - y)^2$ Equation 3

$\dfrac{x+y}{xy} = \dfrac{1}{x} + \dfrac{1}{y}$ $x, y \neq 0$ Equation 4

$\dfrac{x-y}{xy} = \dfrac{1}{y} - \dfrac{1}{x}$ $x, y \neq 0$ Equation 4A

$xy + xz = x(y + z)$ Equation 5

$xy - xz = x(y - z)$ Equation 5A

Examples 1, 3, and 11 can also be solved with the aid of a calculator and some with the aid of a calculator allowing for exponential calculations. However, to illustrate the effectiveness of Math Strategy 4, we did not use the calculator method of solution for these examples.

Use algebra to see patterns.

Example 1

$66^2 + 2(34)(66) + 34^2 =$

(A) 4,730
(B) 5,000
(C) 9,860
(D) 9,950
(E) 10,000

Choice E is correct. Notice that there is a 34 and 66 running through the left side of the equality. To see a pattern, *use algebra*. Substitute *a* for 66 and *b* for 34. You get:

$$66^2 + 2(34)(66) + 34^2 =$$
$$a^2 + 2(b)(a) + b^2$$

But from Equation 2,

$a^2 + 2ab + b^2 =$ $\boxed{1}$

$(a + b)(a + b) =$

$(a + b)^2$

Now substitute the numbers 34 and 66 *back into* $\boxed{1}$ to get:

$$66^2 + 2(34)(66) + 34^2 =$$
$$(66 + 34)(66 + 34) =$$
$$100 \times 100 =$$
$$10,000 \quad (Answer)$$

Example 2

If $(x + y) = 9$ and $xy = 14$, find $\dfrac{1}{x} + \dfrac{1}{y}$.

(Note: $x, y > 0$)

(A) $\dfrac{1}{9}$

(B) $\dfrac{2}{7}$

(C) $\dfrac{9}{14}$

(D) 5

(E) 9

Choice C is correct. We are given:

$(x + y) = 9$ $\boxed{1}$

$xy = 14$ $\boxed{2}$

$x, y > 0$ $\boxed{3}$

I hope that you did not solve $\boxed{2}$ for x (or y), and then substitute it into $\boxed{1}$. If you did, you obtained a quadratic equation.

Here is the FAST method. Use Equation 4:

$\frac{1}{x} + \frac{1}{y} = \frac{x+y}{xy}$ $\boxed{4}$

From $\boxed{1}$ and $\boxed{2}$, we find that $\boxed{4}$ becomes

$\frac{1}{x} + \frac{1}{y} = \frac{9}{14}$ *(Answer)*

Example 3

The value of $100 \times 100 - 99 \times 99 =$

(A) 1

(B) 2

(C) 99

(D) 199

(E) 299

Choice D is correct.

Write a for 100 and b for 99 to see a pattern:

$100 \times 100 - 99 \times 99$

$a \times a - b \times b = a^2 - b^2$. Use Equation 1:

Use the fact that $a^2 - b^2 = (a + b)(a - b)$ $\boxed{1}$

Put back 100 for a and 99 for b in $\boxed{1}$:

$a^2 - b^2 = 100^2 - 99^2 = (100 + 99)(100 - 99) = 199$

Example 4

Use factoring to make problems simpler.

$\frac{8^7 - 8^6}{7} =$

(A) $\frac{8}{7}$

(B) 8^7

(C) 8^6

(D) 8^5

(E) 8^4

Choice C is correct.

Factor: $8^7 - 8^6 = 8^6(8^1 - 1)$ (Equation 5A)

$= 8^6(8 - 1)$

$= 8^6(7)$

So $\frac{8^7 - 8^6}{7} = \frac{8^6(7)}{7} = \frac{8^6(\cancel{7})}{\cancel{7}} = 8^6$

Represented algebraically, the problem would look like this.

Where $a \neq 1$,

$\frac{a^7 - a^6}{a - 1} =$

(A) $\frac{a}{a - 1}$

(B) $\frac{1}{a - 1}$

(C) $a^6 - a^5$

(D) a^5

(E) a^6

Choice E is correct.

Factor: $a^7 - a^6 = a^6(a - 1)$
(Equation 5A)

The expression

$\frac{a^7 - a^6}{a - 1}$

becomes

$\frac{a^6(a - 1)}{a - 1}$

Since $a \neq 1$, this becomes

a^6

Example 5

Use factoring to make problems simpler.

$\sqrt{(88)^2 + (88)^2(3)} =$

(A) 88

(B) 176

(C) 348

(D) 350

(E) 352

Choice B is correct. Factor:

$$(88)^2 + (88)^2(3) = 88^2(1 + 3) = 88^2(4) \qquad \text{(Equation 5)}$$

So:

$$\sqrt{(88)^2 + (88)^2(3)} = \sqrt{88^2(4)}$$
$$= \sqrt{88^2} \times \sqrt{4}$$
$$= 88 \times 2$$
$$= 176$$

Example 6

$$\text{If } y + \frac{1}{y} = 9, \text{ then } y^2 + \frac{1}{y^2} =$$

(A) 76
(B) 77
(C) 78
(D) 79
(E) 81

Choice D is correct.

Square $\left(y + \frac{1}{y}\right) = 9$

Substituting y for x and $\frac{1}{y}$ for y in Equation 2, we get:

$$\left(y + \frac{1}{y}\right)^2 = 81 = y^2 + 2(y)\left(\frac{1}{y}\right) + \left(\frac{1}{y}\right)^2$$
$$= y^2 + 2 + \left(\frac{1}{y}\right)^2$$
$$= y^2 + 2 + \frac{1}{y^2}$$
$$79 = y^2 + \frac{1}{y^2}$$

Example 7

If $a - b = 4$ and $a + b = 7$, then $a^2 - b^2 =$

(A) $5\frac{1}{2}$
(B) 11
(C) 28
(D) 29
(E) 56

Choice C is correct.

Use $(a - b)(a + b) = a^2 - b^2$ \qquad (Equation 1)
$$a - b = 4$$
$$a + b = 7$$
$$(a - b)(a + b) = 28 = a^2 - b^2$$

Example 8

If $x^2 - y^2 = 66$ and $x + y = 6$, what is the value of x?

(A) 11
(B) $\frac{21}{2}$
(C) $\frac{17}{2}$
(D) $\frac{13}{2}$
(E) $\frac{11}{2}$

Choice C is correct. Use

$$x^2 - y^2 = (x + y)(x - y) \qquad \text{(Equation 1)}$$
$$(x + y)(x - y) = 66$$

But we already know $x + y = 6$, so

$$6(x - y) = 66$$
$$x - y = 11$$

Now compare your two equations:

$$x + y = 6$$
$$x - y = 11$$

Adding these equations (see Strategy 13) gets you

$$2x = 17$$
$$x = \frac{17}{2}$$

Example 9

What is the least possible value of $\frac{x + y}{xy}$ if

$2 \leq x < y \leq 11$ and x and y are integers?

(A) $\frac{22}{121}$
(B) $\frac{5}{6}$
(C) $\frac{21}{110}$
(D) $\frac{13}{22}$
(E) 1

Choice C is correct.

Use $\frac{x + y}{xy} = \frac{1}{x} + \frac{1}{y}$ \qquad (Equation 4)

$\frac{1}{x} + \frac{1}{y}$ is *least* when x is *greatest* and y is *greatest*.

Since it was given that x and y are integers and that $2 \leq x < y \leq 11$, the greatest value of x is 10 and the greatest value of y is 11.

So the *least* value of $\frac{1}{x} + \frac{1}{y} = \frac{x+y}{xy} = \frac{10+11}{10 \times 11} = \frac{21}{110}$.

Example 10

If $(a + b)^2 = 20$ and $ab = -3$, then $a^2 + b^2 =$

(A) 14
(B) 20
(C) 26
(D) 32
(E) 38

Choice C is correct.

Use $(a + b)^2 = a^2 + 2ab + b^2 = 20$ (Equation 2)

$ab = -3$

So, $2ab = -6$

Substitute $2ab = -6$ in:

$a^2 + 2ab + b^2 = 20$

We get:

$a^2 - 6 + b^2 = 20$
$\quad a^2 + b^2 = 26$

Example 11

If $998 \times 1,002 > 10^6 - x$, x could be

(A) 4 but not 3
(B) 4 but not 5
(C) 5 but not 4
(D) 3 but not 4
(E) 3, 4, or 5

Choice C is correct.

Use $(a + b)(a - b) = a^2 - b^2$ (Equation 1)

$998 \times 1,002 = (1,000 - 2)(1,000 + 2) =$

$\qquad 1,000^2 - 4 =$

$\qquad (10^3)^2 - 4 =$

$\qquad 10^6 - 4$

So $998 \times 1,002 = 10^6 - 4$

but $998 \times 1,002 > 10^6 - x$ (given)

so $10^6 - 4 > 10^6 - x$

and so $-4 > -x$

Multiply this inequality by -1, which *reverses the inequality sign*, and we get:

$-1(-4 > -x)$

$+4 < +x$

Example 12

If $x^2 + y^2 = 2xy$ and $x > 0$ and $y > 0$, then

(A) $x = 0$ only
(B) $y = 0$ only
(C) $x = 1, y = 1$, only
(D) $x > y > 0$
(E) $x = y$

Choice E is correct. In the given equation $x^2 + y^2 = 2xy$, subtract $2xy$ from both sides to get it to look like what you have in Equation 3.

$x2 + y2 - 2xy = 2xy - 2xy = 0$

$\qquad$ So, $x2 - 2xy + y2 = 0$.

We have:

$x^2 - 2xy + y^2 = (x - y)^2 = 0$ (Equation 3)
$x - y = 0$, and thus $x = y$.

Example 13

If $x + y = 7$ and $xy = 4$, then $x^2 + y^2 =$

(A) 16
(B) 28
(C) 41
(D) 49
(E) 65

Choice C is correct. Since we are trying to find $x^2 + y^2$, square $x + y = 7$ to get

$(x + y)^2 = 49$

Use Equation 2 to get
$x^2 + 2xy + y^2 = 49$

Since $xy = 4$, substitute that quantity into the expanded equation.

We get:

$x2 + 8 + y2 = 49$
$x2 + y2 = 41$

MATH STRATEGY 5

Know how to manipulate averages

Almost all problems involving averages can be solved by remembering that

$$\text{Average} = \frac{\text{Sum of the individual quantities or measurements}}{\text{Number of quantities or measurements}}$$

(*Note:* Average is also called Arithmetic Mean.)

Example 1

The average height of three students is 68 inches. If two of the students have heights of 70 inches and 72 inches respectively, then what is the height (in inches) of the third student?

(A) 60
(B) 62
(C) 64
(D) 65
(E) 66

Choice B is correct. Recall that

$$\text{Average} = \frac{\text{Sum of the individual measurements}}{\text{Number of measurements}}$$

Let x = height (in inches) of the third student. Thus,

$$68 = \frac{70 + 72 + x}{3}$$

Multiplying by 3,

$$204 = 70 + 72 + x$$
$$204 = 142 + x$$
$$x = 62 \text{ inches}$$

Example 2

The average of 30 numbers is 65. If one of these numbers is 65, the sum of the remaining numbers is (A) 65×64

(B) 30×64
(C) 29×30
(D) 29×64
(E) 29×65

Choice E is correct.

$$\text{Average} = \frac{\text{sum of numbers}}{30}$$

Call the numbers a, b, c, d, etc.

$$\text{So } 65 = \frac{a + b + c + d + \cdots}{30}$$

Now immediately get rid of the fractional part: Multiply by 30 to get: $65 \times 30 = a + b + c + d + \ldots$

Since we were told *one of the numbers is 65,* let $a = 65$:

$65 \times 30 = 65 + b + c + d + \ldots$
So $65 \times 30 - 65 = b + c + d + \ldots$
$b + c + d + \ldots$ = sum of remaining numbers

Factor:

$$65 \times 30 - 65 = 65(30 - 1) = \text{sum of remaining numbers}$$
$$65 \times 29 = \text{sum of remaining numbers}$$

Examples 3−6

3. The average length of 6 objects is 25 cm. If 5 objects are each 20 cm in length, what is the length of the sixth object in cm?

(A) 55
(B) 50
(C) 45
(D) 40
(E) 35

4. Scores on five tests range from 0 to 100 inclusive. If Don gets 70 on the first test, 76 on the second, and 75 on the third, what is the minimum score Don may get on the fourth test to average 80 on all five tests?

(A) 76
(B) 79
(C) 82
(D) 89
(E) 99

5. Eighteen students attained an average score of 70 on a test, and 12 students on the same test scored an average of 90. What is the average score for all 30 students on the test?

(A) 78
(B) 80
(C) 82
(D) 85
(E) Cannot be determined.

6. The average length of 10 objects is 25 inches. If the average length of 2 of these objects is 20 inches, what is the average length of the remaining 8 objects?

(A) $22\frac{1}{2}$ inches
(B) 24 inches
(C) $26\frac{1}{4}$ inches
(D) 28 inches
(E) Cannot be determined.

Explanatory answers for examples 3−6

3. (B) *Use the formula:*

$$\text{Average} = \frac{\text{Sum of individual items}}{\text{Number of items}}$$

Now call the length of the sixth item, x. Then:

$$25 = \frac{20 + 20 + 20 + 20 + 20 + x}{6}$$

$$\text{or } 25 = \frac{20 \times 5 + x}{6}$$

Multiply by 6:

$$25 \times 6 = 20 \times 5 + x$$
$$150 = 100 + x$$
$$50 = x$$

4. (B) *Use the formula:*

$$\text{Average} = \frac{\text{Sum of scores on tests}}{\text{Number of tests}}$$

Let x be the score on the fourth test and y be the score on the fifth test.

Then:

$$80 = \text{Average} = \frac{70 + 76 + 75 + x + y}{5}$$

The minimum score x Don can get is the *lowest* score he can get. The higher the score y is, the lower the score x can be. The greatest value of y can be 100. So:

$$80 = \frac{70 + 76 + 75 + x + 100}{5}$$

$$80 = \frac{321 + x}{5}$$

Multiply by 5:

$$400 = 321 + x$$
$$79 = x$$

5. (A) *Use the formula:*

$$\text{Average} = \frac{\text{Sum of scores}}{\text{Number of students}}$$

"Eighteen students attained an average of 70 on a test" translates mathematically to:

$$70 = \frac{\text{sum of scores of 18 students}}{18} \quad \boxed{1}$$

Above "18 students" is the number 30.

"Twelve students on the same test scored an average of 90" translates to:

$$90 = \frac{\text{sum of scores of other 12 students}}{12} \quad \boxed{2}$$

Now what you are looking for is the *average score of all 30 students*. That is, you are looking for:

$$\text{Average of 30 students} = \frac{\text{Sum of scores of all 30 students}}{30} \quad \boxed{3}$$

So, if you can find the *sum of scores of all 30 students*, you can find the required average.

Now, the sum of all 30 students = sum of scores of 18 students + sum of scores of other 12 students.

And this can be gotten from $\boxed{1}$ and $\boxed{2}$:

From $\boxed{1}$: $70 \times 18 = $ sum of scores of 18 students

From $\boxed{2}$: $90 \times 12 = $ sum of scores of other 12 students

So adding:

$70 \times 18 + 90 \times 12 = $ sum of scores of 18 students + sum of scores of other 12 students = sum of scores of 30 students

Put all this in $\boxed{3}$:

$$\text{Average of 30 students} = \frac{70 \times 18 + 90 \times 12}{30}$$

$$= \frac{7\cancel{0} \times 18 + 9\cancel{0} \times 12}{3\cancel{0}}$$

$$= \frac{7 \times 18 + 9 \times 12}{3}$$

$$= \frac{7 \times \overset{6}{\cancel{18}} + \overset{3}{\cancel{9}} \times 12}{\cancel{3}}$$

$$= 42 + 36 = 78$$

6. (C) Denote the lengths of the objects by a, b, c, d, etc. Since the average length of 10 objects is given to be 25 inches, establish an equation for the average length:

sum of 10 lengths

$$\text{Average length} = 25 = \frac{a+b+c+d+\cdots+j}{10} \quad \boxed{1}$$

number of objects

The question also says that the average length of 2 of these objects is 20. Let the lengths of two we choose be a and b. So,

lengths of 2 objects

$$\text{Average length of } a \text{ and } b = 20 = \frac{a+b}{2} \quad \boxed{2}$$

number of objects

Now we want to find the average length of the *remaining* objects. There are 8 remaining objects of lengths c, d, e,...j. Call the average of these lengths x, which is what we want to find.

sum of lengths of remaining objects ($a + b$ are not present because only $c + d + \cdots + j$ remain)

$$\text{Average length} = x = \frac{c+d+e+\cdots+j}{8}$$

number of remaining objects

Use equations $\boxed{1}$ and $\boxed{2}$:

$$25 = \frac{a+b+c+\dots+j}{10} \quad \boxed{1}$$

$$20 = \frac{a+b}{2} \quad \boxed{2}$$

Now, remember, we want to find the value of x:

$$x = \frac{c+d+e+\cdots+j}{8}$$

Multiply Equation $\boxed{1}$ by 10 to get rid of the denominator. We get:

$$25 \times 10 = 250 = a + b + c + \cdots + j$$

Now multiply Equation $\boxed{2}$ by 2 to get rid of the denominator:

$$20 \times 2 = 40 = a + b$$

Subtract these two new equations:

$$250 = a + b + c + \cdots + j$$
$$- [40 = a + b]$$

You get: $210 = c + d + \cdots + j$

Now you just have to divide by 8 to get:

$$\frac{210}{8} = \frac{c + d + \dots + j}{8} = x$$

$$= 26\frac{1}{4}$$

MATH STRATEGY 6

Know How to Manipulate Inequalities

Most problems involving inequalities can be solved by remembering one of the following statements.

If $x > y$, then $x + z > y + z$ | Statement 1 |

If $x > y$ and $w > z$, then $x + w > y + z$ | Statement 2 |

(Note that | Statement 1 | and | Statement 2 | are also true if all the $>$ signs are changed to $<$ signs.)

If $w > 0$ and $x > y$, then $wx > wy$ | Statement 3 |

If $w < 0$ and $x > y$, then $wx < wy$ | Statement 4 |

If $x > y$ and $y > z$, then $x > z$ | Statement 5 |

$x > y$ is the same as $y < x$ | Statement 6 |

$a < x < b$ is the same as both
$a < x$ and $x < b$ | Statement 7 |

If $x > y > 0$ and $w > z > 0$, then
$xw > yz$ | Statement 8 |

If $x > 0$ and $z = x + y$, then $z > y$ | Statement 9 |

If $x < 0$, then $\begin{cases} x^n < 0 \text{ if } n \text{ is odd} & \text{| Statement 10 |} \\ x^n > 0 \text{ if } n \text{ is even} & \text{| Statement 11 |} \end{cases}$

If $xy > 0$, then $x > 0$ and $y > 0$
or $x < 0$ and $y < 0$ | Statement 12 |

If $xy < 0$, then $x > 0$ and $y < 0w$
or $x < 0$ and $y > 0$ | Statement 13 |

Example 1

If $0 < x < 1$, then which of the following must be true?

I. $2x < 2$

II. $x - 1 < 0$

III. $x^2 < x$

(A)   I only

(B)   II only

(C)   I and II only

(D)   II and III only

(E)   I, II, and III

Choice E is correct. We are told that $0 < x < 1$. Using

| Statement 7 |, we have

$$0 < x \qquad \boxed{1}$$
$$x < 1 \qquad \boxed{2}$$

For Item I, we multiply $\boxed{2}$ by 2.

See | Statement 3 |

$$2x < 2$$

Thus, Item I is true.
For Item II, we add -1 to both sides of $\boxed{2}$.

See | Statement 1 | to get

$$x - 1 < 0$$

Thus, Item II is true.

For Item III, we multiply $\boxed{2}$ by x.

See $\boxed{\text{Statement 3}}$ to get

$$x^2 < x$$

Thus, Item III is true.

All items are true, so Choice E is correct.

Example 2

Given that $\dfrac{a}{b}$ is less than 1, $a > 0$, $b > 0$. Which of the following must be greater than 1?

(A) $\dfrac{a}{2b}$

(B) $\dfrac{b}{2a}$

(C) $\dfrac{\sqrt{b}}{a}$

(D) $\dfrac{b}{a}$

(E) $\left(\dfrac{a}{b}\right)^2$

Choice D is correct.

Given: $\dfrac{a}{b} < 1$ $\qquad\qquad$ $\boxed{1}$

$\qquad\quad$ $a > 0$ $\qquad\qquad\qquad$ $\boxed{2}$

$\qquad\quad$ $b > 0$ $\qquad\qquad\qquad$ $\boxed{3}$

See $\boxed{\text{Statement 3}}$ Multiply $\boxed{1}$ by b. We get

$$b\left(\dfrac{a}{b}\right) < b \ (1)$$

$$a < b \qquad\qquad\qquad \boxed{4}$$

Use $\boxed{\text{Statement 3}}$ where $w = \dfrac{1}{a}$. Divide $\boxed{4}$ by a.

We get

$$\dfrac{a}{a} < \dfrac{b}{a}$$

$$1 < \dfrac{b}{a}$$

or

$$\dfrac{b}{a} > 1$$

Example 3

Which combination of the following statements can be used to demonstrate that x is positive?

I. $x > y$

II. $1 < y$

(A) I alone but not II

(B) II alone but not I

(C) I and II taken together but neither taken alone

(D) Both I alone and II alone

(E) Neither I nor II nor both

Choice C is correct. We want to know which of the following

$$x > y \qquad\qquad \boxed{1}$$
$$1 < y \qquad\qquad \boxed{2}$$

is enough information to conclude that

$$x > 0 \qquad\qquad \boxed{3}$$

$\boxed{1}$ alone is not enough to determine $\boxed{3}$ because $0 > x > y$ could be true. (Note: x is greater than y, but they both could be negative.)

$\boxed{2}$ alone is not enough to determine $\boxed{3}$ because we don't know whether x is greater than, less than, or equal to y.

However, if we use $\boxed{1}$ and $\boxed{2}$ together, we can compare the two:

$$1 < y \text{ is the same as } y > 1.$$

Therefore, $x > y$ with $y > 1$ yields $\qquad \boxed{\text{Statement 5}}$

$$x > 1. \qquad\qquad\qquad \boxed{4}$$

Since $1 > 0$ is always true, then from $\boxed{4}$

$$x > 0 \text{ is always true.}$$

Example 4

What are all values of x such that $(x - 7)(x + 3)$ is positive?

(A) $x > 7$

(B) $-7 < x < 3$

(C) $-3 < x < 7$

(D) $x > 7$ or $x < -3$

(E) $x > 3$ or $x < -7$

Choice D is correct.

$$(x - 7)(x + 3) > 0 \text{ when}$$
$$x - 7 > 0 \text{ and } x + 3 > 0 \qquad \boxed{1}$$
$$\text{or} \quad x - 7 < 0 \text{ and } x + 3 < 0 \qquad \boxed{2}$$

$\boxed{\text{Statement 12}}$

From $\boxed{1}$ we have $x > 7$ and $x > -3$ $\qquad \boxed{3}$

Thus $x > 7$ [4]

From [2], we have $x < 7$ and $x < -3$ [5]
Thus $x < -3$ [6]

Example 5

If p and q are nonzero real numbers and if $p^2 + q^3 < 0$ and if $p^3 + q^5 > 0$, which of the following number lines shows the relative positions of p, q, and 0?

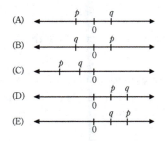

Choice B is correct.

Method 1: Given: $p^2 + q^3 < 0$ [1]
$$p^3 + q^5 > 0$$ [2]

Subtracting p^2 from [1] and q^5 from [2], we have

$$q^3 < -p^2$$ [3]
$$p^3 > -q^5$$ [4]

Since the square of any real number is greater than 0, $p^2 > 0$ and $-p^2 < 0$. [5]

Using | Statement 5 |, combining [3] and [5] we get

$q^3 < -p^2 < 0$ [6]

and get $q^3 < 0$. [7]

Thus, $q < 0$. [8]

From [8], we can say $q^5 < 0$ or $-q^5 > 0$. [9]

Using | Statement 5 |, combining [4] and [9],

$p^3 > -q^5 > 0$ and $p^3 > 0$. Thus $p > 0$. [10]

Using [8] and [10], it is easily seen that Choice B is correct.

Method 2: Use Strategy 6: Know how to manipulate inequalities.

$$\text{Given: } p^2 + q^3 < 0$$ [1]
$$p^3 + q^5 > 0$$ [2]

Since p^2 is always > 0, using this with [1], we know that

$q^3 < 0$ and, therefore, $q < 0$. [3]

If $q^3 < 0$ then $q^5 < 0$. [4]

Using [4] and [2], we know that
$$p^3 > 0, \text{ and therefore } p > 0$$ [5]

Using [3] and [5], only Choice B is correct.

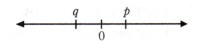

Example 6

Janie is older than Tammy, but she is younger than Lori. Let j, t, and l be the ages in years of Janie, Tammy, and Lori, respectively. Which of the following is true?

(A) $j < t < l$
(B) $t < j < l$
(C) $t < l < j$
(D) $l < j < t$
(E) $l < t < j$

Choice B is correct. *(First, use Strategy 2: Translate English words into mathematical expressions.)* "Janie is older than Tammy, but she is younger than Lori" translates to:

Janie's age $>$ Tammy's age	[1]
Janie's age $<$ Lori's age	[2]
Given: Janie's age $= j$	[3]
Tammy's age $= t$	[4]
Lori's age $= l$	[5]

Substituting [3], [4], and [5] into [1] and [2], we get

$$j > t$$ [6]
$$j < l$$ [7]

Use | Statement 5 |. Reversing [6], we get

$$t < j$$ [8]

Combining [8] and [7], we get

$$t < j < l$$

MATH STRATEGY 7

Use specific numerical examples to prove or disprove your guess

> When you do not want to do a lot of algebra, or when you are unable to prove what you think is the answer, you may want to substitute numbers.

Example 1

The sum of the cubes of any two consecutive positive integers is always

(A) an odd integer
(B) an even integer
(C) the cube of an integer
(D) the square of an integer
(E) the product of an integer and 3

Choice A is correct. Try specific numbers. Call consecutive positive integers 1 and 2.

Sum of cubes:

$$1^3 + 2^3 = 1 + 8 = 9$$

You have now eliminated choices B and C. You are left with choices A, D, and E.

Now try two other consecutive integers: 2 and 3.

$$2^3 + 3^3 = 8 + 27 = 35$$

Choice A is acceptable. Choice D is false. Choice E is false.

Thus, Choice A is the only choice remaining.

Example 2

Jason is now m years old, and Serena is 4 years older than Jason. Which represents Serena's age 6 years ago?

(A) $m + 10$
(B) $m - 10$
(C) $m - 2$
(D) $m - 4$
(E) $4m - 6$

Choice C is correct.

Try a specific number.

Let $m = 10$
Jason is 10 years old.

Serena is 4 years older than Jason, so Serena is 14 years old. Serena's age 6 years ago was 8 years.

Now look for the choice that gives you 8 with $m = 10$.

(A) $m + 10 = 10 + 10 = 20$
(B) $m - 10 = 10 - 10 = 0$
(C) $m - 2 = 10 - 2 = 8$—that's the one

See Math Strategy 2, Example 4 (page 77) for an alternate approach to solving this problem, using a different strategy: *Translate English Words into Mathematical Expressions.*

Example 3

If $x \neq 0$, then $\dfrac{(-3x)^3}{-3x^3} =$

(A) -9
(B) -1
(C) 1
(D) 3
(E) 9

Choice E is correct.

Try a specific number.

Let $x = 1$. Then:

$$\frac{(-3x)^3}{-3x^3} = \frac{(-3(1))^3}{-3(1^3)} = \frac{(-3)^3}{-3} = 9$$

Example 4

If $a = 4b$, then the average of a and b is

(A) $\frac{1}{2}b$

(B) $\frac{3}{2}b$

(C) $\frac{5}{2}b$

(D) $\frac{7}{2}b$

(E) $\frac{9}{2}b$

Choice C is correct.

Try a specific number.

Let $b = 1$. Then $a = 4b = 4$. So the average =

$$\frac{1+4}{2} = \frac{5}{2}.$$

Look at choices where $b = 1$. The only choice that gives $\frac{5}{2}$ is Choice C.

Example 5

The sum of three consecutive even integers is P. Find the sum of the next three consecutive *odd* integers that follow the greatest of the three even integers.

(A) $P + 9$

(B) $P + 15$

(C) $P + 12$

(D) $P + 20$

(E) None of these.

Choice B is correct.

Try specific numbers.
Let the three consecutive even integers be 2, 4, 6.

$$\text{So, } 2 + 4 + 6 = P = 12.$$

The next three consecutive odd integers that follow 6 are:

$$7, 9, 11$$

So the sum of

$$7 + 9 + 11 = 27.$$

Now, where $P = 12$, look for a choice that gives you 27:

(A) $P + 9 = 12 + 9 = 21$—NO

(B) $P + 15 = 12 + 15 = 27$—YES

Example 6

If $3 > a$, which of the following is *not* true?

(A) $3 - 3 > a - 3$

(B) $3 + 3 > a + 3$

(C) $3(3) > a(3)$

(D) $3 - 3 > 3 - a$

(E) $\frac{3}{3} > \frac{a}{3}$

Choice D is correct.

Try specific numbers.
Work backward from Choice E if you wish.

Let $a = 1$.

Choice E:

$$\frac{3}{3} > \frac{a}{3} = \frac{1}{3} \qquad \text{TRUE STATEMENT}$$

Choice D:

$$3 - 3 > 3 - a = 3 - 1, \text{ or } 0 > 2 \quad \text{FALSE STATEMENT}$$

Example 7

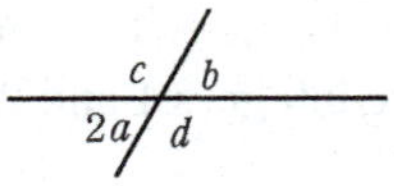

In the figure of intersecting lines above, which of the following is equal to $180 - a$?

(A) $a + d$

(B) $a + 2d$

(C) $c + b$

(D) $b + 2a$

(E) $c + d$

Choice A is correct.

Try a specific number. Let $\boxed{a = 20°}$

Then $2a = 40°$
Be careful now—all of the other angles are now determined, so don't choose any more.

Because vertical angles are equal, $2a = b$, so $\boxed{b = 40°}$

Now $c + b = 180°$, so $c + 40 = 180$ and $\boxed{c = 140°}$

Thus, $\boxed{d = 140°}$ (vertical angles are equal).

Now look at the question:

$$180 - a = 180 - 20 = 160$$

Which is the correct choice?

(A) $a + d = 20 + 140 = 160$—that's the one!

MATH STRATEGY 8

When each choice must be tested, start with choice E and work backward

> If you must check each choice for the correct answer, start with Choice E and work backward. The reason for this is that the test maker of a question *in which each choice must be tested* often puts the correct answer as Choice D or E. The careless student will start testing with Choice A and work downward to Choice E, wasting time. So if you're trying all the choices, start with the last choice, then the next to last choice, etc. See Example 8 for an example of when this strategy should not be used.

Example 1

If p is a positive integer, which *could* be an odd integer?

(A) $2p + 2$
(B) $p^3 - p$
(C) $p^2 + p$
(D) $p^2 - p$
(E) $7p - 3$

Choice E is correct. Start with Choice E first, since you have to *test* out the choices.

Method 1: Try a number for p. Let $p = 1$. Then (starting with Choice E),

$7p - 3 = 7(1) - 3 = 4$. 4 is even, so try another number for p to see whether $7p - 3$ is odd. Let $p = 2$.

$7p - 3 = 7(2) - 3 = 11$. 11 is odd. Therefore, Choice E is correct.

Method 2: Look at Choice E. $7p$ could be even or odd, depending on what p is. If p is even, $7p$ is even. If p is odd, $7p$ is odd. Accordingly, $7p - 3$ is either even or odd. Thus, Choice E is correct.

Note: By using either Method 1 or Method 2, it is not necessary to test the other choices.

Example 2

If $y = x^2 + 3$, then for which value of x is y divisible by 7?

(A) 10
(B) 8
(C) 7
(D) 6
(E) 5

Choice E is correct. Since you must check all of the choices, start with Choice E:

$$y = 5^2 + 3 = 25 + 3 = 28$$
$$28 \text{ is divisible by } 7$$

If you had started with Choice A, you would have had to test four choices instead of one choice before finding the correct answer.

Example 3

Which fraction is greater than $\frac{1}{2}$?

(A) $\frac{4}{9}$

(B) $\frac{17}{35}$

(C) $\frac{6}{13}$

(D) $\frac{12}{25}$

(E) $\frac{8}{15}$

Choice E is correct.

Look at Choice E first.

$$\text{Is } \frac{8}{15} > \frac{1}{2}?$$

Use the cross-multiplication method.

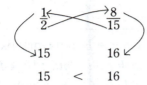

$$15 \quad < \quad 16$$

So, $\frac{1}{2} < \frac{8}{15}$.

You also could have looked at Choice E and said $\frac{8}{16}$ = $\frac{1}{2}$ and realized that $\frac{8}{15} > \frac{1}{2}$ because $\frac{8}{15}$ has a smaller denominator than $\frac{8}{16}$.

Example 4

If n is an even integer, which of the following is an odd integer?

(A) $n^2 - 2$

(B) $n - 4$

(C) $(n - 4)^2$

(D) n^3

(E) $n^2 - n - 1$

Choice E is correct.
Look at Choice E first.

$$n^2 - n - 1$$

$$\text{If } n \text{ is even}$$

$$n^2 \text{ is even}$$

$$n \text{ is even}$$

$$1 \text{ is odd}$$

So, $n^2 - n - 1 = $ even $-$ even $-$ odd $=$ odd.

Example 5

Which of the following is an odd number?

(A) 7×22

(B) $59 - 15$

(C) $55 + 35$

(D) $75 \div 15$

(E) 4^7

Choice D is correct.

Look at Choice E first.

4^7 is even because all positive integral powers of an even number are even.
So now look at Choice D: $\frac{75}{15} = 5$, which is odd.

Example 6

$$\begin{array}{r} 3 \,\#\, 2 \\ \times \quad 8 \\ \hline 28 \,\star\, 6 \end{array}$$

If # and ★ are different digits in the correctly calculated multiplication problem above, then # could be

(A) 1

(B) 2

(C) 3

(D) 4

(E) 6

Choice E is correct.

Try Choice E first.

$$\begin{array}{r} 3 \,\#\, 2 \\ \times \quad 8 \\ \hline 28 \,\star\, 6 \end{array} \qquad \begin{array}{r} 3 \,⑥\, 2 \\ \times \quad 8 \\ \hline 28 \,⑨\, 6 \end{array}$$

9 and 6 are different numbers, so Choice E is correct.

Example 7

Which choice describes a pair of numbers that are *unequal*?

(A) $\frac{1}{6}, \frac{11}{66}$

(B) $3.4, \frac{34}{10}$

(C) $\frac{15}{75}, \frac{1}{5}$

(D) $\frac{3}{8}, 0.375$

(E) $\frac{86}{24}, \frac{42}{10}$

Choice E is correct.

Look at Choice E first.

$$\frac{86}{24} \qquad ? \qquad \frac{42}{10}$$

Cross multiply:

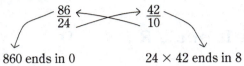

860 ends in 0   24 × 42 ends in 8

Thus, the numbers must be *different* and *unequal*.

When *not* to use this strategy:

If you can spot something in the question that shows you how to solve the problem readily without having to test each choice, there's no need to go through every answer by working backwards.

Example 8

If $|6 - 5y| > 20$, which of the following is a possible value of y?

(A) -3
(B) -1
(C) 1
(D) 3
(E) 5

Choice A is correct.

Instead of plugging in values for y, starting with Choice E, you should realize there will only be one answer listed for which $6 - 5y > 20$. So which choice gives you the largest product for $-5y$? Start by checking the *most negative* choice, or $y = -3$.

This gives you $|6 - 5(-3)| = |6 + 15| = |21|$, which is greater than 20.

MATH STRATEGY 9

Know how to solve problems using the formula R × T = D

Almost every problem involving motion can be solved using the formula

$$R \times T = D$$

or

rate × elapsed time = distance

Example 1

The diagram below shows two paths: Path 1 is 10 miles long, and Path 2 is 12 miles long. If Person X runs along Path 1 at 5 miles per hour and Person Y runs along Path 2 at y miles per hour, and if it takes exactly the same amount of time for both runners to run their whole path, then what is the value of y?

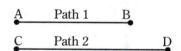

A   Path 1   B

C   Path 2   D

(A) 2
(B) $4\frac{1}{6}$
(C) 6
(D) 20
(E) 24

Choice C is correct. Let T = Time (in hours) for either runner to run the whole path.

Using $R \times T = D$, for Person X, we have

$$\left(\frac{5 \text{ mi}}{\text{hr}}\right)(T \text{ hours}) = 10 \text{ miles}$$

or $5T = 10$ or $\boxed{1}$
        $T = 2$

For Person Y, we have

$$\left(\frac{y \text{ mi}}{\text{hr}}\right)(T \text{ hours}) = 12 \text{ miles}$$

$$\text{or } yT = 12$$

Using $\boxed{1}$ $y(2) = 12$ or $y = 6$.

Example 2

A car traveling at 50 miles per hour for two hours travels the same distance as a car traveling at 20 miles per hour for x hours. What is x?

(A) $\frac{4}{5}$

(B) $\frac{5}{4}$

(C) 5
(D) 2

(E) $\frac{1}{2}$

Choice C is correct.

Use $R \times T = D$. Call the distance both cars travel, D (since distance is the same for both cars).

So we get:

$$50 \times 2 = D = 100 \qquad \boxed{1}$$
$$20 \times x = D = 100 \qquad \boxed{2}$$

Solving $\boxed{2}$ you can see that $x = 5$.

Example 3

John walks at a rate of 4 miles per hour. Sally walks at a rate of 5 miles per hour. If John and Sally both start at the same starting point, how many miles is one person from the other after t hours of walking? (*Note:* Both are walking on the same road in the same direction.)

(A) $\frac{t}{2}$

(B) t
(C) $2t$

(D) $\frac{4}{5}t$

(E) $\frac{5}{4}t$

Choice B is correct.

Draw a diagram:

John (4 mph)   *(t hours)*
D_J

Sally (5 mph)   *(t hours)*
D_S

Let D_J be the distance that John walks in t hours. Let D_S be the distance that Sally walks in t hours.

Then, using $R \times t = D$,

for John: $4 \times t = D_J$
for Sally: $5 \times t = D_S$

The distance between Sally and John after t hours of walking is:

$$D_S - D_J = 5t - 4t = t$$

Example 4

A man rode a bicycle a straight distance at a speed of 10 miles per hour and came back the same distance at a speed of 20 miles per hour. What was the man's total number of miles for the trip back and forth, if his total traveling time was 1 hour?

(A) 15

(B) $7\frac{1}{2}$

(C) $6\frac{1}{3}$

(D) $6\frac{2}{3}$

(E) $13\frac{1}{3}$

Choice E is correct.

Always use $R \times T = D$ (Rate $\times$ Time = Distance) in problems like this. Call the first distance D and the time for the first part T_1. Since he rode at 10 mph:

$$10 \times T_1 = D \qquad \boxed{1}$$

Now for the trip back. He rode at 20 mph. Call the time it took to go back T_2. Since he came back the *same* distance, we can call that distance D also. So for the trip back using $R \times T = D$, we get:

$$20 \times T_2 = D \qquad \boxed{2}$$

Since it was given that the total traveling time was 1 hour, the total traveling time is:

$$T_1 + T_2 = 1$$

Now here's the trick: Let's make use of the fact that $T_1 + T_2 = 1$. Dividing Equation $\boxed{1}$ by 10, we get:

$$T_1 = \frac{D}{10}$$

Dividing $\boxed{2}$ by 20, we get:

$$T_2 = \frac{D}{20}$$

Now add $T_1 + T_2$ and we get:

$$T_1 + T_2 = 1 = \frac{D}{10} + \frac{D}{20}$$

Factor D:

$$1 = D\left(\frac{1}{10} + \frac{1}{20}\right)$$

Add $\frac{1}{10} + \frac{1}{20}$. Remember the fast way of adding fractions?

$$\frac{1}{10} \begin{matrix} \\ + \\ \end{matrix} \frac{1}{20} = \frac{20 + 10}{20 \times 10} = \frac{30}{200}$$

So:

$$1 = (D)\frac{30}{200}$$

Multiply by 200 and divide by 30 and we get:

$$\frac{200}{30} = D; D = 6\frac{2}{3}$$

Don't forget, we're looking for 2D: $2D = 13\frac{1}{3}$

Example 5

What is the average rate of a bicycle traveling at 10 mph a distance of 5 miles and at 20 mph the same distance?

(A) 15 mph

(B) 20 mph

(C) $12\frac{1}{2}$ mph

(D) $13\frac{1}{3}$ mph

(E) 16 mph

Choice D is correct.

Ask yourself, what does *average rate* mean? It *does not* mean the average of the rates! If you thought it did, you would have selected Choice A as the answer (averaging 10 and 20 to get 15)—the "lure" choice.

Average is a word that *modifies* the word *rate* in this case. So you must define the word *rate* first, before you do anything with averaging. Since Rate × Time = Distance,

$$\text{Rate} = \frac{\text{Distance}}{\text{Time}}$$

Then *average* rate must be:

$$\text{Average rate} = \frac{\text{total distance}}{\text{total time}}$$

The *total distance* is the distance covered on the whole trip, which is $5 + 5 = 10$ miles.

The *total time* is the time traveled the first 5 miles at 10 mph added to the time the bicycle traveled the next 5 miles at 20 mph.

Let t_1 be the time the bicycle traveled the first 5 miles.

Let t_2 be the time the bicycle traveled the next 5 miles.

Then the *total time* $= t_1 + t_2$.

Since $R \times T = D$,

$$\text{for the first 5 miles: } 10 \times t_1 = 5$$

$$\text{for the next 5 miles: } 20 \times t_2 = 5$$

Finding t_1: $t_1 = \frac{5}{10}$

Finding t_2: $t_2 = \frac{5}{20}$

So, $t_1 + t_2 = \frac{5}{10} + \frac{5}{20}$

$$= \frac{1}{2} + \frac{1}{4} \quad \text{(remembering how to quickly}$$

$$= \frac{4 + 2}{8} \quad \text{add fractions)}$$

$$= \frac{6}{8} = \frac{3}{4}$$

$$\text{Average rate} = \frac{\text{total distance}}{\text{total time}}$$

$$= \frac{5 + 5}{\frac{3}{4}}$$

$$= (5 + 5) \times \frac{4}{3}$$

$$= 10 \times \frac{4}{3} = \frac{40}{3} = 13\frac{1}{3} \textit{ (Answer)}$$

Here's a formula you can memorize:
If a vehicle travels a certain distance at a mph and travels the same distance at b mph, the *average rate* is

$$\frac{2ab}{a + b}.$$

Try doing the problem using this formula:

$$\frac{2ab}{a + b} = \frac{2 \times (10) \times (20)}{10 + 20} = \frac{400}{30} = 13\frac{1}{3}$$

Caution: Use this formula only when you are looking for *average rate, and when the distance is the same for both speeds.*

MATH STRATEGY 10

Know how to use units of time, distance, area, or volume to find or check your answer

By knowing what the units in your answer must be, you will often have an easier time finding or checking your answer. A very helpful thing to do is to treat the units of time or space as variables (like x or y). Thus, you should substitute, multiply, or divide these units as if they were ordinary variables. The following examples illustrate this idea.

Example 1

What is the distance in miles covered by a car that traveled at 50 miles per hour for 5 hours?

(A) 10
(B) 45
(C) 55
(D) 200
(E) 250

Choice E is correct. Although this is an easy $R \times T = D$ problem, it illustrates this strategy very well.

Recall that

$$\text{rate} \times \text{time} = \text{distance}$$

$$\left(\frac{50 \text{ mi}}{\text{hr}}\right)(5 \text{ hours}) = \text{distance}$$

Notice that when I substituted into $R \times T = D$, *I kept the units of rate and time* (miles/hour and hours). Now I will *treat these units as if they were ordinary variables.* Thus,

$$\text{distance} = \left(\frac{50 \text{ mi}}{\text{hr}}\right)(5 \text{ hours})$$

I have canceled the variable "hour(s)" from the numerator and denominator of the right side of the equation. Hence,

$$\text{distance} = 250 \text{ miles}$$

The distance has units of "miles," as I would expect. In fact, if the units in my answer had been "miles/hour" or "hours," then I would have been in error.

Thus, *the general procedure* for problems using this strategy is:

Step 1. Keep the units given in the question.

Step 2. Treat the units as ordinary variables.

Step 3. Make sure the answer has units that you would expect.

Example 2

How many inches is equivalent to 2 yards, 2 feet, and 7 inches?

(A) 11
(B) 37
(C) 55
(D) 81
(E) 103

Choice E is correct.

Remember that

$$1 \text{ yard } = 3 \text{ feet} \qquad \boxed{1}$$

$$1 \text{ foot } = 12 \text{ inches} \qquad \boxed{2}$$

Treat the units of length as variables! Divide $\boxed{1}$ by 1 yard, and $\boxed{2}$ by 1 foot, to get

$$1 = \frac{3 \text{ feet}}{1 \text{ yard}} \qquad \boxed{3}$$

$$1 = \frac{12 \text{ inches}}{1 \text{ foot}} \qquad \boxed{4}$$

We can multiply any expression by 1 and get the same value. Thus, 2 yards + 2 feet + 7 inches =

$$(2 \text{ yards})(1)(1) + (2 \text{ feet})(1) + 7 \text{ inches} \qquad \boxed{5}$$

Substituting $\boxed{3}$ and $\boxed{4}$ into $\boxed{5}$, 2 yards + 2 feet + 7 inches

$$= 2\,\text{yards}\left(\frac{3\,\text{feet}}{\text{yard}}\right)\left(\frac{12\,\text{inches}}{\text{foot}}\right) + 2\,\text{feet}\left(\frac{12\,\text{inches}}{\text{foot}}\right) + 7\,\text{inches}$$

$$= 72\ \text{inches} + 24\ \text{inches} + 7\ \text{inches}$$

$$= 103\ \text{inches}$$

Notice that the answer is in "inches," as I expected. If the answer had come out in "yards" or "feet," then I would have been in error.

Example 3

A car wash cleans x cars per hour, for y hours, at z dollars per car. How much money in *cents* does the car wash receive?

(A) $\dfrac{xy}{100z}$

(B) $\dfrac{xyz}{100}$

(C) $100xyz$

(D) $\dfrac{100x}{yz}$

(E) $\dfrac{yz}{100x}$

Choice C is correct.

Use units:

$$\left(\frac{x\,\text{cars}}{1\,\text{hour}}\right)(y\ \text{hours})\left(\frac{z\,\text{dollar}}{\text{car}}\right) = xyz\ \text{dollars}$$

Since there are 100 cents to a dollar, we multiply $\boxed{1}$ by 100. We get $100xyz$ cents.

Example 4

There are 3 feet in a yard and 12 inches in a foot. How many yards are there altogether in 1 yard, 1 foot, and 1 inch?

(A) $1\dfrac{1}{3}$

(B) $1\dfrac{13}{36}$

(C) $1\dfrac{11}{18}$

(D) $2\dfrac{5}{12}$

(E) $4\dfrac{1}{12}$

Choice B is correct. **Know how to work with units.**

Given: 3 feet = 1 yard
12 inches = 1 foot

Thus,

$$1\ \text{yard} + 1\ \text{foot} + 1\ \text{inch} =$$

$$1\,\text{yard} + 1\,\text{foot}\left(\frac{1\,\text{yard}}{3\,\text{feet}}\right) + 1\,\text{inch}\left(\frac{1\,\text{foot}}{12\,\text{inches}}\right)\times\left(\frac{1\,\text{yard}}{3\,\text{feet}}\right) =$$

$$\left(1 + \frac{1}{3} + \frac{1}{36}\right)\text{yards} \qquad =$$

$$\left(1 + \frac{12}{36} + \frac{1}{36}\right)\text{yards} \qquad =$$

$$1\frac{13}{36}\ \text{yards}$$

MATH STRATEGY 11

Use new definitions and functions carefully

> Some SAT questions use new symbols, functions, or definitions that were created in the question. At first glance, these questions may seem difficult because you are not familiar with the new symbol, function, or definition. *However, most of these questions can be solved through simple substitution or application of a simple definition.*

Example 1

If the symbol ϕ is defined by the equation

$$a \phi b = a - b - ab$$

for all a and b, then $\left(-\frac{1}{3}\right) \phi (-3) =$

(A) $\frac{5}{3}$

(B) $\frac{11}{3}$

(C) $-\frac{13}{3}$

(D) -4

(E) -5

Choice A is correct. All that is required is substitution:

$$a \phi b = a - b - ab$$

$$\left(-\frac{1}{3}\right) \phi (-3)$$

Substitute $-\frac{1}{3}$ for a and -3 for b in $a - b - ab$:

$$\left(-\frac{1}{3}\right) \phi (-3) = -\frac{1}{3} - (-3) - \left(-\frac{1}{3}\right)(-3)$$

$$= -\frac{1}{3} + 3 - 1$$

$$= 2 - \frac{1}{3}$$

$$= \frac{5}{3} \quad (Answer)$$

Example 2

Let $\boxed{x} = \begin{cases} \frac{5}{2}(x+1) & \text{if } x \text{ is an odd integer} \\ \frac{5}{2}x & \text{if } x \text{ is an even integer} \end{cases}$

Find $\boxed{2y}$, where y is an integer.

(A) $\frac{5y}{2}$

(B) $5y$

(C) $\frac{5}{2}y + 1$

(D) $5y + \frac{5}{2}$

(E) $5y + 5$

Choice B is correct. All we have to do is substitute $2y$ into the definition of $\boxed{x}$. In order to know which definition of $\boxed{x}$ to use, we want to know if $2y$ is even. Since y is an integer, then $2y$ is an even integer. Thus,

$$\boxed{2y} = \frac{5}{2}(2y)$$

or $\boxed{2y} = 5y$ (*Answer*)

Example 3

As in the previous Example 1, ϕ is defined as

$$a \phi b = a - b - ab$$

If $a \phi 3 = 6$, $a =$

(A) $\frac{9}{2}$

(B) $\frac{9}{4}$

(C) $-\frac{9}{4}$

(D) $-\frac{4}{9}$

(E) $-\frac{9}{2}$

Choice E is correct.

$$a \phi b = a - b - ab$$

$$a \phi 3 = 6$$

Substitute a for a, 3 for b:
$$a \phi 3 = a - 3 - a(3) = 6$$
$$= a - 3 - 3a = 6$$
$$= -2a - 3 = 6$$
$$2a = -9$$
$$a = -\frac{9}{2}$$

Example 4

The symbol $\left(\, x \,\right)$ is defined as the greatest integer less than or equal to x.

$\left(\, \text{-3.4} \,\right) + \left(\, 21 \,\right) =$

(A) 16
(B) 16.6
(C) 17
(D) 17.6
(E) 18

Choice C is correct.

$\left(\, \text{-3.4} \,\right)$ is defined as the *greatest integer less than or equal to* -3.4. This is -4, since $-4 < -3.4$.

$\left(\, 21 \,\right)$ is defined as the *greatest integer less than or equal to* 21. That is just 21, since $21 = 21$.

Thus, $-4 + 21 = 17$.

Example 5

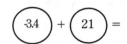 is defined as $xz - yt$

$\begin{pmatrix} 2 & 1 \\ 1 & 1 \end{pmatrix} =$

(A) $\begin{pmatrix} 1 & 1 \\ 1 & 1 \end{pmatrix}$

(B) $\begin{pmatrix} 3 & 2 \\ 2 & 1 \end{pmatrix}$

(C) $\begin{pmatrix} 4 & 3 \\ 2 & 1 \end{pmatrix}$

(D) $\begin{pmatrix} 5 & 4 \\ 4 & 2 \end{pmatrix}$

(E) $\begin{pmatrix} 3 & 1 \\ 1 & 2 \end{pmatrix}$

Choice E is correct.

$\begin{pmatrix} x & y \\ z & t \end{pmatrix} = xz - yt; \begin{pmatrix} 2 & 1 \\ 1 & 1 \end{pmatrix} = ?$

Substituting 2 for x, 1 for z, 1 for y, and 1 for t,

$\begin{pmatrix} 2 & 1 \\ 1 & 1 \end{pmatrix} = (2)(1) - (1)(1)$
$= 1$

Now work from Choice E:

(E) $\begin{pmatrix} 3 & 1 \\ 1 & 2 \end{pmatrix} = xz - yt = (3)(1) - (1)(2)$
$= 3 - 2 = 1$

Example 6

If for all numbers a, b, c, the operation $\bullet$ is defined as
$$a \bullet b = ab - a$$
then
$$a \bullet (b \bullet c) =$$

(A) $a(bc - b - 1)$
(B) $a(bc + b + 1)$
(C) $a(bc - c - b - 1)$
(D) $a(bc - b + 1)$
(E) $a(b - a + c)$

Choice A is correct.
$$a \bullet b = ab - a$$
$$a \bullet (b \bullet c) = ?$$

Find $(b \bullet c)$ first. Use substitution:
$$a \bullet b = ab - a$$
$$\uparrow \quad \uparrow$$
$$b \bullet c$$

Substitute b for a and c for b:
$$b \bullet c = b(c) - b$$

Now, $a \bullet (b \bullet c) = a \bullet (bc - b)$

Use definition $a \bullet b = ab - a$

Substitute a for a and $bc - b$ for b:
$$a \bullet b = ab - a$$
$$a \bullet (bc - b) = a(bc - b) - a$$
$$= abc - ab - a$$
$$= a(bc - b - 1)$$

MATH STRATEGY 12

Try not to make tedious calculations, since there is usually an easier way

In many of the examples given in these strategies, it has been explicitly stated that one should not calculate complicated quantities. In some of the examples, we have demonstrated a fast and a slow way of solving the same problem. On the actual exam, if you find that your solution to a problem involves a tedious and complicated method, then you are probably doing the problem in a long, hard way.* Almost always, there will be an easier way.

Examples 5 and 6 can also be solved with the aid of a calculator and some with the aid of a calculator allowing for exponential calculations. However, to illustrate the effectiveness of Math Strategy 12, we did not use the calculator method of solving these examples.

Example 1

What is the value of $2^1 + 2^2 + 2^3 + 2^4 + 2^5 + 2^6 + 2^7 + 2^8 + 2^9$?

(A) $2^{11} - 2$
(B) 2^{10}
(C) $2^{10} - 2$
(D) $2^{10} - 4$
(E) $2^{10} - 8$

Choice C is correct.

Let $x = 2^1 + 2^2 + 2^3 + 2^4 + 2^5 + 2^6 + 2^7 + 2^8 + 2^9$ $\boxed{1}$

Now multiply $\boxed{1}$ by 2:

$2x = 2(2^1 + 2^2 + 2^3 + 2^4 + 2^5 + 2^6 + 2^7 + 2^8 + 2^9)$

Thus,

$2x = 2^2 + 2^3 + 2^4 + 2^5 + 2^6 + 2^7 + 2^8 + 2^9 + 2^{10}$ $\boxed{2}$

Subtracting $\boxed{1}$ from $\boxed{2}$, we get

$2x - x = x = 2^{10} - 2^1 = 2^{10} - 2$

Example 2

If $16r - 24q = 2$, then $2r - 3q =$

(A) $\frac{1}{8}$
(B) $\frac{1}{4}$
(C) $\frac{1}{2}$
(D) 2
(E) 4

Choice B is correct.

Divide by 8:

$$\frac{16r - 24q}{8} = \frac{2}{8}$$
$$2r - 3q = \frac{1}{4}$$

Example 3

If $(a^2 + a)^3 = x(a + 1)^3$, where $a + 1 \neq 0$, then $x =$

(A) a
(B) a^2
(C) a^3
(D) $\dfrac{a + 1}{a}$
(E) $\dfrac{a}{a + 1}$

* Many times, you can DIVIDE, MULTIPLY, ADD, SUBTRACT, or FACTOR to simplify.

Choice C is correct.

Isolate x first:

$$x = \frac{(a^2 + a)^3}{(a + 1)^3}$$

Now use the fact that $\left(\frac{x^3}{y^3}\right) = \left(\frac{x}{y}\right)^3$:

$$\frac{(a^2 + a)^3}{(a + 1)^3} = \left(\frac{a^2 + a}{a + 1}\right)^3$$

Now factor $a^2 + a = a(a + 1)$

So:

$$\left(\frac{a^2 + a}{a + 1}\right)^3 = \left[\frac{a(a + 1)}{a + 1}\right]^3$$
$$= \left[\frac{a\cancel{(a+1)}}{\cancel{a+1}}\right]^3$$
$$= a^3$$

Example 4

If $\dfrac{p + 1}{r + 1} = 1$ and p, r are nonzero, and p is not equal to -1, and r is not equal to -1, then

(A) $2 > \frac{p}{r} > 1$ always

(B) $\frac{p}{r} < 1$ always

(C) $\frac{p}{r} = 1$ always

(D) $\frac{p}{r}$ can be greater than 2

(E) $\frac{p}{r} = 2$ always

Choice C is correct.

Get rid of the fraction. <u>Multiply</u> both sides of the equation

$$\frac{p + 1}{r + 1} = 1 \text{ by } r + 1$$
$$\left(\frac{p + 1}{\cancel{r+1}}\right)\cancel{r+1} = r + 1$$
$$p + 1 = r + 1$$

Cancel the 1s:

$$p = r$$

So:

$$\frac{p}{r} = 1$$

Example 5

$$\frac{4}{250} =$$

(A) 0.16

(B) 0.016

(C) 0.0016

(D) 0.00125

(E) 0.000125

Choice B is correct.

Don't divide 4 into 250! Multiply:

$$\frac{4}{250} \times \frac{4}{4} = \frac{16}{1,000}$$

Now $\dfrac{16}{100} = .16$, so $\dfrac{16}{1,000} = .016$.

Example 6

$$(3 \times 4^{14}) - 4^{13} =$$

(A) 4

(B) 12

(C) 2×4^{13}

(D) 3×4^{13}

(E) 11×4^{13}

Choice E is correct.

Factor 4^{13} from

$(3 \times 4^{14}) - 4^{13}$

We get $4^{13}[(3 \times 4^1) - 1]$

or $4^{13}(12 - 1) = 4^{13}(11)$

You will see more of the technique of dividing, multiplying, adding, and subtracting in the next strategy, Math Strategy 13.

MATH STRATEGY 13

Know how to find unknown expressions by adding, subtracting, multiplying, or dividing equations or expressions

> When you want to calculate composite quantities like $x + 3y$ or $m - n$, often you can do it by adding, subtracting, multiplying, or dividing the right equations or expressions.

Example 1

If $4x + 5y = 10$ and $x + 3y = 8$, then $\dfrac{5x + 8y}{3} =$

(A) 18
(B) 15
(C) 12
(D) 9
(E) 6

Choice E is correct. Don't solve for x, then for y.

Try to get the quantity $\dfrac{5x + 8y}{3}$ by adding or subtracting the equations. In this case, *add* equations.

$$
\begin{array}{r}
4x + 5y = 10 \\
+\ \ x + 3y = \ 8 \\
\hline
5x + 8y = 18
\end{array}
$$

Now divide by 3:

$\dfrac{5x + 8y}{3} = \dfrac{18}{3} = 6$ (*Answer*)

Example 2

If $25x + 8y = 149$ and $16x + 3y = 89$, then $\dfrac{9x + 5y}{5} =$

(A) 12
(B) 15
(C) 30
(D) 45
(E) 60

Choice A is correct.

We are told

$$25x + 8y = 149 \qquad \boxed{1}$$
$$16x + 3y = \ \ 89 \qquad \boxed{2}$$

The long way to do this problem is to solve $\boxed{1}$ and $\boxed{2}$ for x and y, and then substitute these values into

$$\frac{9x + 5y}{5}$$

The fast way to do this problem is to <u>subtract</u> $\boxed{2}$ from $\boxed{1}$ and get

$$9x + 5y = 60$$
$$\boxed{3}$$

Now all we have to do is to divide $\boxed{3}$ by 5:

$$\frac{9x + 5y}{5} = 12 \quad (\textit{Answer})$$

Example 3

If $21x + 39y = 18$, then $7x + 13y =$

(A) 3
(B) 6
(C) 7
(D) 9
(E) It cannot be determined from the information given.

Choice B is correct. We are given

$$21x + 39y = 18 \qquad \boxed{1}$$

Divide $\boxed{1}$ by 3:

$$7x + 13y = 6 \ (\textit{Answer})$$

Example 4

If $x + 2y = 4$, then $5x + 10y - 8 =$

(A) 10
(B) 12
(C) -10
(D) -12
(E) 0

Choice B is correct.

Multiply $x + 2y = 4$ by 5 to get:

$$5x + 10y = 20$$

Now subtract 8:

$$5x + 10y - 8 = 20 - 8$$
$$= 12$$

Example 5

If $6x^5 = y^2$ and $x = \frac{1}{y}$, then $y =$

(A) x^6

(B) $\frac{x^5}{6}$

(C) $6x^6$

(D) $\frac{6x^5}{5}$

(E) $\frac{x^5}{5}$

Choice C is correct.

Multiply $6x^5 = y^2$ by $x = \frac{1}{y}$ to get:

$$6x^6 = y^2 \times \frac{1}{y} = y$$

Example 6

If $y^8 = 4$ and $y^7 = \frac{3}{x}$, what is the value of y in terms of x?

(A) $\frac{4x}{3}$

(B) $\frac{3x}{4}$

(C) $\frac{4}{x}$

(D) $\frac{x}{4}$

(E) $\frac{12}{x}$

Choice A is correct.

Don't solve for the *value* of y first, by finding $y = 4^{\frac{1}{8}}$.

Just divide the two equations:

$y^8 = 4$ by $y^7 = \frac{3}{x}$

We get

$$\frac{y^8}{y^7} = \frac{4}{\left(\frac{3}{x}\right)}$$

So $y = \dfrac{4}{\left(\frac{3}{x}\right)}$

and so $y = \frac{4x}{3}$ (*Answer*)

Example 7

If $x > 0$, $y > 0$ and $x^2 = 27$ and $y^2 = 3$, then $\frac{x^3}{y^3} =$

(A) 9
(B) 27
(C) 36
(D) 48
(E) 54

Choice B is correct.

Divide: $\dfrac{x^2}{y^2} = \dfrac{27}{3} = 9$

Take square root: $\frac{x}{y} = 3$

So $\left(\frac{x}{y}\right)^3 = \frac{x^3}{y^3} = 3^3 = 27$

Example 8

If $\frac{m}{n} = \frac{3}{8}$ and $\frac{m}{q} = \frac{4}{7}$, then $\frac{n}{q} =$

(A) $\frac{12}{15}$

(B) $\frac{12}{56}$

(C) $\frac{56}{12}$

(D) $\frac{32}{21}$

(E) $\frac{21}{32}$

Choice D is correct.

First get rid of fractions!

Cross-multiply $\frac{m}{n} = \frac{3}{8}$ to get $8m = 3n$.

Now cross-multiply $\frac{m}{q} = \frac{4}{7}$ to get $7m = 4q$. $\boxed{2}$

Now divide Equations $\boxed{1}$ and $\boxed{2}$:

$$\frac{8m}{7m} = \frac{3n}{4q} \qquad \boxed{3}$$

The m's cancel and we get:

$$\frac{8}{7} = \frac{3n}{4q} \qquad \boxed{4}$$

Multiply Equation $\boxed{4}$ by 4 and divide by 3 to get

$$\frac{8 \times 4}{7 \times 3} = \frac{n}{q}$$

$$\text{Thus } \frac{n}{q} = \frac{32}{21}.$$

Example 9

If $\dfrac{a + b + c + d}{4} = 20$

And $\dfrac{b + c + d}{3} = 10$

Then $a =$

(A)   50
(B)   60
(C)   70
(D)   80
(E)   90

Choice A is correct.

We have

$$\frac{a + b + c + d}{4} = 20 \qquad \boxed{1}$$

$$\frac{b + c + d}{3} = 10 \qquad \boxed{2}$$

Multiply Equation $\boxed{1}$ by 4:

We get: $a + b + c + d = 80$ $\boxed{3}$

Now multiply Equation $\boxed{2}$ by 3:

We get: $b + c + d = 30$ $\boxed{4}$

Now subtract Equation $\boxed{4}$ from Equation $\boxed{3}$:

$$a + b + c + d = 80 \qquad \boxed{3}$$
$$- \ (b + c + d = 30) \qquad \boxed{4}$$
$$\overline{}$$
$$\text{We get } a = 50.$$

Example 10

If $y + 2q = 15$, $q + 2p = 5$, and $p + 2y = 7$, then $p + q + y =$

(A)   81
(B)   45
(C)   27
(D)   18
(E)   9

Choice E is correct. There's no need to solve for each variable. Just *add* the equations and divide by 3! To do this, write one equation below the other. Be sure to line up the common variables.

$$
\begin{aligned}
y + 2q &= 15 \\
q + 2p &= 5 \\
+ \ 2y + p &= 7 \\
\hline
3y + 3q + 3p &= 27
\end{aligned}
$$

$$y + 2q + q + 2p + p + 2y = 27$$
$$3y + 3q + 3p = 27$$

Factor by 3:

$$3(y + q + p) = 27$$

So

$$p + q + y = 9$$

Example 11

If $x > 0$, and $xy = 2$, $yz = 5$, and $xz = 10$, then $xyz =$

(A)   10
(B)   17
(C)   50
(D)   100
(E)   200

Choice A is correct. Since we are dealing with multiplication in all of the equations, *multiply* the expressions xy, yz, and xz.

We get:
$(xy)(yz)(xz) = 2 \times 5 \times 10 = 100$

This becomes
$x^2 y^2 z^2 = 100$

This is the same as
$(xyz)^2 = 100$

Take the square root of both sides to get
$xyz = 10$

MATH STRATEGY 14

Draw or extend lines in a diagram to make a problem easier; label unknown quantities

Remember when you took geometry in your early years in high school and the teacher drew a perpendicular line from the top of the triangle to the base of the triangle to prove that "if two sides of a triangle are equal, the base angles are equal"? By drawing this line, the teacher was able to prove the theorem.

Unfortunately, the teacher did not say that whenever you draw a line in a diagram, you usually get more information to work with. If the teacher had said this, you would then use the strategy of drawing lines in diagrams to get more information and results. This strategy is a very powerful one and is used in many questions on tests and in figuring out many geometric problems.

When you see a diagram, be curious as to what lines you can draw to get more information to solve a problem. Also, label lines, angles, etc.

Example 1

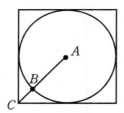

The circle with center A and radius AB is inscribed in the square above. AB is extended to C. What is the ratio of AB to AC?

(A) $\sqrt{2}$

(B) $\dfrac{\sqrt{2}}{4}$

(C) $\dfrac{\sqrt{2}-1}{2}$

(D) $\dfrac{\sqrt{2}}{2}$

(E) None of these.

Choice D is correct. Always draw or extend lines to get more information. Also label unknown lengths, angles, or arcs with letters.

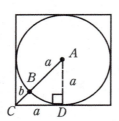

Label $AB = a$ and $BC = b$.

Draw perpendicular AD. Note it is just the radius, a. CD also $= a$, because each side of the square is length $2a$ (the diameter) and CD is $\frac{1}{2}$ the side of the square.

We want to find $\dfrac{AB}{AC} = \dfrac{a}{a+b}$

Now $\triangle ADC$ is an isosceles right triangle, so $AD = CD = a$.

By the Pythagorean Theorem,
$a^2 + a^2 = (a + b)^2$ where $a + b$ is the hypotenuse of a right triangle.

We get: $2a^2 = (a + b)^2$
Divide by $(a + b)^2$:

$$\frac{2a^2}{(a+b)^2} = 1$$

Divide by 2:

$$\frac{a^2}{(a+b)^2} = \frac{1}{2}$$

Take square roots of both sides:

$$\frac{a}{(a+b)} = \frac{1}{\sqrt{2}} =$$

$$= \frac{1}{\sqrt{2}}\left(\frac{\sqrt{2}}{\sqrt{2}}\right)$$

$$= \frac{\sqrt{2}}{2} \quad (Answer)$$

Example 2

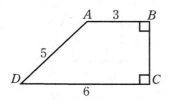

What is the perimeter of the above figure if B and C are right angles?

(A) 14

(B) 16

(C) 18

(D) 20

(E) Cannot be determined.

Choice C is correct.

Draw perpendicular AE. Label side $BC = h$. You can see that $AE = h$.

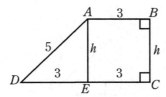

$ABCE$ is a rectangle, so $CE = 3$. This makes $ED = 3$ since the whole $DC = 6$. Now use the Pythagorean Theorem for triangle AED:

$$h^2 + 3^2 = 5^2$$
$$h^2 = 5^2 - 3^2$$
$$h^2 = 25 - 9$$
$$h^2 = 16$$
$$h = 4$$

So the perimeter is $3 + h + 6 + 5 = 3 + 4 + 6 + 5 = 18$. (*Answer*)

Example 3

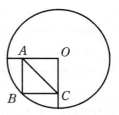

In the figure above, O is the center of a circle with a radius of 6, and $AOCB$ is a square. If point B is on the circumference of the circle, the length of $AC =$

(A) $6\sqrt{2}$

(B) $3\sqrt{2}$

(C) 3

(D) 6

(E) $6\sqrt{3}$

Choice D is correct.

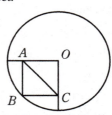

This is tricky if not impossible if you don't draw OB. So draw OB:

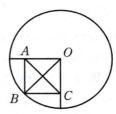

Since $AOCB$ is a square, $OB = AC$; and since $OB =$ radius $= 6$, $AC = 6$.

Example 4

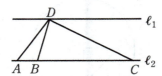

Lines ℓ_1 and ℓ_2 are parallel. $AB = \frac{1}{3}AC$.

$$\frac{\text{The area of triangle } ABD}{\text{The area of triangle } DBC} =$$

(A) $\frac{1}{4}$

(B) $\frac{1}{3}$

(C) $\frac{3}{8}$

(D) $\frac{1}{2}$

(E) Cannot be determined.

Choice D is correct.

$AB = \frac{1}{3}AC$

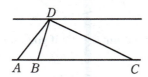

Ask yourself, what is the area of a triangle? It is $\frac{1}{2}$ (height × base). So let's get the heights and the bases of the triangles ABD and DBC. First <u>draw the altitude</u> (call it h).

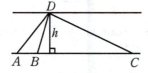

Now label $AB = \frac{1}{3}AC$ (given).

This makes $BC = \frac{2}{3}AC$, since $AB + BC = AC$

Thus the area of $\triangle ABD = \frac{1}{2}h(AB) = \frac{1}{2}h\left(\frac{1}{3}AC\right)$

Area of $\triangle DBC = \frac{1}{2}h(BC) = \frac{1}{2}h\left(\frac{2}{3}AC\right)$

$$\frac{\text{Area of } ABD}{\text{Area of } DBC} = \frac{\frac{1}{2}h\left(\frac{1}{3}AC\right)}{\frac{1}{2}h\left(\frac{2}{3}AC\right)}$$

$$= \frac{\frac{1}{3}}{\frac{2}{3}} = \frac{1}{3} \times \frac{3}{2} = \frac{1}{2}$$

Example 5

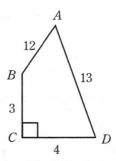

(Note: Figure is not drawn to scale.)

The area of the above figure $ABCD$

(A) is 36

(B) is 108

(C) is 156

(D) is 1,872

(E) Cannot be determined.

Choice A is correct.

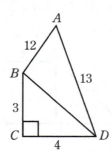

Draw BD. BCD is a 3–4–5 right triangle, so $BD = 5$. Now remember that a 5–12–13 triangle is also a right triangle, so angle ABD is a right angle. The area of triangle BCD is

$\frac{(3 \times 4)}{2} = 6$ and the area of triangle BAD is

$\frac{(5 \times 12)}{2} = 30$, so the total area is 36.

Example 6

In the above figure, two points, *B* and *C*, are placed to the right of point *A* such that $4AB = 3AC$. The value of $\dfrac{BC}{AB}$

(A)   equals $\dfrac{1}{3}$

(B)   equals $\dfrac{2}{3}$

(C)   equals $\dfrac{3}{2}$

(D)   equals 3

(E)   Cannot be determined.

Choice A is correct.

Place *B* and *C* to the right of *A*:

Now label $AB = a$ and $BC = b$:

$$\frac{BC}{AB} = \frac{b}{a} \left(\frac{b}{a} \text{ is what we want to find} \right)$$

We are given $4AB = 3AC$.

So, $4a = 3(a + b)$

Expand: $4a = 3a + 3b$

Subtract $3a$: $a = 3b$

Divide by 3 and a: $\dfrac{1}{3} = \dfrac{b}{a}$

But remember $\dfrac{BC}{AB} = \dfrac{b}{a}$, so $\dfrac{BC}{AB} = \dfrac{1}{3}$

Example 7

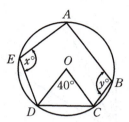

In the figure above, *ABCDE* is a pentagon inscribed in the circle with center at *O*. $\angle DOC = 40°$. What is the value of $x + y$?

(A)   80

(B)   100

(C)   180

(D)   200

(E)   Cannot be determined.

Choice D is correct.

Label degrees in each arc.

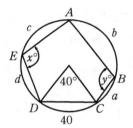

$\angle x$ is measured by $\dfrac{1}{2}$ the arc it cuts.

$$\text{So, } x = \frac{1}{2}(b + a + 40)$$

$$\text{Likewise, } y = \frac{1}{2}(c + d + 40)$$

You want to find $x + y$, so add:

$$x = \frac{1}{2}(b + a + 40)$$
$$+ \; y = \frac{1}{2}(c + d + 40)$$
$$\overline{}$$
$$x + y = \frac{1}{2}(b + a + 40 + c + d + 40)$$

But what is $a + b + c + d + 40$? It is the total number of degrees around the circumference, which is 360.

So, $x + y = \dfrac{1}{2}(\underbrace{b + a + c + d + 40}_{\downarrow} + 40)$

$$= \frac{1}{2}(360 + 40)$$

$$= \frac{1}{2}(400) = 200$$

Example 8

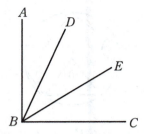

In the above figure, if $\angle ABE = 40°$, $\angle DBC = 60°$, and $\angle ABC = 90°$, what is the measure of $\angle DBE$?

(A) 10°

(B) 20°

(C) 40°

(D) 100°

(E) Cannot be determined.

Choice A is correct.

Label angles first.

$$\text{Now } \angle ABE = 40, \text{ so } a + b = 40$$

$$\angle DBC = 60, \text{ so } b + c = 60$$

$$\angle ABC = 90, \text{ so } a + b + c = 90$$

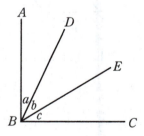

You want to find $\angle DBE$. $\angle DBE = b$, and you want to get the value of b from:

$$a + b = 40 \qquad \boxed{1}$$

$$b + c = 60 \qquad \boxed{2}$$

$$a + b + c = 90 \qquad \boxed{3}$$

$$\text{Add } \boxed{1} \text{ and } \boxed{2}: \quad a + b = 40$$
$$\underline{+\ b + c = 60}$$
$$a + 2b + c = 100$$

$$\text{Subtract } \boxed{3}: \underline{- (a + b + c = 90)}$$
$$b = 10$$

Example 9

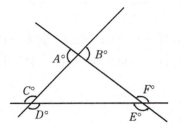

In the figure above, three lines intersect at the points shown. What is the value of $A + B + C + D + E + F$?

(A) 1,080

(B) 720

(C) 540

(D) 360

(E) Cannot be determined.

Choice B is correct.

Relabel, using the fact that *vertical angles are equal.*

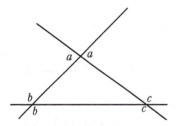

Now use the fact that a straight angle has 180° in it:

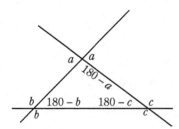

Now use the fact that the sum of the angles of a triangle = 180°:

$$180 - a + 180 - b + 180 - c = 180$$

$$540 - a - b - c = 180$$

$$540 - 180 = a + b + c$$

$$360 = a + b + c$$

Now remember what we are looking to find (the sum):

$$a + a + b + b + c + c = 2a + 2b + 2c$$

But this is just $2(a + b + c) = 2(360) = 720$.

Example 10

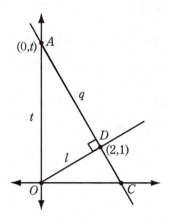

In the figure above, lines l and q are shown to be perpendicular on a coordinate plane. If line l contains the points $(0,0)$ and $(2,1)$, and line q contains the points $(2,1)$ and $(0,t)$, what is the value of t?

(A) -3

(B) -2

(C) 2

(D) 3

(E) 5

Choice E is correct. You want to find the value of t.

Start by drawing line DE, the altitude of $\triangle DOC$. Then label $EC = x$.

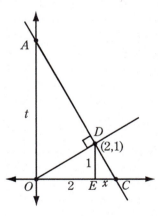

Because the altitude drawn to the hypotenuse of a right triangle forms two similar triangles, $\triangle AOC \sim \triangle DOC \sim \triangle OED$.

This gives $\dfrac{t}{(2 + x)} = \dfrac{2}{1}$ $\boxed{1}$

We need to find the value of x in order to find the value of t.

Look at other similar triangles that involve just the variable x:

$\triangle DEC$ and $\triangle OED$

This gives: $\dfrac{2}{1} = \dfrac{1}{x}$

So, we get: $x = \dfrac{1}{2}$

Plug $x = \dfrac{1}{2}$ into Equation $\boxed{1}$ and we get: $\dfrac{t}{\frac{5}{2}} = \dfrac{2}{1}$

$$t = 5$$

Alternate Method

If the lines are perpendicular, the slope of one line is the negative reciprocal of the other line. **(See Math Refresher 416.)**

Line l contains the points $(0,0)$ and $(2,1)$, so the slope is

$$\frac{(y_2 - y_1)}{(x_2 - x_1)} = \frac{(1 - 0)}{(2 - 0)} = \frac{1}{2}.$$

The slope of line q is $\dfrac{(y_2 - y_1)}{(x_2 - x_1)} = \dfrac{(t - 1)}{(0 - 2)} = \dfrac{(t - 1)}{-2}.$

The slope of line $l = \dfrac{1}{2}$. Since lines l and q are perpendicular, the slope of line q is the negative reciprocal of line l.

$$\frac{t - 1}{-2} = -2$$

$$t - 1 = -2(-2)$$

$$t - 1 = 4$$

$$t = 5$$

Example 11

Here's an example where only a handful of students got the right answer. However, by using two powerful strategies, we can solve it.

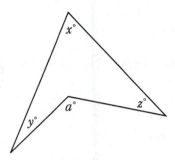

In the figure above, which is true?

(A) $x + y + z = 180 - a$

(B) $2x + y + z = a$

(C) $x - y + x - z = a$

(D) $x + y + z + a = 270$

(E) $x + y + z = a$

This is a classic problem that involves two very powerful strategies. The first is to **draw lines to extend a diagram and label parts (Math Strategy 14).** Draw line BC and label the extra angles, b and c. We get:

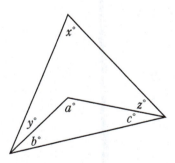

Now use the fact that the sum of the interior angles of any triangle equals $180°$. We get:

$x + y + b + z + c = 180$ for the larger triangle and $\boxed{1}$

$a + b + c = 180$ for the smaller triangle $\boxed{2}$

Now use the second powerful strategy: **Don't just solve for variables, especially when you have many of them. Just add or subtract equations (Math Strategy 13).**

In this case we would subtract equations to reduce the amount of variables.

Subtracting equation $\boxed{2}$ from equation $\boxed{1}$, we get:

$x + y + b + z + c - a - b - c = 180 - 180 = 0$

We end up with: $x + y + z - a = 0$ or

$x + y + z = a$ (Choice E).

MATH STRATEGY 15

Know How to Eliminate Certain Choices

> Instead of working out a lot of algebra, you may be able to eliminate several of the choices at first glance. In this way you can save yourself a lot of work. The key is to remember to use pieces of the given information to eliminate several of the choices at once.

Example 1

The sum of the digits of a three-digit number is 15. If this number is not divisible by 2 but is divisible by 5, which of the following is the number?

(A) 384
(B) 465
(C) 635
(D) 681
(E) 780

Choice B is correct. Use pieces of the given information to eliminate several of the choices.

Which numbers are divisible by 2? Choices A and E are divisible by 2 and, thus, can be eliminated. Of Choices B, C, and D, which are *not* divisible by 5? Choice D can be eliminated because the units digit of the number must be 0 or 5 for the number to be divisible by 5. We are left with Choices B and C.

Only Choice B (465) has the sum of its digits equal to 15. Thus, 465 is the only number that satisfies all the pieces of the given information.

If you learn to use this method well, you can save loads of time.

Example 2

Which of the following numbers is divisible by 5 and 9, but not by 2?

(A) 625
(B) 639
(C) 650
(D) 655
(E) 675

Choice E is correct. Clearly, a number is divisible by 5 if, and only if, its last digit is either 0 or 5. A number is also divisible by 2 if, and only if, its last digit is divisible by 2. *Certain choices are easily eliminated.* Thus we can *eliminate* Choices B and C.

Method 1: To eliminate some more choices, remember that a number is divisible by 9 if, and only if, the sum of its digits is divisible by 9. Thus, Choice E is the only correct answer.

Method 2: If you did not know the test for divisibility by 9, divide the numbers in Choices A, D, and E by 9 to find the answer.

Example 3

If the last digit and the first digit are interchanged in each of the numbers below, which will result in the number with the *largest* value?

(A) 5,243
(B) 4,352
(C) 4,235
(D) 2,534
(E) 2,345

Choice E is correct.
The number with the largest last digit will become the largest number after interchanging.   1

Certain choices are easily eliminated.

Using 1 , we see that Choices C and E each end in 5. All others end in digits less than 5 and may be eliminated. Starting with Choice E (see Strategy 8),

Choice E, 2,345, becomes 5,342.   2
Choice C, 4,235, becomes 5,234.   3
2 is larger than 3 .

Example 4

Which of the following could be the value of 3^x where x is an integer?

(A) 339,066
(B) 376,853
(C) 411,282
(D) 422,928
(E) 531,441

Choice E is correct. Let's look at what 3^x looks like for integral values of x:

$3^1 = 3$

$3^2 = 9$

$3^3 = 27$

$3^4 = 81$

$3^5 = 243$

$3^6 = \ldots 9$

$3^7 = \ldots 7$

$3^8 = \ldots 1$

Note that 3^x always has the *units* digit of 3, 9, 7, or 1. So we can eliminate Choices A, C, and D, since those choices end in numbers other than 3, 9, 7, or 1. We are left with Choices B and E. The number in the correct choice must be exactly divisible by 3, since it is of the form 3^x (= $3 \times 3 \times 3 \ldots$) where x is an integer. This is a good time to use your calculator. Divide the number in Choice B by 3: You get 125,617.66. That's *not* an integer. So the only remaining choice is Choice E.

MATH STRATEGY 16

Watch out for questions that seem very easy but that can be tricky—beware of choice A as a "lure choice"

When questions appear to be solved very easily, think again! Watch out especially for the "lure," Choice A.

Example 1*

$$6:06$$

The diagram above shows a 12-hour digital clock whose hours value is the same as the minutes value. Consider each time when the same number appears for both the hour and the minutes as a "double time" situation. What is the shortest elapsed time period between the appearance of one double time and an immediately succeeding double time?

(A)   61 minutes

(B)   60 minutes

(C)   58 minutes

(D)   50 minutes

(E)   49 minutes

Choice E is correct. Did you think that just by subtracting something like 8:08 from 9:09 you would get the answer (1 hour and 1 minute = 61 minutes)? That's Choice A, which is wrong. So beware, because your answer came too easily for a test like the SAT. You must realize that there is another possibility of "double time" occurrence—12:12 and 1:01, whose difference is 49 minutes. This is Choice E, the correct answer.

Example 2

The letters d and m are integral digits in a certain number system. If $0 \leq d \leq m$, how many different possible values are there for d?

(A) m

(B) $m - 1$

(C) $m - 2$

(D) $m + 1$

(E) $m + 2$

Choice D is correct. Did you think that the answer was m? Do not be careless! The list 1,2,3, ..., m contains m elements. If 0 is included in the list, then there are $m + 1$ elements. Hence, if $0 \leq d \leq m$ where d is integral, then d can have $m + 1$ different values.

---

*   *Note:* This problem also appears in Strategy 1 of the 5 General Strategies on page 62.

Example 3

There are some flags hanging in a horizontal row. Starting at one end of the row, the U.S. flag is 25th. Starting at the other end of the row, the U.S. flag is 13th. How many flags are in the row?

(A) 36
(B) 37
(C) 38
(D) 39
(E) 40

Choice B is correct. **The obvious may be tricky!**

Method 1: Given:

The U.S. flag is 25th from one end. $\boxed{1}$

The U.S. flag is 13th from the other end. $\boxed{2}$

At first glance it may appear that adding $\boxed{1}$ and $\boxed{2}$, 25 + 13 = 38, will be the correct answer. This is WRONG!

The U.S. flag is being counted twice: Once as the 25th and again as the 13th from the other end. The correct answer is

$$25 + 13 - 1 = 37.$$

Method 2:

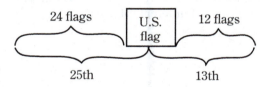

24 flags   U.S. flag   12 flags

25th   13th

$$24 + 12 + \text{U.S. flag} = 36 + \text{U.S. flag} = 37$$

Example 4

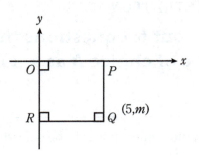

$OR = RQ$ in the figure above. If the coordinates of Q are $(5,m)$, find the value of m.

(A) -5
(B) $-\sqrt{5}$
(C) 0
(D) $\sqrt{5}$
(E) 5

Choice A is correct.

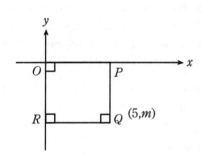

Given: $OR = RQ$ $\boxed{1}$

Coordinates of $Q = (5,m)$ $\boxed{2}$

From $\boxed{2}$, we get $RQ = 5$ $\boxed{3}$

Substitute $\boxed{3}$ into $\boxed{1}$. We get

$$OR = 5$$

The obvious may be tricky! Since Q is below the x-axis, its y-coordinate is negative. Thus $m = -5$.

MATH STRATEGY 17

Use the given information effectively (and ignore irrelevant information)

> You should always use first the piece of information that tells you the most, gives you a useful idea, or brings you closest to the answer.

Example 1

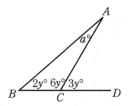

(Note: Figure is not drawn to scale.)

In the figure above, *BD* is a straight line. What is the value of *a*?

(A) 15
(B) 17
(C) 20
(D) 24
(E) 30

Choice C is correct.

Use the piece of information that will give you something definite. You might have first thought of using the fact that the sum of the angles of a triangle = 180°. However, that will give you

$$a + 2y + 6y = 180$$

That's not very useful. However, if you use the fact that the sum of the angles in a straight angle is 180, we get:

$$6y + 3y = 180$$
$$\text{and we get } 9y = 180$$
$$y = 20$$

Now we have gotten something useful. At this point, we can use the fact that the sum of the angles in a triangle is 180.

$$a + 2y + 6y = 180$$

Substituting 20 for *y*, we get

$$a + 2(20) + 6(20) = 180$$
$$a = 20 \quad \textit{(Answer)}$$

Example 2

Avriel, Braden, and Carlos will be seated at random in three chairs, each denoted by X below. What is the probability that Avriel will be seated next to Carlos?

X   X   X

(A) $\frac{1}{8}$

(B) $\frac{1}{3}$

(C) $\frac{3}{8}$

(D) $\frac{5}{8}$

(E) $\frac{2}{3}$

Represent the students as A, B, and C respectively. However, don't make the mistake of representing the students in an unorganized or random fashion, such as ABC, BAC, CAB, and so on, and then try to get all the other possibilities.

Represent the students systematically.

Start with A at the extreme left, B at the extreme left, and then C at the extreme left.

Like this:

ABC
ACB   only two possibilities

BAC
BCA   only two possibilities

CAB
CBA   again only two possibilities

Thus, there are 6 total possibilities: ABC, ACB, BAC, BCA, CAB, CBA.

Probability is defined as the favorable number of ways divided by the total number of ways.

The favorable number of ways is the number of ways where Avriel is seated next to Carlos. This is:

ACB, BAC, BCA, and CAB—4 ways.

Thus, the probability is $\frac{4}{6}$, or $\frac{2}{3}$.

Note that by organizing the information like this, we get all the possibilities in a systemized manner.

Example 3

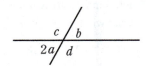

In the figure of intersecting lines above, which of the following is equal to $180 - a$?

(A) $a + d$

(B) $a + 2d$

(C) $c + b$

(D) $b + 2a$

(E) $c + d$

Choice A is correct. Try to get something you can work with. From the diagram,

$$2a + d = 180.$$

So, to find $180 - a$, just subtract a from both sides of the above equation.

$$2a + d - a = 180 - a.$$

You get:

$$a + d = 180 - a.$$

See Math Strategy 7, Example 7 (page 92) for an alternate approach to solving this problem, using a different strategy: **Use Specific Numerical Examples to Prove or Disprove Your Guess**.

Example 4

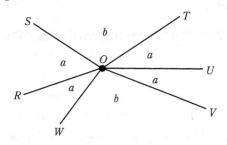

(Note: Figure is not drawn to scale.)

Which of the angles in the figure above has a degree measure that can be determined?

(A) $\angle WOS$

(B) $\angle SOU$

(C) $\angle WOT$

(D) $\angle ROV$

(E) $\angle WOV$

Choice C is correct.

Use information that will get you something useful.

$$4a + 2b = 360 \text{ (sum of all angles} = 360°)$$

Divide by 2 to simplify:

$$2a + b = 180$$

Now try all the choices. You could work backward from Choice E, but we'll start with Choice A:

(A) $\angle WOS = 2a$—You know that $2a + b = 180$ but don't know the value of $2a$.

(B) $\angle SOU = b + a$—You know $2a + b = 180$ but don't know the value of $b + a$.

(C) $\angle WOT = b + 2a$—You know that $2a + b = 180$, so you know the value of $b + 2a$.

Example 5

If a ranges in value from 0.003 to 0.3 and b ranges in value from 3.0 to 300.0, then the minimum value of $\frac{a}{b}$ is

(A) 0.1

(B) 0.01

(C) 0.001

(D) 0.0001

(E) 0.00001

Choice E is correct.

Start by using the definitions of *minimum* and *maximum*.

The minimum value of $\frac{a}{b}$ is when a is *minimum* and b is *maximum*.

The minimum value of $a = .003$
The maximum value of $b = 300$

So the minimum value of $\frac{a}{b} = \frac{.003}{300} = \frac{.001}{100} = .00001$.

Example 6

If $xry = 0$, $yst = 0$, and $rxt = 1$, then which must be 0?

(A) r
(B) s
(C) t
(D) x
(E) y

Choice E is correct.

Use information that will give you something to work with.

$rxt = 1$ tells you that $r \neq 0$, $x \neq 0$, and $t \neq 0$.
So if $xry = 0$ then y must be 0.

Example 7

On a street with 25 houses, 10 houses have *fewer than 6 rooms,* 10 houses have *more than 7 rooms,* and 4 houses have *more than 8 rooms.* What is the total number of houses on the street that are either 6-, 7-, or 8-room houses?

(A) 5
(B) 9
(C) 11
(D) 14
(E) 15

Choice C is correct.

There are three possible situations:

(a) Houses that have *fewer than 6 rooms* (call the number a)
(b) Houses that have *6, 7, or 8 rooms* (call the number b)
(c) Houses that have *more than 8 rooms* (call the number c)

$a + b + c$ must total 25 (given).   ☐1

a is 10 (given).   ☐2

c is 4 (given).   ☐3

Substituting ☐2 and ☐3 in ☐1, we get $10 + b + 4 = 25$. b must therefore be 11.

Example 8

Mr. Martinez's tenth-grade class took a survey to see what activities each student engages in one hour before bed. When the survey was complete, 5 students selected "Play video games" and "Watch TV." 14 students selected "Watch TV," and 8 students selected "Play video games." How many students are in Mr. Martinez's class? (Assume that every student in the class watches TV only, plays video games only, or does both.)

(A) 11
(B) 17
(C) 22
(D) 25
(E) 27

Choice B is correct.

Method 1:

Draw two intersecting circles.

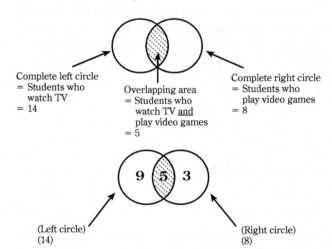

Above, subtracting: all students who watch TV (14) − students who watch TV <u>and</u> also play video games (5), we get 9.

Above, subtracting: all students who play video games (8) − students who watch TV *and* also play video games (5), we get 3.

So the total number of students is 9 + 5 + 3 = 17.

Method 2:

Total number of students are:

(a)   students who only watch TV
(b)   students who only play video games
(c)   students who watch TV *and* also play video games

(a)   There are 14 students who watch TV and 5 students who watch TV *and* play video games, so subtracting, *there are 9 students who watch TV only.*

(b)   There are 8 students who play video games and 5 students who watch TV and also play video games, so subtracting, *there are 3 students who play video games only.*

(c)   The number of students who watch TV and also play video games is 5 (given).

Adding the number of students in (a), (b), and (c) we get 9 + 3 + 5 = 17.

Example 9

Points *A*, *B*, and *X* do not lie on the same line. Point *X* is 5 units from *A* and 3 units from *B*. How many other points in the same plane as *A*, *B*, and *X* are also 5 units from *A* and 3 units from *B*?

(A)   None
(B)   One
(C)   Two
(D)   Four
(E)   More than four

Choice B is correct.

First let's draw the points, making sure *A*, *B*, and *X* do not lie on the same line.

What do we do next? Consider all possibilities. Consider all points that are 5 units from *A*. They would be all points on the circumference of a circle whose radius is 5 units.

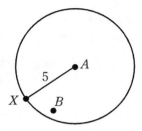

Consider all points that are 3 units from *B*. They would be all points on the circumference of a circle whose radius is 5 units.

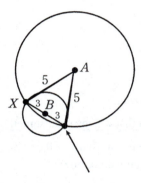

Notice that the two circles intersect at Point *X* and *only one* other point. That point is both 5 units from *A* and 3 units from *B*.

MATH STRATEGY 18

Know and Use Facts about Triangles

> By remembering these facts about triangles, you can often save yourself a lot of time and trouble.

I.

If $a = b$, then $x = y$

The base angles of an isosceles triangle are equal.

If $x = y$, then $a = b$

If the base angles of a triangle are equal, the triangle is isosceles.

II.

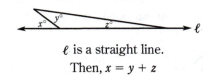

ℓ is a straight line.
Then, $x = y + z$

The measure of an exterior angle is equal to the sum of the measures of the remote interior angles.

III.

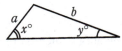

If $a < b$, then $y < x$

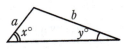

If $y < x$, then $a < b$

In a triangle, the greater angle lies opposite the greater side.

IV.

Similar Triangles

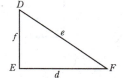

If $\triangle ABC \sim \triangle DEF$, then

$$m\angle A = m\angle D$$

$$m\angle B = m\angle E$$

$$m\angle C = m\angle F$$

and $\dfrac{a}{d} = \dfrac{b}{e} = \dfrac{c}{f}$

V.

$$m\angle A + m\angle B + m\angle C = 180°$$

The sum of the interior angles of a triangle is 180 degrees.

VI.

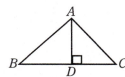

Area of $\triangle ABC = \dfrac{AD \times BC}{2}$

The area of a triangle is one-half the product of the altitude to a side and the side.

Note: If $m\angle A = 90°$,

Area also $= \dfrac{AD \times BC}{2}$

VII.

In a right triangle,
$c^2 = a^2 + b^2$

and $x° + y° = 90°$

VIII.

Memorize the following standard triangles:

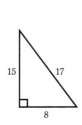

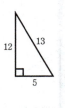

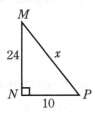

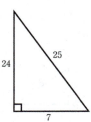

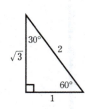

IX.

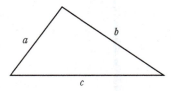

$a + b > c$
$a + c > b$
$b + c > a$

The sum of the lengths of two sides of a triangle is greater than the length of the third side. (This is like saying that the shortest distance between two points is a straight line.)

Example 1

In the diagram below, what is the value of x?

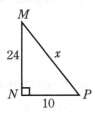

(A) 20
(B) 25
(C) 26
(D) 45
(E) 48

Choice C is correct.

Method 1: Use Statement VII. Then,

$$x^2 = 24^2 + 10^2$$
$$= 576 + 100$$
$$= 676$$

Thus, $x = 26$ (*Answer*)

Method 2: Look at Statement VIII. Notice that $\triangle MNP$ is similar to one of the standard triangles:

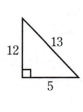 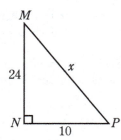

This is true because

$$\frac{12}{24} = \frac{5}{10} \text{ (Look at Statement IV).}$$

Hence, $\frac{12}{24} = \frac{13}{x}$ or $x = 26$ (Answer)

Example 2

If Masonville is 50 kilometers due north of Adamston and Elvira is 120 kilometers due east of Adamston, then the minimum distance between Masonville and Elvira is

(A)   125 kilometers
(B)   130 kilometers
(C)   145 kilometers
(D)   160 kilometers
(E)   170 kilometers

Choice B is correct. *Draw a diagram first.*

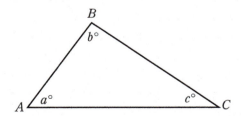

The given information translates into the diagram above. Note Statement VIII. The triangle above is a multiple of the special 5–12–13 right triangle.

$$50 = 10(5)$$
$$120 = 10(12)$$

Thus, $x = 10(13) = 130$ kilometers

(*Note:* The Pythagorean Theorem could also have been used: $50^2 + 120^2 = x^2$.)

Example 3

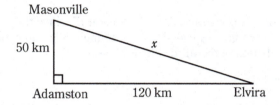

(Note: Figure is not drawn to scale.)

In triangle *ABC*, if $a > c$, which of the following is true?

(A) $BC = AC$
(B) $AB > BC$
(C) $AC > AB$
(D) $BC > AB$
(E) $BC > AC$

Choice D is correct. (*Remember triangle inequality facts.*)
From basic geometry, Statement III, we know that, since $m\angle BAC > m\angle BCA$, then leg opposite $\angle BAC >$ leg opposite $\angle BCA$, or

$$BC > AB$$

Example 4

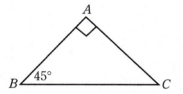

(Note: Figure is not drawn to scale.)

The triangle above has side $BC = 10$, angle $B = 45°$, and angle $A = 90°$. The area of the triangle

(A)   is 15
(B)   is 20
(C)   is 25
(D)   is 30
(E)   Cannot be determined.

Choice C is correct.

First find angle *C* using Statement V.

$$90° + 45° + m\angle C = 180°$$

So $m\angle C = 45°$.

Using Statement I, we find $AB = AC$,

since $m\angle B = m\angle C = 45°$.

Since our right triangle *ABC* has $BC = 10$, using Statement VIII (the right triangle $\frac{\sqrt{2}}{2}, \frac{\sqrt{2}}{2}, 1$), multiply by 10 to get a right triangle:

$$\frac{10\sqrt{2}}{2}, \frac{10\sqrt{2}}{2}, 10$$

Thus side $AB = \frac{10\sqrt{2}}{2} = 5\sqrt{2}$

side $AC = \frac{10\sqrt{2}}{2} = 5\sqrt{2}$

Now the area of triangle *ABC*, according to Statement VI, is

$$\frac{5\sqrt{2} \times 5\sqrt{2}}{2} = \frac{25 \times 2}{2} = 25$$

Example 5

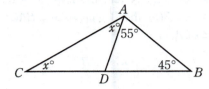

In the figure above, what is the value of x?

(A) 30

(B) 40

(C) 50

(D) 80

(E) 100

Choice B is correct.

<u>Remember triangle facts. Use Statement II.</u>

$\angle ADB$ is an exterior angle of $\triangle ACD$, so

$m\angle ADB = x + x = 2x$ $\boxed{1}$

In $\triangle ADB$, the sum of its angles = 180 (Statement V), so

$$m\angle ADB + 55 + 45 = 180$$

or $\qquad m\angle ADB + 100 = 180$

or $\qquad\qquad m\angle ADB = 80$ $\boxed{2}$

Equating $\boxed{1}$ and $\boxed{2}$ we have

$$2x = 80$$

$$x = 40 \; (\textit{Answer})$$

Example 6

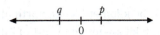

(Note: Figure is not drawn to scale.)

Which of the following represents all of the possibilities for the value of a in the figure above?

(A) $1 < a < 9$

(B) $4 < a < 5$

(C) $0 < a < 9$

(D) $4 < a < 9$

(E) $5 < a < 9$

Choice A is correct. From Statement IX, since the sum of the lengths of two sides of a triangle is greater than the length of the third side, we have:

$a + 5 > 4$ $\boxed{1}$

$a + 4 > 5$ $\boxed{2}$

$5 + 4 > a$ $\boxed{3}$

From $\boxed{2}$ we get:

$$a > 1.$$

From $\boxed{3}$ we get:

$$9 > a.$$

This means that

$$9 > a > 1, \text{ or } 1 < a < 9.$$

MATH STRATEGY 19

When calculating answers, never multiply and/or do long division if you can reduce first

> *Note:* On the SAT exam, because calculators are permitted, you may do the following problems with a calculator also. But it would be wise for you to see the other approach too—how the problem can be solved *without* the use of a calculator.

Example 1

If $w = \dfrac{81 \times 150}{45 \times 40}$, then $w =$

(A) 3

(B) $6\dfrac{3}{4}$

(C) $7\dfrac{1}{4}$

(D) 9

(E) $20\dfrac{1}{4}$

Do not multiply 81×150 and 45×40 to get

$$\frac{12{,}150}{1{,}800}$$

Factor first: $\dfrac{\overset{81}{\overbrace{9 \times 9}} \times \overset{150}{\overbrace{15 \times 10}}}{\underset{45}{\underbrace{9 \times 5}} \times \underset{40}{\underbrace{4 \times 10}}}$

Then cancel like factors in numerator and denominator:

$$\frac{\cancel{9} \times 9 \times 15 \times \cancel{10}}{\cancel{9} \times 5 \times 4 \times \cancel{10}}$$

Reduce further: $\dfrac{9 \times \cancel{5} \times 3}{\cancel{5} \times 4}$

Then simplify: $\dfrac{27}{4} = 6\dfrac{3}{4}$ (*Answer*)

Thus, Choice B is correct.

Example 2

$$\frac{4^2 + 4^2 + 4^2}{3^3 + 3^3 + 3^3} =$$

(A) $\dfrac{16}{27}$

(B) $\dfrac{8}{9}$

(C) $\dfrac{4}{3}$

(D) $\dfrac{64}{27}$

(E) $\dfrac{512}{81}$

Choice A is correct.

$$\frac{4^2 + 4^2 + 4^2}{3^3 + 3^3 + 3^3} =$$

Factor and reduce: $\dfrac{\cancel{3}(4^2)}{\cancel{3}(3^3)} = \dfrac{16}{27}$

Example 3

If $6 \times 7 \times 8 \times 9 = \dfrac{12 \times 14 \times 18}{x}$, then $x =$

(A) $\dfrac{1}{2}$

(B) 1

(C) 4

(D) 8

(E) 12

Choice B is correct.

Given: $6 \times 7 \times 8 \times 9 = \dfrac{12 \times 14 \times 18}{x}$ $\boxed{1}$

so that $x = \dfrac{12 \times 14 \times 18}{6 \times 7 \times 8 \times 9}$ $\boxed{2}$

Do *not* multiply the numbers out in the numerator and denominator of $\boxed{2}$! It is too much work! Rewrite $\boxed{2}$.

Factor and reduce:

$x =$

$\dfrac{12 \times 14 \times 18}{6 \times 7 \times 8 \times 9} = \dfrac{2 \times \cancel{6} \times 2 \times \cancel{7} \times 2 \times \cancel{9}}{\cancel{6} \times \cancel{7} \times 8 \times \cancel{9}}$

$= \dfrac{2 \times 2 \times 2}{8} = \dfrac{\cancel{8}}{\cancel{8}} = 1$ (*Answer*)

Example 4

If $\dfrac{81 \times y}{27} = 21$, then $y =$

(A) $\dfrac{1}{21}$

(B) $\dfrac{1}{7}$

(C) 3

(D) 7

(E) 21

Choice D is correct.

Given: $\dfrac{81 \times y}{27} = 21$

Multiply both sides by 27 to get $81 \times y = 21 \times 27$

$y = \dfrac{21 \times 27}{81}$

Factor and reduce:

$y = \dfrac{3 \cdot 7 \times 3 \cdot \cancel{9}}{9 \cdot \cancel{9}}$

$= \dfrac{\cancel{3} \cdot 7 \times \cancel{3}}{\cancel{3} \cdot \cancel{3}}$

$y = 7$ (*Answer*)

Example 5

Find the value of $\dfrac{y^2 - 7y + 10}{y - 2}$ rounded to the nearest whole number if $y = 8.000001$.

(A) 2

(B) 3

(C) 5

(D) 6

(E) 16

Choice B is correct.

Given: $\dfrac{y^2 - 7y + 10}{y - 2}$ $\boxed{1}$

Factor and reduce:

Factor the numerator of $\boxed{1}$. We get

$\dfrac{(y - 5)\cancel{(y - 2)}}{\cancel{y - 2}} = y - 5$ $\boxed{2}$

Substitute 8.000001 in $\boxed{2}$. We have

$8.000001 - 5 =$

$3.000001 \approx 3$ (*Answer*)

16 VERBAL
(CRITICAL READING)
STRATEGIES

Using Critical-Thinking Skills
in Verbal Questions

(Critical Reading Section)

SENTENCE COMPLETION STRATEGY 1

4 Sentence Completion Strategies

For a Sentence with Only One Blank, Fill in the Blank with Each Choice to See the Best Fit*

Before you decide which is the best choice, fill in the blank with each of the five answer choices to see which word will fit best into the sentence as a whole.

Example 1

He believed that because there is serious unemployment in our auto industry, we should not _____ foreign cars.

- (A) discuss
- (B) regulate
- (C) research
- (D) import
- (E) disallow

EXPLANATORY ANSWER

Choice D is correct. The word "import" means to bring in from another country or place. The sentence now makes good sense. The competition resulting from importation of foreign cars reduces the demand for American-made cars. This throws many American auto workers out of jobs.

Example 2

His attempt to _____ his guilt was betrayed by the tremor of his hand as he picked up the paper.

- (A) extenuate
- (B) determine
- (C) conceal
- (D) intensify
- (E) display

EXPLANATORY ANSWER

Choice C is correct. The word "conceal" means to keep secret or to hide. The sentence now makes good sense. The nervousness caused by his guilty conscience is shown by the shaking of his hand. He is thus prevented in his attempt to hide his guilt.

Example 3

In large cities, the number of family-owned grocery stores has fallen so sharply that the opportunity to shop in such a place is _____ occasion.

- (A) a celebrated
- (B) an old
- (C) a fanciful
- (D) a rare
- (E) an avid

EXPLANATORY ANSWER

Choice D is correct. A rare occasion is one that you seldom have the opportunity to participate in. Shopping in a family-owned grocery store in a large city today is, indeed, a rare occasion.

Example 4

Legal _____ initiated by the government necessitate that manufacturers use _____ in choosing food additives.

- (A) entanglements...knowledge
- (B) devices...intensification
- (C) talents...discretion
- (D) proclivities...moderation
- (E) restraints...caution

---

* Strategy 1 is considered the Master Strategy for *one-blank* Sentence Completion questions because it can be used effectively to answer every *one-blank* Sentence Completion question. However, it is important that you learn all of the other Sentence Completion Strategies because you may need to use them in conjunction with this strategy to find the answer efficiently.

EXPLANATORY ANSWER

Choice E is correct. Although this is a two-blank question, we should still use Sentence Completion Strategy 1. Try the words in each of the choices in the blanks in the sentence.

Another possibility is Choice A. But the point of the sentence evidently is that government prohibitions of certain food additives necessitate care by manufacturers in choosing additives that are permitted. Thus Choice A is not as good as Choice E.

Example 5

It is unthinkable for a prestigious conductor to agree to include _____ musicians in his orchestra.

(A) capable
(B) seasoned
(C) mediocre
(D) recommended
(E) professional

EXPLANATORY ANSWER

Choice C is correct. Ask yourself, "What type of musicians would a prestigious (a highly regarded) conductor <u>not</u> want to include in his or her orchestra?" The conductor would not want to include ordinary, average, or below average musicians. The word "mediocre," which means average or ordinary, fits the sentence. The other choices describe a characteristic higher than ordinary.

Example 6

A desire to be applauded by those in attendance, not his sensitivity to the plight of the underprivileged, was the reason for his _____ at the charity affair.

(A) shyness
(B) discomfort
(C) surprise
(D) arrogance
(E) generosity

Choice E is correct. No other choice makes sense in the sentence. It is clear that the person was primarily interested in being appreciated for his donation.

Example 7

The commentator characterized the electorate as _____ because it was unpredictable and given to constantly shifting moods.

(A) mercurial
(B) corrosive
(C) disingenuous
(D) implacable
(E) phlegmatic

EXPLANATORY ANSWER

Choice A is correct. You can see from the sentence that "unpredictable" and "constantly shifting" describe the electorate.

Look for a word in the choices that describes these words in quotations. In order to do this, you need to associate the first choice "mercurial" with the element in chemistry "mercury." You know that mercury (like that in a thermometer) is a liquid metal that moves around very fast and unpredictably. It is also constantly shifting from one place to another. A logical assumption would be that "mercurial" means "shifting" and "unpredictable."

See also **Vocabulary Strategy 3**.

SENTENCE COMPLETION STRATEGY 2

For a sentence with two blanks, begin by eliminating the initial words that don't make sense in the sentence*

This strategy consists of two steps.

Step 1 Find out which "first words" of the choices make sense in the first blank of the sentence. Don't consider the second word of each pair yet. *Eliminate those choices that contain "first words" that don't make sense in the sentence.*

Step 2 Now consider the *remaining* choices by filling in the pair of words for each choice.

Example 1

The sales assistants in that store are so _____ that it is impossible to even look at a garment without being _____ by their efforts to convince you to purchase.

(A) offensive...considerate
(B) persistent...harassed
(C) extensive...induced
(D) immune...aided
(E) intriguing...evaluated

EXPLANATORY ANSWER

Choice B is correct.

Step 1 [Elimination]

We have eliminated Choice C, extensive...induced, because saying sales assistants are "extensive" ("extensive" meaning covering a large area) does not make sense here. We have eliminated Choice D, immune...aided, because sales assistants who are "immune" ("immune" meaning protected or exempt from) does not make sense here.

Step 2 [Remaining Choices]

This leaves us with these remaining choices to be considered. With Choice A, offensive...considerate, the sentence *does not* make sense. With Choice B, persistent...harassed, the sentence *does* make sense.

With Choice E, intriguing...evaluated, the sentence *does not* make sense.

Example 2

Television in our society is watched so _____ that intellectuals who detest the "tube" are

_____ .

(A) reluctantly...offended
(B) stealthily...ashamed
(C) frequently...revolted
(D) intensely...exultant
(E) noisily...amazed

EXPLANATORY ANSWER

Choice C is correct. We have eliminated Choice A because television is not watched reluctantly in our society. We have eliminated Choice B because television is not watched stealthily in our society. We have eliminated Choice E because it is not common for the viewer to watch television noisily. This leaves us with these remaining choices to be considered. With Choice D, intensely...exultant, the sentence does *not* make sense. With Choice C, frequently...revolted, the sentence *does* make sense.

---

* Strategy 2 is considered the Master Strategy for two-blank Sentence Completion questions because it can be used effectively to answer every two-blank Sentence Completion question. However, it is important to learn all of the other Sentence Completion Strategies because you may need to use them in conjunction with this strategy to find the answer efficiently.

Example 3

In view of the company's _____ claims that its scalp treatment would grow hair on bald heads, the newspaper _____ its advertising.

(A) unproved…banned
(B) interesting…canceled
(C) unreasonable…welcomed
(D) innocent…settled
(E) immune…questioned

EXPLANATORY ANSWER

Choice A is correct. The first step is to examine the first word of each choice. We eliminate Choice D, innocent…, and Choice E, immune…, because "claims" are not innocent or immune. Now we go on to the remaining choices. When you fill in the two blanks of Choice B and of Choice C, the sentence does *not* make sense. So these two choices are also incorrect. Filling in the two blanks of Choice A makes the sentence meaningful.

Example 4

The renowned behaviorist B. F. Skinner believed that those colleges set up to train teachers should _____ change their training philosophy, or else be _____ .

(A) inconsistently…supervised
(B) drastically…abolished
(C) haphazardly…refined
(D) secretly…dedicated
(E) doubtlessly…destroyed

EXPLANATORY ANSWER

Choice B is correct. We can first eliminate Choice A, inconsistently, Choice C, haphazardly, and Choice D, secretly, because these first blank words do *not* make sense in the sentence. This leaves us with Choice B, drastically, and Choice E, doubtlessly. But Choice E, doubtlessly…destroyed, does *not* make sense. Choice B, drastically…abolished, *does* make sense.

Example 5

The report indicates that the crime rate in the United States remains _____ and that one in every three households _____ some form of major crime in any year.

(A) incredible…visualizes
(B) astronomical…experiences
(C) simultaneous…welcomes
(D) unsuccessful…initiates
(E) constant…anticipates

EXPLANATORY ANSWER

Choice B is correct. Examine the first word of each choice. We eliminate Choice C, simultaneous, and Choice D, unsuccessful, because it does not make sense to say that the crime rate remains simultaneous or unsuccessful. Now we consider Choice A, which does *not* make sense in the sentence; Choice B *does* make sense; and Choice E does *not* make sense. Sometimes you can try the "second word" from each choice and see that only one choice fits in the second blank in the sentence.

Example 6

The antithesis of an Olympic athlete, the champion diver was _____ rather than gracious, and unscrupulous rather than _____ .

(A) skillful…discerning
(B) rowdy…deceitful
(C) urbane…resolute
(D) surly…honorable
(E) egotistical…artificial

EXPLANATORY ANSWER

Choice D is correct. In the second blank, we're looking for a word that has the opposite tone as "unscrupulous." But is "unscrupulous" negative or positive? Taking the prefix "anti-" from the first part of the sentence, we can deduce that it can be used to mean "not Olympian" (a negative tone), so we're looking for a *positive*-sounding word. "Honorable" is the most logical choice.

SENTENCE COMPLETION STRATEGY 3

Try to complete the sentence in your own words before looking at the choices

This strategy often works well, especially with one-blank sentences. You may be able to fill in the blank with a word of your own that makes good sense. Then look at the answer choices to see whether any of the choices has the same meaning as your own word.

Example 1

Many buildings with historical significance are now being _____ instead of being torn down.

(A) built
(B) forgotten
(C) destroyed
(D) praised
(E) repaired

EXPLANATORY ANSWER

Choice E is correct. The key words "instead of" constitute an *opposition indicator.* The words give us a good clue—we should fill in the blank with an antonym (opposite) for "torn down." If you used the strategy of trying to complete the sentence *before* looking at the five choices, you might have come up with any of the following appropriate words:

remodeled
reconstructed
remade
renovated

These words all mean the same as the correct Choice E word, "repaired."

Example 2

Wishing to _____ the upset passenger who found a nail in his steak, the flight attendant offered him a complimentary can of soda.

(A) appease
(B) berate
(C) disregard
(D) reinstate
(E) acknowledge

EXPLANATORY ANSWER

Choice A is correct. Since the passenger was upset, the flight attendant wished to do something to make him feel better. If you used the strategy of trying to complete the sentence *before* looking at the five choices, you might have come up with the following words that would have the meaning of "to make someone feel better":

pacify
soothe
satisfy
conciliate
relieve

These words all mean the same as the Choice A word, "appease."

Example 3

Just as the person who is kind brings happiness to others, so does he bring _____ to himself.

(A) wisdom
(B) guidance
(C) satisfaction
(D) stinginess
(E) insecurity

EXPLANATORY ANSWER

Choice C is correct. The words "so does he bring" tell you that you must look for a word that balances with "happiness." Here are some of the words:

joy
goodness
satisfaction
enjoyment

All these words can be linked to Choice C.

Example 4

Actors are sometimes very _____ since they must believe strongly in their own worth and talents.

(A) laconic
(B) unequivocal
(C) tedious
(D) egotistic
(E) reticent

EXPLANATORY ANSWER

Choice D is correct. "Since" signifies *result*. So the second clause of the sentence, starting with "since," really tells us that the missing word or words must be one of the following:

boastful
self-interested
egotistic
self-centered

Thus, Choice D is correct.

Example 5

Hunger has reached epidemic proportions nationwide, leaving up to 20 million people _____ to illness and fear.

(A) agreeable
(B) vulnerable
(C) obvious
(D) acclimated
(E) sensitive

EXPLANATORY ANSWER

Choice B is correct. Ask yourself, "What does **hunger** do to people, and how does it relate to **illness and fear**?" You may answer, it makes people:

susceptible to illness or fear
open to illness or fear
unprotected from illness or fear

The words "susceptible," "open," and "unprotected" all mean about the same as the correct one, Choice B: "vulnerable."

SENTENCE COMPLETION STRATEGY 4

Pay close attention to the key words in the sentence

A key word may indicate what is happening in the sentence. Here are some Examples of key words and what these words may indicate.

Key Word	Indicating
although	
however	
in spite of	
rather than	OPPOSITION
nevertheless	
on the other hand	
but	

Key Word	Indicating
moreover	
besides	
additionally	SUPPORT
furthermore	
in fact	

Key Word	Indicating
therefore	
consequently	
accordingly	RESULT
because	
when	
so	

There are many other words—in addition to these—that can act as key words to help you considerably in getting the right answer. A key word *frequently* appears in the sentence.

Watch for it!

Example 1

Jayden Sanders was frequently intolerant; moreover, his strange behavior caused most of his acquaintances to _____ the composer whenever possible.

(A) contradict
(B) interrogate
(C) shun
(D) revere
(E) tolerate

EXPLANATORY ANSWER

Choice C is correct. The word "moreover" is a *support indicator* in this sentence. As we try each choice word in the blank, we find that "shun" (avoid) is the only logical word that fits. You would avoid a person who was frequently intolerant and avoid a person that had strange behavior. You might have selected Choice A ("contradict"), but very few would seek to contradict an intolerant man with strange behavior.

Example 2

Until we are able to greatly improve the _____ status of the underprivileged in our country, a substantial _____ in our crime rate is remote.

(A) burdensome…harmony
(B) beneficial…gloom
(C) financial…reduction
(D) remarkable…puzzle
(E) questionable…disappointment

EXPLANATORY ANSWER

Choice C is correct. The word "Until" is a *result indicator.* As we try the first word of each choice in the first blank, we find that "burdensome," "financial," and "questionable" all make sense up until the second part of the sentence. We therefore eliminate Choices B and D. Now let us try both words in Choices A, C, and E. We then find that we can eliminate Choices A and E as not making sense in the entire sentence. This leaves us with the correct Choice C, which *does* bring out the result of what is stated in the first part of the sentence.

Example 3

All of the efforts of the teachers will bring about no _____ changes in the scores of the students because the books and other _____ educational materials are not available.

(A) impartial…worthwhile
(B) unique…reflected
(C) spiritual…inspiring
(D) marked…necessary
(E) effective…interrupted

EXPLANATORY ANSWER

Choice D is correct. First use *Sentence Completion Strategy 2: Eliminate the Words That Don't Make Sense.* Let us first eliminate Choices A, impartial…, and C, spiritual…, because we do not speak of "impartial" or "spiritual" changes. Now note that we have a *result* situation here as indicated by the presence of the conjunction "because" in the sentence. Choices B and E do not make sense because "unique" changes have nothing to do with "reflected" educational materials, and "effective" changes have nothing to do with "interrupted" educational materials. Choices B and E certainly do not meet the *result* requirement. Choice D is the only correct choice, because it makes sense to say that there will be no "marked" changes in the scores because the books and other "necessary" educational materials are not available.

Example 4

Being _____ person, he insisted at the conference that when he spoke he was not to be interrupted.

(A) a successful
(B) a delightful
(C) a headstrong
(D) an understanding
(E) a solitary

EXPLANATORY ANSWER

Choice C is correct. The main clause of the sentence—"he insisted…not be interrupted"—*supports* the idea expressed in the first three words of the sentence. If a person insists that he or she not be interrupted, he or she must be a "headstrong" ("stubborn") person. Accordingly, Choice C, "headstrong," is the only correct choice.

Example 5

Although Grete Waitz is a celebrated female marathon runner, she is noted for her _____ .

(A) vigor
(B) indecision
(C) modesty
(D) speed
(E) endurance

EXPLANATORY ANSWER

Choice C is correct. The beginning word "Although" constitutes an *opposition indicator.* We can then expect the second part of the sentence to indicate an idea that is opposite to what is said in the first part of the sentence. Choice C, "modesty," provides the word that gives us the closest to an opposite idea. Since Waitz is celebrated, we expect her to be immodest. The words in the other choices do *not* give us that opposite idea.

For two-blank sentences, look for contrasts or opposition in the two parts of the sentence—then look for opposite relationships in the choices.

Example 6

In spite of the _____ of his presentation, many people were _____ with the speaker's concepts and ideas.

(A) interest...enthralled
(B) power...taken
(C) intensity...shocked
(D) greatness...gratified
(E) strength...bored

EXPLANATORY ANSWER

Choice E is correct. The words *in spite of* at the beginning of the sentence tell you that the two blanks have an *opposite* tone. If the first blank is positive, the second blank is negative. If the first blank is negative, the second blank is positive. Watch for opposites in the choices:

(A) interest...enthralled—NOT OPPOSITE
(B) power...taken—NOT OPPOSITE
(C) intensity...shocked—NOT OPPOSITE
(D) greatness...gratified—NOT OPPOSITE
(E) strength...bored—OPPOSITE

Example 7

The instructor displayed extreme stubbornness; although she _____ the logic of the student's argument, she _____ to acknowledge her conclusion as correct.

(A) accepted...refused
(B) concluded...consented
(C) denounced....declined
(D) asserted....acceded
(E) rejected....preferred

EXPLANATORY ANSWER

Choice A is correct. The word *although* signifies a contrast, so the two blanks will have an *opposite* flavor. Watch for opposites in the choices:

(A) accepted...refused—OPPOSITE
(B) concluded...consented—NOT OPPOSITE
(C) denounced....declined—NOT OPPOSITE
(D) asserted....acceded—NOT OPPOSITE
(E) rejected....preferred—NOT OPPOSITE

Introduction to passage reading

Introduction

Before getting into the detailed strategies, I want to say that the most important way to really understand what you're reading is to *get involved* with the passage—as if a friend of yours was reading the passage to you and you wanted to be interested so you wouldn't hurt your friend's feelings. When you see the passage on paper it is also a good idea to *underline* important parts of the passage, which we'll also go over later in one of the strategies.

So many students ask, How do I answer reading comprehension questions? How do I read the passage effectively? Do I look at the questions before reading the passage? Do I underline things in the passage? Do I have to memorize details and dates? How do I get interested and involved in the passage?

All of these are good questions. They will be answered carefully and in the right sequence.

What reading comprehension questions ask

First of all, it is important to know that most reading comprehension questions ask about one of four things:

1. The MAIN IDEA of the passage.
2. INFORMATION SPECIFICALLY MENTIONED in the passage.
3. INFORMATION IMPLIED (not directly stated) in the passage.
4. The TONE or MOOD of the passage.

For example, following are some typical question stems. Each lets you immediately know which of the above is being asked about.

1. It can be inferred from the passage that… (IMPLIED INFORMATION)

2. According to the author… (MAIN IDEA)

3. The passage is primarily concerned with… (MAIN IDEA)

4. The author's statement that… (SPECIFIC INFORMATION)

5. Which of the following describes the mood of the passage? (TONE or MOOD)

6. The author implies that… (IMPLIED INFORMATION)

7. The use of paper is described in lines 14–16… (SPECIFIC INFORMATION)

8. The main purpose of the passage… (MAIN IDEA)

9. The author's tone is best described as… (TONE or MOOD)

10. One could easily see the author as… (IMPLIED INFORMATION)

Getting involved with the passage

Now, let's first put aside the burning question: Should I read the questions first before reading the passage? The answer is NO! If you have in mind the four main question types given above, you will not likely be in for any big surprises. Many questions, when you get to them, will be reassuringly familiar in the way they're framed and in their intent. You can best answer them by reading the passage first, allowing yourself to become involved with it. To give you an idea of what I mean, look over the following passage. When you have finished, I'll show you how you might read it so as to get involved with it and with the author's intent.

INTRODUCTORY PASSAGE 1

We should also know that "greed" has little to do with the environmental crisis. The two main causes are population pressures, especially the pressures of large metropolitan populations, and the desire—a highly commendable one—to bring a decent living at the lowest possible cost to the largest possible number of people.

The environmental crisis is the result of success—success in cutting down the mortality of infants (which has given us the population explosion), success in raising farm output sufficiently to prevent mass famine (which has given us contamination by pesticides and chemical fertilizers), and success in getting the people out of the tenements of the 19th-century cities and into the greenery and privacy of the single-family home in the suburbs (which has given us urban sprawl and traffic jams). The environmental crisis, in other words, is largely the result of doing too much of the right sort of thing.

To overcome the problems that success always creates, one must build on it. But where to start? Cleaning up the environment requires determined, sustained effort with clear targets and deadlines. It requires, above all, concentration of effort. Up to now we have tried to do a little bit of everything—and tried to do it in the headlines—when what we ought to do first is draw up a list of priorities.

Breakdown and underlining of the passage

Before going over the passage with you, I want to suggest some underlining you might want to make and show what different parts of the passage refer to.

We should also know that "greed" has little to do with the environmental crisis. The two main causes are population pressures, especially the pressures of large metropolitan populations, and the desire—a highly commendable one—to bring a decent living at the lowest possible cost to the largest possible number of people.

Sets stage.

The environmental crisis is the result of success—success in cutting down the mortality of infants (which has given us the population explosion), success in raising farm output sufficiently to prevent mass famine (which has given us contamination by pesticides and chemical fertilizers), and success in getting the people out of the tenements of the 19th-century cities and into the greenery and privacy of the single-family home in the suburbs (which has given us urban sprawl and traffic jams). The environmental crisis, in other words, is largely the result of doing too much of the right sort of thing.

This should interest and surprise you.

Examples of success.

Summary of the success examples.

To overcome the problems that success always creates, one must build on it. But where to start? Cleaning up the environment requires determined, sustained effort with clear targets and deadlines. It requires, above all, concentration of effort. Up to now we have tried to do a little bit of everything—and tried to do it in the headlines—when what we ought to do first is draw up a list of priorities.

Solutions.

Now I'll go over the passage with you, showing you what might go through your mind as you read. This will let you see how to get involved with the passage and how this involvement facilitates answering the questions that follow the passage. In many cases, you'll actually be able to anticipate the questions. Of course, when you are preparing for the SAT, you'll have to develop this skill so that you do it rapidly and almost automatically.

Let's look at the first sentence:

We should also know that "greed" has little to do with the environmental crisis.

Immediately you should say to yourself, "So something else must be involved with the environmental crisis." Read on:

The two main causes are population pressures, especially the pressures of large metropolitan populations, and the desire—a highly commendable one—to bring a decent living at the lowest possible cost to the largest possible number of people.

Now you can say to yourself, "Oh, so population pressures and the desire to help the people in the community caused the environmental crisis." You should also get a feeling that the author is not really against these causes of the environmental crisis, and that he or she believes that the crisis is in part a side effect of worthwhile efforts and enterprises. Read on:

The environmental crisis is the result of success—success in cutting down the mortality of infants (which has given us the population explosion), success in raising farm output sufficiently to prevent mass famine (which has given us contamination by pesticides and chemical fertilizers), and success in getting the people out of the tenements of the 19th-century city and into the greenery and privacy of the single-family home in the suburbs (which has given us urban sprawl and traffic jams).

Now you should say to yourself, "It seems that for every positive thing that the author mentions, there is a negative occurrence that leads to the environmental crisis."

Now read the last sentence of this paragraph:

The environmental crisis, in other words, is largely the result of doing too much of the right sort of thing.

Now you can say to yourself, "Gee, we wanted to do the right thing, but we created something bad. It looks like you can't have your cake and eat it too!"

Now you should anticipate that in the next and final paragraph, the author will discuss what may be done to reduce the bad effects that come from the good. Look at the first sentence of the third paragraph:

To overcome the problems that success always creates, one must build on it.

Now you can say to yourself, "Well, how?" In fact, in the next sentence the author asks the very question you just asked: *But where to start?* Read on to find out the author's answer.

Cleaning up the environment requires determined, sustained effort with clear targets and deadlines. It requires, above all, concentration of effort.

So now you can say to yourself, "Oh, so that's what we need—definite goals, deadlines for reaching those goals, and genuine effort to achieve the goals."

The author then discusses what you may have already thought about:

Up to now we have tried to do a little bit of everything...

What the author is saying (and you should realize this) is that up to now, we haven't concentrated on one particular problem at a time. We used "buckshot instead of bullets." Read on:

—and tried to do it in the headlines—when what we ought to do first is draw up a list of priorities.

So you can now see that, in the author's opinion, making a list of priorities and working on them one at a time, with a target in mind, may get us out of the environmental crisis and still preserve our quality of life.

How to answer reading comprehension questions most effectively

Before we start to answer the questions, let me tell you the best and most effective way of answering passage questions. You should read the question and proceed to look at the choices in the order of Choice A, Choice B, etc. If a choice (such as Choice A) doesn't give you the definite feeling that it is correct, don't try to analyze it further. Go on to Choice B. Again, if that choice (Choice B) doesn't make you feel that it's the right one, and you really have to think carefully about the choice, go on to Choice C and the rest of the choices and choose the best one.

Suppose you have gone through all five choices, and you don't know which one is correct, or you don't see any one that stands out as obviously being correct. Then quickly guess or leave the question blank if you wish and go on to the next question. You can go back after you have answered the other questions relating to the passage. But remember, when you return to the questions you weren't sure of, don't spend too much time on them. Try to forge ahead on the test.

Let's proceed to answer the questions now. Look at the first question:

1. This passage assumes the desirability of

    (A) using atomic energy to conserve fuel
    (B) living in comfortable family lifestyles
    (C) settling disputes peacefully
    (D) combating cancer and heart disease with energetic research
    (E) having greater government involvement in people's daily lives

Look at Choice A. That doesn't seem correct. Now look at Choice B. Do you remember that the author claimed that the environmental crisis is the result of the successful attempt to get people out of their tenements and into a better environment? We can only feel that the author *assumes* this desirability of *living in comfortable family lifestyles* (Choice B), since the author uses the word *success* in describing the transition from living in tenements to living in single-family homes. Therefore, Choice B is correct. You don't need to analyze or even consider the other choices, since we have zeroed in on Choice B.

Let's look at Question 2:

2. According to this passage, one early step in any effort to improve the environment would be to

    (A) return to the exclusive use of natural fertilizers
    (B) put a high tax on profiteering industries
    (C) ban the use of automobiles in the cities
    (D) study successful efforts in other countries
    (E) set up a timetable for corrective actions

Again, let's go through the choices in the order Choice A, Choice B, etc., until we come up with the right choice. Choices A, B, C, and D seem unlikely to be correct. So look at Choice E. We remember that the author said that we should establish clear targets and deadlines to improve the environment. That makes Choice E look like the correct answer.

Let's look at Question 3:

3. The passage indicates that the conditions that led to overcrowded roads also brought about

    (A) more attractive living conditions for many people
    (B) a healthier younger generation
    (C) greater occupational opportunities
    (D) the population explosion
    (E) greater concentration of population pressures

Here we would go back to the part of the passage that discussed overcrowded roads. This is where (second paragraph) the author says that urban sprawl and traffic jams are one result of success in getting people out of tenements and into single-family homes. So you can see that Choice A is correct. Again, there is no need to consider other choices, since you should be fairly comfortable with Choice A.

Let's look at Question 4:

4. It could logically be assumed that the author of this passage would support legislation to

    (A) ban the use of all pesticides
    (B) prevent the use of automobiles in the cities
    (C) build additional conventional power plants immediately
    (D) organize an agency to coordinate efforts to cope with environmental problems
    (E) restrict the press coverage of protests led by environmental groups

This is the type of question that asks you to determine how the author might feel about something else, when you already know something about the author's sentiments on one particular subject.

Choices A, B, and C do not seem correct. But look at Choice D. The author said that the way to get out of the energy crisis is to set targets and deadlines in order to cope with specific problems. The author would therefore probably want to organize an agency to do this. Choice D is correct.

Let's look at another passage, and what I'm going to tell you is what would be going through my mind as I read it. The more you can get involved with the passage in an "active" and not a "passive" way, the faster you'll read it, and the more you'll get out of it.

INTRODUCTORY PASSAGE 2

Some scraps of evidence bear out those who hold a very high opinion of the average level of culture among the Athenians of the great age. The funeral speech of Pericles is the most famous indication from Athenian literature that its level was indeed high. Pericles was, however, a politician, and he may have been flattering his audience. We know that thousands of Athenians sat hour after hour in the theater listening to the plays of the great Greek dramatists. These plays, especially the tragedies, are at a very high intellectual level throughout. There are no letdowns, no concessions to the lowbrows or to the demands of "realism," such as the scene of the gravediggers in *Hamlet*. The music and dancing woven into these plays were almost certainly at an equally high level. Our opera—not Italian opera, not even Wagner, but the restrained, difficult opera of the 18th century—is probably the best modern parallel. The comparison is no doubt dangerous, but can you imagine almost the entire population of an American city (in suitable installments, of course) sitting through performances of Mozart's *Don Giovanni* or Gluck's *Orpheus?* Perhaps the Athenian masses went to these plays because of a lack of other amusements. They could at least understand something of what went on, since the subjects were part of their folklore. For the American people, the subjects of grand opera are not part of their folklore.

Let's start reading the passage:

Some scraps of evidence bear out those who hold a very high opinion of the average level of culture among the Athenians of the great age.

Now this tells you that the author is going to talk about the culture of the Athenians. Thus the stage is set. Go on reading now:

The funeral speech of Pericles is the most famous indication from Athenian literature that its level was indeed high.

At this point you should say to yourself, "That's interesting, and there was an example of the high level of culture."

Read on:

Pericles was, however, a politician, and he may have been flattering his audience.

Now you can say, "So that's why those people were so attentive in listening—they were being flattered."

Read on:

We know that thousands of Athenians sat hour after hour in the theater listening to the plays of the great Greek dramatists. These plays, especially the tragedies, are at a very high intellectual level throughout. There are no letdowns, no concessions to the lowbrows or to the demands of "realism"...

At this point you should say to yourself, "That's strange—it could not have been just flattery that kept them listening hour after hour. How is this possible?" You can almost anticipate that the author will now give examples and contrast what he is saying to our plays and our audiences.

Read on:

The music and dancing woven into these plays were almost certainly at an equally high level. Our opera—not Italian opera...is probably the best modern parallel. The comparison is no doubt dangerous, but can you imagine almost the entire population of an American city...sitting through performances of...

Your feeling at this point should be, "No, I cannot imagine that. Why is that so?" So you should certainly be interested to find out.

Read on:

Perhaps the Athenian masses went to these plays because of a lack of other amusements. They could at least understand something of what went on, since the subjects were part of their folklore.

Now you can say, "So that's why those people were able to listen hour after hour—the material was all part of their folklore!"

Read on:

For the American people, the subjects…are not part of their folklore.

Now you can conclude, "So that's why the Americans cannot sit through these plays and perhaps cannot understand them—they were not part of their folklore!"

Here are the questions that follow the passage:

1. The author seems to question the sincerity of

    (A) politicians
    (B) playwrights
    (C) operagoers
    (D) lowbrows
    (E) gravediggers

2. The author implies that the average American

    (A) enjoys *Hamlet*
    (B) loves folklore
    (C) does not understand grand opera
    (D) seeks a high cultural level
    (E) lacks entertainment

3. The author's attitude toward Greek plays is one of

    (A) qualified approval
    (B) grudging admiration
    (C) studied indifference
    (D) partial hostility
    (E) great respect

4. The author suggests that Greek plays

    (A) made great demands upon their actors
    (B) flattered their audiences
    (C) were written for a limited audience
    (D) were dominated by music and dancing
    (E) stimulated their audiences

Let's try to answer them.

Question 1: Remember the statement about Pericles? This statement was almost unrelated to the passage since it was not discussed or referred to again. And here we have a question about it. Usually, if you see something that you think is irrelevant in a passage you may be pretty sure that a question will be based on that irrelevancy. It is apparent that the author seems to question the sincerity of politicians (*not* playwrights), since Pericles was a politician. Therefore Choice A is correct.

Question 2: We know that it was implied that the average American does not understand grand opera. Therefore Choice C is correct.

Question 3: From the passage, we see that the author is very positive about the Greek plays. Thus the author must have great respect for the plays. Note that the author may not have respect for Pericles, but Pericles was not a playwright; he was a politician. Therefore Choice E (not Choice A) is correct.

Question 4: It is certainly true that the author suggests that the Greek plays stimulated their audiences. They didn't necessarily flatter their audiences—there was only one indication of flattery, and that was by Pericles, who was not a playwright, but a politician. Therefore Choice E (not Choice B) is correct.

EXAMPLE OF UNDERLININGS

Some scraps of evidence bear out those who hold a <u>very high opinion</u>   ← *sets stage*
<u>of the average level of culture among the Athenians</u> of the great
age. <u>The funeral speech</u> of Pericles is the most famous indication   ⎫
from Athenian literature that its level was indeed high. Pericles was,   ⎬ ← *example*
however, <u>a politician</u>, and he may have <u>been flattering his audience.</u>   ⎭
We know that thousands of Athenians sat hour after hour in the
theater listening to the plays of the great Greek dramatists. These
plays, especially the tragedies, are <u>at a very high intellectual</u> level
throughout. There are no letdowns, no concessions to the lowbrows   ← *qualification*
or to the demands of "realism," such as the scene of the gravediggers
in *Hamlet.* The music and dancing woven into these plays were   ← *further examples*
almost certainly at an equally high level. <u>Our opera</u>—not Italian
opera, not even Wagner, but the restrained, difficult opera of the 18th
century—<u>is probably the best modern parallel.</u> The comparison is no   ← *comparison*
doubt dangerous, but can you imagine almost the entire population of
an American city (in suitable installments, of course) sitting through
performances of Mozart's *Don Giovanni* or Gluck's *Orpheus*? <u>Perhaps</u>   ⎫
<u>the Athenian masses went to these plays because of a lack of other</u>   ⎬
<u>amusements. They</u> could at least understand something of what went   ⎬ ← *explanation of previous statements*
on, <u>since the subjects were part of their folklore. For the American</u>   ⎬
<u>people, the subjects of grand opera are not part of their folklore.</u>   ⎭

Now the whole purpose of analyzing this passage the
way I did was to show you that if you get involved and
interested in the passage, you will not only anticipate
many of the questions, but when you answer them
you will be able to zero in on the right question choice
without having to necessarily analyze or eliminate the
wrong choices first. That's a great time-saver on a
standardized test such as the SAT.

Now here's a short passage from which four questions
were derived. Let's see if you can answer them after
you've read the passage.

INTRODUCTORY PASSAGE 3

Sometimes the meaning of glowing water is
ominous. Off the Pacific Coast of North America, it
may mean that the sea is filled with a minute plant
that contains a poison of strange and terrible viru
5 lence. About four days after this minute plant comes
to alter the coastal plankton, some of the fishes
and shellfish in the vicinity become toxic. This is
because in their normal feeding, they have strained
the poisonous plankton out of the water.

1. Fish and shellfish become toxic when they

   (A) swim in poisonous water
   (B) feed on poisonous plants
   (C) change their feeding habits
   (D) give off a strange glow
   (E) take strychnine into their systems

2. One can most reasonably conclude that plankton are

   (A) minute organisms
   (B) mussels
   (C) poisonous fish
   (D) shellfish
   (E) fluids

3. In the context of the passage, the word "virulence"
   in line 4 means

   (A) strangeness
   (B) color
   (C) calamity
   (D) potency
   (E) powerful odor

4. The paragraph preceding this one most probably discussed

    (A) phenomena of the Pacific coastline
    (B) poisons that affect man
    (C) the culture of the early Indians
    (D) characteristics of plankton
    (E) phenomena of the sea

EXPLANATORY ANSWERS

1. Choice B is correct. See the last three sentences. Fish become toxic when they feed on poisonous plants. Don't be fooled by using the first sentence, which seemingly leads to Choice A.

2. Choice A is correct. Since we are talking about *minute* plants (second sentence), it is reasonable to assume that plankton are *minute* organisms.

3. Choice D is correct. We understand that the poison is very strong and toxic. Thus it is "potent," virulent.

4. Choice E is correct. Since the second and not the first sentence was about the Pacific Coast, the paragraph preceding this one probably didn't discuss the phenomena of the Pacific coastline. It might have, if the first sentence—the sentence that links the ideas in the preceding paragraph— were about the Pacific coastline. Now, since we are talking about glowing water being ominous (first sentence), the paragraph preceding the passage is probably about the sea or the phenomena of the sea.

Summary

So in summary

1. Make sure that you get involved with the passage. You may even want to select first the passage that interests you most. For example, if you're interested in science, you may want to choose the science passage first. Just make sure that you make some notation so that you don't mismark your answer sheet by putting the answers in the wrong answer boxes.

2. Pay attention to material that seems unrelated in the passage—there will probably be a question or two based on that material.

3. Pay attention to the mood created in the passage or the tone of the passage. Here again, especially if the mood is striking, there will probably be a question relating to mood.

4. Don't waste valuable time looking at the questions before reading the passage.

5. When attempting to answer the questions (after reading the passage) it is sometimes wise to try to figure out the answer before going through the choices. This will enable you to zero in on the correct answer without wasting time with all of the choices.

6. You may want to underline any information in the passages involving dates, specific names, etc., on your test to have as a ready reference when you come to the questions.

7. Always try to see the overall attempt of the author of the passage or try to get the main gist of why the passage was being written. Try to get involved by asking yourself if you agree or disagree with the author, etc.

About the double-reading passages

On your SAT, you will be given a "double passage" (two separate passages) with about 13 questions. You will also be given a "double paragraph" (two separate paragraphs) with about 4 questions. Some of the questions will be based on *only* the first passage, some will be based on *only* the second passage, and some will be based on *both* passages. Although you may want to read both passages first, then answer all the questions, some of you may find it less anxiety-inducing to **read the first passage, answer those questions relating to the first passage, then read the second passage and answer those questions relating to the second passage, and then finally answer the remaining questions relating to both passages.** By using this approach, since you are reading one passage at a time, the time you would have spent on the second passage could be spent on answering the first set of questions relating to the first passage. This is in case you would have run out of time by reading both passages. The other advantage of this approach is that you do not have to keep both passages in mind at all times when answering the questions. That is, the only time you have to be aware of the content of both passages is when answering only those few questions related to both passages.

9 READING COMPREHENSION STRATEGIES

This section of Reading Comprehension Strategies includes several passages. These passages, though somewhat shorter than the passages that appear on the actual SAT and in the 5 SAT Practice Tests in this book, illustrate the general nature of the "real" SAT reading passages.

Each of the 9 Reading Comprehension Strategies that follow is accompanied by at least two different passages followed by questions and explanatory answers in order to explain how the strategy is used.

READING COMPREHENSION STRATEGY 1

As you read each question, determine the type: main idea, detecting details, inference, or tone/mood

Here are the four major abilities tested in Reading Comprehension questions:

1. **Main Idea**: The main idea of a passage is the central topic of the passage. As you are reading the passage, try to understand the general point of what the author is trying to convey. Try to ascertain the purpose and feel of the piece. The main idea will summarize the complete passage in a short and succinct way.

2. **Detecting Details**: To detect the details of a passage, pay close attention to the specific references and details of the piece. Curious statements such as "Einstein doesn't believe that nature plays dice with the universe" are clues to the details in the passage. When you see a curious statement, underline that statement so you can reference it again easily. Pay close attention when the author describes a specific example.

3. **Inferential Reasoning**: You must be able to ascertain what the author is trying to convey through the passage. For example, in the quote, "Einstein doesn't believe that nature plays dice with the universe," you will have to infer what the author means by this statement. What does the author mean by saying "plays dice with the universe"? You'll need to conclude the author's viewpoint via the passage.

4. **Tone or Mood**: The tone or mood of a passage can be found by determining how the author or narrator *feels* in the passage. Is the passage angry or light, happy or melancholy, humorous or frightening? What feeling do you get from the passage? Knowing this will also give you insight as you are reading the passage, and offer psychological insight into the passage.

Example 1

The fight crowd is a beast that lurks in the darkness behind the fringe of white light shed over the first six rows by the incandescents atop the ring, and is not to be trusted with pop bottles or other hardware.

5   People who go to prize fights are sadistic.

When two prominent pugilists are scheduled to pummel one another in public on a summer's evening, men and women file into the stadium in the guise of human beings, and thereafter become a part of a gray thing that squats in
10   the dark until, at the conclusion of the bloodletting, they may be seen leaving the arena in the same guise they wore when they entered.

As a rule, the mob that gathers to see men fight is unjust, vindictive, swept by intense, unreasoning hatreds, and
15   proud of its swift recognition of what it believes to be sportsmanship. It is quick to greet the purely phony move of the boxer who extends his gloves to his rival who has slipped or been pushed to the floor, and to reward this stimulating but still baloney gesture with a pattering of
20   hands that indicates the following: "You are a good sport. We recognize that you are a good sport, and we know a sporting gesture when we see one. Therefore we are all good sports too. Hurrah for us!"

The same crowd doesn't see the same boxer stick his
25   thumb in his opponent's eye or try to cut him with the laces of his glove, butt him or dig him a low one when the referee isn't in a position to see. It roots consistently for the smaller man, and never for a moment considers the desperate psychological dilemma of the larger of the two. It howls
30   with glee at a good finisher making his kill. The Roman hordes were more civilized. Their gladiators asked them whether the final blow should be administered or not. The main attraction at the modern prize fight is the spectacle of a man clubbing a helpless and vanquished opponent into
35   complete insensibility. The referee who stops a bout to save a slugged and punch-drunken man from the final ignominy is hissed by the assembled sportsmen.

QUESTIONS

1. The tone of the passage is chiefly

    (A) disgusted
    (B) jovial
    (C) matter-of-fact
    (D) satiric
    (E) devil-may-care

2. Which group of words from the passage best indicates the author's opinion?

    (A) "referee," "opponent," "finisher"
    (B) "gladiators," "slugged," "sporting gesture"
    (C) "stimulating," "hissing," "pattering"
    (D) "beast," "lurks," "gray thing"
    (E) "dilemma," "hordes," "spectacle"

3. Apparently, the author believes that boxing crowds find the referee both

    (A) gentlemanly and boring
    (B) entertaining and essential
    (C) blind and careless
    (D) humorous and threatening
    (E) necessary and bothersome

EXPLANATORY ANSWERS

1. Choice A is correct. The author is obviously much offended (disgusted) by the inhuman attitude of the crowd watching the boxing match. For example, see these lines:

    Line 1: "The fight crowd is a beast."
    Line 5: "People who go to prize fights are sadistic."
    Lines 13–14: "…the mob that gathers to see men fight is unjust, vindictive, swept by intense…hatreds."
    Lines 30–31: "The Roman hordes were more civilized."

    To answer this question, you must be able to determine the tone that is dominant in the passage. Accordingly, this is a TONE/MOOD type of question.

2. Choice D is correct. The author's opinion is clearly one of disgust and discouragement because of the behavior of the fight crowd. Accordingly, you would expect the author to use words that were condemnatory, like "beast," and gloom-filled words

like "lurks" and "gray thing." To answer this question, you must see relationships between words and feelings. So, we have here an INFERENTIAL REASONING question type.

3. Choice E is correct. Lines 24–27 show that the referee is *necessary:* "The same crowd doesn't see the same boxer stick his thumb into his opponent's eye…when the referee isn't in a position to see." Lines 35–37 show that the referee is *bothersome:* "The referee who stops a bout…is hissed by the assembled sportsmen." To answer this question, you must have the ability to understand the writer's specific statements. Accordingly, this is a DETECTING DETAILS type of question.

Example 2

Mist continues to obscure the horizon, but above us the sky is suddenly awash with lavender light. At once the geese respond. Now, as well as their cries, a beating roar rolls across the water as if five thousand housewives have
5 taken it into their heads to shake out blankets all at one time. Ten thousand housewives. It keeps up—the invisible rhythmic beating of all those goose wings—for what seems a long time. Even Lonnie is held motionless with suspense.

Then the geese begin to rise. One, two, three hundred—
10 then a thousand at a time—in long horizontal lines that unfurl like pennants across the sky. The horizon actually darkens as they pass. It goes on and on like that, flock after flock, for three or four minutes, each new contingent announcing its ascent with an accelerating roar of cries and
15 wingbeats. Then gradually the intervals between flights become longer. I think the spectacle is over, until yet another flock lifts up, following the others in a gradual turn toward the northeastern quadrant of the refuge.

Finally the sun emerges from the mist; the mist itself
20 thins a little, uncovering the black line of willows on the other side of the wildlife preserve. I remember to close my mouth—which has been open for some time—and inadvertently shut two or three mosquitoes inside. Only a few straggling geese oar their way across the sun's red
25 surface. Lonnie wears an exasperated, proprietary expression, as if he had produced and directed the show himself and had just received a bad review. "It would have been better with more light," he says; "I can't always guarantee just when they'll start moving." I assure him I thought it
30 was a fantastic sight. "Well," he rumbles, "I guess it wasn't too bad."

QUESTIONS

1. In the descriptive phrase "shake out blankets all at one time" (line 5), the author is appealing chiefly to the reader's

(A) background
(B) sight
(C) emotions
(D) thoughts
(E) hearing

2. The mood created by the author is one of

(A) tranquility
(B) excitement
(C) sadness
(D) bewilderment
(E) unconcern

3. The main idea expressed by the author about the geese is that they

(A) are spectacular to watch
(B) are unpredictable
(C) disturb the environment
(D) produce a lot of noise
(E) fly in large flocks

4. Judging from the passage, the reader can conclude that

(A) the speaker dislikes nature's inconveniences
(B) the geese's timing is predictable
(C) Lonnie has had the experience before
(D) both observers are hunters
(E) the author and Lonnie are the same person

EXPLANATORY ANSWERS

1. Choice E is correct. See lines 3–5: "...a beating roar rolls across the water...shake out blankets all at one time." The author, with these words, is no doubt appealing to the reader's hearing. To answer this question, the reader has to identify those words dealing with sound and noise. Therefore, we have here a DETECTING DETAILS type of question. It is also an INFERENTIAL REASONING question type in that the "sound" words such as "beating" and "roar" lead the reader to infer that the author is appealing to the auditory (hearing) sense.

2. Choice B is correct. Excitement courses right through this passage. Here are examples:

Lines 6–7: "...the invisible rhythmic beating of all those goose wings..."
Line 8: "Even Lonnie is held motionless with suspense."
Lines 9–10: "Then the geese begin to rise...a thousand at a time..."
Lines 13–15: "...flock after flock...roar of cries and wingbeats."

To answer this question, you must determine the dominant tone in this passage. Therefore, we have here a TONE/MOOD question type.

3. Choice A is correct. The word "spectacular" means *dramatic, thrilling, impressive.* There is considerable action expressed throughout the passage. Sometimes there is a lull—then the action begins again. See lines 16–17: "I think the spectacle is over, until yet another flock lifts up, following the others..." To answer this question, you must have the ability to judge the general significance of the passage. Accordingly, we have here a MAIN IDEA type of question.

4. Choice C is correct. See lines 25–29: "Lonnie wears an exasperated, proprietary expression...when they'll start moving.'" To answer this question, you must be able to draw a correct inference. Therefore, we have here an INFERENTIAL REASONING type of question.

READING COMPREHENSION STRATEGY 2
Underline the key parts of the reading passage*

The underlinings will help you to answer questions. Practically every question will ask you to detect the following:

a) the main idea

or

b) information that is specifically mentioned in the passage

or

c) information that is implied (not directly stated) in the passage

or

d) the tone or mood of the passage.

If you find out quickly what the question is aiming for, you will more easily arrive at the correct answer by referring to your underlinings in the passage.

Example 1

That one citizen is as good as another is a favorite American axiom, supposed to express the very essence of our Constitution and way of life. But just what do we mean when we utter that platitude? One surgeon is not as good
5 as another. One plumber is not as good as another. We soon become aware of this when we require the attention of either. Yet in political and economic matters we appear to have reached a point where knowledge and specialized training count for very little. A newspaper reporter is sent
10 out on the street to collect the views of various passersby on such a question as "Should the United States defend El Salvador?" The answer of the barfly who doesn't even know where the country is located, or that it is a country, is quoted in the next edition just as solemnly as that of the college
15 teacher of history. With the basic tenets of democracy— that all men are born free and equal and are entitled to life, liberty, and the pursuit of happiness—no decent American can possibly take issue. But that the opinion of one citizen on a technical subject is just as authoritative
20 as that of another is manifestly absurd. And to accept the opinions of all comers as having the same value is surely to encourage a cult of mediocrity.

QUESTIONS

1. Which phrase best expresses the main idea of this passage?

(A) the myth of equality
(B) a distinction about equality
(C) the essence of the Constitution
(D) a technical subject
(E) knowledge and specialized training

---

* Strategy 2 is considered the Master Reading Comprehension Strategy because it can be used effectively in every Reading Comprehension question. However, it is important that you learn the other Reading Comprehension Strategies because you may need to use them in conjunction with this strategy to find the answer efficiently.

2. The author most probably included the example of the question on El Salvador (lines 11–15) in order to

(A) move the reader to rage
(B) show that he is opposed to opinion sampling
(C) show that he has thoroughly researched his project
(D) explain the kind of opinion sampling he objects to
(E) provide a humorous but temporary diversion from his main point

3. The author would be most likely to agree that

(A) some men are born to be masters; others are born to be servants
(B) the Constitution has little relevance for today's world
(C) one should never express an opinion on a specialized subject unless he is an expert in that subject
(D) every opinion should be treated equally
(E) all opinions should not be given equal weight

Explanatory answers

1. Choice B is correct. See lines 1–7: "That one citizen…attention of either." These lines indicate that there is quite a distinction about equality when we are dealing with all the American people.

2. Choice D is correct. See lines 9–15: "A newspaper reporter…college teacher of history." These lines show that the author probably included the example of the question of El Salvador in order to explain the kind of opinion sampling he objects to.

3. Choice E is correct. See lines 18–22: "But that the opinion…to encourage a cult of mediocrity." Accordingly, the author would be most likely to agree that all opinions should *not* be given equal weight.

Example 2

She walked along the river until a policeman stopped her. It was one o'clock, he said. Not the best time to be walking alone by the side of a half-frozen river. He smiled at her, then offered to walk her home. It was the first day of
5 the new year, 1946, eight and a half months after the British tanks had rumbled into Bergen-Belsen.

That February, my mother turned twenty-six. It was difficult for strangers to believe that she had ever been a concentration-camp inmate. Her face was smooth and
10 round. She wore lipstick and applied mascara to her large, dark eyes. She dressed fashionably. But when she looked into the mirror in the mornings before leaving for work, my mother saw a shell, a mannequin who moved and spoke but who bore only a superficial resemblance to her real self.
15 The people closest to her had vanished. She had no proof that they were truly dead. No eyewitnesses had survived to vouch for her husband's death. There was no one living who had seen her parents die. The lack of confirmation haunted her. At night before she went to sleep and during the day as
20 she stood pinning dresses, she wondered if, by some chance, her parents had gotten past the Germans or had crawled out of the mass grave into which they had been shot and were living, old and helpless, somewhere in Poland. What if only one of them had died? What if they had survived and had
25 died of cold or hunger after she had been liberated, while she was in Celle* dancing with British officers?

She did not talk to anyone about these things. No one, she thought, wanted to hear them. She woke up in the mornings, went to work, bought groceries, went to the Jewish
30 Community Center and to the housing office like a robot.

*Celle is a small town in Germany.

Questions

1. The policeman stopped the author's mother from walking along the river because

(A) the river was dangerous
(B) it was the wrong time of day
(C) it was still wartime
(D) it was so cold
(E) she looked suspicious

2. The author states that his mother thought about her parents when she

   (A) walked along the river
   (B) thought about death
   (C) danced with officers
   (D) arose in the morning
   (E) was at work

3. When the author mentions his mother's dancing with the British officers, he implies that his mother

   (A) compared her dancing to the suffering of her parents
   (B) had clearly put her troubles behind her
   (C) felt it was her duty to dance with them
   (D) felt guilty about dancing
   (E) regained the self-confidence she once had

EXPLANATORY ANSWERS

1. Choice B is correct. See lines 1–4: "She walked along…offered to walk her home." The policeman's telling her that it was not the best time to be walking alone indicates clearly that "it was the wrong time of day."

2. Choice E is correct. Refer to lines 19–20: "…and during the day as she stood pinning dresses, she wondered…"

3. Choice D is correct. See lines 24–26: "What if they had survived…dancing with British officers?"

READING COMPREHENSION STRATEGY 3

Look back at the passage when in doubt

Sometimes while you are answering a question, you are not quite sure whether you have chosen the correct answer. Often, the underlinings that you have made in the reading passage will help you to determine whether a certain choice is the only correct choice.

Example 1

All museum adepts are familiar with examples of *ostrakoi*, the oystershells used in balloting. As a matter of fact, these "oystershells" are usually shards of pottery, conveniently glazed to enable the voter to express his wishes
5 in writing. In the Agora, a great number of these have come to light, bearing the thrilling name Themistocles. Into rival jars were dropped the ballots for or against his banishment. On account of the huge vote taken on that memorable date, it was to be expected that many ostrakoi would be found,
10 but the interest of this collection is that a number of these ballots are inscribed in an *identical* handwriting. There is nothing mysterious about it! The Boss was on the job, then as now. He prepared these ballots and voters cast them—no doubt for the consideration of an obol or two.
15 The *ballot box was stuffed.*

How is the glory of the American boss diminished! A vile imitation, he. His methods as old as Time!

QUESTION

1. The title that best expresses the ideas of this passage is

    (A) An Odd Method of Voting
    (B) Themistocles, an Early Dictator
    (C) Democracy in the Past
    (D) Political Trickery—Past and Present
    (E) The Diminishing American Politician

EXPLANATORY ANSWER

1. Choice D is correct. Important ideas that you might have underlined are expressed in lines 12–17: "The Boss was on the job, then as now…His methods as old as Time!"

These underlinings reveal that stuffing the ballot box is a time-honored tradition.

Example 2

But the weather predictions that an almanac always contains are, we believe, mostly wasted on the farmer. He can take a squint at the moon before turning in. He can "smell" snow or tell if the wind is shifting dangerously east.
5 He can register forebodingly an extra twinge in a rheumatic shoulder. With any of these to go by, he can be reasonably sure of tomorrow's weather. He can return the almanac to the nail behind the door and put a last stick of wood in the stove. For an almanac, a zero night or a morning's drifted
10 road—none of these has changed much since Poor Richard wrote his stuff and barns were built along the Delaware.

QUESTION

1. The author implies that, in predicting weather, there is considerable value in

    (A) reading the almanac
    (B) placing the last stick of wood in the stove
    (C) sleeping with one eye on the moon
    (D) keeping an almanac behind the door
    (E) noting rheumatic pains

EXPLANATORY ANSWER

1. Choice E is correct. Important ideas that you might have underlined are the following:

    Lines 2–3: "He can take a squint at the moon."
    Lines 3–4: "He can 'smell' snow…"
    Lines 5–6: "He can register forebodingly an extra twinge in a rheumatic shoulder."

These underlinings will reveal the quote, in lines 5–6, that gives you the correct answer.

READING COMPREHENSION STRATEGY 4

Before you start answering the questions, read the passage carefully

A great advantage of careful reading of the passage is that you will, thereby, get a very good idea of what the passage is about. If a particular sentence is not clear to you as you read, then reread that sentence to get a better idea of what the author is trying to say.

Example 1

The American Revolution is the only one in modern history which, rather than devouring the intellectuals who prepared it, carried them to power. Most of the signatories of the Declaration of Independence were intellectuals.
5 This tradition is ingrained in America, whose greatest statesmen have been intellectuals—Jefferson and Lincoln, for example. These statesmen performed their political function, but at the same time they felt a more universal responsibility, and they actively defined this responsibility.
10 Thanks to them there is in America a living school of political science. In fact, it is at the moment the only one perfectly adapted to the emergencies of the contemporary world, and one that can be victoriously opposed to communism. A European who follows American politics
15 will be struck by the constant reference in the press and from the platform to this political philosophy, to the historical events through which it was best expressed, to the great statesmen who were its best representatives.

[Underlining important ideas as you are reading this passage is strongly urged.]

QUESTIONS

1. The title that best expresses the ideas of this passage is

   (A) Fathers of the American Revolution
   (B) Jefferson and Lincoln—Ideal Statesmen
   (C) The Basis of American Political Philosophy
   (D) Democracy vs. Communism
   (E) The Responsibilities of Statesmen

2. According to the passage, intellectuals who pave the way for revolutions are usually

   (A) honored
   (B) misunderstood
   (C) destroyed
   (D) forgotten
   (E) elected to office

3. Which statement is true according to the passage?

   (A) America is a land of intellectuals.
   (B) The signers of the Declaration of Independence were well educated.
   (C) Jefferson and Lincoln were revolutionaries.
   (D) Adaptability is a characteristic of American political science.
   (E) Europeans are confused by American politics.

EXPLANATORY ANSWERS

1. Choice C is correct. Throughout this passage, the author speaks about the basis of American political philosophy. For example, see lines 5–11: "This tradition is ingrained in America,…a living school of political science."

2. Choice C is correct. See lines 1–3: "The American Revolution is the only one…carried them to power." These lines may be interpreted to mean that intellectuals who pave the way for revolutions—other than the American Revolution—are usually destroyed.

3. Choice D is correct. The word "adaptability" means the ability to adapt—to adjust to a specified use or situation. Now see lines 10–14: "…there is in America…opposed to communism."

Example 2

The microscopic vegetables of the sea, of which the diatoms are most important, make the mineral wealth of the water available to the animals. Feeding directly on the diatoms and other groups of minute unicellular algae
5 are the marine protozoa, many crustaceans, the young of crabs, barnacles, sea worms, and fishes. Hordes of small carnivores, the first link in the chain of flesh eaters, move among these peaceful grazers. There are fierce little dragons half an inch long, the sharp-jawed arrow-worms. There are gooseberry-like comb jellies, armed
10 with grasping tentacles, and there are the shrimplike euphausiids that strain food from the water with their bristly appendages. Since they drift where the currents carry them, with no power or will to oppose that of the sea, this strange community of creatures and the marine plants
15 that sustain them are called *plankton*, a word derived from the Greek, meaning wandering.

[Underlining important ideas as you are reading this passage is strongly urged.]

QUESTIONS

1. According to the passage, diatoms are a kind of

    (A) mineral
    (B) alga
    (C) crustacean
    (D) protozoan
    (E) fish

2. Which characteristic of diatoms does the passage emphasize?

    (A) size
    (B) feeding habits
    (C) activeness
    (D) numerousness
    (E) cellular structure

EXPLANATORY ANSWERS

1. Choice B is correct. See lines 3–5: "Feeding directly on the diatoms…minute unicellular algae are the marine protozoa…" These lines indicate that diatoms are a kind of alga.

2. Choice A is correct. See lines 1–4: "The microscopic vegetables of the sea…minute unicellular algae…." In these lines, the words "microscopic" and "minute" emphasize the small size of the diatoms.

READING COMPREHENSION STRATEGY 5

Get the meanings of "tough" words by using the context method

Suppose you don't know the meaning of a certain word in a passage. Then try to determine the meaning of that word from the context—that is, from the words that are close in position to that word whose meaning you don't know. Knowing the meanings of difficult words in the passage will help you to better understand the passage as a whole.

Example 1

Like all insects, it wears its skeleton on the outside—a marvelous chemical compound called *chitin* which sheathes the whole of its body. This flexible armor is tremendously tough, light, shatterproof, and resistant to alkali and
5 acid compounds that would eat the clothing, flesh, and bones of man. To it are attached muscles so arranged around catapult-like hind legs as to enable the hopper to hop, if so diminutive a term can describe so prodigious a leap as ten or twelve feet—about 150 times the length of the
10 one-or-so-inch-long insect. The equivalent feat for a man would be a casual jump, from a standing position, over the Washington Monument.

QUESTIONS

1. The word "sheathes" (line 2) means

   (A) strips
   (B) provides
   (C) exposes
   (D) encases
   (E) excites

2. The word "prodigious" (line 8) means

   (A) productive
   (B) frightening
   (C) criminal
   (D) enjoyable
   (E) enormous

EXPLANATORY ANSWERS

1. Choice D is correct. The words in line 1: "it wears its skeleton on the outside" give us the idea that "sheathes" probably means "covers" or "encases."

2. Choice E is correct. See the surrounding words in lines 7–10 "enable the hopper to hop...so prodigious a leap as ten or twelve feet—about 150 times the length of the one-or-so-inch-long insect." We may easily infer that the word "prodigious" means "great in size" or "enormous."

Example 2

Since the days when the thirteen colonies, each so jealous of its sovereignty, got together to fight the British soldiers, the American people have exhibited a tendency—a genius— to maintain widely divergent viewpoints in normal times,
5 but to unite and agree in times of stress. One reason the federal system has survived is that it has demonstrated this same tendency. Most of the time the three coequal divisions of the general government tend to compete. In crises they tend to cooperate, and not only during war. A
10 singular instance of cooperation took place in the opening days of the first administration of Franklin D. Roosevelt, when the harmonious efforts of the executive and the legis- lature to arrest the havoc of depression brought the term *rubber-stamp Congress* into the headlines. On the other
15 hand, when in 1937 Roosevelt attempted to bend the judiciary to the will of the executive by "packing" the Supreme Court, Congress rebelled. This frequently proved flexibility—this capacity of both people and government to shift from competition to cooperation and back again as
20 circumstances warrant—suggests that the federal system will be found equal to the very real dangers of the present world situation.

QUESTIONS

1. The word "havoc" (line 13) means

    (A) possession
    (B) benefit
    (C) destruction
    (D) symptom
    (E) enjoyment

2. The word "divergent" (line 4) means

    (A) interesting
    (B) discussed
    (C) flexible
    (D) differing
    (E) appreciated

EXPLANATORY ANSWERS

1. Choice C is correct. The prepositional phrase "of depression," which modifies "havoc," should indicate that this word has an unfavorable meaning. The only choice that has an unfavorable meaning is Choice C—"destruction."

2. Choice D is correct. See lines 3–5: "…the American people…widely divergent viewpoints… but to unite and agree in times of stress." The word "but" in this sentence is an *opposition indicator*. We may, therefore, assume that a "divergent viewpoint" is a "differing" one from the idea expressed in the words "to unite and agree in times of stress."

READING COMPREHENSION STRATEGY 6

Circle transitional words in the passage

There are certain transitional words—also called "bridge" or "key" words—that will help you to discover logical connections in a reading passage. *Circling* these transitional words will help you to get a better understanding of the passage.

Here are examples of commonly used transitional words and what these words may indicate.

Transitional Word	Indicating
although however in spite of rather than nevertheless on the other hand but	OPPOSITION

Transitional Word	Indicating
moreover besides additionally furthermore in fact	SUPPORT

Transitional Word	Indicating
therefore consequently accordingly because when so	RESULT

Example 1

Somewhere between 1860 and 1890, the dominant emphasis in American literature was radically changed. But it is obvious that this change was not necessarily a matter of conscious concern to all writers. In fact, many writers may
5 seem to have been actually unaware of the shifting emphasis. Moreover, it is not possible to trace the steady march of the realistic emphasis from its first feeble notes to its dominant trumpet-note of unquestioned leadership. The progress of realism is to change the figure to that of a small stream,
10 receiving accessions from its tributaries at unequal points along its course, its progress now and then balked by the sandbars of opposition or the diffusing marshes of error and compromise. Again, it is apparent that any attempt to classify rigidly, as romanticists or realists, the writers of
15 this period is doomed to failure, since it is not by virtue of the writer's conscious espousal of the romantic or realistic creed that he does much of his best work, but by virtue of that writer's sincere surrender to the atmosphere of the subject.

QUESTIONS

1. The title that best expresses the ideas of this passage is

(A) Classifying American Writers
(B) Leaders in American Fiction
(C) The Sincerity of Writers
(D) The Values of Realism
(E) The Rise of Realism

2. Which characteristic of writers does the author praise?

(A) their ability to compromise
(B) their allegiance to a "school"
(C) their opposition to change
(D) their awareness of literary trends
(E) their intellectual honesty

EXPLANATORY ANSWERS

1. Choice E is correct. Note some of the transitional words that help you to interpret the passage and see why a title of "The Rise of Realism" would be warranted. In line 6, "Moreover" is a key word that is connected to "realistic emphasis" in line 7. This idea is also connected to the sentence involving the "progress of realism" in lines 8–9. The word "again" in line 13 is also connected with this rise in realism.

2. Choice E is correct. See lines 15–18: "…since it is not by virtue of…but by virtue of that writer's sincere…of the subject." The transitional word "but" helps us to arrive at the correct answer, which is "their intellectual honesty."

Example 2

A humorous remark or situation is, furthermore, always a pleasure. We can go back to it and laugh at it again and again. One does not tire of the *Pickwick Papers,* or of the humor of Mark Twain, any more than the child tires of
5 a nursery tale that he knows by heart. Humor is a feeling, and feelings can be revived. But wit, being an intellectual and not an emotional impression, suffers by repetition. A witticism is really an item of knowledge. Wit, again, is distinctly a gregarious quality, whereas humor may abide
10 in the breast of a hermit. Those who live by themselves almost always have a dry humor. Wit is a city, humor a country, product. Wit is the accomplishment of persons who are busy with ideas; it is the fruit of intellectual cultivation and abounds in coffeehouses, in salons, and in literary
15 clubs. But humor is the gift of those who are concerned with persons rather than ideas, and it flourishes chiefly in the middle and lower classes.

QUESTION

1. It is probable that the paragraph preceding this one discussed the

(A) *Pickwick Papers*
(B) characteristics of literature
(C) characteristics of human nature
(D) characteristics of humor
(E) nature of human feelings

EXPLANATORY ANSWER

1. Choice D is correct. See lines 1–2: "A humorous remark or situation is, furthermore, always a pleasure." The transitional word "furthermore" means "in addition." We may, therefore, assume that something dealing with humor has been discussed in the previous paragraph.

READING COMPREHENSION STRATEGY 7

Don't answer a question on the basis of your own opinion

> Answer each question on the basis of the information given or suggested in the passage itself. Your own views or judgments may sometimes conflict with what the author of the passage is expressing. Answer the question according to what the author believes.

Example 1

The drama critic, on the other hand, has no such advantages. He cannot be selective; he must cover everything that is offered for public scrutiny in the principal playhouses of the city where he works. The column space
5 that seemed, yesterday, so pitifully inadequate to contain his comments on *Long Day's Journey into Night* is roughly the same as that which yawns today for his verdict on some inane comedy that has chanced to find for itself a numskull backer with five hundred thousand dollars to
10 lose. This state of affairs may help to explain why the New York theater reviewers are so often, and so unjustly, stigmatized as baleful and destructive fiends. They spend most of their professional lives attempting to pronounce intelligent judgments on plays that have no aspiration
15 to intelligence. It is hardly surprising that they lash out occasionally; in fact, what amazes me about them is that they do not lash out more violently and more frequently. As Shaw said of his fellow-critics in the 1890s, they are "a culpably indulgent body of men." Imagine the verbal
20 excoriations that would be inflicted if Lionel Trilling, or someone of comparable eminence, were called on to review five books a month of which three were novelettes composed of criminal confessions. The butchers of Broadway would seem lambs by comparison.

QUESTIONS

1. In writing this passage, the author's purpose seems to have been to

    (A) comment on the poor quality of our plays
    (B) show why book reviewing is easier than play reviewing
    (C) point out the opinions of Shaw
    (D) show new trends in literary criticism
    (E) defend the work of the play critic

2. The passage suggests that, as a play, *Long Day's Journey into Night* was

    (A) inconsequential
    (B) worthwhile
    (C) poorly written
    (D) much too long
    (E) much too short

EXPLANATORY ANSWERS

1. Choice E is correct. Throughout the passage, the author is defending the work of the play critic. See, for example, lines 9–14: "This state of affairs…plays that have no aspiration to intelligence." Be sure that you do not answer a question on the basis of your own views. You yourself may believe that the plays presented on the stage today are of poor quality (Choice A) generally. The question, however, asks about the *author's opinion*—not yours.

2. Choice B is correct. See lines 4–9: "The column space…dollars to lose." *Long Day's Journey into Night* is contrasted here with an inane comedy. This implies that *Long Day's Journey into Night* is a worthwhile play. You yourself may believe that it is a bad or underwhelming play (Choice A or C or D or E). But remember—the author's opinion, not yours, is asked for.

Example 2

History has long made a point of the fact that the magnificent flowering of ancient civilization rested upon the institution of slavery, which released opportunity at the top of the art and literature that became the glory of antiq-
5 uity. In a way, the mechanization of the present-day world produces the condition of the ancient in that the enormous development of labor-saving devices and of contrivances that amplify the capacities of mankind affords the base for the leisure necessary for widespread cultural pursuits.
10 Mechanization is the present-day slave power, with the difference that in the mechanized society there is no group of the community that does not share in the benefits of its inventions.

QUESTION

1. The author's attitude toward mechanization is one of

(A) awe
(B) acceptance
(C) distrust
(D) fear
(E) devotion

EXPLANATORY ANSWER

1. Choice B is correct. Throughout the passage, the author's attitude toward mechanization is one of acceptance. Such acceptance on the part of the author is indicated particularly in lines 10–13: "Mechanization is…the benefits of its inventions." You yourself may have a feeling of distrust (Choice C) or fear (Choice D) toward mechanization. But the author does not have such feelings.

READING COMPREHENSION STRATEGY 8

After reading the passage, read each question carefully

Be sure that you read *with care* not only the stem (beginning) of a question, but also *each* of the five choices. Some students select a choice just because it is a true statement—or because it answers part of a question. This can get you into trouble.

Example 1

The modern biographer's task becomes one of discovering the "dynamics" of the personality he is studying rather than allowing the reader to deduce that personality from documents. If he achieves a reasonable likeness, he need
5 not fear too much that the unearthing of still more material will alter the picture he has drawn; it should add dimension to it, but not change its lineaments appreciably. After all, he has had more than enough material to permit him to reach conclusions and to paint his portrait. With this abundance
10 of material he can select moments of high drama and find episodes to illustrate character and make for vividness. In any event, biographers, I think, must recognize that the writing of a life may not be as "scientific" or as "definitive" as we have pretended. Biography partakes of a large part of the
15 subjective side of man; and we must remember that those who walked abroad in our time may have one appearance for us—but will seem quite different to posterity.

QUESTION

1. According to the author, which is the real task of the modern biographer?

   (A) interpreting the character revealed to him by study of the presently available data
   (B) viewing the life of the subject in the biographer's own image
   (C) leaving to the reader the task of interpreting the character from contradictory evidence
   (D) collecting facts and setting them down in chronological order
   (E) being willing to wait until all the facts on his subject have been uncovered

EXPLANATORY ANSWER

1. Choice A is correct. See lines 1–7: "The modern biographer's task…but not change its lineaments appreciably." The word "dynamics" is used here to refer to the physical and moral forces that exerted influence on the main character of the biography. The lines quoted indicate that the author believes that the

real task of the biographer is to study the *presently available data.* Choice D may also appear to be a correct choice since a biographer is likely to consider his job to be collecting facts and setting them down in chronological order. But the passage does not directly state that a biographer has such a procedure.

Example 2

Although patience is the most important quality a treasure hunter can have, the trade demands a certain amount of courage too. I have my share of guts, but make no boast about ignoring the hazards of diving. As all good
5 divers know, the business of plunging into an alien world with an artificial air supply as your only link to the world above can be as dangerous as stepping into a den of lions. Most of the danger rests within the diver himself.

The devil-may-care diver who shows great bravado
10 underwater is the worst risk of all. He may lose his bearings in the glimmering dim light that penetrates the sea and become separated from his diving companions. He may dive too deep, too long and suffer painful, sometimes fatal, bends.

QUESTION

1. According to the author, an underwater treasure hunter needs above all to be

   (A) self-reliant
   (B) adventuresome
   (C) mentally alert
   (D) patient
   (E) physically fit

EXPLANATORY ANSWER

1. Choice D is correct. See lines 1–3: "Although patience is the most important…courage too." Choice E ("physically fit") may also appear to be a correct choice, since an underwater diver certainly has to be physically fit. Nevertheless, the passage nowhere states this directly.

1. You can increase your vocabulary tremendously by learning Latin and Greek roots, prefixes, and suffixes. Knowing the meanings of difficult words will thereby help you to understand a passage better. Sixty percent of all the words in our English language are derived from Latin and Greek. By learning certain Latin and Greek roots, prefixes, and suffixes, you will be able to understand the meanings of more than 150,000 additional English words.

2. Read as widely as possible—novels, nonfiction, newspapers, magazines.

3. Listen to people who speak well. Many TV programs have very fine speakers. You can pick up many new words listening to such programs.

4. Get into the habit of using a dictionary often. You can get a dictionary app for your phone or look up words online.

5. Play word games—crossword puzzles will really build up your vocabulary.

Example 1

Acting, like much writing, is probably a compensation for and release from the strain of some profound maladjustment of the psyche. The actor lives most intensely by proxy. He has to be somebody else to be himself. But it is
5 all done openly and for our delight. The dangerous man, the enemy of nonattachment or any other wise way of life, is the born actor who has never found his way into the Theater, who never uses a stage door, who does not take a call and then wipe the paint off his face. It is the intrusion
10 of this temperament into political life, in which at this day it most emphatically does not belong, that works half the mischief in the world. In every country you may see them rise, the actors who will not use the Theater, and always they bring down disaster from the angry gods who like to
15 see mountebanks in their proper place.

QUESTIONS

1. The meaning of "maladjustment" (lines 2–3) is a

   (A) replacement of one thing for another
   (B) profitable experience in business
   (C) consideration for the feelings of others
   (D) disregard of advice offered by others
   (E) poor relationship with one's environment

2. The meaning of "psyche" (line 3) is

   (A) person
   (B) mind
   (C) personality
   (D) psychology
   (E) physique

3. The meaning of "intrusion" (line 9) is

   (A) entering without being welcome
   (B) acceptance after considering the facts
   (C) interest that has developed after a period of time
   (D) fear as the result of imagination
   (E) refusing to obey a command

4. The meaning of "mountebanks" (line 15) is

   (A) mountain climbers
   (B) cashiers
   (C) high peaks
   (D) fakers
   (E) mortals

EXPLANATORY ANSWERS

1. Choice E is correct. The prefix "mal-" means bad. Obviously a maladjustment is a bad adjustment—that is, a poor relationship with one's environment.

2. Choice B is correct. The root "psyche" means the mind functioning as the center of thought, feeling, and behavior.

3. Choice A is correct. The prefix "in-" means "into" in this case. The root "trud, trus" means "pushing into"—or entering without being welcome.

4. Choice D is correct. The root "mont" means "to climb." The root "banc" means a "bench." A mountebank means literally "one who climbs on a bench." The actual meaning of *mountebank* is a quack (faker) who sells useless medicines from a platform in a public place.

Example 2

The American Museum of Natural History has long por-trayed various aspects of man. Primitive cultures have been shown through habitat groups and displays of man's tools, utensils, and art. In more recent years, there
5   has been a tendency to delineate man's place in nature, displaying his destructive and constructive activities on the earth he inhabits. Now, for the first time, the Museum has taken man apart, enlarged the delicate mechanisms that make him run, and examined him as a biological phenomenon.
10 In the new Hall of the Biology of Man, Museum technicians have created a series of displays that are instructive to a degree never before achieved in an exhibit hall. Using new techniques and new materials, they have been able to produce movement as well as form and color. It is a human
15 belief that beauty is only skin deep. But nature has proved to be a master designer, not only in the matter of man's bilateral symmetry but also in the marvelous packaging job that has arranged all man's organs and systems within his skin-covered case. When these are taken out of the
20 case, greatly enlarged, and given color, they reveal form and design that give the lie to that old saw. Visitors will be surprised to discover that man's insides, too, are beautiful.

QUESTIONS

1. The meaning of "bilateral" (line 17) is

    (A) biological
    (B) two-sided
    (C) natural
    (D) harmonious
    (E) technical

2. The meaning of "symmetry" (line 17) is

    (A) simplicity
    (B) obstinacy
    (C) sincerity
    (D) appearance
    (E) proportion

EXPLANATORY ANSWERS

1. Choice B is correct. The prefix "bi-" means "two." The root "latus" means "side." Therefore, "bilateral" means "two-sided."

2. Choice E is correct. The prefix "sym-" means "together." The root "metr" means "measure." The word "symmetry," therefore, means "proportion," "harmonious relation of parts," "balance."

3 VOCABULARY STRATEGIES

Although *antonyms* (opposites of words) are not on the SAT, it is still important for you to know vocabulary and the strategies to figure out the meanings of words, since there are many questions involving difficult words in all the sections on the verbal part of the SAT, that is, the **sentence completions** and **critical reading parts**.

VOCABULARY STRATEGY 1

Use roots, prefixes, and suffixes to get the meanings of words

You can increase your vocabulary tremendously by learning Latin and Greek roots, prefixes, and suffixes. Sixty percent of all the words in our English language are derived from Latin and Greek. By learning certain Latin and Greek roots, prefixes, and suffixes, you will be able to understand the meanings of more than 150,000 additional English words.

Example 1

Opposite of PROFICIENT:

(A) antiseptic
(B) unwilling
(C) inconsiderate
(D) neglectful
(E) awkward

EXPLANATORY ANSWER

Choice E is correct. The prefix PRO- means *forward, for the purpose of.* The root FIC means *to make* or *to do.* Therefore, PROFICIENT literally means *doing something in a forward way.* The definition of *proficient* is *skillful, adept, capable.* The antonym of *proficient* is, accordingly, *awkward, incapable.*

Example 2

Opposite of DELUDE:

(A) include
(B) guide
(C) reply
(D) upgrade
(E) welcome

EXPLANATORY ANSWER

Choice B is correct. The prefix DE- means *downward, against.* The root LUD means *to play* (a game). Therefore, DELUDE literally means *to play a game against.* The definition of *delude* is *to deceive, to mislead.* The antonym of *delude* is, accordingly, *to guide.*

Example 3

Opposite of LAUDATORY:

(A) vacating
(B) satisfactory
(C) revoking
(D) faultfinding
(E) silent

EXPLANATORY ANSWER

Choice D is correct. The root LAUD means *praise.* The suffix -ORY means a *tendency toward.* Therefore, LAUDATORY means having a *tendency toward praising someone.* The definition of *laudatory* is *praising.* The antonym of laudatory is, accordingly, *faultfinding.*

Example 4

Opposite of SUBSTANTIATE:

(A) reveal
(B) intimidate
(C) disprove
(D) integrate
(E) assist

EXPLANATORY ANSWER

Choice C is correct. The prefix SUB- means *under.* The root STA means *to stand.* The suffix -ATE is a verb form indicating *the act of.* Therefore, SUBSTANTIATE literally means *to perform the act of standing under.* The definition of *substantiate* is *to support* with proof or evidence. The antonym is, accordingly, *disprove.*

Example 5

Opposite of TENACIOUS:

(A) changing
(B) stupid
(C) unconscious
(D) poor
(E) antagonistic

EXPLANATORY ANSWER

Choice A is correct.

TEN = to hold; TENACIOUS = holding—OPPOSITE = *changing*

Example 6

Opposite of RECEDE:

(A) accede
(B) settle
(C) surrender
(D) advance
(E) reform

EXPLANATORY ANSWER

Choice D is correct.

RE- = back; CED = to go; RECEDE = to go back— OPPOSITE = *advance*

Example 7

Opposite of CIRCUMSPECT:

(A) suspicious
(B) overbearing
(C) listless
(D) determined
(E) careless

EXPLANATORY ANSWER

Choice E is correct.

CIRCUM- = around; SPECT = to look or see; CIRCUM-SPECT = to look all around or make sure that you see everything, careful—OPPOSITE = *careless*

Example 8

Opposite of MALEDICTION:

(A) sloppiness
(B) praise
(C) health
(D) religiousness
(E) proof

EXPLANATORY ANSWER

Choice B is correct.

MAL = bad; DICT = to speak; MALEDICTION = to speak badly about—OPPOSITE = *praise*

Example 9

Opposite of PRECURSORY:

(A) succeeding
(B) flamboyant
(C) cautious
(D) simple
(E) cheap

EXPLANATORY ANSWER

Choice A is correct.

PRE- = before; CURS = to run; PRECURSORY = run before—OPPOSITE = *succeeding*

Example 10

Opposite of CIRCUMVENT:

(A) to go the straight route
(B) alleviate
(C) to prey on one's emotions
(D) scintillate
(E) perceive correctly

EXPLANATORY ANSWER

Choice A is correct.

CIRCUM- = around (like a circle); VENT = to come; CIRCUMVENT = to come around—OPPOSITE = *to go the straight route*

VOCABULARY STRATEGY 2

Pay attention to the sound or feeling of the word—whether positive or negative, harsh or mild, big or little, etc.

If the word sounds harsh or terrible, such as "obstreperous," the meaning probably is something harsh or terrible. If you're looking for a word opposite in meaning to "obstreperous," look for a word or words that have a softer sound, such as "pleasantly quiet or docile." The sense of "obstreperous" can also seem to be negative—so if you're looking for a synonym, look for a negative word. If you're looking for an opposite (antonym), look for a positive word.

Example 1

Opposite of BELLIGERENCY

(A) pain
(B) silence
(C) homeliness
(D) elegance
(E) peace

EXPLANATORY ANSWER

Choice E is correct. The word BELLIGERENCY imparts a tone of forcefulness or confusion and means warlike. The opposite would be calmness or peacefulness. The closest choices are B or E, with E a little closer to the opposite in tone for the capitalized word. Of course, if you knew the root BELLI means "war," you could see the opposite as (E) peace.

Example 2

Opposite of DEGRADE

(A) startle
(B) elevate
(C) encircle
(D) replace
(E) assemble

EXPLANATORY ANSWER

Choice B is correct. Here you can think of the DE- in DEGRADE as a prefix that is negative (bad) and means *down,* and in fact DEGRADE does mean to debase or lower. So you should look for an opposite that would be a word with a *positive* (good) meaning. The best word from the choices is (B) elevate.

Example 3

Opposite of OBFUSCATION

(A) illumination
(B) irritation
(C) conviction
(D) minor offense
(E) stable environment

EXPLANATORY ANSWER

Choice A is correct. The prefix OB- is usually negative, as in obstacle or obliterate, and in fact OBFUSCATE means darken or obscure. So since we are looking for an opposite, you would look for a *positive* word. Choices A and E are positive, and you should go for the more positive of the two, which is Choice A.

Example 4

Opposite of MUNIFICENCE

(A) disloyalty
(B) stinginess
(C) dispersion
(D) simplicity
(E) vehemence

EXPLANATORY ANSWER

Choice B is correct because MUNIFICENCE means generosity. Many of the words ending in -ENCE, like OPULENCE, EFFERVESCENCE, LUMINESCENCE, QUINTESSENCE, etc., represent or describe something big or bright. So the opposite of one of these words would denote something small or dark.

You can associate the prefix MUNI- with MONEY, as in "municipal bonds," so the word MUNIFICENCE must deal with money and in a big way. The opposite deals with money in a small way. Choice B fits the bill.

Example 5

Opposite of DETRIMENT

(A) recurrence
(B) disclosure
(C) resemblance
(D) enhancement
(E) postponement

EXPLANATORY ANSWER

Choice D is correct. The prefix DE- can also mean against and is negative, and DETRIMENT means something that causes damage or loss. So you should look for a positive word. The only one is D, enhancement.

Example 6

Opposite of UNDERSTATE

(A) embroider
(B) initiate
(C) distort
(D) pacify
(E) violate

EXPLANATORY ANSWER

Choice A is correct. UNDERSTATE means something said in a restrained or downplayed manner. You see "under" in UNDERSTATE, so look for a choice that gives you the impression of something that is "over," as in "overstated." The only choice is A, embroider, which means to embellish.

Example 7

Opposite of DISHEARTEN

(A) engage
(B) encourage
(C) predict
(D) dismember
(E) misinform

EXPLANATORY ANSWER

Choice B is correct. You see HEART in DISHEARTEN. The DIS- is negative and means "not to," or "not to have heart," and DISHEARTEN does mean to discourage. So you want to look for a *positive* word. Choice B, encourage, fits the bill.

Example 8

Opposite of FIREBRAND

(A) an intellect
(B) one who is charitable
(C) one who makes peace
(D) a philanthropist
(E) one who is dishonest

EXPLANATORY ANSWER

Choice C is correct. You see FIRE in FIREBRAND. So think of something fiery or dangerous. The opposite of FIREBRAND must be something that's calm or safe. The best choice is Choice C.

VOCABULARY STRATEGY 3

Use word associations to determine word meanings and their opposites

Looking at the root or part of any capitalized word may suggest an association with another word that looks similar and whose meaning you know. This new word's meaning may give you a clue as to the meaning of the original word or the opposite in meaning to the original word if you need an opposite. For example, *extricate* reminds us of the word "extract," the opposite of which is "to put together."

Example 1

Opposite of STASIS

(A) stoppage
(B) reduction
(C) depletion
(D) fluctuation
(E) completion

EXPLANATORY ANSWER

Choice D is correct. Think of STATIC or STATIONARY. The opposite would be moving or fluctuating since STASIS means stopping or retarding movement.

Example 2

Opposite of APPEASE

(A) criticize
(B) analyze
(C) correct
(D) incense
(E) develop

EXPLANATORY ANSWER

Choice D is correct. APPEASE means to placate. Think of PEACE in APPEASE. The opposite would be violent or *incense*.

Example 3

Opposite of COMMISERATION

(A) undeserved reward
(B) lack of sympathy
(C) unexpected success
(D) absence of talent
(E) inexplicable danger

EXPLANATORY ANSWER

Choice B is correct. Think of MISERY in the word COMMISERATION. COMMISERATION means the sharing of misery. Choice B is the only appropriate choice.

Example 4

Opposite of JOCULAR

(A) unintentional
(B) exotic
(C) muscular
(D) exaggerated
(E) serious

EXPLANATORY ANSWER

Choice E is correct. Think of JOKE in the word JOCULAR, which means given to joking. The opposite would be *serious*.

Example 5

Opposite of ELONGATE

(A) melt
(B) wind
(C) confuse
(D) smooth
(E) shorten

EXPLANATORY ANSWER

Choice E is correct. Think of the word LONG in ELONGATE, which means to lengthen. The opposite would be short or *shorten*.

Example 6

Opposite of SLOTHFUL

(A) permanent
(B) ambitious
(C) average
(D) truthful
(E) plentiful

EXPLANATORY ANSWER

Choice B is correct. Think of SLOTH, a very, very slow animal. So SLOTHFUL, which means lazy or sluggish, must be slow and unambitious. The opposite would be *ambitious*.

Example 7

Opposite of FORTITUDE

(A) timidity
(B) conservatism
(C) placidity
(D) laxness
(E) ambition

EXPLANATORY ANSWER

Choice A is correct. FORTITUDE means strength in the face of adversity; you should think of FORT or FORTIFY as something strong. The opposite would be weakness or *timidity*.

Example 8

Opposite of LUCID

(A) underlying
(B) abstruse
(C) luxurious
(D) tight
(E) general

EXPLANATORY ANSWER

Choice B is correct. LUCID means easily understood or clear; you should think of LUCITE, a clear plastic. The opposite of clear is hard to see through or abstruse. *Note:* The AB- in ABSTRUSE makes Choice B the only *negative* choice, which is the opposite of the positive word LUCID.

Example 9

Opposite of POTENT

(A) imposing
(B) pertinent
(C) feeble
(D) comparable
(E) frantic

EXPLANATORY ANSWER

Choice C is correct. Think of the word POTENTIAL or POWERFUL. To have potential is to have the ability or power to be able to do something. So the opposite would be feeble. You could also have thought of POTENT as a positive word. The opposite would be a negative word. The only two choices that are negative are choices C and E.

FIVE SAT
PRACTICE TESTS

5 Important reasons for taking these practice tests

Each of the five Practice SATs in the final part of this book is modeled very closely after the actual SAT. You will find that each of these Practice Tests has

a. the same level of difficulty as the actual SAT

and

b. the same question formats as the actual SAT questions.

Accordingly, *taking each of the following tests is like taking the actual SAT.* There are three important reasons for taking each of these Practice SATs:

1. To find out which areas of the SAT you still need to work on.

2. To know just where to concentrate your efforts to eliminate weaknesses.

3. To reinforce the Critical-Thinking Skills—19 Math Strategies and 16 Verbal Strategies—that you learned in the Strategy Section. As we advised you, diligent study of these strategies will result in a sharp rise in your SAT Math and Verbal scores.

These three reasons for taking the five Practice Tests in this section of the book tie in closely with a very important educational principle:

WE LEARN BY DOING!

10 Tips for taking the practice tests

1. Observe the time limits exactly as given.

2. Allow no interruptions.

3. Permit no talking by anyone in the "test area."

4. Use the Answer Sheets provided at the beginning of each Practice Test. Don't make extra marks. Two answers for one question constitute an omitted question.

5. Use scratch paper to figure things out. (On your actual SAT, you are permitted to use the test book for scratchwork.)

6. Omit a question when you start "struggling" with it. Go back to that question later if you have time to do so.

7. Don't get upset if you can't answer several of the questions. You can still get a high score on the test. Even if only 40 to 60 percent of the questions you answer are correct, you will get an average or above-average score.

8. You get the same credit for answering an easy question correctly as you do for answering a tough question correctly.

9. It is advisable to guess if you are sure that at least one of the answer choices is wrong. If you are not sure whether one or more of the answer choices are wrong, statistically it will not make a difference to your total score if you guess or leave the answer blank.

10. *Your SAT score increases by approximately 10 points for every answer you get correct.*

Introduction
To see how you would do on an SAT and what you should do to improve

This SAT Test is very much like the actual SAT. It follows the genuine SAT very closely. Taking this test is like taking the actual SAT. Following is the purpose of taking this test:

1. To find out what you are *weak* in and what you are *strong* in.

2. To know where to concentrate your efforts in order to be fully prepared for the actual test.

Taking this test will prove to be a very valuable TIMESAVER for you. Why waste time studying what you already know? Spend your time profitably by studying what you *don't* know. That is what this test will tell you.

In this book, we do not waste precious pages. We get right down to the business of helping you to increase your SAT scores.

Other SAT preparation books place their emphasis on drill, drill, drill. We do not believe that drill work is of primary importance in preparing for the SAT exam. Drill work has its place. In fact, this book contains a great variety of drill material—2,500 SAT-type multiple-choice questions (Critical Reading and Math and Writing), practically all of which have explanatory answers. But drill work must be coordinated with learning Critical-Thinking Skills. These skills will help you to think clearly and critically so that you will be able to answer many more SAT questions correctly.

Ready? Start taking the test. It's just like the real thing.

SAT PRACTICE TEST 1

ANSWER SHEET FOR PRACTICE TEST 1

Section 1

Begin your essay on this page. If you need more space, continue on the next page. Do not write outside of the essay box.

Continue on the next page if necessary.

Continuation of ESSAY Section 1 from previous page. Write below only if you need more space.

Start with number 1 for each new section. If a section has fewer questions than answer spaces, leave the extra answer spaces blank. Be sure to erase any errors or stray marks completely.

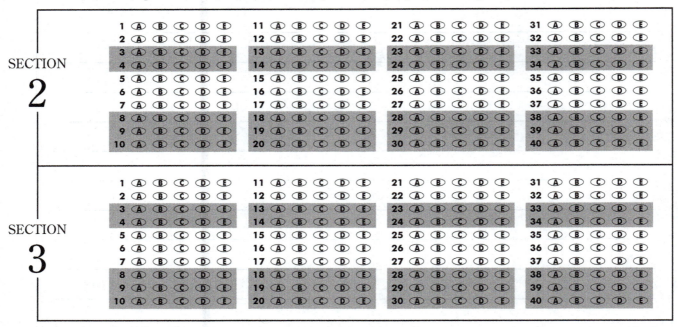

CAUTION Use the answer spaces in the grids below for Section 2 or Section 3 only if you are told to do so in your test book.

Student-Produced Responses

ONLY ANSWERS ENTERED IN THE CIRCLES IN EACH GRID WILL BE SCORED. YOU WILL NOT RECEIVE CREDIT FOR ANYTHING WRITTEN IN THE BOXES ABOVE THE CIRCLES.

Start with number 1 for each new section. If a section has fewer questions than answer spaces, leave the extra answer spaces blank. Be sure to erase any errors or stray marks completely.

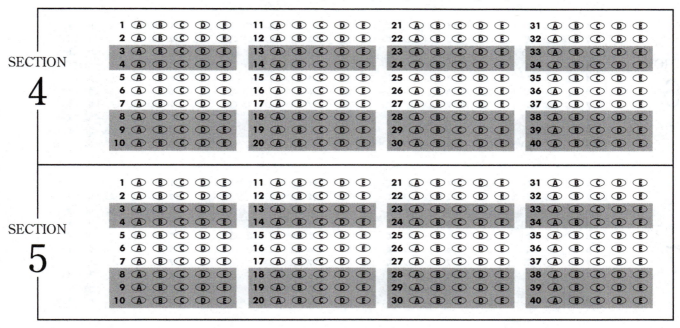

CAUTION   Use the answer spaces in the grids below for Section 2 or Section 3 only if you are told to do so in your test book.

Student-Produced Responses

ONLY ANSWERS ENTERED IN THE CIRCLES IN EACH GRID WILL BE SCORED. YOU WILL NOT RECEIVE CREDIT FOR ANYTHING WRITTEN IN THE BOXES ABOVE THE CIRCLES.

Start with number 1 for each new section. If a section has fewer questions than answer spaces, leave the extra answer spaces blank. Be sure to erase any errors or stray marks completely.

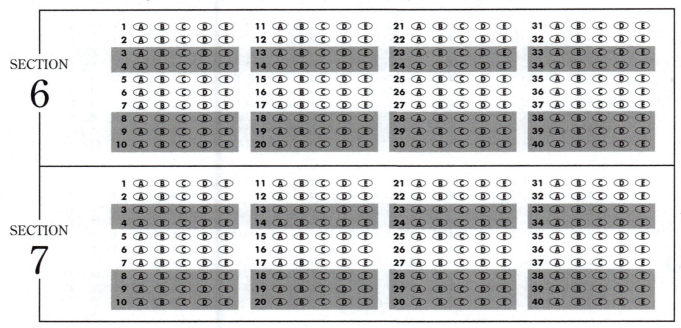

SECTION

6

SECTION

7

CAUTION   Use the answer spaces in the grids below for Section 2 or Section 3 only if you are told to do so in your test book.

Student-Produced Responses

ONLY ANSWERS ENTERED IN THE CIRCLES IN EACH GRID WILL BE SCORED. YOU WILL NOT RECEIVE CREDIT FOR ANYTHING WRITTEN IN THE BOXES ABOVE THE CIRCLES.

9   10   11   12   13

14   15   16   17   18

Start with number 1 for each new section. If a section has fewer questions than answer spaces, leave the extra answer spaces blank. Be sure to erase any errors or stray marks completely.

SECTION 8

1 Ⓐ Ⓑ Ⓒ Ⓓ Ⓔ   11 Ⓐ Ⓑ Ⓒ Ⓓ Ⓔ   21 Ⓐ Ⓑ Ⓒ Ⓓ Ⓔ   31 Ⓐ Ⓑ Ⓒ Ⓓ Ⓔ
2 Ⓐ Ⓑ Ⓒ Ⓓ Ⓔ   12 Ⓐ Ⓑ Ⓒ Ⓓ Ⓔ   22 Ⓐ Ⓑ Ⓒ Ⓓ Ⓔ   32 Ⓐ Ⓑ Ⓒ Ⓓ Ⓔ
3 Ⓐ Ⓑ Ⓒ Ⓓ Ⓔ   13 Ⓐ Ⓑ Ⓒ Ⓓ Ⓔ   23 Ⓐ Ⓑ Ⓒ Ⓓ Ⓔ   33 Ⓐ Ⓑ Ⓒ Ⓓ Ⓔ
4 Ⓐ Ⓑ Ⓒ Ⓓ Ⓔ   14 Ⓐ Ⓑ Ⓒ Ⓓ Ⓔ   24 Ⓐ Ⓑ Ⓒ Ⓓ Ⓔ   34 Ⓐ Ⓑ Ⓒ Ⓓ Ⓔ
5 Ⓐ Ⓑ Ⓒ Ⓓ Ⓔ   15 Ⓐ Ⓑ Ⓒ Ⓓ Ⓔ   25 Ⓐ Ⓑ Ⓒ Ⓓ Ⓔ   35 Ⓐ Ⓑ Ⓒ Ⓓ Ⓔ
6 Ⓐ Ⓑ Ⓒ Ⓓ Ⓔ   16 Ⓐ Ⓑ Ⓒ Ⓓ Ⓔ   26 Ⓐ Ⓑ Ⓒ Ⓓ Ⓔ   36 Ⓐ Ⓑ Ⓒ Ⓓ Ⓔ
7 Ⓐ Ⓑ Ⓒ Ⓓ Ⓔ   17 Ⓐ Ⓑ Ⓒ Ⓓ Ⓔ   27 Ⓐ Ⓑ Ⓒ Ⓓ Ⓔ   37 Ⓐ Ⓑ Ⓒ Ⓓ Ⓔ
8 Ⓐ Ⓑ Ⓒ Ⓓ Ⓔ   18 Ⓐ Ⓑ Ⓒ Ⓓ Ⓔ   28 Ⓐ Ⓑ Ⓒ Ⓓ Ⓔ   38 Ⓐ Ⓑ Ⓒ Ⓓ Ⓔ
9 Ⓐ Ⓑ Ⓒ Ⓓ Ⓔ   19 Ⓐ Ⓑ Ⓒ Ⓓ Ⓔ   29 Ⓐ Ⓑ Ⓒ Ⓓ Ⓔ   39 Ⓐ Ⓑ Ⓒ Ⓓ Ⓔ
10 Ⓐ Ⓑ Ⓒ Ⓓ Ⓔ 20 Ⓐ Ⓑ Ⓒ Ⓓ Ⓔ   30 Ⓐ Ⓑ Ⓒ Ⓓ Ⓔ   40 Ⓐ Ⓑ Ⓒ Ⓓ Ⓔ

SECTION 9

1 Ⓐ Ⓑ Ⓒ Ⓓ Ⓔ   11 Ⓐ Ⓑ Ⓒ Ⓓ Ⓔ   21 Ⓐ Ⓑ Ⓒ Ⓓ Ⓔ   31 Ⓐ Ⓑ Ⓒ Ⓓ Ⓔ
2 Ⓐ Ⓑ Ⓒ Ⓓ Ⓔ   12 Ⓐ Ⓑ Ⓒ Ⓓ Ⓔ   22 Ⓐ Ⓑ Ⓒ Ⓓ Ⓔ   32 Ⓐ Ⓑ Ⓒ Ⓓ Ⓔ
3 Ⓐ Ⓑ Ⓒ Ⓓ Ⓔ   13 Ⓐ Ⓑ Ⓒ Ⓓ Ⓔ   23 Ⓐ Ⓑ Ⓒ Ⓓ Ⓔ   33 Ⓐ Ⓑ Ⓒ Ⓓ Ⓔ
4 Ⓐ Ⓑ Ⓒ Ⓓ Ⓔ   14 Ⓐ Ⓑ Ⓒ Ⓓ Ⓔ   24 Ⓐ Ⓑ Ⓒ Ⓓ Ⓔ   34 Ⓐ Ⓑ Ⓒ Ⓓ Ⓔ
5 Ⓐ Ⓑ Ⓒ Ⓓ Ⓔ   15 Ⓐ Ⓑ Ⓒ Ⓓ Ⓔ   25 Ⓐ Ⓑ Ⓒ Ⓓ Ⓔ   35 Ⓐ Ⓑ Ⓒ Ⓓ Ⓔ
6 Ⓐ Ⓑ Ⓒ Ⓓ Ⓔ   16 Ⓐ Ⓑ Ⓒ Ⓓ Ⓔ   26 Ⓐ Ⓑ Ⓒ Ⓓ Ⓔ   36 Ⓐ Ⓑ Ⓒ Ⓓ Ⓔ
7 Ⓐ Ⓑ Ⓒ Ⓓ Ⓔ   17 Ⓐ Ⓑ Ⓒ Ⓓ Ⓔ   27 Ⓐ Ⓑ Ⓒ Ⓓ Ⓔ   37 Ⓐ Ⓑ Ⓒ Ⓓ Ⓔ
8 Ⓐ Ⓑ Ⓒ Ⓓ Ⓔ   18 Ⓐ Ⓑ Ⓒ Ⓓ Ⓔ   28 Ⓐ Ⓑ Ⓒ Ⓓ Ⓔ   38 Ⓐ Ⓑ Ⓒ Ⓓ Ⓔ
9 Ⓐ Ⓑ Ⓒ Ⓓ Ⓔ   19 Ⓐ Ⓑ Ⓒ Ⓓ Ⓔ   29 Ⓐ Ⓑ Ⓒ Ⓓ Ⓔ   39 Ⓐ Ⓑ Ⓒ Ⓓ Ⓔ
10 Ⓐ Ⓑ Ⓒ Ⓓ Ⓔ 20 Ⓐ Ⓑ Ⓒ Ⓓ Ⓔ   30 Ⓐ Ⓑ Ⓒ Ⓓ Ⓔ   40 Ⓐ Ⓑ Ⓒ Ⓓ Ⓔ

SECTION 10

1 Ⓐ Ⓑ Ⓒ Ⓓ Ⓔ   11 Ⓐ Ⓑ Ⓒ Ⓓ Ⓔ   21 Ⓐ Ⓑ Ⓒ Ⓓ Ⓔ   31 Ⓐ Ⓑ Ⓒ Ⓓ Ⓔ
2 Ⓐ Ⓑ Ⓒ Ⓓ Ⓔ   12 Ⓐ Ⓑ Ⓒ Ⓓ Ⓔ   22 Ⓐ Ⓑ Ⓒ Ⓓ Ⓔ   32 Ⓐ Ⓑ Ⓒ Ⓓ Ⓔ
3 Ⓐ Ⓑ Ⓒ Ⓓ Ⓔ   13 Ⓐ Ⓑ Ⓒ Ⓓ Ⓔ   23 Ⓐ Ⓑ Ⓒ Ⓓ Ⓔ   33 Ⓐ Ⓑ Ⓒ Ⓓ Ⓔ
4 Ⓐ Ⓑ Ⓒ Ⓓ Ⓔ   14 Ⓐ Ⓑ Ⓒ Ⓓ Ⓔ   24 Ⓐ Ⓑ Ⓒ Ⓓ Ⓔ   34 Ⓐ Ⓑ Ⓒ Ⓓ Ⓔ
5 Ⓐ Ⓑ Ⓒ Ⓓ Ⓔ   15 Ⓐ Ⓑ Ⓒ Ⓓ Ⓔ   25 Ⓐ Ⓑ Ⓒ Ⓓ Ⓔ   35 Ⓐ Ⓑ Ⓒ Ⓓ Ⓔ
6 Ⓐ Ⓑ Ⓒ Ⓓ Ⓔ   16 Ⓐ Ⓑ Ⓒ Ⓓ Ⓔ   26 Ⓐ Ⓑ Ⓒ Ⓓ Ⓔ   36 Ⓐ Ⓑ Ⓒ Ⓓ Ⓔ
7 Ⓐ Ⓑ Ⓒ Ⓓ Ⓔ   17 Ⓐ Ⓑ Ⓒ Ⓓ Ⓔ   27 Ⓐ Ⓑ Ⓒ Ⓓ Ⓔ   37 Ⓐ Ⓑ Ⓒ Ⓓ Ⓔ
8 Ⓐ Ⓑ Ⓒ Ⓓ Ⓔ   18 Ⓐ Ⓑ Ⓒ Ⓓ Ⓔ   28 Ⓐ Ⓑ Ⓒ Ⓓ Ⓔ   38 Ⓐ Ⓑ Ⓒ Ⓓ Ⓔ
9 Ⓐ Ⓑ Ⓒ Ⓓ Ⓔ   19 Ⓐ Ⓑ Ⓒ Ⓓ Ⓔ   29 Ⓐ Ⓑ Ⓒ Ⓓ Ⓔ   39 Ⓐ Ⓑ Ⓒ Ⓓ Ⓔ
10 Ⓐ Ⓑ Ⓒ Ⓓ Ⓔ 20 Ⓐ Ⓑ Ⓒ Ⓓ Ⓔ   30 Ⓐ Ⓑ Ⓒ Ⓓ Ⓔ   40 Ⓐ Ⓑ Ⓒ Ⓓ Ⓔ

Section 1

> **Time:** 25 Minutes—Turn to page 142 of your answer sheet to write your ESSAY.

The purpose of the essay is to have you show how well you can express and develop your ideas. You should develop your point of view, logically and clearly present your ideas, and use language accurately.

You should write your essay on the lines provided on your answer sheet. You should not write on any other paper. You will have enough space if you write on every line and if you keep your handwriting to a reasonable size. Make sure that your handwriting is legible to other readers.

You will have 25 minutes to write an essay on the assignment below. *Do not write on any other topic. If you do so, you will receive a score of 0.*

Think carefully about the issue presented in the following excerpt and the assignment below.

> *The well-known proverb "Ignorance is bliss" suggests that people with knowledge of the world's complexities and its limitations are often unhappy, while their less-knowledgeable counterparts remain contented. But how accurate is this folk wisdom? A recent study showed that well-informed people were more likely to report feelings of well-being. In fact, more knowledge leads people to feel better about themselves and more satisfied with their lives.*
>
> –Adapted from Lee Sigelman, "Is Ignorance Bliss? A Reconsideration of the Folk Wisdom"

Assignment: What is your belief on the notion that more knowledge makes one happier? Support your position by citing an example or examples from history, science and technology, literature, the arts, politics, current events, sports, or your observation or experience.

DO NOT WRITE YOUR ESSAY IN YOUR TEST BOOK. You will receive credit only for what you write on your answer sheet.

BEGIN WRITING YOUR ESSAY ON PAGE 142 OF THE ANSWER SHEET.

If you finish before time is called, you may check your work on this section only.
Do not turn to any other section in the test.

Section 2

Time: 25 Minutes – Turn to Section 2 (page 144) of your answer sheet to answer the questions in this section. 20 Questions

Directions: For this section, solve each problem and decide which is the best of the choices given. Fill in the corresponding circle on the answer sheet. You may use any available space for scratchwork.

Notes:

1. The use of a calculator is permitted.

2. All numbers used are real numbers.

3. Figures that accompany problems in this test are intended to provide information useful in solving the problems. They are drawn as accurately as possible EXCEPT when it is stated in a specific problem that the figure is not drawn to scale. All figures lie in a plane unless otherwise indicated.

4. Unless otherwise specified, the domain of any function f is assumed to be the set of all real numbers x for which $f(x)$ is a real number.

REFERENCE INFORMATION

   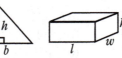

$A = \pi r^2 \quad A = lw \quad A = \frac{1}{2}bh \quad V = lwh \quad V = \pi r^2 h \quad c^2 = a^2 + b^2 \quad \textit{Special Right Triangle.}$
$C = 2\pi r$

The number of degrees of arc in a circle is 360.
The sum of the measures in degrees of the angles of a triangle is 180.

---

1. If a and b are positive integers and $ab = 64$, what is the smallest possible value of $a + b$?

   (A) 65
   (B) 34
   (C) 20
   (D) 16
   (E) 8

2. Find the value of $x + x^3 + x^5 + x^6$ if $x = -1$.

   (A) -4
   (B) -2
   (C) 1
   (D) 2
   (E) 4

GO ON TO THE NEXT PAGE ➤

3.

$$AB$$
$$\underline{+\ BA}$$
$$66$$

If $0 < A < 6$ and $0 < B < 6$ in the addition problem above, how many different integer values of A are possible? (AB and BA both represent two-digit integers.)

(A) Two
(B) Three
(C) Four
(D) Five
(E) Six

4. At 8:00 A.M. the outside temperature was $-15°$F. At 11:00 A.M. the temperature was $0°$F. If the temperature continues to rise at the same uniform rate, what will the temperature be at 5:00 P.M. on the same day?

(A) $-15°$F
(B) $-5°$F
(C) $0°$F
(D) $15°$F
(E) $30°$F

Question 5 refers to the following chart.

Number of Shirts	Total Price
1	$12.00
Box of 3	$22.50
Box of 6	$43.40

5. Which of the following is the closest approximation of the lowest cost per shirt, when a box of shirts is purchased?

(A) $7.10
(B) $7.20
(C) $7.30
(D) $7.40
(E) $7.50

6. If $5x^2 - 15x = 0$ and $x \neq 0$, find the value of x.

(A) -10
(B) -3
(C) 10
(D) 5
(E) 3

GO ON TO THE NEXT PAGE ➤

7. The chickens on a certain farm consumed 600 pounds of feed in half a year. During that time the total number of eggs laid was 5,000. If the feed cost $1.25 per pound, then the feed cost per egg was

(A) $0.0750
(B) $0.1250
(C) $0.15
(D) $0.25
(E) $0.3333

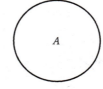

A   B   C

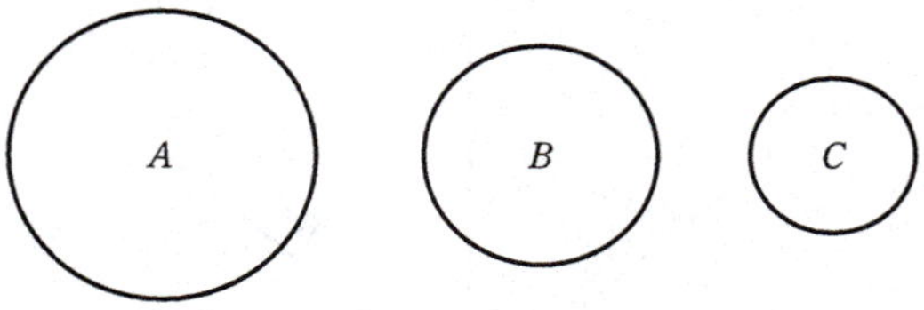

9. In the figure above, there are three circles, *A*, *B*, and *C*. The area of *A* is three times that of *B*, and the area of *B* is three times that of *C*. If the area of *B* is 1, find the sum of the areas of *A*, *B*, and *C*.

(A) 3
(B) $3\frac{1}{3}$
(C) $4\frac{1}{3}$
(D) 5
(E) $6\frac{1}{3}$

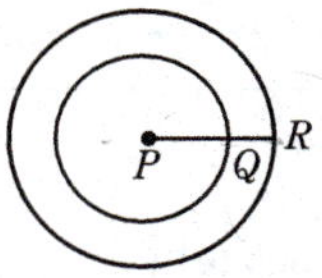

8. If X is the set of negative numbers and Y is the set of positive numbers, then the union of X and Y and 0 is the set of

(A) all real numbers
(B) all integers
(C) all rational numbers
(D) all irrational numbers
(E) all odd integers

Note: Figure not drawn to scale.

10. In the figure above, two concentric circles with center *P* are shown. *PQR,* a radius of the larger circle, equals 9. *PQ,* a radius of the smaller circle, equals 4. If a circle *L* (not shown) is drawn with center at *R* and *Q* on its circumference, find the radius of circle *L*.

(A) 13
(B) 5
(C) 4
(D) 2
(E) It cannot be determined from the information given.

GO ON TO THE NEXT PAGE ➤

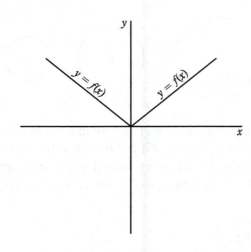

11. The above graph could represent the equation

(A) $y = x$

(B) $y = |x|$

(C) $y = x^2$

(D) $y = x, x > 0$

$y = 0, x = 0$

$y = -|x|, x < 0$

(E) $y = -x$

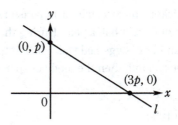

Note: Figure not drawn to scale.

13. What is the slope of line l in the above figure?

(A) -3

(B) $-\dfrac{1}{3}$

(C) 0

(D) $\dfrac{1}{3}$

(E) 3

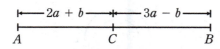

12. Given ACB is a straight line segment, and C is the midpoint of AB, if the two segments have the lengths shown above, then

(A) $a = -2b$

(B) $a = -\dfrac{2}{5}b$

(C) $a = \dfrac{2}{5}b$

(D) $a = b$

(E) $a = 2b$

14. Bus A averages 40 kilometers per gallon of fuel. Bus B averages 50 kilometers per gallon of fuel. If the price of fuel is $3 per gallon, how much less would an 800-kilometer trip cost for Bus B than for Bus A?

(A) $18

(B) $16

(C) $14

(D) $12

(E) $10

GO ON TO THE NEXT PAGE ➤

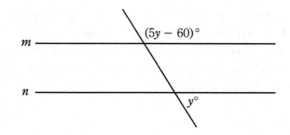

15. $m\|n$ in the figure above. Find y.

   (A) 10
   (B) 20
   (C) 40
   (D) 65
   (E) 175

16. Given 4 percent of $(2a + b)$ is 18 and a is a positive integer, what is the *greatest* possible value of b?

   (A) 450
   (B) 449
   (C) 448
   (D) 43
   (E) 8

17. If an ant runs randomly through an enclosed circular field of radius 2 feet with an inner circle of radius 1 foot, what is the probability that the ant will be in the inner circle at any one time?

   (A) $\frac{1}{8}$
   (B) $\frac{1}{6}$
   (C) $\frac{1}{4}$
   (D) $\frac{1}{2}$
   (E) 1

18. The length and width of a rectangle are $3w$ and w, respectively. The length of the hypotenuse of a right triangle, one of whose acute angles is 30°, is $2w$. What is the ratio of the area of the rectangle to that of the triangle?

   (A) $2\sqrt{3} : 1$
   (B) $\sqrt{3} : 1$
   (C) $1 : \sqrt{3}$
   (D) $1 : 2\sqrt{3}$
   (E) $1 : 6$

GO ON TO THE NEXT PAGE ❯

19. At a certain college, the number of freshmen is three times the number of seniors. If $\frac{1}{4}$ of the freshmen and $\frac{1}{3}$ of the seniors attend a football game, what fraction of the total number of freshmen and seniors attends the game?

(A) $\frac{5}{24}$

(B) $\frac{13}{48}$

(C) $\frac{17}{48}$

(D) $\frac{11}{24}$

(E) $\frac{23}{48}$

20. At Jones College, there are a total of 100 students. If 30 of the students have cars on campus, and 50 have bicycles, and 20 have both cars and bicycles, then how many students have neither a car nor a bicycle on campus?

(A) 80
(B) 60
(C) 40
(D) 20
(E) 0

STOP

If you finish before time is called, you may check your work on this section only.
Do not turn to any other section in the test.

Take a 5 minute break

before starting section 3

Section 3

Time: 25 Minutes – Turn to Section 3 (page 144) of your answer sheet to answer the questions in this section. 20 Questions

Directions: For this section, solve each problem and decide which is the best of the choices given. Fill in the corresponding circle on the answer sheet. You may use any available space for scratchwork.

Notes:

1. The use of a calculator is permitted.

2. All numbers used are real numbers.

3. Figures that accompany problems in this test are intended to provide information useful in solving the problems. They are drawn as accurately as possible EXCEPT when it is stated in a specific problem that the figure is not drawn to scale. All figures lie in a plane unless otherwise indicated.

4. Unless otherwise specified, the domain of any function f is assumed to be the set of all real numbers x for which $f(x)$ is a real number.

REFERENCE INFORMATION

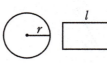 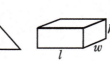 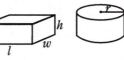

$A = \pi r^2$ $A = lw$ $A = \frac{1}{2}bh$ $V = lwh$ $V = \pi r^2 h$ $c^2 = a^2 + b^2$ *Special Right Triangle.*
$C = 2\pi r$

The number of degrees of arc in a circle is 360.
The sum of the measures in degrees of the angles of a triangle is 180.

1. If $55,555 = y + 50,505$, find the value of $50,505 - 10y$.

    (A) -5.05
    (B) 0
    (C) 5
    (D) 5.05
    (E) 50.5

2. $3x(4x + 2y) =$

    (A) $7x + 5xy$
    (B) $12x + 6xy$
    (C) $12x^2 + 2y$
    (D) $12x^2 + 6xy$
    (E) $12x^2 + 6x$

GO ON TO THE NEXT PAGE ➤

Box Number	Height of Box (in millimeters)
A	1,700
B	2,450
C	2,735
D	1,928
E	2,130

3. Exactly how many of the boxes listed in the table above are more than 20 decimeters high?

   (1 decimeter = 100 millimeters)

   (A) Zero
   (B) One
   (C) Two
   (D) Three
   (E) Four

5. $\dfrac{7}{10} + \dfrac{7}{100} + \dfrac{77}{1,000} =$

   (A) 0.0091
   (B) 0.7777
   (C) 0.784
   (D) 0.847
   (E) 0.854

4. If $a - 3 = 7$, then $2a - 14 =$

   (A) -6
   (B) -4
   (C) 2
   (D) 4
   (E) 6

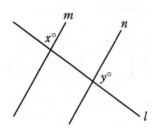

6. Parallel lines m and n are intersected by line l as shown. Find the value of $x + y$.

   (A) 180
   (B) 150
   (C) 120
   (D) 90
   (E) It cannot be determined from the information given.

GO ON TO THE NEXT PAGE ➤

Item	Value
1	P
2	$P \times 3$
3	$(P \times 3) \div 2$
4	$[(P \times 3) \div 2] + 12$
5	$[(P \times 3) \div 2] + 12 - 1$

7. According to the table above, which item has the greatest value when $P = 12$?

   (A) 1

   (B) 2

   (C) 3

   (D) 4

   (E) 5

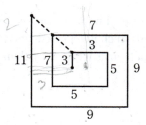

Note: Figure not drawn to scale.

9. In the figure above, each pair of intersecting segments is perpendicular with lengths as shown. Find the length of the dashed line segment.

   (A) 7

   (B) $6\sqrt{3}$

   (C) $4\sqrt{2}$

   (D) $\sqrt{46}$

   (E) $\sqrt{59}$

8. If $\dfrac{3x}{4} = 9$, find $6x$.

   (A) 12

   (B) 18

   (C) 27

   (D) 36

   (E) 72

10. For how many two-digit positive numbers will tripling the tens digit give us a two-digit number that is triple the original number?

   (A) None

   (B) One

   (C) Two

   (D) Three

   (E) Four

GO ON TO THE NEXT PAGE ➤

11. If A is the least positive 5-digit integer with *nonzero* digits, none of which is repeated, and B is the greatest of such positive integers, then $B - A =$

   (A) 41,976
   (B) 66,666
   (C) 86,420
   (D) 86,424
   (E) 89,999

13. Given the volume of a cube is 8 cubic meters, find the distance from any vertex to the center point inside the cube.

   (A) 1 m
   (B) $\sqrt{2}$ m
   (C) $2\sqrt{2}$ m
   (D) $2\sqrt{3}$ m
   (E) $\sqrt{3}$ m

12. At one instant, two meteors are 2,500 kilometers apart and traveling toward each other in straight paths along the imaginary line joining them. One meteor has a velocity of 300 meters per second while the other travels at 700 meters per second. Assuming that their velocities are constant and that they continue along the same paths, how many seconds elapse from the first instant to the time of their collision? (1 kilometer = 1,000 meters)

   (A) 250
   (B) 500
   (C) 1,250
   (D) 2,500
   (E) 5,000

14. The sum of a number of consecutive positive integers will always be divisible by 2 if the number of integers is a multiple of

   (A) 6
   (B) 5
   (C) 4
   (D) 3
   (E) 2

GO ON TO THE NEXT PAGE ❯

15. Find the circumference of a circle that has the same area as a square that has perimeter 2π.

(A) $2\sqrt{2}$

(B) $\pi\sqrt{\pi}$

(C) $\dfrac{\pi}{2}$

(D) $\dfrac{\sqrt{2}}{\pi}$

(E) 2

16. If $\dfrac{a}{b} = \dfrac{1}{4}$, where a is a positive integer, which of the following is a possible value of $\dfrac{a^2}{b}$?

I. $\dfrac{1}{4}$

II. $\dfrac{1}{2}$

III. 1

(A) None

(B) I only

(C) I and II only

(D) I and III only

(E) I, II, and III

17. A plane left airport A and has traveled x kilometers per hour for y hours. In terms of x and y, how many kilometers from airport A had the plane traveled $\dfrac{2}{3}y$ hours ago?

(A) $\dfrac{xy}{6}$

(B) $\dfrac{xy}{3}$

(C) xy

(D) $\dfrac{3xy}{2}$

(E) $\dfrac{xy}{12}$

18. The average (arithmetic mean) of k scores is 20. The average of 10 of these scores is 15. Find the average of the remaining scores in terms of k.

(A) $\dfrac{20k + 150}{10}$

(B) $\dfrac{20k - 150}{10}$

(C) $\dfrac{150 - 20k}{10}$

(D) $\dfrac{150 - 20k}{k - 10}$

(E) $\dfrac{20k - 150}{k - 10}$

GO ON TO THE NEXT PAGE ➤

19. A square has an area of R^2. An equilateral triangle has a perimeter of E. If r is the perimeter of the square and e is a side of the equilateral triangle, then, in terms of R and E, $e + r =$

(A) $\dfrac{E + R}{7}$

(B) $\dfrac{4R + 3E}{3}$

(C) $\dfrac{3E + 4R}{12}$

(D) $\dfrac{12E + R}{3}$

(E) $\dfrac{E + 12R}{3}$

20. Using the formula $C = \dfrac{5}{9}(F - 32)$, if the Celsius (C) temperature increased 35°, by how many degrees would the Fahrenheit (F) temperature be increased?

(A) $19\dfrac{4}{9}^{\circ}$

(B) 31°

(C) 51°

(D) 63°

(E) 82°

STOP

If you finish before time is called, you may check your work on this section only.
Do not turn to any other section in the test.

Take a 5 minute break

before starting section 4

Section 4

Time: 25 Minutes – Turn to Section 4 (page 145) of your answer sheet to answer the questions in this section. 24 Questions

Directions: For each question in this section, select the best answer from among the choices given and fill in the corresponding circle on the answer sheet.

Each sentence below has one or two blanks, each blank indicating that something has been omitted. Beneath the sentence are five words or sets of words labeled A through E. Choose the word or set of words that, when inserted in the sentence, *best* fits the meaning of the sentence as a whole.

Example:

Hoping to _____ the dispute, negotiators proposed a compromise that they felt would be _____ to both labor and management.

(A) enforce...useful

(B) end...divisive

(C) overcome...unattractive

(D) extend...satisfactory

(E) resolve...acceptable

Ⓐ Ⓑ Ⓒ Ⓓ ●

---

1. Because the majority of the evening cable TV programs available dealt with violence and sex, the parents decided that the programs were _____ for the children to watch.

    (A) exclusive
    (B) acceptable
    (C) instructive
    (D) inappropriate
    (E) unnecessary

2. The novel *Uncle Tom's Cabin*, which effectively _____ the unfairness toward African Americans, was a major influence in _____ the antislavery movement.

    (A) portrayed...strengthening
    (B) attacked...pacifying
    (C) glamorized...launching
    (D) viewed...appraising
    (E) exposed...condemning

GO ON TO THE NEXT PAGE ➤

3. Having written 140 books to date, he may well be
    considered one of the most _____ novelists
    of the century.

    (A) eccentric
    (B) controversial
    (C) easygoing
    (D) unheralded
    (E) prolific

4. The articles that he wrote ran the gamut from the
    serious to the lighthearted, from objective to the
    _____, from the innocuous to the _____.

    (A) constant...evil
    (B) casual...realistic
    (C) ridiculous...remote
    (D) argumentative...hostile
    (E) incapacitated...conditioned

5. Because auto repair places charge such _____
    rates, many community colleges have _____
    courses in automotive mechanics.

    (A) shattering...planned
    (B) exorbitant...instituted
    (C) impertinent...discussed
    (D) reasonable...introduced
    (E) intolerable...discontinued

6. Though Socrates was _____ by his students
    who found truth in his teachings, his philosophy
    constituted _____ to the existent government.

    (A) accepted...a benefit
    (B) denied...an innovation
    (C) appraised...an exception
    (D) slighted...a challenge
    (E) revered...a threat

7. The quotation was erroneously _____ to a
    British poet.

    (A) resolved
    (B) attributed
    (C) activated
    (D) relegated
    (E) vitiated

8. Mindful that his hardworking parents _____
    to give him an education, Lopez, now wealthy,
    contributes _____ to scholarship funds for the
    needy.

    (A) planned...needlessly
    (B) skimped...profitably
    (C) squandered...sparingly
    (D) struggled...generously
    (E) regaled...regretfully

GO ON TO THE NEXT PAGE >

Each passage below is followed by questions based on its content. Answer the questions on the basis of what is _stated_ or _implied_ in each passage and in any introductory material that may be provided.

Questions 9–10 are based on the following passage.

Plutarch admired those who could use life for grand purposes and depart from it as grandly, but he would not pass over weaknesses and vices that marred the grandeur. His hero of heroes was Alexander the Great; he admired
5 him above all other men, while his abomination of abominations was bad faith, dishonorable action. Nevertheless he tells with no attempt to extenuate how Alexander promised a safe conduct to a brave Persian army if they surrendered, but then, "even as they were marching away he fell upon
10 them and put them all to the sword," "a breach of his word," Plutarch says sadly, "which is a lasting blemish to his achievements." He adds piteously, "but the only one." He hated to tell that story.

9. Which of the following conclusions is _least_ justified by the passage?

(A) Plutarch considered Alexander basically a great man.

(B) The Persians believed that Alexander was acting in good faith.

(C) The Persians withdrew from the battlefield in orderly array.

(D) The author is familiar with Plutarch's writing.

(E) The author considers Plutarch unfair to Alexander.

10. As used in this passage, the word "extenuate" (line 7) means

(A) interpret
(B) exaggerate
(C) emphasize
(D) excuse
(E) condemn

Questions 11–12 are based on the following passage.

It is no longer needful to labor Dickens's power as a portrayer of modern society nor the seriousness of his "criticism of life." But we are still learning to appreciate his supreme attainment as an artist. Richness of poetic
5 imagery, modulations of emotional tone, subtleties of implication, complex unities of structure, intensities of psychological insight, a panoply of achievement, mount up to overwhelming triumph. Though contemporary readers perhaps still feel somewhat queasy about Dickens's senti-
10 ment, his comedy and his drama sweep all before them. Even his elaborate and multistranded plots are now seen as great symphonic compositions driving forward through theme and variation to the resolving chords on which they close.

11. According to the passage, readers most recently have begun to appreciate Dickens's

(A) feeling for culture
(B) criticisms of life
(C) rhythms
(D) literary references
(E) literary craftsmanship

12. According to the passage, the endings of Dickens's works are most probably characterized by

(A) frequent use of comic relief
(B) unexpected developments
(C) visually effective symbols
(D) a lack of sense of completion
(E) dramatic power

GO ON TO THE NEXT PAGE ➤

Questions 13–24 are based on the following passage.

The passage describes the author's attitude toward transportation.

Many people who are willing to concede that the railroad must be brought back to life are chiefly thinking of bringing this about on the very terms that have robbed us of a balanced transportation network—that is, by treating
5 speed as the only important factor, forgetting reliability, comfort and safety, and seeking some mechanical dodge for increasing the speed and automation of surface vehicles.

My desk is littered with such technocratic fantasies, hopefully offered as "solutions." They range from old-
10 fashioned monorails and jet-propelled hovercraft (now extinct) to a more scientific mode of propulsion at 2,000 miles an hour, from completely automated highway travel in private cars to automated vehicles a government department is now toying with for "facilitating" urban traffic.

15 What is the function of transportation? What place does locomotion occupy in the whole spectrum of human needs? Perhaps the first step in developing an adequate transportation policy would be to clear our minds of technocratic cant. Those who believe that transportation
20 is the chief end of life should be put in orbit at a safe lunar distance from the earth.

The prime purpose of passenger transportation is not to increase the amount of physical movement but to increase the possibilities for human association, coopera-
25 tion, personal intercourse, and choice.

A balanced transportation system, accordingly, calls for a balance of resources and facilities and opportunities in every other part of the economy. Neither speed nor mass demand offers a criterion of social efficiency. Hence such
30 limited technocratic proposals as that for high-speed trains between already overcrowded and overextended urban centers would only add to the present lack of functional balance and purposeful organization viewed in terms of human need. Variety of choices, facilities and destinations,
35 not speed alone, is the mark of an organic transportation system. And, incidentally, this is an important factor of safety when any part of the system breaks down. Even confirmed air travelers appreciate the railroad in foul weather.

If we took human needs seriously in recasting the
40 whole transportation system, we should begin with the human body and make the fullest use of pedestrian move-ment, not only for health but for efficiency in moving large crowds over short distances. The current introduction of shopping malls, free from wheeled traffic, is both a far
45 simpler and far better *technical* solution than the many costly proposals for introducing moving sidewalks or other rigidly automated modes of locomotion. At every stage we should provide for the right type of locomotion, at the right speed, within the right radius, to meet human

50 needs. Neither maximum speed nor maximum traffic nor maximum distance has by itself any human significance.

With the over-exploitation of the particular car comes an increased demand for engineering equipment, to roll ever-wider carpets of concrete over the bulldozed land-
55 scape and to endow the petroleum magnates of some places with fabulous capacities for personal luxury and political corruption. Finally, the purpose of this system, abetted by similar concentration on planes and rockets, is to keep an increasing volume of motorists and tourists
60 in motion, at the highest possible speed, in a sufficiently comatose state not to mind the fact that their distant destination has become the exact counterpart of the very place they have left. The end product everywhere is environmental desolation.

65 If this is the best our technological civilization can do to satisfy genuine human needs and nurture man's further development, it's plainly time to close up shop. If indeed we go farther and faster along this route, there is plenty of evidence to show that the shop will close up without our
70 help. Behind our power blackouts, our polluted environ-ments, our transportation breakdowns, our nuclear threats, is a failure of mind. Technocratic anesthesia has put us to sleep. Results that were predictable—and predicted!— three-quarters of a century ago without awakening any response still find us unready to cope with them—or even
75 to admit their existence.

13.   The author criticizes most railroad advocates because their emphasis is primarily on

(A) monetary costs
(B) speed
(C) traffic flow
(D) reliability
(E) pollution

14.   The author believes that the purpose(s) of transportation is (are)

I.   to move people from place to place efficiently
II.   to increase social contact
III. to open up opportunities

(A) I only
(B) II only
(C) III only
(D) I and II only
(E) I, II, and III

15. A solution advocated by the author for transporting masses of people over short distances involves

    (A) jet-propelled hovercraft
    (B) automated vehicles
    (C) conveyor belts
    (D) moving sidewalks
    (E) pedestrian malls

16. Excessive reliance on the automobile, according to the author, is associated with

    (A) the enrichment of the oil industry
    (B) monopoly power
    (C) our transportation breakdown
    (D) inefficiency in transportation
    (E) a policy of comfort and convenience at all costs

17. It can be inferred that the author would oppose

    (A) a balanced transportation system
    (B) shopping malls
    (C) an expansion of the interstate highway system
    (D) less emphasis on technological solutions
    (E) sacrificing speed for comfort

18. The author predicts that if we continue our present transportation policy

    (A) we will succumb to a technocratic dictatorship
    (B) our society may die
    (C) we will attain a balanced transportation system
    (D) rockets and planes will predominate
    (E) human needs will be surrendered

19. The word "radius" in line 49 refers to

    (A) the distance from the center of a train wheel to the circumference
    (B) the distance of places
    (C) the latitude in connection with human needs
    (D) the traffic in connection with travel
    (E) the time it takes to go from one place to another

20. The author believes that "technocratic" thinking is not consistent with

    (A) technological advances
    (B) the labor relations groups
    (C) faster-moving vehicles
    (D) human interests
    (E) the scientific mode

21. According to the article, the fulfillment of human needs will require

    (A) far greater use of walking
    (B) more resources devoted to transportation
    (C) abandoning the profit system
    (D) a better legislative policy
    (E) automated travel

22. The author believes that the nation has placed too great an emphasis on all of the following *except*

    (A) speed
    (B) traffic flow
    (C) diversity
    (D) maximizing distance
    (E) technological needs

23. It may be inferred that the author is a(n)

    (A) highway engineer
    (B) historian
    (C) railroad industry spokesperson
    (D) lawyer
    (E) oil baron

24. It is stated in the article that safety in transportation is aided by the existence of

    (A) remote air-to-ground control for airplanes
    (B) technological sophistication
    (C) a variety of transport modes
    (D) fail-safe systems
    (E) a combination of surface and subsurface systems

STOP

If you finish before time is called, you may check your work on this section only.
Do not turn to any other section in the test.

Take a 1 minute break

before starting section 5

Section 5

Time: 25 Minutes – Turn to Section 5 (page 145) of your answer sheet to answer the questions in this section. 35 Questions
Directions: For each question in this section, select the best answer from among the choices given and fill in the corresponding circle on the answer sheet.

The following sentences test correctness and effectiveness of expression. Part of each sentence or the entire sentence is underlined; beneath each sentence are five ways of phrasing the under-lined material. Choice A repeats the original phrasing; the other four choices are different. If you think the original phrasing produces a better sentence than any of the alternatives, select Choice A; if not, select one of the other choices.

In making your selection, follow the requirements of standard written English; that is, pay attention to grammar, choice of words, sentence construction, and punctuation. Your selection should result in the most effective sentence—clear and precise, without awkwardness or ambiguity.

EXAMPLE:

Laura Ingalls Wilder published her first book <u>and she was sixty-five years old then</u>.

(A) and she was sixty-five years old then

(B) when she was sixty-five

(C) at age sixty-five years old

(D) upon the reaching of sixty-five years

(E) at the time when she was sixty-five

1. At the top of the hill <u>to the left of the tall oak</u> is where they live.

   (A) to the left of the tall oak
   (B) where the tall oak is to the left of it
   (C) and the tall oak is to the left
   (D) left of the tall oak
   (E) to the tall oak's left

2. Martin pretended to be asleep <u>whenever she came</u> into the room.

   (A) whenever she came
   (B) at the time she comes
   (C) although she came
   (D) since she came
   (E) by the time she came

GO ON TO THE NEXT PAGE ➤

3. Once a person starts taking addictive drugs, <u>it is most likely he will be led to take more.</u>

   (A) it is most likely he will be led to take more
   (B) he will probably take them over and over again
   (C) it is hard to stop him from taking more
   (D) he is likely to continue taking them
   (E) he will have a tendency to continue taking them

4. We have not yet been informed <u>concerning the one who broke the window.</u>

   (A) concerning the one who broke the window
   (B) about the identity of the individual who is responsible for breaking the window
   (C) of the window-breaker
   (D) as to who broke the window
   (E) who broke the window

5. Having the highest marks in his class, <u>the college offered him a scholarship.</u>

   (A) the college offered him a scholarship
   (B) the college offered a scholarship to him
   (C) he was offered a scholarship by the college
   (D) a scholarship was offered him by the college
   (E) a college scholarship was offered to him

6. <u>The government's failing to keep it's pledges</u> will mean disaster.

   (A) The government's failing to keep it's pledges
   (B) The governments failing to keep it's pledges
   (C) The government's failing to keep its pledges
   (D) The government failing to keep it's pledges
   (E) The governments failing to keep their pledges

7. Her father <u>along with her mother and sister insist</u> that she stop smoking.

   (A) along with her mother and sister insist
   (B) along with her mother and sister insists
   (C) along with her mother and sister are insisting
   (D) along with her mother and sister were insisting
   (E) as well as her mother and sister insist

8. Most gardeners like to cultivate <u>these kind of flowers</u> in the early spring.

   (A) these kind of flowers
   (B) these kind of flower
   (C) them kinds of flowers
   (D) those kind of flower
   (E) this kind of flower

9. The doctor informs us that my aunt <u>has not and never will recover</u> from the fall.

   (A) has not and never will recover
   (B) has not recovered and never will
   (C) has not and never would recover
   (D) has not recovered and never will recover
   (E) had not and never will recover

10. The senator was neither in favor of <u>or opposed to the proposed legislation.</u>

    (A) or opposed to the proposed legislation
    (B) and was not opposed to the proposed legislation
    (C) the proposed legislation or opposed to it
    (D) nor opposed to the proposed legislation
    (E) the proposed legislation or opposed to the proposed legislation

11. <u>Glory as well as gain is to be his reward.</u>

    (A) Glory as well as gain is to be his reward
    (B) As his reward, glory as well as gain is to be his
    (C) He will be rewarded by glory as well as gain
    (D) Glory also gain are to be his reward
    (E) First glory, then gain, will be his reward

GO ON TO THE NEXT PAGE ➤

The following sentences test your ability to recognize grammar and usage errors. Each sentence contains either a single error or no error at all. No sentence contains more than one error. The error, if there is one, is underlined and lettered. If the sentence contains an error, select the one underlined part that must be changed to make the sentence correct. If the sentence is correct, select Choice E. In choosing answers, follow the requirements of standard written English.

EXAMPLE:

The other delegates and him immediately
   A   B   C

accepted the resolution drafted by
                          D

the neutral states. No error.
                E

12. The long lines of cars at gasoline stations have
          A

disappeared like as if there were never an
              B   C

energy crisis. No error.
      D   E

13. The man told his son to take the car to the
            A   B

service station because it needed gasoline.
  C   D

No error.
  E

14. The man who's temper is under control at
        A   B

all times is likely to think clearly and to accomplish
  C   D

more in his business and social relations. No error.
                                E

15. Whether nineteenth-century classics should be
                         A

taught in school today has become a matter
 A   B   C

of controversy for students and teachers alike.
                            D

No error.
  E

16. Ethan wanted to finish his homework completely
                             A

before his mother had come home from her
      B   C

sister's house. No error.
  D   E

17. Inflation together with the high interest rates and
soaring oil prices are hurting the nation's
 A   B   C

economy very seriously. No error.
         D   E

18. When one leaves his car to be repaired, he
        A   B

assumes that the mechanic will repair the car
 C

good. No error.
 D   E

19. Carter could easily have gotten a higher score on
               A   B

his college entrance test if he would have read
                       C

more in his school career. No error.
    D   E

GO ON TO THE NEXT PAGE ➤

20. <u>Any</u> modern novelist <u>would be thrilled</u> to have
    A   B

<u>his</u> stories compared <u>with Dickens</u>. <u>No error.</u>
C   D   E

21. The automobile industry <u>is experimenting</u> with a
                        A

new <u>type of a</u> motor that will consume <u>less</u>
    B   C

gasoline and <u>cause</u> much less pollution. <u>No error.</u>
          D   E

22. Savannah planned to pay <u>around</u> a hundred dollars
                      A

<u>for</u> a new spring coat, but when she saw a
B

gorgeous coat <u>that sold</u> for two hundred
           C

dollars, she decided <u>to buy</u> it. <u>No error.</u>
              D   E

23. Had Lincoln <u>have been</u> alive during World War II,
           A

he <u>would have regarded</u> the racial <u>situation in</u>
        B   C

the armed forces as a <u>throwback</u> to pre–Civil
                  D

War days. <u>No error.</u>
        E

24. Members of the staff <u>of the District Attorney</u> made
                  A

more than $100,000 from a <u>get-rich-quick</u> scheme
                  B

in which investors <u>were bilked</u> of about <u>$1 million.</u>
             C   D

<u>No error.</u>
E

25. Since oxygen is <u>indispensable</u> to human life,
            A

scientists <u>are exploring</u> the possibility <u>of providing</u>
        B   C

oxygen for future inhabitants of <u>space</u> stations.
                      D

<u>No error.</u>
E

26. <u>Its</u> my opinion that <u>learning</u> the correct
    A   B

pronunciation <u>should precede</u> any attempt <u>to learn</u>
          C   D

the correct spelling of a word. <u>No error.</u>
                  E

27. If I <u>would have known</u> more <u>about</u> the person
        A   B

<u>whom</u> I was writing to, I would have written a <u>better</u>
C   D

answer. <u>No error.</u>
      E

28. If you <u>compare</u> Seb and Daniel <u>as far as</u> scholarship
        A   B

goes, you will have to conclude that Seb is, <u>without</u>
                        C

any question, the <u>brightest</u>. <u>No error.</u>
          D   E

29. <u>In spite of</u> how very <u>poor</u> Zoe <u>had done</u> in the art
    A   B   C

competition, she was <u>far</u> from discouraged.
              D

<u>No error.</u>
E

GO ON TO THE NEXT PAGE ➤

Directions: The following passage is an early draft of an essay. Some parts of the passage need to be rewritten.

Read the passage and select the best answers for the questions that follow. Some questions are about particular sentences or parts of sentences and ask you to improve sentence structure or word choice. Other questions ask you to consider organization and development. In choosing answers, follow the requirements of standard written English.

Questions 30–35 refer to the following passage.

[1]In fact the Egyptians pushed their cult of cat worship to the point of aberration. [2]Their devotion cost them the loss of a city in 500 BC when the Persians laid siege to Pelusium, a city near the present location of Port Said. [3]All the tactics of the Persian army had been blocked by the fierce resistance of the Egyptians; moreover, Cambyses, the Persian leader, had a brilliant idea. [4]When the moment for the attack came, the Egyptians were appalled to see hundreds of panic-stricken cats surging ahead of the Persian army. [5]To make matters worse, each advancing Persian soldier carried a live cat in his arms. [6]He ordered his soldiers to search out and seize the greatest possible number of cats in the surrounding countryside and to keep them unharmed without hurting them. [7]The Egyptian defenders would not risk harming one cat and the city of Pelusium capitulated without a drop of blood. [8]Animal worship was prevalent during Egyptian times.

30. What should be done with sentence 3?

(A) Moreover and its surrounding punctuation should be replaced with a comma.

(B) Moreover and its surrounding punctuation should be replaced with *when*.

(C) The Persian leader and surrounding commas should be omitted.

(D) The words *fierce resistance* should be changed to bullheadedness.

(E) The sentence should be left as it is except for changing the semicolon in front of moreover to a comma.

31. In sentence 5 To make matters worse should be

(A) changed to It was made worse by

(B) omitted

(C) changed to Plus

(D) left as it is

(E) placed at the end of the sentence

32. The end of sentence 6 would be

(A) improved by adding in the least little way

(B) best if left as it is

(C) clearer if it ended after cats

(D) best if it ended after unharmed

(E) improved if it said unhurt without harming them

33. Sentence 6 should be

(A) placed after sentence 3

(B) omitted

(C) placed after sentence 8, with ordered changed to had ordered

(D) made into two sentences, the first to stop after countryside

(E) joined to sentence 5 with which was because

34. Sentence 7 would be more accurate if

(A) capitulated were changed to crumbled

(B) a drop of blood were changed to further battle

(C) surrendered without fighting at all were substituted for capitulated without a drop of blood

(D) having resisted were substituted for a drop of blood

(E) because of bloodshed were substituted for without a drop of blood

35. Sentence 8 should be

(A) left where it is

(B) placed right after sentence 1

(C) placed before sentence 1

(D) omitted

(E) placed after sentence 5

STOP

If you finish before time is called, you may check your work on this section only.
Do not turn to any other section in the test.

Section 6

Time: 25 Minutes – Turn to Section 6 (page 146) of your answer sheet to answer the questions in this section. 18 Questions

Directions: This section contains two types of questions. You have 25 minutes to complete both types. For questions 1–8, solve each problem and decide which is the best of the choices given. Fill in the corresponding circle on the answer sheet. You may use any available space for scratchwork.

Notes:

1. The use of a calculator is permitted.

2. All numbers used are real numbers.

3. Figures that accompany problems in this test are intended to provide information useful in solving the problems. They are drawn as accurately as possible EXCEPT when it is stated in a specific problem that the figure is not drawn to scale. All figures lie in a plane unless otherwise indicated.

4. Unless otherwise specified, the domain of any function f is assumed to be the set of all real numbers x for which $f(x)$ is a real number.

REFERENCE INFORMATION

 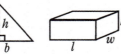

$A = \pi r^2 \quad A = lw \quad A = \frac{1}{2}bh \quad V = lwh \quad V = \pi r^2 h \quad c^2 = a^2 + b^2 \quad \textit{Special Right Triangle.}$

The number of degrees of arc in a circle is 360.
The sum of the measures in degrees of the angles of a triangle is 180.

---

1. If $\sqrt{x}$ is an odd integer, which of the following *MUST* be even?

    (A) x

    (B) $3\sqrt{x}$

    (C) $\sqrt{2x}$

    (D) $2\sqrt{x}$

    (E) x^2

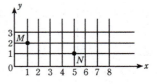

2. If a rectangle is drawn on the grid above with $\overline{MN}$ as one of its diagonals, which of the following could be the coordinates of another vertex of the rectangle?

    (A) (1,0)
    (B) (2,0)
    (C) (3,3)
    (D) (4,3)
    (E) (5,2)

GO ON TO THE NEXT PAGE ➤

x	$f(x)$
0	3
1	4
2	2
3	5
4	8

3. According to the table above, for what value of x does $f(x) = x + 2$?

(A) 0

(B) 1

(C) 2

(D) 3

(E) 4

5. The degree measures of the four angles of a quadrilateral are w, x, y, and z, respectively. If w is the average (arithmetic mean) of x, y, and z, then $x + y + z =$

(A) 45°

(B) 90°

(C) 120°

(D) 180°

(E) 270°

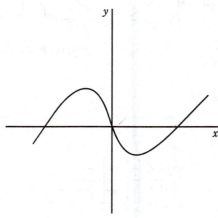

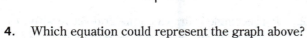

4. Which equation could represent the graph above?

(A) $y = x^3 + 2$

(B) $y = x^3 + 2x + 4$

(C) $y = x^2$

(D) $y = x^3 - x$

(E) $y = x^3 + x^2 - x - 1$

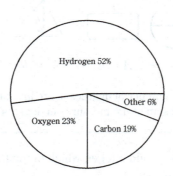

6. A certain mixture contains carbon, oxygen, hydrogen, and other elements in the percentages shown in the graph below. If the total mixture weighs 24 pounds, which number represents the closest number of pounds of carbon that is contained in the mixture?

(A) 5.2

(B) 4.6

(C) 2.1

(D) 1.2

(E) 0.5

GO ON TO THE NEXT PAGE ❯

Bicycle *B*   Bicycle *A*

7. In the figure above, two bicycles are being pedaled in opposite directions around a circular racetrack of circumference = 120 feet. Bicycle *A* is traveling at 5 feet/second in the counterclockwise direction, and Bicycle *B* is traveling at 8 feet/second in the clockwise direction. When Bicycle *B* has completed exactly 600 revolutions, how many complete revolutions will Bicycle *A* have made?

(A) 180
(B) 375
(C) 475
(D) 960
(E) It cannot be determined from the given information.

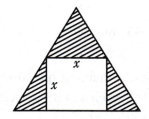

8. A square of side *x* is inscribed inside an equilateral triangle of area $x^2\sqrt{3}$. If a rectangle with width *x* has the same area as the shaded region shown in the figure above, what is the length of the rectangle in terms of *x*?

(A) $\sqrt{3}x - 1$
(B) $x\sqrt{3}$
(C) $\sqrt{3} - x$
(D) $x(\sqrt{3} - 1)$
(E) $x^2\sqrt{3} - x^2$

GO ON TO THE NEXT PAGE ➤

Directions: For Student-Produced Response questions 1–15, use the grids on the following page.

Each of the remaining questions requires you to solve the problem and enter your answer by marking the circles in the special grid, as shown in the examples below. You may use any available space for scratchwork.

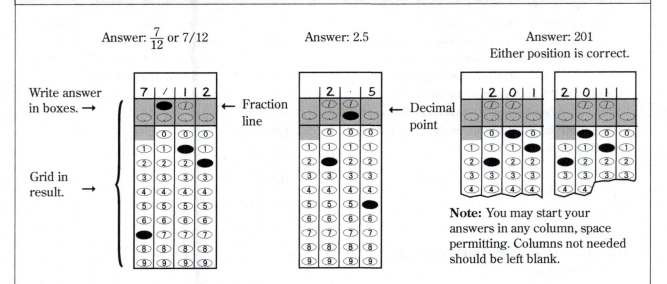

Answer: $\frac{7}{12}$ or 7/12

Write answer in boxes. →   ← Fraction line

Grid in result. →

Answer: 2.5

← Decimal point

Answer: 201
Either position is correct.

Note: You may start your answers in any column, space permitting. Columns not needed should be left blank.

- Mark no more than one oval in any column.

- Because the answer sheet will be machine-scored, **you will receive credit only if the ovals are filled in correctly.**

- Although not required, it is suggested that you write your answer in the boxes at the top of the columns to help you fill in the ovals accurately.

- Some problems may have more than one correct answer. In such cases, grid only one answer.

- No question has a negative answer.

- **Mixed numbers** such as $2\frac{1}{2}$ must be gridded as 2.5 or 5/2. (If ⌗ is gridded, it will be interpreted as $\frac{21}{2}$, not $2\frac{1}{2}$.)

- **Decimal Accuracy:** If you obtain a decimal answer, **enter the most accurate value the grid will accommodate.** For example, if you obtain an answer such as 0.6666..., you should record the result as .666 or .667. **Less accurate values such as .66 or .67 are not acceptable.**

Acceptable ways to grid $\frac{2}{3}$ = .6666...:

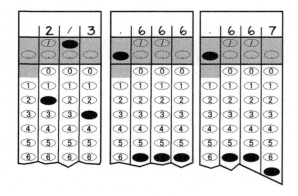

9.   If $\frac{1}{4} < x < \frac{1}{3}$, find one value of x.

10.   Given $3x + y = 17$ and $x + 3y = -1$, find the value of $3x + 3y$.

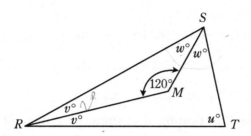

Note: Figure not drawn to scale.

11.   If $\angle RST = 80°$, find u.

12.   There are 22 people on an island. A tram can carry at most 4 people at a time. What is the least number of trips that the tram must make to the mainland to get all the people to the mainland?

13.   Let us define the operation $\odot$ as

$$a \odot b = (a + b)^2 - (a - b)^2$$

Find the value of $\sqrt{18} \odot \sqrt{2}$.

14.   How many ordered pairs of *integers* (x,y) satisfy $x^2 + y^2 < 9$?

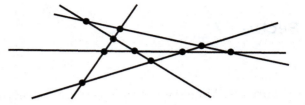

15.   The figure above demonstrates that 5 straight lines can have 10 points of intersection. What is the maximum number of points of intersection of 4 straight lines?

16.   Natalie planned to buy some chocolate bars at 50 cents each but instead decided to purchase 30-cent chocolate bars. If she originally had enough money to buy 21 of the 50-cent bars, how many of the less expensive ones did she buy?

17.   Let d be the least integer greater than 96,666 such that four of d's digits are identical. Find the value of $d - 96,666$.

18.   Find 25 percent of 25 percent of 2.

STOP

If you finish before time is called, you may check your work on this section only.
Do not turn to any other section in the test.

Take a 5 minute break

before starting section 7

Section 7

Time: 25 Minutes – Turn to Section 7 (page 146) of your answer sheet to answer the questions in this section. 24 Questions

Directions: For each question in this section, select the best answer from among the choices given and fill in the corresponding circle on the answer sheet.

Each sentence below has one or two blanks, each blank indicating that something has been omitted. Beneath the sentence are five words or sets of words labeled A through E. Choose the word or set of words that, when inserted in the sentence, best fits the meaning of the sentence as a whole.

Example:

Hoping to _____ the dispute, negotiators proposed a compromise that they felt would be _____ to both labor and management.

(A) enforce…useful

(B) end…divisive

(C) overcome…unattractive

(D) extend…satisfactory

(E) resolve…acceptable

(A) (B) (C) (D) ●

---

1. He tried his hardest to maintain his _____ in the face of the threatening mob.

   (A) synthesis
   (B) analogy
   (C) fraternity
   (D) umbrage
   (E) composure

2. The low-cost apartment buildings, new and well managed, are _____ to those accustomed to living in tenements _____ by shady characters.

   (A) a boon…haunted
   (B) a specter…inhabited
   (C) an exodus…frequented
   (D) an example…viewed
   (E) a surprise…approached

3. Before the inflation _____, one could have had a complete meal in a restaurant for five dollars, including the tip, whereas today a hot dog, coffee, and dessert would _____ add up to two or three times that much.

   (A) spiral…indubitably
   (B) cancellation…rapidly
   (C) problem…improbably
   (D) abundance…consequently
   (E) incidence…radically

GO ON TO THE NEXT PAGE ➤

4. Although the death of his dog had saddened him markedly, his computer designing skills remained completely _____.

(A) twisted
(B) unaffected
(C) incapable
(D) repaired
(E) demolished

5. The guerrillas were so _____ that the general had to develop various strategies to trap them.

(A) distant
(B) wild
(C) unreasonable
(D) elusive
(E) cruel

The two passages below are followed by questions based on their content and on the relationship between the two passages. Answer the questions on the basis of what is <u>stated</u> or <u>implied</u> in the passages and in any introductory material that may be provided.

Questions 6–9 are based on the following passages.

Passage 1

Classical physics is the physics of the macroscopic world (our world which we can see, touch, and hear). It is very appealing to the purist in that there are no uncertainties in measurement of physical quantities. When we set
5   up an apparatus to measure something, the apparatus does not interfere with the measurement. For example, if we want to figure out how fast something is traveling, we can also find out exactly where it is at the time of measurement of its speed. There is certainty in classical physics, the
10   "exact" physics. Thus when a bridge is built, we know exactly what stress the bridge may withstand. When a car is constructed, we know what specifications the engine must have to have the car do what we want.

Passage 2

Modern physics, or physics of the sub-microscopic
15   world (the world of electrons, protons, and neutrons), is very perplexing since there seems to be an apparent violation of cause and effect. There exists only a probability and not certainty in measurement of important physical quantities because the measurement device affects the measurement.
20   For example, if we know exactly in what position an electron is, we cannot determine its speed. Thus the more we know the value of one physical quantity, the less certain we are of a corresponding physical quantity. To paraphrase Albert Einstein, "the universe does not play dice with
25   nature." Ironically, modern physics really controls and determines the outcome of the physics of the macroscopic physics (since the macroscopic world is really made up of constituents in the sub-microscopic realm). Thus modern physics is the foundation of all physics since it contains the
30   basic and fundamental elements used to create all physics.

6. It can be assumed that Albert Einstein believed that

(A) only classical physics existed in nature
(B) there was certainty in all aspects of physics theories
(C) classical physics violates cause and effect
(D) speed and position are not the fundamental characteristics of particles
(E) when a new car is constructed, in order for it to be most efficient, a new physics must be employed

7. Modern physics differs from classical physics chiefly in that

(A) the measurement device does not affect the measurement in classical physics
(B) no quantity in modern physics can be determined
(C) modern physics is not as fundamental as classical physics
(D) classical physics does not deal primarily with measurement
(E) speed is always constant in classical physics

8. Which of the following would resolve the seeming paradox between modern and classical physics?

(A) There could be a third type of physics which would incorporate the phenomena of both classical and modern physics.

(B) One could consider that physics is either macroscopic or microscopic in nature.

(C) One would not consider speed and position as a fundamental set of physical quantity.

(D) Exactness of measurement would not be a requirement in physics.

(E) One could assume that electrons, protons, and neutrons do not exist in nature.

9. Which key elements exist in either classical physics or modern physics but not in both?

(I) existence of cause and effect
(II) probability and not certainty of two quantities
(III) the structure of a bridge

(A) (I) only
(B) (II) only
(C) (III) only
(D) (I) and (II) only
(E) (I), (II), and (III)

Questions 10–15 are based on the following passage.

The following passage tracks the career of the famous artist Vincent van Gogh, and his encounter with another famous artist, Paul Gauguin.

It was at Arles, the small city in the south of France where he stayed from early in 1888 to the spring of 1889, that Vincent van Gogh had his first real bout with madness. After a quarrel with Paul Gauguin, he cut off part of his own
5 ear. Yet Arles was also the scene of an astonishing burst of creativity. Over the short span of 15 months, van Gogh produced some 200 paintings and more than 100 drawings and watercolors, a record that only Picasso has matched in the modern era. Orchards and wheatfields under the
10 glowing sun, neighbors and townspeople, interiors of the Yellow House where he lived, were all subjects of his frenetic brush. The Arles canvases, alive with color—vermilion, emerald green, Prussian blue, and a particularly brilliant yellow—have intensity of feeling that mark the
15 high point of his career, and deeply affected the work of artists to follow, notably the Fauves and the German Expressionists.

Van Gogh went to Arles after two years in Paris, where his beloved younger brother Theo, who supported him psychologically and financially for most of his adult life, was

20 an art dealer. In Paris, Vincent had met Gauguin and other important artists—Lautrec, Degas, Pissarro, and Seurat. Like the last two, he worked in the Neo-Impressionist, or Pointillist, style—applying color in tiny dots or strokes that "mixed" in the viewer's eye to create effects of considerable
25 intensity. But he wanted "gayer" colors than Paris provided, the kind of atmosphere evoked by the Japanese prints he so admired. Then, too, the French capital had exhausted him, mentally and physically. He felt that in Arles, not exactly a bustling arts center, he might find serenity, and even
30 establish an artistic tradition.

It was van Gogh's hope of founding a new artists' colony in the south that made him eager to have Gauguin, whose talent van Gogh readily recognized, join him at Arles. The plan, on Vincent's part, was for Gauguin to
35 stay in Arles for maybe a year, working and sharing with him the small living quarters and studio he had found for himself and dubbed the Yellow House. At first, the two men got along well. But they did not at all agree on judgments of other artists. Still, Gauguin had an influence on van Gogh.
40 Gauguin began pushing the younger artist to paint from memory rather than actuality.

Before the year was up, whether because of Gauguin's attempts to change van Gogh's style, or what, the two men had apparently begun to get on each other's nerves.
45 Gauguin wrote to Theo that he felt he had to return to Paris, citing his and Vincent's "temperamental incompatibility." A letter from Vincent to Theo followed, noting that Gauguin was "a little out of sorts with the good town of Arles, and especially with me."

50 But then, the two apparently made up—but not for long. Gauguin returned to Paris and never saw van Gogh again, although they later had friendly correspondence.

Despite any problem with his relationship with Gauguin, van Gogh maintained his enormous creativity
55 and prolific nature in those months in Arles.

10. Which of the following is the best title for the passage?

(A) Where van Gogh's Art Reached Its Zenith
(B) An Unfortunate Mismatch Between Two Great Artists
(C) Another Tale of a Genius Unable to Adjust to Society
(D) A Prolific Painter Whose Art Will Live On
(E) Van Gogh's Frustration in His Hope to Found a New Artists' Colony

GO ON TO THE NEXT PAGE ➤

11. According to the passage, which of the following statements is not true?

    (A) Fauvism is a movement in painting typified by vivid colors.
    (B) Gauguin was an older man than Theo.
    (C) Pissarro was a painter associated with the Neo-Impressionist school.
    (D) Van Gogh's work began to deteriorate after Gauguin's departure from Arles.
    (E) Van Gogh's behavior was, at times, quite abnormal.

12. For which of the following reasons did van Gogh decide to leave Paris and go to Arles?

    I. He sought a different environment for the kind of painting he wished to do.
    II. He had hopes of forming a new artists' colony.
    III. He wanted a more peaceful location where there was less stress.

    (A) II only
    (B) III only
    (C) I and II only
    (D) I and III only
    (E) I, II, and III

13. The word "frenetic" in line 12 most nearly means

    (A) colorful
    (B) smooth
    (C) bright
    (D) rapid
    (E) frantic

14. Gauguin's attitude toward van Gogh is best described in the passage as one of

    (A) gentle ridicule
    (B) unallayed suspicion
    (C) tolerant acceptance
    (D) open condescension
    (E) resentful admiration

15. Aside from his quarrel with Gauguin, we may infer that a major contributory reason for van Gogh's going to the extreme of cutting off part of his ear was his

    (A) concern about being able to support himself financially
    (B) inability to get along with Gauguin
    (C) failure to form an artists' colony in Arles
    (D) mental and emotional instability
    (E) being upset by Gauguin's attempts to change his style

Questions 16–24 are based on the following passage.

The following passage is excerpted from the essay "Self-Reliance" by the American writer Ralph Waldo Emerson.

Infancy conforms to nobody: all conform to it, so that one babe commonly makes four or five out of the adults who prattle and play to it. So God has armed youth and puberty and manhood no less with its own piquancy and charm, and
5 made it enviable and gracious and its claims not to be put by, if it will stand by itself. Do not think the youth has no force, because he cannot speak to you and me. Hark! in the next room his voice is sufficiently clear and emphatic. It seems he knows how to speak to his contemporaries. Bashful or bold,
10 then, he will know how to make us seniors very unnecessary.

The nonchalance of boys who are sure of a dinner, and would disdain as much as a lord to do or say aught to conciliate one, is the healthy attitude of human nature. A boy is in the parlor what the pit is in the playhouse; inde-
15 pendent, irresponsible, looking out from his corner on such people and facts as pass by, he tries and sentences them on their merits, in the swift, summary way of boys, as good, bad, interesting, silly, eloquent, troublesome. He lumbers himself never about consequences, about interests; he
20 gives an independent, genuine verdict. You must court him: he does not court you. But the man is, as it were, clapped into jail by his consciousness. As soon as he has once acted or spoken with eclat, he is a committed person, watched by the sympathy or the hatred of hundreds, whose affections
25 must now enter into his account. There is no Lethe for this. Ah, that he could pass again into his neutrality.

These are the voices which we hear in solitude, but they grow faint and inaudible as we enter into the world. Society everywhere is in conspiracy against the manhood
30 of every one of its members. Society is a joint-stock company, in which the members agree, for the better securing of his bread to each shareholder, to surrender the liberty and culture of the eater. The virtue in most request is conformity. Self-reliance is its aversion. It loves not reali-
35 ties and creators, but names and customs.

Whoso would be a man must be a nonconformist. He who would gather immortal palms must not be hindered by the name of goodness, but must explore if it be goodness. Nothing is at last sacred but the integrity of your own mind.

No law can be sacred to me but that of my nature.
40 Good and bad are but names very readily transferable to that or this; the only right is what is after my constitution, the only wrong what is against it. A man is to carry himself in the presence of all opposition as if every thing were
45 titular and ephemeral but he. I am ashamed to think how easily we capitulate to badges and names, to large societies and dead institutions. Every decent and well-spoken indi-vidual affects and sways me more than is right. I ought to go upright and vital, and speak the rude truth in all ways.

50 I shun father and mother and wife and brother, when my genius calls me. I would write on the lintels of the doorpost, *Whim.* I hope it is somewhat better than whim at last, but we cannot spend the day in explanation. Expect me not to show cause why I seek or why I exclude company.

55 Then, again, do not tell me, as a good man did to-day, of my obligation to put all poor men in good situations. Are they *my* poor? I tell thee, thou foolish philanthropist, that I grudge the dollar, the dime, the cent, I give to such men as do not belong to me and to whom I do not belong. There
60 is a class of persons to whom by all spiritual affinity I am bought and sold; for them I will go to prison, if need be; but your miscellaneous popular charities; the education at college of fools; the building of meeting-houses to the vain end to which many now stand; alms to sots; and the
65 thousandfold Relief Societies;—though I confess with shame I sometimes succumb and give the dollar, it is a wicked dollar which by and by I shall have the manhood to withhold.

For nonconformity the world whips you with its displeasure. And therefore a man must know how to
70 estimate a sour face. The by-standers look askance on him in the public street or in the friend's parlor. If this aversion had its origin in contempt and resistance like his own, he might well go home with a sad countenance; but the sour faces of the multitude, like their sweet faces, have no
75 deep cause, but are put on and off as the wind blows and a newspaper directs. Yet is the discontent of the multitude more formidable than that of the senate and the college.

The other terror that scares us from self-trust is our consistency; a reverence for our past act or word, because
80 the eyes of others have no other data for computing our orbit than our past acts, and we are loath to disappoint them.

But why should you keep your head over your shoulder? Why drag about this corpse of your memory, lest you contradict somewhat you have stated in this or that
85 public place? Suppose you should contradict yourself; what then?

A foolish consistency is the hobgoblin of little minds, adored by little statesmen and philosophers and divines. With consistency a great soul has simply nothing to do. He may as well concern himself with his shadow on the wall.
90 Speak what you think now in hard words, and to-morrow speak what to-morrow thinks in hard words again, though it contradict everything you said to-day.—"Ah, so you shall be sure to be misunderstood."—Is it so bad, then, to be misunderstood? Pythagoras was misunderstood,
95 and Socrates, and Jesus, and Luther, and Copernicus, and Galileo, and Newton, and every pure and wise spirit that ever took flesh. To be great is to be misunderstood.

16. The main theme of the selection is best expressed as follows:

(A) "A foolish consistency is the hobgoblin of little minds."

(B) "Eternal youth means eternal independence."

(C) "Whoso would be a man must be a noncon-formist."

(D) "Colleges are designed to educate fools."

(E) "Infancy conforms to nobody."

GO ON TO THE NEXT PAGE ➤

17. We are most nonconformist during our period of

   (A) infancy
   (B) puberty
   (C) youth
   (D) manhood
   (E) old age

18. According to the author, "To be great is to be misunderstood" means that

   (A) one should never say exactly what one means
   (B) to be misunderstood is to be great
   (C) all great men have always been misunderstood
   (D) a man should not hesitate to change his mind if he sees the need to, even at the risk of being considered inconsistent
   (E) nice people seldom succeed

19. The refusal of young people to cater to accepted public opinion is, according to the author,

   (A) characteristic of the rebelliousness of youth
   (B) a healthy attitude of human nature
   (C) a manifestation of deep-seated immaturity
   (D) simply bad manners
   (E) part of growing up

20. From the selection, one may infer that the "pit in the playhouse" was

   (A) a section containing the best seats in the theater
   (B) favored by independent, outspoken, unselfconscious playgoers
   (C) an underground theater
   (D) a generally staid, quiet section of the theater, favored by young people only
   (E) the actors' dressing rooms

21. "Society is a joint-stock company," etc., is one way in which the author shows

   (A) that the public is anticulture
   (B) society is highly organized and structured
   (C) how society rejects self-reliance
   (D) that there is no room for solitude in our world
   (E) the public's interest in the stock market

22. The word "eclat" (line 23), as used in this selection, means

   (A) fun-loving and luxury
   (B) violence and force
   (C) disrespect and resistance
   (D) reason and logic
   (E) spirit and enthusiasm

23. "I would write on the lintels of the doorpost, *Whim.*" By this, the author means

   (A) that one should renounce his immediate family
   (B) that signposts have an important educational function in our society
   (C) that an impulsive action may have a subsequent rational explanation
   (D) that one must never be held responsible for what one says and does
   (E) that everyone should do foolish things occasionally

24. The statement that best sums up the spirit and sense of this selection is

   (A) "Nothing is at last sacred but the integrity of your own mind."
   (B) "With consistency a great soul has simply nothing to do."
   (C) "Do not think the youth has no force, because he cannot speak to you and me."
   (D) "The virtue in most request is conformity."
   (E) "A man must know how to estimate a sour face."

STOP

If you finish before time is called, you may check your work on this section only.
Do not turn to any other section in the test.

Section 8

Time: 20 Minutes—Turn to Section 8 (page 147) of your answer sheet to answer the questions in this section. 16 Questions

Directions: For this section, solve each problem and decide which is the best of the choices given. Fill in the corresponding circle on the answer sheet. You may use any available space for scratchwork.

Notes:

1. The use of a calculator is permitted.

2. All numbers used are real numbers.

3. Figures that accompany problems in this test are intended to provide information useful in solving the problems. They are drawn as accurately as possible EXCEPT when it is stated in a specific problem that the figure is not drawn to scale. All figures lie in a plane unless otherwise indicated.

4. Unless otherwise specified, the domain of any function f is assumed to be the set of all real numbers x for which $f(x)$ is a real number.

REFERENCE INFORMATION

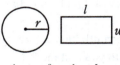

$A = \pi r^2$ $A = lw$ $A = \frac{1}{2}bh$ $V = lwh$ $V = \pi r^2 h$ $c^2 = a^2 + b^2$ *Special Right Triangle.*

The number of degrees of arc in a circle is 360.
The sum of the measures in degrees of the angles of a triangle is 180.

1. Ravi and Ben like to watch their school's baseball team play. Ravi watched $\frac{2}{3}$ of all the games the team played last season. Ben watched 28 games. If Ravi watched more games than Ben did last season, which of the following could be the number of games the team played last season?

    (A) 33
    (B) 36
    (C) 39
    (D) 42
    (E) 45

2. If 8 people share a winning lottery ticket and divide the cash prize equally, what percent of the prize do 2 of them together receive?

    (A) 8%
    (B) 10%
    (C) 20%
    (D) 25%
    (E) 40%

GO ON TO THE NEXT PAGE >

3. An athlete runs 90 laps in 6 hours. This is the same as how many laps per minute?

(A) $\frac{1}{15}$

(B) $\frac{1}{9}$

(C) $\frac{1}{4}$

(D) $\frac{1}{2}$

(E) 1

4. If $x = 16$, $x^{-\frac{3}{4}} =$

(A) $\frac{1}{2}$

(B) $\frac{1}{4}$

(C) $\frac{1}{8}$

(D) $\frac{1}{16}$

(E) $\frac{1}{32}$

5. Which of the following is a graph of $y = 2x - 4$?

(A)

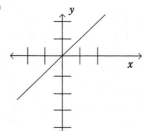

(B)

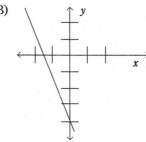

(C)

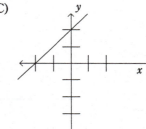

(D)

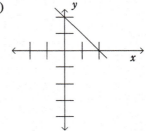

(E)

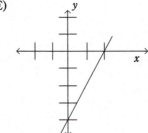

GO ON TO THE NEXT PAGE ➤

6. $[(3a^3b^2)^3]^2 =$

(A) $27a^9b^6$

(B) $54a^9b^6$

(C) $729a^9b^6$

(D) $729a^{18}b^{12}$

(E) $729a^{54}b^{16}$

8.   Paul's average (arithmetic mean) for 3 tests was 85. The average of his scores for the first 2 tests was also 85. What was his score for the third test?

(A)   80

(B)   85

(C)   90

(D)   95

(E)   It cannot be determined from the information given.

7.   Given that $\left(\dfrac{3}{10}\right)^2$ is equal to p hundredths, find the value p.

(A)   5

(B)   6

(C)   9

(D)   12

(E)   32

9.   The operation $\square$ is defined for all numbers x and y by the following: $x \square y = 3 + xy$. For example, $2 \square 7 = 3 + 2(7) = 17$. If $y \neq 0$ and x is a number such that $x \square y = 3$, then find x.

(A)   0

(B) $-\dfrac{3}{y}$

(C) $-y + 3$

(D) $\dfrac{3}{y}$

(E) $y + 3$

GO ON TO THE NEXT PAGE ➤

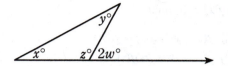

10. In the figure above, one side of a triangle has been extended. What is the value of $w + x + y$?

(A) $3w$
(B) $3z$
(C) $2x + y$
(D) $2x + 2y$
(E) $2w + z$

12. If a certain number has 13 points assigned to it, which of the following statements must be true?

   I. 33 is not in the number.
  II. 34 is in the number.
 III. 43 is in the number.

(A) I only
(B) II only
(C) III only
(D) I and III only
(E) I, II, and III

Questions 11–12 refer to the following game.

A computer generates numbers. Points are assigned as described in the following table each time any of the four number pairs given appears in a number.

Number Pair	Number of Points
"33"	11
"34"	6
"43"	4
"44"	3

11. As an example, the number 4,347 is assigned 4 points for "43" and 6 points more for "34," giving a total of 10 points. Which of the following numbers would be assigned the most points?

(A) 934,432
(B) 464,457
(C) 834,415
(D) 437,934
(E) 336,283

13. The ratio of Suri's age to Bob's age is 3 to 7. The ratio of Suri's age to Javier's age is 4 to 9. The ratio of Bob's age to Javier's age is

(A) 28 to 27
(B) 7 to 9
(C) 27 to 28
(D) 10 to 13
(E) 13 to 10

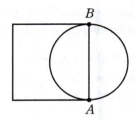

14. The square in the figure above has two sides tangent to the circle. If the area of the circle is $9a^2\pi^2$, find the area of the square in terms of a and π.

(A) $12a^2\pi^2$

(B) $36a^2\pi$

(C) $36a^2\pi^2$

(D) $18a^4\pi^2$

(E) $9a^4\pi^2$

16. If $f(x) = a^x$ then

(A) $f(x + y) = f(x) + f(y)$

(B) $f(x + y) = f(x)f(y)$

(C) $f(x - y) = f(x) - f(y)$

(D) $f(xy) = f(x)f(y)$

(E) $f\left(\frac{x}{y}\right) = \frac{f(x)}{f(y)}$

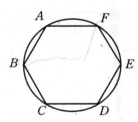

15. Equilateral polygon *ABCDEF* is inscribed in the circle. If the length of arc *BAF* is 14π, find the length of the diameter of the circle.

(A) 7

(B) 14

(C) 7π

(D) 21

(E) 42

STOP

If you finish before time is called, you may check your work on this section only.
Do not turn to any other section in the test.

Section 9

Time: 25 Minutes – Turn to Section 9 (page 147) of your answer sheet to answer the questions in this section. 19 Questions

Directions: For each question in this section, select the best answer from among the choices given and fill in the corresponding circle on the answer sheet.

Each sentence below has one or two blanks, each blank indicating that something has been omitted. Beneath the sentence are five words or sets of words labeled A through E. Choose the word or set of words that, when inserted in the sentence, best fits the meaning of the sentence as a whole.

Example:

Hoping to _____ the dispute, negotiators proposed a compromise that they felt would be _____ to both labor and management.

(A) enforce…useful

(B) end…divisive

(C) overcome…unattractive

(D) extend…satisfactory

(E) resolve…acceptable

Ⓐ Ⓑ Ⓒ Ⓓ ●

---

1. A sense of fairness _____ that the punishment should fit the crime; yet, in actual practice, judicial decisions _____ greatly for the same type of criminal offense.

    (A) assumes…coincide
    (B) relegates…deviate
    (C) accumulates…simplify
    (D) insists…compromise
    (E) dictates…vary

2. The chef made no effort to be _____; she would sometimes add garlic and oregano to the sauce, and other times she would add only basil.

    (A) consistent
    (B) prompt
    (C) amicable
    (D) courteous
    (E) considerate

GO ON TO THE NEXT PAGE ❯

3. As an outstanding contributor to the advancement of technology, Steve Jobs was able to make occasional _____, but his errors were tolerated in view of his tremendous _____.

   (A) appearances…energy
   (B) mistakes…success
   (C) remarks…connections
   (D) enemies…audacity
   (E) conferences…patience

4. Their married life was not _____ since it was fraught with bitter fighting and arguments.

   (A) nubile
   (B) tranquil
   (C) obvious
   (D) cogent
   (E) imminent

5. Because of his _____ driving, the other car was forced to turn off the road or be hit.

   (A) perceptive
   (B) negligent
   (C) resourceful
   (D) placid
   (E) exemplary

6. The _____ in the Bible are both entertaining and instructive.

   (A) syllables
   (B) abatements
   (C) milestones
   (D) parables
   (E) utilities

The two passages below are followed by questions based on their content and on the relationship between the two passages. Answer the questions on the basis of what is <u>stated</u> or <u>implied</u> in the passages and in any introductory material that may be provided.

Questions 7–19 are based on the following passages.

The following two passages describe different time periods. Passage 1 discusses the medieval time period; Passage 2 describes the present and speculates on the future.

Passage 1

To the world when it was half a thousand years younger, the outlines of all things seemed more clearly marked than to us. The contrast between suffering and joy, between adversity and happiness, appeared more striking. All
5　experience had yet to the minds of men the directness and absoluteness of the pleasure and pain of child life. Every event, every action, was still embodied in expressive and solemn forms, which raised them to the dignity of a ritual.

Misfortunes and poverty were more afflicting than at
10　present; it was more difficult to guard against them, and to find solace. Illness and health presented a more striking contrast; the cold and darkness of winter were more real evils. Honors and riches were relished with greater avidity and contrasted more vividly with surrounding misery. We,
15　at the present day, can hardly understand the keenness with which a fur coat, a good fire on the hearth, a soft bed, a glass of wine, were formerly enjoyed.

Then, again, all things in life were of a proud or cruel publicity. Lepers sounded their rattles and went about in
20　processions, beggars exhibited their deformity and their misery in churches. Every order and estate, every rank and profession, was distinguished by its costume. The great lords never moved about without a glorious display of arms and liveries, exciting fear and envy. Executions
25　and other public acts of justice, hawking, marriages and funerals, were all announced by cries and processions, songs and music. The lover wore the colors of his lady; companions the emblem of their brotherhood; parties and servants the badges of their lords. Between town and
30　country, too, the contrast was very marked. A medieval town did not lose itself in extensive suburbs of factories and villas; girded by its walls, it stood forth as a compact whole, bristling with innumerable turrets. However tall and threatening the houses of noblemen or merchants
35　might be, in the aspect of the town, the lofty mass of the churches always remained dominant.

The contrast between silence and sound, darkness and light, like that between summer and winter, was more strongly marked than it is in our lives. The modern town
40　hardly knows silence or darkness in their purity, nor the effect of a solitary light or a single distant cry.

GO ON TO THE NEXT PAGE ➤

All things presenting themselves to the mind in violent contrasts and impressive forms lent a tone of excitement and passion to everyday life and tended to
45 produce that perpetual oscillation between despair and distracted joy, between cruelty and pious tenderness which characterize life in the Middle Ages.

Passage 2

In 1575—over 400 years ago!—the French scholar Louis Le Roy published a learned book in which he voiced
50 despair over the upheavals caused by the social and technological innovations of his time, what we now call the Renaissance. "All is pell-mell, confounded, nothing goes as it should." We, also, feel that our times are out of joint; we even have reason to believe that our descendants
55 will be worse off than we are.

The earth will soon be overcrowded and its resources exhausted. Pollution will ruin the environment, upset the climate, damage human health. The gap in living standards between the rich and the poor will
60 widen and lead the angry, hungry people of the world to acts of desperation including the use of nuclear weapons as blackmail. Such are the inevitable consequences of population and technological growth *if* present trends continue. But what a big *if* this is!

65 The future is never a projection of the past. Animals probably have no chance to escape from the tyranny of biological evolution, but human beings are blessed with the freedom of social evolution. For us, trend is not destiny. The escape from existing trends is now facilitated by
70 the fact that societies anticipate future dangers and take preventive steps against expected upheavals.

Despite the widespread belief that the world has become too complex for comprehension by the human brain, modern societies have often responded effectively
75 to critical situations.

The decrease in birthrates, the partial banning of pesticides, the rethinking of technologies for the production and use of energy are but a few examples illustrating a sudden reversal of trends caused not by political upsets
80 or scientific breakthroughs, but by public awareness of consequences.

Even more striking are the situations in which social attitudes concerning future difficulties undergo rapid changes before the problems have come to pass—witness
85 the heated controversies about the ethics of behavior control and of genetic engineering even though there is as yet no proof that effective methods can be developed to manipulate behavior and genes on a population scale.

One of the characteristics of our times is thus the
90 rapidity with which steps can be taken to change the orientation of certain trends and even to reverse them. Such changes usually emerge from grassroots movements rather than from official directives.

7. Conditions like those described in Passage 1 would most likely have occurred about

(A) A.D. 55
(B) A.D. 755
(C) A.D. 1055
(D) A.D. 1455
(E) A.D. 1755

8. The phrase "with greater avidity" in line 13 is best interpreted to mean with greater

(A) desire
(B) sadness
(C) terror
(D) silence
(E) disappointment

9. In Passage 1, all of the following are stated or implied about towns in the Middle Ages *except*

(A) Towns had no suburbs.
(B) Towns were always quite noisy.
(C) Towns served as places of defense.
(D) Towns always had large churches.
(E) Merchants lived in the towns.

10. The author's main purpose in Passage 1 is to

(A) describe the miseries of the period
(B) show how life was centered on the town
(C) emphasize the uncontrolled and violent course of life at the time
(D) point out how the upper classes mistreated the lower classes
(E) indicate how religious people were in those days

11. According to Passage 1, people at that time, as compared with people today, were

(A) worse off
(B) better off
(C) less intelligent
(D) more subdued
(E) more sensitive to certain events

GO ON TO THE NEXT PAGE ➤

12. In the first paragraph of Passage 2, the mood expressed is one of

    (A) blatant despair
    (B) guarded optimism
    (C) poignant nostalgia
    (D) muted pessimism
    (E) unbridled idealism

13. According to Passage 2, if present trends continue, which one of the following situations will *not* occur?

    (A) New sources of energy from vast coal deposits will be substituted for the soon-to-be-exhausted resources of oil and natural gas.
    (B) The rich will become richer and the poor will become poorer.
    (C) An overpopulated earth will be unable to sustain its inhabitants.
    (D) Nuclear weapons will play a more prominent role in dealings among peoples.
    (E) The ravages of pollution will render the earth and its atmosphere a menace to mankind.

14. Which of the following is the best illustration of the meaning of "trend is not destiny" in line 68?

    (A) Urban agglomerations are in a state of crisis.
    (B) Human beings are blessed with the freedom of social evolution.
    (C) The world has become too complex for comprehension by the human brain.
    (D) Critical processes can overshoot and cause catastrophes.
    (E) The earth will soon be overcrowded and its resources exhausted.

15. According to Passage 2, evidences of the insight of the public into the dangers that surround us can be found in all of the following *except*

    (A) an increase in the military budget by the president
    (B) a declining birthrate
    (C) picketing against expansion of nuclear plants
    (D) opposition to the use of pesticides
    (E) public meetings to complain about dumping chemicals

16. The author's attitude in Passage 2 is one of

    (A) willing resignation
    (B) definite optimism
    (C) thinly veiled cynicism
    (D) carefree abandon
    (E) angry impatience

17. If there is a continuity in history, which of the following situations in Passage 1 is thought to lead to violence in the future of Passage 2?

    (A) the overcrowding of the population
    (B) the executions in public
    (C) the contrast between the social classes
    (D) the contrast between illness and health
    (E) the contrast between religion and politics

18. One can conclude from reading both passages that the difference between the people in Passage 1 and the people in Passage 2 is that

    (A) the people in Passage 2 act on their awareness in contrast to the people in Passage 1
    (B) the people in Passage 2 are more intense and colorful than the people in Passage 1
    (C) there was no controversy between sociology and science in the society in Passage 2 in contrast to the society mentioned in Passage 1
    (D) the people in Passage 1 are far more religious
    (E) sociological changes were faster and more abrupt with the people of Passage 1

19. From a reading of both passages, one may conclude that

    (A) people in both passages are equally subservient to authority
    (B) the future is a mirror to the past
    (C) the topic of biological evolution is of great importance to the scientists of both periods
    (D) the evolution of science has created great differences in the social classes
    (E) the people in Passage 1 are more involved in everyday living, whereas the people in Passage 2 are usually seeking change

STOP

If you finish before time is called, you may check your work on this section only.
Do not turn to any other section in the test.

Section 10

> **Time:** 25 Minutes – Turn to Section 10 (page 147) of your answer sheet to answer the questions in this section. 14 Questions

> **Directions:** For each question in this section, select the best answer from among the choices given and fill in the corresponding circle on the answer sheet.

The following sentences test correctness and effectiveness of expression. Part of each sentence or the entire sentence is underlined; beneath each sentence are five ways of phrasing the underlined material. Choice A repeats the original phrasing; the other four choices are different. If you think the original phrasing produces a better sentence than any of the alternatives, select Choice A; if not, select one of the other choices.

In making your selection, follow the requirements of standard written English; that is, pay attention to grammar, choice of words, sentence construction, and punctuation. Your selection should result in the most effective sentence—clear and precise, without awkwardness or ambiguity.

EXAMPLE:

Laura Ingalls Wilder published her first book <u>and she was sixty-five years old then</u>.

(A) and she was sixty-five years old then

(B) when she was sixty-five

(C) at age sixty-five years old

(D) upon the reaching of sixty-five years

(E) at the time when she was sixty-five

---

1.   She prefers to write poems that describe the slums and <u>study the habits of the underprivileged</u>.

    (A) study the habits of the underprivileged
    (B) study the underprivileged's habits
    (C) studying the habits of the underprivileged
    (D) to study the habits of the underprivileged
    (E) she prefers to study the habits of the underprivileged

2.   <u>By studying during weekends, her grades improved surprisingly.</u>

    (A) By studying during weekends, her grades improved surprisingly.
    (B) By studying during weekends, she improved her grades surprisingly.
    (C) She was surprised to find her grades improved after studying during weekends.
    (D) Her grades, by studying during weekends, improved surprisingly.
    (E) Surprisingly, by studying during weekends, her grades improved.

GO ON TO THE NEXT PAGE ➤

3. The streets here are <u>as dirty as any other city,</u> according to recent research studies.

   (A) as dirty as any other city
   (B) so dirty as any other city
   (C) dirty like any other city
   (D) as dirty as those of any other city
   (E) as those of any city

4. Beau Obama, the first family's dog, is energetic, <u>with bright eyes, and has a pleasant disposition.</u>

   (A) with bright eyes, and has a pleasant disposition
   (B) with eyes so bright, and a pleasant disposition
   (C) bright-eyed, and pleasant
   (D) bright eyes as well as pleasant
   (E) and has bright eyes as well as a pleasant manner

5. Further acquaintance with the memoirs of Elizabeth Barrett Browning and Robert Browning enables us to appreciate the depth of influence that two people <u>of talent can have on one another.</u>

   (A) of talent can have on one another
   (B) of talent can exert on one another
   (C) with talent can have one for the other
   (D) of talent can have on each other
   (E) who are talented can have

6. <u>If you saw the amount of pancakes he consumed</u> at breakfast this morning, you would understand why he is so overweight.

   (A) If you saw the amount of pancakes he consumed
   (B) If you would see the amount of pancakes he consumed
   (C) When you see the amount of pancakes he consumed
   (D) If you saw the number of pancakes he consumed
   (E) If you had seen the number of pancakes he consumed

7. The reality star went to the concert with her <u>boyfriend wearing a sheer blouse.</u>

   (A) The reality star went to the concert with her boyfriend wearing a sheer blouse
   (B) The reality star went to the concert, wearing a sheer blouse, with her boyfriend
   (C) The reality star, wearing a sheer blouse, went to the concert with her boyfriend
   (D) With her boyfriend, wearing a sheer blouse, the reality star went to the concert
   (E) To the concert, wearing a sheer blouse, went the reality star with her boyfriend

8. Briefly the functions of a military staff are to advise the commander, transmit his instructions, <u>and the supervision of the execution of his decisions.</u>

   (A) and the supervision of the execution of his decisions
   (B) also the supervision of the execution of his decisions
   (C) and supervising the execution of his decisions
   (D) and supervise the execution of his decisions
   (E) and have supervision of the execution of his decisions

9. <u>The 15-round decision that the newcomer was given over the champ</u> was not popular with all of the boxing fans.

   (A) The 15-round decision that the newcomer was given over the champ
   (B) the newcomer's 15-round decision over the champ
   (C) The newcomer's 15-round decision over the champ
   (D) The decision of 15 rounds that the newcomer was given over the champ
   (E) The champ's 15-round decision that the newcomer was given over him

GO ON TO THE NEXT PAGE ➤

10. This test was as hard, if not harder than, the one I took last week.

 (A) This test was as hard
 (B) This test was so hard
 (C) This test was as hard as
 (D) This test was so hard as
 (E) This was a test as hard

11. We took a plane from JFK Airport that carried few passengers.

 (A) We took a plane from JFK Airport that carried few passengers
 (B) The plane that was taken by us from JFK Airport carries few passengers
 (C) The plane we took carried few passengers
 (D) We took a plane that carried few passengers from JFK Airport
 (E) The plane that we took from JFK Airport carried few passengers

12. I wanted to and would have gone to the play if I had the money.

 (A) I wanted to and would have gone
 (B) Having wanted to, I would have gone
 (C) I wanted to go and would have gone
 (D) Although I wanted to go and would have gone
 (E) I wanted and would have gone

13. Either I'll go to the store today or tomorrow morning.

 (A) Either I'll go to the store today or tomorrow morning
 (B) Either I'll go to the store today or I'll go tomorrow morning
 (C) I'll go to the store today, or if not today, then tomorrow morning
 (D) I'll go to the store either today or tomorrow morning
 (E) I'll go either today or tomorrow morning to the store

14. For a while the student had a job after school, which caused his grades to suffer.

 (A) which caused his grades to suffer
 (B) and for this reason his grades were suffering
 (C) and this condition caused his grades to suffer
 (D) so his grades suffered as a result of this
 (E) this was the reason his grades suffered

STOP

If you finish before time is called, you may check your work on this section only.
Do not turn to any other section in the test.

How did you do on this test?

Step 1.   Go to the Answer Key

Step 2.   Calculate your "raw score."

Step 3.   Get your "scaled score" for the test by referring to the Raw Score/Scaled Score Conversion Tables.

**THERE'S ALWAYS ROOM
FOR IMPROVEMENT!**

ANSWER KEY FOR PRACTICE TEST 1
Math

Section 2		Correct Answer
1		D
2		B
3		D
4		E
5		B
6		E
7		C
8		A
9		C
10		B
11		B
12		E
13		B
14		D
15		C
16		C
17		C
18		A
19		B
20		C

Number correct

Number incorrect

Section 3		Correct Answer
1		C
2		D
3		D
4		E
5		D
6		A
7		B
8		E
9		C
10		D
11		C
12		D
13		E
14		C
15		B
16		E
17		B
18		E
19		E
20		D

Number correct

Number incorrect

Section 6		Correct Answer
1		D
2		E
3		D
4		D
5		E
6		B
7		B
8		D

Number correct

Number incorrect

Student-Produced Response Questions

9	$\frac{7}{24}$ or x where $.25 <$ $x < .3333$
10	12
11	60
12	6
13	24
14	25
15	6
16	35
17	333
18	$\frac{1}{8}$ or .125

Number correct

Number incorrect

Section 8		Correct Answer
1		E
2		D
3		C
4		C
5		E
6		D
7		C
8		B
9		A
10		A
11		A
12		D
13		A
14		B
15		E
16		B

Number correct

Number incorrect

ANSWER KEY FOR PRACTICE TEST 1
Critical reading

Section 4

	Correct Answer
1	D
2	A
3	E
4	D
5	B
6	E
7	B
8	D
9	E
10	D
11	E
12	E
13	B
14	E
15	E
16	A
17	C
18	B
19	B
20	D
21	A
22	C
23	B
24	C

Number correct

Number incorrect

Section 7

	Correct Answer
1	E
2	A
3	A
4	B
5	D
6	B
7	A
8	A
9	D
10	A
11	D
12	E
13	E
14	C
15	D
16	C
17	A
18	D
19	B
20	B
21	C
22	E
23	C
24	A

Number correct

Number incorrect

Section 9

	Correct Answer
1	E
2	A
3	B
4	B
5	B
6	D
7	D
8	A
9	B
10	C
11	E
12	D
13	A
14	B
15	A
16	B
17	C
18	A
19	E

Number correct

Number incorrect

ANSWER KEY FOR PRACTICE TEST 1
Writing

Section 1

_____

Essay score

Section 5

	Correct Answer
1	A
2	A
3	D
4	D
5	C
6	C
7	B
8	E
9	D
10	D
11	A
12	B
13	D
14	A
15	E
16	C
17	B
18	D
19	C
20	D
21	B
22	A
23	A
24	E
25	E
26	A
27	A
28	D
29	B
30	B
31	D
32	D
33	A
34	B
35	C

Number correct

_____

Number incorrect

Section 10

	Correct Answer
1	D
2	B
3	D
4	C
5	D
6	E
7	C
8	D
9	A
10	C
11	E
12	C
13	D
14	C

Number correct

_____

Number incorrect

Scoring the SAT Practice Test

Check your responses with the correct answers on the previous pages. Fill in the blanks below and do the calculations to get your Math, Critical Reading, and Writing raw scores. Use the table to find your Math, Critical Reading, and Writing scaled scores.

Get Your Math Score

How many Math questions did you get **right**?

Section 2: Questions 1–20   _____

Section 6: Questions 1–18   + _____

Section 8: Questions 1–16   + _____

          Total   = _____ **(A)**

How many Math questions did you get **wrong**?

Section 2: Questions 1–20   _____

Section 6: Questions 1–18   + _____

Section 8: Questions 1–16   + _____

          Total   = _____

         $\times 0.25$ = _____ **(B)**

    A – B   = _____

               Math Raw Score

Round Math raw score to the nearest whole number.

_____

Use the Score Conversion Table to find your Math scaled score.

_____

Get Your Critical Reading Score

How many Critical Reading questions did you get **right**?

Section 4: Questions 1–24   _____

Section 7: Questions 1–24   + _____

Section 9: Questions 1–19   + _____

          Total   = _____ **(A)**

How many Critical Reading questions did you get **wrong**?

Section 4: Questions 1–24   _____

Section 7: Questions 1–24   + _____

Section 9: Questions 1–19   + _____

          Total   = _____

         $\times 0.25$ = _____ **(B)**

    A – B   = _____

           Critical Reading Raw Score

Round Critical Reading raw score to the nearest whole number.

_____

Use the Score Conversion Table to find your Critical Reading scaled score.

_____

Get Your Writing Score

How many multiple-choice Writing questions did you get **right**?

Section 5: Questions 1–35   _____

Section 10: Questions 1–14 + _____

             Total   =   _____ **(A)**

How many multiple-choice Writing questions did you get **wrong**?

Section 5: Questions 1–35   _____

Section 10: Questions 1–14 + _____

             Total   =   _____

           $\times\ 0.25$ =   _____ **(B)**

        A – B   =   _____

             Writing Raw Score

Round Writing raw score to the nearest whole number.

_____

Use the Score Conversion Table to find your Writing multiple-choice scaled score.

_____

Estimate your Essay score using the Essay Scoring Guide.

_____

Use the SAT Score Conversion Table for Writing Composite to find your Writing scaled score. You will need your Writing raw score and your Essay score to use this table.

_____

SAT Score conversion table

Raw Score	Critical Reading Scaled Score	Math Scaled Score	Writing Multiple-Choice Scaled Score*	Raw Score	Critical Reading Scaled Score	Math Scaled Score	Writing Multiple-Choice Scaled Score*
67	800			31	510	550	60
66	800			30	510	540	58
65	790			29	500	530	57
64	770			28	490	520	56
63	750			27	490	520	55
62	740			26	480	510	54
61	730			25	480	500	53
60	720			24	470	490	52
59	700			23	460	480	51
58	690			22	460	480	50
57	690			21	450	470	49
56	680			20	440	460	48
55	670			19	440	450	47
54	660	800		18	430	450	46
53	650	790		17	420	440	45
52	650	760		16	420	430	44
51	640	740		15	410	420	44
50	630	720		14	400	410	43
49	620	710	80	13	400	410	42
48	620	700	80	12	390	400	41
47	610	680	80	11	380	390	40
46	600	670	79	10	370	380	39
45	600	660	78	9	360	370	38
44	590	650	76	8	350	360	38
43	590	640	74	7	340	350	37
42	580	630	73	6	330	340	36
41	570	630	71	5	320	330	35
40	570	620	70	4	310	320	34
39	560	610	69	3	300	310	32
38	550	600	67	2	280	290	31
37	550	590	66	1	270	280	30
36	540	580	65	0	250	260	28
35	540	580	64	−1	230	240	27
34	530	570	63	−2	210	220	25
33	520	560	62	−3	200	200	23
32	520	550	61	−4 and below	200	200	20

This table is for use only with the test in this book.

* The Writing multiple-choice score is reported on a 20–80 scale. Use the SAT Score Conversion Table for Writing Composite for the total writing scaled score.

SAT Score conversion table for writing composite

Writing Multiple-Choice Raw Score	Essay Raw Score						
	0	1	2	3	4	5	6
−12	200	200	200	210	240	270	300
−11	200	200	200	210	240	270	300
−10	200	200	200	210	240	270	300
−9	200	200	200	210	240	270	300
−8	200	200	200	210	240	270	300
−7	200	200	200	210	240	270	300
−6	200	200	200	210	240	270	300
−5	200	200	200	210	240	270	300
−4	200	200	200	230	270	300	330
−3	200	210	230	250	290	320	350
−2	200	230	250	280	310	340	370
−1	210	240	260	290	320	360	380
0	230	260	280	300	340	370	400
1	240	270	290	320	350	380	410
2	250	280	300	330	360	390	420
3	260	290	310	340	370	400	430
4	270	300	320	350	380	410	440
5	280	310	330	360	390	420	450
6	290	320	340	360	400	430	460
7	290	330	340	370	410	440	470
8	300	330	350	380	410	450	470
9	310	340	360	390	420	450	480
10	320	350	370	390	430	460	490
11	320	360	370	400	440	470	500
12	330	360	380	410	440	470	500
13	340	370	390	420	450	480	510
14	350	380	390	420	460	490	520
15	350	380	400	430	460	500	530
16	360	390	410	440	470	500	530
17	370	400	420	440	480	510	540
18	380	410	420	450	490	520	550
19	380	410	430	460	490	530	560
20	390	420	440	470	500	530	560
21	400	430	450	480	510	540	570
22	410	440	460	480	520	550	580

Writing Multiple-Choice Raw Score	Essay Raw Score						
	0	1	2	3	4	5	6
23	420	450	470	490	530	560	590
24	420	460	470	500	540	570	600
25	430	460	480	510	540	580	610
26	440	470	490	520	550	590	610
27	450	480	500	530	560	590	620
28	460	490	510	540	570	600	630
29	470	500	520	550	580	610	640
30	480	510	530	560	590	620	650
31	490	520	540	560	600	630	660
32	500	530	550	570	610	640	670
33	510	540	550	580	620	650	680
34	510	550	560	590	630	660	690
35	520	560	570	600	640	670	700
36	530	560	580	610	650	680	710
37	540	570	590	620	660	690	720
38	550	580	600	630	670	700	730
39	560	600	610	640	680	710	740
40	580	610	620	650	690	720	750
41	590	620	640	660	700	730	760
42	600	630	650	680	710	740	770
43	610	640	660	690	720	750	780
44	620	660	670	700	740	770	800
45	640	670	690	720	750	780	800
46	650	690	700	730	770	800	800
47	670	700	720	750	780	800	800
48	680	720	730	760	800	800	800
49	680	720	730	760	800	800	800

Chart for self-appraisal based on the practice test you have just taken

The Chart for Self-Appraisal below tells you quickly where your SAT strengths and weaknesses lie. Check or circle the appropriate box in accordance with the number of your correct answers for each area of the Practice Test you have just taken.

	Writing (Multiple-Choice)	Sentence Completions	Reading Comprehension	Math Questions*
EXCELLENT	42–49	16–19	40–48	44–54
GOOD	37–41	13–15	35–39	32–43
FAIR	31–36	9–12	26–34	27–31
POOR	20–30	5–8	17–25	16–26
VERY POOR	0–19	0–4	0–16	0–15

*Sections 2, 6, 8 only.

Note: In our tests, we have chosen to have Section 3 as the experimental section. We have also chosen it to be a math section since we felt that students may need more practice in the math area than in the verbal area. Note that on the actual SAT you will take, the order of the sections can vary and you will not know which one is experimental, so it is wise to answer all sections and not to leave any section out.

SAT-I VERBAL AND MATH SCORE/PERCENTILE CONVERSION TABLE

Critical reading and writing

SAT scaled verbal score	Percentile rank
800	99.7+
790	99.5
740–780	99
700–730	97
670–690	95
640–660	91
610–630	85
580–600	77
550–570	68
510–540	57
480–500	46
440–470	32
410–430	21
380–400	13
340–370	6
300–330	2
230–290	1
200–220	0–0.5

Math

SAT scaled math score	Percentile rank
800	99.5+
770–790	99.5
720–760	99
670–710	97
640–660	94
610–630	89
590–600	84
560–580	77
530–550	68
510–520	59
480–500	48
450–470	37
430–440	26
390–420	16
350–380	8
310–340	2
210–300	0.5
200	0

EXPLANATORY ANSWERS FOR PRACTICE TEST 1

THE SAT SCORING GUIDE

Section 1: Essay

Score of 6	Score of 5	Score of 4
An essay in this category is *outstanding*, demonstrating *clear and consistent mastery*, although it may have a few minor errors. A typical essay	An essay in this category is *effective*, demonstrating *reasonably consistent mastery*, although it will have occasional errors or lapses in quality. A typical essay	An essay in this category is *competent*, demonstrating *adequate mastery*, although it will have lapses in quality. A typical essay
• effectively and insightfully develops a point of view on the issue and demonstrates outstanding critical thinking, using clearly appropriate examples, reasons, and other evidence to support its position	• effectively develops a point of view on the issue and demonstrates strong critical thinking, generally using appropriate examples, reasons, and other evidence to support its position	• develops a point of view on the issue and demonstrates competent critical thinking, using adequate examples, reasons, and other evidence to support its position
• is well organized and clearly focused, demonstrating clear coherence and smooth progression of ideas	• is well organized and focused, demonstrating coherence and progression of ideas	• is generally organized and focused, demonstrating some coherence and progression of ideas
• exhibits skillful use of language, using a varied, accurate, and apt vocabulary	• exhibits facility in the use of language, using appropriate vocabulary	• exhibits adequate but inconsistent facility in the use of language, using generally appropriate vocabulary
• demonstrates meaningful variety in sentence structure	• demonstrates variety in sentence structure	• demonstrates some variety in sentence structure
• is free of most errors in grammar, usage, and mechanics	• is generally free of most errors in grammar, usage, and mechanics	• has some errors in grammar, usage, and mechanics

Score of 3	Score of 2	Score of 1
An essay in this category is *inadequate*, but demonstrates *developing mastery*, and is marked by ONE OR MORE of the following weaknesses:	An essay in this category is *seriously-limited*, demonstrating *little mastery*, and is flawed by ONE OR MORE of the following weaknesses:	An essay in this category is *fundamentally lacking*, demonstrating *very little* or *no mastery*, and is severely flawed by ONE OR MORE of the following weaknesses:
• develops a point of view on the issue, demonstrating some critical thinking, but may do so inconsistently or use inadequate examples, reasons, or other evidence to support its position	• develops a point of view on the issue that is vague or seriously limited, demonstrating weak critical thinking, providing inappropriate or insufficient examples, reasons, or other evidence to support its position	• develops no viable point of view on the issue, or provides little or no evidence to support its position
• is limited in its organization or focus, or may demonstrate some lapses in coherence or progression of ideas	• is poorly organized and/or focused, or demonstrates serious problems with coherence or progression of ideas	• is disorganized or unfocused, resulting in a disjointed or incoherent essay
• displays developing facility in the use of language, but sometimes uses weak vocabulary or inappropriate word choice	• displays very little facility in the use of language, using very limited vocabulary or incorrect word choice	• displays fundamental errors in vocabulary
• lacks variety or demonstrates problems in sentence structure	• demonstrates frequent problems in sentence structure	• demonstrates severe flaws in sentence structure
• contains an accumulation of errors in grammar, usage, and mechanics	• contains errors in grammar, usage, and mechanics so serious that meaning is somewhat obscured	• contains pervasive errors in grammar, usage, or mechanics that persistently interfere with meaning

Essays not written on the essay assignment will receive a score of zero.

EXPLANATORY ANSWERS FOR PRACTICE TEST 1

Section 2: Math

When a specific Math Strategy is referred to in the solution, study that strategy, which you will find in "19 Math Strategies."

1. Choice D is correct.

$$\text{Given: } ab = 64 \text{ and } a \text{ and } b \text{ are positive integers} \quad \boxed{1}$$

(Use Strategy 7: Use numerics to help find the answer.)

If $a = 64$, $b = 1$, then $\boxed{1}$ is satisfied
and $a + b = 65$ $\qquad \boxed{2}$

If $a = 32$, $b = 2$, then $\boxed{1}$ is satisfied
and $a + b = 34$ $\qquad \boxed{3}$

If $a = 16$, $b = 4$, then $\boxed{1}$ is satisfied
and $a + b = 20$ $\qquad \boxed{4}$

If $a = 8$, $b = 8$, then $\boxed{1}$ is satisfied
and $a + b = 16$ $\qquad \boxed{5}$

The only other pairs of values that satisfy $\boxed{1}$ are each of the above pairs of values reversed for a and b. Thus $\boxed{5}$, $a + b = 16$, is the smallest value of $a + b$.

2. Choice B is correct.

$$\text{Given: } x + x^3 + x^5 + x^6 \quad \boxed{1}$$
$$x = -1 \quad \boxed{2}$$

Substitute $\boxed{2}$ into $\boxed{1}$. We get

$$-1 + (-1)^3 + (-1)^5 + (-1)^6 =$$
$$-1 - 1 - 1 + 1 = -2$$

3. Choice D is correct.

$$\text{Given:} \quad \begin{array}{r} AB \\ + BA \\ \hline 66 \end{array} \quad \begin{array}{l} 0 < A < 6 \\ 0 < B < 6 \end{array} \quad \begin{array}{l} \boxed{1} \\ \boxed{2} \\ \boxed{3} \end{array}$$

(Use Strategy 17: Use the given information effectively.) From $\boxed{3}$ we see that

$$B + A = 6 \quad \boxed{4}$$

(Use Strategy 7: Use numerics to help find the answer.) Conditions $\boxed{1}$, $\boxed{2}$, and $\boxed{4}$ can be satisfied when:

$$A = 1, B = 5$$
$$A = 2, B = 4$$
$$A = 3, B = 3$$
$$A = 4, B = 2$$
$$A = 5, B = 1$$

Thus, there are five possible values of A.

4. Choice E is correct.

$$\text{Given: Temperature at 11:00 A.M.} = 0°F \quad \boxed{1}$$
$$\text{Temperature at 8:00 A.M.} = -15°F \quad \boxed{2}$$
$$\text{Let } x = \text{Temperature at 5:00 P.M.} \quad \boxed{3}$$
$$y = \text{Temperature rise} \quad \boxed{4}$$

(Use Strategy 13: Find unknowns by sub-tracting.) Subtract $\boxed{2}$ from $\boxed{1}$. We get

$$\text{Temperature rise in 3 hours} = 15°F \quad \boxed{5}$$

Subtract the times in $\boxed{1}$ and $\boxed{3}$. We get

$$\text{Time change} = 6 \text{ hours} \quad \boxed{6}$$

Use $\boxed{4}$, $\boxed{5}$, and $\boxed{6}$ to find temperature rise from 11:00 A.M. to 5:00 P.M. We get

$$\frac{3 \text{ hours}}{6 \text{ hours}} = \frac{15°F}{y}$$
$$3y = 6 \times 15°F$$
$$y = 30°F \quad \boxed{7}$$

Use $\boxed{1}$, $\boxed{3}$, and $\boxed{7}$ to find the final temperature.

$$x = 0°F + 30°F$$
$$x = 30°F$$

5.   Choice B is correct.

Number of Shirts	Total Price
1	$12.00
Box of 3	$22.50
Box of 6	$43.40

From the chart above, we know

6 shirts = $43.40 $\boxed{1}$

(Use Strategy 13: Find unknowns by division.)

Dividing $\boxed{1}$ by 6, we get

$$\frac{6 \text{ shirts}}{6} = \frac{\$43.40}{6}$$
$$1 \text{ shirt } = \$7.23\overline{3}$$
$$\text{Cost per shirt} \approx \$7.20$$

6.   Choice E is correct.

Given: $5x^2 - 15x = 0$ $\boxed{1}$

$x \neq 0$ $\boxed{2}$

(Use Strategy 12: Try not to make tedious calculations.)

Factoring $\boxed{1}$, we get

$$5x(x - 3) = 0$$

$$5x = 0 \text{ or } x - 3 = 0$$

$$x = 0 \text{ or } x = 3 \qquad \boxed{3}$$

Applying $\boxed{2}$ to $\boxed{3}$, we get

$$x = 3$$

7.   Choice C is correct. **(Use Strategy 2: Translate words to algebra.)** In $\frac{1}{2}$ year, 600 pounds of feed were used at a rate of $1.25 per pound. Thus (600 pounds) $\times$ ($1.25 per pound), or $750, was spent. Hence,

$$\text{Feed cost per egg} = \frac{\text{Total cost for feed}}{\text{number of eggs}}$$
$$= \frac{\$750}{5{,}000 \text{ eggs}}$$

(Use Strategy 19: Factor and reduce.)

$$= \frac{\$75 \times 10}{500 \times 10 \text{ eggs}}$$

$$= \frac{\$25 \times 3}{25 \times 20 \text{ eggs}}$$
$$= \frac{\$3}{20} \text{ per egg}$$
$$= \$0.15 \text{ per egg}$$

8.   Choice A is correct. The union of X and Y and 0 is the set of all the elements of X and Y and 0. The elements of all *negative*, *0*, and *positive* numbers is the set of all *real* numbers.

9.   Choice C is correct. **(Use Strategy 2: Translate from words to algebra.)**

Given: Area B = 1 $\boxed{1}$

Area A = 3(Area B) $\boxed{2}$

Area B = 3(Area C) $\boxed{3}$

Substitute $\boxed{1}$ into $\boxed{2}$. We get

Area A = 3(1) = 3 $\boxed{4}$

Substitute $\boxed{1}$ into $\boxed{3}$. We get

$$1 = 3(\text{Area C})$$
$$\frac{1}{3} = \text{Area C} \qquad \boxed{5}$$

Using $\boxed{1}$, $\boxed{4}$, and $\boxed{5}$, we have

Sum of areas A, B, and C $= 3 + 1 + \frac{1}{3}$

Sum of areas A, B, and C $= 4\frac{1}{3}$

10.   Choice B is correct.

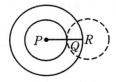

Given: PQR = 9 $\boxed{1}$
PQ = 4 $\boxed{2}$

(Use Strategy 3: The whole equals the sum of its parts.) From the diagram, we see that

$$PQR = PQ + QR \qquad \boxed{3}$$

Substitute $\boxed{1}$ and $\boxed{2}$ into $\boxed{3}$. We get

$$9 = 4 + QR$$
$$5 = QR$$

QR is the radius of a circle with center R and Q on its circumference. (See dotted circle in diagram.)

11. Choice B is correct. $y = f(x)$ is positive or 0 for all x, so only Choices B and C are appropriate. Since $y = f(x)$ represents straight lines, then Choice B is appropriate, while Choice C is eliminated.

12. Choice E is correct.

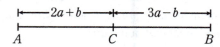

Given: C is the midpoint of AB

Thus, $AC = CB$ $\boxed{1}$

Substituting the lengths from the diagram into $\boxed{1}$, we have

$$2a + b = 3a - b$$
$$b = a - b$$
$$2b = a$$

13. Choice B is correct. **(Use Strategy 17: Use the given information effectively.)** Slope is defined as $\dfrac{y_2 - y_1}{x_2 - x_1}$ where (x_1, y_1) is a point on the line and (x_2, y_2) is another point on the line. We are given that one point is $(0,p)$ and the other point is $(3p,0)$ so,

$$\frac{y_2 - y_1}{x_2 - x_1} = \frac{p - 0}{0 - 3p} = \frac{p}{-3p} = -\frac{1}{3}$$

14. Choice D is correct.

Given: Bus A averages $\dfrac{40 \text{ km}}{\text{gallon}}$ $\boxed{1}$

Bus B averages $\dfrac{50 \text{ km}}{\text{gallon}}$ $\boxed{2}$

Trip distance $= 800$ km $\boxed{3}$

Fuel cost $= \dfrac{\$3}{\text{gallon}}$ $\boxed{4}$

(Use strategy 10: Know how to use units.)

Divide $\boxed{3}$ by $\boxed{1}$. We get

$\dfrac{800 \text{ km}}{40 \text{ km/gallon}} = \dfrac{800}{40} \text{ gallons} = 20 \text{ gallons used by Bus A}$ $\boxed{5}$

Divide $\boxed{3}$ by $\boxed{2}$. We get

$\dfrac{800 \text{ km}}{50 \text{ km/gallon}} = \dfrac{800}{50} \text{ gallons} = 16 \text{ gallons used by Bus B}$ $\boxed{6}$

Multiply $\boxed{5}$ by $\boxed{4}$. We get

$20 \text{ gallons} \times \dfrac{\$3}{\text{gallon}} = \$60 \text{ cost for fuel for Bus A}$ $\boxed{7}$

Multiply $\boxed{6}$ by $\boxed{4}$. We get

$16 \text{ gallons} \times \dfrac{\$3}{\text{gallon}} = \$48 \text{ cost for fuel for Bus B}$ $\boxed{8}$

(Use Strategy 13: Find unknowns by subtracting.)

Subtract $\boxed{8}$ from $\boxed{7}$. We get $\$60 - \$48 = \$12$ difference in the fuel costs between Bus A and Bus B for an 800 km trip.

15. Choice C is correct.

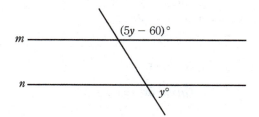

(Use Strategy 17: Use the given information effectively.)

Given: $m \| n$ $\boxed{1}$

From $\boxed{1}$ we know that the two angles are supplementary. Thus,

$$(5y - 60)° + y° = 180°$$
$$6y - 60 = 180°$$
$$6y = 240°$$
$$y = 40°$$

16. Choice C is correct. **(Use Strategy 2: Translate from words to algebra.)**

We have: $\dfrac{4}{100} \times (2a + b) = 18$ $\boxed{1}$

(Use Strategy 13: Find unknowns by multiplication.) Multiply $\boxed{1}$ by $\dfrac{100}{4}$. We get

$$\frac{100}{4}\left(\frac{4}{100} \times (2a + b)\right) = \frac{100}{4}(18)$$

(Use Strategy 19: Factor and reduce.)

$$2a + b = \frac{\cancel{4} \times 25}{\cancel{4}}(18)$$
$$2a + b = 450$$
$$b = 450 - 2a \qquad \boxed{2}$$

(Use Strategy 17: Use the given information effectively.)

b will be greatest when a is smallest.   ☐3
Given: a is a positive integer   ☐4

Applying ☐4 to ☐3, we get

$$a = 1$$ ☐5

Substituting ☐5 into ☐2, we have

$$b = 450 - 2(1)$$
$$= 450 - 2$$
$$b = 448$$

17. Choice C is correct. **(Use Strategy 17: Use the given information effectively.)** The probability is the number of favorable ways divided by the number of total ways. The total ways is the number of points in the large circle of radius 2 feet. We can look at that as the area of the large circle, which is $\pi r^2 = 2 \times 2\pi = 4\pi$. The favorable ways are the number of points in the inner circle, which we can look at as the area of that circle, which is $\pi r^2 = 1 \times 1\pi = 1\pi$. Thus the probability is $\frac{1\pi}{4\pi} = \frac{1}{4}$.

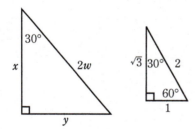

18. Choice A is correct. **(Use Strategy 18: Remember special right triangles.)** The triangle at left (given) is similar to the triangle at right, which is one of the standard triangles.

Corresponding sides of similar triangles are proportional. Thus,

$$\frac{2w}{2} = \frac{y}{1} \text{ and } \frac{2w}{2} = \frac{x}{\sqrt{3}}$$

or $y = w$ and $x = w\sqrt{3}$

$$\text{Area of triangle} = \frac{1}{2}(\text{base})(\text{height})$$

$$= \frac{1}{2}(y)(x)$$

$$= \frac{1}{2}(w)(w\sqrt{3})$$

$$\text{Area of triangle} = \frac{\sqrt{3}}{2}w^2$$ ☐1
$$\text{Area of rectangle} = (3w)(w) = 3w^2$$ ☐2

Using ☐1 and ☐2, we have

$$\frac{\text{area of rectangle}}{\text{area of triangle}} = \frac{3w^2}{\frac{\sqrt{3}}{2}w^2}$$

$$= \frac{3}{\frac{\sqrt{3}}{2}} = 3 \times \frac{2}{\sqrt{3}}$$

$$= \frac{6}{\sqrt{3}} = \frac{6\sqrt{3}}{3} = 2\sqrt{3}$$

or $2\sqrt{3} : 1$ (*Answer*)

19.   Choice B is correct.

(Use Strategy 2: Translate from words to algebra.)

$$\text{Let } f = \text{Number of freshmen}$$
$$s = \text{Number of seniors}$$

We are given $f = 3s$ ☐1

$\frac{1}{4}$ of the freshmen $= \frac{1}{4}f$ ☐2

$\frac{1}{3}$ of the seniors $= \frac{1}{3}s$ ☐3

Total number of freshmen
and seniors $= f + s$ ☐4

(Use Strategy 17: Use the given information effectively.)

The desired fraction uses ☐2, ☐3, and ☐4 as follows:

$$\frac{\frac{1}{4}f + \frac{1}{3}s}{f + s}$$ ☐5

Substituting ☐1 in ☐5, we get

$$\frac{\left(\frac{1}{4}(3s) + \frac{1}{3}s\right)}{3s + s} = \frac{\left(\frac{3}{4}s + \frac{1}{3}s\right)}{4s}$$ ☐6

Multiplying ☐6, numerator and denominator, by 12, we get:

$$\left(\frac{12}{12}\right)\frac{\frac{3}{4}s + \frac{1}{3}s}{4s} =$$

$$\frac{9s + 4s}{48s} =$$

$$\frac{13s}{48s} =$$

$$\frac{13}{48}$$ (*Answer*)

20.   Choice C is correct.

   (Use Strategy 2: Translate from words to algebra.) Set up a Venn diagram:

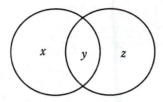

   x = number of students with *only* a car

   z = number of students with *only* a bicycle

   y = number of students having a car and a bicycle

$$\text{Total students} = 100 \qquad \boxed{1}$$
$$\text{We are given: } x + y = 30 \qquad \boxed{2}$$
$$z + y = 50 \qquad \boxed{3}$$
$$y = 20 \qquad \boxed{4}$$

   Substituting $\boxed{4}$ into $\boxed{2}$ and into $\boxed{3}$, we get

$$x = 10, z = 30 \qquad \boxed{5}$$

   Using $\boxed{4}$ and $\boxed{5}$, we have:

$$\text{The sum of } x + y + z =$$
$$10 + 20 + 30 = 60 \qquad \boxed{6}$$

   This is the number of students who have either a car, a bicycle, or both.

   Using $\boxed{1}$ and $\boxed{6}$, we get $100 - 60 = 40$ as the number who have neither a car nor a bicycle.

EXPLANATORY ANSWERS FOR PRACTICE TEST 1

Section 3: Math

> When a specific Math Strategy is referred to in the solution, study that strategy, which you will find in "19 Math Strategies."

1. Choice C is correct. **(Use Strategy 17: Use the given information effectively.)**

$$Given:\ 55,555 = y + 50,505$$
$$5,050 = y \qquad \boxed{1}$$

We need: $50,505 - 10y \qquad \boxed{2}$

Substitute $\boxed{1}$ into $\boxed{2}$. We get

$$50,505 - 10(5,050) =$$
$$50,505 - 50,500 =$$
$$5$$

2. Choice D is correct. Using the distributive property, we get $3x(4x + 2y) = 12x^2 + 6xy$

3. Choice D is correct. **(Use Strategy 17: Use the given information effectively.)**

We are told that 1 decimeter = 100 millimeters. Therefore, 20 decimeters = 2,000 millimeters. E, C, and B are greater than 2,000 millimeters.

4. Choice E is correct.

Given: $\quad a - 3 = 7 \qquad \boxed{1}$

(Use Strategy 13: Find unknowns by addition, subtraction, and multiplication.)

Fast Method: From $\boxed{1}$, we can subtract 7 from both sides, and then add 3 to both sides to get

$$a - 7 = 3 \qquad \boxed{2}$$

Multiplying $\boxed{2}$ by 2, we get

$$2a - 14 = 6 \qquad (Answer)$$

Slow Method: Solve $\boxed{1}$ to get

$$a = 10 \qquad \boxed{3}$$

Now substitute $\boxed{3}$:

$$2a - 14 = 2(10) - 14 = 6 \quad (Answer)$$

5. Choice D is correct.

(Use Strategy 17: Use the given information effectively.)

Change all fractions to decimal form:

$$\frac{7}{10} = 0.7$$

$$\frac{7}{100} = 0.07$$

$$\frac{77}{1,000} = 0.077$$

Adding these, we get 0.847 *(Answer)*

6. Choice A is correct.

(Use Strategy 14: Label unknown quantities to help solve the problem.)

Know the properties of parallel lines. If 2 parallel lines are crossed by a transversal, the pairs of corresponding angles are equal. Thus,

$$x = a \qquad \boxed{1}$$
From the diagram, $a + y = 180 \qquad \boxed{2}$

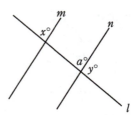

Substituting $\boxed{1}$ into $\boxed{2}$, we get

$$x + y = 180 \qquad (Answer)$$

7. Choice B is correct.

(Use Strategy 7: Use numerics to help find the answer.)

12 must be substituted for P in each of the five expressions and the results evaluated.

Item 1: $P = 12$ 12
Item 2: $P \times 3 = 12 \times 3 =$ 36
Item 3: $(P \times 3) \div 2 = (12 \times 3) \div 2 =$ 18
Item 4: $[(P \times 3) \div 2] + 12 =$
      $[(12 \times 3) \div 2] + 12 =$ 30
Item 5: $[(P \times 3) \div 2] + 12 - 1 =$
      $[(12 \times 3) \div 2] + 12 - 1 =$ 29

Item 2 is greatest in value.

8. Choice E is correct.

Given: $\dfrac{3x}{4} = 9$ $\boxed{1}$

(Use Strategy 13: Find unknowns by multiplication.)

Multiplying $\boxed{1}$ by 4, we get

$$\cancel{4}\left(\frac{3x}{\cancel{4}}\right) = (9)4$$
$$3x = 36 \qquad \boxed{2}$$

Multiply $\boxed{2}$ by 2. We have

$$2(3x) = 2(36)$$
$$6x = 72$$

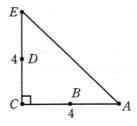

9. Choice C is correct.

From the diagram we find that

$$AB = 2 \qquad \boxed{1}$$
$$BC = 2 \qquad \boxed{2}$$
$$CD = 2 \qquad \boxed{3}$$
$$DE = 2 \qquad \boxed{4}$$

(Use Strategy 3: The whole equals the sum of its parts.)

We know $AB + BC = AC$ $\boxed{5}$

Substituting $\boxed{1}$ and $\boxed{2}$ into $\boxed{5}$, we get

$$2 + 2 = AC$$
$$4 = AC \qquad \boxed{6}$$

We know $CD + DE = CE$. $\boxed{7}$

Substituting $\boxed{3}$ and $\boxed{4}$ into $\boxed{7}$, we get

$$2 + 2 = CE$$
$$4 = CE \qquad \boxed{8}$$

Filling $\boxed{6}$ and $\boxed{8}$ into the diagram and using the fact that all the segments drawn were perpendicular, we have ΔECA is an isosceles right triangle.

(Use Strategy 18: Know and use facts about triangles.)

In the isosceles right triangle, the

$$\text{hypotenuse} = \text{leg}(\sqrt{2}) \qquad \boxed{9}$$

Substituting $\boxed{6}$ or $\boxed{8}$ into $\boxed{9}$, we get

$$EA = 4\sqrt{2} \qquad \boxed{6}$$

10. Choice D is correct.

(Use Strategy 11: Use new definitions carefully.)

Two-digit numbers which have a units digit $= 0$ that can be tripled in value when the tens digit is tripled are the following:

Original number	Tripled tens digit number
10	30
20	60
30	90

The above numbers are the only numbers that result in a two-digit number as defined in the problem. Thus, 3 is the correct answer.

This problem can also be solved using a more sophisticated method.

Call the number $10t + u$ (where t is the tens digit and u is the units digit).

(Use Strategy 2: Translate Words to Math)

In the number $10t + u$, tripling the tens digit gives us the number $10(3t) + u$.

A two-digit number that is triple the original number translates to $3(10t + u)$.

Setting these quantities equal, we get:

$$10(3t) + u = 3(10t + u) \qquad \boxed{1}$$
$$30t + u = 30t + 3u$$
$$u = 3u$$

Therefore $u = 0$.

So the number $10t + u = 10t$, where $t = 1, 2,$ or 3 (three numbers). t can't be more than 3 because $\boxed{1}$ would not give us a two-digit number.

11. Choice C is correct.

(Use Strategy 11: Use new definitions carefully.)

$$\text{By definition, } A = 12,345 \qquad \boxed{1}$$
$$B = 98,765 \qquad \boxed{2}$$

(Use Strategy 13: Find unknowns by subtracting.)

Subtracting $\boxed{1}$ from $\boxed{2}$, we get

$$B - A = 98,765 - 12,345$$
$$B - A = 86,420$$

12. Choice D is correct.

Given:

$$\text{Meteor 1 travels at 300 meters/second} \quad \boxed{1}$$
$$\text{Meteor 2 travels at 700 meters/second} \quad \boxed{2}$$

Draw a diagram:

Let t be the time it takes meteors to meet. Call x the distance Meteor 1 travels. Then $2,500 - x$ is the distance Meteor 2 travels.

(Use Strategy 9: Know Rate, Time, and Distance relationships.)

$$\text{Rate} \times \text{Time} = \text{Distance}$$
$$300 \text{ m/sec} \times t = x \qquad \boxed{3}$$
$$700 \text{ m/sec} \times t = 2500 - x \qquad \boxed{4}$$

(Use Strategy 13: Find unknowns by addition.)

Add $\boxed{3}$ and $\boxed{4}$

$$(300 \text{ m/sec})t + (700 \text{ m/sec})t = 2,500 \text{ km}$$
$$(1,000 \text{ m/sec})t = 2,500 \text{ km} \qquad \boxed{5}$$

(Use Strategy 10: Know how to use units.)

$$1 \text{ km} = 1,000 \text{ m} \qquad \boxed{6}$$

Substitute $\boxed{6}$ in $\boxed{5}$:

$$(1,000 \text{ m/sec})t = 2,500(1,000) \text{ m} \qquad \boxed{7}$$

Divide $\boxed{7}$ by 1,000 m:

$$t/\text{sec} = 2,500$$
$$t = 2,500 \text{ sec}$$

13. Choice E is correct.

(Use Strategy 17: Use the given information effectively.)

The center point inside a cube is the midpoint of an inner diagonal of the cube. Thus, the distance from any vertex to this center point is $\frac{1}{2}$ the length of the inner diagonal.

We know length of inner diagonal of a cube

$$= \sqrt{(edge)^2 + (edge)^2 + (edge)^2}$$
$$\text{inner diagonal} = \sqrt{3(edge)^2} \qquad \boxed{1}$$
$$\text{inner diagonal} = edge\sqrt{3} \qquad \boxed{2}$$
$$\textit{Given:} \quad \text{Volume} = 8 \text{ cubic meters} \qquad \boxed{3}$$

We know volume of a cube $= (edge)^3 \qquad \boxed{4}$

Substituting $\boxed{3}$ into $\boxed{4}$, we get

$$8 \text{ cubic meters} = (edge)^3$$
$$\sqrt[3]{8 \text{ cubic meters}} = \sqrt[3]{(edge)^3}$$
$$2 \text{ meters} = edge \qquad \boxed{5}$$

Substituting $\boxed{5}$ into $\boxed{2}$, we get

$$\text{inner diagonal} = 2\sqrt{3} \text{ meters} \qquad \boxed{6}$$

Using $\boxed{1}$ *and* $\boxed{6}$, we find

$$\text{distance we need} = \frac{1}{2}(\text{inner diagonal})$$
$$= \frac{1}{2}(2\sqrt{3} \text{ meters})$$
$$= \sqrt{3} \text{ meters}$$

$$\text{Distance we need} = \sqrt{3} \text{ m}$$

14. Choice C is correct.

    (Use Strategy 2: Translate from words to algebra.)

    Let a = a positive integer

    Then $a + 1, a + 2, a + 3, a + 4$, etc., are the next positive integers.

    (Use Strategy 13: Find unknowns by addition.)

    Add the first 2 positive integers. We get

    Sum of first 2 positive integers =
    $$a + a + 1 = 2a + 1 \qquad \boxed{1}$$

    $\boxed{1}$ is not divisible by 2.

    Now add the third positive integer, $a + 2$, to $\boxed{1}$. We get

    Sum of first 3 positive integers =
    $$2a + 1 + a + 2 = 3a + 3 \qquad \boxed{2}$$

    $\boxed{2}$ is not divisible by 2.

    Now add the fourth positive integer, $a + 3$, to $\boxed{2}$. We have

    Sum of first 4 positive integers
    $$= 3a + 3 + a + 3$$
    $$= 4a + 6 \qquad \boxed{3}$$

    Since $\boxed{3}$ can be written as $2(2a + 3)$, it is divisible by 2.

    Thus, if the number of integers is a multiple of 4, the sum of the consecutive positive integers will be divisible by 2.

15. Choice B is correct. **(Use Strategy 2: Translate from words to algebra.)**

    Given: Square has perimeter 2π
    $$\boxed{1}$$
    Let S = side of square.
    We know perimeter of a square = $4S$
    $$\boxed{2}$$

    Substitute $\boxed{1}$ into $\boxed{2}$. We get

    $$\text{Perimeter of square} = 4S$$
    $$2\pi = 4S$$
    $$\frac{2\pi}{4} = S$$
    $$\frac{\pi}{2} = S \qquad \boxed{3}$$

We are given that:
$$\text{area of circle} = \text{area of square} \qquad \boxed{4}$$

We know that:
$$\text{area of circle} = \pi r^2 \qquad \boxed{5}$$
$$\text{area of square} = S^2 \qquad \boxed{6}$$

Substituting $\boxed{5}$ and $\boxed{6}$ into $\boxed{4}$, we get
$$\pi r^2 = S^2 \qquad \boxed{7}$$

Substitute $\boxed{3}$ into $\boxed{7}$. We get

$$\pi r^2 = \left(\frac{\pi}{2}\right)^2$$
$$\pi r^2 = \frac{\pi^2}{4}$$
$$r^2 = \frac{\pi^2}{4\pi}$$
$$r^2 = \frac{\pi}{4}$$
$$r = \sqrt{\frac{\pi}{4}} = \frac{\sqrt{\pi}}{2} \qquad \boxed{8}$$

We know the circumference of a circle = $2\pi r$ $\boxed{9}$

Substitute $\boxed{8}$ into $\boxed{9}$. We have

$$\text{Circumference} = 2\pi\left(\frac{\sqrt{\pi}}{2}\right)$$
$$\text{Circumference} = \pi\sqrt{\pi}$$

16. Choice E is correct.

    $$\textit{Given: } \frac{a}{b} = \frac{1}{4} \qquad \boxed{1}$$

    (Use Strategy 13: Find unknowns by multiplying.) Cross-multiply $\boxed{1}$. We have

    $$4a = b \qquad \boxed{2}$$

    Substituting $4a = b$ in the given $\frac{a^2}{b}$, we get

    $$\frac{a^2}{b} = \frac{a^2}{4a} = \frac{a}{4} \qquad \boxed{3}$$

    (Use Strategy 7: Use numerics to help find the answer.) If $a = 1$ is substituted into $\boxed{3}$, we have

    $$\frac{a^2}{b} = \frac{a}{4} = \frac{1}{4}$$

    Thus, Choice I is satisfied. If $a = 2$ is substituted into $\boxed{3}$, we get

    $$\frac{a^2}{b} = \frac{a}{4} = \frac{2}{4} = \frac{1}{2}$$

    Thus, Choice II is satisfied. If $a = 4$ is substituted into $\boxed{3}$, we have

    $$\frac{a^2}{b} = \frac{a}{4} = \frac{4}{4} = 1$$

    Thus Choice III is satisfied.

17. Choice B is correct. **(Use Strategy 2: Translate from words to algebra.)**

Given: Rate of plane $= x \dfrac{\text{km}}{\text{hour}}$ $\boxed{1}$

Time of flight $= y$ hours $\boxed{2}$

Need: Distance plane had flown $\frac{2}{3}y$ hours ago $\boxed{3}$

Subtracting $\boxed{3}$ from $\boxed{2}$, we get

Time plane had flown $\frac{2}{3}y$ hours ago $= y - \frac{2}{3}y$

Time plane had flown $\frac{2}{3}y$ hours ago $= \frac{1}{3}y$ hours $\boxed{4}$

(Use Strategy 9: Know the rate, time, and distance relationship.)

We know: Rate $\times$ Time = Distance $\boxed{5}$

Substitute $\boxed{1}$ and $\boxed{4}$ into $\boxed{5}$. We get

$$x \frac{\text{km}}{\text{hour}} \times \frac{1}{3}y \text{ hours} = \text{Distance}$$

$\dfrac{xy}{3} =$ Distance plane had flown $\frac{2}{3}y$ hours ago.

18. Choice E is correct.

(Use Strategy 5:

$$\textbf{Average} = \frac{\textbf{sum of values}}{\textbf{total number of values}})$$

We know that

$$\text{Average} = \frac{\text{sum of values}}{\text{total number of values}} \quad \boxed{1}$$

Given: Average of k scores is 20 $\boxed{2}$

Substitute $\boxed{2}$ into $\boxed{1}$. We get

$$20 = \frac{\text{sum of } k \text{ scores}}{k}$$

$20k =$ Sum of k scores $\boxed{3}$

Given: Average of 10 of these scores is 15. $\boxed{4}$

Substitute $\boxed{4}$ into $\boxed{1}$. We have

$$15 = \frac{\text{sum of 10 scores}}{10}$$

$150 =$ Sum of 10 scores $\boxed{5}$

There are $k - 10$ scores remaining. $\boxed{6}$

(Use Strategy 3: The whole equals the sum of its parts.)

We know: Sum of 10 scores + Sum of remaining-scores = Sum of k scores $\boxed{7}$

Substituting $\boxed{3}$ and $\boxed{5}$ into $\boxed{7}$, we get

$150 +$ Sum of remaining scores $= 20k$

Sum of remaining scores $= 20k - 150$ $\boxed{8}$

Substituting $\boxed{6}$ and $\boxed{8}$ into $\boxed{1}$, we get

Average of remaining scores $= \dfrac{20k - 150}{k - 10}$

19. Choice E is correct.

Given: Area of square $= R^2$ $\boxed{1}$

Perimeter of equilateral triangle $= E$ $\boxed{2}$

Perimeter of square $= r$ $\boxed{3}$

Side of equilateral triangle $= e$ $\boxed{4}$

(Use Strategy 17: Use the given information effectively.)

We know perimeter of a square $= 4(\text{side})$ $\boxed{5}$

We know area of a square $= (\text{side})^2$ $\boxed{6}$

Substituting $\boxed{1}$ into $\boxed{6}$, we get

$$R^2 = (\text{side})^2$$
$$R = \text{side} \quad \boxed{7}$$

Substituting $\boxed{7}$ and $\boxed{3}$ into $\boxed{5}$, we have

$$r = 4(R)$$
$$r = 4R \quad \boxed{8}$$

We know perimeter of an equilateral triangle $= 3(\text{side})$ $\boxed{9}$

Substituting $\boxed{2}$ and $\boxed{4}$ into $\boxed{9}$, we get

$$E = 3(e)$$
$$E = 3e \quad \boxed{10}$$
$$\frac{E}{3} = e$$

We need $e + r$. $\boxed{11}$

(Use Strategy 13: Find unknowns by addition.) Add $\boxed{8}$ and $\boxed{10}$ to get $\boxed{11}$. We have

$$e + r = \frac{E}{3} + 4R$$

$$= \frac{E}{3} + 4R\left(\frac{3}{3}\right)$$

$$= \frac{E}{3} + \frac{12R}{3}$$

$$e + r = \frac{E + 12R}{3}$$

20. Choice D is correct.

> *Given:* $C = \frac{5}{9}(F - 32)$

Call the number of degrees that the Fahrenheit temperature (F°) increases, x.

(Now use Strategy 17: Use the given information effectively.)

The Celsius temperature (C°) is given as

$$C = \frac{5}{9}(F - 32)$$

This can be rewritten as:

$$C = \frac{5}{9}F - \frac{5}{9}(32) \qquad \boxed{1}$$

When the Celsius temperature increases by 35°, the Fahrenheit temperature increases by $x°$, so we get:

$$C + 35 = \frac{5}{9}[(F + x) - 32]$$
$$C + 35 = \frac{5}{9}F + \frac{5}{9}x - \frac{5}{9}(32) \qquad \boxed{2}$$

(Now use Strategy 13: Find unknowns by subtraction.)

Subtract $\boxed{1}$ from $\boxed{2}$:

$$C + 35 = \frac{5}{9}F + \frac{5}{9}x - \frac{5}{9}(32) \qquad \boxed{2}$$

$$- \qquad C = \frac{5}{9}F - \frac{5}{9}(32) \qquad \boxed{1}$$

$$\overline{\qquad\qquad 35 = \frac{5}{9}x \qquad\qquad} \qquad \boxed{3}$$

Multiply $\boxed{3}$ by 9:

$$35 \times 9 = 5x \qquad \boxed{4}$$

(Use Strategy 19: Don't multiply when reducing can be done first.)

Divide $\boxed{4}$ by 5:

$$\frac{35 \times 9}{5} = x \qquad \boxed{5}$$

Now reduce $\frac{35}{5}$ to get 7 and we get for $\boxed{5}$

$$7 \times 9 = x$$
$$63 = x$$

EXPLANATORY ANSWERS FOR PRACTICE TEST 1

Section 4: Critical reading

As you read these Explanatory Answers, you are advised to refer to "16 Verbal (Critical Reading) Strategies."

1. Choice D is correct. **See Sentence Completion Strategy 4.** The first word, "Because," is a *result indicator*. We can then expect some action to take place after the information about what the evening cable TV programs deal with. The expected action is that parents will consider such programs "inappropriate." Accordingly, only Choice D is correct.

2. Choice A is correct. See **Sentence Completion Strategy 2.** Examine the first word of each choice. Choice (C), glamorized…, and Choice (D) viewed…, do *not* make good sense because a word does not effectively glamorize or effectively view unfairness. Now consider the other choices. Choice (A), portrayed…strengthening, is the only choice which has a word pair that makes sense in the sentence.

3. Choice E is correct. See **Sentence Completion Strategy 1.** The word "prolific" (meaning "producing abundant works or results") completes the sentence so that it makes good sense. The other choices do *not* do that.

4. Choice D is correct. Although this is a two-blank question, we should use **Sentence Completion Strategy 1** (primarily used for one-blank questions). Note that we have a set of three opposites: from the "serious" to the "lighthearted," from the "objective" to the "argumentative," and from the "innocuous" (meaning *harmless, innocent*) to the "hostile." The other choices do *not* have this opposite pattern.

5. Choice B is correct. See **Sentence Completion Strategy 2.** Examine the first word of each choice. Choice (A), shattering…, and Choice (C), impertinent…, do *not* make sense because rates

at a repair place are not aptly called shattering or impertinent. Now consider the other choices. Choices D and E do *not* make sense in the sentence. Choice (B), exorbitant…instituted, *does* make sense.

6. Choice E is correct. See **Sentence Completion Strategy 2.** Examine the first word of each choice. Choice (B), denied…, and Choice (D), slighted…, do *not* make sense because students who found truth in Socrates' teachings would not deny or slight him. Now consider the other choices. Choice (A), accepted…, a benefit and Choice (C), appraised…an exception, do not make sense in the sentence. Choice (E), revered…a threat, *does* make sense in the sentence.

7. Choice B is correct. See **Sentence Completion Strategy 1.** Try each of the choices. The only one that fits is Choice B: The quotation was erroneously *ascribed,* or *credited to,* a British poet.

8. Choice D is correct. See **Sentence Completion Strategy 2.** Examine the first word of each choice. We eliminate Choice (C), squandered, and Choice (E), regaled, because hardworking parents do *not* squander (spend money recklessly) or regale (entertain) to give their son an education. Now consider the other choices. The word pairs of Choice A and Choice B do *not* make sense in the sentence. Choice (D), struggled…generously, *does* make good sense.

9. Choice E is correct. The author describes Plutarch telling of Alexander's achievements as well as the lasting blemish to those achievements, so we wouldn't suspect that the author considers Plutarch unfair to Alexander. Remember, the question requires you to find

the *least* justified reason. Eliminate Choice A because the passage is filled with Plutarch's admiration for Alexander the Great in such phrases as "hero of heroes" and "admired him above all other men." Choice B is incorrect because the Persian army did surrender, believing Alexander's promise of safe conduct. The passage states that the Persian army was "marching away," indicating withdrawal in an orderly fashion, so eliminate Choice C. Choice D is incorrect because the author provides various quotes from Plutarch's writing.

10. Choice D is correct. Even though Alexander is Plutarch's "hero of heroes," he makes "no attempt to extenuate," or excuse, Alexander's betrayal of the Persian army. Given Plutarch's admiration of Alexander, Choices A, B, C, and E are not the best fit with the surrounding context. See also **Reading Comprehension Strategy 5**.

11. Choice E is correct. See lines 4–8: "Richness of poetic imagery…" and lines 10–13: "Even his elaborate and multistranded plots…"

12. Choice E is correct. Look in the last three lines of the passage: "…plots are now seen as great symphonic compositions driving forward…" "A great symphony" can be nothing less than dramatic in power. There is mention of comic relief, surprise, or visually effective symbols, so eliminate Choices A, C, and D. The final line refers to "the resolving chords on which they close," which indicates completion. This eliminates Choice D.

13. Choice B is correct. See the first paragraph: "Many people who are willing to concede that the railroad must be brought back to life are chiefly thinking of bringing this about…by treating speed as the only important factor…"

14. Choice E is correct. See the fourth paragraph: "The prime purpose of passenger transportation is not to increase the amount of physical movement but to increase the possibilities for human association, cooperation, personal intercourse, and choice." Also see the fifth paragraph, sentences 1 and 4. Note that although I is not a prime purpose, it is still a purpose.

15. Choice E is correct. See paragraph 6: "The current introduction of shopping malls…is…a… far better *technical* solution than the many costly proposals for introducing moving sidewalks or other rigidly automated modes of locomotion."

16. Choice A is correct. See the next-to-last paragraph: "With the over-exploitation of the particular car comes an increased demand…to endow the petroleum magnates…with fabulous capacities for personal luxury…"

17. Choice C is correct. See the next-to-last paragraph: "With the over-exploitation of the particular car comes an increased demand…to roll ever-wider carpets of concrete over the bulldozed landscape…"

18. Choice B is correct. See the last paragraph: "If indeed we go farther and faster along this route, there is plenty of evidence to show that the shop will close up without our help."

19. Choice B is correct. From the context of the paragraph, we are talking about distances. Don't get lured into Choice C because you read about "human needs" in the paragraph or Choice D just because you see "traffic" mentioned. See also **Reading Comprehension Strategy 5**.

20. Choice D is correct. From lines 28–32 and other sections of the passage, we can see that the author believes that "technocratic" thinking neither addresses nor is concerned with real human needs.

21. Choice A is correct. See paragraph 6: "If we took human needs seriously…we should…make the fullest use of pedestrian movement…"

22. Choice C is correct. See paragraph 5: "Variety of choices, facilities and destinations, not speed alone, is the mark of an organic transportation system."

23. Choice B is correct. Judging from the time-perspective of the author, and the more general nature of the article, Choice B would be the best answer.

24. Choice C is correct. See paragraph 5: "And… [variety] is an important factor of safety when any part of the system breaks down."

EXPLANATORY ANSWERS FOR PRACTICE TEST 1

Section 5: Writing

1. **(A)** Choice A is correct. Choice B is awkward. The parenthetical effect of Choice C gives the sentence an ungrammatical structure. The ellipsis of "to the" before the beginning of Choice D, is improper. The possessive use ("oak's") in Choice E results in a bad-sounding sentence.

2. **(A)** Choice A is correct. The present tense in Choice B is incorrect. Choices C, D, and E change the meaning of the original sentence.

3. **(D)** Choices A, B, and E are too wordy. Choice C changes the meaning of the original sentence. Choice D is correct.

4. **(D)** Choice A does not come to the point immediately with the use of the expression "concerning the one." Choice B is too wordy. Choice C is not clear. Choice D is correct. Choice E requires an introductory prepositional compound such as "as to."

5. **(C)** Choices A, B, D, and E are incorrect because of a dangling participle error. In these four choices, the participle "Having" must refer to the subject of the sentence. This subject must follow directly after the participial construction ("Having…in his class"). Accordingly, Choice C is the only correct choice.

6. **(C)** Choice A is incorrect because "its" as a possessive pronoun does not take an apostrophe. Choice B is incorrect because the possessive of "government" ("government's") must be used to modify the gerund "failing." Choice C is correct. Choice D is incorrect for the same reason that Choice B is incorrect. Choice E is incorrect for two reasons: (1) it changes the meaning of the original sentence; (2) even if we change the meaning from singularity to plurality, "governments" must correctly be the possessive form "governments'" to modify the gerund "failing."

7. **(B)** The key to getting the correct answer in this question is knowing this grammatical rule: *When explanatory words intervene between the subject and the verb, the number or person of the real subject is not changed.* Note that the subject "father" of the original sentence is singular. Accordingly, Choices A, C, D, and E (each of which has a singular subject, "father") are incorrect with a plural verb. Moreover, Choice D changes the present time of the original sentence to past time. Choice B is correct.

8. **(E)** The demonstrative adjective ("this," "that," "these," "those") must agree in number with the noun ("kind") it modifies. Accordingly, Choices A, B, and D are incorrect. Choice C is incorrect because the personal pronoun "them" may not be used as an adjective. Choice E is correct.

9. **(D)** Choices A, B, C, and E are incorrect because they suffer from incomplete verb comparison. This is a form of improper ellipsis. The corrections would be as follows: Choice A—"has not recovered"; Choice B—"never will recover"; Choice C—(two corrections necessary) "has not recovered" and "never will recover" (the subjunctive "would" should not be used here); Choice E—"has not recovered." Note that in Choice E, the past perfect tense should not be used. Choice D is correct.

10. **(D)** It is important to know that "neither-nor" go together as correlative conjunctions. The pairing of "neither" with "or" is incorrect. Therefore, Choices A, C, and E are incorrect. Choice B is awkward. Choice D is correct.

11. **(A)** Choice A is correct. Note that "Glory" is the singular subject that takes the singular verb "is." "Reward" is the predicate nominative after the copulative verb "is." The other four choices are incorrect because they are indirect and awkward.

12. (B) "...disappeared *as if*..." The correct expression is "as if"—not "like as if." Incidentally, Choice C (*were*) is correct because it is the correct form of the contrary-to-fact conditional.

13. (D) "...because *the car* needed gasoline." The pronoun *it* has an indefinite antecedent. We cannot tell whether *it* refers to the car or the service station. Accordingly, we must be specific by using *car* instead of *it*.

14. (A) "The man *whose* temper is under control..." The contraction (*who's* meaning *who is*) is obviously incorrect here. We need the possessive adjective *whose* to modify the noun (*temper*).

15. (E) All underlined parts are correct.

16. (C) "...before his mother *came* home..." The past perfect tense (*had come*) is used for a past action that occurs before another past action. The mother's coming home did not occur before Ethan wanted to finish his homework. Therefore, the past tense (*came*) should be used—not the past perfect tense (*had come*).

17. (B) "Inflation together with the high interest rates and soaring oil prices *is hurting*..." The subject of the sentence is *Inflation*. This is a singular subject so the verb must be singular—*is hurting* (not *are hurting*). The words *rates* and *prices* are not parts of the subject.

18. (D) "...will repair the car *well*." The erroneous use of "good" (adjective) in place of "well" (adverb) is commonly made. Remember that an adverb describes a verb. The word "well" does not end in the usual "ly" of many adverbs such as "greeted warm<u>ly</u>," "moved deep<u>ly</u>," "dressed beautiful<u>ly</u>." The word "good" is an adjective. Therefore, it cannot be used to modify a verb.

19. (C) "...if he *had read* more..." The "if" clause of a contrary-to-fact past tense requires the verb *had read*—not *would have read*.

20. (D) "...to have his stories compared with *those of* Dickens." We have an improper ellipsis in the original sentence. The additional words (*those of*) are necessary to complete the meaning of the sentence.

21. (B) "...with a new *type* of motor..." Do not use the article *a* or *an* after *kind of, type of, sort of,* etc.

22. (A) "Savannah planned to pay *about*..." *About* means *approximately; around* means *on all sides*.

23. (A) "Had Lincoln *been* alive..." In a past contrary-to-fact situation, the "if" clause verb should take the form *had been*—not *had have been*.

24. (E) All underlined parts are correct.

25. (E) All underlined parts are correct.

26. (A) "*It's* my opinion..." We need the contraction here (*It's* meaning *It is*).

27. (A) "If I *had known* more..." The "if" clause of the past contrary-to-fact conditional statement requires the *had known* form—not the *would have known* form.

28. (D) "If you compare Seb and Daniel...Seb is, without any question, the *brighter*." In comparing two individuals, we use the comparative form (*brighter*)—not the superlative form (*brightest*).

29. (B) "In spite of how *poorly* Zoe had done..." The adverb (*poorly*)—not the adjective (*poor*)—must be used to modify the verb (*had done*).

30. (B) Choice A is incorrect: The removal of the conjunction and replacement with a comma would leave two independent clauses incorrectly joined with only a comma. Choice B is correct: Replacing "moreover" and surrounding punctuation with "when" would correctly make the second clause subordinate to the first and also establish a time sequence for the two pieces of information. Choice C is incorrect because omitting "the Persian leader" would result in an information gap about who Cambyses was. Choice D is incorrect in that "bullheadedness" indicates irrational stubbornness and is, therefore, not an accurate description of the motives of people defending their own city in battle; "fierce resistance" is more appropriate. Choice E is incorrect because "moreover" (meaning "beyond what has been stated, further, or besides") does not furnish an adequate transition between the idea of the first sentence and the idea of the second sentence which need to be related to each other in a time sequence. The comma—instead of the semicolon—would be incorrect punctuation preceding the conjunctive adverb.

31. **(D)** Choice A is incorrect because the introduction of "It was made worse" would create a run-on sentence. Choice B is incorrect in that omitting the phrase would remove a needed transition to carry the action from sentence 4 to sentence 5 by indicating that a second tactic was used. The phrase also furnishes some dramatic reinforcement of the idea that the Egyptians were "appalled." Choice C is incorrect because "plus" can be used as an adjective or a preposition but not, as in this sentence, as a conjunction. Neither the meaning "in addition to" nor "added" fits the structure of the sentence. Choice D is correct because the phrase is useful as a transition and for emphasis. (See explanation for Choice B.) Choice E is incorrect in that placing the phrase at the end of the sentence deprives the phrase of its use as a transition between sentences 5 and 6.

32. **(D)** Choice A is incorrect: "unharmed without hurting them" is redundant; adding "in the least little way" would only compound the repetition. Choice B is incorrect since the redundancy would remain. Choice C is incorrect: The sentence would lose clarity without the information that the soldiers were to keep the cats safely. Choice D is correct because omitting "without hurting them" would cure the redundancy. Choice E is incorrect because the base words "hurt" and "harm" would be merely reversed without eliminating the repetition weakness.

33. **(A)** Choice A is correct: The proper place for sentence 6 is after sentence three. In that position, sentence 6 would show the chronological order of events correctly and the tense of "ordered"

would be accurate. Choice B is incorrect since the omission of the sentence would leave a puzzling information gap about where the cats came from. Choice C is incorrect: Placed at the end of the paragraph, even with an appropriate change in the verb to "had ordered," the sentence would furnish anticlimactic information, well after the time the data was needed. Choice D is incorrect because beginning a new sentence after "countryside" would leave the remaining words as a sentence fragment. Choice E is incorrect not only because it would leave sentence 6 in a position in which chronology is not clearly indicated, but also because inserting "which was because" creates unnecessary wordiness and a pronoun with an ambiguous reference while leaving "ordered" in the wrong tense.

34. **(B)** Choice A is incorrect: "capitulated" is an accurate synonym for "surrendered," while "crumbled" would suggest the physical decay of the city walls or buildings. Choice B is correct: Since previous battle has been suggested in sentence 3 ("the Persian army…blocked by the fierce resistance"), sentence 8 would be more accurate if it ended with "further battle." Choice C is incorrect because, as noted, the Egyptians had previously fought the Persians. Choice D is incorrect: Even though "having resisted" is a complete idea and far preferable to the incomplete idea of "a drop of blood," the substitution is still inaccurate because the Egyptians had previously resisted. Choice E is incorrect because it conveys a totally inaccurate idea of the reason for the surrender of Pelusium.

35. **(C)** Since sentence 8 describes animal worship generally (not specifically), this would lead directly to sentence 1, which is more specific, especially because of the words "In fact" at the beginning of sentence 1.

EXPLANATORY ANSWERS FOR PRACTICE TEST 1
Section 6: Math

> When a specific Math Strategy is referred to in the solution, study that strategy, which you will find in "19 Math Strategies."

1. Choice D is correct.

Method 1: (**Use Strategy 8: When all choices must be tested, start with Choice E.**)

Since $\sqrt{x}$ is odd, then x is odd. $\boxed{1}$
Let us start with solution E.

Choice E: If x is odd (from $\boxed{1}$ above), then x^2 is odd. Choice D: If $\sqrt{x}$ is odd, $2\sqrt{x}$ is *even*, and the solution is found.

(**Use Strategy 7: Use numerics to help you get the answer.**)

Method 2: Choose an odd number for $\sqrt{x}$—for example,

$$\sqrt{x} = 3$$
$$\text{Then } x = 9$$

Choice E: $x^2 = 81$ (odd)

Choice D: $2\sqrt{x} = 2\sqrt{9} = 2(3) = 6$ (even)

The answer is clearly Choice D.

2. Choice E is correct. (**Use Strategy 8: When all choices must be tested, start with Choice E.**) Since we must check all the choices, we should start with Choice E. Clearly, if x is the point whose coordinates are (5,2), then $m\angle MXN = 90°$ and Choice E must be correct.

3. Choice D is correct. You want to find a value of x such that $f(x) = x + 2$, so you look for a value of x in the x-column that makes $f(x)$ in the $f(x)$ column, $x + 2$. You can see that $x = 3$ corresponds to $f(x) = 5$, which is just $x + 2$ (or $3 + 2$).

4. Choice D is correct. (**Use Strategy 15: Certain choices may be easily eliminated.**) Since (according to the graph), $y = 0$ when $x = 0$, Choices A, B, and E are incorrect. Choice C is incorrect since the graph is not a parabola. The only feasible choice is Choice D.

5. Choice E is correct. (**Use Strategy 2: Translate from words to algebra.**) The sum of the degree measures of the 4 angles of any quadrilateral is always 360. Therefore,

$$w + x + y + z = 360° \qquad \boxed{1}$$

(**Use Strategy 5:**

$$\text{Average} = \frac{\text{sum of values}}{\text{total number of values}})$$

If w is the average (arithmetic mean) of x, y, and z, then

$$w = \frac{x + y + z}{3}$$

Multiplying both sides of the above equation by 3, we have

$$3w = x + y + z \qquad \boxed{2}$$

Substituting equation $\boxed{2}$ into equation $\boxed{1}$, we get

$$w + 3w = 360°$$
$$4w = 360°$$
$$w = 90°$$

From equation $\boxed{2}$, we conclude that
$x + y + z = 3w = 3(90) = 270°$

6. Choice B is correct. (**Use Strategy 17: Use the given information effectively.**) The circle graph tells you that 19% of this mixture is carbon. Since the total mixture weighs 24 pounds, 19% of that will be the amount of carbon in the mixture (in pounds). We would multiply 24 lbs × .19. But since the choices are not that close and since we are looking for the *closest* number of pounds, make the problem simpler by multiplying 24 × .20 = 4.8, which is close to 4.6.

7. Choice B is correct. **(Use Strategy 10: Use units of Time, Distance, etc.)** Since the track circumference is 120 feet:

$$\frac{\text{\# of feet}}{120} = \text{\# of revolutions}$$

(Use Strategy 9: Use the Rate × Time = Distance formula.)

Rate × Time = Distance

$$\frac{1}{120}\text{Rate} \times \text{Time} = \frac{1}{120}\text{Distance} = \text{Revolutions}$$

For Bicycle B:

$$\left(\frac{1}{120}\right)8 \times t = 600$$

For Bicycle A:

$$\left(\frac{1}{120}\right)5 \times t = a$$

The key is to realize that the time, t, is identical for both bicycles.

(Use Strategy 13: Find unknowns by dividing equations.)

$$\frac{\left(\frac{1}{120}\right)8 \times t}{\left(\frac{1}{120}\right)5 \times t} = \frac{600}{a}$$

$$\frac{8}{5} = \frac{600}{a}$$

$$8a = 3000$$

$$a = 375$$

8. Choice D is correct. The key to this problem is to find the area of the shaded region in terms of known quantities. **(Use Strategy 3: The whole equals the sum of its parts.)**

Area of shaded region and also the area of the rectangle

= Area of triangle − Area of square

= $x^2\sqrt{3} - x^2$

= $x^2(\sqrt{3} - 1)$

We are given that an unknown rectangle

has width = x $\boxed{1}$

and area = $x^2(\sqrt{3} - 1)$ $\boxed{2}$

Since length × width = area,

length = area ÷ width $\boxed{3}$

Substituting $\boxed{1}$ and $\boxed{2}$ into $\boxed{3}$, we have

length of rectangle = $\dfrac{x^2(\sqrt{3} - 1)}{x}$

length of rectangle = $x(\sqrt{3} - 1)$

9. $\dfrac{7}{24}, \dfrac{2}{7}, \dfrac{3}{10}, \dfrac{3}{11}$, or any number between **0.25** and **.3333**. **(Use Strategy 17: Use the given information effectively.)**

Without a calculator:

Get a common denominator 12. Then write $\frac{1}{4} = \frac{3}{12}$ and $\frac{1}{3} = \frac{4}{12}$ to get a quantity *in between* $\frac{3}{12}$ and $\frac{4}{12}$.

Write $\frac{3}{12} = \frac{6}{24}$ and $\frac{4}{12} = \frac{8}{24}$

Thus $\frac{6}{24} < x < \frac{8}{24}$ and x can be $\frac{7}{24}$.

Or write $\frac{1}{4} = \frac{2}{8}$ and $\frac{1}{3} = \frac{2}{6}$; $\frac{2}{8} < \frac{2}{7} < \frac{2}{6}$, so $\frac{2}{7}$ is an answer. $\frac{3}{10}$ and $\frac{3}{11}$ are also acceptable.

With a calculator:

Calculate $\frac{1}{4} = 0.25$; Calculate $\frac{1}{3} = 0.3333...$

"Grid" any number between 0.25 and 0.3333, like 0.26, 0.27... .332, .333.

10. 12

Given: $3x + y = 17$ $\boxed{1}$
$x + 3y = -1$ $\boxed{2}$

(Use Strategy 13: Find unknowns by adding.)

Adding $\boxed{1}$ and $\boxed{2}$, we get

$$4x + 4y = 16$$ $\boxed{3}$

(Use Strategy 13: Find unknowns by division.) Dividing $\boxed{3}$ by 4, we have

$$x + y = 4$$ $\boxed{4}$

(Use Strategy 13: Find unknowns by multiplying.) Multiply $\boxed{4}$ by 3. We get

$$3x + 3y = 12$$

11. 60

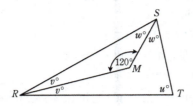

$$Given: \angle M = 120° \quad \boxed{1}$$
$$\angle RST = 80° \quad \boxed{2}$$

(Use Strategy 3: The whole equals the sum of its parts.) From the diagram we see that

$$\angle RST = w + w \quad \boxed{3}$$

Substitute $\boxed{2}$ into $\boxed{3}$. We get

$$80° = w + w$$
$$80° = 2w$$
$$40° = w \quad \boxed{4}$$

We know that in triangle RMS

$$v + w + 120° = 180° \quad \boxed{5}$$

Substituting $\boxed{4}$ into $\boxed{5}$, we get

$$v + 40° + 120° = 180°$$
$$v + 160° = 180°$$
$$v = 20° \quad \boxed{6}$$

From the diagram we see that

$$\angle SRT = v + v \quad \boxed{7}$$

Substitute $\boxed{6}$ into $\boxed{7}$. We get

$$\angle SRT = 20° + 20°$$
$$\angle SRT = 40° \quad \boxed{8}$$

We know that in triangle RST

$$\angle RST + \angle SRT + u = 180° \quad \boxed{9}$$

Substitute $\boxed{2}$ and $\boxed{8}$ into $\boxed{9}$. We get

$$80° + 40° + u = 180°$$
$$120° + u = 180°$$
$$u = 60°$$

12. 6 **(Use Strategy 17: Use the given information effectively.)** If the tram carries its maximum of 4 people then

$$\frac{22 \text{ people}}{4 \text{ people}}{\text{trip}} = 5\frac{1}{2} \text{ trips}$$

(Use Strategy 16: The obvious may be tricky!) There is no such thing as $\frac{1}{2}$ a trip. The $\frac{1}{2}$ arises because the last trip, the *6th* trip only, takes 2 people. So there are 6 trips.

13. 24 *Method 1:* **(Use Strategy 4: Remember classic expressions.)**

$$(a + b)^2 = a^2 + 2ab + b^2 \quad \boxed{1}$$
$$(a - b)^2 = a^2 - 2ab + b^2 \quad \boxed{2}$$

(Use Strategy 11: Use new definitions carefully. These problems are generally easy.)

Using $\boxed{1}$ and $\boxed{2}$, we have

$$a \odot b = (a + b)^2 - (a - b)^2$$
$$= a^2 + 2ab + b^2 - (a^2 - 2ab + b^2)$$
$$= 4ab \quad \boxed{3}$$

When we use $\boxed{3}$ with $a = \sqrt{18}$ and $b = \sqrt{2}$, we get

$$\sqrt{18} \odot \sqrt{2} = 4(\sqrt{18})(\sqrt{2})$$
$$= 4(\sqrt{36})$$
$$= 4(6)$$
$$= 24$$

Method 2: $a \odot b = (a + b)^2 - (a - b)^2$

$$2\sqrt{18} \odot \sqrt{2}$$
$$= (\sqrt{18} + \sqrt{2})^2 - (\sqrt{18} - \sqrt{2})^2$$
$$= 18 + 2\sqrt{36} + 2 - (18 - 2\sqrt{36} + 2)$$
$$= 18 + 12 + 2 - 18 + 12 - 2$$
$$= 24$$

The calculations in Method 2 are much more complex!

14. 25 If you have patience, it is not too hard to list all ordered pairs of integers (x,y) such that

$$x^2 + y^2 < 9$$

(Use Strategy 17: Use the given information effectively.)

However, to save time, try listing the possible values of each variable.

$x = -2, -1, 0, 1, 2$

$y = -2, -1, 0, 1, 2$

Since each variable has 5 possible values, the total number of ordered pairs for which $x^2 + y^2 < 9$ is:

(# of values for x) (# of values for y) = $5 \times 5 = 25$

Another way to do this problem is to note that $x^2 + y^2 = 9$ is the equation of a circle of radius 3 whose center is at (0, 0).

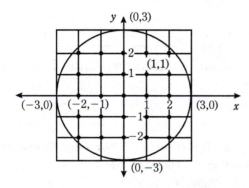

Thus, $x^2 + y^2 < 9$ is the region inside the circle. We want to find the number of ordered pairs of integers (x,y) inside the circle. As we can count from the picture above, there are 25 such ordered pairs.

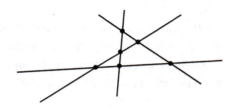

15. 6 (Use Strategy 17: Use the given information effectively.)

Method 1: You can just take out one line and you will have 6 points (see above).

Method 2: There is a formula for finding the maximum number of points of intersection of n straight line segments.

$$\text{It is } \frac{n(n-1)}{2} \qquad \boxed{1}$$

Substituting 4 into $\boxed{1}$, we get

$$\frac{4(4-1)}{2} = \frac{4(3)}{2} =$$
$$\frac{12}{2} = 6$$

16. 35 (Use Strategy 2: Translate from words to algebra.) Natalie originally had enough money to buy 21 bars at 50¢ per bar. Thus, she had 21×50 = 1,050 cents = $10.50. Therefore,

Number of 30¢ bars she bought

$$= \frac{\text{total amount she had}}{\text{price of each bar}}$$

$$= \frac{\$10.50}{\$.30}$$

$$= 35 \text{ bars}$$

17. 333

(Use Strategy 16: The obvious may be tricky!) From the problem, we see that

$$d = 96,999; \; not \; 97,777$$

Thus, $d - 96,666 = 333$

18. $\frac{1}{8}$ or .125

(Use Strategy 2: Remember the definition of percent.) 25 percent of 2 is

$$\frac{25}{100} \times 2$$

Thus, 25 percent of 25 percent of 2 is

$$\frac{25}{100} \times \frac{25}{100} \times 2 = \frac{1}{4} \times \frac{1}{4} \times 2$$
$$= \frac{2}{16}$$
$$= \frac{1}{8}$$

EXPLANATORY ANSWERS FOR PRACTICE TEST 1
Section 7: Critical reading

As you read these Explanatory Answers, you are advised to refer to "16 Verbal (Critical Reading) Strategies."

1. Choice E is correct. See **Sentence Completion Strategy 1.** Try each choice. Bear in mind that in the face of a threatening mob, you would probably try to keep (maintain) your calm, poise, or composure. Choices A, B, C, and D do not do that.

2. Choice A is correct. See **Sentence Completion Strategy 2.** Examine the first word of each choice. Choice B, a specter…, and Choice C, an exodus…, do *not* make sense because a nice apartment building is not a specter (ghost) or an exodus (a departure). Now consider the other choices. Choice A, a boon…haunted, is the only choice that makes sense in the sentence. The word "haunted" here means "visited frequently."

3. Choice A is correct. See **Sentence Completion Strategy 2.** Examine the first word of each choice. Choice B, cancellation…, and Choice D, abundance…, do *not* make sense because we do not refer to an inflation cancellation or an inflation abundance. Now consider the other choices. Choice A, spiral…indubitably (meaning "unquestionably, certainly"), is the only choice which has a word pair that makes sense in the sentence.

4. Choice B is correct. See **Sentence Completion Strategy 4.** The first word, "although," is an *opposition indicator.* After the subordinate clause "although…markedly," we can expect an opposing idea in the main clause that follows and completes the sentence. Choice B, unaffected, gives us the word that brings out the opposition thought that we expect in the sentence. Choices A, C, D, and E do not give us a sentence that makes sense.

5. Choice D is correct. See **Sentence Completion Strategy 1.** The word "elusive" means "cleverly or skillfully; able to avoid being caught." Therefore, Choice D, elusive, is the only correct choice. Don't assume that *guerrillas* are *gorillas.* A general (of an army) would not be involved with trapping gorillas!

6. Choice B is correct. In line 24, the statement "the universe does not play dice with nature" illustrates that Einstein believes that there is certainty and not mere probability in all aspects of physics.

7. Choice A is correct. See lines 4–6 and lines 17–19 about measurement devices. Choice B is incorrect because in lines 20–21, we may know the exact position of an electron but not its exact speed. Choice C is incorrect: See lines 28–30. Choice D is incorrect because in lines 4–6, it just explains that the apparatus does not interfere with measurement, not that we don't deal with measurement.

8. Choice A is correct. Since classical and modern physics seem to be somewhat contradictory, there could exist a "unified" physics that would incorporate both without retaining the paradoxes inherent in classical and modern physics. The other choices do not resolve the issue.

9. Choice D is correct. For (I), it is seen that cause and effect exist in classical physics but not in modern physics; for (II), probability exists in modern physics whereas certainty exists in classical physics; for (III), the structure of a bridge is apparent in both modern and classical

physics since the subatomic make-up of the bridge and the macroscopic structure of the supports, etc., also exists. Thus only (I) and (II) are true and Choice D is correct.

10. Choice A is correct. The passage deals mainly with van Gogh's 15-month stay in Arles. It was in this small French town that his art, in fact, did reach its zenith. See lines 5–9: "Yet Arles…in the modern era." Although Choices B, C, D, and E have some association with the passage, none of these choices represents the best title for the passage as a whole. Therefore, these choices are incorrect.

11. Choice D is correct. Answer Choice D is neither stated nor implied in the passage; therefore, it is the correct choice. First see lines 42–45: "Before the year was up…had to return to Paris." Note that Gauguin had stayed in Arles *less* than a year. Now see lines 5–9: "Yet Arles was also the scene…in the modern era." Choice A is true—therefore an incorrect choice. See lines 12–16: "The Arles canvases, alive with color… notably the Fauves." Choice B is true—therefore an incorrect choice. First see lines 17–20: "Van Gogh went to Arles…beloved younger brother Theo…an art dealer." Now see lines 39–41: "… Gauguin had an influence on van Gogh…pushing the younger artist…than actuality." Choice C is true—therefore an incorrect choice. See lines 20–23: "In Paris…Neo-Impressionist…style." Choice E is true—therefore incorrect. See lines 1–5: "It was at Arles…cut off part of his own ear."

12. Choice E is correct. Let us consider each of the three Roman numeral items. Item I is true. See lines 25–27: "But he wanted 'gayer' colors… Japanese prints he so admired."

    Item II is true. First see lines 28–30: "He felt that in Arles…establish an artistic tradition." Now see lines 31–34: "It was van Gogh's hope…join him at Arles."

    Item III is true. See lines 27–30: "Then, too, the French capital…an artistic tradition."

    Accordingly, Choice E is the only correct choice.

13. Choice E is correct. In the context in the sentence "…under the glowing sun…," it would appear that the word "frenetic" should mean "frantic." Choice A is incorrect because the author would not be likely to repeat the word "colorful" in the next sentence.

14. Choice C is correct. Gauguin's attitude of tolerant acceptance of van Gogh is indicated in the following lines of the passage. Lines 37–41: "At first…rather than actuality." Lines 45–49: "Gauguin wrote to Theo…especially with me." Lines 50–52: "But then…they later had friendly correspondence." Choices A, B, D, and E are incorrect because the passage does not give evidence of the attitudes mentioned in these choices.

15. Choice D is correct. The passage indicates that there was a buildup of stresses and strains on van Gogh that he was eventually unable to cope with because of his mental and emotional instability. This condition led him to such acts as cutting off a piece of his ear. Finally—though the passage does not include this fact—van Gogh committed suicide in Paris on July 29, 1890, by shooting himself in the chest. The following lines in the passage are related to van Gogh's mental and emotional instability. Lines 1–3: "It was at Arles…had his first real bout with madness." Lines 17–20: "Van Gogh went to Arles…supported him psychologically and financially…art dealer." Lines 45–46: "Gauguin wrote to Theo…'temperamental incompatibility.'"

    Choices B and E are incorrect because these were not the basic reasons for van Gogh's extreme action. The basic reason was van Gogh's mental and emotional instability (Choice D). Choice C is incorrect because the passage mentions nothing about van Gogh's failure to form an artists' colony in Arles.

16. Choice C is correct. The theme of this essay, "Self-Reliance," by the American writer Ralph Waldo Emerson (1803–1882), is expressed in various other ways throughout the essay. For example: in referring to the independence of opinion that one loses with one's loss of early youth; in condemning our surrender of the

freedom of solitude to the group actions of
society at large; and in encouraging us not to
fear the consequences of being inconsistent and
misunderstood.

17. Choice A is correct. The infant can be, and is
expected to be, completely irresponsible. "Infancy
conforms to nobody: all conform to it, so that
one babe commonly makes four or five out of the
adults who prattle and play to it."

18. Choice D is correct. "Speak what you think
now in hard words, and to-morrow speak what
to-morrow thinks in hard words again, though
it contradict everything you said to-day." The
misunderstanding will occur because what you
say may be the opposite of conventional opinion,
or may be ahead of its time. But the risk is worth
it.

19. Choice B is correct. It is a natural prerogative of
youth to give "an independent, genuine verdict."
He naturally cares very little about what older
people may think because "It seems he knows
how to speak to his contemporaries. Bashful or
bold, then, he will know how to make us seniors
very unnecessary."

20. Choice B is correct. The "pit" or gallery in a
theater usually contains the least expensive
seats. Consequently, it is favored by those less
economically endowed, and, according to the
author, less committed to conventional manners
and highly dignified behavior. In effect, these are
the people who go to the theater to see, rather
than to be seen.

21. Choice C is correct. When people desert solitude
(or individual action) to join society (group
action), they surrender a large part of individual
freedom in exchange for a livelihood. They thus
become more reliant and dependent on others
than on themselves. The metaphor of the joint-
stock company is a good one because such a
company is faceless and without identity. No one
member stands out above any other member.

22. Choice E is correct. "Spirit and enthusiasm" are
something individualistic and definite. To be
spirited and enthusiastic is to be spontaneous,
natural, and uninhibited. One must (according
to the author) be committed and courageous
"As soon as he has once acted or spoken with
eclat...." See also **Reading Comprehension
Strategy 5.**

23. Choice C is correct. To act out of whim is to
act impulsively and in an unpremeditated,
spontaneous (and generally sincere) manner. The
author, however, is not endorsing *whimsical* action
simply because it is uninhibited ("I hope it is
somewhat better than whim at last, but we cannot
spend the day in explanation"), but because it is a
way of speaking freely, and usually with complete
honesty.

24. Choice A is correct. The essence of true
self-reliance and genuine nonconformity is,
as Shakespeare put it, "To thine own self be
true." If one is dishonest with oneself, one will
be dishonest with others; if one is honest with
oneself, one will be honest with others.

EXPLANATORY ANSWERS FOR PRACTICE TEST 1

Section 8: Math

> When a specific Math Strategy is referred to in the solution, study that strategy, which you will find in "19 Math Strategies."

1. Choice E is correct.

(Use Strategy 2: Translate from words to algebra.)

Let g = number of games the team played

28 = number of games Ben watched

$\frac{2}{3}g$ = number of games Ravi watched

We are given

$$\frac{2}{3}g > 28 \qquad \boxed{1}$$

Multiplying $\boxed{1}$ by $\frac{3}{2}$, we get

$$\left(\frac{3}{2}\right)\frac{2}{3}g > 28\left(\frac{3}{2}\right)$$
$$g > 42$$

Only Choice E satisfies this relationship.

2. Choice D is correct.

Given: 8 people divide a cash prize equally $\boxed{1}$

(Use Strategy 2: Translate from words to algebra.)

From $\boxed{1}$ we get:

Each person receives $\frac{1}{8}$ of the total prize $\boxed{2}$

2 people receive $\frac{2}{8} = \frac{1}{4}$ of the prize $\boxed{3}$

To change $\boxed{3}$ to a percent we multiply by 100.

$$100\left(\frac{1}{4}\right) = \frac{100}{4}$$
$$= 25\%$$

3. Choice C is correct.

(Use Strategy 10: Know how to use units.)

We are given his rate is $\frac{90 \text{ laps}}{6 \text{ hours}}$

$$\frac{90 \text{ laps}}{6 \text{ hours}} \times \frac{1 \text{ hour}}{60 \text{ minutes}} = \frac{90 \text{ laps}}{360 \text{ minutes}}$$

$\frac{1}{4}$ lap per minute (*Answer*)

4. Choice C is correct. $x^{-\frac{3}{4}} = \frac{1}{x^{\frac{3}{4}}} = \frac{1}{(\sqrt[4]{x})^3}$

$$x^{-\frac{3}{4}} = \frac{1}{(\sqrt[4]{16})^3}$$
$$= \frac{1}{(2)^3}$$
$$= \frac{1}{8}$$

5. Choice E is correct. **(Use Strategy 15: Know how to eliminate certain choices.)** The graph $y = 2x - 4$ is a straight line such that when $x = 0$, $y = -4$ and when $y = 0$, $2x - 4 = 0$ and thus $x = 2$. So we look for a line that cuts the y-axis (vertical axis where $x = 0$) at $y = -4$, and cuts the x-axis (horizontal axis where $y = 0$) at $x = 2$.

6. Choice D is correct. **(Use Strategy 17: Use the given information effectively.)**

$$[(3a^3b^2)^3]^2 =$$
$$(3a^3b^2)^6 = 3^6a^{18}b^{12}$$

Checking the choices, we find only Choice D has $a^{18}b^{12}$ and must be correct.

Note: We did not have to calculate 3^6!

7. Choice C is correct. **(Use Strategy 17: Use the given information effectively.)**

$$\left(\frac{3}{10}\right)^2 = \frac{9}{100} = \frac{p}{100}$$

Thus $p = 9$.

8. Choice B is correct.

Given: Paul's average on 3 tests = 85 $\boxed{1}$

Paul's average on first 2 tests = 85 $\boxed{2}$

(Use Strategy 5:

$$\textbf{Average} = \frac{\textbf{sum of values}}{\textbf{total number of values}}\Bigg)$$

We know Average = $\dfrac{\text{sum of values}}{\text{total number of values}}$ $\boxed{3}$

Let x be the first test score $\boxed{4}$
y be the second test score $\boxed{5}$
z be the third test score $\boxed{6}$

Substituting $\boxed{1}$, $\boxed{4}$, $\boxed{5}$, and $\boxed{6}$ into $\boxed{3}$, we have

$$85 = \frac{x + y + z}{3} \qquad \boxed{7}$$

(Use Strategy 13: Find unknowns by multiplication.)

Multiply $\boxed{7}$ by 3. We get

$$3(85) = \left(\frac{x + y + z}{3}\right)\cancel{3}$$
$$255 = x + y + z \qquad \boxed{8}$$

Substituting $\boxed{2}$, $\boxed{4}$, and $\boxed{5}$ into $\boxed{3}$, we have

$$85 = \frac{x + y}{2} \qquad \boxed{9}$$

Multiplying $\boxed{9}$ by 2, we get

$$2(85) = \left(\frac{x + y}{2}\right)\cancel{2}$$
$$170 = x + y \qquad \boxed{10}$$

Substituting $\boxed{10}$ into $\boxed{8}$, we get

$$225 = 170 + z$$
$$85 = z$$

9. Choice A is correct.

(Use Strategy 11: Use new definitions carefully.)

Given: $x \,\square\, y = 3 + xy$ $\boxed{1}$

$y \neq 0$ $\boxed{2}$

$x \,\square\, y = 3$ $\boxed{3}$

Substituting $\boxed{3}$ into $\boxed{1}$, we get

$$3 = 3 + xy$$
$$0 = xy \qquad \boxed{4}$$

Noting $\boxed{2}$, we divide $\boxed{4}$ by y

$$\frac{0}{y} = \frac{xy}{y}$$
$$0 = x$$

10. Choice A is correct.

(Use Strategy 3: The whole equals the sum of its parts.)

From the given diagram, it is clear that

$$z + 2w = 180 \qquad \boxed{1}$$

Since the sum of the measures of the angles of a triangle is 180, then

$$x + y + z = 180 \qquad \boxed{2}$$

(Use Strategy 13: Find unknowns by subtracting equations.)

Subtracting $\boxed{2}$ from $\boxed{1}$,

$$2w - (x + y) = 0$$
or $\qquad 2w = x + y \qquad \boxed{3}$

Using $\boxed{3}$, we calculate the unknown expression,

$$w + x + y = w + 2w$$
$$= 3w$$

11. Choice A is correct.

(Use Strategy 11: Use new definitions carefully.)

All choices must be evaluated using the definition.

Choice A, 934,432, would be assigned $6 + 3 + 4 = 13$ points, while the other choices all receive fewer than 13 points.

Number Pair	Number of Points
"33"	11
"34"	6
"43"	4
"44"	3

12. Choice D is correct.

Given: A certain number has 13 points.

(Use Strategy 11: Use new definitions carefully.)

From the chart, the only ways to accumulate 13 points are:

$$6 + 4 + 3 \qquad \boxed{1}$$
$$3 + 3 + 3 + 4 \qquad \boxed{2}$$

I.   33 is not in the number is always true.
II. 34 is in the number is *not* always true.
III. 43 is in the number is always true.

Thus, I and III are always true.

13. **Choice A is correct.**

    (Use Strategy 2: Translate from words to algebra.)

    "The ratio of Suri's age to Bob's age is 3 to 7" becomes

    $$\frac{\text{Suri's age } (S)}{\text{Bob's age } (B)} = \frac{3}{7}$$

    or $\qquad \dfrac{S}{B} = \dfrac{3}{7} \qquad \boxed{1}$

    "The ratio of Suri's age to Javier's age is 4 to 9" becomes

    $$\frac{S}{J} = \frac{4}{9} \qquad \boxed{2}$$

    Cross multiplying $\boxed{1}$, we have $7S = 3B$

    or $\qquad \dfrac{7S}{3} = B \qquad \boxed{3}$

    Cross multiplying $\boxed{2}$, we have $9S = 4J$

    or $\qquad \dfrac{9S}{4} = J \qquad \boxed{4}$

    We need the ratio of Bob's age to Javier's age. $\boxed{5}$

    Substituting $\boxed{3}$ and $\boxed{4}$ into $\boxed{5}$, we get

    $$\frac{\text{Bob's age}}{\text{Javier's age}} = \frac{\dfrac{7S}{3}}{\dfrac{9S}{4}}$$

    $$= \frac{7S}{3} \div \frac{9S}{4}$$

    $$= \frac{7S}{3} \times \frac{4}{9S}$$

    $$\frac{\text{Bob's age}}{\text{Javier's age}} = \frac{28}{27}$$

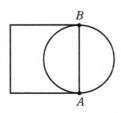

14. **Choice B is correct.**

    (Use Strategy 17: Use the given information effectively.)

    Given: Area of circle $= 9a^2\pi^2 \qquad \boxed{1}$
    Two sides of square are
    tangent to the circle $\qquad \boxed{2}$

    We know that the area of a circle $= \pi r^2$ where r is the radius. $\qquad \boxed{3}$

    Substituting $\boxed{1}$ into $\boxed{3}$, we have

    $$9a^2\pi^2 = \pi r^2 \qquad \boxed{4}$$

    Dividing by π, we get

    $$9a^2\pi = r^2 \qquad \boxed{5}$$

    Since $2r$ is the side of the square, the area of the square is

    $$(2r)^2 = 4r^2$$

    From $\boxed{5}$, multiplying both sides of the equation by 4, we get

    $$4(9a^2\pi) = 4r^2$$

    Thus $36a^2\pi = 4r^2 =$ area of square

15. **Choice E is correct.**

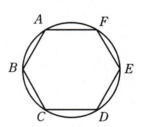

    Given: $\overparen{BAF} = 14\pi \qquad \boxed{1}$

    $ABCDEF$ is equilateral $\qquad \boxed{2}$

    From $\boxed{2}$ we know that all 6 sides are equal. $\boxed{3}$

    From $\boxed{3}$ we know that all 6 arcs are equal. $\boxed{4}$

    From $\boxed{1}$ and $\boxed{4}$ and noting that $\overparen{AB}$ equals $\frac{1}{2}\overparen{BAF}$, we find

    $$\overparen{AB} = \overparen{BC} = \overparen{CD} = \overparen{DE} = \overparen{EF} = \overparen{FA} = 7\pi \qquad \boxed{5}$$

    (Use Strategy 3: The whole equals the sum of its parts.)

Circumference of circle =

$6 \times 7\pi$ (since there are 6 arcs) $\boxed{6}$

We know circumference = $2\pi r$ $\boxed{7}$

Using $\boxed{6}$ and $\boxed{7}$, we get

$$2\pi r = 6 \times 7\pi$$
$$2\pi r = 42\pi$$
$$2r = 42 \qquad \boxed{8}$$

We know diameter = $2 \times$ radius $\boxed{9}$
So diameter = 42

16. Choice B is correct.

(Use Strategy 13: Know how to find unknown expressions.)

$f(x) = a^x$

so $f(x + y) = a^{x+y}$

$a^{x+y} = a^x a^y = f(x)f(y)$

EXPLANATORY ANSWERS FOR PRACTICE TEST 1
Section 9: Critical reading

> As you read these Explanatory Answers, you are advised to refer to "16 Verbal (Critical Reading) Strategies."

1. Choice E is correct. See **Sentence Completion Strategy 2.** Examine the first word of each choice. Choice B, relegates…(meaning to banish or to assign to a lower position), and Choice C, accumulates…, do *not* make sense since we do not say that a sense of fairness relegates or accumulates. Now consider the other choices. Choice E, dictates…vary, is the only choice that makes sense in the sentence. This is because if you say *a sense of fairness dictates that the punishment should fit the crime*, the opposite (because of the word *yet*) would indicate that there are different punishments for the same crime. That is, the *punishments* (or judgments) *vary* greatly.

2. Choice A is correct. See **Sentence Completion Strategy 1.** The chef's inconsistency in making sauce is obvious in the manner in which she adds spices—sometimes garlic and oregano and other times only basil. There are no clues in the sentence that would lead to Choice B, C, D, or E.

3. Choice B is correct. See **Sentence Completion Strategy 2.** Let us first examine the first word of each choice. We can then eliminate Choice C, remarks…, and Choice E, conferences…, because an outstanding contributor's being able to make occasional remarks or occasional conferences does not make good sense. Now we go on to the three remaining choices. When you fill in the two blanks of Choice A and of Choice D, the sentence does not make sense. So these two choices are also incorrect. Filling in the two blanks of Choice B makes the sentence meaningful.

4. Choice B is correct. See **Sentence Completion Strategies 1 and 4.** Try each choice being aware that "since" is a *result indicator*. Their married life was not *smooth and content*.

5. Choice B is correct. See **Sentence Completion Strategies 1 and 4.** Try each choice, being aware that "because" is a *result indicator*. This happened because of his *careless, indifferent* driving.

6. Choice D is correct. See **Sentence Completion Strategy 1.** Try each choice. Parables are *stories* or fables that illustrate a moral or ethical point while relating a simple incident.

7. Choice D is correct. Line 1 ("To the world when it was half a thousand years younger…") indicates that the author is describing the world roughly five hundred years ago. Choice D—A.D. 1455—is therefore the closest date. Although Choice C is also in the Middle Ages, it is almost a thousand years ago. So it is an incorrect choice. Choices A, B, and E are obviously incorrect choices.

8. Choice A is correct. We can see that "with greater avidity" is an adverbial phrase telling the reader how "honors and riches" were enjoyed and desired. See lines 14–17: "We, at the present day…formerly enjoyed." The reader thus learns that even simple pleasures such as a glass of wine were more keenly enjoyed then. Choices B, C, D, and E are incorrect because the passage does *not* state or imply that "with greater avidity" means "with greater sadness *or* terror *or* silence *or* disappointment." See also **Reading Comprehension Strategy 5.**

9. Choice B is not true—therefore it is the correct choice. See lines 37–39: "The contrast between silence and sound…than it is in our lives." The next sentence states that the modern town hardly knows silence. These two sentences together imply that the typical town of the Middle Ages did have periods of silence.

Choice A is true—therefore an incorrect choice. See lines 30–32: "A medieval town…in extensive suburbs of factories and villas." Choice C is true—therefore an incorrect choice. See lines 32–33: "…it [a medieval town] stood forth…with innumerable turrets."

Choice D is true—therefore an incorrect choice. See lines 35–36: "…the lofty mass of the churches always remained dominant."

Choice E is true—therefore an incorrect choice. See lines 33–35: "However tall…in the aspect of the town."

10. Choice C is correct. Throughout Passage 1, the author is indicating the strong, rough, uncontrolled forces that pervaded the period. See, for example, the following references. Lines 9–10: "Misfortunes and poverty were more afflicting than at present." Lines 18–19: "Then, again, all things in life…cruel publicity." Lines 24–27: "Executions…songs and music." Therefore, Choice C is correct. Choice A is incorrect because the passage speaks of joys as well as miseries. See lines 14–17: "We, at the present day…formerly enjoyed." Choice B is incorrect for this reason: Although the author contrasts town and country, he gives no indication as to which was dominant in that society. Therefore, Choice B is incorrect. Choice D is incorrect. The author contrasts how it felt to be rich or poor, but he does not indicate that the rich mistreated the poor. Choice E is incorrect because the pious nature of the people in the Middle Ages is only one of the many elements discussed in the passage.

11. Choice E is correct. See lines 4–6: "All experience…pain of child-life." Throughout the passage, this theme is illustrated with specific examples. Choices A and B are incorrect because they are one-sided. In the passage, many conditions that may make the Middle Ages seem worse than today are matched with conditions that may make the Middle Ages seem better than today. Choice C is incorrect because nowhere in the passage is intelligence mentioned or implied. Choice D is incorrect because the third paragraph indicates that, far from being subdued, people went about their lives with a great deal of show and pageantry.

12. Choice D is correct. Choice A is incorrect because the author stops short of outright despair in the last sentence of the first paragraph by tempering the outbursts of the Renaissance scholar with the milder "our times are out of joint." Choices B and E are incorrect because there is no positive feeling expressed in the first paragraph. Choice C is incorrect because there is no feeling of attraction toward an earlier age. Choice D is correct because the negative feeling is not quite full-bodied.

13. Choice A is correct. There is no mention of energy sources at any point in the selection. Therefore this answer is correct. Choices B, C, D, and E are mentioned in paragraph 2.

14. Choice B is correct. The positive outlook of the words "trend is not destiny" is best exemplified by Choice B, which implies that man can improve his situation. The other statements are negative or pessimistic pronouncements.

15. Choice A is correct. The author cites Choices B, C, D, and E in paragraph 5 as examples of renewed public awareness. The reference to the president's increase in the military budget does not indicate evidence of the public's insight regarding a danger.

16. Choice B is correct. Choices A and C are incorrect because the author is consistently expressing optimism in man's ability to learn from past mistakes. Choice B is the correct answer. Accordingly, Choice D contradicts the realistic tone of the essay. Choice E is not at all characteristic of the writer's attitude.

17. Choice C is correct. See lines 13–14 and lines 56–59. Note that the author of Passage 2 states that *if* present trends continue, the gap in living standards between the rich and the poor will lead to acts of desperation, including the use of nuclear weapons.

    Choice A is correct. See lines 73–78. We don't see this acting on awareness in the first passage.

    Choice B cannot be correct because there is no evidence that the people in Passage 2 are more intense and colorful than the people in Passage 1 as is evident in lines 41–46.

18. Choice C is incorrect. See lines 82–84: "Even more striking are the situations in which social attitudes concerning future difficulties undergo rapid changes before the problems have come to pass—witness the heated controversies..."

    Choice D is incorrect because there is no evidence that the people in Passage 1 are more religious than those in Passage 2.

    Choice E cannot be correct looking at the evidence in lines 85–88: "...the ethics of behavior control and of genetic engineering even though there is as yet no proof that effective methods can be developed to manipulate behavior and genes..."

19. Choice E is correct because there is ample evidence throughout Passage 1 (see lines 41–46) that shows people are more involved in everyday living than the people in Passage 2 (see lines 73–90), who are more involved in seeking change. There is no evidence to support the conclusions that are presented in Choices A, B, C, and D.

EXPLANATORY ANSWERS FOR PRACTICE TEST 1
Section 10: Writing

1. Choice D is correct. Choices A, B, and C are incorrect because they lack parallelism. Note that the infinitive phrase "to write poems" should balance with the infinitive phrase "to study the habits." Choice D, which does have the parallelism required, is correct. Choice E is too wordy.

2. Choice B is correct. This question is concerned with the correct position of the gerund phrase "By studying." Choice A is incorrect because "grades" have been doing the "studying" with such sentence structure. Choices C, D, and E are incorrect for the same reason. Choice B is correct since "she" is obviously the one who is doing the "studying."

3. Choice D is correct. Choice A is incorrect because of the improper omission of the demonstrative pronoun "those." Choices B and C are incorrect for the same reason. Choice D is correct. Choice E is incorrect because we must bring out the comparison with *another* city.

4. Choice C is correct. Parallelism is the important consideration here: "Beau Obama...is energetic, with bright eyes, and has a pleasant disposition" is not parallel in construction. Choice C is the only option that fulfills the requirements of parallel structure: "...energetic, bright-eyed, and pleasant."

5. Choice D is correct. The expression "one another" refers to three or more; "each other" refers to two only. Therefore, Choices A and B are incorrect and Choice D is correct. Choice C is awkward. Choice E changes the meaning of the original sentence.

6. Choice E is correct. The past contrary-to-fact conditional form is "had seen." Therefore, Choices A, B, C, and D are all incorrect. Choice

E is correct. Moreover, Choice C has the wrong tense and the wrong tense sequence. It should also be seen that when you speak of *pancakes* you speak of *number* of *pancakes*. If you speak of *flour*, you speak of *amount* of *flour*.

7. Choice C is correct. A misplaced modifier may create a very embarrassing situation—so we can observe in the original sentence. We certainly don't want the boyfriend wearing a sheer blouse. Such a blouse clearly belongs on the female. Choices A and D are, therefore, incorrect. Choice B is incorrect because it may appear that the concert is wearing the sheer blouse. Choice C is, of course, correct. Choice E is not acceptable because (1) the phrase "wearing a sheer blouse" is a "squinting" modifier, and (2) the sentence would be inappropriately poetic.

8. Choice D is correct. We are looking for *balanced construction* in this question. Note that the correct Choice D gives us a balanced infinitive construction: "to advise," "(to) transmit," and "(to) supervise." None of the other choices offers this balanced construction.

9. Choice A is correct. Choices B and C are incorrect because the newcomer did not "own" the decision—it was rendered by the judges and the referee. Choice D is too roundabout. Choice E changes the meaning of the original sentence—and it is too roundabout.

10. Choice C is correct. Choices A, B, and E suffer from incomplete comparison. The conjunction (a second "as") is required to complete the comparison: "This test was as hard...*as* the one I took last week." Choice D is incorrect because the conjunction "so" should be used in a negative construction: "This test was *not* so hard..." Choice C is correct because it completes the comparison.

11. Choice E is correct. Choice A is incorrect because the plane and *not* JFK Airport carried few passengers. Choice B is incorrect because there is a lack of agreement in the verb tenses. Also the active voice should be used. See correct Choice E. Choice C does not include a reference to JFK Airport, which is necessary to the meaning of the original sentence. Choice D is ambiguous. Choice E is correct.

12. Choice C is correct. Choice A is incorrect because the word "go" is needed after the word "to" (otherwise the sentence means "I wanted to gone"). Choice B also requires the word "go" after "to." Choice C is correct. In Choice D, the word "although" changes the original sentence to a fragment. Choice E requires the words "to go" after "wanted."

13. Choice D is correct. Choices A and B are incorrect because "either" should be placed right before "today." This is because you are describing when you will go to the store, and the word you use should be linked right next to the time (today or tomorrow morning). Choice C is too wordy, and Choice E is awkward.

14. Choice C is correct. Choice A is incorrect because "which" should be used to refer to a noun or pronoun and *not* a clause, as it is used here. In Choice B, there is a lack of agreement in the verb tenses. Choice C is correct. Choice D is awkward. Choice E is a complete sentence, making the original a run-on sentence.

SAT PRACTICE
TEST 2

ANSWER SHEET FOR PRACTICE TEST 2

Section 1

Begin your essay on this page. If you need more space, continue on the next page. Do not write outside of the essay box.

Continue on the next page if necessary.

Continuation of ESSAY Section 1 from previous page. Write below only if you need more space.

Start with number 1 for each new section. If a section has fewer questions than answer spaces, leave the extra answer spaces blank. Be sure to erase any errors or stray marks completely.

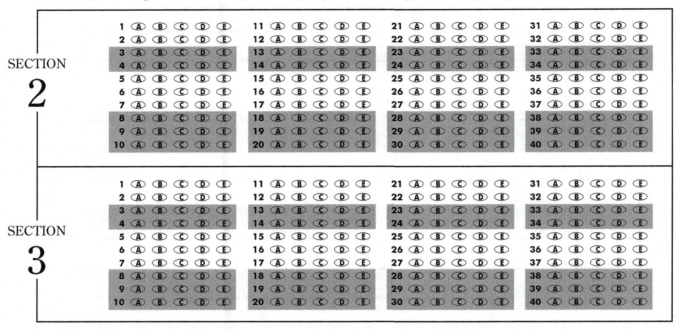

CAUTION Use the answer spaces in the grids below for Section 2 or Section 3 only if you are told to do so in your test book.

Student-Produced Responses

ONLY ANSWERS ENTERED IN THE CIRCLES IN EACH GRID WILL BE SCORED. YOU WILL NOT RECEIVE CREDIT FOR ANYTHING WRITTEN IN THE BOXES ABOVE THE CIRCLES.

Start with number 1 for each new section. If a section has fewer questions than answer spaces, leave the extra answer spaces blank. Be sure to erase any errors or stray marks completely.

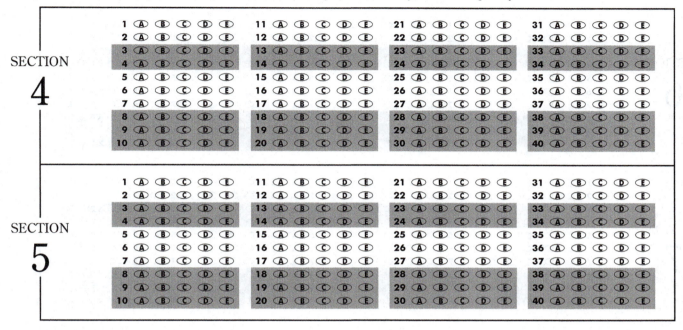

SECTION

4

SECTION

5

CAUTION   Use the answer spaces in the grids below for Section 2 or Section 3 only if you are told to do so in your test book.

Student-Produced Responses   ONLY ANSWERS ENTERED IN THE CIRCLES IN EACH GRID WILL BE SCORED. YOU WILL NOT RECEIVE CREDIT FOR ANYTHING WRITTEN IN THE BOXES ABOVE THE CIRCLES.

9   **10**   **11**   **12**   **13**

14   **15**   **16**   **17**   **18**

Start with number 1 for each new section. If a section has fewer questions than answer spaces, leave the extra answer spaces blank. Be sure to erase any errors or stray marks completely.

SECTION

6

1 Ⓐ Ⓑ Ⓒ Ⓓ Ⓔ	11 Ⓐ Ⓑ Ⓒ Ⓓ Ⓔ	21 Ⓐ Ⓑ Ⓒ Ⓓ Ⓔ	31 Ⓐ Ⓑ Ⓒ Ⓓ Ⓔ
2 Ⓐ Ⓑ Ⓒ Ⓓ Ⓔ	12 Ⓐ Ⓑ Ⓒ Ⓓ Ⓔ	22 Ⓐ Ⓑ Ⓒ Ⓓ Ⓔ	32 Ⓐ Ⓑ Ⓒ Ⓓ Ⓔ
3 Ⓐ Ⓑ Ⓒ Ⓓ Ⓔ	13 Ⓐ Ⓑ Ⓒ Ⓓ Ⓔ	23 Ⓐ Ⓑ Ⓒ Ⓓ Ⓔ	33 Ⓐ Ⓑ Ⓒ Ⓓ Ⓔ
4 Ⓐ Ⓑ Ⓒ Ⓓ Ⓔ	14 Ⓐ Ⓑ Ⓒ Ⓓ Ⓔ	24 Ⓐ Ⓑ Ⓒ Ⓓ Ⓔ	34 Ⓐ Ⓑ Ⓒ Ⓓ Ⓔ
5 Ⓐ Ⓑ Ⓒ Ⓓ Ⓔ	15 Ⓐ Ⓑ Ⓒ Ⓓ Ⓔ	25 Ⓐ Ⓑ Ⓒ Ⓓ Ⓔ	35 Ⓐ Ⓑ Ⓒ Ⓓ Ⓔ
6 Ⓐ Ⓑ Ⓒ Ⓓ Ⓔ	16 Ⓐ Ⓑ Ⓒ Ⓓ Ⓔ	26 Ⓐ Ⓑ Ⓒ Ⓓ Ⓔ	36 Ⓐ Ⓑ Ⓒ Ⓓ Ⓔ
7 Ⓐ Ⓑ Ⓒ Ⓓ Ⓔ	17 Ⓐ Ⓑ Ⓒ Ⓓ Ⓔ	27 Ⓐ Ⓑ Ⓒ Ⓓ Ⓔ	37 Ⓐ Ⓑ Ⓒ Ⓓ Ⓔ
8 Ⓐ Ⓑ Ⓒ Ⓓ Ⓔ	18 Ⓐ Ⓑ Ⓒ Ⓓ Ⓔ	28 Ⓐ Ⓑ Ⓒ Ⓓ Ⓔ	38 Ⓐ Ⓑ Ⓒ Ⓓ Ⓔ
9 Ⓐ Ⓑ Ⓒ Ⓓ Ⓔ	19 Ⓐ Ⓑ Ⓒ Ⓓ Ⓔ	29 Ⓐ Ⓑ Ⓒ Ⓓ Ⓔ	39 Ⓐ Ⓑ Ⓒ Ⓓ Ⓔ
10 Ⓐ Ⓑ Ⓒ Ⓓ Ⓔ	20 Ⓐ Ⓑ Ⓒ Ⓓ Ⓔ	30 Ⓐ Ⓑ Ⓒ Ⓓ Ⓔ	40 Ⓐ Ⓑ Ⓒ Ⓓ Ⓔ

SECTION

7

1 Ⓐ Ⓑ Ⓒ Ⓓ Ⓔ	11 Ⓐ Ⓑ Ⓒ Ⓓ Ⓔ	21 Ⓐ Ⓑ Ⓒ Ⓓ Ⓔ	31 Ⓐ Ⓑ Ⓒ Ⓓ Ⓔ
2 Ⓐ Ⓑ Ⓒ Ⓓ Ⓔ	12 Ⓐ Ⓑ Ⓒ Ⓓ Ⓔ	22 Ⓐ Ⓑ Ⓒ Ⓓ Ⓔ	32 Ⓐ Ⓑ Ⓒ Ⓓ Ⓔ
3 Ⓐ Ⓑ Ⓒ Ⓓ Ⓔ	13 Ⓐ Ⓑ Ⓒ Ⓓ Ⓔ	23 Ⓐ Ⓑ Ⓒ Ⓓ Ⓔ	33 Ⓐ Ⓑ Ⓒ Ⓓ Ⓔ
4 Ⓐ Ⓑ Ⓒ Ⓓ Ⓔ	14 Ⓐ Ⓑ Ⓒ Ⓓ Ⓔ	24 Ⓐ Ⓑ Ⓒ Ⓓ Ⓔ	34 Ⓐ Ⓑ Ⓒ Ⓓ Ⓔ
5 Ⓐ Ⓑ Ⓒ Ⓓ Ⓔ	15 Ⓐ Ⓑ Ⓒ Ⓓ Ⓔ	25 Ⓐ Ⓑ Ⓒ Ⓓ Ⓔ	35 Ⓐ Ⓑ Ⓒ Ⓓ Ⓔ
6 Ⓐ Ⓑ Ⓒ Ⓓ Ⓔ	16 Ⓐ Ⓑ Ⓒ Ⓓ Ⓔ	26 Ⓐ Ⓑ Ⓒ Ⓓ Ⓔ	36 Ⓐ Ⓑ Ⓒ Ⓓ Ⓔ
7 Ⓐ Ⓑ Ⓒ Ⓓ Ⓔ	17 Ⓐ Ⓑ Ⓒ Ⓓ Ⓔ	27 Ⓐ Ⓑ Ⓒ Ⓓ Ⓔ	37 Ⓐ Ⓑ Ⓒ Ⓓ Ⓔ
8 Ⓐ Ⓑ Ⓒ Ⓓ Ⓔ	18 Ⓐ Ⓑ Ⓒ Ⓓ Ⓔ	28 Ⓐ Ⓑ Ⓒ Ⓓ Ⓔ	38 Ⓐ Ⓑ Ⓒ Ⓓ Ⓔ
9 Ⓐ Ⓑ Ⓒ Ⓓ Ⓔ	19 Ⓐ Ⓑ Ⓒ Ⓓ Ⓔ	29 Ⓐ Ⓑ Ⓒ Ⓓ Ⓔ	39 Ⓐ Ⓑ Ⓒ Ⓓ Ⓔ
10 Ⓐ Ⓑ Ⓒ Ⓓ Ⓔ	20 Ⓐ Ⓑ Ⓒ Ⓓ Ⓔ	30 Ⓐ Ⓑ Ⓒ Ⓓ Ⓔ	40 Ⓐ Ⓑ Ⓒ Ⓓ Ⓔ

CAUTION Use the answer spaces in the grids below for Section 2 or Section 3 only if you are told to do so in your test book.

Student-Produced Responses

ONLY ANSWERS ENTERED IN THE CIRCLES IN EACH GRID WILL BE SCORED. YOU WILL NOT RECEIVE CREDIT FOR ANYTHING WRITTEN IN THE BOXES ABOVE THE CIRCLES.

9   10   11   12   13

14   15   16   17   18

Start with number 1 for each new section. If a section has fewer questions than answer spaces, leave the extra answer spaces blank. Be sure to erase any errors or stray marks completely.

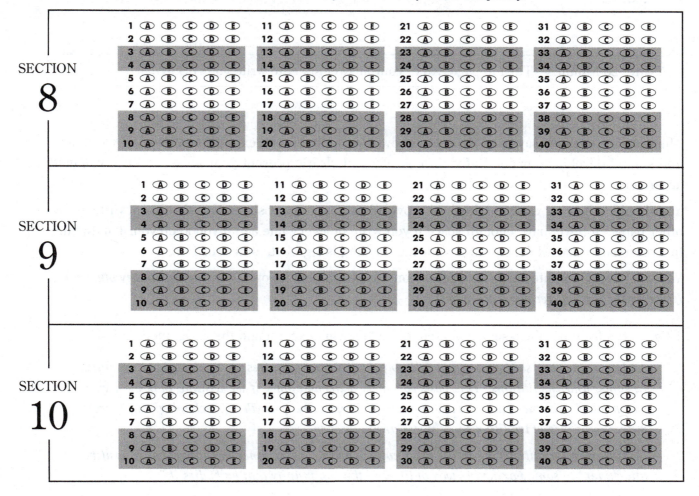

Section 1

> **Time:** 25 Minutes—Turn to page 240 of your answer sheet to write your ESSAY.

The purpose of the essay is to have you show how well you can express and develop your ideas. You should develop your point of view, logically and clearly present your ideas, and use language accurately.

You should write your essay on the lines provided on your answer sheet. You should not write on any other paper. You will have enough space if you write on every line and if you keep your handwriting to a reasonable size. Make sure that your handwriting is legible to other readers.

You will have 25 minutes to write an essay on the assignment below. *Do not write on any other topic. If you do so, you will receive a score of 0.*

Think carefully about the issue presented in the following excerpt and the assignment below.

> *"It has been often said that rapid technological change requires us to change our morals, customs, and institutions. This observation is believable only if we assume that humanity was made for the machine, not the machine for humanity. If anything, technological progress makes our sense of tradition more necessary than ever.*
>
> *"Maintaining traditions is not (or need not be) merely a resistance to change, but a positive attachment to some particular way of life and the community that embodies it."*
>
> –ADAPTED FROM KARL JAHN, "TRADITION AND PROGRESS"

Assignment: In the above excerpt, Jahn argues that we do not have to change our traditions to keep pace with technological changes. To what extent do you agree or disagree with his position? Support your position with reasons and examples from your own experience, reading, and observations.

DO NOT WRITE YOUR ESSAY IN YOUR TEST BOOK. You will receive credit only for what you write on your answer sheet.

BEGIN WRITING YOUR ESSAY ON PAGE 240 OF THE ANSWER SHEET.

If you finish before time is called, you may check your work on this section only.
Do not turn to any other section in the test.

Section 2

Time: 25 Minutes – Turn to Section 2 (page 242) of your answer sheet to answer the questions in this section. 20 Questions

Directions: For this section, solve each problem and decide which is the best of the choices given. Fill in the corresponding circle on the answer sheet. You may use any available space for scratchwork.

Notes:

1. The use of a calculator is permitted.

2. All numbers used are real numbers.

3. Figures that accompany problems in this test are intended to provide information useful in solving the problems. They are drawn as accurately as possible EXCEPT when it is stated in a specific problem that the figure is not drawn to scale. All figures lie in a plane unless otherwise indicated.

4. Unless otherwise specified, the domain of any function f is assumed to be the set of all real numbers x for which $f(x)$ is a real number.

REFERENCE INFORMATION

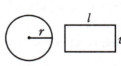

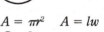

$A = \pi r^2$ $A = lw$ $A = \frac{1}{2}bh$ $V = lwh$ $V = \pi r^2 h$ $c^2 = a^2 + b^2$ *Special Right Triangle.*
$C = 2\pi r$

The number of degrees of arc in a circle is 360.
The sum of the measures in degrees of the angles of a triangle is 180.

---

1. Given that $500w = 3 \times 700$, find the value of w.

    (A) $\frac{5}{21}$

    (B) 2

    (C) $\frac{11}{5}$

    (D) $\frac{21}{5}$

    (E) 7

2. If $\frac{3+y}{y} = 7$, then $y =$

    (A) 4

    (B) 3

    (C) 2

    (D) 1

    (E) $\frac{1}{2}$

GO ON TO THE NEXT PAGE ➤

3. The positive integer x is a multiple of 9 and also a multiple of 12. The smallest possible value of x is

    (A) 3
    (B) 12
    (C) 21
    (D) 36
    (E) 72

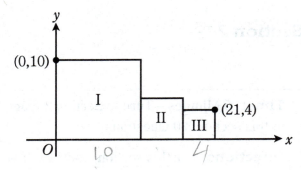

Note: Figure is not drawn to scale.

5. In the figure above, squares I, II, and III are situated along the x-axis as shown. Find the area of square II.

    (A) 16
    (B) 25
    (C) 49
    (D) 100
    (E) 121

4. Find $(r - s)(t - s) + (s - r)(s - t)$ for all numbers r, s, and t.

    (A) 0
    (B) 2
    (C) $2rt$
    (D) $2(s - r)(t - s)$
    (E) $2(r - s)(t - s)$

6. A certain cup holds 100 grams of butter. If a cake requires 75 grams of butter and a pie requires 225 grams of butter, then 4 cups of butter is *not* enough for any of the following *except*

    (A) 6 cakes
    (B) 2 pies
    (C) 3 cakes and 1 pie
    (D) 2 cakes and 2 pies
    (E) 2 cakes and 1 pie

GO ON TO THE NEXT PAGE ➤

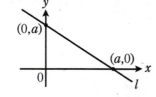

Note: Figure is not drawn to scale.

7. In the rectangular coordinate system above, which of the following is true about line ℓ?

I. the slope is −1

II. the distance of point $(0,a)$ to point $(a,0)$ is equal to $a\sqrt{2}$

III. the acute angle that line ℓ makes with the x-axis is 45°

(A) I only
(B) II only
(C) III only
(D) II and III only
(E) I, II, and III

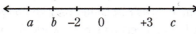

8. In the above number line, *a*, *b*, and *c* are real numbers. Which is true?

(A) $b > -1$
(B) $|b| < 2$
(C) $-|c| = c$
(D) $|b| > |a|$
(E) $|a| > |b|$

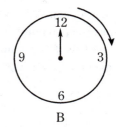

9. If the sum of the four terms in each of the diagonal rows is the same, then $A =$

(A) 4
(B) 5
(C) 6
(D) 7
(E) 8

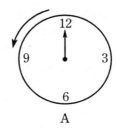

10. The two dials shown above operate simultaneously in the following manner. The hand in A turns *counterclockwise* while the hand in B turns *clockwise*. In the first move, the hand of A moves to 9 at exactly the same moment that the hand of B moves to 3. In the second move, the hand of A moves to 6 at exactly the same moment that the hand of B moves to 6, and so on. If each hand starts at 12, where will each hand be at the end of 17 moves?

(A) Both at 12
(B) Both at 9
(C) A at 3 and B at 12
(D) A at 3 and B at 9
(E) A at 9 and B at 3

GO ON TO THE NEXT PAGE ➤

11. Given that $w = 7r + 6r + 5r + 4r + 3r$, which of the terms listed below may be added to w so that the resulting sum will be divisible by 7 for every positive integer r?

   (A) $7r$
   (B) $6r$
   (C) $5r$
   (D) $4r$
   (E) $3r$

13. Which of the following is always true for real numbers a, b, x, y?

   I. $(a^x)^y = a^{xy}$

   II. $a^{x+y} = a^x a^y$

   III. $(ab)^x = a^x b^x$

   (A) I only
   (B) II only
   (C) III only
   (D) I and II only
   (E) I, II, and III

12. S is a set of positive, odd, whole numbers in which no two numbers are the same. If the sum of all of its members is 64, then what is the maximum number of members that S can have?

   (A) 10
   (B) 13
   (C) 6
   (D) 8
   (E) 7

14. A painter earns $10 an hour for all hours spent on a job. For a certain job, he worked from 7:00 A.M. until 5:00 P.M. on Monday, Tuesday, and Thursday, and from 1:00 P.M. until 7:00 P.M. on Wednesday, Friday, and Saturday. How much did he earn for the entire job?

   (A) $420
   (B) $450
   (C) $480
   (D) $510
   (E) $540

GO ON TO THE NEXT PAGE ➤

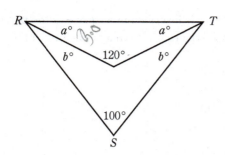

Note: Figure is not drawn to scale.

15.   Given △*RST* above, what is the value of *b*?

(A) 50°
(B) 40°
(C) 30°
(D) 20°
(E) 10°

17. If ⓐ ⓑ = $\dfrac{a+1}{b-1}$ where *a* and *b* are positive integers and *b* > 1, which of the following is largest?

(A) ②③
(B) ③③
(C) ③⑤
(D) ④⑤
(E) ⑤③

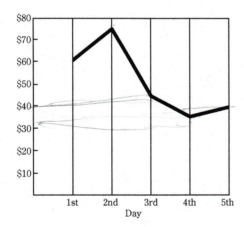

16. John works for 5 days. His daily earnings are displayed on the above graph. If John earned $35 on the sixth day, what would be the difference between the median and the mode of the wages for the six days?

(A) $5.50
(B) $6.50
(C) $7.50
(D) $8.50
(E) $9.50

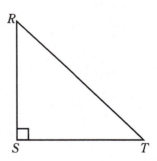

18. In △*RST* above, *RS* and *ST* have lengths equal to the same integer. All of the following could be the area of triangle *RST* *except*

(A) $\dfrac{1}{2}$

(B) 2

(C) $4\dfrac{1}{2}$

(D) $12\dfrac{1}{2}$

(E) 20

GO ON TO THE NEXT PAGE ➤

19. A rectangular solid has dimensions of 2 feet × 2 feet × 1 foot. If it is sliced in small cubes, each of edge 0.1 foot, what is the maximum number of such cubes that can be formed?

    (A) 40
    (B) 500
    (C) 1,000
    (D) 2,000
    (E) 4,000

20. A circle is inscribed in a square. If the perimeter of the square is 40, what is the area of the circle?

    (A) 100π
    (B) 50π
    (C) 40π
    (D) 25π
    (E) 5π

STOP

If you finish before time is called, you may check your work on this section only.
Do not turn to any other section in the test.

Take a 5 minute break

before starting section 3

Section 3

Time: 25 Minutes – Turn to Section 3 (page 242) of your answer sheet to answer the questions in this section. 18 Questions

Directions: For this section, solve each problem and decide which is the best of the choices given. Fill in the corresponding circle on the answer sheet. You may use any available space for scratchwork.

Notes:

1. The use of a calculator is permitted.

2. All numbers used are real numbers.

3. Figures that accompany problems in this test are intended to provide information useful in solving the problems. They are drawn as accurately as possible EXCEPT when it is stated in a specific problem that the figure is not drawn to scale. All figures lie in a plane unless otherwise indicated.

4. Unless otherwise specified, the domain of any function f is assumed to be the set of all real numbers x for which $f(x)$ is a real number.

REFERENCE INFORMATION

 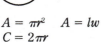

$A = \pi r^2$ $A = lw$ $A = \frac{1}{2}bh$ $V = lwh$ $V = \pi r^2 h$ $c^2 = a^2 + b^2$ *Special Right Triangle.*
$C = 2\pi r$

The number of degrees of arc in a circle is 360.
The sum of the measures in degrees of the angles of a triangle is 180.

---

1. If 3 is added to a number and this sum is divided by 4, the result is 6. What is the number?

    (A) 5
    (B) 7
    (C) 12
    (D) 21
    (E) 27

2. Given that $\frac{3}{4} < x < \frac{4}{5}$, which of the following is a possible value of x?

    (A) $\frac{7}{16}$

    (B) $\frac{13}{20}$

    (C) $\frac{31}{40}$

    (D) $\frac{16}{20}$

    (E) $\frac{6}{7}$

GO ON TO THE NEXT PAGE ➤

3. If the perimeter of a square is 20 meters, how many square meters are contained in its area?

(A) 100
(B) 25
(C) 20
(D) 10
(E) 5

5. If x is a positive integer, which of the following must be an even integer?

(A) $x + 2$
(B) $2x + 1$
(C) $3x + 1$
(D) $x^2 + x + 1$
(E) $x^2 + x + 2$

4. Given that $80 + a = -32 + b$, find the value of $b - a$.

(A) -112
(B) -48
(C) 2.5
(D) 48
(E) 112

6. If $ax = r$ and $by = r - 1$, then which of the following is a correct expression for x?

(A) $\dfrac{by + 1}{a}$

(B) $\dfrac{by - 1}{a}$

(C) $\dfrac{by + r}{a}$

(D) $by + ar$

(E) $ab + ry$

GO ON TO THE NEXT PAGE ➤

7. Container A holds twice as much as container B, and container C holds as much as A and B put together. If we start with A and B full, and C empty, and pour half the contents of A and a third of the contents of B into container C, what fraction of C's capacity will be filled?

(A) $\frac{5}{6}$

(B) $\frac{4}{9}$

(C) $\frac{5}{12}$

(D) $\frac{7}{12}$

(E) $\frac{7}{18}$

8. What is the diameter of a wheel which, when rotating at a speed of 10 revolutions per minute, takes 12 seconds to travel 16 feet?

(A) 4π feet

(B) $\frac{4}{\pi}$ feet

(C) 8π feet

(D) $\frac{8}{\pi}$ feet

(E) $\frac{16}{\pi}$ feet

9. If $\frac{5}{8}$ of a number is 3 less than $\frac{3}{4}$ of the number, what is the number?

10. Let $\boxed{n\!\!\rangle}$ represent the greatest even integer less than n that divides n, for any positive integer n. For example, $\boxed{24\!\!\rangle} = 12$. Find the value of $\boxed{20\!\!\rangle}$.

Directions: For Student-Produced Response questions 9–18, use the grids on the following page.

Each of the remaining questions requires you to solve the problem and enter your answer by marking the circles in the special grid, as shown in the examples below. You may use any available space for scratchwork.

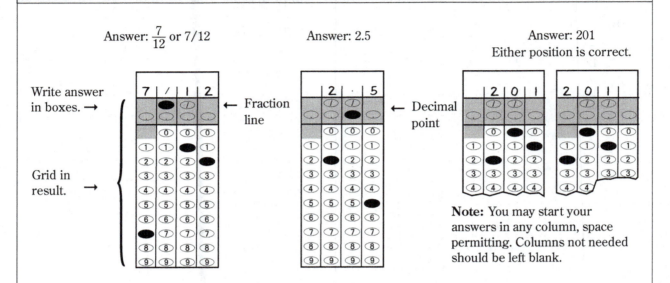

Answer: $\frac{7}{12}$ or 7/12

Write answer in boxes. → ← Fraction line

Grid in result. →

Answer: 2.5

← Decimal point

Answer: 201
Either position is correct.

Note: You may start your answers in any column, space permitting. Columns not needed should be left blank.

- Mark no more than one oval in any column.

- Because the answer sheet will be machine-scored, **you will receive credit only if the ovals are filled in correctly.**

- Although not required, it is suggested that you write your answer in the boxes at the top of the columns to help you fill in the ovals accurately.

- Some problems may have more than one correct answer. In such cases, grid only one answer.

- No question has a negative answer.

- **Mixed numbers** such as $2\frac{1}{2}$ must be gridded as 2.5 or 5/2. (If $\boxed{2\ 1\ /\ 2}$ is gridded, it will be interpreted as $\frac{21}{2}$, not $2\frac{1}{2}$.)

- **Decimal Accuracy:** If you obtain a decimal answer, **enter the most accurate value the grid will accommodate.** For example, if you obtain an answer such as 0.6666..., you should record the result as .666 or .667. **Less accurate values such as .66 or .67 are not acceptable.**

Acceptable ways to grid $\frac{2}{3}$ = .6666...:

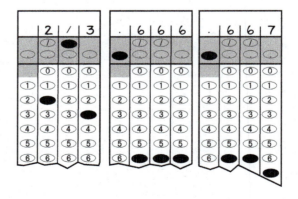

GO ON TO THE NEXT PAGE ❯

11. If $m = 94$ and $n = 6$, then find the value of $23m + 23n$.

12. A horizontal line has a length of 100 yards. A vertical line is drawn at one of its ends. If lines are drawn every ten yards thereafter, until the other end is reached, how many vertical lines are finally drawn?

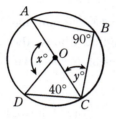

Note: Figure not drawn to scale

13. In the circle above with center O, diameter AC, and $AB = BC$, find the value of $x + y$.

14. In a certain class containing 60 students, the average (arithmetic mean) age is 20. In another class containing 20 students, the average age is 40. Find the average age of all 80 students.

15. In the addition problem shown below, if □ is a constant, what must □ equal in order for the answer to be correct?

$$
\begin{array}{r}
\square\ 1 \\
6\ \square \\
+\ \square\ 9 \\
\hline
1\ 5\ \square
\end{array}
$$

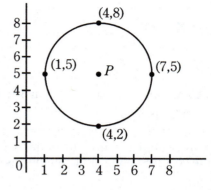

16. Given the circle above, with center P, what is the length of its radius?

17. A lawn covers 108.6 square feet. Regan mowed all of the lawn in three evenings. She mowed $\frac{2}{9}$ of the lawn during the first evening. She mowed twice that amount on the second evening. On the third and final evening she mowed the remaining lawn. How many square feet were mowed the third evening?

18. If 9 people are standing in a straight line in a circle, what is the *smallest* number of people who must move so that all 9 will be standing on the circumference of another circle?

STOP

If you finish before time is called, you may check your work on this section only.
Do not turn to any other section in the test.

Section 4

Time: 25 Minutes – Turn to Section 4 (page 243) of your answer sheet to answer the questions in this section. 24 Questions

Directions: For each question in this section, select the best answer from among the choices given and fill in the corresponding circle on the answer sheet.

Each sentence below has one or two blanks, each blank indicating that something has been omitted. Beneath the sentence are five words or sets of words labeled A through E. Choose the word or set of words that, when inserted in the sentence, best fits the meaning of the sentence as a whole.

Example:

Hoping to _____ the dispute, negotiators proposed a compromise that they felt would be _____ to both labor and management.

(A) enforce...useful

(B) end...divisive

(C) overcome...unattractive

(D) extend...satisfactory

(E) resolve...acceptable

(A) (B) (C) (D) ●

---

1. Though the student was a highly skilled computer programmer, she had little or no _____ in designing educational software.

    (A) emotion
    (B) opportunity
    (C) structure
    (D) competition
    (E) creativity

2. They are some of the most _____ professors that we have ever had, with a _____ knowledge of their subjects and a thoroughness in their teaching.

    (A) capable...limited
    (B) tantamount...tremendous
    (C) collegiate...remarkable
    (D) scholarly...profound
    (E) active...carefree

3. Because the people of India were _____ under British rule, many went over to the Japanese side during World War II.

    (A) employed
    (B) deported
    (C) educated
    (D) abused
    (E) satisfied

GO ON TO THE NEXT PAGE ➤

4. The author told the publisher that the royalty payment specified in the contract was _____ because the research costs, including traveling for writing the book, were far more than the royalties projected for a year.

(A) rational
(B) precarious
(C) payable
(D) insufficient
(E) incomprehensible

5. The dean was quite _____ about having the students keep their books neatly in their lockers; yet her desk was very _____.

(A) indifferent…comfortable
(B) perplexed…weird
(C) firm…disorderly
(D) considerate…modern
(E) humorous…attractive

6. Those who were invited to Hunter's party had to come dressed in _____ clothes, thus convincing all the guests of his _____ inclination.

(A) sonorous…imaginative
(B) tawdry…humble
(C) raucous…peace-loving
(D) tattered…nightmarish
(E) old-fashioned…nostalgic

7. Her devotion to music _____ his own interest in an art he had once loved as a child.

(A) belied
(B) revived
(C) defiled
(D) reviled
(E) exiled

8. President Obama, disregarding _____ criticism from both sides of the House, _____ accepted an invitation to meet with the Speaker of the House to help resolve the matter.

(A) categorical…previously
(B) blemished…stiffly
(C) charismatic…meticulously
(D) acrimonious…formally
(E) malignant…plaintively

GO ON TO THE NEXT PAGE ➤

Each passage below is followed by questions on its content. Answer the questions on the basis of what is <u>stated</u> or <u>implied</u> in each passage and in any introductory material that may be provided.

Questions 9–10 are based on the following passage.

A legendary island in the Atlantic Ocean beyond the Pillars of Hercules was first mentioned by Plato in the *Timaeus*. Atlantis was a fabulously beautiful and prosperous land, the seat of an empire nine thousand years before Solon.
5 Its inhabitants overran parts of Europe and Africa, Athens alone being able to defy them. Because of the impiety of its people, the island was destroyed by an earthquake and inundation. The legend may have existed before Plato and may have sprung from the concept of Homer's Elysium.
10 The possibility that such an island once existed has caused much speculation, resulting in a theory that pre-Columbian civilizations in America were established by colonists from the lost island.

9. According to the passage, we may most safely conclude that the inhabitants of Atlantis

(A) were known personally to Homer
(B) were ruled by Plato
(C) were a religious and superstitious people
(D) used the name Columbia for America
(E) left no recorded evidence of their existence

10. According to the legend, Atlantis was destroyed because the inhabitants

(A) failed to obtain an adequate food supply
(B) failed to conquer Greece
(C) failed to respect their gods
(D) believed in Homer's Elysium
(E) had become too prosperous

Questions 11–12 are based on the following passage.

Lithography is the art of drawing with a greasy substance, usually crayon, on a stone, metal, or paper surface, and then printing. It is based on the fact that grease attracts grease and is repelled by water. It is the most direct of
5 all the graphic arts, for in practicing it the artist first sees the exact value of each line that he draws and then has his drawing reproduced so accurately that it may truly be said to have been multiplied. In making either an etching, a process in which a drawing is engraved on a metal plate
10 through a thin film of wax, or a woodblock, in which the drawing is carved in wood, the artist must wait for a print to estimate his work fairly. When a lithograph is made, the artist's drawing grows in definite values under his eyes and he can make changes in it as he works.

11. A great advantage of lithography as a means of reproducing drawings is that it

(A) is quicker and neater than other methods
(B) gives faithful reproductions
(C) requires a metal plate
(D) requires no special materials
(E) is less expensive than other methods

12. Many artists like to use lithography to reproduce their drawings because they

(A) know in advance the value of each picture
(B) often get unexpected results
(C) get higher prices for lithographs than for etchings
(D) can get clearer enlargements
(E) can make alterations and corrections

GO ON TO THE NEXT PAGE ❯

Questions 13–24 are based on the following passage.

The following passage discusses advanced technological institutions and their relation to the workforce, with social implications.

A second major hypothesis would argue that the most important dimension of advanced technological institutions is the social one; that is, the institutions are agencies of highly centralized and intensive social control. Technology
5 conquers nature, as the saying goes. But to do so it must first conquer man. More precisely, it demands a very high degree of control over the training, mobility, and skills of the workforce. The absence (or decline) of direct controls or of coercion should not serve to obscure from our view the reality
10 and intensity of the social controls which are employed (such as the internalized belief in inequality of opportunity, indebtedness through credit, advertising, selective service channeling, and so on).

Advanced technology has created a vast increase in occu-
15 pational specialties, many of them requiring many, many years of highly specialized training. It must motivate this training. It has made ever more complex and "rational" the ways in which these occupational specialties are combined in our economic and social life. It must win passivity and obedience to this
20 complex activity. Formerly, technical rationality had been employed only to organize the production of rather simple physical objects, for example, aerial bombs. Now technical rationality is increasingly employed to organize all of the processes necessary to the utilization of physical objects, such
25 as bombing systems, maintenance, intelligence and supply systems. For this reason it seems a mistake to argue that we are in a "post-industrial" age, a concept favored by the *laissez innover* school. On the contrary, the rapid spread of technical rationality into organizational and economic life and, hence,
30 into social life is more aptly described as a second and much more intensive phase of the industrial revolution. One might reasonably suspect that it will create analogous social problems.

Accordingly, a third major hypothesis would argue that there are very profound social antagonisms or contra-
35 dictions not less sharp or fundamental than those ascribed by Marx to the development of nineteenth-century industrial society. The general form of the contradictions might be described as follows: a society characterized by the employment of advanced technology requires an ever more
40 socially disciplined population, yet retains an ever declining capacity to enforce the required discipline.

One may readily describe four specific forms of the same general contradiction. Occupationally, the workforce must be overtrained and underutilized. Here, again, an
45 analogy to classical industrial practice serves to shorten and simplify the explanation. I have in mind the assembly line. As a device in the organization of the work process, the assembly line is valuable mainly in that it gives management a high degree of control over the pace of the work
50 and, more to the point in the present case, it divides the work process into units so simple that the quality of the work performed is readily predictable. That is, since each operation uses only a small fraction of a worker's skill,

there is a very great likelihood that the operation will be
55 performed in a minimally acceptable way. Alternately, if each operation taxed the worker's skill, there would be frequent errors in the operation, frequent disturbance of the work flow, and a thoroughly unpredictable quality to the end product. The assembly line also introduces standardization in work skills and thus makes for a high
60 degree of interchangeability among the workforce.

For analogous reasons the workforce in advanced technological systems must be relatively overtrained or, what is the same thing, its skills relatively underused. My impres-
65 sion is that this is no less true now of sociologists than of welders, of engineers than of assemblers. The contradiction emerges when we recognize that technological progress requires a continuous increase in the skill levels of its workforce, skill levels which frequently embody a fairly rich
70 scientific and technical training, while at the same time the advance of technical rationality in work organization means that those skills will be less and less fully used.

Economically, there is a parallel process at work. It is commonly observed that the workforce within techno-
75 logically advanced organizations is asked to work not less hard but more so. This is particularly true for those with advanced training and skills. Brzezinski's conjecture that technical specialists undergo continuous retraining is off the mark only in that it assumes such retraining only for
80 a managing elite. To get people to work harder requires growing incentives. Yet the prosperity which is assumed in a technologically advanced society erodes the value of economic incentives (while of course, the values of craftsmanship are "irrational"). Salary and wage increases and
85 the goods they purchase lose their overriding importance once necessities, creature comforts, and an ample supply of luxuries are assured. As if in confirmation of this point, it has been pointed out that among young people, one can already observe a radical weakening in the power of such
90 incentives as money, status, and authority.

13. The term "technical rationality" in line 20 is used in conjunction with

(A) a 20th-century euphemism for the industrial revolution
(B) giving credibility to products of simple technology
(C) the incorporation of unnecessary skills into economic social living
(D) effective organization of production processes
(E) safeguarding against technological over-acceleration

GO ON TO THE NEXT PAGE ➤

14. The author states that advanced technological institutions exercise control by means of

 (A) assembly-line work process
 (B) advertising, selective service channeling, etc.
 (C) direct and coercive pressures
 (D) salary incentives
 (E) authoritarian managerial staffs

15. The word "taxed" in line 56 means

 (A) a burdensome or excessive demand on the worker
 (B) a financial obstacle the worker must endure
 (C) the speed at which the worker must complete the job
 (D) the efficiency of the worker's performance on the job
 (E) the standardization in work skills of the workforce

16. The passage indicates that technologically advanced institutions

 (A) fully utilize worker skills
 (B) fare best under a democratic system
 (C) necessarily overtrain workers
 (D) find it unnecessary to enforce discipline
 (E) are operated by individuals motivated by traditional work incentives

17. The value of the assembly line is that it

 I. minimizes the frequency of error
 II. allows for interchangeability among the workforce
 III. allows for full utilization of workers' skills

 (A) I and III only
 (B) I and II only
 (C) II and III only
 (D) I, II, and III
 (E) I only

18. Technologies cannot conquer nature unless

 (A) there is unwavering worker allegiance to the goals of the institutions
 (B) there is strict adherence to a *laissez innover* policy
 (C) worker and management are in concurrence
 (D) there is another more intense, industrial revolution
 (E) the institutions have control over the training, mobility, and skills of the workforce

19. The article states that the workforce within the framework of a technologically advanced organization is

 (A) expected to work less hard
 (B) segregated into levels defined by the degree of technical training
 (C) familiarized with every process of production
 (D) expected to work harder
 (E) isolated by the fact of its specialization

20. From the tone of the article, it can be inferred that the author is

 (A) an eloquent spokesman for technological advancement
 (B) in favor of increased employee control of industry
 (C) a social scientist objectively reviewing an industrial trend
 (D) vehemently opposed to the increase of technology
 (E) skeptical of the workings of advanced technological institutions

21. According to the author, economic incentives

 (A) are necessary for all but the managerial elite
 (B) are bigger and better in a society made prosperous by technology
 (C) cease to have importance beyond a certain level of luxury
 (D) are impressive only to new members of the workforce
 (E) are impressive to all but the radical young

GO ON TO THE NEXT PAGE ➤

22. The "managing elite" in line 80 refers to

    (A) all the "blue" collar workers
    (B) the assembly-line workers only
    (C) the craftsman only
    (D) the owners of the organizations
    (E) the top technical specialists

23. According to the article, technological progress requires

    I.   increasing skill levels of workforce
    II. less utilization of work skills
    III. rich scientific and technical training

    (A) I and II only
    (B) II and III only
    (C) I and III only
    (D) III only
    (E) I, II, and III

24. The article states that money, status, and authority

    (A) will always be powerful work incentives
    (B) are not powerful incentives for the young
    (C) are unacceptable to radical workers
    (D) are incentives that are a throwback to 19th-century industrial society
    (E) are incentives evolving out of human nature

STOP

If you finish before time is called, you may check your work on this section only.
Do not turn to any other section in the test.

Take a 1 minute break

before starting section 5

Section 5

Time: 25 Minutes – Turn to Section 5 (page 243) of your answer sheet to answer the questions in this section. 35 Questions

Directions: For each question in this section, select the best answer from among the choices given and fill in the corresponding circle on the answer sheet.

The following sentences test correctness and effectiveness of expression. Part of each sentence or the entire sentence is underlined; beneath each sentence are five ways of phrasing the underlined material. Choice A repeats the original phrasing; the other four choices are different. If you think the original phrasing produces a better sentence than any of the alternatives, select Choice A; if not, select one of the other choices.

In making your selection, follow the requirements of standard written English; that is, pay attention to grammar, choice of words, sentence construction, and punctuation. Your selection should result in the most effective sentence—clear and precise, without awkwardness or ambiguity.

EXAMPLE:

Laura Ingalls Wilder published her first book <u>and she was sixty-five years old then</u>.

(A)   and she was sixty-five years old then

(B)   when she was sixty-five

(C)   at age sixty-five years old

(D)   upon the reaching of sixty-five years

(E)   at the time when she was sixty-five

---

1.   Although I know this house and this neighborhood as well as I know myself, <u>and although my friend here seems not hardly to know them at all,</u> nevertheless he has lived here longer than I.

(A)   and although my friend here seems not hardly to know them at all

(B)   and even though my friend here seems hardly to know them at all

(C)   and in spite of the fact that my friend doesn't hardly seem to know them at all

(D)   and because my friend here hardly seems to know them at all

(E)   my friend here seems hardly to know them at all

2.   So I leave it with all of you: Which came out of the open door—<u>the lady or the tiger.</u>

(A)   the lady or the tiger.

(B)   the lady or the Tiger!

(C)   the Tiger or the lady.

(D)   the Lady or the tiger.

(E)   the lady or the tiger?

GO ON TO THE NEXT PAGE ➤

3. The machine is not easy to fool, <u>it isn't altogether foolproof either</u>.

(A) it isn't altogether foolproof either
(B) or is it foolproof
(C) and it isn't completely fooled by anyone
(D) nor is it entirely foolproof
(E) so it isn't altogether foolproof

4. The police and agents of the F.B.I. <u>arrested the owner of a Madison Avenue art gallery yesterday</u> and charged him with receiving paintings stolen last November.

(A) arrested the owner of a Madison Avenue art gallery yesterday
(B) yesterday arrested the owner of a Madison Avenue art gallery
(C) arrested the owner yesterday of a Madison Avenue art gallery
(D) had the owner of a Madison Avenue art gallery yesterday arrested
(E) arranged the arrest yesterday of a Madison Avenue art gallery owner

5. <u>Deciding whether Shakespeare's plays or his sonnets are better poetry, that is a task</u> only for those prepared to examine the texts closely and able to distinguish subtle differences in the use of poetic devices.

(A) Deciding whether Shakespeare's plays or his sonnets are better poetry, that is a task
(B) In deciding whether Shakespeare's plays or his sonnets are better poetry is a task
(C) In order to decide whether Shakespeare's plays or his sonnets are better poetry is a task
(D) Deciding whether Shakespeare's plays or his sonnets are the best poetry is a task
(E) Deciding whether Shakespeare's plays or his sonnets are better poetry is a task

6. <u>Go where they may,</u> they are the life of the party.

(A) Go where they may,
(B) Where they may go,
(C) Wherever they go,
(D) Wherever they may happen to go,
(E) Whatever they do,

7. At first we were willing to support him, <u>afterwards it occurred to us that</u> he ought to provide for himself.

(A) afterwards it occurred to us that
(B) that wasn't the thing to do since
(C) but we came to realize that
(D) we came to the conclusion, however, that
(E) then we decided that

8. <u>The statistics were checked and the report was filed.</u>

(A) The statistics were checked and the report was filed.
(B) The statistics and the report were checked and filed.
(C) The statistics were checked and the report filed.
(D) The statistics and the report were checked and filed respectively.
(E) Only after the statistics were checked was the report filed.

9. Cody was awarded a medal for bravery <u>on account he risked his life</u> to save the drowning child.

(A) on account he risked his life
(B) being that he risked his life
(C) when he risked his life
(D) the reason being on account of his risking his life
(E) since he had risked his life

10. The teacher asked the newly admitted student <u>which was the country that she came from.</u>

(A) which was the country that she came from.
(B) from which country she had come from.
(C) the origin of the country she had come from.
(D) which country have you come from?
(E) which country she was from.

11. If Jack <u>would have listened to his financial consultant</u>, he would not have bought those worthless stocks.

(A) would have listened to his financial consultant
(B) would listen to his financial consultant
(C) had listened to his financial consultant
(D) listened to what his financial consultant had said
(E) would have listened to his financial consultant's advice

GO ON TO THE NEXT PAGE ➤

The following sentences test your ability to recognize grammar and usage errors. Each sentence contains either a single error or no error at all. No sentence contains more than one error. The error, if there is one, is underlined and lettered. If the sentence contains an error, select the one underlined part that must be changed to make the sentence correct. If the sentence is correct, select Choice E. In choosing answers, follow the requirements of standard written English.

EXAMPLE:

<u>The other</u> delegates and <u>him</u> <u>immediately</u>
  A   B   C

accepted the resolution <u>drafted by</u>
                              D

the neutral states. <u>No error.</u>
                        E

12. The girl <u>who won</u> the beauty contest is <u>nowhere</u>
              A   B
    <u>near</u> as beautiful <u>as</u> my mother <u>was</u> when she was
     C   D
    a bride. <u>No error.</u>
                 E

13. Sitting <u>opposite</u> my sister and <u>me</u> in the subway
             A   B
    were <u>them</u> same men who walked <u>alongside</u> us
          C   D
    and tried to speak to us on Fifth Avenue. <u>No error.</u>
                                                   E

14. <u>Even if</u> Detroit could provide <u>nonpolluting</u> cars by
     A   B
    the original deadline to meet <u>prescribed</u> federal
                                       C
    standards for clean air, the effect in big cities would
    be slight because <u>only</u> new cars would be properly
                           D
    equipped. <u>No error.</u>
                  E

15. Of the two cars that the Smiths <u>have</u>, the Plymouth
                                       A
    is, <u>without any question</u>, the <u>cheapest</u> to <u>run</u>.
          B   C   D
    <u>No error.</u>
        E

16. Man <u>cannot</u> live <u>by bread</u> alone, <u>or</u> can he <u>live</u>
          A   B   C   D
    without bread. <u>No error.</u>
                       E

17. <u>Having swam</u> <u>two-thirds</u> of the distance <u>across</u>
     A   B   C
    the English Channel, Dixon <u>could not give up</u> now.
                                    D
    <u>No error.</u>
        E

18. In the discussion, one speaker <u>held</u> that, since we
                                       A
    live in a <u>money-oriented</u> society, the average
                   B
    individual cares <u>little</u> about solving <u>anyone's else</u>
                         C   D
    problems. <u>No error.</u>
                  E

GO ON TO THE NEXT PAGE ➤

19. Due to the meat boycott, the butchers were doing

    A   B

about half of the business that they were doing

       C

previous to the boycott. No error.

  D   E

20. We requested the superintendent of the building

to clean up the storage room in the basement

  A   B

so that the children had enough space for their

  C   D

bicycles. No error.

      E

21. Lidocaine's usefulness as a local anesthetic

  A   B

was discovered by two Swedish chemists who

repeatedly tested the drug's effects on their

    C   D

bodies. No error.

     E

22. After Mo Farah won the marathon relatively easily,

        A   B

he decided to continue his training program and

  C

even to enter more races. No error.

    D   E

23. Learning by doing, long a guiding principal of

      A   B   C

many educators, has been somewhat neglected

                D

during the current back-to-basics boom. No error.

                          E

24. The Watergate scandal may be a thing of the past,

              A   B

but the Republicans will feel it's effects for a long

                C   D

time to come. No error.

      E

25. If we had began our vacation a day earlier, we

      A   B

wouldn't have had so much trouble getting a plane

  C   D

reservation. No error.

         E

26. All of the class presidents but Jerry, Alice, and

              A

I were at the meeting to select the delegates for next

B   C

month's convention. No error.

  D   E

27. Everyone who attends a concert at the sports

    A   B

arena knows that they will be searched for drugs

              C

before entering. No error.

    D   E

28. Our professor assigned us to write a short story,

                A   B

but I found I could not write one quick. No error.

                  C   D   E

29. One of the key suspects in the killing of a

      A   B

United States drug agent were captured early

  C   D

today by the police. No error.

        E

GO ON TO THE NEXT PAGE ➤

Directions: The following passage is an early draft of an essay. Some parts of the passage need to be rewritten.

Read the passage and select the best answers for the questions that follow. Some questions are about particular sentences or parts of sentences and ask you to improve sentence structure or word choice. Other questions ask you to consider organization and development. In choosing answers, follow the requirements of standard written English.

Questions 30–35 refer to the following passage.

[1]The typical Miwok Indian village was compromised of both private family dwellings and communal dwellings. [2]One was a men's sweathouse. [3]In the sweathouse, grown men and adolescent boys who were learning to be hunters sat around a small, open fire. [4]Sometimes exchanging information and anecdotes and sometimes preparing themselves for the hunt to come by fasting, sweating and silent contemplation. [5]Occasionally a woman past childbearing age would be admitted to the sweathouse. [6]Adolescent girls learned to weave baskets and cook. [7]When one of these older women was accepted into the membership of the Miwok men's "clubhouse," her acceptance was by popular acclaim and was based on her ability to tell entertaining or enlightening stories. [8]As far as anthropologists know, no equal accommodations were made for males to enter the communal women's house, which was set aside for menstruating or pregnant women.

30. What should be done with sentence 1?

    (A) It should be omitted.
    (B) Was compromised of should be changed to included.
    (C) It should be joined to sentence 2 with a semicolon.
    (D) It should not be changed.
    (E) The words was and of should be omitted.

31. Sentence 2 should

    (A) be left as it is
    (B) begin with there instead of one
    (C) be joined to sentence 1 with and, omitting one was
    (D) omitted
    (E) begin with among the latter instead of one

32. Sentence 3 would be most improved by

    (A) connecting it to sentence 2 with where and omitting in the sweat house
    (B) omitting adolescent
    (C) placing learning to be hunters before grown men and omitting who were
    (D) connecting it to sentence 2 with a semicolon
    (E) beginning with It was there

33. Sentence 4 ought to

    (A) be made into two sentences, the first to end with anecdotes
    (B) begin with Sometimes they exchanged
    (C) be improved by substituting once in a while for the second sometimes
    (D) be connected to sentence 3 with a comma
    (E) have or substituted for and sometimes after anecdotes

34. What is the best thing to do with sentence 6?

    (A) Place it in parentheses in sentence 3, after adolescent boys.
    (B) Place it before sentence 5.
    (C) Omit it.
    (D) Place it after sentence 7.
    (E) Leave it as it is.

35. Sentence 8 should

    (A) stop after house
    (B) be placed after sentence 5
    (C) be made into two sentences, the first to end after house
    (D) begin a new paragraph
    (E) have ladies substituted for women

STOP

If you finish before time is called, you may check your work on this section only.
Do not turn to any other section in the test.

Section 6

Time: 25 Minutes – Turn to Section 6 (page 244) of your answer sheet to answer the questions in this section. 18 Questions

Directions: This section contains two types of questions. You have 25 minutes to complete both types. For questions 1–8, solve each problem and decide which is the best of the choices given. Fill in the corresponding circle on the answer sheet. You may use any available space for scratchwork.

Notes:

1. The use of a calculator is permitted.

2. All numbers used are real numbers.

3. Figures that accompany problems in this test are intended to provide information useful in solving the problems. They are drawn as accurately as possible EXCEPT when it is stated in a specific problem that the figure is not drawn to scale. All figures lie in a plane unless otherwise indicated.

4. Unless otherwise specified, the domain of any function f is assumed to be the set of all real numbers x for which $f(x)$ is a real number.

REFERENCE INFORMATION

$A = \pi r^2$ $A = lw$ $A = \frac{1}{2}bh$ $V = lwh$ $V = \pi r^2 h$ $c^2 = a^2 + b^2$ *Special Right Triangle.*
$C = 2\pi r$

The number of degrees of arc in a circle is 360.
The sum of the measures in degrees of the angles of a triangle is 180.

---

1. If a, b are odd numbers, and c is even, which of the following is an even number?

   (A) $ab + c$
   (B) $a(b + c)$
   (C) $(a + b) + (b + c)$
   (D) $(a + b) - c$
   (E) $a + bc$

2. Distribution of Stamps in Harry's Collection

English	22%
French	18%
South American	25%
U.S.	35%

   (Continued on next page)

GO ON TO THE NEXT PAGE ➤

2. (Continued)

Distribution of U.S. Stamps in Harry's Collection

Commemoratives	52%
Special Delivery	10%
Postage Due	15%
Air Mail	23%

According to the table above, of Harry's collection, U.S. Air Mail stamps make up

(A) 4.00%

(B) 8.05%

(C) 15.50%

(D) 16.00%

(E) 21.35%

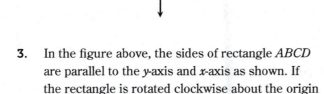

3.   In the figure above, the sides of rectangle *ABCD* are parallel to the *y*-axis and *x*-axis as shown. If the rectangle is rotated clockwise about the origin through 90°, what are the new coordinates of *B*?

(A) $(3,-5)$

(B) $(-3,5)$

(C) $(-3,-5)$

(D) $(5,-3)$

(E) $(-5,3)$

4.   The half-life of a certain radioactive substance is 6 hours. In other words, if you start with 8 grams of the substance, 6 hours later you will have 4 grams. If a sample of this substance contains *x* grams, how many grams remain after 24 hours?

(A) $\frac{x}{32}$

(B) $\frac{x}{16}$

(C) $\frac{x}{8}$

(D) $2x$

(E) $4x$

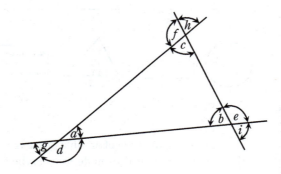

5.   In the figure above, what is the sum of the degree measures of the marked angles?

(A) 360°

(B) 720°

(C) 900°

(D) 1080°

(E) The answer cannot be determined from the information given.

GO ON TO THE NEXT PAGE ➤

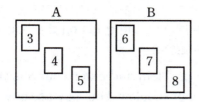

6. Box A contains 3 cards, numbered 3, 4, and 5.
    Box B contains 3 cards, numbered 6, 7, and 8. If
    one card is drawn from each box and their sum is
    calculated, how many different numerical results
    are possible?

    (A) eight
    (B) seven
    (C) six
    (D) five
    (E) four

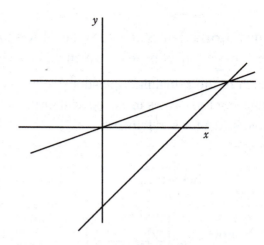

7. Which of the following equations could *not*
    represent any of the above graphs?

    (A) $2y = x$
    (B) $y = 2$
    (C) $y = 2x - 6$
    (D) $y = 2x + 4$
    (E) $y = 4$

8. If $f(x) = |x| - x$, which of the following is true?

    (A) $f(x) = f(-x)$
    (B) $f(2x) = 2f(x)$
    (C) $f(x + y) = f(x) + f(y)$
    (D) $f(x) = -f(-x)$
    (E) $f(x - y) = 0$

GO ON TO THE NEXT PAGE ➤

Directions: For Student-Produced Response questions 9–18, use the grids on the bottom of the answer sheet page on which you have answered questions 1-8.

Each of the remaining questions requires you to solve the problem and enter your answer by marking the circles in the special grid, as shown in the examples below. You may use any available space for scratchwork.

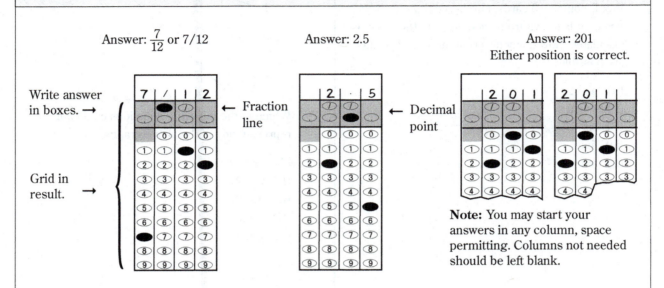

Answer: $\frac{7}{12}$ or 7/12

Write answer in boxes. →

← Fraction line

Answer: 2.5

← Decimal point

Answer: 201
Either position is correct.

Grid in result. →

Note: You may start your answers in any column, space permitting. Columns not needed should be left blank.

- Mark no more than one oval in any column.

- Because the answer sheet will be machine-scored, **you will receive credit only if the ovals are filled in correctly.**

- Although not required, it is suggested that you write your answer in the boxes at the top of the columns to help you fill in the ovals accurately.

- Some problems may have more than one correct answer. In such cases, grid only one answer.

- No question has a negative answer.

- **Mixed numbers** such as $2\frac{1}{2}$ must be gridded as 2.5 or 5/2. (If [2 1/2] is gridded, it will be interpreted as $\frac{21}{2}$, not $2\frac{1}{2}$.)

- **Decimal Accuracy:** If you obtain a decimal answer, **enter the most accurate value the grid will accommodate.** For example, if you obtain an answer such as 0.6666..., you should record the result as .666 or .667. **Less accurate values such as .66 or .67 are not acceptable.**

Acceptable ways to grid $\frac{2}{3}$ = .6666...:

9. If f is a linear function and $f(5) = 6$ and $f(7) = 8$, what is the slope of the graph of f in the xy plane?

11. If 12 is the average (arithmetic mean) of 5 different integers, each integer > 0, then what is the greatest that any one of the integers could be?

10. A bag contains exactly 4 blue marbles, 7 green marbles, and 8 yellow marbles. Fred draws marbles at random from the bag without replacement, one by one. If he does not look at the marbles he draws out, what is the smallest number of marbles he will have to draw out before he knows for sure that on his *next* draw he will have marbles in every color?

12. A classroom has 12 seated students, 5 students at the board, and 7 empty seats. If 3 students leave the room, 2 enter, and all now in the room are seated, how many empty seats will there be?

GO ON TO THE NEXT PAGE ➤

13. How many different *pairs* of parallel edges are there on a rectangular solid?

_____

14. If the sum of $2r$ and $2r + 3$ is less than 11, find a positive value of r.

_____

15. Given the sum of two angles of a quadrilateral is 90°, find the average (arithmetic mean) of the measures of the other two angles. (Disregard the degree sign when gridding in your answer.)

_____

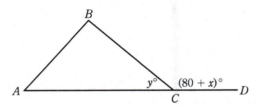

Note: Figure is not drawn to scale.

16. If AD is a straight line segment in the figure above, find the value of $x + y$.

_____

17. If $x^2 + 2xy + y^2 = 25$, $x + y > 0$ and $x - y = 1$, then find the value of x.

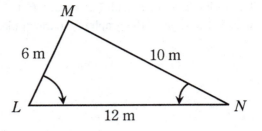

18. In the figure above, if sides LM and NM are cut apart from each other at point M creating 2 free-swinging segments and each is folded down to LN in the directions shown by the arrows, what will be the length, in meters, of the overlap of the 2 segments? (Disregard the thickness of the segments.)

STOP

If you finish before time is called, you may check your work on this section only.
Do not turn to any other section in the test.

Take a 5 minute break

before starting section 7

Section 7

> **Time:** 25 Minutes – Turn to Section 7 (page 244) of your answer sheet to answer the questions in this section. 19 Questions
>
> **Directions:** For each question in this section, select the best answer from among the choices given and fill in the corresponding circle on the answer sheet.

Each sentence below has one or two blanks, each blank indicating that something has been omitted. Beneath the sentence are five words or sets of words labeled A through E. Choose the word or set of words that, when inserted in the sentence, <u>best</u> fits the meaning of the sentence as a whole.

Example:

Hoping to _____ the dispute, negotiators proposed a compromise that they felt would be _____ to both labor and management.

(A) enforce…useful

(B) end…divisive

(C) overcome…unattractive

(D) extend…satisfactory

(E) resolve…acceptable

Ⓐ Ⓑ Ⓒ Ⓓ ⬤

---

1. The foreman's leniency, especially in being overfriendly, had its _____, one of which was _____ workmanship.

   (A) compensations…unacceptable
   (B) innuendoes…superior
   (C) drawbacks…shoddy
   (D) frequencies…attractive
   (E) cancellations…mediocre

2. Although the physical setup of the high school's lunchroom seems rundown in many respects, it was enlarged and _____ quite recently.

   (A) visited
   (B) examined
   (C) occupied
   (D) renovated
   (E) criticized

3. The activities that interested Jack were those that provided him with _____ pleasure, like dancing, feasting, and partying.

   (A) questionable
   (B) distant
   (C) immediate
   (D) limited
   (E) delayed

4. His current inability to complete his assignments in a timely and efficient manner has resulted in a feeling of _____ even in his most _____ backers.

   (A) urgency…lackadaisical
   (B) flexibility…hostile
   (C) expectancy…cautious
   (D) dizziness…visible
   (E) disappointment…fervent

5. The two performers taking the parts of shy, romantic teenagers were quite _____ in their roles even though they were in their forties.

   (A) convincing
   (B) flippant
   (C) amateurish
   (D) personable
   (E) boring

The two passages below are followed by questions based on their content and on the relationship between the two passages. Answer the questions on the basis of what is stated or implied in the passages and in any introductory material that may be provided.

Questions 6–9 are based on the following passages.

Passage 1

To keep clear of concealment, to keep clear of the need of concealment, to do nothing which one might not do out in a crowded street of onlookers in the heart of a city at the middle of the day—I cannot say to me how more and more
5 it seems to me to be the glory of a young man's life. It is an awful hour when the first necessity of hiding anything comes. The whole life is different thereafter. When there are questions to be feared and eyes to be avoided and subjects which must not be touched, then the bloom of
10 life is gone. Put off that day as long as possible. Put it off forever if you can.

Passage 2

Keeping things to yourself is an art. It is indeed a virtue to be able to hold back and not share what you would otherwise be tempted to convey. We must protect ourselves
15 from invaders that will use what we tell them and make us vulnerable to the slings and arrows of life. Who knows how what we tell them they will use for our detriment and what consequences will occur in all lives which touch us. There is no better time for concealment than today.

6. The title below that best expresses the ideas of both passages is:

   (A) A Time for Concealment
   (B) Fear and Vulnerability
   (C) A Code for Living
   (D) Penalties for Procrastination
   (E) Youth vs. Age

7. A description of the two paragraphs would be best noted as

   (A) Pro and con
   (B) Contrasting and authoritarian
   (C) Procrastinating and tenacious
   (D) Optimistic and cautious
   (E) Encouraging and dangerous

8. Which aspects do the authors of both paragraphs *not* discuss?

   (A) How the authors show the reader to accomplish what they advocate
   (B) The consequences of not conforming to the author's caution
   (C) When to abide by the author's admonition
   (D) The dangers of not conforming to the author's warnings
   (E) The element of fear and timing

9. Which lines describe analogies?

   (A) lines 1 and 12
   (B) lines 2, 3, and 15
   (C) lines 6 and 18
   (D) lines 8 and 19
   (E) lines 9 and 16

GO ON TO THE NEXT PAGE >

Questions 10–15 are based on the following passage.

The following passage describes the development of tumors, differentiating between the process of formation of malignant and benign ones.

Neoplasia, or the development of tumors, is the abnormal biological process in which some intrinsic cellular change within a group of normal cells produces a group of cells which no longer respond to the mechanisms which
5 regulate normal cells. As a result, this group of cells increases in number but fails to achieve the specialized characteristics associated with normal cells. The degree to which neoplastic cells resemble their normal counterpart cells, both in appearance and behavior, allows us to classify
10 tumors as either benign or malignant. Benign tumors look and behave like their normal tissue of origin, are usually slow-growing, are rarely fatal and remain localized. Malignant tumors, on the other hand, look very little like their tissue of origin and behave in such a manner that the
15 animal which bears the tumor frequently succumbs.

The characteristic which most strikingly separates malignant tumors from benign tumors is the ability of malignant cells to become widely disseminated and to estab-lish secondary sites of tumor far distant from the original
20 tumor. This process of widespread dissemination, which is called metastasis, is not well understood; however, some of the features of the process have been ascertained. Before metastasis can occur, the malignant cells must invade the surrounding normal tissue. Initial attempts to invade are
25 inhibited by the normal tissue. With time, the neoplastic cells undergo changes which allow them to overcome this inhibition, and tumor cells leave the primary mass of tumor. The entire process of inhibition by normal tissue and the eventual breakdown of inhibition is undoubtedly complex.

30 Malignant cells are characteristically less adhesive, one to another, than are normal cells. The outer membrane of the malignant cells contains less calcium than the membrane of normal cells. The malignant cell also acquires a greater negative electrical charge. After malignant cells
35 have invaded the surrounding normal tissue, they ulti-mately enter the bloodstream where most of the cells die. Those cells which survive will form a metastasis at a distant site only if they can adhere to the wall of a small blood vessel. The factors which govern this adherence include
40 the size of the malignant cell or a clump of these cells, the diameter of the blood vessel and the stickiness of the blood vessel wall. Stickiness of the blood vessel wall is at least partially due to the status of blood clotting components in the blood. In addition to these mechanical considerations,
45 some patterns of metastasis are explicable only on the basis of a receptive chemical environment or "soil" in which the malignant cell can grow. Finally, although a number of the characteristics of malignant neoplastic cells have been elucidated as described above, it still must be stated that
50 many aspects of their behavior remain a mystery.

10. The main topic of this passage is

   (A) the meaning of neoplasia
   (B) the inhibition of tumor metastasis by normal tissue
   (C) the transformation of benign tumors into malignant tumors
   (D) the manner in which malignant tumors behave in the body
   (E) the fate of malignant cells after they enter the bloodstream

11. Before malignant cells can be disseminated to widespread parts of the body, they must first

   (A) acquire new outer membrane characteristics
   (B) inhibit the lethal effects of components of the blood
   (C) penetrate the surrounding normal tissue
   (D) locate the proper chemical environment in which to grow
   (E) achieve sufficient size to become lodged in a blood vessel

12. According to the passage, the property of a malignant cell that most greatly enhances its metastatic potential is

   (A) its ability to choose the proper "soil"
   (B) its ability to invade the surrounding tissue
   (C) the amount of calcium in the outer membrane of the cell
   (D) the extent of deviation from the appearance of a normal cell
   (E) its ability to attach itself to the wall of a small blood vessel

13. It can be concluded from the passage that

   (A) benign tumors usually progress to malignant tumors
   (B) malignant cells reach distant tissues by routes yet to be ascertained
   (C) if the wall of a blood vessel is "sticky," a tumor metastasis has a better chance to develop
   (D) the outer membrane of malignant cells is the same as that of normal cells
   (E) the pattern of metastasis of a particular tumor is predictable with considerable accuracy

GO ON TO THE NEXT PAGE ➤

14. According to this passage, characteristics that distinguish malignant neoplastic cells from normal cells include all of the following *except*

   (A) their growth rate

   (B) their physical appearance

   (C) their outer membrane characteristics

   (D) their normal tissue of origin

   (E) their ability to invade surrounding tissue and metastasize

15. The word "explicable" in line 45 means

   (A) withdrawn

   (B) with exception

   (C) created

   (D) explainable

   (E) malignant

Questions 16–24 are based on the following passage.

The following passage is about the old Middle West and its influence on modern society.

The old Middle West is gone. However, it still lives in song and story. Give most children the choice of visiting Valley Forge or Dodge City…Dodge City wins. It is more glamorous in their imagination than Valley Forge.

5   The old Middle West developed a strong, compassionate people out of the hardships and suffering of the destructive blizzards of earlier generations—"northern" that swept over it with white clouds of blinding snow and ice—and southern winds that brought the black blizzards 10 of dust storms.

The Middle West is realistic about the nation's domestic and international affairs. It views both with intense interest and anxiety, for it knows that—although stubborn resistance to change can lead to catastrophe— 15 change often does have unforeseen ramifications.

This caution is still—especially on political major questions—present in the modern Middle West and is its particular contribution to our national relationships.

I think the Middle West's strength is in its customary 20 cautious approach to the day of reckoning in our complex industrial structure and what should be put forward for its solution. That solution will take time, for slapdash approaches never work.

It took thirty years for our great country to recover 25 from the upheaval of the Civil War. It took thirty years for our country to discard the Democrat policy that the way to settle economic troubles was with fiat money. It made inflation the prime issue in 1936. It still is.

Our era has seen some fifty years of war and interna- 30 tional tension piled on top of World War I, and enormous industrial development.

The new West is more worldly minded than the old Middle West was, and, in general, is a balance between the East Coast—with alignment toward Europe and the 35 Atlantic countries—and the West Coast—with its interests in Asian affairs.

There is still a noticeable difference between the atmosphere in the Middle West and that of the Eastern states. It is more free and easy. There are not as many old families 40 with local supremacy. The East's "money power"—as the old Middle West called it—is now the "Establishment."

The parallel factor is the desire on the part of many heads of families in many lines of activity to change from the tensions and insecurity of life in the big cities to the 45 pleasure and comfort that come from the security of living in smaller towns. In the Middle West, it has increasingly taken the form of people remaining in the smaller cities and giving them new life and intelligence. This has strengthened smaller communities and offset the flow of Middle 50 Westerners to the big cities. There are, however, signs that cities in general are no longer content to be corrupt. There is pragmatic awakening that can mean a new leadership—with a growing understanding of their problems and responsibilities. This newly awakened urban leadership, 55 joining the Midwest and small city leadership in the quest for stability, may just possibly be the salvation of the big cities.

That is a reversal of the trend that started some years ago that seemed to threaten the stagnation of the Middle West by the tide of migration to the big metropolitan areas.

60   The Jews are almost the only people in America today—or, in the world, for that matter—that, during Passover, recall to the memory of the present generation their tremendous racial achievements, their leadership and their heroes of long ago.

65   On the other hand, the freedom of communications—the easy movement of Americans around their great country—and the ease of changing occupations are remarkable in the United States. All contribute to breaking down ethnic and religious group prejudices.

70   Possibly one reason we have so much difficulty in resolving our problems of a complex society is that we have tended to lose not only a sense of national identity, but a sense of pride in and a strong feeling for the special qualities of our local area.

75   What Americans must find is a way to square their diversification, and the freedom upon which it is based, with the older sense of identity and of stability. Perhaps the contemporary Middle West offers the answer in its freer acceptance of people as they are, and as they are capable 80 of becoming—a surviving characteristic of mutual helpfulness, willingness to accept change—not for change's sake, but on its merits.

GO ON TO THE NEXT PAGE ➤

16. The author would agree that the "old Middle West" remains

    (A) intact in only a few areas
    (B) only in tales that are told
    (C) unchanged in many small towns
    (D) in spirit but is lost in practice
    (E) a reality only to children who view it on television

17. The author feels that the strength of the Middle West lies in its

    (A) tolerance of differences of opinion
    (B) worldliness
    (C) cautiousness
    (D) free and easy atmosphere
    (E) ability to recover from strife

18. A current trend that the author finds encouraging is

    (A) a gradual reduction in inflation
    (B) the increasing complexity of the national industrial structure
    (C) realism in domestic and international affairs
    (D) people staying in the smaller towns and cities
    (E) a growing sense of national identity

19. The character of the old Middle West was formed by

    I.   weather hardships
    II. the Gold Rush of 1849
    III. the Civil War

    (A) I only
    (B) II only
    (C) III only
    (D) I and II only
    (E) I and III only

20. The word "pragmatic" in line 51 means

    (A) lethargic
    (B) anticipatory
    (C) flippant
    (D) practical
    (E) governmental

21. The author feels that we have had trouble in solving the problems of a complex society because

    (A) of fiat money
    (B) city governments are corrupt
    (C) our cities are too large to be managed
    (D) we have lost our attachment to local areas
    (E) of the breakdown of ethnic and religious groups

22. It can be inferred that the author is

    (A) a wealthy Middle West businessman
    (B) a radical reformer
    (C) a former political candidate
    (D) a Middle West farmer
    (E) a suburbanite

23. The word "diversification" in line 76 most likely refers to

    (A) jobs
    (B) income
    (C) social stature
    (D) intelligence
    (E) race or religion

24. The author states that the following have been factors leading to the breakdown of ethnic and religious prejudices:

    I.   Ease of communications
    II. Increased education at school and on the job
    III. Ease of changing occupations

    (A) I only
    (B) II only
    (C) III only
    (D) I and II only
    (E) I and III only

STOP

If you finish before time is called, you may check your work on this section only.
Do not turn to any other section in the test.

Section 8

Time: 25 Minutes – Turn to Section 8 (page 245) of your answer sheet to answer the questions in this section. 16 Questions

Directions: For this section, solve each problem and decide which is the best of the choices given. Fill in the corresponding circle on the answer sheet. You may use any available space for scratchwork.

Notes:

1. The use of a calculator is permitted.

2. All numbers used are real numbers.

3. Figures that accompany problems in this test are intended to provide information useful in solving the problems. They are drawn as accurately as possible EXCEPT when it is stated in a specific problem that the figure is not drawn to scale. All figures lie in a plane unless otherwise indicated.

4. Unless otherwise specified, the domain of any function f is assumed to be the set of all real numbers x for which $f(x)$ is a real number.

REFERENCE INFORMATION

$A = \pi r^2$ $A = lw$ $A = \frac{1}{2}bh$ $V = lwh$ $V = \pi r^2 h$ $c^2 = a^2 + b^2$ *Special Right Triangle.*
$C = 2\pi r$

The number of degrees of arc in a circle is 360.
The sum of the measures in degrees of the angles of a triangle is 180.

---

1. If x inversely varies with y and when $x = 5$, $y = 4$, find x when $y = 10$.

    (A) 2
    (B) 3
    (C) 4
    (D) 5
    (E) The answer cannot be determined from the information given.

2. The projected sales of a music book per month is 4,000 at \$1; 1,000 at \$2; 250 at \$4; and 160 at \$5. If x is the price of the book, what are the expected sales per month in terms of x?

    (A) $\dfrac{1,000}{x^2}$

    (B) $\dfrac{1,000}{x}$

    (C) $\dfrac{2,000}{x^2}$

    (D) $\dfrac{4,000}{x^2}$

    (E) $\dfrac{4,000}{x}$

GO ON TO THE NEXT PAGE ➤

3. If $x^{-3} = 27$, what is the value of $x^{\frac{1}{2}}$?

(A) $\frac{1}{3}$

(B) $\sqrt{2}$

(C) $\sqrt{3}$

(D) $\frac{\sqrt{3}}{3}$

(E) $\frac{\sqrt{3}}{4}$

5. The graphs of $y = x + 2$ and $y = x^2 + 4x + 4$ intersect at

(A) $x = 2, x = -1$
(B) $x = -2$ only
(C) $x = -1$ only
(D) $x = -1, x = -2$
(E) $x = 2, x = 1$

4. If $f(x) = 2x + 3^x$, what is the value of $f(2)$?

(A) 9
(B) 10
(C) 11
(D) 12
(E) 13

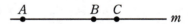

6. Points A, B, and C are on line m, as shown above, such that $AC = \frac{4}{3}AB$. What is the ratio of BC to AB?

(A) $\frac{1}{4}$

(B) $\frac{1}{3}$

(C) $\frac{1}{2}$

(D) $\frac{2}{3}$

(E) The answer cannot be determined from the given information.

GO ON TO THE NEXT PAGE ➤

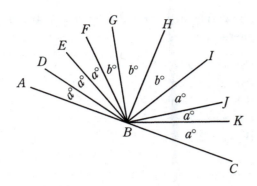

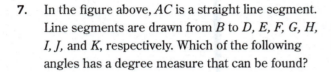

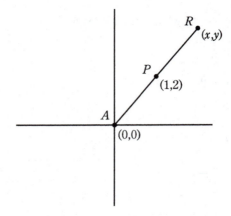

Note: Figure is not drawn to scale.

7. In the figure above, *AC* is a straight line segment. Line segments are drawn from *B* to *D, E, F, G, H, I, J,* and *K,* respectively. Which of the following angles has a degree measure that can be found?

   (A) ∠*FBG*

   (B) ∠*EBG*

   (C) ∠*DBG*

   (D) ∠*GBI*

   (E) ∠*GBJ*

9. If points (1,2) and (*x,y*) are on the line represented in the above diagram, which of the following could represent the value of *x* and *y*?

   (A) $x = 3, y = 5$

   (B) $x = 4, y = 8$

   (C) $x = 5, y = 11$

   (D) $x = 6, y = 15$

   (E) $x = 7, y = 17$

8. Given $8r + 3s = 12$ and $7r + 2s = 9$, find the value of $5(r + s)$.

   (A) 5

   (B) 10

   (C) 15

   (D) 20

   (E) 25

10. If *p* is the average of *x* and *y,* and if *q* is the average of *y* and *z,* and if *r* is the average of *x* and *z,* then what is the average of *x, y,* and *z*?

   (A) $\dfrac{p + q + r}{3}$

   (B) $\dfrac{p + q + r}{2}$

   (C) $\dfrac{2}{3}(p + q + r)$

   (D) $p + q + r$

   (E) $\dfrac{3}{2}(p + q + r)$

GO ON TO THE NEXT PAGE ➤

11. In order to obtain admission into a special school program, all applicants must take a special exam, which is passed by three out of every five applicants. Of those who pass the exam, one-fourth are finally accepted. What is the percentage of all applicants who *fail* to gain admission into the program?

(A) 55
(B) 60
(C) 75
(D) 85
(E) 90

12. Which of the following represents a possible length of the hypotenuse of a triangle whose perpendicular sides are both integers?

(A) $\sqrt{44}$
(B) $\sqrt{45}$
(C) $\sqrt{46}$
(D) $\sqrt{47}$
(E) $\sqrt{48}$

13. In a certain school, special programs in French and Spanish are available. If there are N students enrolled in the French program, and M students enrolled in the Spanish program, including P students who enrolled in both programs, how many students are taking only one (but not both) of the language programs?

(A) $N + M$
(B) $N + M - P$
(C) $N + M + P$
(D) $N + M - 2P$
(E) $N + M + 2P$

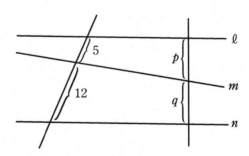

14. Lines ℓ and n are parallel to each other, but line m is parallel to neither of the other two. Find $\dfrac{p}{q}$ if $p + q = 13$.

(A) $\dfrac{13}{5}$
(B) $\dfrac{12}{5}$
(C) $\dfrac{7}{6}$
(D) $\dfrac{1}{5}$
(E) The answer cannot be determined from the information given.

GO ON TO THE NEXT PAGE ➤

15. Ross wants to make up 3 letter combinations. He wants each combination to have exactly 3 of the following letters: *A, B, C,* and *D.* No letter can be used more than once. For example, "*AAB*" is not acceptable. What is the maximum number of such triplets that Ross can make up? (The order of the letters must be considered. Example: "*ABC*" and "*CBA*" are acceptable triplets.)

(A) 6
(B) 9
(C) 24
(D) 27
(E) 64

16. The tables below show the number of uniforms ordered at two schools and the cost of the types of uniforms ordered in child and adult sizes. Find the total cost of all the uniforms in child sizes ordered at School B.

Number of child uniforms ordered

	Type A	Type B	Type C
School A	20	50	40
School B	30	60	50

Cost of uniforms

	Child	Adult
Type A	$9	$12
Type B	$10	$14
Type C	$11	$16

(A) $30
(B) $140
(C) $1,420
(D) $1,480
(E) $1,490

STOP

If you finish before time is called, you may check your work on this section only.
Do not turn to any other section in the test.

Section 9

Time: 20 Minutes – Turn to Section 9 (page 245) of your answer sheet to answer the questions in this section. 19 Questions

Directions: For each question in this section, select the best answer from among the choices given and fill in the corresponding circle on the answer sheet.

Each sentence below has one or two blanks, each blank indicating that something has been omitted. Beneath the sentence are five words or sets of words labeled A through E. Choose the word or set of words that, when inserted in the sentence, best fits the meaning of the sentence as a whole.

Example:

Hoping to _____ the dispute, negotiators proposed a compromise that they felt would be _____ to both labor and management.

(A) enforce...useful

(B) end...divisive

(C) overcome...unattractive

(D) extend...satisfactory

(E) resolve...acceptable

Ⓐ Ⓑ Ⓒ Ⓓ ⬤

1. He was _____ about a rise in the value of the stocks he had recently purchased and was eager to make a change in his investment portfolio.

    (A) fearful
    (B) unconcerned
    (C) hesitant
    (D) amused
    (E) dubious

2. Nature's brute strength is never more _____ than during a major earthquake, when the earth shifts with a sickening sway.

    (A) frightening
    (B) effective
    (C) replaceable
    (D) placating
    (E) complete

3. Instead of providing available funds to education and thus _____ the incidence of crime, the mayor is _____ the funds to the building of more prisons.

    (A) disdain...denying
    (B) revoke...assigning
    (C) abolish...confining
    (D) reduce...diverting
    (E) nourish...planning

4. The dancer excelled neither in grace nor technique, but the _____ musical accompaniment gives the performance a(n) _____ of excellence.

    (A) gradual...sensation
    (B) soothing...mandate
    (C) well-rehearsed...diction
    (D) superb...aura
    (E) chronic...effervescence

GO ON TO THE NEXT PAGE ➤

5. Her fine reputation as a celebrated actress was
_____ by her appearance in a TV soap opera.

(A) enhanced
(B) blemished
(C) appreciated
(D) concluded
(E) intensified

6. The dictator's slow, easy manner and his air of
gentility _____ his firm intention to ensure no
opposition to his planned _____ policies.

(A) revealed...eager
(B) accepted...professional
(C) belied...drastic
(D) disregarded...inane
(E) animated...crude

The two passages below are followed by questions based on their content and on the relationship between the two passages. Answer the questions on the basis of what is <u>stated</u> or <u>implied</u> in the passages and in any introductory material that may be provided.

Questions 7–19 are based on the following passages.

The following passages represent two different views of living—the views of living in the country and of living in the city.

Passage 1

The snow falls gently on our quiet meadow sloping down to Penobscot Bay, with spruce trees back against the gray of the water. A raven croaks from a nearby treetop. Two gulls sail over the house and squawk unintelligibly together. The
5   only other sounds are the wood fire snapping, the kettle steaming on the stove and Pusso purring.

There is no phone to ring, no radio to turn on, no television to watch. We need don no city disguise and ride subways, catch trains, attend cocktail parties or dinners.
10 We can choose and make our own music, reread our favorite books, wear our old clothes, eat when and what we like from a well-stocked root cellar, or happily abstain from food, if we wish, the whole day. There is wood to cut, snow to shovel, mail to answer, but all in our own good time. No
15 one is pushing, no one shoving, no one ordering about. There is no job to lose; we make our own jobs. Free men? Almost.

A neighbor may amble in on snowshoes and bring us word of his horse's health or wife's pregnancy. Over a glass of cider we may talk of snowmobile incursions or hunters'
20 depredations. He may bring us a huge cabbage he has grown and we send him back with a bottle of our rose hips juice and a knitted doll for his little daughter. In our chat beside the fire we will probably not touch on the outside world, though we are not unaware of what stirs the nation.

25 The newspaper, reaching us by mail, brings us echoes of an inconsequential election between two shadow-boxing candidates for an office no one should covet. We read that two high officials, the Episcopal Bishop of New York and the chief of the Russian delegation to the United Nations,

30 have separately been held up in daylight and robbed by armed men in Central Park. We learn that invaders are entering classrooms in Manhattan's public schools and at knife or gunpoint relieving teachers of their cash and trinkets before their open-mouthed pupils.

35 We thank our lucky stars that we live out in the wilderness, that we are not on congested streets and highways or clustered in high-rise city rookeries, with jangling noise and turmoil all about, that we are not in smog, that we can drink clean clear water, not fluoridized or chlorinated, from
40 our bubbling spring, that our homegrown food is not stale, preserved or embalmed and bought from the supermarket.

We are thankful for what the wilderness makes possible. Peace, progress, prosperity? We prefer peace, quiet, and frugality.

Passage 2

45 You look out the window of your one-bedroom apartment and see swarms of people in the streets as if the day never ends. You live with the interminable sounds of the cars, trucks, and repair services and hassles encountered. But there is an excitement that makes you alive. You can leave
50 your apartment at three in the morning and go to a coffee shop which remains open. You can lose your identity and forget about your problems by mingling during the day with the thousands of people roaming the streets. You may be walking right next to a famous celebrity or a lowly degen-
55 erate. But it doesn't matter. It is the excitement that counts, the fact that you can call anybody anytime by phone, get up-to-the-minute news through radio, TV, or Internet. You can choose from hundreds of international restaurants, and although the food may not be homegrown, you certainly
60 have the exciting ambience of a packed restaurant with constant movement. You can choose from the best of hospitals and doctors, although it may take you some time to get an appointment with a doctor or get to the hospital because of traffic. But the noise, the inconveniences, the muggings,

GO ON TO THE NEXT PAGE ➤

65 all this goes with the territory—with the excitement. You
can always escape to the country by train, car, bus, or even
plane if you need to. However, city living is certainly not
for everyone. And your ability to live or even survive in a
city depends on your temperament, your principles, your
70 occupation and your interests. But for many, the trade-off
for a vibrant life, a pulse which never ends, and access to
almost every cultural event almost at any time is certainly
a lure to live in the city environment.

7. The general feeling running through Passage 1 is
one of

(A) guarded resentment
(B) tolerable boredom
(C) restless indecision
(D) peaceful satisfaction
(E) marked indifference

8. Which of the following is the most appropriate
title for Passage 1?

(A) Winter in the Country
(B) The Frills Aren't Needed
(C) Peace, Progress, and Prosperity
(D) Life Goes On
(E) A Lack of Conveniences

9. The author's reference to "an inconsequential
election between two shadow-boxing candidates"
(lines 26–27) indicates that the author

(A) has no faith in politicians
(B) is opposed to professional prizefighting
(C) does not believe in having any elections
(D) prefers that people govern themselves
(E) is of the opinion that all elections are fixed

10. The author of Passage 1 states or implies that

(A) there is no work to be done
(B) he is a completely free man
(C) his wife is pregnant
(D) he reads no newspapers
(E) he has a farm

11. Of the states below, the location of the author's
home in Passage 1 is most likely in the state of

(A) Arizona
(B) Florida
(C) Maine
(D) Louisiana
(E) Georgia

12. It can be inferred from Passage 2 that the author
believes that in the city

(A) many people live in one-bedroom apartments
(B) when eating out, you'll never get homegrown
food
(C) you can meet rich and poor at the most
expensive restaurants
(D) losing one's identity is considered a "plus"
(E) friendliness is a "way of life"

13. The word "interminable" in line 47 means

(A) loud
(B) harsh
(C) ongoing
(D) bright
(E) close

14. The passages differ in that

(A) in Passage 2, there is more of a tendency to
qualify the good with the bad
(B) in Passage 1 there are no hospitals in the village, whereas there are many in Passage 2
(C) the author of Passage 1 believes that everyone should live in the country, whereas in
Passage 2 the author believes that everyone
would do well in the city
(D) in Passage 1 there are no post offices to
deliver mail
(E) in Passage 1 the author never reads newspapers, whereas the author in Passage 2 is
interested in up-to-the-minute news

15. Which is more likely to be surprising to the
respective author?

(A) Passage 1 author: reading a headline in a
news paper: "Scientists Find Cancer Cure"
(B) Passage 2 author: speaking with a famous
movie celebrity in the street
(C) Passage 2 author: finding a movie at two in
the morning
(D) Passage 1 author: seeing some people skip a
few meals
(E) Passage 2 author: hearing someone complain
about city living

GO ON TO THE NEXT PAGE ➤

16. The word "frugality" in line 44 means

    (A) progress
    (B) stinginess
    (C) wastefulness
    (D) poverty
    (E) quiet

17. The word "don" in line 8 is related to

    (A) motion
    (B) purchasing goods
    (C) clothing
    (D) eating
    (E) fishing

18. We can infer from the authors of each passage that

    (A) the author of Passage 1 believes most news is bad whereas the author of Passage 2 believes most news is good
    (B) the author of Passage 1 believes politics and elections are useless whereas the author in Passage 2 believes they are necessary
    (C) the author of Passage 1 believes that city schools are dangerous and prefers not to have his or her children attend them whereas the author of Passage 2 may agree but accepts the situation
    (D) the author of Passage 1 believes only the parks in the cities are safe whereas the author of Passage 2 believes that crime "goes with the territory"
    (E) one author likes home-grown food, whereas the other does not

19. Which situation or condition is described or mentioned in one passage but not in the other?

    (I) The sociable and friendly nature of the people
    (II) The positive effects of the environment
    (III) The impossibility of attaining any news from outside locations or sources

    (A) I only
    (B) II only
    (C) III only
    (D) I and II only
    (E) I, II, and III

STOP

If you finish before time is called, you may check your work on this section only.
Do not turn to any other section in the test.

Section 10

Time: 10 Minutes – Turn to Section 10 (page 245) of your answer sheet to answer the questions in this section. 14 Questions

Directions: For each question in this section, select the best answer from among the choices given and fill in the corresponding circle on the answer sheet.

The following sentences test correctness and effectiveness of expression. Part of each sentence or the entire sentence is underlined; beneath each sentence are five ways of phrasing the underlined material. Choice A repeats the original phrasing; the other four choices are different. If you think the original phrasing produces a better sentence than any of the alternatives, select Choice A; if not, select one of the other choices.

In making your selection, follow the requirements of standard written English; that is, pay attention to grammar, choice of words, sentence construction, and punctuation. Your selection should result in the most effective sentence—clear and precise, without awkwardness or ambiguity.

EXAMPLE:

Laura Ingalls Wilder published her first book <u>and she was sixty-five years old then</u>.

(A) and she was sixty-five years old then

(B) when she was sixty-five

(C) at age sixty-five years old

(D) upon the reaching of sixty-five years

(E) at the time when she was sixty-five

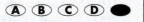

1. The bank robber approached the teller quietly, cautiously, <u>and in an unpretentious manner</u>.

   (A) and in an unpretentious manner
   (B) and with no pretense
   (C) and by acting unpretentious
   (D) and by acting unpretentiously
   (E) and unpretentiously

2. The conduct of the judge <u>with the accused</u> seemed very unfair to the jury.

   (A) with the accused
   (B) toward the accused
   (C) as to the man who was accused
   (D) and the accused
   (E) as far as the accused was concerned

GO ON TO THE NEXT PAGE ➤

3. Every IT support technician in the office <u>except she</u> was out sick at least one day during the past month.

   (A) except she
   (B) except her
   (C) excepting she
   (D) but not her
   (E) outside of her

4. Max is a professor of theoretical physics, <u>while his brothers are architects</u> with outstanding reputations.

   (A) while his brothers are architects
   (B) also his brothers are architects
   (C) his brothers architects
   (D) as his brothers are architects
   (E) and his brothers are architects

5. A reward was offered <u>to whoever would return the dog to its owner</u>.

   (A) to whoever would return the dog to its owner
   (B) to whomever would return the dog to its owner
   (C) to whosoever would return the dog to its owner
   (D) to whomsoever would return the dog to its owner
   (E) to whichever person would return the dog to its owner

6. <u>Irregardless of the outcome of the battle</u>, neither side will be able to claim a decisive victory.

   (A) Irregardless of the outcome of the battle
   (B) Irregardless of how the battle ends
   (C) Regardless of the outcome of the battle
   (D) Despite the outcome of the battle
   (E) Irregardless of the battle

7. One of the finest examples of early Greek sculpture <u>are to be found in the British Museum</u> in London.

   (A) are to be found in the British Museum
   (B) were to be found in the British Museum
   (C) are found in the British Museum
   (D) is to be found in the British Museum
   (E) are in the British Museum

8. <u>We were surprised at him canceling the order with-out giving any previous indication of his intentions.</u>

   (A) We were surprised at him canceling the order without giving any previous indication of his intentions.
   (B) We were surprised that he canceled the order and didn't tell anyone.
   (C) His canceling the order surprised us all.
   (D) We were surprised at his canceling the order without giving any previous indication of his intentions.
   (E) We were surprised at him canceling the order and not letting anyone know about it.

9. When going for an interview, <u>a high school graduate should be prepared to answer the questions that will be asked of him without hesitation</u>.

   (A) a high school graduate should be prepared to answer the questions that will be asked of him without hesitation
   (B) a high school graduate should without hesitation be prepared to answer the questions that will be asked of him
   (C) a high school graduate should be prepared without hesitation to answer the questions that will be asked of him
   (D) a high school graduate should be prepared to answer without hesitation the questions that will be asked of him
   (E) a high school graduate should be prepared to answer the questions without hesitation that will be asked of him

10. When a student learns a foreign language, he or she must not only learn to speak and write it, <u>but understand the culture of those who speak it</u>.

    (A) but understand the culture of those who speak it
    (B) and he or she must understand the culture of those who speak it
    (C) he or she must understand the culture of those who speak it
    (D) but must also understand the culture of those who speak it
    (E) but in addition he or she must also understand the culture of those who speak it

GO ON TO THE NEXT PAGE ➤

11. The paintings of Dali, <u>like many artists</u>, have been both applauded as great masterpieces and dismissed as rubbish.

   (A) like many artists
   (B) like most other artists
   (C) like the paintings of many artists
   (D) like many other paintings
   (E) like those of many other artists

12. <u>Because the patient laid in bed</u> for several months, she developed pneumonia.

   (A) Because the patient laid in bed
   (B) Because the patient had laid in bed
   (C) Because the patient had lain in bed
   (D) Because the patient is laying in bed
   (E) Because the patient lies in bed

13. The pollution bills recently passed by the House are <u>different than those</u> that were vetoed earlier.

   (A) different than those
   (B) different from those
   (C) different to those
   (D) different from the earlier ones
   (E) different to the ones

14. <u>Neither you nor I are going to agree</u> with the speaker; sometimes, however, it is a good idea to listen to someone whom one may disagree with.

   (A) Neither you nor I are going to agree
   (B) Neither of us are going to agree
   (C) Neither you nor me is going to agree
   (D) Neither you nor I am going to agree
   (E) Neither I nor you am going to agree

STOP

If you finish before time is called, you may check your work on this section only.
Do not turn to any other section in the test.

How did you do on this test?

Step 1.   Go to the Answer Key

Step 2.   Calculate your "raw score."

Step 3.   Get your "scaled score" for the test by referring to the Raw Score/Scaled Score Conversion Tables.

**THERE'S ALWAYS ROOM
FOR IMPROVEMENT!**

ANSWER KEY FOR PRACTICE TEST 2

Math

Section 2

	Correct Answer
1	D
2	E
3	D
4	E
5	C
6	E
7	E
8	E
9	B
10	E
11	E
12	D
13	E
14	C
15	E
16	C
17	E
18	E
19	E
20	D

Number correct

Number incorrect

Section 3

	Correct Answer
1	D
2	C
3	B
4	E
5	E
6	A
7	B
8	D

Number correct

Number incorrect

Student-Produced Response Questions

9	24
10	10
11	2300
12	11
13	125
14	25
15	4
16	3
17	36.2
18	7

Number correct

Number incorrect

Section 6

	Correct Answer
1	D
2	B
3	A
4	B
5	B
6	D
7	D
8	B

Number correct

Number incorrect

Section 8

Student-Produced Response Questions

9	$\frac{1}{1}$, 1, 1.0, etc.
10	15
11	50
12	3
13	18
14	1.999, 1.998... .001, or any number r such that $0 < r < 2$, like $\frac{1}{2}, \frac{1}{4}$, etc.
15	135
16	100
17	3
18	4

Number correct

Number incorrect

Section 8

	Correct Answer
1	A
2	D
3	D
4	E
5	D
6	B
7	C
8	C
9	B
10	A
11	D
12	B
13	D
14	E
15	C
16	C

Number correct

Number incorrect

ANSWER KEY FOR PRACTICE TEST 2

Critical reading

Section 4

	Correct Answer
1	E
2	D
3	D
4	D
5	C
6	E
7	B
8	D
9	E
10	C
11	B
12	E
13	D
14	B
15	A
16	C
17	B
18	E
19	D
20	E
21	C
22	E
23	E
24	B

Number correct

Number incorrect

Section 7

	Correct Answer
1	C
2	D
3	C
4	E
5	A
6	C
7	B
8	A
9	E
10	D
11	C
12	E
13	C
14	D
15	D
16	B
17	C
18	D
19	A
20	D
21	D
22	C
23	E
24	E

Number correct

Number incorrect

Section 9

	Correct Answer
1	E
2	A
3	D
4	D
5	B
6	C
7	D
8	B
9	A
10	E
11	C
12	D
13	C
14	A
15	A
16	B
17	C
18	C
19	A

Number correct

Number incorrect

ANSWER KEY FOR PRACTICE TEST 2
Writing

Section 1

_____

Essay score

Section 5

	Correct Answer
1	B
2	E
3	D
4	B
5	E
6	C
7	C
8	A
9	E
10	E
11	C
12	B
13	C
14	E
15	C
16	C
17	A
18	D
19	A
20	D
21	E
22	A
23	C
24	C
25	A
26	B
27	C
28	D
29	D
30	B
31	E
32	A
33	D
34	C
35	D

_____

Number correct

_____

Number incorrect

Section 10

	Correct Answer
1	E
2	B
3	B
4	E
5	A
6	C
7	D
8	D
9	D
10	D
11	E
12	C
13	B
14	D

_____

Number correct

_____

Number incorrect

Scoring the SAT Practice Test

Check your responses with the correct answers on the previous pages. Fill in the blanks below and do the calculations to get your Math, Critical Reading, and Writing raw scores. Use the table to find your Math, Critical Reading, and Writing scaled scores.

Get Your Math Score

How many Math questions did you get **right**?

Section 2: Questions 1–20   _____

Section 6: Questions 1–18   + _____

Section 8: Questions 1–16   + _____

Total   = _____ **(A)**

How many Math questions did you get **wrong**?

Section 2: Questions 1–20   _____

Section 6: Questions 1–18   + _____

Section 8: Questions 1–16   + _____

Total   = _____

$\times$ 0.25   = _____ **(B)**

A – B   = _____

Math Raw Score

Round Math raw score to the nearest whole number.

_____

Use the Score Conversion Table to find your Math scaled score.

_____

Get Your Critical Reading Score

How many Critical Reading questions did you get **right**?

Section 4: Questions 1–24   _____

Section 7: Questions 1–24   + _____

Section 9: Questions 1–19   + _____

Total   = _____ **(A)**

How many Critical Reading questions did you get **wrong**?

Section 4: Questions 1–24   _____

Section 7: Questions 1–24   + _____

Section 9: Questions 1–19   + _____

Total   = _____

$\times$ 0.25   = _____ **(B)**

A – B   = _____

Critical Reading Raw Score

Round Critical Reading raw score to the nearest whole number.

_____

Use the Score Conversion Table to find your Critical Reading scaled score.

_____

Get Your Writing Score

How many multiple-choice Writing questions did you get **right**?

Section 5: Questions 1–35 _____

Section 10: Questions 1–14 + _____

Total = _____ **(A)**

How many multiple-choice Writing questions did you get **wrong**?

Section 5: Questions 1–35 _____

Section 10: Questions 1–14 + _____

Total = _____

$\times$ 0.25 = _____ **(B)**

A – B = _____

Writing Raw Score

Round Writing raw score to the nearest whole number.

_____

Use the Score Conversion Table to find your Writing multiple-choice scaled score.

_____

Estimate your Essay score using the Essay Scoring Guide.

_____

Use the SAT Score Conversion Table for Writing Composite to find your Writing scaled score. You will need your Writing raw score and your Essay score to use this table.

_____

SAT Score conversion table

Raw Score	Critical Reading Scaled Score	Math Scaled Score	Writing Multiple-Choice Scaled Score*	Raw Score	Critical Reading Scaled Score	Math Scaled Score	Writing Multiple-Choice Scaled Score*
67	800			31	510	550	60
66	800			30	510	540	58
65	790			29	500	530	57
64	770			28	490	520	56
63	750			27	490	520	55
62	740			26	480	510	54
61	730			25	480	500	53
60	720			24	470	490	52
59	700			23	460	480	51
58	690			22	460	480	50
57	690			21	450	470	49
56	680			20	440	460	48
55	670			19	440	450	47
54	660	800		18	430	450	46
53	650	790		17	420	440	45
52	650	760		16	420	430	44
51	640	740		15	410	420	44
50	630	720		14	400	410	43
49	620	710	80	13	400	410	42
48	620	700	80	12	390	400	41
47	610	680	80	11	380	390	40
46	600	670	79	10	370	380	39
45	600	660	78	9	360	370	38
44	590	650	76	8	350	360	38
43	590	640	74	7	340	350	37
42	580	630	73	6	330	340	36
41	570	630	71	5	320	330	35
40	570	620	70	4	310	320	34
39	560	610	69	3	300	310	32
38	550	600	67	2	280	290	31
37	550	590	66	1	270	280	30
36	540	580	65	0	250	260	28
35	540	580	64	−1	230	240	27
34	530	570	63	−2	210	220	25
33	520	560	62	−3	200	200	23
32	520	550	61	−4 and below	200	200	20

This table is for use only with the test in this book.

* The Writing multiple-choice score is reported on a 20–80 scale. Use the SAT Score Conversion Table for Writing Composite for the total writing scaled score.

SAT Score conversion table for writing composite

Writing Multiple-Choice Raw Score	Essay Raw Score						
	0	1	2	3	4	5	6
−12	200	200	200	210	240	270	300
−11	200	200	200	210	240	270	300
−10	200	200	200	210	240	270	300
−9	200	200	200	210	240	270	300
−8	200	200	200	210	240	270	300
−7	200	200	200	210	240	270	300
−6	200	200	200	210	240	270	300
−5	200	200	200	210	240	270	300
−4	200	200	200	230	270	300	330
−3	200	210	230	250	290	320	350
−2	200	230	250	280	310	340	370
−1	210	240	260	290	320	360	380
0	230	260	280	300	340	370	400
1	240	270	290	320	350	380	410
2	250	280	300	330	360	390	420
3	260	290	310	340	370	400	430
4	270	300	320	350	380	410	440
5	280	310	330	360	390	420	450
6	290	320	340	360	400	430	460
7	290	330	340	370	410	440	470
8	300	330	350	380	410	450	470
9	310	340	360	390	420	450	480
10	320	350	370	390	430	460	490
11	320	360	370	400	440	470	500
12	330	360	380	410	440	470	500
13	340	370	390	420	450	480	510
14	350	380	390	420	460	490	520
15	350	380	400	430	460	500	530
16	360	390	410	440	470	500	530
17	370	400	420	440	480	510	540
18	380	410	420	450	490	520	550
19	380	410	430	460	490	530	560
20	390	420	440	470	500	530	560
21	400	430	450	480	510	540	570
22	410	440	460	480	520	550	580

Writing Multiple-Choice Raw Score	Essay Raw Score						
	0	1	2	3	4	5	6
23	420	450	470	490	530	560	590
24	420	460	470	500	540	570	600
25	430	460	480	510	540	580	610
26	440	470	490	520	550	590	610
27	450	480	500	530	560	590	620
28	460	490	510	540	570	600	630
29	470	500	520	550	580	610	640
30	480	510	530	560	590	620	650
31	490	520	540	560	600	630	660
32	500	530	550	570	610	640	670
33	510	540	550	580	620	650	680
34	510	550	560	590	630	660	690
35	520	560	570	600	640	670	700
36	530	560	580	610	650	680	710
37	540	570	590	620	660	690	720
38	550	580	600	630	670	700	730
39	560	600	610	640	680	710	740
40	580	610	620	650	690	720	750
41	590	620	640	660	700	730	760
42	600	630	650	680	710	740	770
43	610	640	660	690	720	750	780
44	620	660	670	700	740	770	800
45	640	670	690	720	750	780	800
46	650	690	700	730	770	800	800
47	670	700	720	750	780	800	800
48	680	720	730	760	800	800	800
49	680	720	730	760	800	800	800

Chart for self-appraisal based on the practice test you have just taken

The Chart for Self-Appraisal below tells you quickly where your SAT strengths and weaknesses lie. Check or circle the appropriate box in accordance with the number of your correct answers for each area of the Practice Test you have just taken.

	Writing (Multiple-Choice)	Sentence Completions	Reading Comprehension	Math Questions*
EXCELLENT	42–49	16–19	40–48	44–54
GOOD	37–41	13–15	35–39	32–43
FAIR	31–36	9–12	26–34	27–31
POOR	20–30	5–8	17–25	16–26
VERY POOR	0–19	0–4	0–16	0–15

*Sections 2, 6, 8 only.

Note: In our tests, we have chosen to have Section 3 as the experimental section. We have also chosen it to be a math section since we felt that students may need more practice in the math area than in the verbal area. Note that on the actual SAT you will take, the order of the sections can vary and you will not know which one is experimental, so it is wise to answer all sections and not to leave any section out.

SAT-I VERBAL AND MATH SCORE/PERCENTILE CONVERSION TABLE

Critical reading and writing

SAT scaled verbal score	Percentile rank
800	99.7+
790	99.5
740–780	99
700–730	97
670–690	95
640–660	91
610–630	85
580–600	77
550–570	68
510–540	57
480–500	46
440–470	32
410–430	21
380–400	13
340–370	6
300–330	2
230–290	1
200–220	0–0.5

Math

SAT scaled math score	Percentile rank
800	99.5+
770–790	99.5
720–760	99
670–710	97
640–660	94
610–630	89
590–600	84
560–580	77
530–550	68
510–520	59
480–500	48
450–470	37
430–440	26
390–420	16
350–380	8
310–340	2
210–300	0.5
200	0

EXPLANATORY ANSWERS FOR PRACTICE TEST 2

THE SAT SCORING GUIDE

Section 1: Essay

Score of 6	Score of 5	Score of 4
An essay in this category is *outstanding*, demonstrating *clear and consistent mastery*, although it may have a few minor errors. A typical essay	An essay in this category is *effective*, demonstrating *reasonably consistent mastery*, although it will have occasional errors or lapses in quality. A typical essay	An essay in this category is *competent*, demonstrating *adequate mastery*, although it will have lapses in quality. A typical essay
• effectively and insightfully develops a point of view on the issue and demonstrates outstanding critical thinking, using clearly appropriate examples, reasons, and other evidence to support its position	• effectively develops a point of view on the issue and demonstrates strong critical thinking, generally using appropriate examples, reasons, and other evidence to support its position	• develops a point of view on the issue and demonstrates competent critical thinking, using adequate examples, reasons, and other evidence to support its position
• is well organized and clearly focused, demonstrating clear coherence and smooth progression of ideas	• is well organized and focused, demonstrating coherence and progression of ideas	• is generally organized and focused, demonstrating some coherence and progression of ideas
• exhibits skillful use of language, using a varied, accurate, and apt vocabulary	• exhibits facility in the use of language, using appropriate vocabulary	• exhibits adequate but inconsistent facility in the use of language, using generally appropriate vocabulary
• demonstrates meaningful variety in sentence structure	• demonstrates variety in sentence structure	• demonstrates some variety in sentence structure
• is free of most errors in grammar, usage, and mechanics	• is generally free of most errors in grammar, usage, and mechanics	• has some errors in grammar, usage, and mechanics

Score of 3	Score of 2	Score of 1
An essay in this category is *inadequate*, but demonstrates *developing mastery*, and is marked by ONE OR MORE of the following weaknesses:	An essay in this category is *seriously-limited*, demonstrating *little mastery*, and is flawed by ONE OR MORE of the following weaknesses:	An essay in this category is *fundamentally lacking*, demonstrating *very little* or *no mastery*, and is severely flawed by ONE OR MORE of the following weaknesses:
• develops a point of view on the issue, demonstrating some critical thinking, but may do so inconsistently or use inadequate examples, reasons, or other evidence to support its position	• develops a point of view on the issue that is vague or seriously limited, demonstrating weak critical thinking, providing inappropriate or insufficient examples, reasons, or other evidence to support its position	• develops no viable point of view on the issue, or provides little or no evidence to support its position
• is limited in its organization or focus, or may demonstrate some lapses in coherence or progression of ideas	• is poorly organized and/or focused, or demonstrates serious problems with coherence or progression of ideas	• is disorganized or unfocused, resulting in a disjointed or incoherent essay
• displays developing facility in the use of language, but sometimes uses weak vocabulary or inappropriate word choice	• displays very little facility in the use of language, using very limited vocabulary or incorrect word choice	• displays fundamental errors in vocabulary
• lacks variety or demonstrates problems in sentence structure	• demonstrates frequent problems in sentence structure	• demonstrates severe flaws in sentence structure
• contains an accumulation of errors in grammar, usage, and mechanics	• contains errors in grammar, usage, and mechanics so serious that meaning is somewhat obscured	• contains pervasive errors in grammar, usage, or mechanics that persistently interfere with meaning

Essays not written on the essay assignment will receive a score of zero.

EXPLANATORY ANSWERS FOR PRACTICE TEST 2

Section 2: Math

> When a specific Math Strategy is referred to in the solution, study that strategy, which you will find in "19 Math Strategies."

1.   Choice D is correct.

$$Given: 500w = 3 \times 700 \qquad \boxed{1}$$

(Use Strategy 13: Find an unknown by dividing.)

Divide $\boxed{1}$ by 500, giving

$$\frac{500w}{500} = \frac{3 \times 700}{500}$$

(Use Strategy 19: Factor and reduce first. Then multiply.)

$$w = \frac{3 \times 7 \times \cancel{100}}{5 \times \cancel{100}}$$

$$w = \frac{21}{5}$$

2.   Choice E is correct.

$$Given: \frac{3+y}{y} = 7 \qquad \boxed{1}$$

(Use Strategy 13: Find an unknown by multiplying.)

Multiply $\boxed{1}$ by y, to get

$$\cancel{y}\left(\frac{3+y}{\cancel{y}}\right) = (7)y$$

$$3 + y = 7y$$
$$3 = 6y$$
$$\frac{3}{6} = y$$
$$\frac{1}{2} = y$$

3.   Choice D is correct. **(Use Strategy 2: Translate from words to algebra.)**

x is a multiple of 9, gives

$$x \in \{9, 18, 27, 36, 45, 54, \ldots \} \qquad \boxed{1}$$

x is a multiple of 12, gives

$$x \in \{12, 24, 36, 48, 60, 72, \ldots \} \qquad \boxed{2}$$

The smallest value that appears in both sets $\boxed{1}$ and $\boxed{2}$ is 36.

4.   Choice E is correct.

Method 1:

$$Given: \quad (r-s)(t-s)$$
$$+ (s-r)(s-t) \qquad \boxed{1}$$

(Use Strategy 17: Use the given information effectively.)

Recognizing that $(s-r) = -1(r-s) \qquad \boxed{2}$

$$(s-t) = -1(t-s) \qquad \boxed{3}$$

Substituting $\boxed{2}$ and $\boxed{3}$ into $\boxed{1}$, we get

$$(r-s)(t-s) + [-1(r-s)][-1(t-s)] =$$
$$(r-s)(t-s) + (-1)(-1)(r-s)(t-s) =$$
$$2(r-s)(t-s)$$

Method 2:

$$Given: (r-s)(t-s) + (s-r)(s-t) \qquad \boxed{1}$$

Multiply both pairs of quantities from $\boxed{1}$, giving

$$rt - rs - st + s^2 + s^2 - st - rs + rt =$$
$$2rt - 2rs - 2st + 2s^2 =$$
$$2(rt - rs - st + s^2) =$$
$$2[r(t-s) - s(t-s)] =$$
$$2(r-s)(t-s)$$

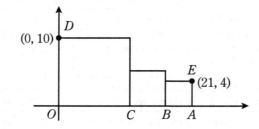

5.   Choice C is correct.

We want to find the area of the middle square, which is $(CB)^2$. (**Use Strategy 3: The whole equals the sum of its parts.**)

$$OA = OC + CB + BA \qquad \boxed{1}$$

From the diagram, we get

$$OA = 21 \qquad \boxed{2}$$
$$AE = 4 \qquad \boxed{3}$$
$$OD = 10 \qquad \boxed{4}$$

Since each figure is a square, we get

$$BA = AE \qquad \boxed{5}$$
$$OC = OD \qquad \boxed{6}$$

Substituting $\boxed{5}$ into $\boxed{3}$, we get

$$AE = BA = 4 \qquad \boxed{7}$$

Substituting $\boxed{6}$ into $\boxed{4}$, we get

$$OD = OC = 10 \qquad \boxed{8}$$

Substituting $\boxed{2}$, $\boxed{7}$, and $\boxed{8}$ into $\boxed{1}$, we get

$$21 = 10 + CB + 4$$
$$21 = 14 + CB$$
$$7 = CB \qquad \boxed{9}$$

Area of square II = $(CB)^2$
Area of square II = 7^2 (From $\boxed{9}$)
Area of square II = 49

6.   Choice E is correct.

Given: 1 cup = 100 grams $\boxed{1}$
1 cake = 75 grams $\boxed{2}$
1 pie = 225 grams $\boxed{3}$

Using $\boxed{1}$, we get

4 cups = 4(100 grams)
4 cups = 400 gramsww $\boxed{4}$

(**Using Strategy 8: When all choices must be tested, start with E and work backward.**)

2 cakes and 1 pie is Choice E. $\boxed{5}$

Substituting $\boxed{2}$ and $\boxed{3}$ in $\boxed{5}$, we get

2(75 grams) + 225 grams =
150 grams + 225 grams =
375 grams $\boxed{6}$

Since $\boxed{6}$ is less than $\boxed{4}$, there *is enough* in 4 cups. So Choice E is correct.

7.   Choice E is correct.

I: Slope is defined as $\frac{y_2 - y_1}{x_2 - x_1}$ where (x_1,y_1) and (x_2,y_2) are points on the line. Thus here $0 = x_1$, $a = y_1$, $a = x_2$, and $0 = y_2$.

Thus $\frac{y_2 - y_1}{x_2 - x_1} = \frac{0 - a}{a - 0} = -1$: I is therefore true.

(**Use Strategy 18: Know and use facts about triangles.**)

II: The triangle created is an isosceles right triangle with sides a, a, $a\sqrt{2}$. Thus II is true.

III: In an isosceles right triangle, the interior angles of the triangle are 90-45-45 degrees. Thus III is true.

8.   Choice E is correct. (**Use Strategy 8: When all choices must be tested, start with E and work backward.**) Choice A is incorrect: On the number line b is to the left of -2, so this implies that b is less than -2 (written as $b < -2$). Since $b < -2$, b is certainly less than -1 (written as $b < -1$). Thus Choice A is incorrect. Choice B is false because if $b < -2$, the absolute value of b (denoted as $|b|$) must be greater than 2. Choice C is false: c is positive ($c > +3 > 0$) so $c \neq -|c|$, since $-|c|$ is negative. Choice D is false: Since a and b are negative numbers and since $a < b$, $|a| > |b|$. Choice E is correct and Choice D is incorrect.

9.   Choice B is correct. (**Use Strategy 2: Translate from words to algebra.**) We are told:

$$A + 8 + A + 1 + A + 2$$
$$= A + A + 1 + A + 2 + A + 3 \qquad \boxed{1}$$

(**Use Strategy 1: Cancel expressions that appear on both sides of an equation.**)

Each side contains an A, $A + 1$, and $A + 2$. Canceling each of these from each side, we get

$$\cancel{A} + 8 + \cancel{A} + \cancel{1} + \cancel{A} + \cancel{2} = \cancel{A} + \cancel{A} + \cancel{1} +$$
$$\cancel{A} + \cancel{2} + A + 3.$$

$$\text{Thus, } 8 = A + 3$$
$$5 = A$$

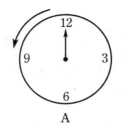
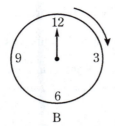

A   B

10. Choice E is correct. **(Use Strategy 11: New definitions lead to easy questions.)**

By the definition of a move, every 4 moves brings each hand back to 12.

Thus, after 4, 8, 12, and 16 moves, respectively, each hand is at 12.

Hand A, moving counterclockwise, moves to 9 on its 17th move.

Hand B, moving clockwise, moves to 3 on its 17th move.

11. Choice E is correct. **(Use Strategy 17: Use the given information effectively.)**

$$Given: w = 7r + 6r + 5r + 4r + 3r$$
$$Then, w = 25r \qquad \boxed{1}$$

We are told we must add something to w so that the resulting sum will be divisible by 7 for every positive integer r.

Check the choices. **(Use Strategy 8: Start with Choice E.)** Add $3r$ to $\boxed{1}$

$$25r + 3r = 28r = 7(4r)$$

will always be divisible by 7. Thus, Choice E is correct.

12. Choice D is correct. **(Use Strategy 7: Use numerics to help find the answer.)** To obtain the maximum number of members of S, choose the numbers as small as possible; hence $1 + 3 + 5 + 7 + 9 + 11 + 13 + 15 = 64$.

Hence, the maximum is 8.

13. Choice E is correct. **(Use Strategy 7: Use numerics to help find the answer.)** I, II, and III are correct.

Examples: $(2^3)^2 = 2^6 = 64,$

$2^{3+2} = 2^3 \, 2^2 = 32; \; (2 \times 3)^2 = 2^2 \, 3^2 = 36.$

14. Choice C is correct. **(Use Strategy 2: Translate from words to algebra.)**

The number of hours from 7:00 A.M. to 5:00 P.M. is 10.

The number of hours from 1:00 P.M. to 7:00 P.M. is 6.

He worked 10 hours for 3 days and 6 hours for 3 days. Thus,

$$\text{Total hours} = 3(10) + 3(6)$$
$$= 30 + 18$$
$$\text{Total hours} = 48 \qquad \boxed{1}$$
$$\text{Total earnings} = \text{Hours worked} \times$$
$$\text{Hourly rate} \qquad \boxed{2}$$
Given: He earns \$10 per hour $\qquad \boxed{3}$

Substituting $\boxed{1}$ and $\boxed{3}$ into $\boxed{2}$, we get

Total earnings $= 48 \times \$10$
Total earnings $= \$480$

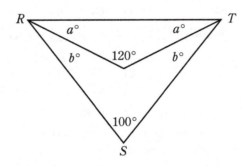

15. Choice E is correct. **(Use Strategy 3: The whole equals the sum of its parts.)**

The sum of the angles in a $\Delta = 180$. For the small triangle we have

$$120 + a + a = 180$$
$$120 + 2a = 180$$
$$2a = 60$$
$$a = 30 \qquad \boxed{1}$$

For $\Delta\, RST$, we have

$$100 + m\angle SRT + m\angle STR = 180 \qquad \boxed{2}$$

From the diagram, we get

$$m\angle SRT = a + b \qquad \boxed{3}$$
$$m\angle STR = a + b \qquad \boxed{4}$$

Substituting $\boxed{3}$ and $\boxed{4}$ into $\boxed{2}$, we get

$$100 + a + b + a + b = 180$$
$$100 + 2a + 2b = 180$$
$$2a + 2b = 80 \qquad \boxed{5}$$

Substituting $\boxed{1}$ into $\boxed{5}$, we get

$$2(30) + 2b = 80$$
$$60 + 2b = 80$$
$$2b = 20$$
$$b = 10$$

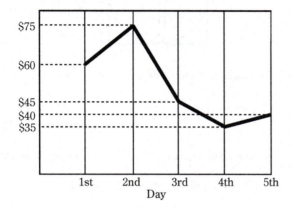

16. Choice C is correct. In ascending order, the wages for the six days are:

$35
$35
$40
$45
$60
$75

The median is the middle number. But wait! There is no middle number. So we average the two middle numbers, 40 and 45, to get 42.5.

The mode is the number appearing most frequently, that is, 35. So $42.50 - 35 = 7.50 = 7.50.

17. Choice E is correct. **(Use Strategy 11: Use new definitions carefully. Use Strategy 8: When all choices must be tested, start with E and work backward.)**

$$\text{Given:} \quad ⓐⓑ = \frac{a+1}{b-1}$$

$$\text{Choice E:} \quad ⑤③ = \frac{5+1}{3-1} = \frac{6}{2} = 3$$

Note that the other choices have b as either 3 or 5, which makes the denominator $b - 1$ as either 2 or 4. Since all the other choices (D, C, B, A) have a less than 5, the fraction in Choice E is greatest.

The remaining choices are shown below.

$$\text{Choice D:} \quad ④⑤ = \frac{4+1}{5-1} = \frac{5}{4} = 1\frac{1}{4}$$

$$\text{Choice C:} \quad ③⑤ = \frac{3+1}{5-1} = \frac{4}{4} = 1$$

$$\text{Choice B:} \quad ③③ = \frac{3+1}{3-1} = \frac{4}{2} = 2$$

$$\text{Choice A:} \quad ②③ = \frac{2+1}{3-1} = \frac{3}{2} = 1\frac{1}{2}$$

18. Choice E is correct. **(Use Strategy 17: Use the given information effectively.)**

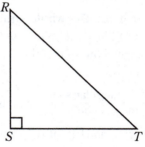

We know that area of $\Delta = \frac{1}{2} \times$ base $\times$ height $\boxed{1}$

We are given that $RS = ST =$ an integer $\boxed{2}$

Substituting $\boxed{2}$ into $\boxed{1}$, we get

Area $\Delta RST = \frac{1}{2} \times$ (An integer) $\times$ (same integer)

Area $\Delta RST = \frac{1}{2} \times$ (An integer)^2 $\boxed{3}$

Multiplying $\boxed{3}$ by 2, we have

2(Area ΔRST) $=$ (An integer)^2 $\boxed{4}$

(Use Strategy 8: When all choices must be tested, start with E and work backward.)

Substituting Choice E, 20, into $\boxed{4}$, we get

$2(20) =$ (An integer)^2

$40 =$ (An integer)^2 $\boxed{5}$

$\boxed{5}$ is *not* possible, since 40 isn't the square of an integer.

19. Choice E is correct. **(Use Strategy 17: Use the given information effectively.)**

Volume of rectangular solid = $l \times w \times h$ ☐1

Substituting the given dimensions into ☐1, we get

Volume of solid = 2 feet × 2 feet × 1 foot

Volume of solid = 4 cubic feet   ☐2

Volume of cube = (edge)³   ☐3

Substituting edge = 0.1 foot into ☐3, we get

Volume of cube = (0.1 foot)³

Volume of cube = 0.001 cubic feet   ☐4

(Use Strategy 3: The whole equals the sum of its parts.) Since the volume of the rectangular solid must equal the sum of the small cubes, we need to know

$$\frac{\text{volume of rectangular solid}}{\text{volume of cube}} = \text{Number of cubes} \;\; ☐5$$

Substituting ☐2 and ☐4 into ☐5, we get

$$\frac{4 \text{ cubic feet}}{0.001 \text{ cubic feet}} = \text{Number of cubes}$$

$$\frac{4}{0.001} = \text{Number of cubes}$$

Multiplying numerator and denominator by 1,000, we get

$$\frac{4}{0.001} \times \frac{1,000}{1,000} = \text{Number of cubes}$$

$$\frac{4,000}{1} = \text{Number of cubes}$$

$$4,000 = \text{Number of cubes}$$

20. Choice D is correct. **(Use Strategy 2: Translate from words to algebra. Use Strategy 17: Use the given information effectively.)**

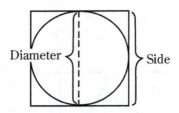

Given the perimeter of the square = 40

Thus, 4(side) = 40

side = 10   ☐1

A side of the square = length of diameter of circle.

Thus, diameter = 10 from ☐1

Since diameter = 2(radius)

10 = 2(radius)

5 = radius   ☐2

Area of a circle = πr^2 ☐3

Substituting ☐2 into ☐3, we have

Area of circle = $\pi 5^2$

Area of circle = 25π

EXPLANATORY ANSWERS FOR PRACTICE TEST 2

Section 3: Math

When a specific Math Strategy is referred to in the solution, study that strategy, which you will find in "19 Math Strategies."

1. Choice D is correct. (**Use Strategy 2: Translate from words to algebra.**)

Let n = the number.

Then $\dfrac{n+3}{4} = 6$

Multiplying both sides by 4, we have

$$4\left(\dfrac{n+3}{4}\right) = (6)4$$
$$n + 3 = 24$$
$$n = 21$$

2. Choice C is correct. (**Use Strategy 17: Use the given information effectively.**)

Given: $\dfrac{3}{4} < x < \dfrac{4}{5}$

Change both fractions to fractions with the same denominator. Thus,

$$\dfrac{3}{4} < x < \dfrac{4}{5}$$

becomes

$$\dfrac{15}{20} < x < \dfrac{16}{20}$$

(**Use Strategy 15: Certain choices may be easily eliminated.**)

Choice B = $\dfrac{13}{20}$ can be instantly eliminated.

Choice D = $\dfrac{16}{20}$ can be instantly eliminated.

Change both fractions to 40ths to compare Choice C. Thus,

$$\dfrac{30}{40} < x < \dfrac{32}{40}$$

Choice C = $\dfrac{31}{40}$ is a possible value of x.

3. Choice B is correct. (**Use Strategy 2: Translate from words to algebra.**)

Perimeter of a square = $4 \times$ side. $\boxed{1}$
We are given that perimeter = 20 meters $\boxed{2}$

Substituting $\boxed{2}$ into $\boxed{1}$, we get

20 meters = $4 \times$ side
5 meters = side $\boxed{3}$
Area of square = $(\text{side})^2$ $\boxed{4}$

Substituting $\boxed{3}$ into $\boxed{4}$, we get

Area of square = $(5 \text{ meters})^2$
Area of square = 25 square meters

4. Choice E is correct. (**Use Strategy 17: Use the given information effectively.**)

Given: $80 + a = -32 + b$

Subtract a from both sides, getting

$$\begin{array}{r} 80 + a = -32 + b \\ \underline{-a \qquad -a} \\ 80 \quad = -32 + b - a \end{array}$$

Add 32 to both sides, giving

$$\begin{array}{r} 80 = -32 + b - a \\ \underline{+\ 32 \quad +\ 32} \\ 112 = \qquad b - a \end{array}$$

5. Choice E is correct. (**Use Strategy 8: When all choices must be tested, start with E and work backward.**)

Choice E is $x^2 + x + 2$

(**Use Strategy 7: Use specific number examples.**)

Let $x = 3$ (an odd positive integer)

Then $x^2 + x + 2 =$

$$3^2 + 3 + 2 =$$
$$9 + 3 + 2 =$$
$$14 = \text{(an even result)}$$

Now let $x = 2$ (an even positive integer)

$$\text{Then } x^2 + x + 2 =$$
$$2^2 + 2 + 2 =$$
$$4 + 2 + 2 =$$
$$8 = \text{(an even result)}$$

Whether x is odd or even, Choice E is even.

The more sophisticated way of doing this is to use **Strategy 8: When all choices must be tested, start with Choice E and work backward.**

Choice E is $x^2 + x + 2$.

(Use Strategy 4: Factor quantities.)

$$x^2 + x + 2 = x(x + 1) + 2.$$

Note that since x is an integer, $x(x + 1)$ is always the product of an even integer multiplied by an odd integer. So $x(x + 1)$ is even and thus 2 times an integer. 2 is even, so $x(x + 1) + 2$ is even. And since $x(x + 1) + 2 = x^2 + x + 2$, then $x^2 + x + 2$ is even.

6.   Choice A is correct. **(Use Strategy 17: Use the given information effectively.)**

Given: $ax = r$ 1
$by = r - 1$ 2

The quick method is to substitute 1 into 2, giving

$$by = ax - 1$$
$$by + 1 = ax$$
$$\frac{by + 1}{a} = x$$

7.   Choice B is correct. **(Use Strategy 2: Translate from words to algebra.)** Let the capacity of container B be x. Then the capacity of container A will be $2x$, and that of container C will be $3x$. The amount poured into container C is equal to half of $2x$ plus one-third of x, or $\frac{2x}{2} + \frac{x}{3} = x + \frac{x}{3} = \frac{4x}{3}$. Dividing this amount by the total capacity of container C, we find the fraction that was filled:

$$\frac{\left(\frac{4x}{3}\right)}{3x} = \frac{4}{9}.$$

8.   Choice D is correct. **(Use Strategy 17: Use the given information effectively.)** In 12 seconds, the wheel travels through 2 revolutions (since 12 seconds is $\frac{1}{5}$ of the minute it would take for ten revolutions). Since this distance is equal to 16 feet, the wheel travels 8 feet per revolution; thus, 8 feet must be the circumference of the wheel. To find the diameter, we divide this figure by π (because the circumference of a circle is π times its diameter). Thus, the diameter is $\frac{8}{\pi}$ feet.

9.   24 **(Use Strategy 2: Translate from words to algebra.)**

Let $n = $ the number

We are given:

$$\frac{5}{8}n = \frac{3}{4}n - 3 \qquad \boxed{1}$$

(Use Strategy 13: Find unknowns by multiplication.) Multiply $\boxed{1}$ by 8. We get

$$8\left(\frac{5}{8}n\right) = 8\left(\frac{3}{4}n - 3\right)$$
$$5n = \frac{24}{4}n - 24$$
$$5n = 6n - 24$$
$$24 = n \qquad \text{(Answer)}$$

10.   10 **(Use Strategy 11: Use new definitions carefully.)**

By definition $\boxed{20} = 10$

11.   2300 **(Use Strategy 12: Try not to make tedious calculations.)**

$$23m + 23n = 23(m + n)$$
$$= 23(94 + 6)$$
$$= 23(100)$$
$$= 2300$$

Multiplying $23(94)$ and $23(6)$ and adding would be time-consuming and therefore tedious.

12. 11 Since lines are drawn every 10 yards after the first one, $\frac{100}{10}$ lines, or 10 additional lines, are drawn.

(Use Strategy 2: Translate from words to algebra.) The total number of lines on the field = the original line + the number of additional lines

$$= 1 + 10 = 11$$

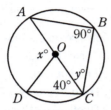

13. 125 (Use Strategy 18: Know and use facts about triangles.) Since $AB = BC$ in $\triangle ABC$, it is isosceles, and the opposite angles are equal. So

$$m\angle A = y \qquad \boxed{1}$$

(Use Strategy 3: The whole equals the sum of its parts.) The sum of the angles in a triangle is 180°, so

$$m\angle A + y + 90 = 180$$

Subtracting 90 from both sides gives

$$m\angle A + y = 90 \qquad \boxed{2}$$

From $\boxed{1}$, the angles are equal, so substituting y for $m\angle A$ in $\boxed{2}$ gives

$$y + y = 90$$
$$\frac{2y}{2} = \frac{90}{2}$$
$$y = 45 \qquad \boxed{3}$$

$x°$ is a central angle, so it is measured by the intercepted arc AD. $\angle DCA = 40°$ is an inscribed angle and measures $\frac{1}{2}$ its intercepted arc AD. Therefore, the intercepted arc $AD = 80°$. So $x = 80$; therefore $x + y = 80 + 45 = 125$.

14. 25

(Use Strategy 5:

$$\mathbf{Average = \frac{sum\ of\ values}{total\ number\ of\ values}}\Big)$$

Average age of students in a class

$$= \frac{\text{sum of the ages of students in the class}}{\text{number of students in the class}} \qquad \boxed{1}$$

Thus,

Average age of all 80 students

$$= \frac{\text{sum of the ages of the 80 students}}{80} \qquad \boxed{2}$$

Using $\boxed{1}$, we know that

$$20 = \frac{\text{sum of the ages of the 60 students}}{60}$$

and $40 = \dfrac{\text{sum of the ages of the 20 students}}{20}$

Thus,

the sum of the ages of the 60 students

$$= (60)(20) = 1{,}200$$

and the sum of the ages of the 20 students

$$= (40)(20) = 800$$

Hence, the sum of the ages of the 80 students

$$= \text{sum of the ages of the 60 students}$$
$$+ \text{sum of the ages of the 20 students}$$
$$= 1{,}200 + 800 = 2{,}000 \qquad \boxed{3}$$

Substituting $\boxed{3}$ into $\boxed{2}$, we get

$$\frac{2{,}000}{80} = 25$$

Average age of all 80 students = 25 *(Answer)*

15. 4 By trial and error, it can be seen that 4 is the answer. A second way of approaching this problem is as follows:

Let $\square = x$. Then we have

$$\begin{array}{r} x\,1 \\ 6\,x \\ x\,9 \\ \hline 1\,5\,x \end{array}$$

We get $1 + x + 9 = 10 + x$. So we carry the 1 and get $1 + x + 6 + x = 15$. So $7 + 2x = 15$; $2x = 8$; $x = 4$.

A third way to approach this problem (and the most sophisticated way) is: Let $\square = x$. Then $\square 1$ is $x\,1$, which is $10x + 1$ since $\square$ is in the tens column. (Any number XY is $10X + Y$; any number XYZ is $100X + 10Y + Z$.) $6\,\square = 6\,x = 60 + x$. $\square 9 = x\,9 = 10x + 9$.

So adding, we get

$10x + 1 + 60 + x + 10x + 9 = 21x + 70.$

This must equal $15\square = 15 x =$

$100 + 50 + x = 150 + x.$

So $21x + 70 = 150 + x$ and $20x = 80$; $x = 4$.
(Use Strategy 17: Use the given information effectively.)

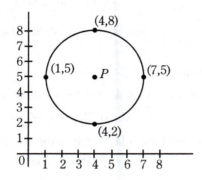

16. **3 (Use Strategy 17: Use the given information effectively.)** The coordinates of the center P are $(4,5)$. By definition, the length of a radius is the distance from the center to any point on the circle. Therefore,

radius = distance from $(7,5)$ to $(4,5)$
$= 7 - 4$
radius $= 3$

17. **36.2 (Use Strategy 2: Translate from words to algebra.)**

Fraction mowed during evening $1 = \frac{2}{9}$
$\boxed{1}$

Fraction mowed during evening $2 = 2\left(\frac{2}{9}\right) = \frac{4}{9}$
$\boxed{2}$

Adding $\boxed{1}$ and $\boxed{2}$, we get

Total fraction mowed during
first two evenings $= \frac{2}{9} + \frac{4}{9}$

$= \frac{6}{9}$

Total fraction mowed during
first two evenings $= \frac{2}{3}$

(Use Strategy 3: The whole equals the sum of its parts.)

Amount left for evening 3 =
1 whole lawn $- \frac{2}{3}$ already mowed
Amount left for evening 3 $= \frac{1}{3}$
$\boxed{3}$

Given: Lawn area = 108.6 square feet
$\boxed{4}$

Multiplying $\boxed{3}$ by $\boxed{4}$, we get

Amount left for evening 3 $= \frac{1}{3} \times 108.6$ square feet

Amount left for evening 3 = 36.2 square feet

18. **7** All nine people are on a straight line in a circle, and we want to have the least number of people move so that all nine are on the circumference of *another* circle. **(Use Strategy 17: Use the given information effectively.)** Draw the situation:

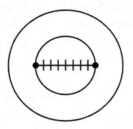

You can see that since two people are already on the circumference of the inner circle, you need to move the other seven to be on the circumference of the inner circle, so all nine will be on the circumference of the *same* circle.

EXPLANATORY ANSWERS FOR PRACTICE TEST 2

Section 4: Critical reading

As you read these Explanatory Answers, you are advised to refer to "16 Verbal (Critical Reading) Strategies."

1. Choice E is correct. See **Sentence Completion Strategy 4.** The first word, "Though," is an *opposition indicator.* The beginning of the sentence speaks positively about the computer programmer. We must find a word that gives us a negative idea about her. Choice E, creativity, is the appropriate word. The other choices are incorrect because their words are not appropriate to give us that opposite feeling.

2. Choice D is correct. See **Sentence Completion Strategy 2.** Examine the first word of each choice. Choice B, tantamount (meaning equivalent to)…, and Choice C, collegiate…, do *not* make sense because we do not speak of tantamount professors or collegiate professors. Now consider the other choices. Choice D, scholarly…profound, is the only choice which has a word pair that makes sense in the sentence.

3. Choice D is correct. See **Sentence Completion Strategy 1.** The beginning word "Because" is a *result indicator.* We may expect, then, a reason in the first part of the sentence for the Indian people to escape from British rule and join the Japanese. The word "abused" (Choice D) provides the reason. The words in the other choices do not make sense in the sentence.

4. Choice D is correct. See **Sentence Completion Strategy 1.** The author is obviously not satisfied with the royalty payment specified, as the sentence refers to the high research costs necessary for writing the book. The other choices do not fit this situation.

5. Choice C is correct. See **Sentence Completion Strategy 2.** The first step is to examine the first word of each choice. We eliminate Choice B, perplexed, and Choice D, considerate, because the first part of the sentence makes no sense with these choices. Now we go to the remaining choices. Choice A and Choice E do *not* make sense in the sentence and are therefore incorrect. Choice C *does* make sense in the sentence.

6. Choice E is correct. See **Sentence Completion Strategy 2.** The first step is to examine the first word of each choice. We eliminate Choice A and Choice C because there are no such things as "sonorous clothes" or "raucous clothes." Now we go to the remaining choices. Choice B, tawdry… humble, and Choice D, tattered…nightmarish, do *not* make sense in the sentence. Choice E, old-fashioned…nostalgic, *does* make sense in the sentence.

7. Choice B is correct. See **Sentence Completion Strategy 1.** Try each choice one by one. Choices C and D are very negative in connotation and do not make sense given "her devotion to music." His own interest in music would not be "belied" (contradicted, negated) or "banished" (exiled) by her devotion to the same art, Choices A and E. Choice B is the most appropriate word for this sentence: "revived" (renewed).

8. Choice D is correct. See **Sentence Completion Strategy 2.** Look at the first word of each choice. The first words in Choices C and E do not quite sound right in the sentence. So eliminate Choices C and E. Now try both words in each of the remaining choices in the sentence. You can

see that Choice D fits best: President Obama disregarded sharp or bitter criticism—that is, *acrimonious* criticism. He accepted the Speaker's invitation in accordance with conventional requirements—that is, *formally.*

9. Choice E is correct. Throughout the passage there was no evidence for the existence of the inhabitants of Atlantis. There was only a theory that was discussed in lines 11–13.

10. Choice C is correct. See lines 6–7. The word "impiety" provides the answer. It means a lack of reverence or respect.

11. Choice B is correct. See lines 6–8: "...his drawing reproduced so accurately that it may truly be said to have been multiplied." The other answers do not give great advantage to lithography.

12. Choice E is correct. See lines 12–14: "...the artist's drawing grows in definite values under his eyes and he can make changes in it as he works." This sentence identifies the reason why artists like to use lithography. There is no evidence in the passage that favors the other answer choices.

13. Choice D is correct. See paragraph 2: "Formerly, technical rationality had been employed only to organize the production of rather simple physical objects.... Now technical rationality is increasingly employed to organize all of the processes necessary to the utilization of physical objects...."

14. Choice B is correct. See paragraph 1: "The absence of direct controls or of coercion should not serve to obscure from our view the... social controls which are employed (such as... advertising, selective service channeling, and so on)."

15. Choice A is correct. It can be seen from the context of the sentence: "...there would be frequent errors...." Choice A is correct. See also **Reading Comprehension Strategy 5.**

16. Choice C is correct. See paragraph 5: "...the workforce must be relatively over-trained...."

17. Choice B is correct. See paragraph 4: "The assembly line also introduced standardization in work skills and thus makes for a high degree of interchangeability among the workforce....If each operation taxed the workers still there would be frequent errors...."

18. Choice E is correct. See paragraph 1: "Technology conquers nature...to do so it must first conquer man...it demands a very high degree of control over the training, mobility, and skills of the workforce."

19. Choice D is correct. See paragraph 6: "...the workforce within technologically advanced organizations is asked to work not less hard but more so."

20. Choice E is correct. See paragraph 3: "... there are very profound social antagonisms or contradictions...." This article is one of skepticism. It frequently points out the contradictions, irrationality, and coercive tactics exhibited by advanced technological institutions.

21. Choice C is correct. See paragraph 6: "Salary and wage increases...lose their...importance...once... an ample supply of luxuries are assured."

22. Choice E is correct. We link "technical specialists" with "such retraining only for a managing elite." Therefore Choice E is correct. See also **Reading Comprehension Strategy 5.**

23. Choice E is correct. See paragraph 5: "... technological progress requires a continuous increase in the skill levels of its workforce, skill levels which frequently embody a fairly rich scientific and technical training...those skills will be less and less fully used."

24. Choice B is correct. See paragraph 6: "...among young people one can already observe a radical weakening in the power of such incentives as money, status, and authority."

EXPLANATORY ANSWERS FOR PRACTICE TEST 2

Section 5: Writing

1. **(B)** Avoid the double negative. Choices A and C suffer from the double-negative fault. Choice B is correct. Choice D changes the meaning of the original sentence. Choice E creates a run-on sentence.

2. **(E)** The original sentence is interrogative. Accordingly, the sentence must end with a question mark. Choice E is correct.

3. **(D)** Choice A is incorrect because it creates a run-on sentence. Choice B fails to include the all-inclusive ("altogether," "completely," "entirely") idea of the original sentence. Choice C changes the meaning of the original sentence. Choice D is correct. Choice E changes the meaning of the original sentence.

4. **(B)** The adverb "yesterday" should, in this sentence, be placed before the modified verb ("arrested"). The time should be placed close to the event, so "yesterday" should not be next to "gallery." Therefore, Choices A and C are incorrect and Choice B is correct. Choices D and E are too roundabout.

5. **(E)** Choice A is incorrect because "that" is redundant; "deciding" is the subject and "that" merely repeats it. Choices B and C are incorrect because they have no subject. Prepositional phrases cannot act as subjects of sentences. Choice D is incorrect because only two items are being compared, so the comparative ("better"), not the superlative ("best"), is needed. Choice E is correct because a gerund ("deciding") can act as the subject of a sentence.

6. **(C)** Choice A is out-of-date. Choice B does not give the meaning intended in the original sentence. Choice C is correct. Choice D is too wordy. Choice E changes the meaning of the original sentence.

7. **(C)** Choices A, B, D, and E are incorrect because each choice begins its own new sentence. Each of these choices, therefore, creates a run-on sentence. Choice C is correct.

8. **(A)** Choice A is correct. Choices B and E change the meaning of the original sentence. Choice C is incorrect grammatically because the verb ellipsis is improper—"the report *was* filed." Choice D is too involved.

9. **(E)** The expression "on account" in Choice A cannot be used as a subordinate conjunction. The expression "being that" in Choice B is always incorrect. Choice C changes the meaning of the original sentence. Choice D is too wordy. Choice E is correct.

10. **(E)** Choice A is too wordy. The double use of the preposition "from" in Choice B is incorrect. Choice C is too wordy. Choice D, as direct discourse, would be correct with the proper punctuation: "…student, 'Which country have you come from?'" Choice E is correct.

11. **(C)** Sequence of tenses in contrary-to-fact past situations requires the "had listened" form of the verb. Choice C is therefore correct and all the other choices are incorrect. Moreover, in Choice E, there is no need to use the word "advice" since the rest of the choice implies that advice has been given.

12. **(B)** The word "nowhere" indicates location. The author is not talking about a place but the beauty of a person. Therefore, it would be more appropriate to use the phrase "not nearly" rather than "nowhere near." This is not an interchangeable phrase.

13. **(C)** "…where *those* same men…." The demonstrative pronoun-adjective form (*those*)—not the personal pronoun form (*them*)—must be used to modify the noun *men*.

14. **(E)** All underlined parts are correct.

15. **(C)** "...the *cheaper* to run." Since we are comparing two things, we must use the comparative degree—not the superlative degree (*cheapest*).

16. **(C)** "...*nor* can he live without bread." The coordinate conjunction *nor* is used when the alternative statement is negative.

17. **(A)** "*Having swam* two-thirds of the distance..." is the incorrect use of the verb. The past tense of the verb *to swim* is *swam*. The past participle form of *to swim* is *swum*, as in *having swum*.

18. **(D)** "...about solving *anyone else's* problems." Say *anyone else's, somebody else's,* etc. Do *not* say *anyone's else, somebody's else.*

19. **(A)** "*Because of* the meat boycott...." Do not begin a sentence with the words *due to. Due* is an adjective. As an adjective, it must have a noun to modify.

20. **(D)** "...so that the children *would have* enough space...." In a clause expressing purpose, the subjunctive form of the verb (*would have*)—not the indicative form (*had*)—should be used.

21. **(E)** All underlined parts are correct.

22. **(A)** "After Mo Farah *had won* the marathon...he decided...." The past perfect tense (*had won*)—not the past tense (*won*)—is necessary when an action in the past has taken place *before* another action in the past.

23. **(C)** "...long a guiding *principle* of many educators...." *Principal* applies to a chief or the chief part of something. *Principle* applies to a basic law.

24. **(C)** "...the Republicans will feel *its* effects...." The possessive adjective *its* does not have an apostrophe. (There is another word, *it's*, that means *it is*.)

25. **(A)** "If we *had begun* our vacation...." The past perfect tense of *to begin* is *had begun*—not *had began*.

26. **(B)** "All of the class presidents but Jerry, Alice, and *me*...." The preposition (*but*) must take an object form (*me*)—not a subject form (*I*).

27. **(C)** "Everyone who attends...knows that *he or she* will be searched...." A pronoun must agree with its antecedent in number. Therefore, the singular pronoun *he or she*—not *they*—must be used because the antecedent of the pronoun is singular (*everyone*).

28. **(D)** "...write one *quickly*." The adverb form is needed to modify the verb *could not write*.

29. **(D)** "One of the key suspects...*was captured*...." *One* is the singular subject of the sentence. The verb, therefore, must be singular (*was captured*). The plural verb (*were captured*) is incorrect.

30. **(B)** Choice A is incorrect because the sentence is needed to communicate information vital to understanding the paragraph. Choice B is correct, since "compromised" is not the same as "comprised." Choice C is incorrect: Joining the two sentences with a semicolon would be all right, but the faulty diction of "compromised" would remain. Choices D and E are incorrect because the misused word is not changed.

31. **(E)** Choice A is incorrect: The pronoun "one" is ambiguous in its reference, failing to make the fact perfectly clear that the men's sweathouse was one of the communal dwellings. Choice B is incorrect in that beginning the sentence with "there" makes no transition at all between sentence 1 and sentence 2, failing completely to indicate the communal nature of the sweathouse. Choice C is incorrect because joining "a men's sweathouse" to "family dwellings and communal dwellings" with "and" makes the sense appear to be that there are three classes of buildings, rather than indicating that the sweathouse belongs in the second group of buildings. Choice D is incorrect: The sentence cannot be omitted since it furnishes a necessary piece of information for understanding sentence 3. Choice E is correct because substituting "among the latter" for "one" makes the reference entirely clear that the sweathouse is one of the communal buildings.

32. **(A)** Choice A is correct: Changing sentence 3 into a dependent clause beginning with "where" improves the sentence by doing away with the awkward repetition of "sweathouse" at the end of sentence 2 and the beginning of sentence 3. Choice B is incorrect in that omitting the adjective "adolescent" serves only to reduce the accuracy and clarity of the information about how old the boys were. Choice C is incorrect: Placing the modifier before "grown men" indicates that both the men and boys were learning, a meaning that common sense dictates as improbable. Choice D is incorrect: The sentence would not be improved by being joined to sentence 2 with a semicolon since the awkward repetition of "sweathouse" would remain. Choice E is incorrect: While "it was there" would eliminate the repetition of "sweathouse," almost no sentence is improved by adding an unnecessary "it was" or "there was"; in this case, since "where" is available as a transition in Choice A, this is the choice that offers the greatest improvement.

33. **(D)** Choice A is incorrect: Since "sentence" 4 is already a fragment, breaking it into two portions would only compound the present error. Choice B is incorrect: Beginning with "sometimes they exchanged" would furnish a subject and verb predicate for the sentence but would result in a lack of parallel structure when followed by "sometimes preparing themselves." Choice C is incorrect because the substitution would not correct the sentence fragment. Choice D is correct in that connecting the fragment to sentence 3 with a comma would make the words function properly as modifying phrases. Choice E is incorrect in that the suggested substitution does not correct the sentence fragment.

34. **(C)** Choice A is incorrect: Placing the sentence after "boys" in sentence 3 merely interrupts the sequence of ideas in that sentence with extraneous information which does not belong in that context. Choice B is incorrect since introducing the information in sentence 6 between sentences 4 and 5 is distracting and serves no purpose. Choice C is correct because the information in sentence 6 does not belong in the paragraph at all since it has no relevance to the topic of the men's sweathouse. Choice D is incorrect because placement after sentence 7 would not make the information any more relevant to the paragraph than the present placement does. Choice E is incorrect because the sentence does not belong in the paragraph.

35. **(D)** Choice A is incorrect: It would be merely prudish to stop the sentence before naming the uses of the women's house since the uses of the men's house have been named. Choice B is incorrect: Placing sentence 8 after sentence 5 would interrupt the sequence of information about the admission of women to the sweathouse. Choice C is incorrect because if the first sentence ended with "house," the remaining words would constitute a sentence fragment. Choice D is correct: The sentence introduces a new topic, that of the women's communal house, and should, therefore, start a new paragraph. Choice E is incorrect: The word "lady" connotes a woman of breeding and refinement and may even suggest a distinction in a social hierarchy. Because of these connotations, the word should not be used to denote a female person generically.

EXPLANATORY ANSWERS FOR PRACTICE TEST 2
Section 6: Math

When a specific Math Strategy is referred to in the solution, study that strategy, which you will find in "19 Math Strategies."

1. Choice D is correct.

   Method 1: Remember that

   1. The sum of two odd numbers is even.

   2. The sum, difference, and product of two even numbers is even.

   3. The product of two odd numbers is odd.

      Given: a is odd, b is odd, c is even. Therefore, $a + b$ is even.

   $$(a + b) - c \text{ is even.}$$

   Method 2: Choose a numerical example.

   (Use Strategy 7: Use number examples.)

   Let $a = 3$, $b = 5$, and $c = 4$

   (Use Strategy 8: When all choices must be tested, start with Choice E and work backward.)

   Then Choice E $(a + bc) = 23$

   Therefore, Choice E is odd.

   Choice D $(a + b) - c = 4$

   Therefore, Choice D is even.

2. Choice B is correct. **(Use Strategy 2: Translate words to numbers.)** 35% of all of Harry's stamps are American, and 23% of these are Air Mail. 23% of 35% equals

   $$\frac{23}{100} \times \frac{35}{100} = \frac{805}{10,000} = \frac{8.05}{100}$$

   which equals 8.05%.

3. Choice A is correct. **(Use Strategy 14: Draw lines to help solve the problem.)** Before the rotation, we have

   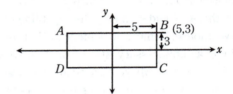

   After the rotation, we have

   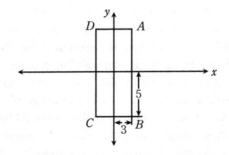

   Note that the new y-coordinate of B is negative because B is below the x-axis. Since B is to the right of the y-axis, its x-coordinate is positive. By looking at the second diagram, we see that the coordinates of B are:

   $$(3, -5).$$

4. Choice B is correct. **(Use Strategy 11: Use new definitions carefully.)**

   After 6 hours $\frac{x}{2}$ grams remain.

   After 12 hours, $\frac{1}{2}\left(\frac{x}{2}\right)$ grams remain.

   After 18 hours, $\frac{1}{2}\left(\frac{1}{2}\right)\left(\frac{x}{2}\right)$ grams remain.

   After 24 hours, $\frac{1}{2}\left(\frac{1}{2}\right)\left(\frac{1}{2}\right)\left(\frac{x}{2}\right) = \frac{x}{16}$ grams remain.

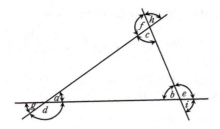

5.   Choice B is correct.

Method I: Shortest method:

$$a + b + c = 180 \qquad \boxed{1}$$
$$g + d = 180 \qquad \boxed{2}$$
$$e + i = 180 \qquad \boxed{3}$$
$$f + h = 180 \qquad \boxed{4}$$

(Use Strategy 13: Find unknowns by adding equations.)

Adding $\boxed{1} + \boxed{2} + \boxed{3} + \boxed{4}$, we get

$$a + b + c + g + d + e + i + f + h = 720$$

Method II:

From the diagram, we get

$$a + d = 180 \qquad \boxed{1}$$
$$b + e = 180 \qquad \boxed{2}$$
$$c + f = 180 \qquad \boxed{3}$$

(Use Strategy 13: Find unknowns by adding equations.)

Adding $\boxed{1} + \boxed{2} + \boxed{3}$, we get

$$a + b + c + d + e + f = 540 \qquad \boxed{4}$$

(Use Strategy 3: The whole equals the sum of its parts.)

The sum of the angles of a $\Delta = 180$

Thus, $a + b + c = 180 \qquad \boxed{5}$

From the diagram (vertical angles), we have

$$a = g, \, b = i, \, c = h \qquad \boxed{6}$$

Substituting $\boxed{6}$ into $\boxed{5}$, we get

$$g + i + h = 180 \qquad \boxed{7}$$

Adding $\boxed{4} + \boxed{7}$, we get

$$a + b + c + d + e + f + g + i + h = 720$$

Method III:

Let X be the value of $a + b + c + d + e + f + g + h + i$.

Label the unmarked angles j, k, and l.

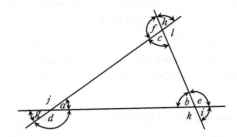

We know that the sum of the angles in a circle is $360°$. So we get:

$$a + d + g + j = 360 \qquad \boxed{8}$$
$$b + e + i + k = 360 \qquad \boxed{9}$$
$$c + f + h + l = 360 \qquad \boxed{10}$$

(Use Strategy 13: Add equations.)

$$X + j + k + l = 3(360) \qquad \boxed{11}$$

We know that the sum of angles in a straight line is $180°$. So we get:

$$j + a = 180 \qquad \boxed{12}$$
$$k + b = 180 \qquad \boxed{13}$$
$$l + c = 180 \qquad \boxed{14}$$

By adding equations $\boxed{12}$, $\boxed{13}$, and $\boxed{14}$ together, we get:

$$j + k + l + a + b + c = 3(180) \qquad \boxed{15}$$

And since the angles of a triangle $= 180°$

$$a + b + c = 180 \qquad \boxed{16}$$

Substituting $\boxed{16}$ into $\boxed{15}$, we get:

$$j + k + l + 180 = 3(180)$$
$$j + k + l = 3(180) - 180 = 2(180) = 360 \qquad \boxed{17}$$

Substituting $\boxed{17}$ into $\boxed{11}$, we get:

$$X + 360 = 3(360)$$
$$X = 3(360) - 360 = 2(360) = 720$$

6.   Choice D is correct. **(Use Strategy 11: Use new definitions carefully.)** The smallest sum occurs when we choose 3 from A and 6 from B.

Therefore, the minimum sum $= 3 + 6 = 9$

The largest sum occurs when we choose 5 from A and 8 from B.

Therefore, the maximum sum $= 5 + 8 = 13$

All numbers from 9 to 13 inclusive can be sums.

Thus, there are 5 different sums possible.

7. Choice D is correct. **(Use Strategy 8: When all choices must be tested, start with Choice E and work backward.)** The equation that does not represent any of the illustrated graphs is $y = 2x + 4$ because none of the illustrated graphs has a slope of 2 and crosses the y-axis ($x = 0$) at $y = 4$.

8. Choice B is correct. $f(2x) = |2x| - 2x = 2|x| - 2x = 2f(x)$.

9. $\frac{1}{1}$, 1, 1.0, etc. **(Use Strategy 17: Use the given information effectively.)** This means that when $x = 5$, $y = 6$ and when $x = 7$, $y = 8$.

The slope is $\frac{(y_2 - y_1)}{(x_2 - x_1)}$. Thus $\frac{(y_2 - y_1)}{(x_2 - x_1)} = \frac{(8-6)}{(7-5)} = \frac{1}{1}$.

See diagram below:

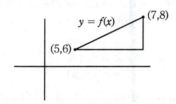

10. 15 **(Use Strategy 17: Use the given information effectively.)**

Given: a bag with 4 blue, 7 green, and 8 yellow marbles.

Fred could draw 15 marbles and have only green and yellow marbles ($8 + 7$). On his next pick, however, he would be sure of having one of each color.

(Use Strategy 16: The obvious may be tricky!)

It is his sixteenth draw that gets Fred one of each color, but the question asks how many Fred would have drawn, so that on his *next* draw he will have 1 marble of every color.

He would have drawn *15*. The sixteenth is the next draw, but not the answer to the question.

The correct answer is 15.

11. 50 **(Use Strategy 5: Remember**

$$\text{average} = \frac{\text{sum of values}}{\text{total number of values}}\bigg)$$

We are told that the average of 5 different integers is 12. Thus,

$$\frac{x + y + z + w + v}{5} = 12 \qquad \boxed{1}$$

Multiplying $\boxed{1}$ by 5, we get

$$5\left(\frac{x + y + z + w + v}{5}\right) = 5(12)$$

$$x + y + z + w + v = 60 \qquad \boxed{2}$$

(Use Strategy 17: Use the given information effectively.)

For one of the integers to be the greatest, the other four must be as small as possible. Thus,

$$\begin{array}{ll} \text{let } x = 1 & \boxed{3} \\ \text{let } y = 2 & \boxed{4} \\ \text{let } z = 3 & \boxed{5} \\ \text{let } w = 4 & \boxed{6} \end{array}$$

The four smallest possible different integers > 0.

Substituting $\boxed{3}$, $\boxed{4}$, $\boxed{5}$, and $\boxed{6}$ into $\boxed{2}$, we get

$$1 + 2 + 3 + 4 + v = 60$$
$$10 + v = 60$$
$$v = 50$$

Thus, the greatest possible value for any of the integers is 50.

12. 3 **(Use Strategy 2: Translate from words to algebra.)**

Given: 12 seated students, 5 students at board

This translates to $12 + 5 = 17$ students in all. $\boxed{1}$

Given: 12 seated students, 7 empty seats

This translates to $12 + 7 = 19$ seats in all. $\boxed{2}$

Subtracting $\boxed{1}$ from $\boxed{2}$ gives

$19 - 17 = 2$ vacant seats when all are seated $\boxed{3}$

Given: 3 leave and 2 enter

This translates to $-3 + 2$

$= -1$, or a net loss of 1 student. $\boxed{4}$

Combining $\boxed{4}$ and $\boxed{3}$, we have

$2 + 1 = 3$ vacant seats.

13. 18

Method I:

(Use Strategy 14: Draw lines to help solve the problem.)

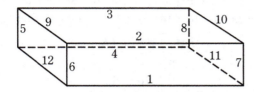

Above is a rectangular solid with each of its edges numbered 1 through 12, respectively. There are 3 groups of 4 parallel edges each.

1, 2, 3, and 4 are parallel.
5, 6, 7, and 8 are parallel.
9, 10, 11, and 12 are parallel.

Within each group of 4 parallel edges, there are 6 pairs of parallel edges. For example, within the first group listed above, 1 and 2 are parallel, 1 and 3 are parallel, etc. Because there are 3 groups and each group has 6 pairs of parallel edges, there are $3 \times 6 = 18$ different pairs of parallel edges in all. Below is a listing of all the pairs:

1–2	2–3	5–6	6–7
1–3	2–4	5–7	6–8
1–4	3–4	5–8	7–8

9–10	10–11
9–11	10–12
9–12	11–12

Method II:

A rectangular solid exists in three dimensions; within each dimension, there are four edges that run parallel to each other. Therefore the combinations of parallel edges for *one* dimension, taken two at a time, is:

$$_4C_2 = \frac{(4 \times 3)}{(2 \times 1)} = 6$$

Since there are three dimensions, the total number of combinations is:

$$3(_4C_2) = 3(6) = 18$$

14. 1.999, 1.998... .001, or any number

$0 < r < 2$, like $\frac{1}{2}, \frac{1}{4}$ etc. (Use Strategy 2: Translate from words to algebra.)

$$2r + 2r + 3 < 11$$
$$4r + 3 < 11$$
$$4r < 8$$
$$r < 2 \qquad \boxed{1}$$

15. 135 (Use Strategy 3: The whole equals the sum of its parts.)

The sum of the four angles in a quadrilateral $= 360°$ $\qquad \boxed{1}$

Given: the sum of two angles $= 90°$ $\qquad \boxed{2}$

Let a and b represent the two remaining angles. $\qquad \boxed{3}$

Substituting $\boxed{2}$ and $\boxed{3}$ into 1, we get

$$90° + a + b = 360°$$
$$a + b = 270° \qquad \boxed{4}$$

(Use Strategy 5:

$$\textbf{Average} = \frac{\textbf{sum of values}}{\textbf{total number of values}}\bigg)$$

Average of a and $b = \dfrac{a+b}{2}$ $\qquad \boxed{5}$

Applying $\boxed{5}$ to $\boxed{4}$, we get

$$\frac{a+b}{2} = \frac{270°}{2}$$

Average of $a + b = 135°$

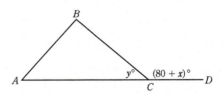

16. 100 (Use Strategy 3: The whole equals the sum of its parts.)

$$m\angle ACB + m\angle BCD = m\angle ACD \qquad \boxed{1}$$

We are given that AD is a straight line segment. We know that

$$m\angle ACD = 180 \qquad \boxed{2}$$
$$\textit{Given: } m\angle ACB = y \qquad \boxed{3}$$
$$m\angle BCD = 80 + x \qquad \boxed{4}$$

We substitute $\boxed{2}$, $\boxed{3}$, and $\boxed{4}$ into $\boxed{1}$

Thus, $y + 80 + x = 180$
Subtract 80: $y + x = 100$

17. **3 (Use Strategy 4: Remember classic expressions.)**

$$x^2 + 2xy + y^2 = (x + y)^2 \qquad \boxed{1}$$

$$\text{Given: } x^2 + 2xy + y^2 = 25 \qquad \boxed{2}$$

Substitute $\boxed{1}$ into $\boxed{2}$, giving

$$(x + y)^2 = 25$$

$$x + y = \pm 5 \qquad \boxed{3}$$

$$\text{Given: } x + y > 0 \qquad \boxed{4}$$

Using $\boxed{3}$ and $\boxed{4}$ together, we conclude that

$$x + y = +5 \qquad \boxed{5}$$

$$\text{Given: } x - y = 1 \qquad \boxed{6}$$

(Use Strategy 13: Find an unknown by adding equations.)

Adding $\boxed{5}$ and $\boxed{6}$, we have

$$2x = 6$$

$$x = 3$$

18. **4 (Use Strategy 17: Use the given information effectively.)**

Method I:

Remembering that the sum of 2 sides of a triangle is greater than the third side, we know that

$$LM + MN > LN$$
$$6 + 10 > 12$$
$$16 > 12$$

The difference between 16 and 12: $16 - 12 = 4$ is the amount of overlap.

Method 2: **(Use Strategy 14: Draw lines when appropriate.)**

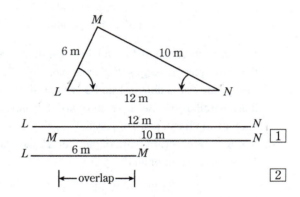

In the figure above, the segments have been redrawn so that the result can be easily discovered.

In $\boxed{1}$, the distance $LM = 12\,\text{m} - 10\,\text{m} = 2\,\text{m}$ $\boxed{3}$

Subtracting $\boxed{3}$ from the distance LM in $\boxed{2}$, we get $6\,\text{m} - 2\,\text{m} = 4\,\text{m}$ overlap.

EXPLANATORY ANSWERS FOR PRACTICE TEST 2

Section 7: Critical reading

As you read these Explanatory Answers, you are advised to refer to "16 Verbal (Critical Reading) Strategies."

1. Choice C is correct. See **Sentence Completion Strategy 2.** The first step is to examine the first word of each choice. We eliminate Choice B, innuendoes, Choice D, frequencies, and Choice E, cancellations, because the foreman's leniency did not have innuendoes or frequencies or cancellations. Now we go to the remaining choices. Choice A, compensations... unacceptable, does *not* make sense in the sentence. Choice C, drawbacks...shoddy, makes the sentence meaningful.

2. Choice D is correct. See **Sentence Completion Strategy 4.** The word "Although" at the beginning of the sentence is an *opposition indicator*. As a contrast to the rundown condition of the school, the word "renovated" is the acceptable choice.

3. Choice C is correct. See **Sentence Completion Strategy 1.** Ask yourself, "What do dancing, feasting, and partying have in common?" What kind of pleasure would they give? "Immediate" pleasure is the most appropriate choice. Choices A, B, D, and E have too negative a connotation to be correct.

4. Choice E is correct. See **Sentence Completion Strategy 2.** The first words of Choice B (flexibility) and Choice D (dizziness) do not make sense in the first part of the sentence. Therefore, we eliminate these two choices. When we try the two words in each of the remaining choices, only Choice E (disappointment...fervent) makes good sense in the sentence as a whole.

5. Choice A is correct. See **Sentence Completion Strategy 4.** The *opposition indicator* "even though" should lead us to the correct Choice A with the fill-in word "convincing."

6. Choice C is correct. Although what is mentioned in (A), (B), and (D) is mentioned in both passages, the passages describe essentially a code for living life and dealing with people.

7. Choice B is correct. The passages are contrasting in that one proposes concealing and the other openness, and the tone is didactic and authoritarian. Although you may have thought that Choice A was correct, the passages are not really pro and con to something.

8. Choice A is correct. The authors do not show the reader *how* to conceal or not conceal. For Choices B and D: The authors do show the consequences and danger of not conforming to the authors' advice: In passage 1, lines 9–10: "bloom of life is gone." In passage 2, lines 15–16: "make us vulnerable to the slings and arrows of life." For Choice C, both passages really say that one should abide by the authors' admonition as soon as possible; see line 10: "Put off that day as long as possible" and lines 18–19: "There is no better time for concealment than today." For Choice E: In both passages the fear is addressed and, as in Choice C, timing is addressed.

9. Choice E is correct. In Passage 1: Note line 9—"*bloom of life* is gone." In Passage 2: Note lines 15–16, "make us vulnerable to the *slings and arrows of life*." The phrases in italics describe analogies: *bloom,* as in a flower, and *slings and arrows,* as in weapons.

10. Choice D is correct. Beginning with lines 12–13 ("Malignant tumors, on the other hand...") the passage is primarily concerned with the manner in which malignant tumors behave in the body. Choice A is incorrect because the definition of neoplasia is confined only to the first sentence: "Neoplasia...normal cells." Choice B is incorrect because the inhibition of tumor metastasis is discussed only in lines 22–29. Choice C does not occur and is not discussed in the passage. Therefore, Choice C is incorrect. Choice E is not discussed until lines 34–36. "After malignant cells...most of the cells die." Therefore, Choice E is not correct.

11. Choice C is correct. See lines 22–24: "Before metastasis can occur...surrounding normal tissue." Choice A is incorrect because the passage does not indicate that malignant cells shed their original membrane in order to acquire a new membrane. The passage simply states in lines 31–33: "The outer membrane...of normal cells." Choice B is incorrect because the passage nowhere states that malignant cells "inhibit the lethal effects of the components of the blood." Choices D and E are incorrect because the passage does not indicate in any way what these two choices state.

12. Choice E is correct. See lines 37–39: "Those cells which survive...small blood vessel." Although the passage does refer to Choices A, B, C, and D, none of these choices represents a characteristic of a malignant cell that most greatly enhances its metastatic potential. Therefore, these four choices are all incorrect.

13. Choice C is correct. See lines 37–42: "Those cells which survive...stickiness of the blood vessel wall." Choice A is incorrect because the passage does not indicate that benign tumors become malignant tumors. Choice B is incorrect. See lines 20–22: "This process...have been ascertained." Choice D is incorrect. See lines 31–33: "The outer membrane...of normal cells." Choice E is incorrect. See lines 49–50: "...it still must be stated...a mystery."

14. Choice D is correct. First see lines 10–11: "Benign tumors...tissue of origin." Now see lines 12–13: "Malignant tumors...tissue of origin." Choice A is incorrect. See lines 10–11: "Benign tumors... are usually slow-growing." We infer, therefore, that malignant cells are fast growing. Choice B is incorrect. See lines 12–13: "Malignant tumors... tissue of origin..." Choice C is incorrect. See lines 31–33: "The outer membrane...of normal cells." Choice E is incorrect. See lines 16–20: "The characteristic...the original tumor."

15. Choice D is correct. From the context of the rest of the sentence, it can be seen that the word "explicable" means "explainable." See also **Reading Comprehension Strategy 5.**

16. Choice B is correct. See lines 1–2: "The old Middle West is gone. However, it still lives in song and story." Choices A, C, D, and E are incorrect because the passage makes no reference to what these choices state.

17. Choice C is correct. See lines 19–20: "I think the Middle West's strength is in its customary cautious approach...." Choice D (line 39) is incorrect because it is not cited as the strength of the Middle West. Choices A, B, and E may be true, but they are not indicated in the passage.

18. Choice D is correct. See lines 46–49: "In the Middle West it has...taken the form of people remaining in the smaller cities and giving them new life and intelligence. This has strengthened smaller communities...." Choices A, B, C, and E are incorrect because the passage does not indicate these choices as current trends.

19. Choice A is correct. See lines 5–10: "The old Middle West developed...out of...destructive blizzards...and...dust storms." Therefore, Item I is true. Items II and III cannot be accepted because the passage says nothing about the Gold Rush of 1849 and the Civil War as factors in the formation of the Middle West. Accordingly, Choices B, C, D, and E are incorrect.

20. Choice D is correct. From the context of the sentence—"…with a growing understanding of their problems and responsibilities"—the best meaning of "pragmatic" would be "practical." See also **Reading Comprehension Strategy 5**.

21. Choice D is correct. See the next-to-last paragraph: "…so much difficulty in resolving our problems of a complex society is that we have tended to lose…a strong feeling for the special qualities of our local area."

22. Choice C is correct. See paragraph 6: "It made inflation the prime issue in 1936…." Also see paragraph 4:
"especially on political major questions" and the flavor and content of the rest of the passage.

23. Choice E is correct. Given the context of the sentence with the ideas expressed throughout the passage, "diversification" refers to race or religion. See also **Reading Comprehension Strategy 5**.

24. Choice E is correct. See the second-from-last paragraph: "…freedom of communications…and the ease of changing occupations…contribute to breaking down ethnic and religious group prejudices."

EXPLANATORY ANSWERS FOR PRACTICE TEST 2

Section 8: Math

> When a specific Math Strategy is referred to in the solution, study that strategy, which you will find in "19 Math Strategies."

1. Choice A is correct. **(Use Strategy 2: Translate from words to algebra.)** "x varies inversely with y" means that xy = constant. We are given that $x = 5$ and $y = 4$, so $5 \times 4 = 20$ and 20 is therefore the *constant*. Thus $xy = 20$. So when $y = 10$, $x(10) = 20$ and thus $x = 2$.

2. Choice D is correct. We write a table:

	Sales	Cost per book
(1)	4,000	$1
(2)	1,000	$2
(3)	250	$4
(4)	160	$5

(Use Strategy 8: When all choices must be tested, start with Choice E and work backward.)

For Choice E:

For (1): $\dfrac{4,000}{1} = 4,000$; for (2): $\dfrac{4,000}{2} = 2,000$— doesn't check with sales of (2), which is 1,000. So try Choice D:

For (1): $\dfrac{4,000}{1^2} = 4,000$

For (2): $\dfrac{4,000}{2^2} = 1,000$ (checks with (2))

For (3): $\dfrac{4,000}{4^2} = 250$ (checks with (3))

For (4): $\dfrac{4,000}{5^2} = 160$ (checks with (4))

Choice D is correct.

3. Choice D is correct. **(Use Strategy 16: The obvious may be tricky.)** If $x^{-3} = 27$, then $\dfrac{1}{x^3} = 27$, so $\dfrac{1}{27} = x^3$ and $\dfrac{1}{3^3} = x^3$. Thus $x = \dfrac{1}{3}$; $x^{\frac{1}{2}} = \left(\dfrac{1}{3}\right)^{\frac{1}{2}} = \dfrac{1}{\sqrt{3}}$. Multiply numerator and denominator by $\sqrt{3}$ (rationalizing the denominator) and we get $x^{\frac{1}{2}} = \dfrac{1}{\sqrt{3}} = \dfrac{\sqrt{3}}{\sqrt{3}(\sqrt{3})} = \dfrac{\sqrt{3}}{3}$.

4. Choice E is correct. We substitute $x = 2$. So $f(2) = 2(2) + 3^2 = 4 + 9 = 13$

5. Choice D is correct. **(Use Strategy 17: Use the given information effectively.)**

    We set $x + 2 = x^2 + 4x + 4$.

    Since $x^2 + 4x + 4 = (x + 2)(x + 2)$,
    we have $x + 2 = (x + 2)(x + 2)$
    Thus $x = -2$ or $1 = x + 2$
    Therefore $x = -2$ or $x = -1$

    Or, for a more straightforward approach:
    $$x + 2 = x^2 + 4x + 4$$
    $$0 = x^2 + 3x + 2$$

    Factoring, we get:
    $$0 = (x + 1)(x + 2)$$

    We get:
    $$x + 1 = 0 \text{ or } x + 2 = 0.$$

    Thus $x = -1$ or $x = -2$

6. Choice B is correct.

$$\text{Given: } AC = \frac{4}{3}(AB) \qquad \boxed{1}$$

(Use Strategy 13: Find unknowns by multiplication.)

Multiply $\boxed{1}$ by 3. We get

$$3(AC) = 4(AB) \qquad \boxed{2}$$

(Use Strategy 3: The whole equals the sum of its parts.)

From the diagram, we see that

$$AC = AB + BC \qquad \boxed{3}$$

Substituting $\boxed{3}$ into $\boxed{2}$, we have

$$3(AB + BC) = 4(AB)$$
$$3AB + 3BC = 4AB$$
$$3BC = 1AB \qquad \boxed{4}$$

(Use Strategy 13: Find unknowns by division.)

Dividing $\boxed{4}$ by $3AB$, we get

$$\frac{3BC}{3AB} = \frac{1AB}{3AB}$$
$$\frac{BC}{AB} = \frac{1}{3}$$

7. Choice C is correct.

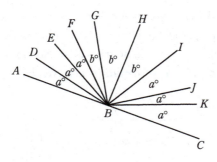

(Use Strategy 3: The whole equals the sum of its parts.) The whole straight angle ABC is equal to the sum of the individual angles.

$$\text{Thus, } m\angle ABC = a + a + a + b + b +$$
$$b + a + a + a$$
$$m\angle ABC = 6a + 3b \qquad \boxed{1}$$

We know $m\angle ABC = 180°$ $\qquad \boxed{2}$

Substituting $\boxed{2}$ into $\boxed{1}$, we get

$$180° = 6a + 3b \qquad \boxed{3}$$

(Use Strategy 13: Find an unknown expression by dividing.) Dividing both sides of $\boxed{3}$ by 3, we have

$$60° = 2a + b \qquad \boxed{4}$$

Choice C, $m\angle DBG = 2a + b$, so its measure can be determined. It is 60° (from $\boxed{4}$).

8. Choice C is correct.

$$\text{Given: } 8r + 3s = 12 \qquad \boxed{1}$$
$$7r + 2s = 9 \qquad \boxed{2}$$

(Use Strategy 13: Find unknowns by subtracting.)

Subtracting $\boxed{2}$ from $\boxed{1}$, we get

$$r + s = 3 \qquad \boxed{3}$$

Multiplying $\boxed{3}$ by 5, we get

$$5(r + s) = (3)5$$
$$5(r + s) = 15$$

9. Choice B is correct. **(Use Strategy 17: Use the given information effectively.)** Since the slope of the line is constant, the *ratio* of the *difference* in y-coordinates to the *difference* in x-coordinates must be constant for any two points on the line. For points P and A, this ratio is

$$\frac{2 - 0}{1 - 0} = 2$$

The only choice of x and y which gives the ratio 2 for point R and point A is Choice B, since if $x = 4$ and $y = 8$,

$$\frac{8 - 0}{4 - 0} = 2.$$

All the other choices give a different ratio from 2.

10. Choice A is correct.

(Use Strategy 5:

$$\textbf{Average} = \frac{\textbf{sum of values}}{\textbf{total number of values}})$$

$$p = \frac{x + y}{2} \qquad \boxed{1}$$

$$q = \frac{y + z}{2} \qquad \boxed{2}$$

$$r = \frac{x + z}{2} \qquad \boxed{3}$$

(Use Strategy 13: Find unknown expressions by adding equations.) Adding $\boxed{1}$, $\boxed{2}$, and $\boxed{3}$, we get

$$p + q + r = \frac{x+y}{2} + \frac{y+z}{2} + \frac{x+z}{2}$$

$$= \frac{2x + 2y + 2z}{2}$$

$$p + q + r = x + y + z \qquad \boxed{4}$$

The average of x, y, and $z = \dfrac{x+y+z}{3}$ $\qquad \boxed{5}$

Substitute $\boxed{4}$ into $\boxed{5}$. We have

The average of x, y, and $z = \dfrac{p+q+r}{3}$ (Answer)

11. Choice D is correct. (Use Strategy 17: Use the given information effectively.) Two-fifths, or 40%, of the applicants fail on the examination. Of the 60% remaining, three-fourths fail to get into the program. $\frac{3}{4} \times 60\% = 45\%$. Thus, the total number of failures is equal to 40% + 45%, or 85%.

Or, to solve it algebraically:

Let x be the number of applicants.

$\frac{3}{5}x$ = applicants who passed the exam

$\dfrac{\frac{3}{5}x}{4} = \frac{3}{20}x$ = applicants who passed the exam and were accepted

$\dfrac{\frac{3}{20}x}{x} = \frac{3}{20}$ = % of all applicants who gain admission

$1 - \frac{3}{20} = \frac{17}{20} = 85\%$ = % who *fail* to gain admission

12. Choice B is correct. (Use Strategy 18: Know and use facts about triangles.) Let the two perpendicular sides equal a and b, and the hypotenuse be c. By the Pythagorean theorem, $a^2 + b^2 = c^2$. Thus, c^2 must be the sum of two square numbers; but our only possible choices for c^2 are 44, 45, 46, 47, and 48. Listing the square numbers which do not exceed these, we find 1, 4, 9, 16, 25, and 36. The only choice which can be broken down into the sum of two of these squares is 45, which equals 36 + 9. (To show that we cannot

so break down the others, we need only notice that 36 + 16 = 52 is too large, 36 + 4 = 40 is too small; 25 + 25 = 50 is too large, 25 + 16 = 41 is too small; and there are no other values in between, so 36 + 9 = 45 is the only choice). Since $c^2 = 45$, c must equal $\sqrt{45}$.

13. Choice D is correct. (Use Strategy 17: Use the given information effectively.) Of the N French students, P are in both programs, so only $(N-P)$ are in the French program alone; similarly, $(M-P)$ students are in the Spanish program alone. Thus, the number of students in only one language program is equal to $(N-P)+(M-P)$, which equals $N + M - 2P$. (Note: The following diagram may help you to visualize the answer better.)

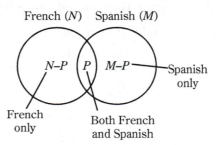

14. Choice E is correct. Since we know only that $\overleftrightarrow{m}$ is not parallel to either $\overleftrightarrow{\ell}$ or $\overleftrightarrow{n}$, both of the following situations could be true. (Use Strategy 17: Use the given information effectively.)

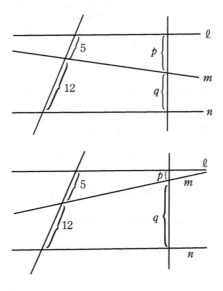

(Note: $p + q = 13$ is still true in both cases in the drawings above.) Clearly, the value of $\frac{p}{q}$ is different for each case. Hence, $\frac{p}{q}$ cannot be determined unless we know more about $\overleftrightarrow{m}$.

15. Choice C is correct. **(Use Strategy 17: Use the given information effectively.)** There are 4 choices for the first letter of the 3-letter combinations. Since each letter cannot be used more than once in a combination, there are only 3 choices for the second letter and only 2 choices for the third letter. Thus, the maximum number of 3-letter combinations that Ross can make up is

$$= 4 \cdot 3 \cdot 2$$
$$= 24$$

16. Choice C is correct. **(Use Strategy 17: Use the given information effectively (and ignore irrelevant information).)** To find the total cost of all uniforms in *child* sizes at *School B*, we would multiply the number of uniforms at School B of Type A with the Child's Type A cost, multiply the number of uniforms at School B of Type B with the Child's Type B cost, and multiply the number of uniforms at School B of Type C with the Child's Type C cost, and add those three quantities. That is: $30 \times \$9 + 60 \times \$10 + 50 \times \$11 = \$1,420$.

EXPLANATORY ANSWERS FOR PRACTICE TEST 2
Section 9: Critical reading

As you read these Explanatory Answers, you are advised to refer to "16 Verbal (Critical Reading) Strategies."

1. Choice E is correct. See **Sentence Completion Strategy 1.** The fact that the investor was eager to make an investment change points to his being "dubious" about his current investment—the stocks he had recently purchased. A rise in the value of the stocks would be a positive occurrence, so the investor would not be "fearful, unconcerned, hesitant, or amused" about it happening. Therefore, Choices A, B, C, and D are incorrect.

2. Choice A is correct. See **Sentence Completion Strategy 4.** The word "when" is a *support indicator* in this sentence. As we try each choice, we find that "frightening" is the only word that fits in this sentence. The fact that "the earth shifts with a sickening sway" reinforces the initial idea that "nature's brute strength is never more frightening."

3. Choice D is correct. See **Sentence Completion Strategy 2.** Consider the first word of each choice. We can thus eliminate Choice A, disdain, because one doesn't "disdain" the incidence of crime, and we can eliminate Choice B, revoke, because one doesn't "revoke" the incidence of crime. Now consider the other three choices. Choice D, with its two fill-in words "reduce" and "diverting," is the only choice that makes sense in the sentence.

4. Choice D is correct. See **Sentence Completion Strategy 2.** Consider the first word of each choice. We can first eliminate Choice A, gradual, because "gradual" musical accompaniment does not make sense, and we can eliminate Choice E, chronic, because the "chronic" musical accompaniment

does not make sense. Now consider the other three choices. Choice D, with its two fill-in words "superb" and "aura," is the only choice that makes sense in the sentence.

5. Choice B is correct. See **Sentence Completion Strategy 4.** The first part of the sentence about her fine reputation as a celebrated actress is obviously in opposition to her appearance in a TV soap opera. Accordingly, the word "blemished" is the only possible choice.

6. Choice C is correct. See **Sentence Completion Strategy 2.** First, let us examine the first words in each choice. We eliminate Choice B because one's manner does not "accept" his intention. We eliminate Choice D because one's manner does not "disregard" his intention. We eliminate Choice E because one's manner does not "animate" his intention. This leaves us with Choice A (revealed… eager), which does *not* make good sense, and Choice C (belied…drastic), which *does* make good sense.

7. Choice D is correct. The author is definitely satisfied and happy with the simple life he and his partner are leading. See lines such as the following: "We thank our lucky stars that we live out in the wilderness" (lines 35–36) and "We are thankful for what the wilderness makes possible" (lines 42–43). Choices A, B, C, and E are incorrect because the author gives no indication that the lifestyle, as he describes it, is marked by resentment, boredom, indecision, or indifference.

8. Choice B is correct. Throughout the passage, the author is showing that frills are not necessary for a happy life. Example: "There is no phone to ring,

no radio to turn on, no television to watch" (lines 7–8). Choices A and D are incorrect because they are much too general. Choice C is an inappropriate title because progress and prosperity are not of interest to the author. Choice E is an inappropriate title because the author is not concerned about conveniences such as a phone, radio, or television. He has what he needs—"peace, quiet, and frugality" (lines 43–44).

9. Choice A is correct. The author indicates that the typical election is inconsequential—that is, unproductive, of no use. One may conclude, then, that the author has no faith in the typical candidates who run for office. Choices B, C, D, and E are incorrect because the author does not express these sentiments in the passage— although he may agree with those choices.

10. Choice E is correct. The author must have a farm because he says: "…our homegrown food is not stale, preserved or embalmed and bought from the supermarket" (lines 40–41). Choice A is incorrect because the author states: "There is wood to cut, snow to shovel…" (lines 13–14). Choice B is incorrect. See lines 14–16: "No one is pushing, no one shoving…we make our own jobs. Free men? Almost." Therefore, the author is not *completely* a free man. Choice C is incorrect because it is his neighbor's wife who may be pregnant (line 18). Choice D is incorrect. See line 25: "The newspaper, reaching us by mail…"

11. Choice C is correct. Maine is the only one of the five states listed that would likely have snow (line 1) and spruce (evergreen) trees (line 2). Therefore, Choices A, B, D, and E are incorrect.

12. Choice D is correct. Choice A is incorrect. From line 45, you cannot conclude that the author believes that even though he or she lives in a one-bedroom apartment, much of the population in the city lives in one-bedroom apartments. Choice B is incorrect. Although the author says in line 59 that food may not be homegrown, the author doesn't say that you'll never get homegrown food. Choice C is incorrect. Although the author states that you may bump into rich and poor on a street, the author doesn't claim that both eat at the most expensive restaurants. Choice D is correct. In lines 51–52 the author links losing one's identity with forgetting about problems. Thus it can be assumed that losing one's identity is a plus. Choice E is incorrect. There is no reference to friendliness as a way of life.

13. Choice C is correct. The word "interminable" (line 47) refers to *sounds of cars, trucks, repair, services,* and *hassles encountered.* Thus the word cannot be "loud" (Choice A), "bright" (Choice D), "harsh" (Choice B), or "close" (Choice E). It makes sense that *interminable* relates to *time* (Choice C). Note that "term" has to do with a specific length of time, and the prefix "in" here means "not," so *interminable* must mean "not having a specific term or length of time," that is, *ongoing.* See also **Reading Comprehension Strategy 5**.

14. Choice A is correct. Note that in Passage 2, the author mentions in many instances the good with the bad: excitement, hassles, services, traffic, and so on.

15. Choice A is correct. The author of Passage 1 seems to feel (lines 25–34) that all or most news is bad, so the author would be surprised at seeing a headline as described in Choice A. Choice B is incorrect. The author of Passage 2 (line 54) may bump into a celebrity in the street and indeed talk with the celebrity. Choice C is incorrect. The author believes that he or she can go to a coffee shop at three in the morning, so a movie theater is also probably open at two in the morning. Choice D is incorrect. See line 12. Choice E is incorrect. The author of Passage 2 acknowledges that certain types of people may not enjoy living in the city (lines 67–70), and the author admits that there are negative aspects about city living.

16. Choice B is correct. Note the comparison in lines 43–44. "Peace, progress, prosperity? We prefer peace, quiet, and frugality." Thus "frugality" must relate to "prosperity" with a somewhat *opposite* meaning and obviously not have too negative a connotation since the author is striving for this. The only word that makes sense is "stinginess." See also **Reading Comprehension Strategy 5**.

17. Choice C is correct. In lines 8–9 the author links "don" with "city disguise, cocktail parties, dinners." It is logical to assume that "don" relates to "clothing." See also **Reading Comprehension Strategy 5**.

18. Choice C is correct. See lines 31–34. Choice A is incorrect: Although the author of Passage 1 may believe that most news is bad, there is no reference to the author of Passage 2's believing that most news is good. Choice B is incorrect: Although it is true that the author of Passage 1 may believe that most elections are useless, there is no reference to the author of Passage 2's believing that they are necessary. Choice D is incorrect: We cannot infer that the author of Passage 1 believes that the parks in cities are safe (see lines 27–31 about Central Park). The author of Passage 2 may agree that crime "goes with the territory." However, Choice D in its entirety is incorrect. Choice E is incorrect. We cannot assume that one author does not like home-grown food (even though, for example, the author of Passage 2 may not get to eat it).

19. Choice A is correct. For (I), see lines 17–23. This type of friendly socialization is not mentioned in Passage 2. For (II), see lines 35–43 and lines 70–74. Positive effects are mentioned in both passages. For (III), see line 25: "The newspaper, reaching us by mail…" and lines 56–57: "get up-to-the-minute news through radio or TV…" Thus this condition is described in both passages.

EXPLANATORY ANSWERS FOR PRACTICE TEST 2
Section 10: Critical reading

1. **(E)** Choice E is the only correct choice since the other choices lack parallelism. Remember that a *parallel structure* or a *parallelism* is the repetition of a chosen grammatical form within a sentence. By making each compared item or idea in your sentence follow the same grammatical pattern, you create a parallel construction. Since the first two words describing the robber's approach are "...*quietly, cautiously*" (both adverbs), it is only fitting that the next word in the list would be "*unpretentiously*" (another adverb). The other choices are not parallel in structure. Choice D is incorrect for an additional reason—the predicate adjective "unpretentious" (not the adverb "unpretentiously") should be used after the copulative verbal "acting."

2. **(B)** Choice A is incorrect because it is unidiomatic; that is, it is not how we express ourselves in the English language. Choice B is correct. Choices C and E are incorrect because they are too wordy. Choice D improperly omits "conduct of the (accused)."

3. **(B)** The object form of the pronoun must be used for the object of any preposition. Therefore, Choices A and C are incorrect and Choice B is correct. Choice D is incorrect because we need the nominative form of the personal pronoun ("she") as the subject ("but not she"). Choice E is incorrect because it is too informal for the context.

4. **(E)** Choice A is incorrect because "while" pertains to time and should not be substituted loosely for "and." Choice B is incorrect because it does not tie up grammatically with the rest of the sentence. Choice C is incorrect for the same reason. Choice D is incorrect because the subordinate conjunction "as" does not make sense here. Choice E is correct.

5. **(A)** Choice A is correct. Choice B wrongly substitutes the objective case "whomever" for the nominative "whoever," the subject of the verb "would return." Choice C uses the form "whosoever," which, while correct, is legalistic and not needed here. Choice D again uses the objective case. Choice E is awkward.

6. **(C)** The word "irregardless" does not exist in the English language. Therefore Choices A, B, and E cannot be right. The correct word should be "regardless," which means having or showing no regard or being without concern. "Despite" in Choice D does not give the same meaning as "regardless." Choice C is the correct one.

7. **(D)** Choice A wrongly uses the plural verb "are to be found" after the subject of the sentence, "One." (The plural word "examples" is not the subject of the prepositional phrase "of the finest examples.") Choice B simply uses the same plural verb in the past tense instead of the present. Choice C does not correct the error. Choice D does, by using the singular verb "is." Choice E is incorrect because of the use of the plural verb "are."

8. **(D)** Choice A fails to use the possessive case of the pronoun that governs a gerund. Choice B changes the meaning of the sentence. Choice C corrects the error but omits a necessary part of the meaning. Choice D is correct. Choice E retains the error of Choice A and, in addition, distorts the meaning of the sentence.

9. **(D)** Choices A, B, C, and E should place the adverbial phrase "without hesitation" after the infinitive it modifies, "to answer." Since the meaning is to "answer without hesitation," the phrase "without hesitation" should be placed right after the infinitive "to answer." This is done in Choice D.

10. **(D)** Choice A is incorrect because the expression "not only" must be accompanied by "but also." B is also incorrect for this reason. C is a complete sentence, making the original a run-on sentence. Choice D is correct. In Choice E, the words "in addition" are unnecessary.

11. **(E)** The subject of the sentence is, in fact, "The paintings of Dali…" It is not Dali himself, but his paintings that are the subject of the sentence. Choice A, "like many artists," would imply that the artist is the subject—we know that to not be true. Choice B has the same issue as Choice A. Choice C unnecessarily repeats "…the paintings." Choice D omits any mention of artists and so is not the best choice. Choice E uses "those" (the possessive pronoun) and also includes "other artists." It is therefore the most suitable answer.

12. **(C)** Choice A is incorrect because "laid" is the past tense of the verb "to lay," and the verb required is "to lie." Choice B is incorrect because "had laid" is the past perfect tense of the verb "to lay." Choice C is correct; Choice D is incorrect because it is in the present tense and it also is a form of the verb "to lay." Choice E is in the present tense—it should be in the past perfect tense.

13. **(B)** In making a comparison, the word "different" is followed by the word "from" rather than by the word "than." For this reason, Choices A, C, and E are incorrect. Choice D uses the word "from" correctly but the choice includes the unnecessary repetition of "earlier." Choice B is, of course, correct.

14. **(D)** Choices A and E are incorrect because in a "neither-nor" construction, the verb agrees with the noun or pronoun that follows "nor." Choice B is incorrect because "neither" must be followed by a singular verb. Choice C is incorrect because the nominative form of the pronoun ("Neither you nor *I*") should be used, since "I" is a subject in the sentence. Choice D is correct.

SAT PRACTICE
TEST 3

ANSWER SHEET FOR PRACTICE TEST 3

Section 1

Begin your essay on this page. If you need more space, continue on the next page. Do not write outside of the essay box.

Continue on the next page if necessary.

Continuation of ESSAY Section 1 from previous page. Write below only if you need more space.

Start with number 1 for each new section. If a section has fewer questions than answer spaces, leave the extra answer spaces blank. Be sure to erase any errors or stray marks completely.

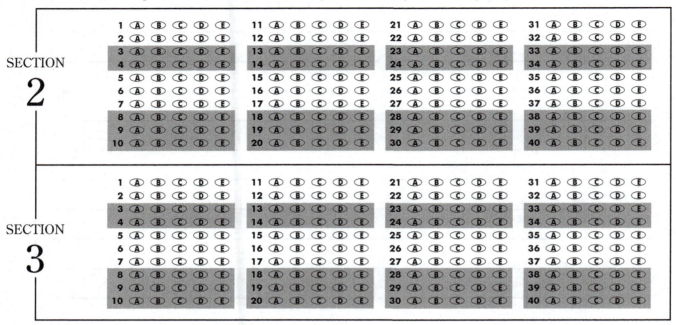

SECTION 2

SECTION 3

CAUTION Use the answer spaces in the grids below for Section 2 or Section 3 only if you are told to do so in your test book.

Student-Produced Responses

ONLY ANSWERS ENTERED IN THE CIRCLES IN EACH GRID WILL BE SCORED. YOU WILL NOT RECEIVE CREDIT FOR ANYTHING WRITTEN IN THE BOXES ABOVE THE CIRCLES.

Start with number 1 for each new section. If a section has fewer questions than answer spaces, leave the extra answer spaces blank. Be sure to erase any errors or stray marks completely.

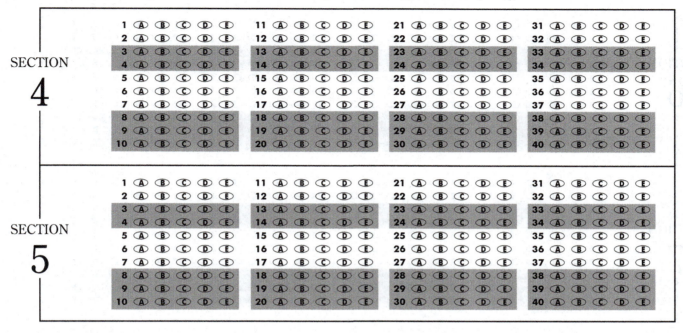

SECTION 4

SECTION 5

CAUTION Use the answer spaces in the grids below for Section 2 or Section 3 only if you are told to do so in your test book.

Student-Produced Responses ONLY ANSWERS ENTERED IN THE CIRCLES IN EACH GRID WILL BE SCORED. YOU WILL NOT RECEIVE CREDIT FOR ANYTHING WRITTEN IN THE BOXES ABOVE THE CIRCLES.

Start with number 1 for each new section. If a section has fewer questions than answer spaces, leave the extra answer spaces blank. Be sure to erase any errors or stray marks completely.

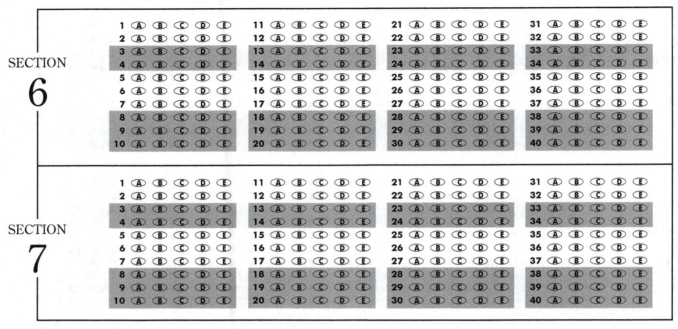

SECTION

6

SECTION

7

CAUTION Use the answer spaces in the grids below for Section 2 or Section 3 only if you are told to do so in your test book.

Student-Produced Responses

ONLY ANSWERS ENTERED IN THE CIRCLES IN EACH GRID WILL BE SCORED. YOU WILL NOT RECEIVE CREDIT FOR ANYTHING WRITTEN IN THE BOXES ABOVE THE CIRCLES.

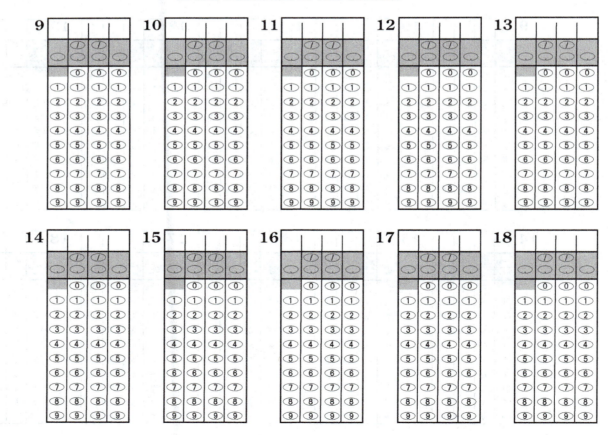

Start with number 1 for each new section. If a section has fewer questions than answer spaces, leave the extra answer spaces blank. Be sure to erase any errors or stray marks completely.

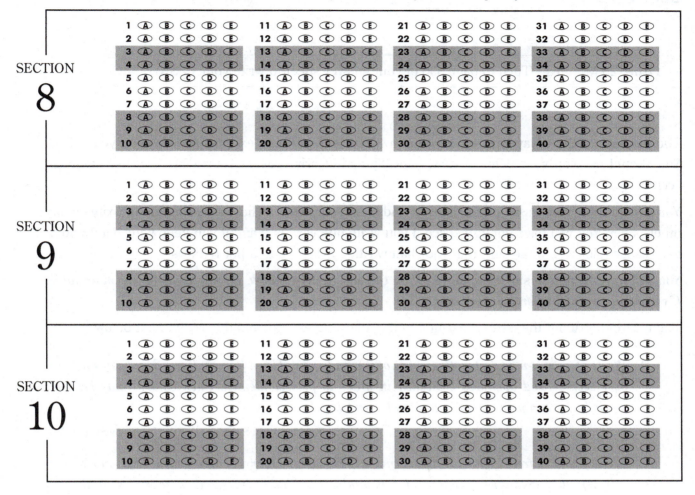

Section 1

> **Time:** 25 Minutes—Turn to page 336 of your answer sheet to write your ESSAY.

The purpose of the essay is to have you show how well you can express and develop your ideas. You should develop your point of view, logically and clearly present your ideas, and use language accurately.

You should write your essay on the lines provided on your answer sheet. You should not write on any other paper. You will have enough space if you write on every line and if you keep your handwriting to a reasonable size. Make sure that your handwriting is legible to other readers.

You will have 25 minutes to write an essay on the assignment below. *Do not write on any other topic. If you do so, you will receive a score of 0.*

Think carefully about the issue presented in the following excerpt and the assignment below.

1. *While secrecy can be destructive, some of it is indispensable in human lives. Some control over secrecy and openness is needed in order to protect identity. Such control may be needed to guard privacy, intimacy, and friendship.*

   –ADAPTED FROM SISSELA BOK, "THE NEED FOR SECRECY"

2. *Secrecy and a free, democratic government, President Harry Truman once said, don't mix. An open exchange of information is vital to the kind of informed citizenry essential to healthy democracy.*

   –EDITORIAL, "OVERZEALOUS SECRECY THREATENS DEMOCRACY"

Assignment: Do you believe that people need to keep secrets, or do you believe that secrecy is harmful? Write an essay in which you develop your point of view on this issue. Support your position with reasoning and examples based on your own reading, observations, and experiences.

DO NOT WRITE YOUR ESSAY IN YOUR TEST BOOK. You will receive credit only for what you write on your answer sheet.

BEGIN WRITING YOUR ESSAY ON PAGE 336 OF THE ANSWER SHEET.

If you finish before time is called, you may check your work on this section only.
Do not turn to any other section in the test.

Section 2

Time: 25 Minutes – Turn to Section 2 (page 338) of your answer sheet to answer the questions in this section. 20 Questions

Directions: For this section, solve each problem and decide which is the best of the choices given. Fill in the corresponding circle on the answer sheet. You may use any available space for scratchwork.

Notes:

1. The use of a calculator is permitted.

2. All numbers used are real numbers.

3. Figures that accompany problems in this test are intended to provide information useful in solving the problems. They are drawn as accurately as possible EXCEPT when it is stated in a specific problem that the figure is not drawn to scale. All figures lie in a plane unless otherwise indicated.

4. Unless otherwise specified, the domain of any function f is assumed to be the set of all real numbers x for which $f(x)$ is a real number.

REFERENCE INFORMATION

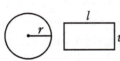

$A = \pi r^2$ $A = lw$ $A = \frac{1}{2}bh$ $V = lwh$ $V = \pi r^2 h$ $c^2 = a^2 + b^2$ *Special Right Triangle.*
$C = 2\pi r$

The number of degrees of arc in a circle is 360.
The sum of the measures in degrees of the angles of a triangle is 180.

---

1. A certain number is divided by 3, but its value remains the same. What is this number?

   (A) -1

   (B) $-\frac{1}{2}$

   (C) 0

   (D) $\frac{1}{2}$

   (E) 1

2. A man walks a certain distance in the direction 30° south of west, stops, and then turns 35° to his right. In what new direction is he facing?

   (A) 65° north of west

   (B) 35° north of west

   (C) $32\frac{1}{2}^{\circ}$ north of west

   (D) 30° north of west

   (E) 5° north of west

GO ON TO THE NEXT PAGE ➤

3. What is the value of $\frac{1}{5}K$ if $\frac{9}{5}K = 18$?

(A) $\frac{1}{9}$

(B) $\frac{1}{5}$

(C) 2

(D) 5

(E) 10

5. Let x, y, and z be negative numbers such that $x < y < z$. Which expression is the smallest?

(A) $(z)(z)$

(B) $(y)(z)$

(C) $(x)(z)$

(D) $(y)(x)$

(E) $(x)(x)$

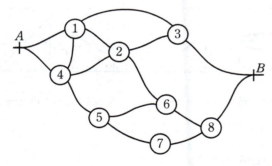

4. The figure above is a piece of fishnet. Which of the following statements must be true about an ant crawling on the net from Point A to Point B?

(A) If it goes through 2, it must go through 7.

(B) If it goes through 3, it must go through 1.

(C) Its route must go through either 2 or 7.

(D) If it goes through 4, it must go through 3 or 5.

(E) If it goes through 8, it must go through 2 or 5.

6. A sequence of integers is defined as follows: The first term is 2, and every additional term is obtained by subtracting 2 from the previous term and tripling the resulting difference. For example, the second term would be 0. Which of the following is a true statement about this sequence?

(A) The terms behave as follows: even, even, odd, odd, even, even, odd, odd,...

(B) The terms behave as follows: even, odd, even, odd, even, odd,...

(C) The terms behave as follows: even, even, even, odd, odd, odd, even, even, even,...

(D) All of the terms, except for the first one, are odd.

(E) All of the terms are even.

GO ON TO THE NEXT PAGE ➤

$$A = \left\{ \frac{3}{8}, 2, \frac{3}{2}, 6, \frac{13}{2}, 8 \right\}$$

$$B = \left\{ \frac{3}{8}, \frac{8}{3}, 6, 8 \right\}$$

7. If n is a member of both the sets A and B above, which of the following must be true?

    I. n is an integer
    II. $8n$ is an integer
    III. $n = 6$

    (A) None
    (B) I only
    (C) II only
    (D) III only
    (E) I and II only

9. If x and y are integers such that $1 < |x| < 5$ and $2 < |y| < 7$, what is the least possible value of $x + y$?

    (A) -10
    (B) -8
    (C) -5
    (D) 5
    (E) 10

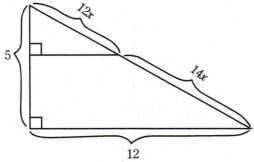

8. If the segments shown in the diagram have the indicated lengths, find the value of x.

    (A) 13
    (B) 12
    (C) 5
    (D) 2
    (E) $\frac{1}{2}$

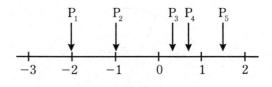

10. For the five numbers marked above by arrows, the best approximation to their product is

    (A) $\frac{1}{3}$
    (B) $\frac{2}{3}$
    (C) $\frac{3}{2}$
    (D) 3
    (E) -3

GO ON TO THE NEXT PAGE ➤

11. If K is the sum of three consecutive even integers and y is the sum of the greatest three consecutive *odd* integers that precede the least of the three even integers, express y in terms of K.

(A) $y = K - 5$
(B) $y = K - 10$
(C) $y = K - 15$
(D) $y = K - 20$
(E) The answer cannot be determined from the information given.

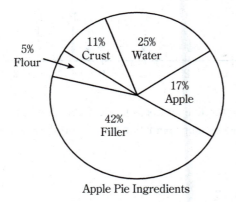

Apple Pie Ingredients

12. If John buys a 2 lb apple pie with ingredients distributed as shown, how much of his pie is water?

(A) $\frac{1}{4}$ lb

(B) $\frac{1}{2}$ lb

(C) $\frac{3}{4}$ lb

(D) 1 lb

(E) $1\frac{1}{4}$ lb

13. The number of subsets of the set $\{1,2,3\}$ is

(A) 4
(B) 5
(C) 6
(D) 7
(E) 8

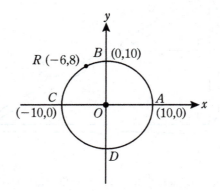

14. In the figure above, S is a point (not shown) such that segment RS divides the area of circle O into two equal parts. What are the coordinates of S?

(A) $(6,-8)$
(B) $(6,8)$
(C) $(8,-6)$
(D) $(-6,-8)$
(E) $(8,6)$

GO ON TO THE NEXT PAGE ➤

	First Place (6 points)	Second Place (4 points)	Third Place (2 points)
Game 1			
Game 2		Arisa	
Game 3			Arisa

15. The figure above is a partially filled-in score card for a video game contest. Isaac, Arisa, and Dylan each played in all of the three games. There were no ties. What is the *minimum* possible score for Dylan in this tournament?

(A) 2

(B) 6

(C) 8

(D) 12

(E) The answer cannot be determined from the information given.

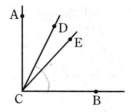

Note: Figure is not drawn to scale.

17. Given that $AC \perp BC$, $\angle DCB = 62°$, and $\angle ACE = 37°$, find $\angle DCE$ in degrees.

(A) 5°

(B) 9°

(C) 13°

(D) 25°

(E) 27°

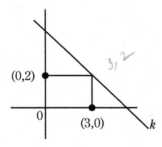

16. In the above figure, if line k has a slope of -1, what is the y-intercept of k?

(A) 4

(B) 5

(C) 6

(D) 7

(E) 8

18. Over the first few weeks of the baseball season, the league's five leading pitchers had the following won–lost records. (All games ended in a win or loss for that pitcher.)

	Won	Lost
Pitcher A	4	2
Pitcher B	3	2
Pitcher C	4	1
Pitcher D	2	2
Pitcher E	3	1

At the time these statistics were compiled, which pitcher was leading the league in winning percentage? (That is, which pitcher had won the greatest percentage of his games?)

(A) Pitcher A

(B) Pitcher B

(C) Pitcher C

(D) Pitcher D

(E) Pitcher E

GO ON TO THE NEXT PAGE ➤

19. In the watch shown above, the normal numbers 1, 2, 3,..., 12 have been replaced by the letters A, B, C,..., L. In terms of these letters, a correct reading of the time shown would be

(A) I minutes after L

(B) 3E minutes before A

(C) 5C minutes after L

(D) I minutes before A

(E) None of the above

20. 27 equal cubes, each with a side of length r, are arranged so as to form a single larger cube with a volume of 81. If the larger cube has a side of length s, then r divided by s equals

(A) $\frac{1}{3}$

(B) $\frac{1}{\sqrt{3}}$

(C) $\frac{1}{2}$

(D) $\frac{1}{8}$

(E) $\frac{1}{27}$

STOP

If you finish before time is called, you may check your work on this section only.
Do not turn to any other section in the test.

Take a 5 minute break

before starting section 3

Section 3

Time: 25 Minutes – Turn to Section 3 (page 338) of your answer sheet to answer the questions in this section. 20 Questions

Directions: For this section, solve each problem and decide which is the best of the choices given. Fill in the corresponding circle on the answer sheet. You may use any available space for scratchwork.

Notes:

1. The use of a calculator is permitted.

2. All numbers used are real numbers.

3. Figures that accompany problems in this test are intended to provide information useful in solving the problems. They are drawn as accurately as possible EXCEPT when it is stated in a specific problem that the figure is not drawn to scale. All figures lie in a plane unless otherwise indicated.

4. Unless otherwise specified, the domain of any function f is assumed to be the set of all real numbers x for which $f(x)$ is a real number.

REFERENCE INFORMATION

$A = \pi r^2$ $A = lw$ $A = \dfrac{1}{2}bh$ $V = lwh$ $V = \pi r^2 h$ $c^2 = a^2 + b^2$ *Special Right Triangle.*
$C = 2\pi r$

The number of degrees of arc in a circle is 360.
The sum of the measures in degrees of the angles of a triangle is 180.

---

1. A piece of rope is lying on a number line. One of its ends is at coordinate −4, and the other is at coordinate 7. What is the length of the rope?

   (A) 3
   (B) 5
   (C) 7
   (D) 9
   (E) 11

2. A long jumper has jumps of 8.4 meters, 8.1 meters, and 9.3 meters. What is the average (arithmetic mean) of these jumps?

   (A) 8.5
   (B) 8.6
   (C) 8.7
   (D) 8.8
   (E) 8.9

GO ON TO THE NEXT PAGE ➤

3. If $x + 9 = -11 - x$, then $x =$

    (A) -10
    (B) -2
    (C) 2
    (D) 10
    (E) 20

5. Jayden deposited $50 in a savings bank at the beginning of the year. Jayden's money earns him interest at the rate of 8 percent of the amount deposited, for each year that Jayden leaves his money in the bank. If Jayden leaves his $50 in the bank for exactly one year and then decides to withdraw all of his money, how much money (including interest) can he withdraw? (The interest is not compounded.)

    (A) $50.04
    (B) $50.08
    (C) $54.00
    (D) $54.08
    (E) $58.00

4. If $3y = 12$ and $\frac{10}{x} = 5$, then $\frac{y + 11}{x + 15} =$

    (A) $\frac{7}{10}$
    (B) $\frac{3}{4}$
    (C) $\frac{15}{17}$
    (D) 1
    (E) $\frac{17}{15}$

6. If $(x + 6)^2 = 12x + 72$, then $x =$

    (A) 0
    (B) ± 1
    (C) ± 3
    (D) ± 6
    (E) ± 12

GO ON TO THE NEXT PAGE ➤

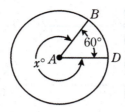

Note: Figure is not drawn to scale.

7. In the circle above, A is the center of the circle. Find the value of $x - 60$.

(A) 60
(B) 120
(C) 240
(D) 300
(E) 360

8. To the nearest hundred, how many minutes are there in a week?

(A) 1,000
(B) 1,100
(C) 10,000
(D) 10,100
(E) 11,000

9. If $\sqrt{x}$ is defined by the equation $\sqrt{x} = \dfrac{x^3}{4}$ for real numbers x, which of the following equals 16?

(A) $\sqrt{2}$
(B) $\sqrt{4}$
(C) $\sqrt{8}$
(D) $\sqrt{16}$
(E) $\sqrt{64}$

| 42 | 27 | 56 | x | y |

10. 200 pieces of candy have been randomly put into five jars. The number of pieces of candy in three of the five jars is shown in the figure above. What is the maximum possible value of x? (x is the number of pieces of candy in the fourth jar.)

(A) 69
(B) 75
(C) 102
(D) 144
(E) 200

GO ON TO THE NEXT PAGE ➤

11. There are 16 pages in a booklet. Last night, Ron read $\frac{1}{4}$ of the booklet. This morning, Ron read $\frac{1}{4}$ of the remaining pages. How many pages does Ron still have left to read?

   (A) 7
   (B) 8
   (C) 9
   (D) 10
   (E) 11

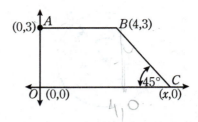

13. What is the area of quadrilateral *ABCO* in the figure above?

   (A) 10.5
   (B) 14.5
   (C) 16.5
   (D) 21.0
   (E) The answer cannot be determined from the information given.

12. A different candle was lit at noon each day between December 9 and December 21, inclusive. How many candles were lit during this period?

   (A) 10
   (B) 11
   (C) 12
   (D) 13
   (E) 14

14. The difference between the sum of two numbers and the difference of the two numbers is 6. Find the larger of the two numbers if their product is 15.

   (A) 3
   (B) 5
   (C) 17
   (D) 20
   (E) 23

GO ON TO THE NEXT PAGE >

15. If $\frac{1}{a} + \frac{1}{b} = 10$, what is the value of $a + b$?

(A) $\frac{1}{10}$

(B) $\frac{2}{5}$

(C) 1

(D) 10

(E) The answer cannot be determined from the information given.

17. Brayden had b marbles and Carlos had c marbles. After Brayden gave 6 marbles to Carlos, Brayden still had 18 more marbles than Carlos. Find $c - b$.

(A) 30

(B) 12

(C) 3

(D) -12

(E) -30

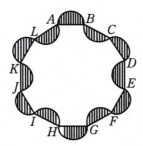

16. In the figure above, *ABCDEFGHIJKL* is a regular dodecagon (a regular twelve-sided polygon). The curved path is made up of 12 semicircles, each of whose diameters is a side of the dodecagon. If the perimeter of the dodecagon is 24, find the area of the shaded region.

(A) 6π

(B) 12π

(C) 24π

(D) 36π

(E) 48π

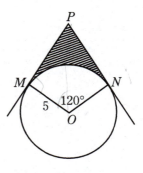

18. $\overline{PM}$ and $\overline{PN}$ are tangent to circle O at M and N, respectively; $m \angle MON = 120°$ and $OM = ON = 5$. Find the perimeter of the shaded region.

(A) $10 + 10\pi$

(B) $5\sqrt{3} + 10\pi$

(C) $5\sqrt{3} + \frac{10}{3}\pi$

(D) $10\sqrt{3} + \frac{10\pi}{3}$

(E) $10\sqrt{3} + 10\pi$

19. If $x + y + z = 3(a + b)$, which of the following is the average (arithmetic mean) of x, y, z, a, and b in terms of a and b?

(A) $\dfrac{a + b}{5}$

(B) $\dfrac{4(a + b)}{15}$

(C) $\dfrac{a + b}{2}$

(D) $\dfrac{4(a + b)}{5}$

(E) $a + b$

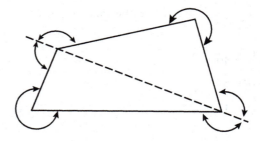

20. The arrows in the diagram above represent all of the exterior angles of the figure. The sum of the degree measures of these angles is

(A) 720

(B) 1,080

(C) 1,440

(D) 1,800

(E) The answer cannot be determined from the information given.

STOP

If you finish before time is called, you may check your work on this section only.
Do not turn to any other section in the test.

Section 4

Time: 25 Minutes – Turn to Section 4 (page 339) of your answer sheet to answer the questions in this section. 24 Questions

Directions: For each question in this section, select the best answer from among the choices given and fill in the corresponding circle on the answer sheet.

Each sentence below has one or two blanks, each blank indicating that something has been omitted. Beneath the sentence are five words or sets of words labeled A through E. Choose the word or set of words that, when inserted in the sentence, *best* fits the meaning of the sentence as a whole.

Example:

Hoping to _____ the dispute, negotiators proposed a compromise that they felt would be _____ to both labor and management.

(A) enforce…useful

(B) end…divisive

(C) overcome…unattractive

(D) extend…satisfactory

(E) resolve…acceptable

Ⓐ Ⓑ Ⓒ Ⓓ ⬤

1. As a general dealing with subordinates, he was like two sides of a coin: _____ yet known for his severity, _____ yet a man of few words.

    (A) agreeable…talkative
    (B) brilliant…handsome
    (C) fair…outgoing
    (D) understanding…candid
    (E) harsh…pleasant

2. The profession of a major-league baseball player involves more than _____ in these times when astronomical salaries and _____ contract bargaining are commonplace.

    (A) skill…astute
    (B) agitation…traditional
    (C) practice…minimal
    (D) enthusiasm…whimsical
    (E) intellect…mystical

GO ON TO THE NEXT PAGE ➤

3. Internal dissension in this congressional committee can _____ affirmative action for months and increase the chances of racial _____.

   (A) encourage...regard
   (B) complicate...agreement
   (C) induce...movement
   (D) apply...validity
   (E) delay...upheaval

4. Although there was considerable _____ among the members of the panel as to the qualities essential for a champion, Sugar Ray Robinson was _____ voted the greatest fighter of all time.

   (A) suspicion...quietly
   (B) disagreement...overwhelmingly
   (C) discussion...incidentally
   (D) sacrifice...happily
   (E) research...irrelevantly

5. The police commissioner insisted on severity in dealing with the demonstrators rather than the _____ approach that his advisers suggested.

   (A) arrogant
   (B) defeatist
   (C) violent
   (D) conciliatory
   (E) retaliatory

6. Feeling no particular affection for either of his two acquaintances, he was able to judge their dispute very _____.

   (A) impartially
   (B) accurately
   (C) immaculately
   (D) heatedly
   (E) judiciously

7. His choice for the new judge won the immediate _____ of city officials, even though some of them had _____ about him.

   (A) acclaim...reservations
   (B) disdain...information
   (C) apprehension...dilemmas
   (D) vituperation...repercussions
   (E) enmity...preconceptions

8. There are some individuals who thrive on action and, accordingly, cannot tolerate a _____ lifestyle.

   (A) passive
   (B) chaotic
   (C) brazen
   (D) grandiose
   (E) vibrant

GO ON TO THE NEXT PAGE >

Each passage below is followed by questions on its content. Answer the questions on the basis of what is <u>stated</u> or <u>implied</u> in each passage and in any introductory material that may be provided.

Questions 9–10 are based on the following passage.

A cliché is made, not born. The process begins when someone hits upon a bright new way of stating a common experience. At that point, the remark is an epigram. But if it is particularly apt as well as catchy, the saying receives
5 wide circulation as verbal coin. Soon it is likely to be suffering from overwork. It has then arrived at cliché-hood. The dictionary records the doom of the successful epigram in defining a cliché: "A trite phrase; a hackneyed expression." For the epigrammatist, the only cheer in
10 this process is that it proves his expression was good. Even this situation is covered by a cliché: "Imitation is the sincerest form of flattery."

9. The writer suggests that an epigram is

(A) fresh
(B) trite
(C) ordinary
(D) cheerful
(E) noble

10. According to the author, the chief difference between an epigram and a cliché is in their

(A) origin
(B) length
(C) meaning
(D) use
(E) purpose

Questions 11–12 are based on the following passage.

In the ordinary course of nature, the great beneficent changes come slowly and silently. The noisy changes, for the most part, mean violence and disruption. The roar of storms and tornadoes, the explosions of volcanoes, the
5 crash of thunder, are the result of a sudden break in the equipoise of the elements; from a condition of comparative repose and silence they become fearfully swift and audible. The still small voice is the voice of life and growth and perpetuity. In the history of a nation it is the same.

11. As used in the passage, the word "equipoise" (line 6) most nearly means

(A) stress
(B) balance
(C) course
(D) slowness
(E) condition

12. The author implies that growth and perpetuity in nature and in history are the result of

(A) quiet changes
(B) a period of silence
(C) undiscovered action
(D) storms and tornadoes
(E) violence and disruptions

Questions 13–24 are based on the following passage.

The following passage is about the Depression, which was caused by the stock market crash of 1929, whose effect lasted into the subsequent decade.

The American people were dismayed by the sudden proof that something had gone wrong with their economic system, that it lacked stability and was subject to crises of unpredictable magnitude. They had encountered hard
5 times and temporary depressions before, and such reverses had tended for over a century to broaden out and to become international misfortunes. But the depression that began in 1929 proved so severe, so general, and so difficult to arrest, that it caused a "loss of nerve."

10 Students of economics pointed out that periods of inflation and deflation, of "boom and bust," had alternated for generations. Any strong stimulus such as a war might force the economy of the Western world into high gear; when the fighting ceased, reconstruction and a "backlog" of consumers'
15 orders unfilled in wartime might for a time keep the machines running at full speed; but within a decade the market was likely to become satiated and a fall in demand would then cause a recession. Adjustment and recovery were certain to come in time, and come the sooner if a new stimulus developed. The
20 threat of another war, or war itself, that put millions of men in uniform and created a demand for munitions, was one such stimulus. War provided a limitless market for expendable goods, the type of goods the machines were best fitted to supply, and solved unemployment by creating more military
25 and civilian jobs. Such reasoning as this brought no comfort, however, for it implied a choice between war and depression, and the cure was worse than the disease. "Is modern industry a sick giant that can rouse itself only to kill?" one critic asked. There was no clear answer. But the American people were not
30 willing to accept such a grim diagnosis and insisted that there must be some method of coordinating a supply and demand within the framework of a peacetime economy.

The problem appeared to be as much psychological as economic. In prosperous times business expanded, prices
35 rose, wages increased, and the expectation that the boom would continue indefinitely tempted people to live beyond their means. They purchased goods on credit, confident that they could meet the payments later. The increasing prosperity, in part genuine but overstimulated by optimism and artificial
40 elements, encouraged farmers and manufacturers to over-produce until the supply exceeded the capacity of the market to absorb it. Then when business confidence began to falter, and stock quotations began to drop, panic set in. Speculators who saw their "paper profits" vanishing began to unload their
45 securities with a disastrous effect on prices. Dealers with overloaded shelves slashed their prices to keep their goods moving, and canceled outstanding orders. Manufacturers, seeing orders shrink, reduced output. All down the line the contraction of business left employees without jobs, and
50 lacking wages they could not meet their debts. Once started, this spiral of deflation seemed to have no limit.

It is natural for people to blame others when misfortune strikes, and after 1929 the American people became

suddenly critical of their business leaders, who had failed
55 to foresee or avert the swift transition from prosperity to privation. The conviction spread that the heads of great banks and corporations, the promoters and financiers and stockbrokers, had misled the public. Demands raised earlier in American history were revived, demands for
60 "cheap" money with which to pay off debts, demands that the great trusts and monopolies be investigated, demands that the federal government intervene to correct business abuses and aid the destitute. More and more people began to feel that the system of free business enterprise, of
65 unregulated economic competition, so highly praised in the 1920s, must be wrong if it could lead to crises that brought such widespread misery and unemployment.

But President Hoover was firm in his conviction that the American economic system was fundamentally sound
70 and that it would be a mistake for the government to interfere unduly. Government supervision and regulation of business, he felt, would stifle freedom and lead to government control of activities that should be left to private initiative. "You cannot extend the mastery of the government over
75 the daily life of a people," he warned, "without somewhere making it master of people's souls and thoughts." He believed that the government's role should be limited to helping business help itself, and to this end he supported an act (1932) which created the Reconstruction Finance
80 Corporation to aid ailing businesses, as well as hard-pressed states, with government loans. Hoover also inaugurated a public works program which he hoped would effectively relieve unemployment. But beyond such indirect measures as these he did not believe the federal government should
85 go. Meanwhile the burden of providing direct relief for the millions of unemployed and their families was exhausting the resources of state and local governments and private agencies—and still the breadlines formed as jobs and savings went.

13. According to the passage, President Hoover

  (A) urged more and more government regulation

  (B) did little or nothing to aid ailing business

  (C) made efforts to relieve unemployment

  (D) had sincere doubts about the soundness of the American economic system

  (E) expressed the belief that we should convert gradually to a socialistic form of government

14. The author indicates that recovery from a recession most likely comes about

  (A) during wartime

  (B) during peacetime

  (C) by decreasing manufacturing

  (D) by lowering wages

  (E) by raising the interest rate

GO ON TO THE NEXT PAGE ▶

15. Which of the following was *not* a cause of the 1929 Depression?

    (A) too much buying on credit
    (B) rising prices
    (C) overproduction of goods
    (D) lack of economic stability
    (E) political unrest throughout the world

16. According to the passage, when the stock quotations began to drop,

    (A) manufacturers immediately increased output
    (B) unemployment decreased
    (C) there was a reduction of business
    (D) dealers increased their prices
    (E) speculators held on to their securities

17. As used in line 56, the word "privation" means

    (A) solitude
    (B) lack of basic necessities
    (C) strictness
    (D) a smooth transition
    (E) a reduction in the usual business sales rate

18. The word "inaugurated" in line 81 means

    (A) stifled
    (B) amalgamated
    (C) began
    (D) commemorated
    (E) oversaw

19. According to the passage, the Reconstruction Finance Corporation

    (A) remodeled old private and government buildings
    (B) served as a price-regulating organization
    (C) helped the unemployed to find jobs during the Depression
    (D) gave government loans to certain businesses
    (E) supported the unemployed by public relief programs

20. Which statement would the author *not* agree to?

    (A) There will continue to be economic crises.
    (B) The end of the spiral of deflation was usually in sight.
    (C) War tends to reduce unemployment.
    (D) War is not the answer to avoiding economic depression.
    (E) The Depression of 1929 had psychological roots.

21. As seen from the passage, as a result of the Depression

    (A) the value of the free enterprise system was questioned
    (B) more people demanded that the government stay out of business
    (C) people put more trust in business leaders
    (D) a third of the population was unemployed
    (E) the government was forced to increase taxes

22. The author would agree that war is economically advantageous in that

    (A) it implies a choice between war and depression
    (B) it increases unemployment
    (C) the market becomes satiated
    (D) it solves bouts of inflation
    (E) it increases aggregate demand

23. After 1929, the following demands were raised *except*

    (A) abolition of the great financial cartels
    (B) cheap money
    (C) investigation of trusts and monopolies
    (D) intervention of the federal government to correct business abuses
    (E) intervention of the federal government to aid the poor

24. As seen by the passage, the contraction of business in 1929 led to

    (A) war fever
    (B) increased unemployment
    (C) payment of debts
    (D) demand exceeding supply
    (E) skyrocketing prices

STOP

**If you finish before time is called, you may check your work on this section only.
Do not turn to any other section in the test.**

Section 5

Time: 25 Minutes – Turn to Section 5 (page 339) of your answer sheet to answer the questions in this section. 35 Questions

Directions: For each question in this section, select the best answer from among the choices given and fill in the corresponding circle on the answer sheet.

The following sentences test correctness and effectiveness of expression. Part of each sentence or the entire sentence is underlined; beneath each sentence are five ways of phrasing the underlined material. Choice A repeats the original phrasing; the other four choices are different. If you think the original phrasing produces a better sentence than any of the alternatives, select Choice A; if not, select one of the other choices.

In making your selection, follow the requirements of standard written English; that is, pay attention to grammar, choice of words, sentence construction, and punctuation. Your selection should result in the most effective sentence—clear and precise, without awkwardness or ambiguity.

EXAMPLE:

Laura Ingalls Wilder published her first book <u>and she was sixty-five years old then</u>.

(A)   and she was sixty-five years old then

(B)   when she was sixty-five

(C)   at age sixty-five years old

(D)   upon the reaching of sixty-five years

(E)   at the time when she was sixty-five

---

1.   The most primitive boat of all is the dugout canoe, <u>being carved from a tree trunk</u>.

   (A)   being carved from a tree trunk
   (B)   carving from a tree trunk
   (C)   carved from a tree trunk
   (D)   having been carved from a tree trunk
   (E)   its being carved from a tree trunk

2.   <u>Whether you can find a place to park your car</u> is probably the hardest part of the day's outing.

   (A)   Whether you can find a place to park your car
   (B)   Finding a place to park your car
   (C)   To park your car in a place
   (D) Taking your car to a place where you can park it
   (E)   Finding a car parking place near you

3.   The trustee resigned <u>in protest from the town board against its approval</u> of the rent control law.

   (A)   in protest from the town board against its approval
   (B)   protesting against the approval by the town board
   (C)   from the town board in protest against its approval
   (D)   against the town board, protesting its approval
   (E)   in protest from the town board, protesting its approval

GO ON TO THE NEXT PAGE ➤

4. In the summer, the number of injuries <u>from ladder falls</u> soars.

   (A) from ladder falls
   (B) coming from people falling off their ladders
   (C) because of falls from ladders
   (D) caused by falls from ladders
   (E) which come from the result of falls from ladders

5. Thousands of people are blind <u>because their glaucoma</u> has reached an advanced stage.

   (A) because their glaucoma
   (B) due to their glaucoma
   (C) since they have their glaucoma and it
   (D) having their glaucoma
   (E) from their glaucoma

6. Driving a racing car on a speedway <u>is in some ways like when you are riding</u> a horse on a bridle path.

   (A) is in some ways like when you are riding
   (B) in some ways is in the same class as riding
   (C) is in some ways similar to when you are riding
   (D) is in some ways similar to riding
   (E) is like a ride in some ways of

7. <u>Seeing the security guard, the cigarettes were immediately concealed by the workers.</u>

   (A) Seeing the security guard, the cigarettes were immediately concealed by the workers
   (B) The security guard being seen by them, the workers immediately concealed the cigarettes
   (C) The workers having seen the security guard, the cigarettes were concealed immediately
   (D) When the workers saw the security guard, they immediately concealed the cigarettes
   (E) When the security guard was seen, the workers immediately concealed the cigarettes

8. <u>Henry VIII had many wives, Henry VI one,</u> but each is remembered not for his women but for his talent.

   (A) Henry VIII had many wives, Henry VI one
   (B) Henry VIII had many wives, Henry VI having one
   (C) Henry VIII having many wives, Henry VI just one
   (D) Henry VIII has had many wives, but Henry VI only one
   (E) Henry VIII had many wives, Henry VI had only one wife

9. Biologists often say that <u>it is not chemists or physicists but that they have</u> the answer to the improvement of life on earth.

   (A) it is not chemists or physicists but that they have
   (B) it is not chemists or physicists but they have
   (C) they, and not chemists or physicists have
   (D) it is not chemists or physicists but it is they who have
   (E) it is they, not chemists or physicists, who have

10. The underprivileged student is getting a better <u>education, there are better teachers for them</u> and better facilities.

    (A) education, there are better teachers for them
    (B) education; he has better teachers
    (C) education; they have better teachers
    (D) education, he has better teachers
    (E) education; because he has better teachers

11. <u>When the university administration changed its role from that of a judge and prosecutor to that of an adviser and friend</u>, not only did the students stop their demonstrations but they also sided with the administration against the outsiders.

    (A) When the university administration changed its role from that of a judge and prosecutor to that of an adviser and friend
    (B) When the university administration changed its role from that of a judge and prosecutor to an adviser and friend
    (C) When the university administration changed its role from that of a judge and prosecutor to one of an adviser and friend
    (D) As a result of the administration's changing its role from judge and prosecutor to that of adviser and friend
    (E) As to the university administration, in changing its role from that of a judge and prosecutor to that of an adviser and friend

GO ON TO THE NEXT PAGE ➤

The following sentences test your ability to recognize grammar and usage errors. Each sentence contains either a single error or no error at all. No sentence contains more than one error. The error, if there is one, is underlined and lettered. If the sentence contains an error, select the one underlined part that must be changed to make the sentence correct. If the sentence is correct, select Choice E. In choosing answers, follow the requirements of standard written English.

EXAMPLE:

The other delegates and him immediately
    A   B   C

accepted the resolution drafted by
                      D

the neutral states. No error.
            E

12. You <u>may not</u> realize <u>it</u> but the weather in
      A   B

Barbados <u>during Christmas</u> is <u>like New York</u> in
           C   D

June. <u>No error</u>.
        E

13. Stores were <u>jammed</u> with <u>last-minute</u> Christmas
           A   B

shoppers, and the festive spirit was <u>greatly</u>
                             C

disrupted by homemade bombs that <u>exploded</u> at
                          D

two department stores. <u>No error</u>.
                 E

14. The teacher did not encourage the student <u>any</u>
                             A

even though the boy began <u>to weep</u> when he
                   B

<u>was told</u> that his poor marks would likely <u>hold up</u>
 C   D

his graduation. <u>No error</u>.
          E

15. Allen <u>has stated</u> that he <u>has always had</u> a great
      A   B

<u>interest and</u> admiration for the <u>work</u> of the British
   C   D

economist Keynes. <u>No error</u>.
           E

16. <u>Besides</u> my job as a legal secretary, I also have a job
   A

<u>as</u> a condominium manager <u>that</u> requires me to
 B   C

solve a large <u>amount</u> of problems. <u>No error</u>.
         D   E

17. <u>Who's</u> to decide that certain <u>terminally-ill</u> patients
  A   B

should be taken <u>off</u> life-support systems <u>while</u> others
          C   D

should remain dependent upon machines? <u>No error</u>.
                          E

18. When the results of the polls <u>were published</u> in the
                    A

paper, my brother, who was a <u>candidate for</u> mayor,
                    B

was not discouraged <u>any</u> because he was <u>among</u>
             C   D

the top four candidates. <u>No error</u>.
             E

19. A mother <u>along with</u> her five children <u>were rescued</u>
       A   B

from the burning apartment building by a postal

worker <u>who</u> was making his daily deliveries earlier
    C

<u>than</u> usual. <u>No error</u>.
 D   E

GO ON TO THE NEXT PAGE ➤

20. My partner in the computer class <u>worked on</u> the
                                        A
same programs as <u>I,</u> but his method of solving the
                 B
problems was <u>quite</u> <u>different than</u> mine. <u>No error.</u>
             C   D   E

21. The school board members did <u>like</u> <u>they</u> <u>were</u>
                                    A   B   C
<u>expected</u> to do when they decided to increase the
   C
length of the school day <u>rather than</u> the length of
                          D
the school year. <u>No error.</u>
                      E

22. A <u>woman</u> perished on Sunday when the hot air
         A
balloon in which she <u>had rode</u> <u>caught</u> fire as it
                      B   C
<u>touched</u> down. <u>No error.</u>
   D   E

23. From every community <u>comes</u> reports <u>that</u> there
                            A   B
<u>has been</u> an increase in vandalism by <u>teenagers.</u>
   C   D
<u>No error.</u>
    E

24. When the hurricane <u>struck</u>, the people who
                          A
<u>had gone</u> to the shelter found that there <u>wasn't</u>
   B   C
scarcely enough food for <u>everyone</u>. <u>No error.</u>
                          D   E

25. By the time I <u>graduate</u> <u>from</u> law school, my sister
                     A   B
<u>will have been practicing</u> law <u>for three years.</u>
              C   D
<u>No error.</u>
    E

26. I had to borrow a book <u>off of</u> my English instructor
                              A
<u>since</u> the campus bookstore <u>had</u> <u>sold all</u> the copies
   B   C   D
of the required text. <u>No error.</u>
                           E

27. Neither the school board members <u>or</u> the city
                                        A
<u>council</u> wanted <u>to change</u> the school boundaries
   B   C
<u>in order</u> to reduce the over-enrollment. <u>No error.</u>
   D   E

28. When my neighbor, <u>who</u> cannot <u>swim</u>, was a
                         A   B
teenager, he <u>had rescued</u> a <u>drowning</u> swimmer by
             C   D
pulling him into his rowboat. <u>No error.</u>
                                   E

29. <u>As</u> an incentive <u>to attend</u> the local college, our
        A   B
father told my brother and <u>I</u> that we could use his
                            C
company car <u>for</u> transportation. <u>No error.</u>
            D   E

GO ON TO THE NEXT PAGE ➤

> **Directions:** The following passage is an early draft of an essay. Some parts of the passage need to be rewritten.
>
> Read the passage and select the best answers for the questions that follow. Some questions are about particular sentences or parts of sentences and ask you to improve sentence structure or word choice. Other questions ask you to consider organization and development. In choosing answers, follow the requirements of standard written English.

Questions 30–35 refer to the following passage.

[1]We know that a proportion of our sleeping time is spent dreaming. [2]This is true for everyone, whether you are the kind of person who ordinarily remembers your dreams or not. [3]Often our dreams show us "the other side of the picture," making us aware of things we have failed to take conscious note of during the day. [4]Moreover, if you dream that your new boss, who seems gruff and unfriendly during waking hours, is smiling at you and praising you for your work, perhaps you have subliminally picked up signals that day that his bark is worse than his bite.

[5]All of us need our dreams, and the younger we are, the more necessary they appear to be. [6]Babies spend nearly half their sleep in the dreaming phase. [7]When adult subjects in an experiment were given drugs that eliminated their dreaming for several nights, they became increasingly irritable and anxious, and often began having difficulty concentrating. [8]Too much dreaming appears to have its drawbacks too. [9]If you doze late on Sunday morning, you often wake up feeling tired. [10]The reason is that the longer you sleep, the longer your dreams become. [11](Dreaming periods are short during the first part of the night and lengthen as your sleep progresses.)

30. The word <u>Moreover,</u> in sentence 4 should be

   (A) left as it is

   (B) changed to <u>However,</u>

   (C) changed to <u>For instance,</u>

   (D) changed to <u>In short,</u>

   (E) changed to <u>Some people believe</u>

31. Sentence 8 would be improved if

   (A) it were joined to sentence 7 with a semicolon

   (B) it were joined to sentence 7 with <u>and</u>

   (C) it began with <u>Although</u>

   (D) it began with <u>Yet</u>

   (E) it were placed after sentence 9

32. Sentence 10 should be

   (A) eliminated

   (B) joined to sentence 9 with a semicolon

   (C) joined to sentence 9 with a comma

   (D) placed at the end of the paragraph

   (E) shortened to read <u>The longer you sleep, the longer your dreams become</u>

33. Which of the following sentences would make the best introductory sentence to the passage?

   (A) Dreams have fascinated man since ancient times.

   (B) Many people dismiss dreams as unimportant.

   (C) You do not need a psychoanalyst to learn something from your dreams.

   (D) Socrates said dreams represented the voice of our consciences; Freud called them "the royal road to the unconscious."

   (E) New research indicates that, night and day, dreams play an important part in all of our lives.

34. In sentence 7, the word <u>When</u> should be

   (A) left as it is

   (B) changed to <u>If</u>

   (C) changed to <u>Only</u>

   (D) changed to <u>Before</u>

   (E) changed to <u>Nevertheless</u>

35. What should be done with sentence 11?

   (A) The parentheses should be eliminated.

   (B) An exclamation point should be used instead of a period.

   (C) The sentence should be italicized.

   (D) The sentence should be made into two sentences without the parentheses.

   (E) It should be left as it is.

STOP

If you finish before time is called, you may check your work on this section only.
Do not turn to any other section in the test.

Section 6

Time: 25 Minutes – Turn to Section 6 (page 340) of your answer sheet to answer the questions in this section. 18 Questions
Directions: This section contains two types of questions. You have 25 minutes to complete both types. For questions 1–8, solve each problem and decide which is the best of the choices given. Fill in the corresponding circle on the answer sheet. You may use any available space for scratchwork.

Notes:

1. The use of a calculator is permitted.

2. All numbers used are real numbers.

3. Figures that accompany problems in this test are intended to provide information useful in solving the problems. They are drawn as accurately as possible EXCEPT when it is stated in a specific problem that the figure is not drawn to scale. All figures lie in a plane unless otherwise indicated.

4. Unless otherwise specified, the domain of any function f is assumed to be the set of all real numbers x for which $f(x)$ is a real number.

REFERENCE INFORMATION

 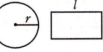 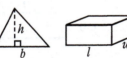

$A = \pi r^2$ $A = lw$ $A = \frac{1}{2}bh$ $V = lwh$ $V = \pi r^2 h$ $c^2 = a^2 + b^2$ *Special Right Triangle.*
$C = 2\pi r$

The number of degrees of arc in a circle is 360.
The sum of the measures in degrees of the angles of a triangle is 180.

---

1. From the equations $7a = 4$ and $7a + 4b = 12$, one can conclude that b is

    (A) -1
    (B) 0
    (C) 1
    (D) 2
    (E) any integer

2. How many values of x satisfy $-\frac{1}{2} < \frac{x}{3} < -\frac{1}{4}$ where x is an integer?

    (A) none
    (B) one
    (C) two
    (D) three
    (E) infinitely many

GO ON TO THE NEXT PAGE ➤

3. If r and s are negative numbers, then all of the following must be positive *except*

(A) $\frac{r}{s}$

(B) rs

(C) $(rs)^2$

(D) $r + s$

(E) $-r - s$

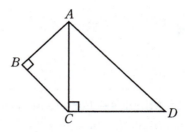

5. In the figure above, $AB = BC$ and $AC = CD$. How many of the angles have a measure of 45 degrees?

(A) none

(B) two

(C) three

(D) four

(E) five

4. If $f(x) = x^2 + 2x + 1$, then $f(x - 1) =$

(A) $x^2 + 2x$

(B) 0

(C) 1

(D) x^2

(E) $2x + 1$

6. Which of the rectangles below has a length of $\frac{4}{3}$, if each has an area of 4?

(A)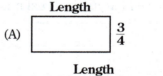
Length $\frac{3}{4}$

(B)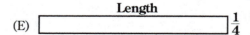
Length 3

(C)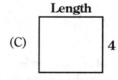
Length 4

(D)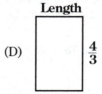
Length $\frac{4}{3}$

(E)
Length $\frac{1}{4}$

Note: Figures are not drawn to scale.

GO ON TO THE NEXT PAGE ▶

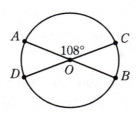

7. O is the center of a circle of diameter 20 and $\angle AOC = 108°$. Find the sum of the lengths of minor arcs $\overarc{AC}$ and $\overarc{DB}$.

(A) 5π

(B) 8π

(C) 10π

(D) 12π

(E) 15π

8. Which is true of the graphs $y = 2x^2$ and $y = -2x^2$?

I.   They have only one point in common.

II.   The shapes of both are the same but one is right side up and the other is upside down.

III. They both represent linear functions.

(A) I only

(B) II only

(C) III only

(D) I and II only

(E) I, II, and III

GO ON TO THE NEXT PAGE ❯

Directions: For Student-Produced Response questions 9–18, use the grids on the bottom of the answer sheet page on which you have answered questions 1-8.

Each of the remaining questions requires you to solve the problem and enter your answer by marking the circles in the special grid, as shown in the examples below. You may use any available space for scratchwork.

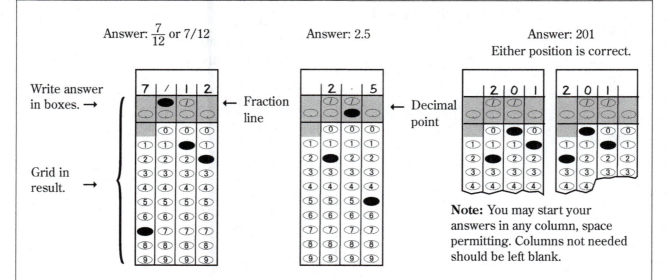

Answer: $\frac{7}{12}$ or 7/12   Answer: 2.5   Answer: 201
Either position is correct.

Write answer in boxes. →   ← Fraction line   ← Decimal point

Grid in result. →

Note: You may start your answers in any column, space permitting. Columns not needed should be left blank.

- Mark no more than one oval in any column.

- Because the answer sheet will be machine-scored, **you will receive credit only if the ovals are filled in correctly.**

- Although not required, it is suggested that you write your answer in the boxes at the top of the columns to help you fill in the ovals accurately.

- Some problems may have more than one correct answer. In such cases, grid only one answer.

- No question has a negative answer.

- **Mixed numbers** such as $2\frac{1}{2}$ must be gridded as 2.5 or 5/2. (If $2\frac{1}{2}$ is gridded, it will be interpreted as $\frac{21}{2}$, not $2\frac{1}{2}$.)

- **Decimal Accuracy:** If you obtain a decimal answer, **enter the most accurate value the grid will accommodate.** For example, if you obtain an answer such as 0.6666..., you should record the result as .666 or .667. **Less accurate values such as .66 or .67 are not acceptable.**

Acceptable ways to grid $\frac{2}{3}$ = .6666...:

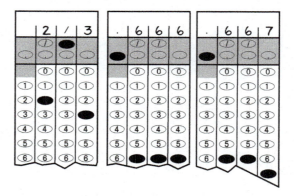

9. Sophie has 3 times as many jelly beans as Mia, and Riley has 18 times as many jelly beans as Mia. What is the ratio

$$\frac{\text{Riley's jelly beans}}{\text{Sophie's jelly beans}}?$$

10. If two cubes have edges of 1 and 2, what is the sum of their volumes?

11. If the numerical value of the binomial coefficient $\left(\dfrac{n}{2}\right)$ is given by the formula $\dfrac{n(n-1)}{2}$, then what is the numerical value of $\left(\dfrac{15}{2}\right)$?

12. The letters r and s represent numbers satisfying $r^2 = 9$ and $s^2 = 25$. What is the difference between the greatest possible values of $s - r$ and $r - s$?

GO ON TO THE NEXT PAGE ➤

13. According to the graph, what percent of the people in the group had brown eyes?

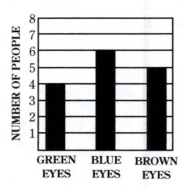

15. In the figure above, the hand of dial Z moves in a clockwise direction. When its hand makes one complete revolution, it causes the hand of dial Y to move 1 number in the counterclockwise direction. How many complete revolutions of the hand of dial Z are needed to move the hand of dial Y 3 complete revolutions?

Dial Y   Dial Z

$$\begin{array}{r} N\,5 \\ \times\ LM \\ \hline 3\,8\,5 \\ 3\,8\,5 \\ \hline 4{,}2\,3\,5 \end{array}$$

14. In the multiplication problem above, L, M, and N each represent one of the digits 0 through 9. If the problem is computed correctly, find N.

16. To make enough paste to hang 6 rolls of wallpaper, a $\frac{1}{4}$ pound package of powder is mixed with $2\frac{1}{2}$ quarts of water. How many pounds of powder are needed to make enough of the same mixture of paste to hang 21 rolls of paper?

17. On a mathematics test, the average score for a certain class was 90. If 40 percent of the class scored 100 and 10 percent scored 80, what was the average score for the remainder of the class?

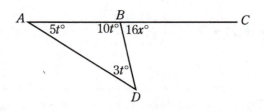

18. In the figure above, ABC is a line segment. What is the value of x?

STOP

If you finish before time is called, you may check your work on this section only.
Do not turn to any other section in the test.

Take a 5 minute break

before starting section 7

Section 7

Time: 25 Minutes – Turn to Section 7 (page 340) of your answer sheet to answer the questions in this section. 24 Questions

Directions: For each question in this section, select the best answer from among the choices given and fill in the corresponding circle on the answer sheet.

Each sentence below has one or two blanks, each blank indicating that something has been omitted. Beneath the sentence are five words or sets of words labeled A through E. Choose the word or set of words that, when inserted in the sentence, <u>best</u> fits the meaning of the sentence as a whole.

Example:

Hoping to _____ the dispute, negotiators proposed a compromise that they felt would be _____ to both labor and management.

(A) enforce...useful

(B) end...divisive

(C) overcome...unattractive

(D) extend...satisfactory

(E) resolve...acceptable

Ⓐ Ⓑ Ⓒ Ⓓ ⬤

1. The girl's extreme state of _____ aroused in him a feeling of pity.

    (A) disapproval
    (B) exultation
    (C) enthusiasm
    (D) degradation
    (E) jubilation

2. Although our team was aware that the Raiders' attack power was _____ as compared with that of our players, we were stupid to be so _____.

    (A) calculated...alert
    (B) sluggish...easygoing
    (C) acceptable...serious

    (D) determined...detailed
    (E) premeditated...willing

3. The _____ prime minister caused the downfall of the once _____ country.

    (A) heroic...important
    (B) respected...rich
    (C) incompetent...powerful
    (D) vacillating...confidential
    (E) insightful...unconquerable

GO ON TO THE NEXT PAGE ❯

4. The main character in the novel was dignified and _____, a man of great reserve.

   (A) garrulous
   (B) aloof
   (C) boring
   (D) hypocritical
   (E) interesting

5. The nonsmoker's blood contains _____ amounts of carbon monoxide; on the other hand, the smoker's blood contains _____ amounts.

   (A) frequent…extensive
   (B) heavy…adequate
   (C) minute…excessive
   (D) definite…puzzling
   (E) bland…moderate

The two passages below are followed by questions based on their content and on the relationship between the two passages. Answer the questions on the basis of what is <u>stated</u> or <u>implied</u> in the passages and in any introductory material that may be provided.

Questions 6–9 are based on the following passages.

Passage 1

Classical music is termed "classical" because it can be heard over and over again without the listener tiring of the music. A symphony of Brahms can be heard and heard again with the same or even heightened enjoyment a few months
5 later. It is unfortunate that the sales of classical music are dismal compared to other types of music. Perhaps this is because many people in our generation were not exposed to classical music at an early age and therefore did not get to know the music.

Passage 2

10 Contemporary nonclassical music has a high impact on the listener but unfortunately is not evergreen. Its enjoyment lasts only as long as there is current interest in the topic or emotion that the music portrays, and that only lasts for three months or so until other music replaces it, especially when another bestselling song comes out.
15 The reason why the impact of this type of music is not as great when it first comes out is thought to be because technically the intricacy of the music is not high and not sophisticated, although many critics believe it is because
20 the music elicits a particular emotional feeling that gradually becomes worn out in time.

6. According to the passage, it can be assumed that the majority of younger people do not like classical music because they

   (A) buy only the bestselling songs
   (B) do not have the sophistication of a true music lover
   (C) grow tired of classical music
   (D) did not hear that type of music in their youth
   (E) are more restless than the older generation

7. The reason that the enjoyment of a particular piece of contemporary music may not last as long as a piece of classical music is due to the

   (A) emotion of a person, which is thought to change in time
   (B) high sophistication of the classical music and its technical intricacy
   (C) fact that there is always another piece of contemporary music that replaces the one before it
   (D) youth desiring something new
   (E) economy and marketing of the songs

8. The term "evergreen" in line 11 most nearly means

   (A) colorful
   (B) lasting
   (C) current
   (D) likeable
   (E) encompassing

9. Which of the following is addressed in one passage but not the other?

   (A) The time period of enjoyment of the music
   (B) The type of music
   (C) A specific example illustrating a point
   (D) The instruments used in the music
   (E) The musicians playing the music

GO ON TO THE NEXT PAGE ➤

Questions 10–15 are based on the following passage.

The following passage is excerpted from the Brahmin's life, Siddhartha.

Siddhartha was now pleased with himself. He could have dwelt for a long time yet in that soft, well-upholstered hell, if this had not happened, this moment of complete hopelessness and despair and the tense moment when he was ready
5 to commit suicide. Was it not his Self, his small, fearful and proud Self, with which he had wrestled for many years, which had always conquered him again and again, which robbed him of happiness and filled him with fear?

Siddhartha now realized why he had struggled in
10 vain with this Self when he was a Brahmin and an ascetic. Too much knowledge had hindered him; too many holy verses, too many sacrificial rites, too much mortification of the flesh, too much doing and striving. He had been full of arrogance; he had always been the cleverest, the
15 most eager—always a step ahead of the others, always the learned and intellectual one, always the priest or the sage. His Self had crawled into his priesthood, into this arrogance, into this intellectuality. It sat there tightly and grew, while he thought he was destroying it by fasting and penitence. Now he understood it and realized that the
20 inward voice had been right, that no teacher could have brought him salvation. That was why he had to go into the world, to lose himself in power, women and money; that was why he had to be a merchant, a dice player, a drinker and a man of property, until the priest and Samana in him
25 were dead. That was why he had to undergo those horrible years, suffer nausea, learn the lesson of the madness of an empty, futile life till the end, till he reached bitter despair, so that Siddhartha the pleasure-monger and Siddhartha the man of property could die. He had died and a new
30 Siddhartha had awakened from his sleep. He also would grow old and die. Siddhartha was transitory, all forms were transitory, but today he was young, he was a child—the new Siddhartha—and he was very happy.

These thoughts passed through his mind. Smiling, he
35 listened thankfully to a humming bee. Happily he looked into the flowing river. Never had a river attracted him as much as this one. Never had he found the voice and appearance of flowing water so beautiful. It seemed to him as if the river had something special to tell him, something
40 which he did not know, something which still awaited him. The new Siddhartha felt a deep love for this flowing water and decided that he would not leave it again so quickly.

10. The "soft, well-upholstered hell" (line 2) is a reference to

(A) an attractive yet uncomfortable dwelling where Siddhartha resided
(B) Siddhartha's lifestyle, which made him an unhappy person
(C) a place to which Siddhartha went when he wished to be completely by himself
(D) Siddhartha's abode in a previous life not referred to in the passage
(E) a figment of Siddhartha's imagination that used to haunt him

11. Which of the following best describes the relation between the second and third paragraphs?

(A) Paragraph 3 shows how much happier one can be by living alone than in living with others, as brought out in paragraph 2.
(B) Paragraph 3 discusses the advantages of a simple life as opposed to the more complicated lifestyle discussed in paragraph 2.
(C) Paragraph 3 contrasts the life of a person without wealth and a formal religion with a person who has wealth and a formal religion, as in paragraph 2.
(D) Paragraph 3 demonstrates the happiness that can come as a result of giving up the power and the worldly pleasures referred to in paragraph 2.
(E) Paragraph 3 generalizes about the specific points made in paragraph 2.

12. Which of the following questions does the passage answer?

(A) What is the meaning of a Brahmin?
(B) Why did Siddhartha decide to commit suicide?
(C) Where did Siddhartha own property?
(D) For how many years was Siddhartha a member of the priesthood?
(E) Where did Siddhartha go to school?

GO ON TO THE NEXT PAGE ➤

13. The word "transitory" in line 31 most likely means

(A) quick on one's feet

(B) invisible

(C) short-lived

(D) going from one place to another

(E) frozen

14. Which statement best expresses the main idea of this passage?

(A) Arrogance constitutes a great hindrance for one who seeks to lead a peaceful life.

(B) One has to discipline himself so that he will refrain from seeking pleasures that will prove harmful later.

(C) The quest for knowledge is commendable provided that search has its limitations.

(D) There is a voice within a person that can advise him how to attain contentment.

(E) Peace and quiet are more important than wealth and power in bringing happiness.

15. What is the meaning of "Self," as it is referred to in the passage?

(A) one's love of nature

(B) one's own lifestyle

(C) one's inner voice

(D) one's remembrances

(E) one's own interests

Questions 16–24 are based on the following passage.

The following passage explores how brilliant people think, how they may come up with their theories, and what motivates their thinking and creativity.

The discoveries made by scientific geniuses, from Archimedes through Einstein, have repeatedly revolutionized both our world and the way we see it. Yet no one really knows how the mind of a genius works. Most people think
5 that a very high IQ sets the great scientist apart. They assume that flashes of profound insight like Einstein's are the product of mental processes so arcane that they must be inaccessible to more ordinary minds.

But a growing number of researchers in psychology,
10 psychiatry, and the history of science are investigating the way geniuses think. The researchers are beginning to give us tantalizing glimpses of the mental universe that can produce the discoveries of an Einstein, an Edison, a Da Vinci—or any Nobel Prize winner.
15 Surprisingly, most researchers agree that the important variable in genius is not the IQ but creativity. Testers start with 135 as the beginning of the "genius" category,

but the researchers seem to feel that, while an IQ above a certain point—about 120—is very helpful for a scientist,
20 having an IQ that goes much higher is not crucial for producing a work of genius. All human beings have at least four types of intelligence. The great scientist possesses the ability to move back and forth among them—the logical-mathematical, the spatial, which includes visual perception,
25 the linguistic, and the bodily kinesthetic.

Some corroboration of these categories comes from the reports of scientists who describe thought processes centered on images, sensations, or words. Einstein reported a special "feeling at the tips of the fingers" that told him
30 which path to take through a problem. The idea for a self-starting electric motor came to Nikola Tesla one evening as he was reciting a poem by Goethe and watching a sunset. Suddenly he imagined a magnetic field rapidly rotating inside a circle of electromagnets.
35 Some IQ tests predict fairly accurately how well a person will do in school and how quickly he or she will master knowledge, but genius involves more than knowledge. The genius has the capacity to leap significantly beyond his present knowledge and produce something
40 new. To do this, he sees the relationship between facts or pieces of information in a new or unusual way.

The scientist solves a problem by shifting from one intelligence to another, although the logical-mathematical intelligence is dominant. Creative individuals seem to be
45 marked by a special fluidity of mind. They may be able to think of a problem verbally, logically, and also spatially.

Paradoxically, fluid thinking may be connected to another generally agreed-upon trait of the scientific genius—persistence, or unusually strong motivation to
50 work on a problem. Persistence kept Einstein looking for the solution to the question of the relationship between the law of gravity and his special theory of relativity. Yet surely creative fluidity enabled him to come up with a whole new field that included both special relativity and gravitation.
55 Many scientists have the ability to stick with a problem even when they appear not to be working on it. Werner Heisenberg discovered quantum mechanics one night during a vacation he had taken to recuperate from the mental jumble he had fallen into trying to solve the atomic-
60 spectra problem.

16. Which statement is true, according to the passage?

(A) The law of gravity followed the publication of Einstein's theory of relativity.

(B) Nikola Tesla learned about magnets from his research of the works of Goethe.

(C) Archimedes and Einstein lived in the same century.

(D) Most scientists have IQ scores above 120.

(E) We ought to refer to intelligences rather than to intelligence.

GO ON TO THE NEXT PAGE ❯

17. The author believes that, among the four intelligences he cites, the most important one for the scientist is

    (A) spatial
    (B) bodily kinesthetic
    (C) linguistic
    (D) logical-mathematical
    (E) not singled out

18. The author focuses on the circumstances surrounding the work of great scientists in order to show that

    (A) scientific geniuses are usually eccentric in their behavior
    (B) the various types of intelligence have come into play during their work
    (C) scientists often give the impression that they are relaxing when they are really working on a problem
    (D) scientists must be happy to do their best work
    (E) great scientific discoveries are almost always accidental

19. The passage can best be described as

    (A) a comparison of how the average individual and the great scientist think
    (B) an account of the unexpected things that led to great discoveries by scientists
    (C) an explanation of the way scientific geniuses really think
    (D) a criticism of intelligence tests as they are given today
    (E) a lesson clarifying scientific concepts such as quantum mechanics and relativity

20. The passage suggests that a college football star who is majoring in literature is quite likely to have which intelligences to a high degree?

    I. logical-mathematical
    II. spatial
    III. linguistic
    IV. bodily kinesthetic

    (A) I only
    (B) II only
    (C) III only

    (D) I, II, and III only
    (E) II, III, and IV only

21. Which statement would the author most likely *not* agree with?

    (A) Most people believe that IQ is what makes the scientist brilliant.
    (B) Some scientists may come up with a solution to a problem when they are working on something else.
    (C) Creativity is much more important than basic intelligence in scientific discovery.
    (D) Scientists and artists may think alike in their creative mode.
    (E) Scientists usually get the answer to a problem fairly quickly, and if they get stuck they usually go on to another problem.

22. "Fluidity" as described in lines 52–54 can best be defined as

    (A) persistence when faced with a problem
    (B) having a flighty attitude in dealing with scientific problems
    (C) being able to move from one scientific area to another
    (D) having an open mind in dealing with scientific phenomena
    (E) being able to generate enormous excitement in the scientist's work

23. The word "paradoxically" in line 47 means

    (A) ironically
    (B) seemingly contradictorily
    (C) in a manner of speaking
    (D) experimentally
    (E) conditionally

24. The author's attitude toward scientists in this passage can be seen as one of

    (A) objective intrigue
    (B) grudging admiration
    (C) subtle jealousy
    (D) growing impatience
    (E) boundless enthusiasm

STOP

If you finish before time is called, you may check your work on this section only.
Do not turn to any other section in the test.

Section 8

Time: 20 Minutes – Turn to Section 8 (page 341) of your answer sheet to answer the questions in this section. 16 Questions

Directions: For this section, solve each problem and decide which is the best of the choices given. Fill in the corresponding circle on the answer sheet. You may use any available space for scratchwork.

Notes:

1. The use of a calculator is permitted.

2. All numbers used are real numbers.

3. Figures that accompany problems in this test are intended to provide information useful in solving the problems. They are drawn as accurately as possible EXCEPT when it is stated in a specific problem that the figure is not drawn to scale. All figures lie in a plane unless otherwise indicated.

4. Unless otherwise specified, the domain of any function f is assumed to be the set of all real numbers x for which $f(x)$ is a real number.

REFERENCE INFORMATION

   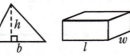

$A = \pi r^2$ $A = lw$ $A = \frac{1}{2}bh$ $V = lwh$ $V = \pi r^2 h$ $c^2 = a^2 + b^2$ *Special Right Triangle.*
$C = 2\pi r$

The number of degrees of arc in a circle is 360.
The sum of the measures in degrees of the angles of a triangle is 180.

1. A box of candy contains 0.6 of a pound of caramels and 3.6 pounds of coconut. What percent of the contents of the box, by weight, consists of caramels?

    (A) 6%

    (B) $14\frac{2}{7}$%

    (C) $16\frac{2}{3}$%

    (D) 25%

    (E) $33\frac{1}{3}$%

GO ON TO THE NEXT PAGE ➤

Distribution of $100,000 Land Improvement
Funds to Five High Schools

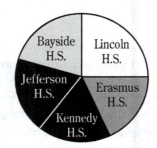

2.   The circle graph above describes the distribution
of $100,000 to five high schools for land
improvement. Which high school received an
amount closest to $25,000?

(A) Bayside H.S.
(B) Lincoln H.S.
(C) Erasmus H.S.
(D) Kennedy H.S.
(E) Jefferson H.S.

3.   If $y = r - 6$ and $z = r + 5$, which of the following
is an expression representing r in terms of y and
z?

(A) $\dfrac{y + z + 1}{2}$

(B) $\dfrac{y + z - 1}{2}$

(C) $y + z - 1$

(D) $y + z$

(E) $y + z + 1$

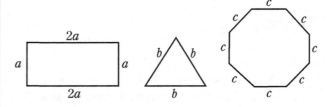

Note: Figures are not drawn to scale.

4.   Which of the following is true if the three
polygons above have equal perimeters?

(A) $b < a < c$
(B) $a < c < b$
(C) $a < b < c$
(D) $c < b < a$
(E) $c < a < b$

Town A Town B Town C

5.   A car travels from Town A to Town B in 3 hours.
It travels from Town B to Town C in 5 hours. If
the distance AB is equal to the distance BC, what
is the ratio of the car's average speed between A
and B to its average speed for the whole distance
AC?

(A) $5 : 3$
(B) $4 : 3$
(C) $1 : 1$
(D) $1 : 3$
(E) $1 : 5$

GO ON TO THE NEXT PAGE ❯

6. Given that ax is an integer and bx is an integer, which of the following must also be an integer?

I. a and b

II. x

III. $(a + b)x$

(A) None

(B) I only

(C) III only

(D) II and III only

(E) I, II, and III

8. The function $f(x) = \dfrac{x-3}{2x+4}$ is not defined at

I. $x = 3$

II. $x = 2$

III. $x = -2$

(A) I only

(B) II only

(C) III only

(D) I and II only

(E) I and III only

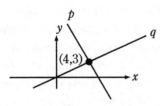

7. In the xy-coordinate system above, the lines q and p are perpendicular. The point $(3,a)$ is on line p. What is the value of a?

(A) 3

(B) 4

(C) $4\frac{1}{3}$

(D) $4\frac{2}{3}$

(E) $5\frac{1}{3}$

9. A sphere is inscribed in a cube whose volume is 64. What is the diameter of the sphere?

(A) 2

(B) $2\sqrt{2}$

(C) 8

(D) $4\sqrt{2}$

(E) 4

GO ON TO THE NEXT PAGE ❯

10. If $\frac{m}{n} = \frac{x}{m}$, then $x =$

(A) $\frac{m^2}{n}$

(B) $\frac{m}{n}$

(C) $\frac{n}{m^2}$

(D) $\frac{1}{n}$

(E) n

12. The number of boys in a certain class exceeds the number of girls by 7. If the number of boys is $\frac{5}{4}$ of the number of girls, how many boys are there in the class?

(A) 21

(B) 28

(C) 35

(D) 42

(E) 63

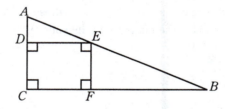

11. The rectangle $CDEF$ has been inscribed in the right triangle ABC, as shown in the figure above. If $CD = \frac{3}{4}AC$ and $CF = \frac{2}{7}BC$, what is the ratio of the area of $\triangle ABC$ to the area of $\square CDEF$?

(A) $\frac{14}{3}$

(B) $\frac{7}{3}$

(C) $\frac{7}{6}$

(D) $\frac{1}{6}$

(E) The answer cannot be determined from the information given.

13. In 2009, the population of Smithdale was 900. Every year, the population of Smithdale had a net increase of 100. For example, in 2010, the population of Smithdale was 1,000. In which of the following periods was the percent increase in population of Smithdale the greatest?

(A) 2009–2010

(B) 2010–2011

(C) 2011–2012

(D) 2012–2013

(E) The answer cannot be determined from the information given.

GO ON TO THE NEXT PAGE ❯

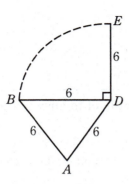

14. Arc *BE* is a quarter circle with radius 6, and *C*, which is not shown, is an arbitrary point on arc *BE*. If *AB* = *BD* = *AD* = 6, then all of the possible values of the perimeter *P* of the quadrilateral *ABCD* are

(A) $P = 18$

(B) $12 < P \leq 18$

(C) $18 < P \leq 24$

(D) $18 < P \leq 18 + 6\sqrt{2}$

(E) $18 < P \leq 30$

15. If $x > 0$ and $y > 0$ and $x^9 = 4$ and $x^7 = \dfrac{9}{y^2}$, which of the following is an expression for the value of *x* in terms of *y*?

(A) $\dfrac{4}{9}y$

(B) $\dfrac{2}{3}y$

(C) $\dfrac{3}{2}y^2$

(D) $6y$

(E) $36y^2$

16. When Ethan received 10*x* DVDs, he then had 5*y* + 1 times as many DVDs as he had originally. In terms of *x* and *y*, how many DVDs did Ethan have originally?

(A) $10x(5y + 1)$

(B) $\dfrac{5y + 1}{10x}$

(C) $\dfrac{2x}{y}$

(D) $\dfrac{10}{5y + 1}$

(E) None of the above

STOP

If you finish before time is called, you may check your work on this section only.
Do not turn to any other section in the test.

Section 9

Time: 20 Minutes – Turn to Section 9 (page 341) of your answer sheet to answer the questions in this section. 19 Questions

Directions: For each question in this section, select the best answer from among the choices given and fill in the corresponding circle on the answer sheet.

Each sentence below has one or two blanks, each blank indicating that something has been omitted. Beneath the sentence are five words or sets of words labeled A through E. Choose the word or set of words that, when inserted in the sentence, best fits the meaning of the sentence as a whole.

Example:

Hoping to _____ the dispute, negotiators proposed a compromise that they felt would be _____ to both labor and management.

(A) enforce...useful

(B) end...divisive

(C) overcome...unattractive

(D) extend...satisfactory

(E) resolve...acceptable

Ⓐ Ⓑ Ⓒ Ⓓ ●

---

1. As a truly objective person, Mr. Moy allows neither _____ attempts to please him nor open _____ on the part of his students to influence his marks.

   (A) unearned...respect
   (B) condescending...humor
   (C) sincere...reliance
   (D) backward...offense
   (E) hypocritical...defiance

2. Because the subject matter was so technical, the instructor made every effort to use _____ terms to describe it.

   (A) candid
   (B) simplified
   (C) discreet
   (D) specialized
   (E) involved

3. Violent crime has become so _____ in our cities that hardly a day goes by when we are not made aware of some _____ act on our local news broadcasts.

   (A) scarce...momentous
   (B) pervasive...benign
   (C) conclusive...serious
   (D) common...heinous
   (E) ridiculous...unacceptable

4. Although they are _____ by intense police patrols, burglars _____ to prowl the subways.

   (A) incited...decline
   (B) enlivened...attempt
   (C) hindered...cease
   (D) persuaded...refuse
   (E) impeded...continue

GO ON TO THE NEXT PAGE ➤

5. Britain's seizure of American ships and _____ of our sailors to serve in the British Navy were two major causes of the War of 1812.

(A) compelling
(B) recruiting
(C) bribing
(D) enlisting
(E) deriding

6. Since she had not worked very hard on her project, the student was quite _____ upon learning that she had won the contest.

(A) annoyed
(B) apathetic
(C) rebuffed
(D) dismayed
(E) elated

The two passages below are followed by questions based on their content and on the relationship between the two passages. Answer the questions on the basis of what is <u>stated</u> or <u>implied</u> in the passages and in any introductory material that may be provided.

Questions 7–19 are based on the following passages.

The following two passages are about science. The first describes science in general, and the second focuses on the subject of physics, one of the disciplines of science.

Passage 1

Science, like everything else that man has created, exists, of course, to gratify certain human needs and desires. The fact that it has been steadily pursued for so many centuries, that it has attracted an ever-wider extent of attention, and
5 that it is now the dominant intellectual interest of mankind, shows that it appeals to a very powerful and persistent group of appetites. It is not difficult to say what these appetites are, at least in their main divisions. Science is valued for its practical advantages, it is valued because it
10 gratifies curiosity, and it is valued because it provides the imagination with objects of great aesthetic charm. This last consideration is of the least importance, so far as the layman is concerned, although it is probably the most important consideration of all to scientific men. It is quite
15 obvious, on the other hand, that the bulk of mankind value science chiefly for the practical advantages it brings with it.

This conclusion is borne out by everything we know about the origin of science. Science seems to have come into existence merely for its bearings on practical life.

20 More than two thousand years before the beginning of the Christian era, both the Babylonians and the Egyptians were in possession of systematic methods of measuring space and time. They had a rudimentary geometry and a rudimentary astronomy. This rudimentary science arose to
25 meet the practical needs of an agricultural population. Their geometry resulted from the measurements made necessary by the problems of land surveying. The cultivation of crops, dependent on the seasons, made a calendar almost a necessity. The day, as a unit of time, was, of course, imposed by
30 nature. The movement of the moon conveniently provided another unit, the month, which was reckoned from one new moon to the next. Twelve of these months were taken to constitute a year, and the necessary adjustments were made from time to time by putting in extra months.

Passage 2

35 Let's be honest right at the start. Physics is neither particularly easy to comprehend nor easy to love, but then again, *what*—or for that matter, *who*—is? For most of us it is a new vision, a different way of understanding with its own scales, rhythms, and forms. And yet, as with *Macbeth, Mona Lisa,*
40 or *La Traviata,* physics has its rewards. Surely you have already somehow prejudged this science. It's all too easy to compartmentalize our human experience: science in one box; and music, art, and literature in other boxes.

The Western mind delights in little boxes—life is
45 easier to analyze when it's presented in small pieces in small compartments (we call it specialization). It is our traditional way of seeing the trees and missing the forest. The label on the box for physics too often reads "Caution: Not for Common Consumption" or "Free from Sentiment."
50 If you can, please tear off that label and discard the box or we will certainly, sooner or later, bore each other to death. There is nothing more tedious than the endless debate between humanist and scientist on whose vision is truer; each of us is less for what we lack of the other.

55 It is pointless and even worse to separate physics from the body of all creative work, to pluck it out from history, to shear it from philosophy, and then to present it pristine, pure, all-knowing, and infallible. We know nothing of what will be with absolute certainty. There is no scientific tome
60 of unassailable, immutable truth. Yet what little we do know about physics reveals an inspiring grandeur and intricate beauty.

GO ON TO THE NEXT PAGE ➤

7. The main idea of Passage 1 is that

    (A) science originated and developed because of the practical advantages it offers
    (B) the Egyptians and the Babylonians used scientific methods to meet the practical needs of feeding their people
    (C) the use of geometry and astronomy are very important for agricultural development
    (D) science has a different value for scientists than it does for the rest of the population
    (E) science is valued not only for its practical contributions to mankind but also for its potential to stir the imagination

8. According to Passage 1,

    (A) the Babylonians and the Egyptians were the first to use scientific methods
    (B) the Christians were the first to have a calendar
    (C) a 12-month calendar was first used by the Egyptians and Babylonians
    (D) the Christians preceded the Babylonians and Egyptians
    (E) scientists are probably more attracted to the charm of science than to its practical benefits

9. The author of Passage 1 implies that scientists are generally

    (A) sociable
    (B) imaginative
    (C) practical
    (D) philosophical
    (E) arrogant

10. The word "rudimentary" in line 23 means

    (A) sophisticated
    (B) flawed
    (C) unworkable
    (D) basic
    (E) coarse

11. According to the author of Passage 2, what does the label on the box for physics suggest about physics?

    (A) It is a dangerous area of study.
    (B) It is a cause for great excitement.
    (C) It is uninteresting to the ordinary person.
    (D) It is difficult to understand because it is completely subjective.
    (E) It is a subject that should be elective but not required.

12. What statement does the author of Passage 2 make about physics?

    (A) It should be recognized for its unique beauty.
    (B) It is a boring course of study.
    (C) It appeals only to the Western mind.
    (D) It is superior to music, art, and literature.
    (E) It is unpopular with people who are romantic.

13. What is the main idea of Passage 2?

    (A) Scientists contribute more to mankind than do humanists.
    (B) The Western mind is more precise than other minds.
    (C) Complete vision needs both the scientist and the humanist.
    (D) Humanists and scientists share no common ground.
    (E) Physics is as important as other science.

14. In which manner does the author of Passage 2 address his audience?

    (A) affectionately
    (B) arrogantly
    (C) humorously
    (D) cynically
    (E) frankly

GO ON TO THE NEXT PAGE ❯

15. In line 47, the phrase "seeing the trees and missing the forest" means

(A) putting experiences into categories
(B) viewing the world too narrowly
(C) analyzing scientific discoveries
(D) making judgments too hastily
(E) ignoring the beauty of natural surroundings

16. The author of Passage 2 leaves out an important aspect of the subject that is addressed in Passage 1. This aspect is the

(A) reaction of laymen to physics
(B) specialization in science
(C) purity of physics
(D) practical applications of physics
(E) arguments between humanists and scientists

17. Which device or method does the author of Passage 2 use that is not used by the author of Passage 1?

(A) analogy through objects
(B) critique
(C) contrast with respect to perceived values
(D) historical referencing
(E) examples to support a claim

18. Which subject is not directly mentioned in either passage?

(A) agriculture
(B) astronomy
(C) art
(D) philosophy
(E) chemistry

19. The word "intricate" in line 61 means

(A) eloquent
(B) complicated
(C) devastating
(D) uninteresting
(E) pointless

STOP
If you finish before time is called, you may check your work on this section only.
Do not turn to any other section in the test.

Section 10

Time: 10 Minutes – Turn to Section 10 (page 341) of your answer sheet to answer the questions in this section. 14 Questions

Directions: For each question in this section, select the best answer from among the choices given and fill in the corresponding circle on the answer sheet.

The following sentences test correctness and effectiveness of expression. Part of each sentence or the entire sentence is underlined; beneath each sentence are five ways of phrasing the underlined material. Choice A repeats the original phrasing; the other four choices are different. If you think the original phrasing produces a better sentence than any of the alternatives, select Choice A; if not, select one of the other choices.

In making your selection, follow the requirements of standard written English; that is, pay attention to grammar, choice of words, sentence construction, and punctuation. Your selection should result in the most effective sentence—clear and precise, without awkwardness or ambiguity.

EXAMPLE:

Laura Ingalls Wilder published her first book <u>and she was sixty-five years old then</u>.

(A) and she was sixty-five years old then

(B) when she was sixty-five

(C) at age sixty-five years old

(D) upon the reaching of sixty-five years

(E) at the time when she was sixty-five

1. In the next booklet, <u>the sales manager and personnel director will tell you something about his work</u>.

   (A) the sales manager and personnel director will tell you something about his work
   (B) the sales manager who is also director of personnel will tell you something about their work
   (C) the sales manager who is also personnel director will tell you something
   (D) the sales manager and personnel director will tell you something as it applies to his work
   (E) the sales manager and the personnel director will tell you something about what his work is

2. I have enjoyed the study of the Spanish language not only because of its beauty but also <u>to make use of it in business</u>.

   (A) to make use of it in business
   (B) because of its use in business
   (C) on account it is useful in business
   (D) one needs it in business
   (E) since all business people use it

GO ON TO THE NEXT PAGE ➤

3. Known to every man, woman, and child in the town, <u>friends were never lacking to my grandfather.</u>

(A) friends were never lacking to my grandfather
(B) my grandfather was not lacking to his friends
(C) friends never lacked my grandfather
(D) my grandfather never lacked no friends
(E) my grandfather never lacked friends

4. No sooner had he entered the room <u>when the lights went out</u> and everyone began to scream.

(A) when the lights went out
(B) than the lights went out
(C) and the lights went out
(D) but the lights went out
(E) the lights went out

5. John, whose mother is a teacher, <u>is not so good a student as many other friends</u> I have with no academic background in their families.

(A) is not so good a student as many other friends
(B) is not as good a student like many other friends
(C) is not quite the student as are other friends
(D) as a student is not as good as many other friends
(E) does not have the studious qualities of many other friends

6. After Sal had spent twenty minutes giving an answer, Pamela found he had given her only one item of information <u>beyond what she already knew.</u>

(A) beyond what she already knew
(B) beyond what she knows already
(C) beyond her knowledge at the current time
(D) to add to what she knew already presently
(E) in addition to her present knowledge then

7. When the members of the committee are at odds, <u>and when also, in addition, they are in the process</u> of offering their resignations, problems become indissoluble.

(A) and when also, in addition, they are in the process
(B) and also when they are in the process
(C) and when, in addition, they are in the process
(D) they are in the process
(E) and when the members of the committee are in the process

8. <u>There is no objection to him joining the party</u> if he is willing to fit in with the plans of the group.

(A) There is no objection to him joining the party
(B) There is no objection on him joining the party
(C) There is no objection to his joining the party
(D) No objection will be raised upon him joining the party
(E) If he decides to join the party, there will be no objection

9. As no one knows the truth <u>as fully as him, no one but him</u> can provide the testimony needed to clear the accused of the very serious charges.

(A) as fully as him, no one but him
(B) as fully as he, no one but him
(C) as fully as he, no one but he
(D) as fully as he does, no one but he
(E) as fully as he does, no one but he alone

10. <u>After having completed her experiments on cancer,</u> the scientist tried to determine if her findings could be used to help prevent this dreaded disease.

(A) After having completed her experiments on cancer
(B) As soon as she completed her experiments on cancer
(C) Having completed her experiments on cancer
(D) After the experiments of the scientist on cancer were completed
(E) When her experiments on cancer are completed

11. The principal, as well as the students and faculty, <u>is trying to affect</u> constructive changes in the school curriculum.

(A) is trying to affect
(B) try to affect
(C) are trying to effect
(D) is trying to effect
(E) does try to encourage

GO ON TO THE NEXT PAGE ➤

12. Because of the recent General Motors strike, <u>less workers will be hired in the coming year</u>.

    (A) less workers will be hired in the coming year
    (B) not as many workers will be hired in the coming year as before
    (C) in the coming year less workers will be hired
    (D) few workers will be hired in the coming year
    (E) fewer workers will be hired in the coming year

13. <u>If the director would have changed</u> some of the dialogue in the script, the scene would have worked better.

    (A) If the director would have changed
    (B) If changes had been made in
    (C) If the director had changed
    (D) Had there been changes made in
    (E) If there would have been changes in

14. <u>Neither Ella nor Mila had their money with them.</u>

    (A) Neither Ella nor Mila had their money with them.
    (B) Neither of the girls had their money with them.
    (C) Neither Ella or Mila had her money with her.
    (D) Neither girl had her money with her.
    (E) Neither Ella nor Mila had her money with her.

How did you do on this test?

Step 1.   Go to the Answer Key

Step 2.   Calculate your "raw score."

Step 3.   Get your "scaled score" for the test by referring to the Raw Score/Scaled Score Conversion Tables.

**THERE'S ALWAYS ROOM
FOR IMPROVEMENT!**

ANSWER KEY FOR PRACTICE TEST 3
Math

Section 2	Correct Answer
1	C
2	E
3	C
4	E
5	A
6	E
7	C
8	E
9	A
10	B
11	C
12	B
13	E
14	A
15	C
16	B
17	B
18	C
19	B
20	A

Number correct

Number incorrect

Section 3	Correct Answer
1	E
2	B
3	A
4	C
5	C
6	D
7	C
8	D
9	B
10	B
11	C
12	D
13	C
14	B
15	E
16	A
17	E
18	D
19	D
20	B

Number correct

Number incorrect

Section 6	Correct Answer
1	D
2	B
3	D
4	D
5	D
6	B
7	D
8	D

Number correct

Number incorrect

Student-Produced Response Questions

9	$\frac{6}{1}$, 6, or $\frac{12}{2}$
10	9
11	105
12	0
13	$33\frac{1}{3}$ or 33.3
14	5
15	24
16	$\frac{7}{8}$ or .875
17	84
18	5

Number correct

Number incorrect

Section 8	Correct Answer
1	B
2	B
3	A
4	E
5	B
6	C
7	C
8	C
9	E
10	A
11	B
12	C
13	A
14	D
15	B
16	C

Number correct

Number incorrect

ANSWER KEY FOR PRACTICE TEST 3
Critical reading

Section 4		Section 7		Section 9	
	Correct Answer		Correct Answer		Correct Answer
1	C	1	D	1	E
2	A	2	B	2	B
3	E	3	C	3	D
4	B	4	B	4	E
5	D	5	C	5	A
6	A	6	D	6	E
7	A	7	A	7	A
8	A	8	B	8	E
9	A	9	C	9	B
10	D	10	B	10	D
11	B	11	D	11	C
12	A	12	B	12	A
13	C	13	C	13	C
14	A	14	E	14	E
15	E	15	E	15	B
16	C	16	E	16	D
17	B	17	D	17	A
18	C	18	B	18	E
19	D	19	C	19	B
20	B	20	E		
21	A	21	E		
22	E	22	C		
23	A	23	B		
24	B	24	A		

Section 9:

Number correct

_____

Number incorrect

Section 4:

Number correct

_____

Number incorrect

Section 7:

Number correct

_____

Number incorrect

ANSWER KEY FOR PRACTICE TEST 3
Writing

Section 1

_____

Essay score

Section 5

	Correct Answer
1	C
2	B
3	C
4	D
5	A
6	D
7	D
8	A
9	E
10	B
11	A
12	D
13	E
14	A
15	C
16	D
17	E
18	C
19	B
20	D
21	A
22	B
23	A
24	C
25	E
26	A
27	A
28	C
29	C
30	C
31	D
32	B
33	E
34	A
35	E

_____

Number correct

_____

Number incorrect

Section 10

	Correct Answer
1	A
2	B
3	E
4	B
5	A
6	A
7	C
8	C
9	B
10	C
11	D
12	E
13	C
14	E

_____

Number correct

_____

Number incorrect

Scoring the SAT Practice Test

Check your responses with the correct answers on the previous pages. Fill in the blanks below and do the calculations to get your Math, Critical Reading, and Writing raw scores. Use the table to find your Math, Critical Reading, and Writing scaled scores.

Get Your Math Score

How many Math questions did you get **right**?

Section 2: Questions 1–20   _____

Section 6: Questions 1–18 + _____

Section 8: Questions 1–16 + _____

             Total = _____ **(A)**

How many Math questions did you get **wrong**?

Section 2: Questions 1–20   _____

Section 6: Questions 1–18 + _____

Section 8: Questions 1–16 + _____

           Total = _____

         $\times 0.25$ = _____ **(B)**

     A – B = _____

          Math Raw Score

Round Math raw score to the nearest whole number.

_____

Use the Score Conversion Table to find your Math scaled score.

_____

Get Your Critical Reading Score

How many Critical Reading questions did you get **right**?

Section 4: Questions 1–24   _____

Section 7: Questions 1–24 + _____

Section 9: Questions 1–19 + _____

            Total = _____ **(A)**

How many Critical Reading questions did you get **wrong**?

Section 4: Questions 1–24   _____

Section 7: Questions 1–24 + _____

Section 9: Questions 1–19 + _____

          Total = _____

       $\times 0.25$ = _____ **(B)**

   A – B = _____

     Critical Reading Raw Score

Round Critical Reading raw score to the nearest whole number.

_____

Use the Score Conversion Table to find your Critical Reading scaled score.

_____

Get Your Writing Score

How many multiple-choice Writing questions did you get **right**?

Section 5: Questions 1–35 _____

Section 10: Questions 1–14 + _____

Total = _____ **(A)**

How many multiple-choice Writing questions did you get **wrong**?

Section 5: Questions 1–35 _____

Section 10: Questions 1–14 + _____

Total = _____

$\times$ 0.25 = _____ **(B)**

A – B = _____

Writing Raw Score

Round Writing raw score to the nearest whole number.

_____

Use the Score Conversion Table to find your Writing multiple-choice scaled score.

_____

Estimate your Essay score using the Essay Scoring Guide.

_____

Use the SAT Score Conversion Table for Writing Composite to find your Writing scaled score. You will need your Writing raw score and your Essay score to use this table.

_____

SAT Score conversion table

Raw Score	Critical Reading Scaled Score	Math Scaled Score	Writing Multiple-Choice Scaled Score*	Raw Score	Critical Reading Scaled Score	Math Scaled Score	Writing Multiple-Choice Scaled Score*
67	800			31	510	550	60
66	800			30	510	540	58
65	790			29	500	530	57
64	770			28	490	520	56
63	750			27	490	520	55
62	740			26	480	510	54
61	730			25	480	500	53
60	720			24	470	490	52
59	700			23	460	480	51
58	690			22	460	480	50
57	690			21	450	470	49
56	680			20	440	460	48
55	670			19	440	450	47
54	660	800		18	430	450	46
53	650	790		17	420	440	45
52	650	760		16	420	430	44
51	640	740		15	410	420	44
50	630	720		14	400	410	43
49	620	710	80	13	400	410	42
48	620	700	80	12	390	400	41
47	610	680	80	11	380	390	40
46	600	670	79	10	370	380	39
45	600	660	78	9	360	370	38
44	590	650	76	8	350	360	38
43	590	640	74	7	340	350	37
42	580	630	73	6	330	340	36
41	570	630	71	5	320	330	35
40	570	620	70	4	310	320	34
39	560	610	69	3	300	310	32
38	550	600	67	2	280	290	31
37	550	590	66	1	270	280	30
36	540	580	65	0	250	260	28
35	540	580	64	−1	230	240	27
34	530	570	63	−2	210	220	25
33	520	560	62	−3	200	200	23
32	520	550	61	−4 and below	200	200	20

This table is for use only with the test in this book.

* The Writing multiple-choice score is reported on a 20–80 scale. Use the SAT Score Conversion Table for Writing Composite for the total writing scaled score.

SAT Score conversion table for writing composite

Writing Multiple-Choice Raw Score	Essay Raw Score						
	0	**1**	**2**	**3**	**4**	**5**	**6**
−12	200	200	200	210	240	270	300
−11	200	200	200	210	240	270	300
−10	200	200	200	210	240	270	300
−9	200	200	200	210	240	270	300
−8	200	200	200	210	240	270	300
−7	200	200	200	210	240	270	300
−6	200	200	200	210	240	270	300
−5	200	200	200	210	240	270	300
−4	200	200	200	230	270	300	330
−3	200	210	230	250	290	320	350
−2	200	230	250	280	310	340	370
−1	210	240	260	290	320	360	380
0	230	260	280	300	340	370	400
1	240	270	290	320	350	380	410
2	250	280	300	330	360	390	420
3	260	290	310	340	370	400	430
4	270	300	320	350	380	410	440
5	280	310	330	360	390	420	450
6	290	320	340	360	400	430	460
7	290	330	340	370	410	440	470
8	300	330	350	380	410	450	470
9	310	340	360	390	420	450	480
10	320	350	370	390	430	460	490
11	320	360	370	400	440	470	500
12	330	360	380	410	440	470	500
13	340	370	390	420	450	480	510
14	350	380	390	420	460	490	520
15	350	380	400	430	460	500	530
16	360	390	410	440	470	500	530
17	370	400	420	440	480	510	540
18	380	410	420	450	490	520	550
19	380	410	430	460	490	530	560
20	390	420	440	470	500	530	560
21	400	430	450	480	510	540	570
22	410	440	460	480	520	550	580

Writing Multiple-Choice Raw Score	Essay Raw Score						
	0	**1**	**2**	**3**	**4**	**5**	**6**
23	420	450	470	490	530	560	590
24	420	460	470	500	540	570	600
25	430	460	480	510	540	580	610
26	440	470	490	520	550	590	610
27	450	480	500	530	560	590	620
28	460	490	510	540	570	600	630
29	470	500	520	550	580	610	640
30	480	510	530	560	590	620	650
31	490	520	540	560	600	630	660
32	500	530	550	570	610	640	670
33	510	540	550	580	620	650	680
34	510	550	560	590	630	660	690
35	520	560	570	600	640	670	700
36	530	560	580	610	650	680	710
37	540	570	590	620	660	690	720
38	550	580	600	630	670	700	730
39	560	600	610	640	680	710	740
40	580	610	620	650	690	720	750
41	590	620	640	660	700	730	760
42	600	630	650	680	710	740	770
43	610	640	660	690	720	750	780
44	620	660	670	700	740	770	800
45	640	670	690	720	750	780	800
46	650	690	700	730	770	800	800
47	670	700	720	750	780	800	800
48	680	720	730	760	800	800	800
49	680	720	730	760	800	800	800

Chart for self-appraisal based on the practice test you have just taken

The Chart for Self-Appraisal below tells you quickly where your SAT strengths and weaknesses lie. Check or circle the appropriate box in accordance with the number of your correct answers for each area of the Practice Test you have just taken.

	Writing (Multiple-Choice)	Sentence Completions	Reading Comprehension	Math Questions*
EXCELLENT	42–49	16–19	40–48	44–54
GOOD	37–41	13–15	35–39	32–43
FAIR	31–36	9–12	26–34	27–31
POOR	20–30	5–8	17–25	16–26
VERY POOR	0–19	0–4	0–16	0–15

*Sections 2, 6, 8 only.

Note: In our tests, we have chosen to have Section 3 as the experimental section. We have also chosen it to be a math section since we felt that students may need more practice in the math area than in the verbal area. Note that on the actual SAT you will take, the order of the sections can vary and you will not know which one is experimental, so it is wise to answer all sections and not to leave any section out.

SAT-I VERBAL AND MATH SCORE/PERCENTILE CONVERSION TABLE

Critical reading and writing

SAT scaled verbal score	Percentile rank
800	99.7+
790	99.5
740–780	99
700–730	97
670–690	95
640–660	91
610–630	85
580–600	77
550–570	68
510–540	57
480–500	46
440–470	32
410–430	21
380–400	13
340–370	6
300–330	2
230–290	1
200–220	0–0.5

Math

SAT scaled math score	Percentile rank
800	99.5+
770–790	99.5
720–760	99
670–710	97
640–660	94
610–630	89
590–600	84
560–580	77
530–550	68
510–520	59
480–500	48
450–470	37
430–440	26
390–420	16
350–380	8
310–340	2
210–300	0.5
200	0

EXPLANATORY ANSWERS FOR PRACTICE TEST 3

THE SAT SCORING GUIDE
Section 1: Essay

Score of 6	Score of 5	Score of 4
An essay in this category is *outstanding,* demonstrating *clear and consistent mastery,* although it may have a few minor errors. A typical essay	An essay in this category is *effective,* demonstrating *reasonably consistent mastery,* although it will have occasional errors or lapses in quality. A typical essay	An essay in this category is *competent,* demonstrating *adequate mastery,* although it will have lapses in quality. A typical essay
• effectively and insightfully develops a point of view on the issue and demonstrates outstanding critical thinking, using clearly appropriate examples, reasons, and other evidence to support its position	• effectively develops a point of view on the issue and demonstrates strong critical thinking, generally using appropriate examples, reasons, and other evidence to support its position	• develops a point of view on the issue and demonstrates competent critical thinking, using adequate examples, reasons, and other evidence to support its position
• is well organized and clearly focused, demonstrating clear coherence and smooth progression of ideas	• is well organized and focused, demonstrating coherence and progression of ideas	• is generally organized and focused, demonstrating some coherence and progression of ideas
• exhibits skillful use of language, using a varied, accurate, and apt vocabulary	• exhibits facility in the use of language, using appropriate vocabulary	• exhibits adequate but inconsistent facility in the use of language, using generally appropriate vocabulary
• demonstrates meaningful variety in sentence structure	• demonstrates variety in sentence structure	• demonstrates some variety in sentence structure
• is free of most errors in grammar, usage, and mechanics	• is generally free of most errors in grammar, usage, and mechanics	• has some errors in grammar, usage, and mechanics

Score of 3	Score of 2	Score of 1
An essay in this category is *inadequate,* but demonstrates *developing mastery,* and is marked by ONE OR MORE of the following weaknesses:	An essay in this category is *seriously-limited,* demonstrating *little mastery,* and is flawed by ONE OR MORE of the following weaknesses:	An essay in this category is *fundamentally lacking,* demonstrating *very little* or *no mastery,* and is severely flawed by ONE OR MORE of the following weaknesses:
• develops a point of view on the issue, demonstrating some critical thinking, but may do so inconsistently or use inadequate examples, reasons, or other evidence to support its position	• develops a point of view on the issue that is vague or seriously limited, demonstrating weak critical thinking, providing inappropriate or insufficient examples, reasons, or other evidence to support its position	• develops no viable point of view on the issue, or provides little or no evidence to support its position
• is limited in its organization or focus, or may demonstrate some lapses in coherence or progression of ideas	• is poorly organized and/or focused, or demonstrates serious problems with coherence or progression of ideas	• is disorganized or unfocused, resulting in a disjointed or incoherent essay
• displays developing facility in the use of language, but sometimes uses weak vocabulary or inappropriate word choice	• displays very little facility in the use of language, using very limited vocabulary or incorrect word choice	• displays fundamental errors in vocabulary
• lacks variety or demonstrates problems in sentence structure	• demonstrates frequent problems in sentence structure	• demonstrates severe flaws in sentence structure
• contains an accumulation of errors in grammar, usage, and mechanics	• contains errors in grammar, usage, and mechanics so serious that meaning is somewhat obscured	• contains pervasive errors in grammar, usage, or mechanics that persistently interfere with meaning

Essays not written on the essay assignment will receive a score of zero.

EXPLANATORY ANSWERS FOR PRACTICE TEST 3

Section 2: Math

> When a specific Math Strategy is referred to in the solution, study that strategy, which you will find in "19 Math Strategies."

1. Choice C is correct. **(Use Strategy 2: Translate from words to algebra.)** Let n = the number. We are told

$$\frac{n}{3} = n \qquad \boxed{1}$$

Subtracting $\frac{n}{3}$ from both sides of $\boxed{1}$,

$$n - \frac{n}{3} = 0 \qquad \boxed{2}$$

Multiplying $\boxed{2}$ by 3, we get

$$3\left(n - \frac{n}{3}\right) = 0$$
$$3n - n = 0$$
$$2n = 0$$
$$n = 0$$

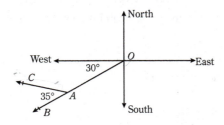

2. Choice E is correct. **(Use Strategy 14: Draw lines to help solve the problem.)**

Originally, the man is facing in the direction of OA. After he turns, he is facing in the direction of $\overrightarrow{AC}$, where $m\angle CAB = 35$. We want to find out the direction of $\overrightarrow{AC}$ with respect to the North–South–East–West axes. In other words, when we redraw the above diagram with $\ell \| W\text{-}E$ axis, and $m \| N\text{-}S$ axis, then $\overrightarrow{AC}$ is $x°$ north of west. $\qquad \boxed{1}$

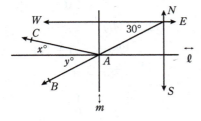

Since $m\angle CAB = 35$, then

$$x + y = 35 \qquad \boxed{2}$$

Since $\ell \| W\text{-}E$ axis, then

$$y = 30° \qquad \boxed{3}$$

Subtracting $\boxed{3}$ from $\boxed{2}$,

$$x = 5° \qquad \boxed{4}$$

Thus, using $\boxed{4}$ and $\boxed{1}$, $\overrightarrow{AC}$ is 5° north of west.

3. Choice C is correct.

Short Method: Given $\frac{9}{5}K = 18 \qquad \boxed{1}$

(Use Strategy 13: Find unknowns by division.)

Dividing $\boxed{1}$ by 9, we have

$$\left(\frac{1}{9}\right)\frac{9}{5}K = \overset{2}{\cancel{18}}\left(\frac{1}{\cancel{9}}\right)$$

$$\frac{1}{5}K = 2 \text{ (Answer)}$$

Long Method: Given $\frac{9}{5}K = 18 \qquad \boxed{1}$

Multiply $\boxed{1}$ by $\frac{5}{9}$, getting

$$\left(\frac{\cancel{5}}{\cancel{9}}\right)\frac{\cancel{9}}{\cancel{5}}K = \overset{2}{\cancel{18}}\left(\frac{5}{\cancel{9}}\right)$$

Finding $K = 10 \qquad \boxed{2}$

Multiplying $\boxed{2}$ by $\frac{1}{5}$ gives

$$\frac{1}{5}K = \overset{2}{\cancel{10}}\left(\frac{1}{\cancel{5}}\right)$$

$$\frac{1}{5}K = 2 \text{ (Answer)}$$

4. Choice E is correct. **(Use Strategy 8: When all choices must be tested, start with E and work backward.)** The only way to solve this question is to test the choices one by one. We start with Choice E, and it is correct.

5. Choice A is correct.

$$\text{Given: } x, y, z < 0 \qquad \boxed{1}$$
$$x < y \qquad \boxed{2}$$
$$y < z \qquad \boxed{3}$$

(Use Strategy 6: Know how to manipulate inequalities.)

Method 1: When you multiply an inequality by a negative number, you must reverse the inequality. For example, multiplying $\boxed{2}$ and $\boxed{3}$ by x, we get

$$x^2 > xy \qquad \boxed{4}$$
$$xy > xz \qquad \boxed{5}$$

multiplying $\boxed{2}$ and $\boxed{3}$ by z, we get

$$xz > yz \qquad \boxed{6}$$
$$yz > z^2 \qquad \boxed{7}$$

Comparing $\boxed{4}$, $\boxed{5}$, $\boxed{6}$, and $\boxed{7}$, we have

$$x^2 > xy > xz > yz > z^2$$

Thus, Choice A is correct.

(Use Strategy 7: Use numerics to help.)

Method 2: Choose specific numeric values for x, y, z satisfying $\boxed{1}$, $\boxed{2}$, and $\boxed{3}$.

For example, let $x = -3$, $y = -2$, $z = -1$
The choices become

(A) 1
(B) 2
(C) 3
(D) 6
(E) 9

Choice A is correct.

6. Choice E is the correct answer. **(Use Strategy 11: Use new definitions carefully. These problems are generally easy.)** The first few terms of the sequence are found as follows:

Given: Term 1 = 2

By definition, Term 2 = (Term 1 − 2)3
$$= (2 - 2)3$$
$$= (0)3$$
Term 2 = 0

Term 3 = (Term 2 − 2)3
$$= (0 - 2)3$$
$$= (-2)3$$
$$= -6$$

Term 4 = (Term 3 − 2)3
$$= (-6 - 2)3$$
$$= (-8)3$$
$$= -24$$

and so on.
2, 0, −6, and −24 are all even, so Choices A, B, C, and D can be eliminated.

7. Choice C is correct. **(Use Strategy 17: Use the given information effectively.)** $n = \frac{3}{8}$ is a member of both sets. Note that n is not an integer in this case, and certainly in this case n is not equal to 6. Thus I and III are not true for this case. Members of both sets are $\frac{3}{8}$, 6, and 8. So for any of these members, $8n$ is an integer. Thus II is always true.

8. Choice E is correct.

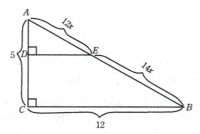

Method 1: **(Use Strategy 18: Remember right triangle facts.)** Triangle BCA is a right triangle, so we can use the Pythagorean Theorem:

$$(AB)^2 = (AC)^2 + (BC)^2$$
$$(12x + 14x)^2 = 5^2 + 12^2$$
$$(26x)^2 = 25 + 144$$
$$676x^2 = 169$$
$$x^2 = \frac{169}{676}$$

(Use Strategy 19: Factor and reduce.)

$$x^2 = \frac{\cancel{13} \times \cancel{13}}{\cancel{13} \times \cancel{13} \times 4} = \frac{1}{4}$$

$$x = \frac{1}{2}$$

Method 2: **(Use Strategy 18: Remember special right triangles.)** Triangle *BCA* is a right triangle with legs 5 and 12. 5–12–13 is a special right triangle. Thus, *AB* must = 13

Therefore $12x + 14x = 13$

$$26x = 13$$
$$x = \frac{13}{26}$$
$$x = \frac{1}{2}$$

9.   Choice A is correct. **(Use Strategy 6: Know how to manipulate inequalities.)** The least possible value of $x + y$ is when x is least and y is least. You can see that the smallest value of x is -4 (not 2 or -2) in the inequality $1 < |x| < 5$. The smallest value of y is -6 (not 3 or -3) in the inequality $2 < |y| < 7$. Thus the smallest value of $x + y = -10$.

10.   Choice B is correct. **(Use Strategy 17: Use the given information effectively.)** By looking at the diagram, we have

$$P_1 = -2$$
$$P_2 = -1$$

We can approximate the other numbers by looking at their positions on the number line:

$$P_3 \approx \frac{1}{3}$$

$$P_4 \approx \frac{2}{3}$$

$$P_5 \approx \frac{3}{2}$$

Thus,

$$P_1 P_2 P_3 P_4 P_5 \approx (-2)(-1)\left(\frac{1}{\cancel{3}}\right)\left(\frac{\cancel{2}}{\cancel{3}}\right)\left(\frac{\cancel{3}}{\cancel{2}}\right)$$
$$P_1 P_2 P_3 P_4 P_5 \approx \frac{2}{3}$$

11.   Choice C is correct. **(Use Strategy 2: Translate from words to algebra.)** Let the 3 consecutive even integers be

$$x, x + 2, x + 4 \qquad \boxed{1}$$

where x is even. We are told that

$$x + x + 2 + x + 4 = K$$
or $\qquad 3x + 6 = K \qquad \boxed{2}$

From $\boxed{1}$, we know that

$$x - 5, x - 3, x - 1$$

must be the 3 consecutive odd integers immediately preceding x. We are told that

$$x - 5 + x - 3 + x - 1 = y$$
or $\qquad 3x - 9 = y \qquad \boxed{3}$

(Use Strategy 13: Find unknown expressions by subtraction.) Subtracting $\boxed{3}$ from $\boxed{2}$, we get

$$15 = K - y$$
or $\qquad y = K - 15$

12.   Choice B is correct. **(Use Strategy 2: Translate from words to math.)** From the diagram we can see that 25% is water, so $0.25 \times 2 \text{ lb} = \frac{1}{2} \text{ lb}$ is water.

13.   Choice E is correct. **(Use Strategy 16: Watch out for questions that can be tricky.)** The subsets of {1,2,3} are {1}, {2}, {3}, {1,2}, {1,3}, {2,3}, {1,2,3}, and { }.

14.   Choice A is correct. **(Use Strategy 17: Use the given information effectively.)** A segment that divides the area of a circle into two equal parts must be a diameter. Thus, segment *RS* must go through point *O*.

Since *ROS* is a diameter, then $RO = OS$, each segment being a radius.

Since *R* is in the 2nd quadrant, *S* must be in the 4th quadrant.

You can see that the *x*-coordinate of *S* must be positive and the *y*-coordinate of S must be negative.

$$S = (-1(-6), -1(8))$$
$$S = (6, -8)$$

	First Place (6 points)	Second Place (4 points)	Third Place (2 points)
Game 1			
Game 2		Arisa	
Game 3			Arisa

15. Choice C is correct. **(Use Strategy 17: Use the given information effectively.)** Dylan can attain the *minimum* possible score by placing third in Game 1 and Game 2 and second in Game 3.

From the chart he would have 2, 2, and 4 points for each of these finishes.

Thus, minimum score = 2 + 2 + 4

minimum score = 8 points

16. Choice B is correct. **(Use Strategy 17: Use the given information effectively.)** Use $y = mx + b$ for representation of line k. m is the slope of the line and b is the y-intercept (that is, the value of y when $x = 0$). You can see that a point on the graph is at $x = 3$ and $y = 2$ from the points $(0,2)$ and $(3,0)$. Thus, substituting $x = 3$ and $y = 2$ into $y = mx + b$, we get $2 = m(3) + b$. Since m is the slope of the graph and is equal to -1, we get

$$2 = (-1)(3) + b.$$

$$2 = -3 + b$$

and so $5 = b$.

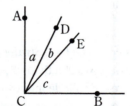

17. Choice B is correct. **(Use Strategy 14: Label unknown quantities.)**

Label angles as above with a, b, c.

You are given that

$$a + b + c = 90 \qquad \boxed{1}$$

$$b + c = 62 \qquad \boxed{2}$$

$$a + b = 37 \qquad \boxed{3}$$

You want to find $\angle DCE = b$

(Use Strategy 13: Find unknown expressions by adding or subtracting.)

First add $\boxed{2}$ and $\boxed{3}$:
We get:

$$a + 2b + c = 62 + 37 = 99 \qquad \boxed{4}$$

Now subtract $\boxed{1}$ from $\boxed{4}$:

$$\begin{array}{r} a + 2b + c = 99 \\ a + b + c = 90 \\ \hline b \phantom{{}+ c} = 9 \end{array}$$

18. Choice C is correct. **(Use Strategy 2: Remember how to calculate percent.)**

Winning percentage =

$$\frac{\text{\# of games won}}{\text{total \# of games played}} \times 100$$

For example,

Winning % for pitcher A

$$= \frac{4}{4+2} \times 100 = \frac{4}{6} \times 100$$

$$= \frac{\cancel{2} \times 2}{\cancel{2} \times 3} \times 100$$

$$= \frac{200}{3} = 66\frac{2}{3}\%$$

For each pitcher, we have

Pitcher	Winning Percentage
A	$66\frac{2}{3}\%$
B	60%
C	80%
D	50%
E	75%

Pitcher C has the highest winning percentage.

19. Choice B is correct. **(Use Strategy 11: Use new definitions carefully.)**

Given: A, B, C, ..., L =

1, 2, 3, ..., 12 (respectively) $\boxed{1}$

The time on the watch is 15 minutes before 1. $\boxed{2}$

From $\boxed{1}$, we know that

E = 5 and A = 1 $\boxed{3}$

Substituting $\boxed{3}$ into $\boxed{2}$, we have

3E minutes before A.

20. Choice A is correct.

Volume of cube = (side)^3

Thus, volume of each small cube= r^3 $\boxed{1}$

Volume of larger cube= s^3 $\boxed{2}$

and sum of the volumes of the

27 cubes= $27r^3$ $\boxed{3}$

(Use Strategy 3: The whole equals the sum of its parts.) We are told that the sum of the volumes of the 27 cubes = the volume of the larger cube

= 81 $\boxed{4}$

From $\boxed{2}$, $\boxed{3}$, and $\boxed{4}$ together, we have

$27r^3 = 81$ $\boxed{5}$

$s^3 = 81$ $\boxed{6}$

(Use Strategy 13: Find unknown expressions by division.) Dividing $\boxed{5}$ by $\boxed{6}$, we get

$27\dfrac{r^3}{s^3} = 1$ $\boxed{7}$

Multiplying $\boxed{7}$ by $\dfrac{1}{27}$, we get

$\dfrac{r^3}{s^3} = \dfrac{1}{27}$

or $\dfrac{r}{s} = \dfrac{1}{3}$

EXPLANATORY ANSWERS FOR PRACTICE TEST 3
Section 3: Math

> When a specific Math Strategy is referred to in the solution, study that strategy, which you will find in "19 Math Strategies."

1. Choice E is correct.

The distance between points on a number line is found by:

$$|a - b| = |-4 - (7)| =$$
$$|-4 - 7| = |-11| = 11$$

2. Choice B is correct.

(Use Strategy 5:

$$\textbf{Average} = \frac{\textbf{sum of values}}{\textbf{total number of values}})$$

The average is found by $\dfrac{8.4 + 8.1 + 9.3}{3} =$

$$\frac{25.8}{3} =$$
$$8.6$$

3. Choice A is correct. **(Use Strategy 13: Find unknowns by addition.)**

Given: $x + 9 = -11 - x$ $\boxed{1}$

Adding $x - 9$ to both sides of $\boxed{1}$,

$$2x = -20$$
$$x = -10$$

4. Choice C is correct. **(Use Strategy 17: Use the given information effectively.)**

Given: $3y = 12$ and $\dfrac{10}{x} = 5$ $\boxed{1}$

Solving $\boxed{1}$ for x and y:

$$y = 4 \text{ and } x = 2 \qquad \boxed{2}$$

Substitute equation $\boxed{2}$ into unknown expression.

$$\frac{y + 11}{x + 15} = \frac{4 + 11}{2 + 15}$$
$$= \frac{15}{17}$$

5. Choice C is correct. **(Use Strategy 10: Know how to use units.)**

Interest = rate × time × amount deposited

$$= \frac{8\%}{\text{year}} \times 1 \text{ year} \times \$50$$
$$= .08 \times 1 \times \$50$$
$$= \$4$$

(Use Strategy 3: The whole equals the sum of its parts.)

Total amount = Deposit + Interest
$$= \$50 + \$4$$
$$= \$54$$

6. Choice D is correct.

Given: $(x + 6)^2 = 12x + 72$ $\boxed{1}$

(Use Strategy 17: Use the given information effectively.)

Complete the squaring operation on the left side of the equation:

$$(x + 6)^2 = x^2 + 12x + 36$$

Continue the equation with $\boxed{1}$

$$x^2 + 12x + 36 = 12x + 72 \qquad \boxed{2}$$

(Use Strategy 1: Cancel numbers and expressions that appear on both sides of an equation.)

We get: $x^2 + 36 = 72$
Therefore, $x^2 = 36$
$$x = \pm 6$$

7. Choice C is correct. (**Use Strategy 3: The whole equals the sum of its parts.**)

From the diagram, we see that

$$x + 60 = 360 \qquad \boxed{1}$$

Subtracting 60 from both sides of $\boxed{1}$, we get

$$x = 300 \qquad \boxed{2}$$

Subtracting 60 from both sides of $\boxed{2}$, we get

$$x - 60 = 240$$

8. Choice D is correct. (**Use Strategy 10: Know how to use units.**)

Since 60 min = 1 hour, 24 hours = 1 day, and 7 days = 1 week, we have

$$\left(\frac{60 \text{ min}}{\text{hour}}\right)\left(\frac{24 \text{ hours}}{\text{day}}\right)\left(\frac{7 \text{ days}}{\text{week}}\right) = 10,080$$

or 1 week = 10,080 minutes. To the nearest hundred, 1 week ≈ 10,100 minutes.

9. Choice B is correct. (**Use Strategy 11: Use new definitions carefully.**)

Method 1: By definition, $\boxed{\!\!\bigtriangledown\!\!} = \dfrac{x^3}{4}$

We are looking for

$$\frac{x^3}{4} = 16 \qquad \boxed{1}$$

(**Use Strategy 13: Find unknowns by multiplication.**)

Multiplying $\boxed{1}$ by 4, we have

$$x^3 = 64$$
$$x = 4$$

Method 2: Calculate each of the choices, A through E, until you find the one whose value is 16.

10. Choice B is correct. (**Use Strategy 2: Translate from words to algebra.**)

We are given:

$$42 + 27 + 56 + x + y = 200$$
$$125 + x + y = 200$$
$$x + y = 75$$
$$x = 75 - y \qquad \boxed{1}$$

(**Use Strategy 17: Use the given information effectively.**)

From $\boxed{1}$, it is clear that x is a maximum when y is a minimum. Since y is the number of pieces of candy in a jar, its minimum value is

$$y = 0 \qquad \boxed{2}$$

Substituting $\boxed{2}$ into $\boxed{1}$,

$$x = 75$$

11. Choice C is correct. (**Use Strategy 2: Translate from words to algebra.**)

Number of pages Ron read last night
$$= \frac{1}{4} \times 16 = 4$$

(**Use Strategy 3: The whole equals the sum of its parts.**)

Number of pages remaining immediately after Ron finished reading last night = 16 − 4 = 12

Number of pages read this morning $= \frac{1}{4} \times 12 = 3$

Pages still not read

$$= \text{Remaining pages} - \text{pages read this morning}$$
$$= 12 - 3$$

Pages still not read = 9

12. Choice D is correct. (**Use Strategy 16: Watch out for questions that can be tricky.**)

Number of candles lit = Number of days between December 9 and 21, *inclusive* = 13

Not 21 − 9 = 12, which is just the difference.

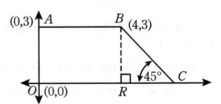

13. Choice C is correct.

Method 1: (**Use Strategy 17: Use the given information effectively.**)

The above figure has AB parallel to the x-axis. (Both A and B have y-coordinates of 3.) Thus, the figure is a trapezoid.

Its height (*OA*) is 3   ☐1

Its top base is 4   ☐2

(Use Strategy 14: Draw lines when appropriate.)

Draw *BR* perpendicular to the *x*-axis.

$$BR = OA = 3 \text{ and } AB = OR = 4$$

(Use Strategy 18: Remember isosceles triangle facts.)

Triangle *BRC* is an isosceles right triangle.

Thus, $BR = RC = 3$

The bottom base of the trapezoid

$$= OC = OR + RC = 4 + 3 = 7 \quad ☐3$$

The area of a trapezoid

$$=\frac{1}{2}h(\text{base 1} + \text{base 2}) \quad ☐4$$

Substituting ☐1, ☐2, and ☐3 into ☐4, we have

Area of trapezoid $= \frac{1}{2}(3)(4 + 7) = \frac{1}{2}(3)(11)$

$$= 16.5$$

Method 2: **(Use Strategy 14: Draw lines when appropriate.)**

Draw *BR* perpendicular to the *x*-axis.

ABRO is a rectangle and *BRC* is an isosceles triangle.

$$\text{Area } ABRO = (\text{base}) \times (\text{height})$$
$$= 4 \times 3$$
$$= 12 \quad ☐1$$
$$\text{Area } BRC = \frac{1}{2} \times (\text{base}) \times (\text{height})$$
$$= \frac{1}{2} \times 3 \times 3$$
$$= 4.5 \quad ☐2$$

(Use Strategy 3: The whole equals the sum of its parts.)

Using ☐1 and ☐2, the total area of figure *ABCO*

$$= \text{Area of } ABRO + \text{Area of } BRC$$
$$= 12 + 4.5$$
$$= 16.5$$

14. Choice B is correct. **(Use Strategy 2: Translate from words to algebra.)**

Let $x + y = $ sum of the 2 numbers   ☐1

$x - y = $ difference of the 2 numbers   ☐2

$xy = $ product of the 2 numbers   ☐3

We are told that the difference between their sum and their difference is 6.   ☐4

Substituting ☐1 and ☐2 into ☐4, we have

$$x + y - (x - y) = 6$$
$$x + y - x + y = 6$$
$$2y = 6$$
$$y = 3 \quad ☐5$$

Substituting ☐5 into ☐3, we get

$$x(3) = 15$$
$$x = 5$$

Clearly, 5 is the larger number.

15. Choice E is correct.

Given:

$$\frac{1}{a} + \frac{1}{b} = 10 \quad ☐1$$

Method 1: You should suspect that $a + b$ does not have a unique value because ☐1 is one equation in two variables, and thus a and b are not uniquely determined. To prove that $a + b$ is not uniquely determined, you can use the next method.

(Use Strategy 7: Use numerics to help find the answer.)

Method 2: Choose values of a and b satisfying ☐1, and calculate $a + b$.

EXAMPLE 1

$$a = \frac{1}{4} \qquad b = \frac{1}{6}$$

$$a + b = \frac{5}{12}$$

EXAMPLE 2

$$a = \frac{1}{5} \qquad b = \frac{1}{5}$$

$$a + b = \frac{2}{5}$$

Thus, $a + b$ has at least two different values.

16. Choice A is correct. **(Use Strategy 3: The whole equals the sum of its parts.)**

The area between the curved path and the dodecagon is simply the sum of the areas of the 12 semicircles.

Since   area of circle $= \pi r^2$

then   area of semicircle $= \frac{1}{2}\pi r^2$

where r is the radius of the circle.

Thus, area of shaded region $= 12\left(\frac{1}{2}\pi r^2\right)$

$$= 6\pi r^2 \qquad \boxed{1}$$

We are told diameter of semicircle = side of dodecagon. $\qquad \boxed{2}$

Since each side of a regular dodecagon has the same length, then

length of a side of dodecagon =

$$\frac{\text{perimeter of dodecagon}}{12} =$$

$$\frac{24}{12} = 2$$

From $\boxed{2}$, we know that

diameter of semicircle = 2

Thus, radius of semicircle = 1 $\qquad \boxed{3}$

Substituting $\boxed{3}$ into $\boxed{1}$,

area of shaded region $= 6\pi$

17. Choice E is correct. **(Use Strategy 2: Translate from words to algebra.)** From what we are told in the problem, notice that

$b - 6 =$ the number of Brayden's marbles after Brayden gave 6 away

$c + 6 =$ the number of Carlos's marbles after Brayden gave 6 away

We are told

$$b - 6 = c + 6 + 18$$
$$\text{or} \quad b - 6 = c + 24 \qquad \boxed{1}$$

(Use Strategy 13: Find unknowns by adding equations or expressions.) Adding $-b - 24$ to both sides of $\boxed{1}$, we get

$$c - b = -30$$

18. Choice D is correct. **(Use Strategy 3: The whole equals the sum of its parts.)** The perimeter of the shaded region

$$= PM + PN + \text{length of } \overset{\frown}{MN} \qquad \boxed{1}$$

From basic geometry, we know that if two tangents to a circle meet at a point, the lengths of the tangents from that point to where they touch the circle are equal. If a radius is drawn from the center of a circle to the point where the tangent

touches the circle, the angle of the radius line is perpendicular to the tangent. Thus,

$$PM = PN \qquad m\angle PMO = 90 \qquad \boxed{2}$$

and that OP bisects $\angle MON$. **(Use Strategy 14: Draw additional lines.)** Thus, we can redraw the diagram. **(Use Strategy 18: Remember standard right triangles.)**

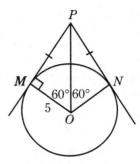

ΔPMO is similar to one of the standard triangles previously discussed.

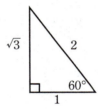

Corresponding sides of similar triangles are *in proportion*, so that

$$\frac{\sqrt{3}}{1} = \frac{PM}{5}$$

$$\text{or } PM = 5\sqrt{3} = PN \qquad \boxed{3}$$

It is always true that the length of $\overset{\frown}{MN}$

$$= \frac{m\angle MON}{360} \times \text{circumference of the circle}$$

$$= \frac{m\angle MON}{360} \times 2\pi(5)$$

$$= \frac{120}{360} \times 2\pi(5)$$

(Use Strategy 19: Factor and reduce.)

$$= \frac{12 \times \cancel{10}}{36 \times \cancel{10}} \times 2\pi(5)$$

$$= \frac{\cancel{12}}{\cancel{12} \times 3} \times 2\pi(5)$$

$$= \frac{10\pi}{3} \qquad \boxed{4}$$

Substituting $\boxed{4}$ and $\boxed{3}$ into $\boxed{1}$, we get the perimeter of shaded region $= 10\sqrt{3} + \frac{10\pi}{3}$

19. Choice D is correct.

(Use Strategy 5:

$$\text{Average} = \frac{\text{sum of values}}{\text{total number of values}}\Big)$$

We want to find

$$\frac{x + y + z + a + b}{5} \quad \boxed{1}$$

We are given

$$x + y + z = 3(a + b) \quad \boxed{2}$$

By substituting $\boxed{2}$ into $\boxed{1}$, the unknown expression becomes

$$\frac{3(a + b) + a + b}{5}$$

$$= \frac{3a + 3b + a + b}{5}$$

$$= \frac{4a + 4b}{5}$$

$$= \frac{4(a + b)}{5}$$

20. Choice B is correct.

Method I:

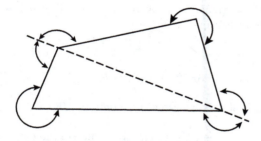

(Use Strategy 3: The whole equals the sum of its parts).
What we really have here is $4 \times 360°$ (four circles) minus the sum of the internal angles in the quadrilateral.
That is: $4 \times 360 - 360$
This is equal to $3 \times 360 = 1,080$

Method II:

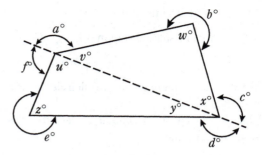

(Use Strategy 14: Label unknown quantities.)
With the diagram labeled as above, we want to find

$$a + b + c + d + e + f \quad \boxed{1}$$

(Use Strategy 3: The whole equals the sum of its parts.) Looking at the diagram, we see

$$a + f + u + v = 360 \quad \boxed{2}$$
$$b + w = 360 \quad \boxed{3}$$
$$c + d + x + y = 360 \quad \boxed{4}$$
$$e + z = 360 \quad \boxed{5}$$

(Use Strategy 13: Find unknown quantities by addition.) Adding equations $\boxed{2}$ through $\boxed{5}$,

$$a + b + c + d + e + f$$
$$+ u + v + w + x + y + z$$
$$= 1,440 \quad \boxed{6}$$

Since the sum of the measures of the angles of a triangle is 180, then

$$v + w + x = 180 \quad \boxed{7}$$
$$u + y + z = 180 \quad \boxed{8}$$

Substituting $\boxed{7}$ and $\boxed{8}$ into $\boxed{6}$

$$a + b + c + d + e + f + 180 + 180 = 1,440$$
$$\text{or } a + b + c + d + e + f = 1,080$$

EXPLANATORY ANSWERS FOR PRACTICE TEST 3
Section 4: Critical reading

> As you read these Explanatory Answers, you are advised to refer to "16 Verbal (Critical Reading) Strategies."

1. Choice C is correct. See **Sentence Completion Strategy 4.** Since the general "was like two sides of a coin," we have an *opposition indicator* to guide us. It is not ordinary for a man who is fair to be a man of severity. Nor is it ordinary for a man who is outgoing to be a man of few words.

2. Choice A is correct. See **Sentence Completion Strategy 2.**

STEP 1 [ELIMINATION]

We have eliminated Choices B and E because "agitation" and "intellect" do not make sense in the first blank.

STEP 2 [REMAINING CHOICES]

This leaves us with the remaining choices to be considered. The sentence *does not* make sense with the second word "minimal" of Choice C and the second word "whimsical" of Choice D. The sentence *does* make sense with the words "skill" and "astute" (meaning "cunning") of Choice A.

3. Choice E is correct. See **Sentence Completion Strategy 4.** "Internal dissension" is likely to have a negative effect on "affirmative action." We, accordingly, have an *opposition indicator.* Therefore, we eliminate Choice A, encourage, Choice C, induce, and Choice D, apply. This leaves us with Choice B, complicate, and Choice E, delay. Choice B, complicate…agreement, *does not* make sense. Choice E, delay…upheaval, *does* make sense.

4. Choice B is correct. See **Sentence Completion Strategy 2.** We can first eliminate Choice A, suspicion…, and Choice D, sacrifice…, because these first blank words do not make sense in the sentence. This leaves us with Choice B,

disagreement, Choice C, discussion, and Choice E, research. However, Choice C, discussion… incidentally, and Choice E, research…irrelevantly, *do not* make sense. Choice B, disagreement… overwhelmingly, *does* make sense.

5. Choice D is correct. See **Sentence Completion Strategies 3 and 4.** The key words "rather than" tell us that a word *opposite* to "severity" is needed to fill in the blank space. If you used the strategy of trying to complete the sentence *before* looking at the five choices, you might have chosen for your blank fill-in one of these appropriate words: easy, friendly, diplomatic, pleasing, soothing. Each of these words has a meaning much like that of the word "conciliatory." The words of the other four choices are *not* appropriate in the sentence. Therefore, these choices are incorrect.

6. Choice A is correct. See **Sentence Completion Strategy 1.** Try each choice. He would be able to be impartial, or unbiased, only as a result of not being emotionally attached to either acquaintance; he would not necessarily be able to be accurate (Choice B) or judicious (Choice E).

7. Choice A is correct. See **Sentence Completion Strategy 4.** This sentence calls for two words of contrasting nature, as shown by the words "even though." The only pair that has this contrast in meaning is Choice A.

8. Choice A is correct. The word "passive" means "submissive, not participating, accepting without objection." See **Sentence Completion Strategy 1.** A person who loves action certainly cannot tolerate a passive lifestyle. Choices B, C, D, and

E are incorrect because an action-loving person may, indeed, tolerate a chaotic or brazen or grandiose or vibrant lifestyle.

9. Choice A is correct. See lines 2–3: "hits upon a bright new way…At that point, the remark is an epigram." In other words, we can say that a "bright new way" is a "fresh" idea that will eventually develop into a "cliché."

10. Choice D is correct. See lines 5–7: "Soon it is likely to be suffering from overwork. It has then arrived at clichéhood." This indicates how the epigram is used.

11. Choice B is correct. From the context in the sentence, "…the crash of thunder, are the result of a sudden break in the equipoise…," you can see that "equipoise" must relate to "status quo" or "balance."

12. Choice A is correct. See lines 8–9: "The still small voice is the voice of life and growth and perpetuity…" The answer cannot be Choice B since "the small voice" is not a silence. The answer cannot be Choice D or E because the passage states that these are a "roar" and "a sudden break in the equipoise of the elements," not a "small voice." There is nothing in the passage to support Choice C.

13. Choice C is correct. See paragraph 5, lines 81–82: "Hoover also inaugurated…relieve unemployment."

14. Choice A is correct. See paragraph 2, lines 19–22: "The threat of another war…was one such stimulus."

15. Choice E is correct. According to the passage, political unrest was the result—not the cause—of the 1929 Depression.

16. Choice C is correct. See paragraph 3, lines 48–50: "All down the line…not meet their debts."

17. Choice B is correct. From the context of the sentence, we see that we should look for a word or phrase opposite in meaning or in contrast to the word "prosperity." Choice B is perfect. See also **Reading Comprehension Strategy 5.**

18. Choice C is correct. Given the context of the rest of the sentence, "inaugurated" must have to do with having begun something. Therefore, Choice C is correct. See also **Reading Comprehension Strategy 5.**

19. Choice D is correct. See paragraph 5, lines 79–81: "…Reconstruction Finance Corporation…with government loans."

20. Choice B is correct. See paragraph 3, last sentence: "Once started, this spiral of deflation seemed to have no limit."

21. Choice A is correct. See paragraph 4, lines 63–67: "More and more…brought such widespread misery and unemployment."

22. Choice E is correct. See paragraph 2: "War provided a limitless market for expendable goods."

23. Choice A is correct. See paragraph 4: All are mentioned except A.

24. Choice B is correct. See paragraph 3: "…the contraction of business left employees without jobs…"

EXPLANATORY ANSWERS FOR PRACTICE TEST 3

Section 5: Writing

1. **(C)** Choices A and B are incorrect uses of the present participle form to modify the noun *canoe*. Choice C is the correct use of the past participle. Choice D is incorrect because, in this sentence, it is an awkward use of the past participle. Choice E is an incorrect use of the present participle preceded by the inappropriate possessive pronoun *its*.

2. **(B)** What we are looking for here is a group of words to be used as a subject. Choice A is incorrect because the clause beginning with *whether* conveys an uncertainty, which is not the meaning of the sentence. Choice B is correct as a positive statement. It is a gerund phrase followed by an infinitive phrase. Choices C, D, and E are incorrect because they are awkward and vague.

3. **(C)** Choice A is incorrect because the phrases are misplaced, resulting in an unclear statement. Choices B and D are incorrect. They are awkwardly constructed and omit the fact that the trustee resigned from the town board. Choice C is correct. Choice E is incorrect because it is repetitious and awkward.

4. **(D)** Choice A is incorrect because the meaning of the phrase is unclear. Choice B is incorrect because the use of the participial form *coming* is awkward. Choice C is incorrect because it is too vague. Choice D is correct. Choice E is incorrect because it is too wordy.

5. **(A)** Choice A is correct. Choice B is incorrect. The use of *due to* calls for a participle, *having reached,* while the sentence contains a finite verb *has reached*. Choice E is incorrect also because the structure of the phrase calls for the use of a participle. Choice C is incorrect because it is awkward and wordy. Choice D is incorrect because it makes the sentence ungrammatical.

6. **(D)** Choice A is incorrect because "like when" is ungrammatical. Choice B is incorrect because it is too indirect. Choice C is incorrect because "similar to when" is ungrammatical. Choice D is correct. Choice E is incorrect because it is awkwardly expressed.

7. **(D)** Even if we were to simply read out loud this sentence, it would sound confusing. In a roundabout way, we can understand what is being stated. However, it is important that you remember that this section of the SAT wants to see if you can identify the best, clearest way of stating something. The present participle "Seeing" is incorrectly modifying "the cigarettes." Choices B, C, and E are long-winded and still create confusion. Choice D is the only choice that provides the clearest understanding of the sentence.

8. **(A)** Choice A is correct. Choice B is incorrect because the nominative absolute construction "Henry VI having one" throws the sentence out of balance. Choice C is incorrect because we need a finite verb ("had"), not the participle "having." Choice D is incorrect because the present perfect tense ("has had") should be replaced by the past tense ("had"). Choice E is too wordy.

9. **(E)** Choice A is incorrect because it is awkward and because the pronoun "they" has an indefinite antecedent. Choice B is incorrect for the same reason. Choice C is incorrect—it would be correct if changed to "they, not chemists and physicists, have." Choice D is too wordy. Choice E is correct.

10. **(B)** Choice A is incorrect because we have a run-on sentence. The comma should be replaced by a semicolon or a period. Choice A is incorrect for another reason: the singular pronoun "him" (not "them") should be used because the

antecedent ("student") of the pronoun is singular. Choice B is correct. Choice C is incorrect because the pronoun "they" should be singular. Choice D is incorrect because it creates a run-on sentence. Choice E is incorrect—the semicolon should be eliminated.

11.   (A) Choice A is correct. Choice B is incorrect because of the improper ellipsis of the words "that of" which should precede "an adviser and friend." Choice C is incorrect, because the word "one" should be replaced by the words "that of." Choices D and E are incorrect because they are too indirect. Moreover, in Choice D, right after the words "its role" we should place the words "that of."

12.   (D) "...is like *that of* New York in June." We have an improper ellipsis here. An ellipsis is an omission from a sentence of one or more words that would complete or clarify it. We must include the words *that of,* meaning *the weather of.*

13.   (E) All underlined parts are correct.

14.   (A) "The teacher did not encourage the student *in any way* even though..." We cannot properly use the indefinite pronoun *any* to modify the verb (*did not encourage*). The adverbial phrase *in any way* should be used for this purpose.

15.   (C) "...a great interest *in* and admiration for the work of..." We are not permitted to omit the preposition *in* since it is necessary to introduce the object of the preposition (*work*).

16.   (D) "...requires me to solve a large *number* of problems." *Amount* is used to refer to things in bulk. *Number* is used to refer to things or people that can be counted.

17.   (E) All underlined parts are correct.

18.   (C) "...my brother...was not discouraged *in any way*..." We cannot properly use the indefinite pronoun *any* to modify the adjective (*discouraged*). The adverbial phrase *in any way* should be used for this purpose.

19.   (B) "Mother" is the subject of the sentence, and "mother" is singular. Therefore, it would be incorrect to state: "The mother *were* rescued." This is an easy error to make because at first glance, the subject might *seem* plural: "A mother *along with her children*," but on closer look, you will realize it does not state: "A mother *and her children*..." The words "along with" prevent this phrase from becoming a compound subject (a subject that is formed by more than one noun phrase). Therefore, the correct sentence would read: "A mother along with her children *was rescued*..."

20.   (D) "...his method...was quite *different from* mine." *Different from* is always the correct form; *different than* is always incorrect.

21.   (A) "The school board members did *as* they were expected..." The conjunction (*as*) should be used to introduce the dependent clause (*as they were expected to*)—not the preposition (*like*).

22.   (B) "...in which she *had ridden*..." The past perfect tense of *to ride* is *had ridden*—not *had rode.*

23.   (A) "From every community *come* reports..." The plural form of the verb (*come*) must be used to agree with the plural subject *reports.* "From every community" is an introductory prepositional phrase.

24.   (C) "...there *was* scarcely enough food..." The word *scarcely* is considered a negative. Remember that a double negative will create a positive: "I am *not not* going to the party" means "I *am* going to the party." Therefore, "wasn't," or "was not," and "scarcely" would negate each other, changing the meaning of the sentence.

25.   (E) All underlined parts are correct.

26.   (A) "...to borrow a book *from*..." One borrows *from* someone. The phrase *off of* is always incorrect.

27.   (A) "Neither the school board members *nor* the city council..." Correlative conjunctions are always used in pairs. The correlative conjunction pair is *neither...nor*—not *neither...or.*

28. (C) We must preserve sequence of tenses. When two different parts of a sentence refer to the same period of time, the same tense must be used in each case. In this sentence, when the neighbor *was* (past tense) a teenager, he *rescued* (past tense) a swimmer.

29. (C) "…our father told my brother and *me*…" The indirect object of a clause or sentence must be in the objective case and, accordingly, must take the objective form (*me*—not *I*).

30. (C) The word *Moreover* is misused in the sentence as it stands; it means "besides." Thus Choice A is incorrect. Choice B is wrong since far from showing contrast to sentence 3, sentence 4 gives a specific example to show what the previous sentence means. Therefore, Choice C is correct: It is the only suggestion that shows an example is coming up. Choice D is wrong since *In short* implies that a summary statement is to follow (nor is sentence 4 particularly brief!). Although it is the second best answer, Choice E is inappropriate since it suggests that there is doubt about sentence 4. The writer has stated sentence 3 as a fact (having qualified it with the word *often*); therefore sentence 4 should be stated more definitely. Note too that sentence 4 is already qualified by the word *perhaps;* beginning the sentence *Some people believe* would water down the example to the point that it means almost nothing.

31. (D) Since sentence 8 has nothing to do with what has been said in sentence 7, it should not be joined to this sentence with either a semicolon or *and*. Therefore Choices A and B are both incorrect. Choice C is wrong as well, since if the sentence began with *Although,* it would be a fragment. Choice D is correct: *Yet* is a transitional word that sets up the contrast with sentence 7, but, unlike *Although,* leaves it a complete sentence. Choice E is incorrect—if the sentence were moved, sentence 9 would be a complete non sequitur after sentence 7. Nor would the transition *The reason is* in sentence 10 follow logically after sentence 8.

32. (B) Choice A is incorrect since, if the sentence were eliminated, no explanation would be given for sentence 9 and the reader would have to guess at it from sentence 11. Choice B is correct—since sentences 8, 9, and 10 are all quite short, it would be good to combine two of them. The semicolon is the correct form of punctuation to join two complete sentences. Choice C is incorrect: If sentence 10 were joined to sentence 9 with a comma, the result would be a run-on sentence. Choice D is incorrect since, if sentence 10 were moved to the end of the paragraph, it would refer not to sentence 9 but to sentence 11. Choice E is wrong because it would leave out the helpful transition *The reason is,* which shows the relationship between sentences 9 and 10.

33. (E) Although Choices A, B, C, and D would all make good introductory sentences for a general passage on dreams, Choice E is the only one that applies directly to this particular passage. Note how "New research indicates" leads smoothly into the beginning of the next sentence: "We know that…" The intention of the entire passage is to show us that dreams "play an important part in all of our lives." Choice C is probably the next best choice, but it would apply only to sentences 3 and 4.

34. (A) Since we are concerned with timing, that is, adults at a certain time are given drugs, we use the word *When*. None of the other choices serve what the author is trying to get across.

35. (E) Sentence 11 further explains and clarifies the previous sentence and should therefore be in parentheses. None of the other choices describe anything that would be useful or better clarify the passage.

EXPLANATORY ANSWERS FOR PRACTICE TEST 3

Section 6: Math

> When a specific Math Strategy is referred to in the solution, study that strategy, which you will find in "19 Math Strategies."

1. Choice D is correct. (**Use Strategy 17: Use the given information effectively.**)

   Given:

   $$7a = 4 \qquad \boxed{1}$$
   $$7a + 4b = 12 \qquad \boxed{2}$$

   Substituting $\boxed{1}$ into $\boxed{2}$,

   $$4 + 4b = 12$$
   $$4b = 8$$
   $$b = 2$$

2. Choice B is correct. (**Use Strategy 6: Know how to manipulate inequalities.**)

   Multiply the string of inequalities

   $-\frac{1}{2} < \frac{x}{3} < -\frac{1}{4}$ by 3 to get x alone:

   $$3\left[-\frac{1}{2} < -\frac{x}{3} < -\frac{1}{4} \right] =$$
   $$-\frac{3}{2} < x < -\frac{3}{4} \qquad \boxed{1}$$

   Only one integer, $x = -1$, will satisfy $\boxed{1}$

3. Choice D is correct.

   Method 1: By inspection, Choice D is the sum of two negatives, which must be negative.

   Method 2: (**Use Strategy 7: Try numerics to help find the answer.**)

   Let $r = -1, s = -2$

   (**Use Strategy 8: When all choices must be tested, start with E and work backward.**)

   Choice E is $-r - s = -(-1) - (-2)$
   $$= 1 + 2$$
   $$= 3$$

Choice D is $r + s = -1 + (-2) = -3$
Thus D is negative and the answer.

4. Choice D is correct. $f(x - 1) =$
   $$(x - 1)^2 + 2(x - 1) + 1 =$$
   $$x^2 - 2x + 1 + 2x - 2 + 1 = x^2$$

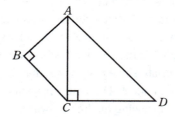

5. Choice D is correct. (**Use Strategy 18: Remember the isosceles right triangle.**)

   Given: $AB = BC$ $\qquad \boxed{1}$
   $ AC = CD$ $\qquad \boxed{2}$

   From $\boxed{1}$ we get that ΔABC is an isosceles right triangle. Therefore, $\angle BAC$ and $\angle BCA$ are each 45-degree angles.

   From $\boxed{2}$ we get that ΔACD is an isosceles right triangle. Therefore, $\angle CAD$ and $\angle CDA$ are each 45-degree angles.

   Thus, there are four 45-degree angles.

6. Choice B is correct. (**Use Strategy 2: Translate from words to algebra.**)

   We know that:

   Area of rectangle = length × width $\qquad \boxed{1}$

   We are given: Area = 4 $\qquad \boxed{2}$

   $$\text{length} = \frac{4}{3} \qquad \boxed{3}$$

Substituting $\boxed{2}$ and $\boxed{3}$ into $\boxed{1}$, we get

$$4 = \frac{4}{3} \times \text{width} \qquad \boxed{4}$$

(Use Strategy 13: Find unknowns by multiplication.)

Multiply $\boxed{4}$ by $\frac{3}{4}$. We get

$$\frac{3}{4}(4) = \frac{3}{4}\left(\frac{4}{3} \times \text{width}\right)$$

$$3 = \text{width}$$

7. Choice D is correct.

Since vertical angles are equal, then

$$m\angle AOC = m\angle DOB = 108 \qquad \boxed{1}$$

Thus, from $\boxed{1}$, we get length of

$$\text{minor } \overset{\frown}{AC} = \text{length of minor } \overset{\frown}{DB} \qquad \boxed{2}$$

From geometry we know

$$\text{length of minor } \overset{\frown}{AC} = \frac{108}{360} \times \text{circumference of circle}$$

$$= \frac{108}{360} \times \pi(\text{diameter})$$

$$= \frac{108}{360} \times \pi(20)$$

(Use Strategy 19: Factor and reduce.)

$$\text{length of minor } \overset{\frown}{AC} = \frac{18 \times 6}{18 \times 20} \times \pi(20)$$

$$\text{length of minor } \overset{\frown}{AC} = 6\pi \qquad \boxed{3}$$

Length $\overset{\frown}{AC}$ + Length $\overset{\frown}{DB}$ can be found using $\boxed{2}$ and $\boxed{3}$

Length $\overset{\frown}{AC}$ + Length $\overset{\frown}{DB} = 6\pi + 6\pi$

Length $\overset{\frown}{AC}$ + Length $\overset{\frown}{DB} = 12\pi$

8. Choice D is correct. The graphs are represented as follows: Plot $x = 0$, $y = 0$.

For $y = 2x^2$, when $x = \pm 1$, $y = 2$; when $x = \pm 2$, $y = 8$

For $y = -2x^2$, when $x = \pm 1$, $y = -2$; when $x = \pm 2$, $y = -8$

The graphs are represented as follows:

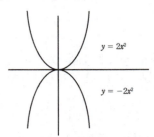

Thus, I and II are true. III is false. A linear function is of the form $y = mx + b$.

9. $\frac{6}{1}$ or 6 or $\frac{12}{2}$

(Use Strategy 2: Translate from words to algebra.)

Let M = number of Mia's jelly beans $\boxed{1}$

Let S = number of Sophie's jelly beans $\boxed{2}$

And R = number of Riley's jelly beans $\boxed{3}$

We are looking for $\dfrac{\text{Riley's jelly beans}}{\text{Sophie's jelly beans}}$ $\boxed{4}$

According to the given, $S = 3M$ $\boxed{5}$

Also given, $R = 18M$ $\boxed{6}$

Dividing $\boxed{6}$ by $\boxed{5}$, we get

$$\frac{R}{S} = \frac{6}{1}$$

10. 9

$$\text{Volume of cube} = (\text{side})^3$$

Thus, the volume of a cube whose edge has length of $1 = 1^3 = 1$.

The volume of a cube whose edge has the length of $2 = 2^3 = 8$. Thus the sum of the volumes of the two cubes $= 8 + 1 = 9$.

11. 105

(Use Strategy 11: Use new definitions carefully. These problems are generally easy.)

$$\text{Given: } \left(\frac{n}{2}\right) = \frac{n(n-1)}{2}$$

$$\text{Thus } \left(\frac{15}{2}\right) = \frac{15(15-1)}{2}$$

$$= \frac{15(14)}{2}$$

$$= 105$$

12. 0

Given: $\quad r^2 = 9 \qquad \boxed{1}$
$\qquad\qquad\quad s^2 = 25 \qquad \boxed{2}$

(Use Strategy 17: Use the given information effectively.) From $\boxed{1}$ and $\boxed{2}$, we have

$$r = 3 \text{ or } -3 \qquad \boxed{3}$$
$$s = 5 \text{ or } -5 \qquad \boxed{4}$$

The greatest possible value of $s - r$ occurs when s is a maximum and r is a minimum or

$$5 - (-3) = 8 \qquad \boxed{5}$$

The greatest possible value of $r - s$ occurs when r is a maximum and s is a minimum or

$$3 - (-5) = 8 \qquad \boxed{6}$$

The answer to this question is the difference between $\boxed{5}$ and $\boxed{6}$:

$$8 - 8 = 0$$

13. $33\frac{1}{3}$, which translates to 33.3 in "grid" form.

(Use Strategy 2: Translate from words to algebra.) According to the graph, 4 people had green eyes, 6 people had blue eyes, and 5 had brown eyes, so there were 15 people in the group. The percentage, x, can be found by setting up the ratio $\frac{x}{100} = \frac{5}{15} = \frac{1}{3}$, or $x = 33\frac{1}{3}$. $33\frac{1}{3}\%$ had brown eyes.

14. 5

$$\begin{array}{r} N5 \\ \times\ LM \\ \hline 385 \\ +\ 385 \\ \hline 4235 \end{array}$$

(Use Strategy 17: Use the given information effectively.) From the given problem we see that

$$N5 \times M = 385$$

(Use Strategy 7: Use numerical examples.)

Try $N = 1$

$$15 \times M = 385$$

M must be greater than 10, which is incorrect.

Try $N = 2$

$$25 \times M = 385$$

M must be greater than 10, which is incorrect.

Try $N = 3$

$$35 \times M = 385$$

M must be greater than 10, which is incorrect.

Try $N = 4$

$$45 \times M = 385$$

M is not an integer.

Try $N = 5$

$$55 \times M = 385. \text{ Thus, } M = 7$$

Therefore, L can be equal to 7 to give:

$$\begin{array}{r} 55 \\ \times\ 77 \\ \hline 385 \\ +\ 385 \\ \hline 4235 \end{array}$$

ALTERNATE METHOD

The number "$N5$" can be written as $10N + 5$. For example, "25" $= 10 \times 2 + 5$. So in the multiplication example given, we have

$$(10N + 5) \times M = 385 \qquad \boxed{1}$$

(Use Strategy 12: *Factor* to make problem simpler.)

$$10N + 5 = 5(2N + 1)$$

So from $\boxed{1}$, $5(2N + 1) \times M = 385$

Now divide by 5:

$$(2N + 1)M = 77$$

Because the only two integers that can give us 77 when multiplied are 11 and 7, or 77 and 1, and because N and M are integers, each must be less than 10, $2N + 1 = 11$, $M = 7$.

If $2N + 1 = 11$, then $N = 5$.

15. 24

(Use Strategy 11: Use new definitions carefully.)

By definition, the hand of dial Y moves one number for each complete revolution of the hand of dial Z. $\boxed{1}$

The hand of Dial Y must move 8 numbers to complete one of its own revolutions. Therefore, it must move 24 numbers to complete 3 of its revolutions.

From $\boxed{1}$ above, 24 numbers on dial Y correspond to 24 complete revolutions on dial Z.

16. $\dfrac{7}{8}$ or .875

(Use Strategy 17: Use the given information effectively.)

Given: 6 rolls uses $\frac{1}{4}$ pound of powder $\boxed{1}$

6 rolls uses $2\frac{1}{2}$ quarts of water $\boxed{2}$

Number $\boxed{2}$ is not necessary to solve the problem!

We need to know how much powder is needed for the same mixture for 21 rolls. Let x = number of pounds for 21 rolls. We set up a proportion:

$$\frac{6 \text{ rolls}}{\frac{1}{4} \text{ pound}} = \frac{21 \text{ rolls}}{x}$$

(Use Strategy 10: Know how to use units.)

$$(6 \text{ rolls})x = (21 \text{ rolls}) \times \left(\tfrac{1}{4} \text{ pound}\right)$$

$$6x = 21 \times \tfrac{1}{4} \text{ pound} \qquad \boxed{3}$$

(Use Strategy 13: Find unknowns by multiplication.) Multiply $\boxed{3}$ by $\frac{1}{6}$. We get

$$\tfrac{1}{6}(6x) = \tfrac{1}{6}\left(21 \times \tfrac{1}{4} \text{ pound}\right)$$

$$x = \tfrac{1}{6} \times 21 \times \tfrac{1}{4} \text{ pound}$$

$$x = \tfrac{21}{24} \text{ pound}$$

$$x = \tfrac{7}{8} \text{ of a pound}$$

17. 84

(Use Strategy 5:

$$\text{Average} = \frac{\text{sum of values}}{\text{total number of values}}\Big)$$

Method I: The simplest math and the quickest solution:

Suppose there are 10 students in the class.

Since 40% of the class scored 100, 4 students scored 100.

Since 10% of the class scored 80, 1 student scored 80.

That leaves us with 50% of the class, or 5 students, who scored an average of d.

The overall average was 90, so

$$90 = \frac{(4 \times 100) + (1 \times 80) + (5 \times d)}{10}$$

$$90 = \frac{400 + 80 + 5d}{10}$$

$$900 = 400 + 80 + 5d = 480 + 5d$$

$$420 = 5d$$

$$d = 84$$

Method II: How a mathematician would solve this

Let N be the number of students.

Then $0.4N$ = Number of students scoring 100

$0.1N$ = Number of students scoring 80

(Use Strategy 3: The whole equals the sum of its parts.)

We know that 50% of the class has been accounted for, so

$0.5N$ = Number of students remaining

Let d be the average score for the remaining students.

The overall average was 90, so

$$90 = \frac{(0.4N \times 100) + (0.1N \times 80) + (0.5N \times d)}{N}$$

$$= \frac{40N + 8N + (0.5N \times d)}{N}$$

$$= \frac{48N + (0.5N \times d)}{N}$$

$$90 = 48 + (.5 \times d) = 48 + \frac{d}{2}$$

$$42 = \frac{d}{2}$$

$$d = 84$$

18. **5 (Use Strategy 3: The whole equals the sum of its parts.)** The sum of the angles in a triangle $= 180°$.

$$\text{Therefore } 3t° + 5t° + 10t° = 180$$
$$18t = 180$$
$$t = 10 \qquad \boxed{1}$$

Since ABC is a line segment, straight angle $ABC = 180°$. $\qquad \boxed{2}$

(Use Strategy 3: The whole equals the sum of its parts.)

$$\angle ABC = \angle ABD + \angle DBC \qquad \boxed{3}$$

Substituting the given and $\boxed{2}$ in $\boxed{3}$ gives

$$180 = 10t + 16x \qquad \boxed{4}$$

Substituting $\boxed{1}$ in $\boxed{4}$, we have

$$180 = 10(10) + 16x$$
$$180 = 100 + 16x$$
$$80 = 16x$$
$$5 = x$$

As you read these Explanatory Answers, you are advised to refer to "16 Verbal (Critical Reading) Strategies."

1.   Choice D is correct. See **Sentence Completion Strategy 1.** The word "degradation" means deterioration, a lowering of position. The sight of a person in such a state would generally bring about a feeling of pity. Choices A, B, C, and E do *not* make good sense in the sentence. Therefore, these choices are incorrect.

2.   Choice B is correct. See **Sentence Completion Strategy 4.** The key word "although" in this sentence indicates that there is opposition or difference between the first part of the sentence and the last part. Since our team knew that the opponents (the Raiders) were "sluggish," we were stupid—we should have pushed hard instead of being so "easygoing." The other four choices are incorrect because their word pairs do not make sense in the sentence.

3.   Choice C is correct. See **Sentence Completion Strategy 2.** We first examine the first word of each choice. We eliminate Choice A, heroic, Choice B, respected, and Choice E, insightful, because a prime minister with any of these positive qualities would hardly be expected to cause a downfall of his country. So Choices A, B, and E are incorrect.

We now consider the remaining choices. Choice D, vacillating...confidential, does not make sense in the sentence because we cannot refer to a country as confidential. Therefore, Choice D is also incorrect. Choice C, incompetent...powerful, makes sense and is the correct choice.

4.   Choice B is correct. See **Sentence Completion Strategy 1.** The word "aloof" means "withdrawn, distant, uninvolved." A character who is dignified and who is a man of reserve is likely to be aloof.

5.   Choice C is correct. See **Sentence Completion Strategy 2.** Let us first examine the first word of each choice. We can eliminate Choice A, frequent, Choice B, heavy, and Choice E, bland, because saying that blood contains frequent or heavy or bland amounts does not make sense. So Choices A, B, and E are incorrect.

We now consider the remaining choices. Choice D, definite...puzzling, does *not* make sense because blood does not contain puzzling amounts. Therefore, Choice D is also incorrect. Choice C, minute (pronounced "mine-yute"—meaning exceptionally small)...excessive, makes sense and *is* the correct choice.

6.   Choice D is correct. See lines 7–9 where it states that many people in our generation were not exposed to classical music. Don't be lured into the distractor Choice A, even though there was mention of sales.

7.   Choice A is correct. See lines 19–21 where it mentions that the emotional feeling gradually wears out in time.

8.   Choice B is correct. Since the next sentence after the word "evergreen" qualifies that enjoyment lasts only for a short time, "lasting" would be an appropriate definition of "evergreen" in this context. Be careful of the distractor choice "colorful."

9.   Choice C is correct. Note that only in Passage 1, lines 3–5, is an example of a symphony of Brahms

illustrating the point. No specific examples are presented in Passage 2. In Choice A, the time period is addressed in *both* passages. In Choice B the types of music are presented in *both* passages (classical in Passage 1 and contemporary in Passage 2). In Choice D, no instrument is addressed in either passage and in Choice E, specific musicians are not mentioned in either passage.

10.   Choice B is correct. See lines 25–29: "That was why…till he reached bitter despair…the man of property could die." The "well-upholstered hell" constituted the lifestyle that almost caused him to commit suicide. The passage shows no justification for Choices A, C, D, or E.

11.   Choice D is correct. Throughout paragraph 3 we see the evidence of Siddhartha's happiness as a result of his renouncing the "power, women and money" (lines 22–23) as well as the arrogance and intellectuality referred to in line 17. Choices A, B, and C are incorrect because, though the passage discusses these choices, they do not really *pinpoint* the relation between the third and fourth paragraphs. Choice E is incorrect because paragraph 3 does not generalize about the specific points made in paragraph 2.

12.   Choice B is correct. His "complete hopelessness and despair" (lines 3–4) led to Siddhartha's decision to commit suicide. The passage does not answer the questions expressed in Choices A, C, D, and E. Therefore, these choices are incorrect.

13.   Choice C is correct. From the context of the sentence and the one preceding it, we can see that the word "transitory" means short-lived. (We are dealing with time.) See also **Reading Comprehension Strategy 5.**

14.   Choice E is correct. The unhappiness that may result from wealth and power is brought out clearly throughout the second paragraph. In contrast, peace and quiet are likely to assure a happy life. The last paragraph demonstrates this conclusively. Although Choices A, B, C, and D are vital points, none of the choices is sufficiently inclusive to be considered the *main*

idea of the passage. References to these choices follow. Choice A—lines 13–21: "He had been full of arrogance…brought him salvation." Choice B—lines 5–8: "Was it not his Self…filled him with fear?" Choice C—lines 10–11: "Too much knowledge had hindered him." Choice D—lines 19–21: "Now he understood…brought him salvation."

15.   Choice E is correct. The word "Self" as it is used in this passage means one's own interests, welfare, or advantage; self-love. By an extension of these definitions, "Self" may be considered selfishness. See lines 5–8: "Was it not his Self… filled him with fear?" See also lines 16–17. Accordingly, Choices A, B, C, and D are incorrect.

16.   Choice E is correct. See lines 21–22: "All human beings have at least four types of intelligence." Choice A is incorrect. See lines 50–52: "Persistence kept Einstein looking for the solution to the question of the relationship between the law of gravity and his special theory of relativity." Isaac Newton (1642–1727) formulated the law of gravitation. Choice B is incorrect. The passage simply states: "The idea for a self-starting electric motor came to Nikola Tesla one evening as he was reciting a poem by Goethe and watching a sunset" (lines 30–33). Choice C is incorrect. The author indicates a span of time when he states: "The discoveries made by scientific geniuses, from Archimedes through Einstein…" (lines 1–2). Archimedes was an ancient Greek mathematician, physicist, and inventor (287–212 BC), whereas Einstein was, of course, a modern scientist (1879–1955). Choice D is incorrect. The passage states: "…while an IQ above a certain point— about 120—is very helpful for a scientist,…[it] is not crucial for producing a work of genius" (lines 18–21). The passage does not specifically say that most scientists have IQ scores above 120.

17.   Choice D is correct. See lines 42–44: "The scientist solves a problem by shifting from one intelligence to another, although the logical-mathematical intelligence is dominant." Accordingly, Choices A, B, C, and E are incorrect.

18. Choice B is correct. When the author describes the work experiences of Einstein and Tesla, he refers to their use of one or more of the four types of intelligence. Moreover, lines 26–28 state: "Some corroboration of these [four intelligence] categories comes from the reports of scientists who describe thought processes centered on images, sensations, or words." Choices A, C, D, and E are incorrect because the author does not refer to these choices in the passage.

19. Choice C is correct. The author indicates that great scientists use to advantage four intelligences—logical-mathematical, spatial, linguistic, and bodily- kinesthetic. See lines 22–25: "The great scientist possesses the ability to move back and forth among them—the logical-mathematical, the spatial, which includes visual perception, the linguistic, and the bodily kinesthetic." Choices B and D are brought out in the passage but not at any length. Therefore, Choices B and D are incorrect. Choice A is incorrect because the author nowhere compares the thinking of the average individual and that of the great scientist. Choice E is incorrect because though the concepts are mentioned, they are certainly not clarified in the passage.

20. Choice E is correct. As a football star, he would certainly have to have a high level of (a) spatial intelligence [II], which involves space sensitivity as well as visual perception, and (b) bodily kinesthetic intelligence [IV], which involves the movement of muscles, tendons, and joints. As a literature major, he would certainly have to have a high level of linguistic intelligence [III], which involves the ability to read, write, speak, and listen. Whether he would have logical-mathematical intelligence to a high degree is questionable. It follows that Choices A, B, C, and D are incorrect.

21. Choice E is correct. According to what is stated in lines 50–56, persistence is an important characteristic of the scientist. Thus the author would probably not agree with the statement in Choice E. The author would agree with the statement in Choice A: See lines 4–5. Note that although the author may not agree that IQ is what makes the scientist brilliant, he believes that *most* people feel that way. The author would agree with the statement in Choice B. See lines 30–32 and lines 56–60. The author would agree with the statement in Choice C. See lines 15–16 in the context of the rest of the passage. The author would probably not disagree with the statement in Choice D since the author does not appear to distinguish artists from scientists in their thinking process even though the passage is primarily about the scientists: See lines 9–14.

22. Choice C is correct. See lines 52–54. Note that although persistence is mentioned in lines 47–52, the passage states that fluid thinking may be connected to persistence, not defined as persistence. Thus Choice A is incorrect. See also **Reading Comprehension Strategy 5**.

23. Choice B is correct. Given the context in lines 47–54, the word "paradoxically" means seemingly contradictorily. See also **Reading Comprehension Strategy 5**.

24. Choice A is correct. It can be seen in the passage that the author is intrigued by and interested in the way the scientist thinks but at the same time feels that the scientist reports the findings very objectively.

EXPLANATORY ANSWERS FOR PRACTICE TEST 3
Section 8: Math

When a specific Math Strategy is referred to in the solution, study that strategy, which you will find in "19 Math Strategies."

1. Choice B is correct. (**Use Strategy 2: Know the definition of percent.**)

$$\text{Percent of Caramels} =$$

$$\frac{\text{weight of caramels}}{\text{total weight}} \times 100 \qquad \boxed{1}$$

Given:

Weight of Caramels = 0.6 pounds $\qquad \boxed{2}$

Weight of Coconuts = 3.6 pounds $\qquad \boxed{3}$

Adding $\boxed{2}$ and $\boxed{3}$, we get

Total Weight = 0.6 pounds + 3.6 pounds

Total Weight = 4.2 pounds $\qquad \boxed{4}$

Substituting $\boxed{2}$ and $\boxed{4}$ into $\boxed{1}$, we have

$$\text{Percent of Caramels} = \frac{0.6 \text{ pounds}}{4.2 \text{ pounds}} \times 100$$

$$= \frac{.6}{4.2} \times 100$$

$$= \frac{6}{42} \times 100$$

$$= \frac{600}{42} = \frac{300}{21} =$$

$$\text{Percent of Caramels} = 14\frac{2}{7}$$

2. Choice B is correct. Notice that $25,000 is one-fourth of $100,000 (the total funds). (**Use Strategy 17: Use the given information effectively.**)

That is, $\frac{25,000}{100,000} = \frac{1}{4}$.

So look for the piece or part of the circle that is closest to $\frac{1}{4}$ of the whole circle. $\frac{1}{4}$ of the whole circle ($360°$) is $90°$. Lincoln H.S. represents about $\frac{1}{4}$ of the whole circle, or $90°$.

3. Choice A is correct.

Given: $\qquad y = r - 6 \qquad \boxed{1}$
$\qquad\qquad\qquad z = r + 5 \qquad \boxed{2}$

(**Use Strategy 13: Find unknown expressions by addition of equations.**)

Adding $\boxed{1}$ and $\boxed{2}$, we get

$$y + z = 2r - 1$$
$$y + z + 1 = 2r$$
$$\frac{y + z + 1}{2} = r$$

4. Choice E is correct. (**Use Strategy 2: Translate from words to algebra.**)

Given: The 3 polygons have equal perimeters, which gives us

$$6a = 3b \qquad \boxed{1}$$
$$8c = 6a \qquad \boxed{2}$$

Dividing $\boxed{1}$ by 6, we get

$$a = \frac{3}{6}b = \frac{1}{2}b \qquad \boxed{3}$$

Thus, $a < b$

Dividing $\boxed{2}$ by 8, we get

$$c = \frac{6}{8}a = \frac{3}{4}a \qquad \boxed{4}$$

Thus, $c < a$

(**Use Strategy 6: Know how to use inequalities.**)

Using the Transitive Property of Inequalities with $\boxed{3}$ and $\boxed{4}$, we have $c < a < b$.

5. Choice B is correct. (**Use Strategy 9: Know the formula for rate, time, and distance.**)

Rate $\times$ Time = Distance $\qquad \boxed{1}$

Given: Time from A to B = 3 hours ⬛②

Time from B to C = 5 hours ⬛③

Distance from A to B =
Distance from B to C ⬛④

Using ④, let Distance from A to B =
Distance from B to C = D ⬛⑤

Substituting ② and ⑤ into ①, we get

$\text{Rate}_{AB} \times 3 = D$

$\text{Rate}_{AB} = \dfrac{D}{3}$ ⬛⑥

Substituting ③ and ⑤ into ①, we get

$\text{Rate}_{BC} \times 5 = D$

$\text{Rate}_{BC} = \dfrac{D}{5}$ ⬛⑦

From ⑤ we get the whole distance from
A to C = $2D$ ⬛⑧

From ② and ③ we get the time for the
whole trip = $3 + 5 = 8$ ⬛⑨

Substituting ⑧ and ⑨ into ①, we get

$\text{Rate}_{AC} \times 8 = 2D$

$\text{Rate}_{AC} = \dfrac{2D}{8}$

$\text{Rate}_{AC} = \dfrac{D}{4}$ ⬛⑩

We are asked to find the ratio

$\dfrac{\text{average speed from } A \text{ to } B}{\text{average speed from } A \text{ to } C}$ ⬛⑪

Substituting ⑥ and ⑩ into ⑪, we have

$\dfrac{\text{average speed from } A \text{ to } B}{\text{average speed from } A \text{ to } C} =$

$\dfrac{\dfrac{D}{3}}{\dfrac{D}{4}} =$

$\dfrac{D}{3} \div \dfrac{D}{4} =$

$\dfrac{D}{3} \times \dfrac{4}{D} =$

$\dfrac{4}{3} = 4 : 3$

6. Choice C is correct. **(Use Strategy 7: Use number examples.)**

If $a = \dfrac{2}{3}$, $b = \dfrac{4}{3}$, and $x = \dfrac{3}{2}$ ⬛①

Then, substituting from ①, we get

$ax = \dfrac{2}{3}\left(\dfrac{3}{2}\right) \qquad bx = \dfrac{4}{3}\left(\dfrac{3}{2}\right) = \dfrac{4}{2}$

$ax = 1 \qquad\qquad bx = 2$

Neither a nor b nor x is an integer, but both ax and bx are integers.

Thus, Choices B, D, and E are eliminated.

(Use Strategy 13: Find unknown expressions by addition of equations.)

Adding ax to bx, we get

$ax + bx =$
$(a + b)x$ ⬛②

Since ax and bx are integers, ② is an integer. Thus, Choice C is correct.

7. Choice C is correct. **(Use Strategy 17: Use the given information effectively.)** For line q, $y = mx + b_1$. Since the line q crosses the origin where $x = 0$ and $y = 0$, b_1 must $= 0$. Thus for line q, $y = mx$. Now since (4,3) is on line q, this means when $x = 4$, $y = 3$, so if $y = mx$, $3 = m(4)$ and $m = \dfrac{3}{4}$. Now let's look at line p. For this line, $y = Mx + b$. Since the lines p and q are perpendicular, the slope of one is the **negative reciprocal** of the other. Thus $m = -\dfrac{1}{M}$. Since $m = \dfrac{3}{4}$, $\dfrac{3}{4} = -\dfrac{1}{M}$ and so $M = -\dfrac{4}{3}$.

Thus for line p, $y = -\left(\dfrac{4}{3}\right)x + b$. The point (4,3) is also on line p so substituting $x = 4$ and $y = 3$ in the equation $y = -\left(\dfrac{4}{3}\right)x + b$, we get: $3 = -\left(\dfrac{4}{3}\right)(4) + b$. We get $3 = -\dfrac{16}{3} + b$, and thus $3 + \dfrac{16}{3} = b$ and $b = \dfrac{25}{3}$.

Thus for line p, $y = -\left(\dfrac{4}{3}\right)x + \dfrac{25}{3}$. If (3,$a$) is on line p, then substituting $x = 3$ and $y = a$, we get $a = -\left(\dfrac{4}{3}\right)3 + \dfrac{25}{3} = -4 + \dfrac{25}{3} = \dfrac{13}{3} = 4\dfrac{1}{3}$.

8. Choice C is correct. The function $f(x)$ is not defined when the denominator is 0. So if $2x + 4 = 0$, $2x = -4$ and $x = -2$. Thus only III is the case where the function is not defined.

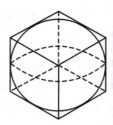

9. Choice E is correct. (**Use Strategy 17: Use the given information effectively.**)

Clearly, we can see from the picture above that the diameter of the sphere has the same length as a side of the cube. We know

Volume of cube = (length of side)^3 $\boxed{1}$

We are given

Volume of cube = 64 $\boxed{2}$

Substituting $\boxed{2}$ into $\boxed{1}$, 64 = (length of side)^3

Thus,

length of side = 4 = diameter of sphere

10. Choice A is correct.

Given: $\frac{m}{n} = \frac{x}{m}$ $\boxed{1}$

(**Use Strategy 13: Find unknowns by multiplication.**)

Multiplying $\boxed{1}$ by m, we have

$$m\left(\frac{m}{n}\right) = \left(\frac{x}{m}\right)m$$

$$\frac{m^2}{n} = x$$

11. Choice B is correct. (**Use Strategy 17: Use the given information effectively.**) We are given

$$CD = \frac{3}{4}AC \qquad \boxed{1}$$

$$CF = \frac{2}{7}BC \qquad \boxed{2}$$

We want to find

$$\frac{\text{area of } \triangle ABC}{\text{area of rectangle } CDEF}$$

We know that the area of rectangle CDEF

$$= (CD)(CF) \qquad \boxed{3}$$

and area of $\triangle ABC$

$$= \frac{1}{2}(AC)(BC) \qquad \boxed{4}$$

Substituting $\boxed{1}$ and $\boxed{2}$ into $\boxed{3}$,

Area of rectangle CDEF

$$= \left(\frac{3}{4}AC\right)\left(\frac{2}{7}BC\right) = \frac{3}{14}(AC)(BC) \qquad \boxed{5}$$

Substituting $\boxed{4}$ and $\boxed{5}$ into the unknown expression,

$$\frac{\text{area of } \triangle ABC}{\text{area of rectangle } CDEF} =$$

$$\frac{\frac{1}{2}(AC)(BC)}{\frac{3}{14}(AC)(BC)}$$

$$= \frac{1}{2} \times \frac{14}{3} = \frac{14}{6} = \frac{7}{3} \text{ (Answer)}$$

12. Choice C is correct. (**Use Strategy 2: Translate from words to algebra.**)

Let b = number of boys
g = number of girls

We are given

$$b = g + 7 \qquad \boxed{1}$$

$$b = \frac{5}{4}g \qquad \boxed{2}$$

(**Use Strategy 13: Find unknowns by multiplication.**) Multiplying $\boxed{2}$ by $\frac{4}{5}$,

$$\frac{4}{5}b = g \qquad \boxed{3}$$

Substituting $\boxed{3}$ into $\boxed{1}$,

$$b = \frac{4}{5}b + 7 \qquad \boxed{4}$$

Multiplying $\boxed{4}$ by 5,

$$5b = 4b + 35$$

or $\qquad b = 35$

13. Choice A is correct. (**Use Strategy 2: Translate words to algebra—see translation table for percent increase.**)

Percent increase = $\frac{\text{amount of increase}}{\text{original amount}}$ $\boxed{1}$

Amount of increase is given as 100 per year $\boxed{2}$

Substituting $\boxed{2}$ into $\boxed{1}$, we get

% increase = $\frac{100}{\text{original amount}}$ $\boxed{3}$

(**Use Strategy 12: Try not to make tedious calculations.**) The greatest % increase will occur when the original amount is least.

Since the population is increasing by 100 every year, it is least at the beginning, in 2009.

Thus $\boxed{3}$ will be greatest from 2009–2010.

14.   Choice D is correct.

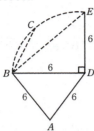

(Use Strategy 14: Draw lines where appropriate.)

Given: $AB = BD = AD = 6$ $\boxed{1}$

C can be any point on arc $\overset{\frown}{BE}$, not just where it appears in the drawing above. For any point C on arc $\overset{\frown}{BE}$

$$CD = 6 \qquad \boxed{2}$$
because CD = radius of the circular arc.

(Use Strategy 3: The whole equals the sum of its parts.) We want to find P = perimeter of

$$ABCD = AB + BC + CD + AD \qquad \boxed{3}$$

Substituting $\boxed{2}$ and $\boxed{1}$ into $\boxed{3}$,

$$P = 18 + BC \qquad \boxed{4}$$

We cannot find BC, but we can find the highest and lowest possible values for BC. Clearly, since BC is a side of a quadrilateral,

$$BC > 0 \qquad \boxed{5}$$

By looking at the diagram, we see that the highest possible value of BC occurs when C coincides with E.

$$BC \le BE \qquad \boxed{6}$$

must be true. BE can easily be found. ΔEDB is similar to one of the standard triangles discussed before. **(Use Strategy 18: Remember special right triangles.)**

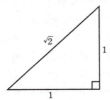

Corresponding sides of similar triangles are proportional, so that

$$\frac{\sqrt{2}}{1} = \frac{BE}{6}$$
or
$$BE = 6\sqrt{2} \qquad \boxed{7}$$

Substituting $\boxed{7}$ into $\boxed{6}$,

$$BC \le 6\sqrt{2} \qquad \boxed{8}$$

Comparing $\boxed{4}$ and $\boxed{8}$,

$$P = 18 + BC \le 18 + 6\sqrt{2} \qquad \boxed{9}$$

Comparing $\boxed{4}$ and $\boxed{5}$,

$$P = 18 + BC > 18 \qquad \boxed{10}$$

From $\boxed{9}$ and $\boxed{10}$ together,

$$18 < P \le 18 + 6\sqrt{2}$$

15.   Choice B is correct.

Given: $x^9 = 4$ $\boxed{1}$

$\qquad\qquad x^7 = \dfrac{9}{y^2}$ $\boxed{2}$

$\qquad\qquad x > 0$ and $y > 0$

(Use Strategy 13: Find unknown by division of equations.)

Divide $\boxed{1}$ by $\boxed{2}$. We get

$$\frac{x^9}{x^7} = \frac{4}{\frac{9}{y^2}}$$

$$x^2 = 4 \times \frac{y^2}{9}$$

$$x^2 = \frac{4}{9}y^2$$

$$\sqrt{x^2} = \sqrt{\frac{4}{9}y^2}$$

$$x = \frac{2}{3}y$$

(*Note:* This is the only solution because $x > 0$ and $y > 0$.)

16.   Choice C is correct. **(Use Strategy 2: Translate from words to algebra.)** Let s = the number of DVDs Ethan originally had.

Thus, $s + 10x$ = the number of DVDs Ethan had after receiving $10x$ DVDs.

We are told

$$s + 10x = (5y + 1)s$$
$$s + 10x = 5ys + s$$
$$10x = 5ys$$
$$s = \frac{10x}{5y}$$
$$s = \frac{2x}{y}$$

EXPLANATORY ANSWERS FOR PRACTICE TEST 3
Section 9: Critical reading

As you read these Explanatory Answers, you are advised to refer to "16 Verbal (Critical Reading) Strategies."

1. Choice E is correct. See **Sentence Completion Strategy 2.** Let us first examine the first word of each choice. We can then eliminate Choice A, unearned, and Choice D, backward, because saying unearned attempts to please or backward attempts to please *does not* make sense. So Choices A and D are incorrect.

   Let us now consider the remaining choices. The second words of Choice B, ...humor, and Choice C, ...reliance, *do not* make sense in the sentence. Choice E, hypocritical...defiance, makes sense and is the correct choice.

2. Choice B is correct. See **Sentence Completion Strategy 3.** If you used this strategy of trying to complete the sentence *before* looking at the five choices, you might have come up with any of the following words:

simple	ordinary
understandable	common
easy-to-understand	

   These words all mean about the same as the correct Choice B, simplified. Therefore, Choices A, C, D, and E are incorrect.

3. Choice D is correct. See **Sentence Completion Strategy 2.** We first examine the first word of each choice. We can then eliminate Choice C, conclusive, and Choice E, ridiculous, because violent crime does not become conclusive or ridiculous. Now we go on to the three remaining choices. When you fill in the two blanks with Choice A and with Choice B, the sentence does not make sense. So these two choices are also incorrect. Filling in the two blanks with Choice D makes the sentence acceptable.

4. Choice E is correct. See **Sentence Completion Strategy 4.** We have an *opposition indicator* here with the first word "Although." We can now assume that the opening clause of the sentence— "Although...patrols"—will contradict the thought expressed in the rest of the sentence. Choice E, impeded...continue, fills in the blanks so that the sentence makes sense. The other choices are incorrect because their word-pairs do not make sense.

5. Choice A is correct. See **Sentence Completion Strategy 3.** This strategy suggests that you try to complete the sentence *before* looking at the five choices. Doing this, you might have come up with any of the following words that indicate an additional type of force or injury besides "seizure":

coercing	forcing	pressuring

   These words all come close to the meaning of correct Choice A, compelling. Therefore, Choices B, C, D, and E are incorrect.

6. Choice E is correct. See **Sentence Completion Strategy 4.** We have an *opposition indicator* here—the student's not working hard and her winning the contest. We, therefore, look for a definitely positive word as our choice to contrast with the negative thought embodied in her not working hard. That positive word is "elated" (Choice E), which means delighted beyond measure. Accordingly Choices A, B, C, and D are incorrect.

7. Choice A is correct. The main idea of the passage is expressed in lines 18–19: "Science seems to have come into existence merely for its bearings on practical life." This main idea is also expressed in other parts of the passage. For example—lines 1–2: "Science, like everything else…needs and desires." Also lines 15–16: "…the bulk of mankind…advantages it brings with it." Finally, all through the last paragraph of the passage we learn how the Babylonians and the Egyptians reaped practical benefits with the help of science. Choices B, C, D, and E are true, but they are too confining to be considered the main idea of the passage. Therefore, these choices are incorrect.

8. Choice E is correct. See lines 8–14: "Science is valued…most important consideration of all to scientific men." Choice A is incorrect. The passage does not indicate that this choice is true. Furthermore, others *before* the Babylonians and the Egyptians also used scientific methods. Choice B is incorrect. See lines 27–29: "The cultivation of crops…made a calendar almost a necessity [for the Babylonians and Egyptians]." Choice C is incorrect. First see lines 20–23: "More than two thousand years before…measuring space and time." Now see lines 32–34: "Twelve of these months…putting in extra months." Choice D is incorrect. See lines 20–23 again.

9. Choice B is correct. See lines 8–14: "Science is valued…provides the imagination…most important consideration of all to scientific men." Choices A, C, D, and E are incorrect because the author does not imply in any way that scientists are sociable, practical, philosophical, or arrogant people.

10. Choice D is correct. You can see from lines 20–25 that "rudimentary" must be related to something fundamental or basic. In fact in lines 24–25, this rudimentary science met the practical needs of the population, so Choices B, C, and E would have been ruled out anyway. See also **Reading Comprehension Strategy 5.**

11. Choice C is correct. The two labels (lines 48–49) obviously have negative implications about the value of physics and thus indicate that physics is uninteresting and pointless to the ordinary person. Accordingly, Choice C is correct. It follows, then, that Choice B—which states that physics "is a cause for great excitement"—is incorrect. Choices A, D, and E are incorrect because none of these choices is stated or implied in the passage.

12. Choice A is correct. See lines 60–62: "Yet what little we do know…grandeur and intricate beauty." Choices B, C, D, and E are incorrect because none of these choices is brought up in the passage.

13. Choice C is correct. See lines 52–54: "There is nothing…what we lack of the other." Also see lines 55–58: "It is pointless…all-knowing, and infallible." None of the other choices is indicated in the passage. Accordingly, Choices A, B, D, and E are incorrect.

14. Choice E is correct. See the very first sentence of the passage: "Let's be honest right at the start." This frankness on the part of the author pervades the entire passage. Choices A, B, C, and D are, therefore, incorrect.

15. Choice B is correct. The author is, in effect, saying that one must appreciate the forest as a whole—not merely certain individual trees. He therefore implies that we should not separate physics from the body of all creative work. See lines 55–56: "It is pointless…all creative work…" Choices A, C, D, and E are incorrect because they are not justified by the content of the passage.

16. Choice D is correct. The practical use of science is discussed in lines 20–34 of Passage 1 but not in Passage 2. Choice A is incorrect: lines 44–51 imply the way laymen view physics. Choice B is incorrect: specialization in science is mentioned in lines 44–47 of Passage 2. Choice C is incorrect: purity of physics is mentioned in line 58 of Passage 2. Choice E is incorrect: lines 51–54 address the arguments between humanists and scientists.

17. Choice A is correct. See lines 44–51 of Passage 2: "boxes." Choices B, C, D, and E are incorrect: critique is certainly used by both authors. The author in Passage 1 contrasts with respect to perceived values in lines 8–16. Historical referencing and examples to support a claim are used in Passage 1 in lines 20–34.

18. Choice E is correct. Choice A, agriculture, is mentioned in line 25. Choice B, astronomy, is mentioned in line 24. Choice C, art, is mentioned in line 43. Choice D, philosophy, is mentioned in line 57. However, Choice A, chemistry, is not directly mentioned.

19. Choice B is correct. Choice A can be immediately ruled out because it repeats the meaning of "grandeur" and would make it redundant (line 61). Since the author described physics as complex, "complicated" would be a good choice. Note that Choices D and E are incorrect because the author believes that although the outside world may view physics as uninteresting or pointless, it is not the real characteristic of physics. It would be unlikely that the noun "beauty" (line 62) would be described by a negative adjective or word (especially because it is also associated with the positive word "grandeur"). Thus it is unlikely that "complicated" is a negative word such as *devastating, uninteresting,* or *pointless,* ruling out Choices C, D, and E. See also **Reading Comprehension Strategy 5**.

EXPLANATORY ANSWERS FOR PRACTICE TEST 3
Section 5: Writing

1. **(A)** Choice A is correct. If you are questioning the singularity of the possessive adjective "his," it is correct. The subject of the sentence consists of a singular compound subject, "the sales manager and personnel director." If we wanted to indicate plurality here, we would have to insert the article "the" before the second member ("personnel director") of the compound subject. Choice B is incorrect because "their" must refer to a plural antecedent. Choice C is incorrect because it changes the meaning of the original sentence. Choice D is awkward. Choice E is too wordy.

2. **(B)** Choice A is incorrect because it does not parallel the structure of "not only because of its beauty." Choice B is correct. Choices C, D, and E are incorrect for the same reason that Choice A is incorrect—the lack of parallel structure. Moreover, Choice C is incorrect because "on account" cannot be used as a subordinate conjunction.

3. **(E)** The past participle "known" must modify the subject of the sentence. Choices A and C are, therefore, incorrect because the subject must be "grandfather"—he is the one (not "friends") that is "known to every man, woman, and child in the town." Choice B changes the meaning of the original sentence. Choice D has a double negative ("never...no..."). Choice E is correct.

4. **(B)** "No sooner...than" is the correct expression. Have you ever heard the expression *"No sooner said than done?"* Sometimes it is easier to bring to mind the more common phrases to remind us of the correct construction of certain phrases. The phrase "no sooner...than" can only be constructed as such and therefore the other choices are to be eliminated.

5. **(A)** Choice A is correct. Choice B is incorrect for two reasons: (1) We use the adverb "so" instead of "as" in a negative comparison; (2) "like" may not be used instead of "as" in this type of comparison. Choice C is awkward. Choice D is roundabout. Choice E changes the meaning of the original sentence.

6. **(A)** Choice A is correct. It is very direct and gets the point across clearly. Choice B is awkward ("knows already"). Choice C should be more direct ("current time" is awkward). Choice D is too wordy, confusing, and redundant ("already presently"). Choice E is awkward ("to her present knowledge then").

7. **(C)** Choice A is incorrect because in this sentence "also" means the same as "in addition." Choice B is awkward. Choice C is correct as a subordinate clause which parallels the preceding subordinate clause. Choice D creates a run-on sentence. Choice E is too wordy.

8. **(C)** Choices A, B, and D are incorrect because of the use of "him joining." The word "joining" is a gerund in this sentence. Its possessive adjective must be "his"—not "him." Choice B, moreover, has the unidiomatic expression "objection on." Choice C is correct. Choice E changes the meaning of the original sentence.

9. **(B)** Choice A is incorrect because the nominative form ("he") is required: "as fully as him" is wrong. Choice B is correct. Choices C, D, and E are incorrect because the object of the preposition must have an objective case form—the preposition "but" must be followed by the object case form "him."

10. **(C)** Choice A is incorrect because the verb should be the past perfect form ("had completed") to indicate an action that took place prior to "tried." Choice B changes the meaning of the original sentence. Choice C is correct. Choice D is awkward. Choice E changes the tense of the original sentence.

11. **(D)** Choice A uses the word "affect" incorrectly. It means "to influence" and in the original sentence it is incorrectly used to mean "to bring about." Choice B also uses the word "affect" incorrectly and in addition the verb needed is "is trying" as it refers to the principal *only*. Choice C is incorrect because the singular verb is required. Choice D is correct. Choice E is not correct because it changes the meaning of the original sentence.

12. **(E)** Choice A is incorrect because the word "fewer" should be used instead of "less," because "less" denotes amount or degree and "fewer" denotes number. Choice B is not correct because "as before" is superfluous. Choice C is incorrect for the same reason as Choice A (above). Choice D changes the meaning of the original sentence. Choice E is correct.

13. **(C)** Choice A is incorrect because in this past contrary-to-fact situation, the verb of the "if" clause should be expressed in the past perfect tense ("had changed"). Choice B does not include a reference to the director, which is necessary to the meaning of the original sentence. Choice C is correct. Choice D is incorrect because it does not include a reference to the director, which, as indicated previously, is necessary to the meaning of the original sentence. Choice E omits a reference to the director and also uses "would have been" incorrectly.

14. **(E)** Choices A and B are incorrect because when two singular antecedents are joined by "nor," they should be referred to by a singular pronoun. Also, Choice B does not include the names of the girls, which were included in the original sentence. Choice C uses the word "or" incorrectly, rather than "nor." Choice D does not include the names of the girls and so it changes the meaning of the original sentence. Choice E is correct.

SAT PRACTICE
TEST 4

ANSWER SHEET FOR PRACTICE TEST 4

Section 1

Begin your essay on this page. If you need more space, continue on the next page. Do not write outside of the essay box.

Continue on the next page if necessary.

Continuation of ESSAY Section 1 from previous page. Write below only if you need more space.

Start with number 1 for each new section. If a section has fewer questions than answer spaces, leave the extra answer spaces blank. Be sure to erase any errors or stray marks completely.

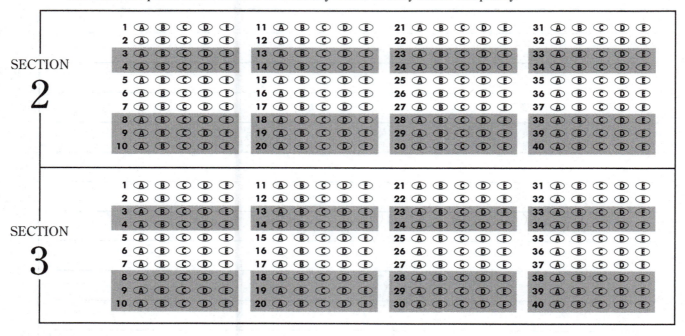

SECTION 2

SECTION 3

CAUTION Use the answer spaces in the grids below for Section 2 or Section 3 only if you are told to do so in your test book.

Student-Produced Responses

ONLY ANSWERS ENTERED IN THE CIRCLES IN EACH GRID WILL BE SCORED. YOU WILL NOT RECEIVE CREDIT FOR ANYTHING WRITTEN IN THE BOXES ABOVE THE CIRCLES.

9   10   11   12   13

14   15   16   17   18

Start with number 1 for each new section. If a section has fewer questions than answer spaces, leave the extra answer spaces blank. Be sure to erase any errors or stray marks completely.

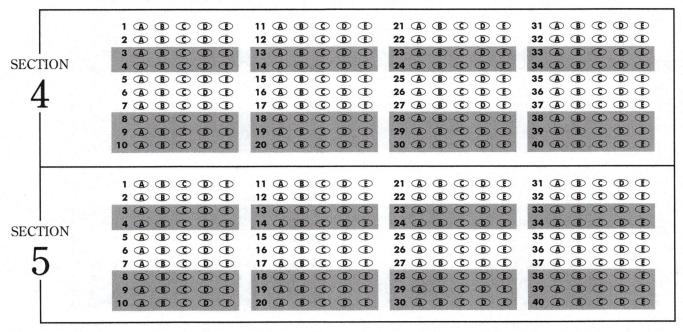

CAUTION Use the answer spaces in the grids below for Section 2 or Section 3 only if you are told to do so in your test book.

Student-Produced Responses

ONLY ANSWERS ENTERED IN THE CIRCLES IN EACH GRID WILL BE SCORED. YOU WILL NOT RECEIVE CREDIT FOR ANYTHING WRITTEN IN THE BOXES ABOVE THE CIRCLES.

Start with number 1 for each new section. If a section has fewer questions than answer spaces, leave the extra answer spaces blank. Be sure to erase any errors or stray marks completely.

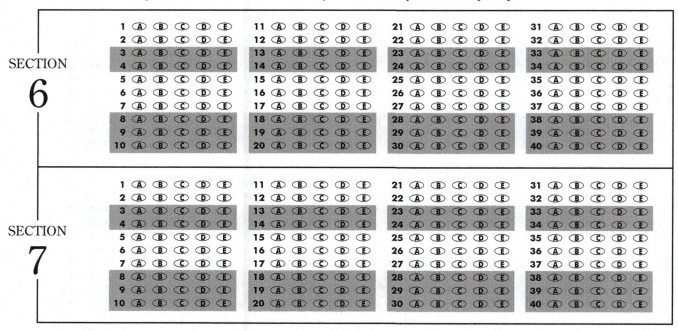

CAUTION Use the answer spaces in the grids below for Section 2 or Section 3 only if you are told to do so in your test book.

Student-Produced Responses

ONLY ANSWERS ENTERED IN THE CIRCLES IN EACH GRID WILL BE SCORED. YOU WILL NOT RECEIVE CREDIT FOR ANYTHING WRITTEN IN THE BOXES ABOVE THE CIRCLES.

Start with number 1 for each new section. If a section has fewer questions than answer spaces, leave the extra answer spaces blank. Be sure to erase any errors or stray marks completely.

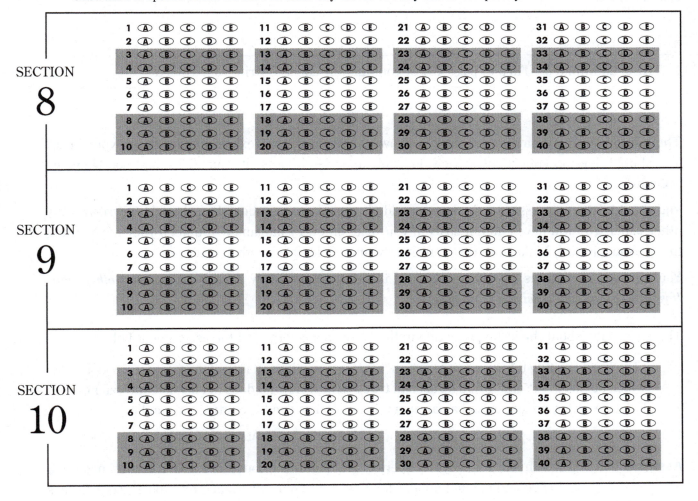

Section 1

Time: 25 Minutes—Turn to page 434 of your answer sheet to write your ESSAY.

The purpose of the essay is to have you show how well you can express and develop your ideas. You should develop your point of view, logically and clearly present your ideas, and use language accurately.

You should write your essay on the lines provided on your answer sheet. You should not write on any other paper. You will have enough space if you write on every line and if you keep your handwriting to a reasonable size. Make sure that your handwriting is legible to other readers.

You will have 25 minutes to write an essay on the assignment below. *Do not write on any other topic. If you do so, you will receive a score of 0.*

Think carefully about the issue presented in the following excerpt and the assignment below.

> "The most exciting thing we can experience is the mysterious. It is the fundamental emotion which stands at the cradle of true art and true science. He who does not know it and can no longer wonder, no longer feel amazement, is as good as dead, a snuffed-out candle."
>
> –Adapted from Albert Einstein, "What I Believe."

Assignment: In which ways have you experienced "the mysterious" and how has that made you feel alive and excited about life? Based on your experience or experiences, discuss how the above quote rings true and how science or art illustrates the "mysterious."

DO NOT WRITE YOUR ESSAY IN YOUR TEST BOOK. You will receive credit only for what you write on your answer sheet.

BEGIN WRITING YOUR ESSAY ON PAGE 434 OF THE ANSWER SHEET.

If you finish before time is called, you may check your work on this section only.
Do not turn to any other section in the test.

Section 2

Time: 25 Minutes – Turn to Section 2 (page 436) of your answer sheet to answer the questions in this section. 20 Questions

Directions: For this section, solve each problem and decide which is the best of the choices given. Fill in the corresponding circle on the answer sheet. You may use any available space for scratchwork.

Notes:

1. The use of a calculator is permitted.

2. All numbers used are real numbers.

3. Figures that accompany problems in this test are intended to provide information useful in solving the problems. They are drawn as accurately as possible EXCEPT when it is stated in a specific problem that the figure is not drawn to scale. All figures lie in a plane unless otherwise indicated.

4. Unless otherwise specified, the domain of any function f is assumed to be the set of all real numbers x for which $f(x)$ is a real number.

REFERENCE INFORMATION

$A = \pi r^2$ $A = lw$ $A = \frac{1}{2}bh$ $V = lwh$ $V = \pi r^2 h$ $c^2 = a^2 + b^2$ *Special Right Triangle.*
$C = 2\pi r$

The number of degrees of arc in a circle is 360.
The sum of the measures in degrees of the angles of a triangle is 180.

---

1. What is another expression for 8 less than the quotient of x and 3?

   (A) $\frac{x-8}{3}$

   (B) $\frac{x}{3} - 8$

   (C) $8 - 3x$

   (D) $3x - 8$

   (E) $3(8 - x)$

2. Each of Phil's buckets has a capacity of 11 gallons. Each of Mark's buckets can hold 8 gallons. How much more water, in gallons, can 7 of Phil's buckets hold than 7 of Mark's buckets?

   (A) 3

   (B) 7

   (C) 21

   (D) 24

   (E) 56

GO ON TO THE NEXT PAGE ➤

3. Which of the following is equal to $\frac{|x|}{|y|}$ for all real numbers x and y?

(A) $\frac{x}{y}$

(B) $\frac{|x|}{y}$

(C) $\frac{x}{|y|}$

(D) $\left|\frac{x}{y}\right|$

(E) $-\left|\frac{x}{y}\right|$

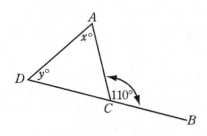

5. In the figure above, $m\angle ACB = 110°$ and $AC = CD$. What is the value of $2y$?

(A) 45
(B) 70
(C) 90
(D) 110
(E) 140

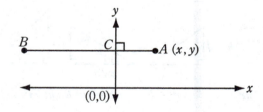

4. If $3AC = BC$ in the figure above, what are the coordinates of B?

(A) $(x, 3y)$
(B) $(-x, 3y)$
(C) $(3x, y)$
(D) $(-3x, y)$
(E) $(-3x, 3y)$

6. If $(x + y)^2 = 9$, what is $x + y$?

(A) 0
(B) 3
(C) 9
(D) 27
(E) The answer cannot be determined from the information given.

GO ON TO THE NEXT PAGE ❯

7. The average (arithmetic mean) of five numbers is 34. If three of the numbers are 28, 30, and 32, what is the sum of the other two?

(A) 40
(B) 50
(C) 60
(D) 70
(E) 80

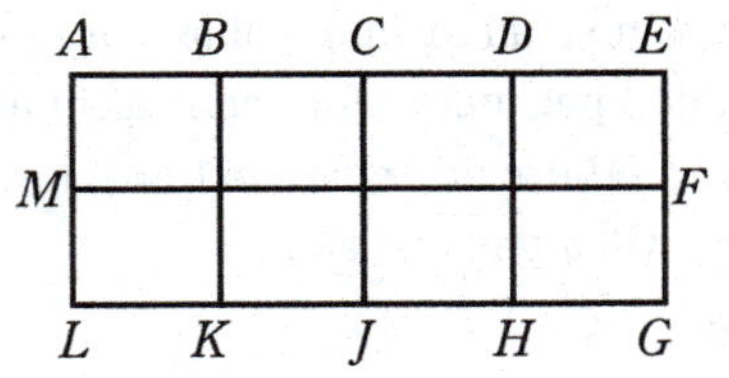

9. For any positive integer, x, $\circledS = \dfrac{x^2}{3}$ and $\boxed{x} = \dfrac{9}{x}$. What is an expression for $\circledS \times \boxed{x}$?

(A) $3x$
(B) x
(C) 1
(D) $\dfrac{x^3}{64}$
(E) $27x^3$

8. In the figure above, rectangle $AEGL$ has been divided into 8 congruent squares. If the perimeter of one of these squares is 16, what is the value of $AE + MF + LG + AL + BK + CJ + DH + EG$?

(A) 32
(B) 44
(C) 88
(D) 128
(E) 176

10. If each of the 3 distinct points A, B, and C are the same distance from point D, which of the following could be true?

I. A, B, C, and D are the four vertices of a square.
II. A, B, C, and D lie on the circumference of a circle.
III. A, B, and C lie on the circumference of the circle whose center is D.

(A) I only
(B) II only
(C) III only
(D) II and III only
(E) I, II, and III

GO ON TO THE NEXT PAGE ➤

11. Of the following five diagrams below, which diagram describes the dark region as the set of elements that belongs to all of the sets A, B, and C?

(A)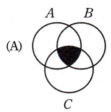

(B)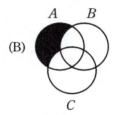

(C)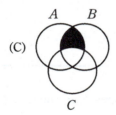

(D)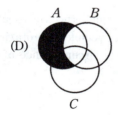

(E)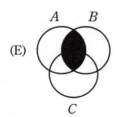

12. If the points (1,3), (3,5), and (6,y) all lie on the same line, the value of y is

(A) 8
(B) 7
(C) 6
(D) 5
(E) 4

13. In a certain small town, p gallons of gasoline are needed per month for each car in town. At this rate, if there are r cars in town, how long, in months, will q gallons last?

(A) $\frac{pq}{r}$

(B) $\frac{qr}{p}$

(C) $\frac{r}{pq}$

(D) $\frac{q}{pr}$

(E) pqr

GO ON TO THE NEXT PAGE ➤

The next two questions refer to the following definition:

The *l*-length of the segment from point A to point B is $B - A$.

14. What is the *l*-length from -3 to 3?

(A) -6
(B) -3
(C) 0
(D) 3
(E) 6

16. If the sum of 5 consecutive positive integers is w, in terms of w, which of the following represents the sum of the next 5 consecutive positive integers?

(A) $w + 5$
(B) $5w + 5$
(C) $5w + 25$
(D) $w + 25$
(E) $w^2 + 25$

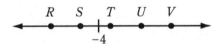

15. Of all segments beginning at -4 and ending at one of the integers indicated above on the number line, which segment has the *least* *l*-length?

(A) From -4 to R
(B) From -4 to S
(C) From -4 to T
(D) From -4 to U
(E) From -4 to V

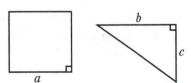

17. If the area of the square is twice the area of the triangle and $bc = 100$, then find a^2.

(A) 400
(B) 200
(C) 100
(D) 50
(E) 25

GO ON TO THE NEXT PAGE ➤

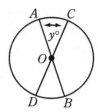

Note: Figure is not drawn to scale

18. In the figure above, $\overline{AB}$ and $\overline{CD}$ are diameters of the circle whose center is O. If the radius of the circle is 2 inches and the sum of the lengths of arcs $\overarc{AD}$ and $\overarc{BC}$ is 3π inches, then $y =$

(A) 45
(B) 60
(C) 75
(D) 90
(E) 120

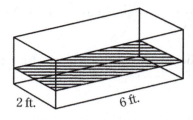

2 ft.   6 ft.

20. The figure above shows water in a tank whose base is 2 feet by 6 feet. If a rectangular solid whose dimensions are 1 foot by 1 foot by 2 feet is totally immersed in the water, how many *inches* will the water rise?

(A) $\frac{1}{6}$
(B) 1
(C) 2
(D) 3
(E) 12

19. Five years ago, Ross was N times as old as Amanda was. If Amanda is now 19 years old, how old is Ross now in terms of N?

(A) $14N - 5$
(B) $14N + 5$
(C) $19N + 5$
(D) $15N + 5$
(E) $19N - 5$

STOP

If you finish before time is called, you may check your work on this section only.
Do not turn to any other section in the test.

Take a 5 minute break

before starting section 3

Section 3

Time: 25 Minutes – Turn to Section 3 (page 436) of your answer sheet to answer the questions in this section. 18 Questions

Directions: For this section, solve each problem and decide which is the best of the choices given. Fill in the corresponding circle on the answer sheet. You may use any available space for scratchwork.

Notes:

1. The use of a calculator is permitted.

2. All numbers used are real numbers.

3. Figures that accompany problems in this test are intended to provide information useful in solving the problems. They are drawn as accurately as possible EXCEPT when it is stated in a specific problem that the figure is not drawn to scale. All figures lie in a plane unless otherwise indicated.

4. Unless otherwise specified, the domain of any function f is assumed to be the set of all real numbers x for which $f(x)$ is a real number.

REFERENCE INFORMATION

$A = \pi r^2$ $A = lw$ $A = \dfrac{1}{2}bh$ $V = lwh$ $V = \pi r^2 h$ $c^2 = a^2 + b^2$ *Special Right Triangle.*
$C = 2\pi r$

The number of degrees of arc in a circle is 360.
The sum of the measures in degrees of the angles of a triangle is 180.

---

1. If $x + by = 3x + y = 5$ and $y = 2$, then $b =$

   (A) 0
   (B) 1
   (C) 2
   (D) 3
   (E) 4

2. There are 2 boys and 3 girls in the class. The ratio of boys to girls in the class is equal to all of the following *except*

   (A) $4:6$
   (B) $9:12$
   (C) $6:9$
   (D) $12:18$
   (E) $18:27$

GO ON TO THE NEXT PAGE ➤

3. What fraction of 1 week is 24 min?

    (A) $\frac{1}{60}$

    (B) $\frac{1}{168}$

    (C) $\frac{1}{420}$

    (D) $\frac{1}{1,440}$

    (E) $\frac{1}{10,080}$

5. Jaxon spent $\frac{2}{5}$ of his allowance on candy and $\frac{5}{6}$ of the remainder on ice cream. If his allowance is $30, how much money did he have left after buying the candy and ice cream?

    (A) $1
    (B) $2
    (C) $3
    (D) $5
    (E) $10

4. $2 \times 10^{-5} \times 8 \times 10^{2} \times 5 \times 10^{2} =$

    (A) .00008
    (B) .008
    (C) .08
    (D) 8
    (E) 800

Questions 6–7 refer to the following diagram:

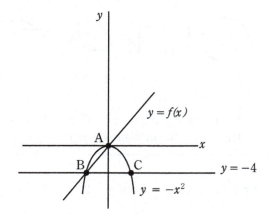

6. The x-coordinate of point B is

    (A) -2
    (B) -3
    (C) -4
    (D) -5
    (E) -6

GO ON TO THE NEXT PAGE ❯

7. The graph of the equation $y = f(x)$ is of the form $y = mx + b$, where b is

(A) 0
(B) 1
(C) 2
(D) 3
(E) 4

8. At how many points does the graph of the equation $y = x^4 + x^3$ intersect the x-axis?

(A) 0
(B) 1
(C) 2
(D) 3
(E) 4

GO ON TO THE NEXT PAGE ➤

Directions: For Student-Produced Response questions 9–18, use the grids on the bottom of the answer sheet page on which you have answered questions 1-8.

Each of the remaining questions requires you to solve the problem and enter your answer by marking the circles in the special grid, as shown in the examples below. You may use any available space for scratchwork.

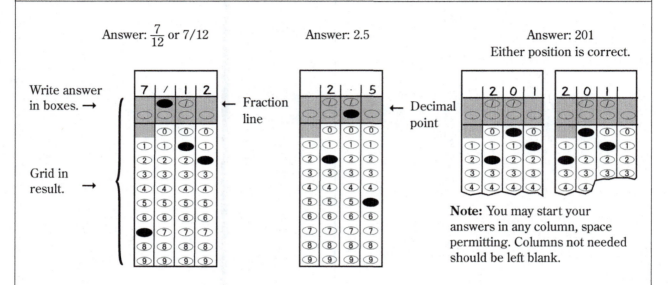

Answer: $\frac{7}{12}$ or 7/12   Answer: 2.5   Answer: 201
Either position is correct.

Write answer in boxes. →   ← Fraction line   ← Decimal point

Grid in result. →

Note: You may start your answers in any column, space permitting. Columns not needed should be left blank.

- Mark no more than one oval in any column.

- Because the answer sheet will be machine-scored, **you will receive credit only if the ovals are filled in correctly.**

- Although not required, it is suggested that you write your answer in the boxes at the top of the columns to help you fill in the ovals accurately.

- Some problems may have more than one correct answer. In such cases, grid only one answer.

- No question has a negative answer.

- **Mixed numbers** such as $2\frac{1}{2}$ must be gridded as 2.5 or 5/2. (If [2 1/2] is gridded, it will be interpreted as $\frac{21}{2}$, not $2\frac{1}{2}$.)

- **Decimal Accuracy:** If you obtain a decimal answer, **enter the most accurate value the grid will accommodate.** For example, if you obtain an answer such as 0.6666..., you should record the result as .666 or .667. **Less accurate values such as .66 or .67 are not acceptable.**

Acceptable ways to grid $\frac{2}{3}$ = .6666...:

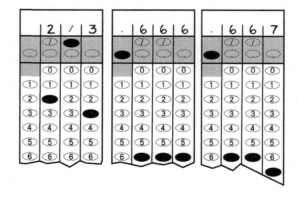

9. If $\frac{5}{8}$ of x is 40, then find the value of $\frac{3}{8}$ of x.

10. A piece of wire is bent to form a circle of radius 3 feet. How many pieces of wire, each 2 feet long, can be made from the wire?

11. Ana spent $7 in order to buy baseballs and tennis balls. If baseballs are 70¢ each and tennis balls are 60¢ each, what is the greatest possible number of tennis balls that Ana could have bought?

12. Let $f(x)$ be defined for all x by the equation $f(x) = 12x + 8$. Thus, $f(2) = 32$. If $f(x) \div f(0) = 2x$, then find the value of x.

ABA	*BBB*	*CBA*	*BBA*
ACC	*CBC*	*CCC*	*ACA*
BAC	*ABC*	*BCA*	*CAB*
CBB	*BCA*	*AAB*	*ACC*

13. In the triple arrangement of letters above, a triple has a value of 1 if exactly 2 of the letters in the triple are the same. Any other combination has a value of 0. The value of the entire arrangement is the sum of the values of each of the triples. What is the value of the above arrangement?

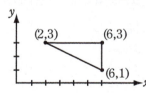

14. In the figure above, what is the area of the triangle?

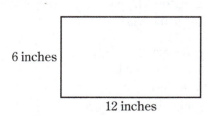

6 inches

12 inches

15. How many squares with 2-inch sides can be placed, without overlapping, into the rectangle shown above?

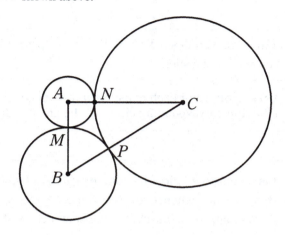

16. The circles having their centers at *A*, *B*, and *C* have radii of 1, 2, and 3, respectively. The circles are tangent at points *M*, *N*, and *P* as shown above. What is the product of the lengths of the sides of the triangle?

17. If the average (arithmetic mean) of 4 numbers is 8,000 and the average (arithmetic mean) of 3 of the 4 numbers is 7,500, then what must the fourth number be?

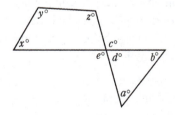

18. Five line segments intersect to form the figure above. What is the value of $x + y + z$ if $c = 100$?

GO ON TO THE NEXT PAGE ➤

Section 4

Time: 25 Minutes – Turn to Section 4 (page 437) of your answer sheet to answer the questions in this section. 24 Questions
Directions: For each question in this section, select the best answer from among the choices given and fill in the corresponding circle on the answer sheet.

Each sentence below has one or two blanks, each blank indicating that something has been omitted. Beneath the sentence are five words or sets of words labeled A through E. Choose the word or set of words that, when inserted in the sentence, <u>best</u> fits the meaning of the sentence as a whole.

Example:

Hoping to _____ the dispute, negotiators proposed a compromise that they felt would be _____ to both labor and management.

(A) enforce...useful

(B) end...divisive

(C) overcome...unattractive

(D) extend...satisfactory

(E) resolve...acceptable

Ⓐ Ⓑ Ⓒ Ⓓ ⬤

1. In a rising tide of _____ in public education, Ms. Anderson was an example of an informed and _____ teacher—a blessing to children and an asset to the nation.

   (A) compromise...inept
   (B) pacifism...inspiring
   (C) ambiguity...average
   (D) mediocrity...dedicated
   (E) oblivion...typical

2. It is _____ that primitive man considered eclipses to be _____ .

   (A) foretold...spectacular
   (B) impossible...ominous
   (C) understandable...magical
   (D) true...rational
   (E) glaring...desirable

3. By _____ the conversation, the girl had once again proved that she had overcome her shyness.

   (A) appreciating
   (B) recognizing
   (C) hearing
   (D) initiating
   (E) considering

4. Only an authority in that area would be able to _____ such highly _____ subject matter included in the book.

   (A) understand...general
   (B) confuse...simple
   (C) read...useless
   (D) comprehend...complex
   (E) misconstrue...sophisticated

GO ON TO THE NEXT PAGE ➤

5. The professor displayed extreme stubbornness; not only did he _____ the logic of the student's argument, but he _____ to acknowledge that the textbook conclusion was correct.

    (A) amplify…hesitated
    (B) reject…refused
    (C) clarify…consented
    (D) justify…expected
    (E) ridicule…proposed

6. The _____ of the explorers was reflected in their refusal to give up.

    (A) tenacity
    (B) degradation
    (C) greed
    (D) harassment
    (E) sociability

7. Ironically, the protest held in order to strengthen the labor movement served to _____ it.

    (A) justify
    (B) coddle
    (C) weaken
    (D) invigorate
    (E) appease

8. In spite of David's tremendous intelligence, he was frequently _____ when confronted with practical matters.

    (A) coherent
    (B) baffled
    (C) cautious
    (D) philosophical
    (E) pensive

Each passage below is followed by questions on its content. Answer the questions on the basis of what is stated or implied in each passage and in any introductory material that may be provided.

Questions 9–10 are based on the following passage.

In the South American rain forest abide the greatest acrobats on earth. The monkeys of the Old World, agile as they are, cannot hang by their tails. It is only the monkeys of America that possess this skill. They are called ceboids
5   and their unique group includes marmosets, owl monkeys, sakis, spider monkeys, squirrel monkeys and howlers. Among these the star gymnast is the skinny, intelligent spider monkey. Hanging head down like a trapeze artist from the loop of a liana, he may suddenly give a short
10 swing, launch himself into space and, soaring outward and downward across a 50-foot void of air, lightly catch a bough on which he spied a shining berry. Owl monkeys cannot match his leap, for their arms are shorter, their tails untalented. The marmosets, smallest of the tribe, tough noisy
15 hoodlums that travel in gangs, are also capable of leaps into space, but their landings are rough: smack against a tree trunk with arms and legs spread wide.

9. Which of the following titles best expresses the ideas of this selection?

    (A) The Star Gymnast
    (B) Monkeys and Trees
    (C) Travelers in Space
    (D) The Uniqueness of Monkeys
    (E) Ceboid Acrobats

10. Compared to monkeys of the Old World, American monkeys are

    (A) smaller
    (B) quieter
    (C) more dexterous
    (D) more protective of their young
    (E) less at home in their surroundings

GO ON TO THE NEXT PAGE ➤

Questions 11–12 are based on the following passage.

A critic of politics finds himself driven to deprecate the power of words while using them copiously in warning against their influence. It is indeed in politics that their influence is most dangerous, so that one is almost tempted
5 to wish that they did not exist, and that society might be managed silently, by instinct, habit, and ocular perception, without this supervening Babel of reports, arguments, and slogans.

11.   The author implies that critics of misused language

    (A) become fanatical on this subject

    (B) are guilty of what they criticize in others

    (C) are clever in contriving slogans

    (D) tell the story of the Tower of Babel

    (E) rely too strongly on instincts

12.   Which statement is true according to the passage?

    (A) Critics of politics are often driven to take desperate measures.

    (B) Words, when used by politicians, have the greatest capacity for harm.

    (C) Politicians talk more than other people.

    (D) Society would be better managed if mutes were in charge.

    (E) Reports and slogans are not to be trusted

Questions 13–24 are based on the following passage.

The following passage deals with the importance of castles in medieval Europe and how they affected the society at that time.

Medieval Europe abounded in castles. Germany alone had ten thousand and more, most of them now vanished; all that a summer journey in the Rhineland and the southwest now can show are a handful of ruins and a few nineteenth
5 century restorations. Nevertheless, anyone journeying from Spain to the Dvina, from Calabria to Wales, will find castles rearing up again and again to dominate the open landscape. There they still stand, in desolate and uninhabited districts where the only visible forms of life are herdsmen and
10 their flocks, with hawks circling the battlements, far from the traffic and comfortably distant even from the nearest small town: these were the strongholds of the European aristocracy.

The weight of aristocratic dominance was felt in
15 Europe until well after the French Revolution; political and social structure, the Church, the general tenor of thought and feeling were all influenced by it. Over the centuries, consciously or unconsciously, the other classes of this older European society—the clergy, the bourgeoisie and
20 the "common people"—adopted many of the outward characteristics of the aristocracy, who became their model, their standard, their ideal. Aristocratic values and ambitions

were adopted alongside aristocratic manners and fashions of dress. Yet the aristocracy were the object of much
25 contentious criticism and complaint; from the thirteenth century onwards their military value and their political importance were both called in question. Nevertheless, their opponents continued to be their principal imitators. In the eleventh and twelfth centuries, the reforming Papacy
30 and its clerical supporters, although opposed to the excessively aristocratic control of the Church (as is shown by the Investiture Contest), nevertheless themselves first adopted and then strengthened the forms of this control. Noblemen who became bishops or who founded new Orders helped
35 to implant aristocratic principles and forms of government deep within the structure and spiritual life of the Church. Again, in the twelfth and thirteenth centuries the urban bourgeoisie, made prosperous and even rich by trade and industry, were rising to political power as the servants
40 and legal proteges of monarchy. These "patricians" were critical of the aristocracy and hostile towards it. Yet they also imitated the aristocracy, and tried to gain admittance to the closed circle and to achieve equality of status. Even the unarmed peasantry, who usually had to suffer more
45 from the unrelieved weight of aristocratic dominance, long remained tenaciously loyal to their lords, held to their allegiance by that combination of love and fear, *amor et timor*, which was so characteristic of the medieval relationship between lord and servant, between God and man.

13.   According to the passage, class conflict in the Middle Ages was kept in check by

    (A) the fact that most people belonged to the same class

    (B) tyrannical suppressions of rebellions by powerful monarchs

    (C) the religious teachings of the church

    (D) the fact that all other classes admired and attempted to emulate the aristocracy

    (E) the fear that a relatively minor conflict would lead to a general revolution

14.   According to the author, the urban bourgeoisie was hostile to the aristocracy because

    (A) the bourgeoisie was prevented by the aristocracy from seeking an alliance with the kings

    (B) aristocrats often confiscated the wealth of the bourgeoisie

    (C) the bourgeoisie saw the aristocracy as their rivals

    (D) the aristocrats often deliberately antagonized the bourgeoisie

    (E) the bourgeoisie felt that the aristocracy was immoral

GO ON TO THE NEXT PAGE ➤

15. According to the passage, castles were originally built

  (A) as status symbols
  (B) as strongholds against invaders
  (C) as simple places to live in
  (D) as luxurious chateaux
  (E) as recreation centers for the townspeople

16. One of the groups that invaded central Europe during the Middle Ages from the ninth century on was the

  (A) Magyars
  (B) Franks
  (C) Angles
  (D) Celts
  (E) Welsh

17. It can be seen from the passage that the aristocracy was originally

  (A) the great landowners
  (B) members of the clergy
  (C) the king's warriors
  (D) merchants who became wealthy
  (E) slaves who had rebelled

18. The reform popes eventually produced an aristocratic church because

  (A) they depended on the aristocracy for money
  (B) they themselves were more interested in money than in religion
  (C) they were defeated by aristocrats
  (D) many aristocrats entered the structure of the church and impressed their values on it
  (E) the aristocrats were far more religious than other segments of the population

19. The word "contentious" in line 25 is best interpreted to mean

  (A) careful
  (B) solid
  (C) controversial
  (D) grandiose
  (E) annoying

20. According to the passage, hunting served the dual purpose of

  (A) preparing for war and engaging in sport
  (B) preparing for war and getting meat
  (C) learning how to ride and learning how to shoot
  (D) testing horses and men
  (E) getting furs and ridding the land of excess animals

21. The phrase "amor et timor" in line 47 is used to describe

  (A) the rivalry between the bourgeoisie and the aristocracy
  (B) the Church's view of man and his relationship to God
  (C) the peasant's loyalty to the aristocracy
  (D) the adaptation of aristocratic manners and dress
  (E) the payment of food in exchange for protection

22. The passage indicates that protection of the peasantry was implemented by

  (A) the king's warriors
  (B) the Magyar mercenaries
  (C) the replacement of wood towers by stone donjons
  (D) the princes of the Church
  (E) the ruling monarchy

23. According to the passage, the effectiveness of the Church and king was diminished by

  (A) the ambition of the military
  (B) conflicts and weaknesses within the Church and Royal house
  (C) peasant dissatisfaction
  (D) the inherent flaws of feudalism
  (E) economic instability

24. "Retinue," the last word in the passage, refers to

  (A) food
  (B) all material goods
  (C) money
  (D) attendants
  (E) family

STOP

**If you finish before time is called, you may check your work on this section only.
Do not turn to any other section in the test.**

Section 5

Time: 25 Minutes – Turn to Section 5 (page 437) of your answer sheet to answer the questions in this section. 35 Questions

Directions: For each question in this section, select the best answer from among the choices given and fill in the corresponding circle on the answer sheet.

The following sentences test correctness and effectiveness of expression. Part of each sentence or the entire sentence is underlined; beneath each sentence are five ways of phrasing the underlined material. Choice A repeats the original phrasing; the other four choices are different. If you think the original phrasing produces a better sentence than any of the alternatives, select Choice A; if not, select one of the other choices.

In making your selection, follow the requirements of standard written English; that is, pay attention to grammar, choice of words, sentence construction, and punctuation. Your selection should result in the most effective sentence—clear and precise, without awkwardness or ambiguity.

EXAMPLE:

Laura Ingalls Wilder published her first book <u>and she was sixty-five years old then</u>.

(A)   and she was sixty-five years old then

(B)   when she was sixty-five

(C)   at age sixty-five years old

(D)   upon the reaching of sixty-five years

(E)   at the time when she was sixty-five

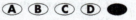

---

1.   <u>After the defendant charged him with being prejudiced</u>, the judge withdrew from the case.

 (A)   After the defendant charged him with being prejudiced

 (B)   On account of the defendant charged him with being prejudiced

 (C)   Charging the defendant with being prejudiced

 (D)   Upon the defendant charging him with being prejudiced

 (E)   The defendant charged him with being prejudiced

2.   <u>Although the mourners differed in nationality and in dress</u>, they all sat silently together for an hour to honor Whitney M. Young Jr.

 (A)   Although the mourners differed in nationality and in dress

 (B)   Because the mourners differed in nationality and in dress

 (C)   The mourners having differed in nationality and in dress

 (D)   When the mourners differed in nationality and in dress

 (E)   The mourners differed in nationality and in dress

GO ON TO THE NEXT PAGE ➤

3. To avoid the hot sun, our plans were that we would travel at night.

    (A) To avoid the hot sun, our plans were that we would travel at night.
    (B) To try to avoid the hot sun, our plans were for travel at night.
    (C) Our plans were night travel so that we could avoid the hot sun.
    (D) We planned to travel at night, that's how we would avoid the hot sun.
    (E) To avoid the hot sun, we made plans to travel at night.

4. Whatever she had any thoughts about, they were interrupted as the hotel lobby door opened.

    (A) Whatever she had any thoughts about
    (B) Whatever her thoughts
    (C) Whatever be her thoughts
    (D) What her thoughts were
    (E) What thoughts

5. The use of cell phones and the Internet make it possible for school administrators to easily maintain contact with parents at all times.

    (A) make it possible
    (B) makes it possible
    (C) allows the possibility
    (D) makes possible
    (E) make it a possibility

6. Irregardless what reasons or excuses are offered, there is only one word for his behavior: cowardice.

    (A) Irregardless what reasons or excuses are offered
    (B) Regardless about what reasons or excuses he may offer
    (C) Since he offered reasons and excuses
    (D) Nevertheless he offered reasons and excuses
    (E) No matter what reasons and excuses are offered

7. What a man cannot state, he does not perfectly know.

    (A) What a man cannot state, he does not perfectly know.
    (B) A man cannot state if he does not perfectly know.
    (C) A man cannot perfectly know if he does not state.
    (D) That which a man cannot state is that which he cannot perfectly know.
    (E) What a man cannot state is the reason he does not perfectly know.

8. Professional writers realize that they cannot hope to effect the reader precisely as they wish without care and practice in the use of words.

    (A) they cannot hope to effect
    (B) they cannot hope to have an effect on
    (C) they cannot hope to affect
    (D) they cannot hope effecting
    (E) they cannot try to affect

9. I've met two people whom, I believe, were police officers.

    (A) whom, I believe
    (B) who, I believe
    (C) each, I believe
    (D) and I believe they
    (E) who

10. Such people never have and never will be trusted.

    (A) never have and never will be trusted
    (B) never have and will be trusted
    (C) never have trusted and never will trust
    (D) never have been trusted and never will be trusted
    (E) never have had anyone trust them and never will have anyone trust them

11. Your employer would have been inclined to favor your request if you would have waited for an occasion when he was less busy.

    (A) if you would have waited for an occasion
    (B) if you would only have waited for an occasion
    (C) if you were to have waited for an occasion
    (D) if you waited for an occasion
    (E) if you had waited for an occasion

GO ON TO THE NEXT PAGE ➤

The following sentences test your ability to recognize grammar and usage errors. Each sentence contains either a single error or no error at all. No sentence contains more than one error. The error, if there is one, is underlined and lettered. If the sentence contains an error, select the one underlined part that must be changed to make the sentence correct. If the sentence is correct, select Choice E. In choosing answers, follow the requirements of standard written English.

EXAMPLE:

The other delegates and him immediately
    A   B   C

accepted the resolution drafted by
                         D

the neutral states. No error.
                E

---

12. Because of the bomb threat, everyone was asked
    A   B
to evacuate the bank but a security guard,
                C
a fireman, and I. No error.
          D   E

13. Having drank almost all the lemonade that his
    A   B
wife had made for the picnic, Mike could not face
       C   D
her. No error.
    E

14. The wealthy socialite decided that her fortune
would be left to whomever of her relatives
    A   B
could present her with the best plan for dispensing
    C
part of the money to deserving charities. No error.
                     D   E

15. Shortly after arriving at the amusement park with
            A
the eager third-graders, the parents realized that
                        B
they had brought nowhere near the number of
              C   D
chaperones required to control the children.
No error.
    E

16. The board members along with the chairman were
                  A   B
planning a series of speakers to lecture on different
    B   C
dividend plans for their employees. No error.
                D   E

17. Due to his not studying and not attending review
    A B
sessions, Paul got a failing mark in his bar exam,
             C
resulting in a retraction of the job offer from the
    D
law firm. No error.
         E

18. When I was in high school, I worked hard to buy
        A   B
the kind of a car that most of my friends were
      C   D
also driving. No error.
         E

19. The literature professor has complained that
many
                          A
student poets are so conceited that they compare
            B
their poems with Robert Frost. No error.
    C   D   E

GO ON TO THE NEXT PAGE ➤

20. I appreciate <u>you</u> offering <u>to help</u> me with my
             A   B

research project, but the honor system <u>prevents</u>
                                   C

students from giving and receiving <u>assistance.</u>
                                   D

<u>No error.</u>
E

21. In the final heat of the mile race, <u>only two</u> runners
                                   A

finished the race, but even the <u>slowest</u> of the
                               B

two <u>was able</u> to break the school record that
     C

<u>had been set</u> a decade earlier. <u>No error.</u>
    D   E

22. Passing the <u>written</u> test <u>that</u> is required for a
               A   B

driver's license is usually <u>easier</u> than <u>to pass</u> the
                       C   D

driving test. <u>No error.</u>
         E

23. All the <u>aspiring</u> young writers submitted their
        A

<u>stories,</u> each <u>hoping</u> that <u>they</u> would win first prize.
  B   C   D

<u>No error.</u>
E

24. Her answer <u>to</u> the essay question on the test was
          A

<u>all together</u> incorrect, but because it was very
 B

<u>well written</u> she received <u>partial</u> credit for her work.
    C   D

<u>No error.</u>
E

25. When I introduced Scott and Wilma, <u>they</u> acted
                             A

<u>as if</u> they never <u>met</u> before <u>even though</u> they had
 B   C   D

gone to the same high school. <u>No error.</u>
                       E

26. The realtor felt <u>badly</u> about not <u>being able</u> to sell
             A   B

<u>their</u> house because they were in a big hurry
C

<u>to move to</u> their condominium. <u>No error.</u>
   D   E

27. The president of the newly formed nation <u>took</u>
                                A

steps <u>to encourage</u> <u>several thousands</u> of people to
      B   C

<u>immigrate into</u> the country. <u>No error.</u>
    D   E

28. The governor asked the attorney <u>to head</u> the
                         A

committee because <u>he</u> <u>was convinced</u> <u>that</u> the
              B   C   D

committee needed to start work immediately.

<u>No error.</u>
E

29. <u>Both</u> my sisters <u>participate</u> in sports, but my <u>older</u>
  A   B   C

sister is the <u>better</u> athlete. <u>No error.</u>
      D   E

GO ON TO THE NEXT PAGE ➤

Directions: The following passage is an early draft of an essay. Some parts of the passage need to be rewritten.

Read the passage and select the best answers for the questions that follow. Some questions are about particular sentences or parts of sentences and ask you to improve sentence structure or word choice. Other questions ask you to consider organization and development. In choosing answers, follow the requirements of standard written English.

Questions 30–35 refer to the following passage.

[1]It has been proven beyond doubt that using seat belts in automobiles and wearing helmets while riding motorcycles can save lives. [2]The federal government has passed laws requiring the installation of seat belts in all new cars. [3]Still, there are people who argue that government has no right to interfere with individual comfort and freedom by mandating the installation and use of these safety devices. [4]In many states, laws prohibit motorcyclists from riding without helmets. [5]What these people fail to realize is that, although wearing a seat belt may be somewhat uncomfortable or confining, it is not as uncomfortable as broken bones nor as confining as a wheelchair or a coffin. [6]Motorcyclists who refuse to wear helmets may enjoy a degree of pleasure in feeling the free wind blow through their hair, but, if thrown in an accident, their heads can be as easily squashed as "free and natural" cantaloupes. [7]These safety devices may limit pleasure and freedom in small ways because they greatly increase the opportunity to live pleasant and free lives in more important ways.

30. What should be done with sentence 4?

(A) It should be placed before sentence 1.

(B) It should be attached to sentence 3 with and.

(C) Nothing should be done with it.

(D) It should be placed after sentence 2.

(E) It should be attached to sentence 5 with a semicolon.

31. In sentence 3, mandating should be

(A) omitted

(B) left as it is

(C) changed to prohibiting

(D) placed before individual

(E) changed to issuing directions that are in favor of

32. In sentence 6, what change is needed?

(A) These riders are should be inserted before thrown.

(B) Cantaloupes should be changed to balloons.

(C) They should be substituted for their heads.

(D) Commas should be placed around who refuse to wear helmets.

(E) Degree should be changed to measure.

33. Sentence 7 would be improved by

(A) turning it into two sentences, the first to end after small ways

(B) putting a comma after devices

(C) beginning the sentence with while

(D) omitting in more important ways

(E) changing because to but

34. Which would get the author's point across more effectively?

(A) Inserting a sentence that would describe statistics about the danger of not wearing seat belts or helmets.

(B) Describing the mechanics of how a seat belt works and how a helmet protects the head.

(C) Describing the governmental agency that enforced the laws.

(D) Pinpointing the states that enforce the helmet law.

(E) Citing the safest cars and motorcycles.

35. To begin the author's paragraph,

(A) sentence 2 should be placed first

(B) sentence 4 should be placed first

(C) sentence 6 should be placed first

(D) sentence 7 should be placed first, deleting the first word, "These," in that sentence

(E) sentence 1 should remain as the introductory sentence

STOP

If you finish before time is called, you may check your work on this section only.
Do not turn to any other section in the test.

Section 6

Time: 25 Minutes – Turn to Section 6 (page 438) of your answer sheet to answer the questions in this section. 18 Questions

Directions: For this section, solve each problem and decide which is the best of the choices given. Fill in the corresponding circle on the answer sheet. You may use any available space for scratchwork.

Notes:

1. The use of a calculator is permitted.

2. All numbers used are real numbers.

3. Figures that accompany problems in this test are intended to provide information useful in solving the problems. They are drawn as accurately as possible EXCEPT when it is stated in a specific problem that the figure is not drawn to scale. All figures lie in a plane unless otherwise indicated.

4. Unless otherwise specified, the domain of any function f is assumed to be the set of all real numbers x for which $f(x)$ is a real number.

REFERENCE INFORMATION

$A = \pi r^2$ $A = lw$ $A = \frac{1}{2}bh$ $V = lwh$ $V = \pi r^2 h$ $c^2 = a^2 + b^2$ *Special Right Triangle.*
$C = 2\pi r$

The number of degrees of arc in a circle is 360.
The sum of the measures in degrees of the angles of a triangle is 180.

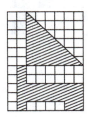

1. If each square in the grid above has a side of length 1, find the sum of the areas of the shaded regions.

    (A) 55
    (B) 46
    (C) 37
    (D) 30
    (E) 24

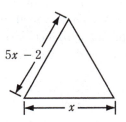

2. The figure above is an equilateral triangle. What is its perimeter?

    (A) $\frac{1}{4}$ (D) $3\frac{1}{2}$

    (B) $\frac{1}{2}$ (E) The answer cannot be determined from the information given.

    (C) $1\frac{1}{2}$

GO ON TO THE NEXT PAGE ➤

3. If w waves pass through a certain point in s seconds, how many waves would pass through that point in t seconds?

   (A) wst

   (B) $\frac{t}{s}$

   (C) $\frac{ws}{t}$

   (D) $\frac{ts}{w}$

   (E) $\frac{tw}{s}$

5. A box contains exactly 24 coins—nickels, dimes, and quarters. The probability of selecting a nickel by reaching into the box without looking is $\frac{3}{8}$. The probability of selecting a dime by reaching into the box without looking is $\frac{1}{8}$. How many quarters are in the box?

   (A) 6
   (B) 8
   (C) 12
   (D) 14
   (E) 16

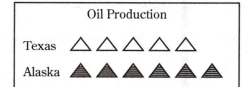

Oil Production

Texas, Alaska

4. In the chart above, the amount represented by each shaded triangle is three times that represented by each unshaded triangle. What fraction of the total production represented by the chart was produced in Alaska?

   (A) $\frac{6}{11}$

   (B) $\frac{18}{5}$

   (C) $\frac{18}{23}$

   (D) $\frac{12}{17}$

   (E) $\frac{23}{17}$

6. Which of the following designs *can* be formed by combining rectangles with size and shading the same as that shown above if overlap is not permitted?

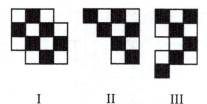

      I   II   III

   (A) I only
   (B) II only
   (C) III only
   (D) I and II only
   (E) II and III only

GO ON TO THE NEXT PAGE ➤

7. If $f(x) = (x - 1)^2 + (x - 2)^2 + (x - 3)^2$, then $f(x + 2) =$

(A) $3x^2 + 4x + 2$

(B) $3x$

(C) $(x + 2)^2 + x^2 + (x - 2)^2$

(D) $3x^2 + 2$

(E) $4x^2 + 4$

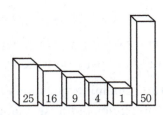

8. Six containers, whose capacities in cubic centimeters are shown, appear in the figure above. The 25-cubic-centimeter container is filled with flour, and the rest are empty. The contents of the 25-cubic-centimeter container are used to fill the 16-cubic-centimeter container, and the excess is dumped into the 50-cubic-centimeter container. Then the 16-cubic-centimeter container is used to fill the 9-cubic-centimeter container, and the excess is dumped into the 50-cubic-centimeter container. The process is repeated until all containers, except the 1-cubic-centimeter and the 50-cubic-centimeter containers, are empty. What percent of the 50-cubic-centimeter container is *empty*?

(A) 24%   (D) 52%

(B) 48%   (E) 76%

(C) 50%

GO ON TO THE NEXT PAGE ➤

Directions: For Student-Produced Response questions 9–18, use the grids on the bottom of the answer sheet page on which you have answered questions 1-8.

Each of the remaining questions requires you to solve the problem and enter your answer by marking the circles in the special grid, as shown in the examples below. You may use any available space for scratchwork.

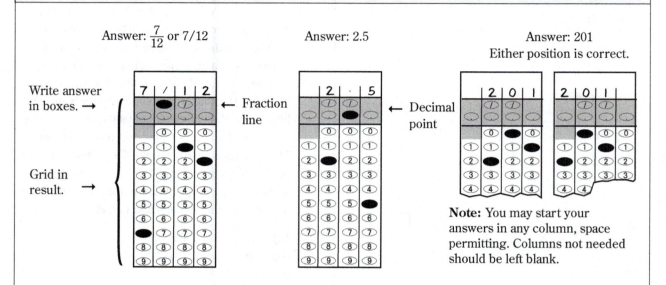

Answer: $\frac{7}{12}$ or 7/12   Answer: 2.5   Answer: 201
Either position is correct.

Write answer in boxes. →   ← Fraction line   ← Decimal point

Grid in result. →

Note: You may start your answers in any column, space permitting. Columns not needed should be left blank.

- Mark no more than one oval in any column.

- Because the answer sheet will be machine-scored, **you will receive credit only if the ovals are filled in correctly.**

- Although not required, it is suggested that you write your answer in the boxes at the top of the columns to help you fill in the ovals accurately.

- Some problems may have more than one correct answer. In such cases, grid only one answer.

- No question has a negative answer.

- **Mixed numbers** such as $2\frac{1}{2}$ must be gridded as 2.5 or 5/2. (If $\boxed{2\ |\ 1\ /\ 2}$ is gridded, it will be interpreted as $\frac{21}{2}$, not $2\frac{1}{2}$.)

- **Decimal Accuracy:** If you obtain a decimal answer, **enter the most accurate value the grid will accommodate.** For example, if you obtain an answer such as 0.6666..., you should record the result as .666 or .667. **Less accurate values such as .66 or .67 are not acceptable.**

Acceptable ways to grid $\frac{2}{3}$ = .6666...:

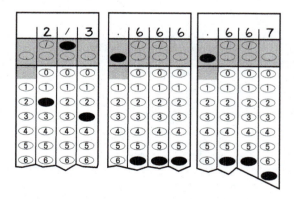

9. If $ab = 40$, $\frac{a}{b} = \frac{5}{2}$, and a and b are positive numbers, find the value of a.

10. Stephanie earned $x while working 10 hours. Evelyn earned $y while working 20 hours. If they both earn the same hourly wage and $x + y = 60$, how many dollars did Stephanie earn?

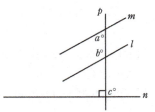

11. In the figure above, m is parallel to l and p is perpendicular to n. Find the value of $a + b + c$.

12. The difference of the areas of two circles is 21π. If their radii are $r + 3$ and r, find the radius of the *larger* circle.

	FIRST PLACE	SECOND PLACE	THIRD PLACE
	(8 points)	(4 points)	(2 points)
EVENT ①	TEAM A	TEAM B	TEAM C
EVENT ②	TEAM B	TEAM A	TEAM C

13. The results of two games involving 3 teams are shown above. Thus, we have the following standings: A and B both have 12 points, and C has 4 points. Assuming no ties, what is the least number of additional games that Team C will have to play in order to have the highest total score?

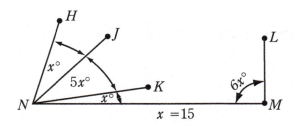

Note: Figure is not drawn to scale.

14. If the figure above were drawn to scale and all line segments were extended indefinitely in *both directions*, how many intersection points would there be in addition to N and M?

15. If a is 10 percent greater than b, and ac is 32 percent greater than bd, then c is what percent greater than d?

16. Since one gross = 12 dozen, what fraction of a gross of eggs is 3 eggs?

17. The figure above represents a layer of bricks, where each brick has a volume of 40 cubic inches. If all bricks are stacked in layers as shown, and the final pile of bricks occupies 8,000 cubic inches, how many layers are there in the final pile of bricks?

18. Let x be the smallest possible 3-digit number greater than or equal to 100 in which no digit is repeated. If y is the largest positive 3-digit number that can be made using all of the digits of x, what is the value of $y - x$?

STOP

If you finish before time is called, you may check your work on this section only.
Do not turn to any other section in the test.

Take a 5 minute break

before starting section 7

Section 7

Time: 25 Minutes – Turn to Section 7 (page 438) of your answer sheet to answer the questions in this section. 24 Questions

Directions: For each question in this section, select the best answer from among the choices given and fill in the corresponding circle on the answer sheet.

Each sentence below has one or two blanks, each blank indicating that something has been omitted. Beneath the sentence are five words or sets of words labeled A through E. Choose the word or set of words that, when inserted in the sentence, <u>best</u> fits the meaning of the sentence as a whole.

Example:

Hoping to _____ the dispute, negotiators proposed a compromise that they felt would be _____ to both labor and management.

(A) enforce...useful

(B) end...divisive

(C) overcome...unattractive

(D) extend...satisfactory

(E) resolve...acceptable

Ⓐ Ⓑ Ⓒ Ⓓ ●

---

1. Governor Edwards combined _____ politics with administrative skills to dominate the state; in addition to these assets, he was also _____.

   (A) corrupt...glum
   (B) inept...civil
   (C) incriminating...sincere
   (D) astute...dapper
   (E) trivial...lavish

2. After four years of _____ curbs designed to protect the American auto industry, the government cleared the way for foreign countries to _____ more cars to the United States.

   (A) profitable...drive
   (B) flexible...produce
   (C) motor...direct
   (D) import...ship
   (E) reciprocal...sell

3. UNICEF reports about the 2011 crisis in the Horn of Africa demonstrate the _____ of drought, poor land use, and overpopulation.

   (A) consequences
   (B) prejudices
   (C) inequities
   (D) indications
   (E) mortalities

GO ON TO THE NEXT PAGE ➤

4. Amid the _____ of a country constantly under threat from terrorist attacks, the United States is set to bolster national _____.

(A) treaties…silence
(B) advantages…relations
(C) differences…amity
(D) tensions…security
(E) commerce…decision

5. The union struck shortly after midnight after its negotiating committee _____ a company offer of a 3% raise.

(A) applauded
(B) rejected
(C) considered
(D) postponed
(E) accepted

Each passage below is followed by questions on its content. Answer the questions on the basis of what is stated or implied in each passage and in any introductory material that may be provided.

Questions 6–9 are based on the following passages.

Passage 1

Homeschooling is becoming more and more desirable because children do not have the burden of traveling to school and becoming exposed to other children's sickness and everything else that goes with being in a crowded
5   room. There is also the individual attention that the parent or tutor can give the student, which creates a better and more efficient learning environment. As standards become more and more flexible, homeschooling may in fact be the norm of the future.

Passage 2

10 In many studies, it was shown that students benefit in a classroom setting since the interaction and dialogue with other students creates a stimulating learning environment. The more students who are in a class, the more diversity within the group and the more varied the feedback. With
15 a good teacher and facilitator, a classroom can be very beneficial for the student's cognitive development.

6. In Passage 1, the author's condition for an effective learning condition is based on

(A) flexible standards
(B) the closeness of a parent and a child
(C) the reduction of travel time
(D) a one-on-one learning experience
(E) the sanitary conditions in the learning environment

7. Which of the following is *not* addressed in Passage 2?

(A) The advantage of classroom learning with the student interacting and sharing ideas with other students
(B) The student exposed to multicultural ways in approaching the learning experience

(C) The teacher's playing an active role in the learning experience
(D) The more students in the classroom leading to the more feedback each student can receive
(E) The positive relationship between the different types of students and learning

8. Which criterion is the same in homeschooling and regular classroom schooling?

(A) the health condition
(B) the burden of traveling
(C) the feedback with other students
(D) the diversity of the students
(E) the learning experience

9. Which of the following adjustments would make an ideal environment for learning, according to what is addressed in both passages?

(A) In homeschooling, the student could travel on weekends to cultural areas.
(B) In school, the teacher could occasionally work with the student on an individual basis.
(C) In homeschooling, the student could be exposed to and interact with other students on a regular basis.
(D) The student could spend one-half of his educational time in school and one-half of his educational time at home.
(E) The student could learn at home and go to school to socialize.

GO ON TO THE NEXT PAGE ➤

Questions 10–15 are based on the following passage.

The following passage is about the literature of the African American culture and its impact on society.

The literature of an oppressed people is the conscience of man, and nowhere is this seen with more intense clarity than in the literature of African Americans. An essential element of African American literature is that the literature
5 as a whole—not the work of occasional authors—is a movement against concrete wickedness. In African American literature, accordingly, there is a grief rarely to be found elsewhere in American literature, and frequently a rage rarely to be found in American letters: a rage different in
10 quality, more profound, more towering, more intense—the rage of the oppressed. Whenever an African American artist picks up pen or horn, his target is likely to be American racism, his subject the suffering of his people, and the core element his own grief and the grief of his people. Almost
15 all of African American literature carries the burden of this protest.

The cry for freedom and the protest against injustice indicate a desire for the birth of the New Man, a testament to the New Unknown World to be discovered, to be created by man. African American literature is, as a body, a declara-
20 tion that despite the perversion and cruelty that cling like swamp roots to the flesh of man's feet, man has options for freedom, for cleanliness, for wholeness, for human harmony, for goodness: for a human world. Like the spirituals that are a part of it, African American literature is a passionate asser-
25 tion that man will win freedom. Thus, African American literature rejects despair and cynicism; it is a literature of realistic hope and life affirmation. This is not to say that no African American literary work reflects cynicism or despair, but rather that the basic theme of African American
30 literature is that man's goodness will prevail.

African American literature is a statement against death, a statement as to what life should be: life should be vivacious, exuberant, wholesomely uninhibited, sensual, sensuous, constructively antirespectable; life should
35 abound and flourish and laugh; life should be passionately lived and man should be loving; life should be not a sedate waltz or foxtrot but a vigorous breakdance. Thus, when the African American writer criticizes America for its cruelty, the criticism implies that America is drawn to death and
40 repelled by what should be the human style of life, the human way of living.

African American literature in America is, then, a setting forth of man's identity and destiny; an investigation of man's iniquity and a statement of belief in his potential
45 godliness; a prodding of man toward exploring and finding deep joy in his humanity.

10. The author states or implies that

(A) a separate-but-equal doctrine is the answer to American racism
(B) African American literature is superior to American literature
(C) hopelessness and lack of trust are the key-notes of African American literature
(D) standing up for one's rights and protesting about unfairness are vital
(E) traditional forms of American-type dancing should be engaged in

11. When the author, in referring to African American literature, states that "life should be… constructively antirespectable" (lines 32–34), it can be inferred that people ought to

(A) do their own thing provided what they do is worthwhile
(B) show disrespect for others when they have the desire to do so
(C) be passionate in public whenever the urge is there
(D) shun a person because he is of another race or color
(E) be enraged if their ancestors have been unjustly treated

12. With reference to the passage, which of the following statements are true about African American literature?

I. It expresses the need for nonviolent opposition to antiracism.
II. It urges a person to have respect for himself and for others.
III. It voices the need for an active, productive, and satisfying life.

(A) I only
(B) II only
(C) I and III only
(D) II and III only
(E) I, II, and III

13. The tone of the passage is one of

 (A) anger and vindictiveness
 (B) hope and affirmation
 (C) forgiveness and charity
 (D) doubt and despair
 (E) grief and cruelty

14. Which of the following constitute(s) the author's view of a "human world?"

  I. harmony
  II. cleanliness
  III. wholeness

 (A) I only
 (B) I and II only
 (C) II and III only
 (D) I and III only
 (E) I, II, and III

15. The word "iniquity" (line 44) means

 (A) potential
 (B) creation
 (C) wickedness
 (D) cleverness
 (E) greatness

Questions 16–24 are based on the following passage.

The following passage is based on B. F. Skinner's book About Behaviorism *and discusses the pros and cons of Skinner's work on behaviorism and the various points made by Skinner.*

In his compact and modestly titled book *About Behaviorism*, Dr. B. F. Skinner, the noted behavioral psychologist, lists the 20 most salient objections to "behaviorism or the science of behavior," and he has gone on to answer them
5 both implicitly and explicitly. He has answers and explanations for everyone.

 For instance, to those who object that behaviorists "deny the existence of feelings, sensations, ideas, and other features of mental life," Dr. Skinner concedes that "a
10 good deal of clarification" is in order. What such people are really decrying is "methodological behaviorism," an earlier stage of the science whose goal was precisely to close off mentalistic explanations of behavior, if only to counteract the 2,500-year-old influence of mentalism. But Dr. Skinner
15 is a "radical behaviorist." "Radical behaviorism…takes a different line. It does not deny the possibility of self-observation or self-knowledge or its possible usefulness… It restores introspection…."

 For instance, to those who object that behaviorism
20 "neglects innate endowment and argues that all behavior is

acquired during the lifetime of the individual," Dr. Skinner expresses puzzlement. Granted, "A few behaviorists… have minimized if not denied a genetic contribution, and in their enthusiasm for what may be done through the
25 environment, others have no doubt acted as if a genetic endowment were unimportant, but few would contend that behavior is 'endlessly malleable.'" And Dr. Skinner himself, sounding as often as not like some latter-day Social Darwinist, gives as much weight to the "contingencies of
30 survival" in the evolution of the human species as to the "contingencies of reinforcement" in the lifetime of the individual.

 For instance, to those who claim that behaviorism "cannot explain creative achievements—in art, for example,
or in music, literature, science, or mathematics"—Dr.
35 Skinner provides an intriguing ellipsis. "Contingencies of reinforcement also resemble contingencies of survival in the production of novelty….In both natural selection and operant conditioning the appearance of 'mutations' is crucial. Until recently, species evolved because of random
40 changes in genes or chromosomes, but the geneticist may arrange conditions under which mutations are particularly likely to occur. We can also discover some of the sources of new forms of behavior which undergo selection by prevailing contingencies or reinforcement, and fortunately
45 the creative artist or thinker has other ways of introducing novelties."

 And so go Dr. Skinner's answers to the 20 questions he poses—questions that range all the way from asking if behaviorism fails "to account for cognitive processes" to
50 wondering if behaviorism "is indifferent to the warmth and richness of human life, and…is incompatible with the… enjoyment of art, music, and literature and with love for one's fellow men."

 But will it wash? Will it serve to silence those critics who have characterized B. F. Skinner variously as a mad,
55 manipulative doctor, as a naïve 19th-century positivist, as an unscientific technician, and as an arrogant social engineer? There is no gainsaying that *About Behaviorism* is an unusually compact summary of both the history and "the philosophy of the science of human behavior" (as Dr.
60 Skinner insists on defining behaviorism). It is a veritable artwork of organization. And anyone who reads it will never again be able to think of behaviorism as a simplistic philosophy that reduces human beings to black boxes responding robotlike to external stimuli.

65 Still, there are certain quandaries that *About Behaviorism* does not quite dispel. For one thing, though Dr. Skinner makes countless references to the advances in experiments with human beings that behaviorism has made since it first began running rats through mazes many
70 decades ago, he fails to provide a single illustration of these advances. And though it may be true, as Dr. Skinner argues, that one can extrapolate from pigeons to people, it would be reassuring to be shown precisely how.

 More importantly, he has not satisfactorily rebutted
75 the basic criticism that behaviorism "is scientistic rather

GO ON TO THE NEXT PAGE ➤

than scientific. It merely emulates the sciences." A true science doesn't predict what it will accomplish when it is firmly established as a science, not even when it is posing as "the philosophy of that science." A true science simply
80 advances rules for testing hypotheses.

But Dr. Skinner predicts that behaviorism will produce the means to save human society from impending disaster. Two key concepts that keep accreting to that prediction are "manipulation" and "control." And so, while he reassures
85 us quite persuasively that his science would practice those concepts benignly, one can't shake off the suspicion that he was advancing a science just in order to save society by means of "manipulation" and "control." And that is not so reassuring.

16. According to the passage, Skinner would be most likely to agree that

(A) studies of animal behavior are applicable to human behavior

(B) introspection should be used widely to analyze conscious experience

(C) behaviorism is basically scientistic

(D) behavioristic principles and techniques will be of no use in preventing widespread disaster

(E) an individual can form an infinite number of sentences that he has never heard spoken

17. The reader may infer that

(A) Skinner's philosophy is completely democratic in its methodology

(B) behaviorism, in its early form, and mentalism were essentially the same

(C) the book *About Behaviorism* is difficult to understand because it is not well structured

(D) methodological behaviorism preceded both mentalism and radical behaviorism

(E) the author of the article has found glaring weaknesses in Skinner's defense of behaviorism

18. When Skinner speaks of "contingencies of survival" (line 29) and "contingencies of reinforcement" (lines 30–31), the word "contingency" most accurately means

(A) frequency of occurrence

(B) something incidental

(C) a quota

(D) dependence on chance

(E) one of an assemblage

19. The author of the article says that Skinner sounds "like some latter-day Social Darwinist" (line 28) most probably because Skinner

(A) is a radical behaviorist who has differed from methodological behaviorists

(B) has predicted that human society faces disaster

(C) has been characterized as a 19th-century positivist

(D) has studied animal behavior as applicable to human behavior

(E) believes that the geneticist may arrange conditions for mutations to occur

20. It can be inferred from the passage that "extrapolate" (line 72) means

(A) to gather unknown information by extending known information

(B) to determine how one organism may be used to advantage by another organism

(C) to insert or introduce between other things or parts

(D) to change the form or the behavior of one thing to match the form or behavior of another thing

(E) to transfer an organ of a living thing into another living thing

21. One *cannot* conclude from the passage that

(A) Skinner is a radical behaviorist but not a methodological behaviorist

(B) *About Behavior* does not show how behaviorists have improved in experimentation with human beings

(C) only human beings are used in experiments conducted by behaviorists

(D) methodological behaviorism rejects the introspective approach

(E) the book being discussed is to the point and well organized

22. In Skinner's statement that "few would contend that behavior is 'endlessly malleable'" (lines 26–27), he means that

    (A) genetic influences are of primary importance in shaping human behavior

    (B) environmental influences may be frequently supplemented by genetic influences

    (C) self-examination is the most effective way of improving a behavior pattern

    (D) the learning process continues throughout life

    (E) psychologists will never come to a common conclusion about the best procedure for studying and improving human behavior

23. According to the author, which of the following are true concerning *scientistic* and *scientific* disciplines?

    I.   The scientific one develops the rules for testing the theory; the scientistic one does not.

    II.   There is no element of prediction in scientistic disciplines.

    III. Science never assumes a philosophical nature.

    (A) I only

    (B) I and III only

    (C) I and II only

    (D) II and III only

    (E) I, II, and III

24. The word "veritable" (line 60) means

    (A) abundant

    (B) careful

    (C) political

    (D) true

    (E) believable

Section 8

Time: 20 Minutes – Turn to Section 8 (page 439) of your answer sheet to answer the questions in this section. 16 Questions

Directions: For this section, solve each problem and decide which is the best of the choices given. Fill in the corresponding circle on the answer sheet. You may use any available space for scratchwork.

Notes:

1. The use of a calculator is permitted.

2. All numbers used are real numbers.

3. Figures that accompany problems in this test are intended to provide information useful in solving the problems. They are drawn as accurately as possible EXCEPT when it is stated in a specific problem that the figure is not drawn to scale. All figures lie in a plane unless otherwise indicated.

4. Unless otherwise specified, the domain of any function f is assumed to be the set of all real numbers x for which $f(x)$ is a real number.

REFERENCE INFORMATION

$A = \pi r^2$ $A = lw$ $A = \dfrac{1}{2}bh$ $V = lwh$ $V = \pi r^2 h$ $c^2 = a^2 + b^2$ *Special Right Triangle.*
$C = 2\pi r$

The number of degrees of arc in a circle is 360.
The sum of the measures in degrees of the angles of a triangle is 180.

1. If $5x = 3$, then $(5x + 3)^2 =$

   (A) 0
   (B) 9
   (C) 25
   (D) 36
   (E) 64

2. The ratio of girls to boys in a class is $8 : 7$. The number of students in the class could be any of the following *except*

   (A) 15
   (B) 45
   (C) 50
   (D) 60
   (E) 90

GO ON TO THE NEXT PAGE ❯

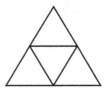

3. The above figure is an equilateral triangle divided into four congruent, smaller, equilateral triangles. If the perimeter of a smaller triangle is 1, then the perimeter of the whole large triangle is

(A) 2
(B) 4
(C) 6
(D) 8
(E) 16

5. Given $\dfrac{4^3 + 4^3 + 4^3 + 4^3}{4^y} = 4$, find y.

(A) 3
(B) 4
(C) 8
(D) 12
(E) 64

4. Matías has $15.25 and spent $7.50 at the sporting goods store. How much money does he have left?

(A) $0.25
(B) $1.75
(C) $6.75
(D) $7.75
(E) $8.25

6. If $\dfrac{2x^2 + x - 5}{x^3 + 4x^2} = \dfrac{1}{2}$ then which of the following is true?

(A) $x^3 - 2x = 10$
(B) $x^3 + 2x = 10$
(C) $x^3 - 2x = -10$
(D) $x^3 + 2x = -10$
(E) $x^3 + 2x + 2x^2 = 10$

GO ON TO THE NEXT PAGE ➤

7. A population that starts at 100 and doubles after eight years can be expressed as the following, where t stands for the number of years that have elapsed from the start:

   (A) 100×2^t

   (B) $100 \times 2^{\frac{t}{7}}$

   (C) $100 \times 2^{t-8}$

   (D) $100 \times 2^{\frac{t}{8}}$

   (E) 100×2^{16t}

9. If $a^b = x$ and $x^b = y$, then

   (A) $a^{2b} = y$

   (B) $a^{b^2} = y$

   (C) $b^a = y$

   (D) $(ax)^b = y$

   (E) $(ax)^b = x$

8. Find the solution set in positive integers of $2x + 5 < 5$.

   (A) $\{1, 2, 3, 4\}$

   (B) $\{1, 2\}$

   (C) $\{0\}$

   (D) $\{\ \}$

   (E) infinity

10. Two lines in a plane are represented by $y = x - 1$ and $2x + 5y = 9$. The coordinates of the point at which the lines intersect are

   (A) $(2,1)$

   (B) $(1,2)$

   (C) $(2,5)$

   (D) $(5,2)$

   (E) $(3,3)$

GO ON TO THE NEXT PAGE ➤

$$C = md + t$$

11. The cost, C, of a business trip is represented by the equation above, where m is a constant, d is the number of days of the complete trip, and t is the cost of transportation, which does not change. If the business trip was increased by 5 days, how much more did the business trip cost than the original planned trip?

(A) $5d$

(B) $5m$

(C) $5t$

(D) $d(m - 3)$

(E) $m(d - 3)$

$$4x - 3y = 9$$
$$8x + ky = 19$$

13. For which value of k will the system of equations above have *no* solution?

(A) $+6$

(B) $+3$

(C) 0

(D) -3

(E) -6

12. Which of the following represents x on a number line if $(x - 3) \le 0$?

(A)

(B)

(C)

(D)

(E)

14. Given that $r \ne 0$ and $r = 5w = 7a$, find the value of $r - w$ in terms of a.

(A) $\dfrac{1a}{7}$

(B) $\dfrac{7a}{5}$

(C) $3a$

(D) $\dfrac{28a}{5}$

(E) $28a$

GO ON TO THE NEXT PAGE ➤

15. The figure above consists of equal semicircles each touching the other at the ends of their diameters. If the radius of each circle is 2, what is the *total enclosed* area?

(A) $\dfrac{\sqrt{3}}{4} + \pi$

(B) $\sqrt{3} + 2\pi$

(C) $4\sqrt{3} + 6\pi$

(D) 6π

(E) $\dfrac{\sqrt{2}}{4} + 4\pi$

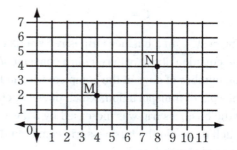

16. Which of the following points, when plotted on the grid above, will be three times as far from $M(4,2)$ as from $N(8,4)$?

(A) (2,1)
(B) (4,4)
(C) (6,3)
(D) (7,1)
(E) (10,5)

STOP

If you finish before time is called, you may check your work on this section only.
Do not turn to any other section in the test.

Section 9

Time: 20 Minutes – Turn to Section 9 (page 439) of your answer sheet to answer the questions in this section. 19 Questions

Directions: For each question in this section, select the best answer from among the choices given and fill in the corresponding circle on the answer sheet.

Each sentence below has one or two blanks, each blank indicating that something has been omitted. Beneath the sentence are five words or sets of words labeled A through E. Choose the word or set of words that, when inserted in the sentence, best fits the meaning of the sentence as a whole.

Example:

Hoping to _____ the dispute, negotiators proposed a compromise that they felt would be _____ to both labor and management.

(A) enforce…useful

(B) end…divisive

(C) overcome…unattractive

(D) extend…satisfactory

(E) resolve…acceptable

ⓐ ⓑ ⓒ ⓓ ●

1. Illegally parked vehicles block hydrants and crosswalks, _____ the flow of traffic when double-parked, and _____ the law.

(A) stem…enforce

(B) expedite…violate

(C) reduce…resist

(D) drench…challenge

(E) impede…flout

2. With social media _____, Facebook and other suchlike websites are changing the way millions around the world use their _____ time.

(A) advertising…canceled

(B) suffering…valuable

(C) stabilizing…extra

(D) recording…unused

(E) booming…leisure

3. The fact that the _____ of confrontation is no longer as popular as it once was _____ progress in race relations.

(A) practice…inculcates

(B) reticence…indicates

(C) glimmer…foreshadows

(D) insidiousness…reiterates

(E) technique…presages

4. The _____ of scarcity amidst plenty characterizes even a rich country in a time of inflation.

(A) coherence

(B) tedium

(C) facet

(D) sequence

(E) paradox

GO ON TO THE NEXT PAGE ➤

5. The scientist averred that a nuclear war could
_____ enough smoke and dust to blot out the
sun and freeze the earth.

(A) pervert
(B) extinguish
(C) generate
(D) evaluate
(E) perpetrate

6. Until his death he remained _____ in the belief
that the world was conspiring against him.

(A) ignominious
(B) taciturn
(C) tantamount
(D) obdurate
(E) spurious

The two passages below are followed by questions based on their content and on the relationship
between the two passages. Answer the questions on the basis of what is <u>stated</u> or <u>implied</u> in the
passages and in any introductory material that may be provided.

Questions 7–19 are based on the following passages.

The following two passages are about violence. The first discusses televised violence; the second attempts to address the history of violence in general.

Passage 1

Violence is alive and well on television. Yet there
appears to be a difference in the quality, variety, and
pervasiveness of today's televised violence. Some observers
believe that, as a result of more than three decades of
5 television, viewers have developed a kind of immunity to
the horror of violence. By the age of 16, for example, the
average young person will have seen some 18,000 murders
on television. One extension of this phenomenon may be an
appetite for more varied kinds of violence. On the basis of
10 the amount of exposure, certain things that initially would
have been beyond the pale have become more readily
accepted.

Violence on TV has been more prevalent in recent
years, in large measure because there are fewer situation
comedies and more action series, but also because some
15 25 million of the nation's 85 million homes with television
now receive one of the cable services that routinely show
uncut feature films containing graphic violence as early as
8:00 in the evening.

The evidence is becoming overwhelming that just as
20 witnessing violence in the home may contribute to children
learning and acting out violent behavior, violence on TV and
in the movies may lead to the same result. Studies have shown
that a steady diet of watching graphic violence or sexually
violent films such as those shown on cable TV has caused some
25 men to be more willing to accept violence against women,
such as rape and wife-beating. Not only actual violence,
but the kind of violence coming through the television
screen is causing concern. One of the principal developments is the increasing sophistication of the weaponry. The

30 simple gunfight of the past has been augmented by high-
tech crimes like terrorist bombings. A gunfighter shooting
down a sheriff is one thing. When you have terrorist bombs,
the potential is there for hundreds to die. Programs in the
past used the occasional machine gun, but such weapons as
35 the M-60 machine gun and Uzi semiautomatic have become
commonplace today on network shows.

Many people are no longer concerned about televised
violence because they feel it is the way of the world. It is
high time that broadcasters provide public messages on
40 TV screens that would warn viewers about the potentially
harmful effects of viewing televised violence.

Passage 2

We have always been a lawless and a violent people.
Thus, our almost unbroken record of violence against the
Indians and all others who got in our way—the Spaniards
45 in the Floridas, the Mexicans in Texas; the violence of the
vigilantes on a hundred frontiers; the pervasive violence
of slavery (a "perpetual exercise," Jefferson called it,
"of the most boisterous passions"); the lawlessness of
the Ku Klux Klan during Reconstruction and after; and
50 of scores of race riots from those of Chicago in 1919 to
those of New Orleans in the 1960s. Yet, all this violence,
shocking as it doubtless was, no more threatened the
fabric of our society or the integrity of the Union than did
the lawlessness of Prohibition back in the Twenties. The
55 explanation for this is to be found in the embarrassing fact
that most of it was official, quasi-official, or countenanced
by public opinion: exterminating the Indian; flogging the
slave; lynching the outlaw; exploiting women and children
in textile mills and sweatshops; hiring Pinkertons to shoot
60 down strikers; condemning immigrants to fetid ghettos;
punishing blacks who tried to exercise their civil or political
rights. Most of this was socially acceptable—or at least
not wholly unacceptable—just as so much of our current

GO ON TO THE NEXT PAGE ➤

65 violence is socially acceptable: the many thousands of automobile deaths every year; the mortality rate for black babies at twice that for white; the deaths from cancer induced by cigarettes or by air pollution; the sadism of our penal system and the horrors of our prisons; the violence of some police against the so-called "dangerous classes of society."

70 What we have now is the emergence of violence that is not acceptable either to the Establishment, which is frightened and alarmed, or to the victims of the Establishment, who are no longer submissive and who are numerous and powerful. This is now familiar "crime in the streets," or it 75 is the revolt of the young against the economy, the politics, and the wars of the established order, or it is the convulsive reaction of the blacks to a century of injustice. But now, too, official violence is no longer acceptable to its victims—or to their ever more numerous sympathizers: the violence 80 of great corporations and of government itself against the natural resources of the nation; the long drawn-out violence of the white majority against blacks and other minorities; the violence of the police and the National Guard against the young; the massive violence of the military against the 85 peoples of other countries. These acts can no longer be absorbed by large segments of our society. It is this new polarization that threatens the body politic and the social fabric much as religious dissent threatened them in the Europe of the sixteenth and seventeenth centuries.

7. The title that best summarizes the content of Passage 1 is

(A) TV's Role in the Rising Crime Rate
(B) Violence on TV—Past and Present
(C) TV Won't Let Up on Violence
(D) Violence Raises the TV Ratings
(E) Violence Galore on Cable TV

8. Which of the following types of TV programs would the author of Passage 1 be *least* likely to approve of?

(A) A cowboy Western called "Have Gun, Will Travel"
(B) A talk show dealing with teenage pregnancy caused by rape
(C) A documentary dealing with Vietnam veterans suffering from the aftereffects of herbicide spraying during the war
(D) A movie showing a bomb exploding in a bus carrying civilians on their way to work
(E) A soap opera in which a jealous husband is shown murdering his wife's lover, then his own wife

9. According to Passage 1,

(A) television programs are much different today from what they were a generation ago
(B) a very large percentage of the viewers are presently worried about the showing of violence on television
(C) situation comedy programs are more popular on TV now than ever before
(D) broadcasting stations are considering notifying viewers about possible dangers of watching programs that include violence
(E) violence on the television screen is more extreme than it was about 20 years ago

10. As an illustration of current "socially acceptable" violence, the author of Passage 2 would probably include

(A) National Guard violence at Kent, Ohio, during the Vietnam War
(B) the Vietnam War
(C) the cruelties of our prison system
(D) the police behavior in Chicago at the 1968 Democratic Convention
(E) "crime in the streets"

11. It can be inferred that the author's definition of violence (Passage 2)

(A) includes the social infliction of harm
(B) is limited to nongovernmental acts of force
(C) is confined to governmental acts of illegal force
(D) is synonymous with illegal conduct by either government or citizen
(E) is shared by the FBI

12. The author of Passage 2 describes current violence as

I. acceptable neither to the authorities nor to the victims
II. carried out primarily by corporations
III. increasingly of a vigilante nature

(A) I only
(B) II only
(C) III only
(D) I and II only
(E) II and III only

GO ON TO THE NEXT PAGE ➤

13. The author of Passage 2 mentions all of the following forms of violence in the nineteenth century *except*

    (A) the activities of the Klan during Reconstruction
    (B) wiping out the Indians
    (C) the New York City draft riots of the 1860s
    (D) the Annexation of Texas and Florida
    (E) the practice of slavery

14. Which action or activity would the author of Passage 2 be most likely to disapprove of?

    (A) trying to prevent a mugging
    (B) reading a science fiction story
    (C) watching a rock music TV performance
    (D) attending a Super Bowl football game
    (E) participating in a country square dance

15. The word "pervasiveness" in line 2 of Passage 1 (also note "pervasive" in line 46 of Passage 2) means

    (A) variety
    (B) televised
    (C) seeping through
    (D) quality
    (E) terribleness

16. Which of the following, according to the author of Passage 1, is a contributing factor to the marked increase of violent deaths?

    I.   cable television
    II. present feature films
    III. technology

    (A) I only
    (B) II only
    (C) II and III only
    (D) I and II only
    (E) I, II, and III

17. The author of Passage 2 would probably argue with the author of Passage 1 in the resolution of violence (lines 37–41) that

    (A) if violence were curtailed on television, it would pop up elsewhere
    (B) television does not show a significant amount of violence to warrant warnings against such programs
    (C) television can also influence the public toward nonviolence
    (D) there are more dangers to television than the portrayal of violence
    (E) violence is inbred in television

18. From the passages, which can we assume to be *false*?

    (A) Unlike the author of Passage 1, the author of Passage 2 believes that society is disgusted with violence.
    (B) The author of Passage 1 believes that sophisticated weaponry causes increased violence, whereas the author of Passage 2 believes that violence is inherent in society.
    (C) The type of violence discussed by the author of Passage 2 is much more encompassing than the type of violence discussed by the author of Passage 1.
    (D) Both authors propose a direct resolution for at least a start to the end of violence.
    (E) Both authors believe either that violence is a part of daily living or at least that many feel that violence is a part of daily living.

19. The word "polarization" in line 87 means

    (A) electrical tendencies
    (B) governments in different parts of the world
    (C) completely opposing viewpoints
    (D) extreme religious differences
    (E) cold climatic conditions

STOP

If you finish before time is called, you may check your work on this section only.
Do not turn to any other section in the test.

Section 10

Time: 10 Minutes – Turn to Section 10 (page 439) of your answer sheet to answer the questions in this section. 14 Questions

Directions: For each question in this section, select the best answer from among the choices given and fill in the corresponding circle on the answer sheet.

The following sentences test correctness and effectiveness of expression. Part of each sentence or the entire sentence is underlined; beneath each sentence are five ways of phrasing the underlined material. Choice A repeats the original phrasing; the other four choices are different. If you think the original phrasing produces a better sentence than any of the alternatives, select Choice A; if not, select one of the other choices.

In making your selection, follow the requirements of standard written English; that is, pay attention to grammar, choice of words, sentence construction, and punctuation. Your selection should result in the most effective sentence—clear and precise, without awkwardness or ambiguity.

EXAMPLE:

Laura Ingalls Wilder published her first book <u>and she was sixty-five years old then</u>.

(A) and she was sixty-five years old then

(B) when she was sixty-five

(C) at age sixty-five years old

(D) upon the reaching of sixty-five years

(E) at the time when she was sixty-five

---

1. I find Henry James' prose style more difficult to read than James Joyce.

(A) I find Henry James's prose style more difficult to read than James Joyce.

(B) I find Henry Jame's prose style more difficult to read than James Joyce'.

(C) I find Henry James's prose style more difficult to read than James Joyce's.

(D) I find the prose style of Henry James more difficult to read than James Joyce.

(E) Henry James' prose style I find more difficult to read than I find James Joyce.

2. Neither Dr. Conant nor his followers knows what to do about the problem.

(A) Neither Dr. Conant nor his followers knows what to do about the problem.

(B) Neither Dr. Conant or his followers knows what to do about the problem.

(C) Neither Dr. Conant nor his followers know what to do about the problem.

(D) Neither Dr. Conant nor his followers know what to do as far as the problem goes.

(E) As to the problem, neither Dr. Conant nor his followers know what to do.

GO ON TO THE NEXT PAGE ➤

3. <u>The students requested a meeting with the chancellor</u> since they desired a greater voice in university policy.

  (A) The students requested a meeting with the chancellor

  (B) A meeting with the chancellor was requested by the students

  (C) It occurred to the students to request a meeting with the chancellor

  (D) The chancellor was the one with whom the students requested a meeting

  (E) The students insisted upon a meeting with the chancellor

4. Three American scientists were jointly awarded the Nobel Prize in Medicine <u>for their study of viruses which led to discoveries</u>.

  (A) for their study of viruses which led to discoveries

  (B) for their discoveries concerning viruses

  (C) as a prize for their discoveries about viruses

  (D) the discovery into viruses being the reason

  (E) for their virus discoveries

5. <u>You must convince me of promptness in returning the money</u> before I can agree to lend you $100.

  (A) You must convince me of promptness in returning the money

  (B) The loan of the money must be returned promptly

  (C) You must understand that you will have to assure me of a prompt money return

  (D) You will have to convince me that you will return the money promptly

  (E) You will return the money promptly

6. Because Bob was an outstanding athlete in high school, <u>in addition to a fine scholastic record</u>, he was awarded a scholarship at Harvard.

  (A) in addition to a fine scholastic record

  (B) also a student of excellence

  (C) and had amassed an excellent scholastic record

  (D) his scholastic record was also outstanding

  (E) as well as a superior student

7. Although pre-season odds against the Mets had been 100 to 1, <u>the Orioles were trounced by them in the World Series</u>.

  (A) the Orioles were trounced by them in the World Series

  (B) the World Series victors were the Mets who trounced the Orioles

  (C) they won the World Series by trouncing the Orioles

  (D) which is hard to believe since the Orioles were trounced in the World Series

  (E) it was the Mets who trounced the Orioles in the World Series

8. Before you can make a fresh fruit salad, <u>you must buy oranges, bananas, pineapples and peaches are necessary</u>.

  (A) you must buy oranges, bananas, pineapples and peaches are necessary

  (B) you must buy oranges and bananas and pineapples and peaches

  (C) you must buy oranges and bananas. And other fruit such as pineapples and peaches

  (D) you must buy oranges and bananas and other fruit. Such as pineapples and peaches

  (E) you must buy oranges, bananas, pineapples, and peaches

9. The physical education department of the school offers instruction <u>to learn how to swim, how to play tennis, and how to defend oneself</u>.

  (A) to learn how to swim, how to play tennis, and how to defend oneself

  (B) in swimming, playing tennis, and defending oneself

  (C) in regard to how to swim, how to play tennis, and how to defend oneself

  (D) for the purpose of swimming, playing tennis, and defending oneself

  (E) in swimming, playing tennis, and to defend oneself

GO ON TO THE NEXT PAGE ➤

10. He is not only chairman of the Ways and Means Committee, but also of the Finance Committee.

    (A) He is not only chairman of the Ways and Means Committee, but also of the Finance Committee.

    (B) He is the chairman not only of the Ways and Means Committee, but also of the Finance Committee.

    (C) He is the chairman of the Ways and Means Committee and the chairman of the Finance Committee.

    (D) Not only is he the chairman of the Ways and Means Committee, but also of the Finance Committee.

    (E) Both the Finance Committee and the Ways and Means Committee are committees in which he is the chairman.

11. First the student did research in the library, and then his English composition was written.

    (A) and then his English composition was written

    (B) and then the English composition was written by the student

    (C) and following this he then wrote his English composition

    (D) and then he wrote his English composition

    (E) then he wrote his English composition

12. Two candidates for the U.S. Senate, Buckley and him, made speeches to the group.

    (A) Two candidates for the U.S. Senate, Buckley and him, made speeches to the group.

    (B) Two candidates for the U.S. Senate, Buckley and he, made speeches to the group.

    (C) Buckley and him, two candidates for the U.S. Senate, made speeches to the group.

    (D) Speeches to the group were made by Buckley and he, two candidates for the U.S. Senate.

    (E) Buckley and he made speeches to the group.

13. A student of American history for many years, Stephen Douglas and his economic policies were thoroughly familiar to him.

    (A) A student of American history for many years

    (B) After having been a student of American history for many years

    (C) He was a student of American history for many years

    (D) Being that he was student of American history for many years

    (E) Since he was a student of American history for many years

14. Does anyone know to who this book belongs?

    (A) to who this book belongs

    (B) to whom this book belongs to

    (C) to whom this book belongs

    (D) who this book belongs to

    (E) to whom this belongs

STOP

If you finish before time is called, you may check your work on this section only.
Do not turn to any other section in the test.

How did you do on this test?

Step 1. Go to the Answer Key

Step 2. Calculate your "raw score."

Step 3. Get your "scaled score" for the test by referring to the Raw Score/Scaled Score Conversion
Tables.

**THERE'S ALWAYS ROOM
FOR IMPROVEMENT!**

ANSWER KEY FOR PRACTICE TEST 4

Math

Section 2	Correct Answer
1	B
2	C
3	D
4	D
5	D
6	E
7	E
8	C
9	A
10	C
11	A
12	A
13	D
14	E
15	A
16	D
17	C
18	A
19	B
20	C

Number correct

Number incorrect

Section 3	Correct Answer
1	C
2	B
3	C
4	D
5	C
6	A
7	A
8	C

Number correct

Number incorrect

Student-Produced Response Questions

9	24
10	9
11	7
12	2
13	8
14	4
15	18
16	60
17	9500
18	280

Number correct

Number incorrect

Section 6	Correct Answer
1	C
2	C
3	E
4	C
5	C
6	C
7	D
8	D

Number correct

Number incorrect

Student-Produced Response Questions

9	10
10	20
11	270
12	5
13	2
14	2
15	20
16	$\frac{1}{48}$ or .020 or .021
17	5
18	108

Number correct

Number incorrect

Section 8	Correct Answer
1	D
2	C
3	A
4	D
5	A
6	C
7	D
8	D
9	B
10	A
11	B
12	D
13	E
14	D
15	C
16	E

Number correct

Number incorrect

ANSWER KEY FOR PRACTICE TEST 4

Critical reading

Section 4

	Correct Answer
1	D
2	C
3	D
4	D
5	B
6	A
7	C
8	B
9	E
10	C
11	B
12	B
13	D
14	C
15	B
16	A
17	C
18	D
19	C
20	B
21	C
22	A
23	B
24	D

Number correct

Number incorrect

Section 7

	Correct Answer
1	D
2	D
3	A
4	D
5	B
6	D
7	B
8	E
9	C
10	D
11	A
12	D
13	B
14	E
15	C
16	A
17	E
18	D
19	D
20	A
21	C
22	B
23	A
24	D

Number correct

Number incorrect

Section 9

	Correct Answer
1	E
2	E
3	E
4	E
5	C
6	D
7	C
8	D
9	E
10	C
11	A
12	A
13	C
14	D
15	C
16	E
17	A
18	D
19	C

Number correct

Number incorrect

ANSWER KEY FOR PRACTICE TEST 4
Writing

Section 1

_____

Essay score

Section 5

	Correct Answer
1	A
2	A
3	E
4	B
5	B
6	E
7	A
8	C
9	B
10	D
11	E
12	D
13	A
14	B
15	C
16	E
17	A
18	C
19	D
20	A
21	B
22	D
23	D
24	B
25	C
26	A
27	E
28	B
29	E
30	D
31	B
32	A
33	E
34	A
35	E

_____

Number correct

_____

Number incorrect

Section 10

	Correct Answer
1	C
2	C
3	A
4	B
5	D
6	E
7	E
8	E
9	B
10	B
11	D
12	B
13	E
14	C

_____

Number correct

_____

Number incorrect

Scoring the SAT Practice Test

Check your responses with the correct answers on the previous pages. Fill in the blanks below and do the calculations to get your Math, Critical Reading, and Writing raw scores. Use the table to find your Math, Critical Reading, and Writing scaled scores.

Get Your Math Score

How many Math questions did you get **right**?

Section 2: Questions 1–20   _____

Section 6: Questions 1–18   + _____

Section 8: Questions 1–16   + _____

Total   =   _____ **(A)**

How many Math questions did you get **wrong**?

Section 2: Questions 1–20   _____

Section 6: Questions 1–18   + _____

Section 8: Questions 1–16   + _____

Total   =   _____

× 0.25   =   _____ **(B)**

A – B   =   _____

Math Raw Score

Round Math raw score to the nearest whole number.

_____

Use the Score Conversion Table to find your Math scaled score.

_____

Get Your Critical Reading Score

How many Critical Reading questions did you get **right**?

Section 4: Questions 1–24   _____

Section 7: Questions 1–24   + _____

Section 9: Questions 1–19   + _____

Total   =   _____ **(A)**

How many Critical Reading questions did you get **wrong**?

Section 4: Questions 1–24   _____

Section 7: Questions 1–24   + _____

Section 9: Questions 1–19   + _____

Total   =   _____

× 0.25   =   _____ **(B)**

A – B   =   _____

Critical Reading Raw Score

Round Critical Reading raw score to the nearest whole number.

_____

Use the Score Conversion Table to find your Critical Reading scaled score.

_____

Get Your Writing Score

How many multiple-choice Writing questions did you get **right**?

Section 5: Questions 1–35 _____

Section 10: Questions 1–14 + _____

Total = _____ **(A)**

How many multiple-choice Writing questions did you get **wrong**?

Section 5: Questions 1–35 _____

Section 10: Questions 1–14 + _____

Total = _____

$\times$ 0.25 = _____ **(B)**

A – B = _____

Writing Raw Score

Round Writing raw score to the nearest whole number.

_____

Use the Score Conversion Table to find your Writing multiple-choice scaled score.

_____

Estimate your Essay score using the Essay Scoring Guide.

_____

Use the SAT Score Conversion Table for Writing Composite to find your Writing scaled score. You will need your Writing raw score and your Essay score to use this table.

_____

SAT Score conversion table

Raw Score	Critical Reading Scaled Score	Math Scaled Score	Writing Multiple-Choice Scaled Score*	Raw Score	Critical Reading Scaled Score	Math Scaled Score	Writing Multiple-Choice Scaled Score*
67	800			31	510	550	60
66	800			30	510	540	58
65	790			29	500	530	57
64	770			28	490	520	56
63	750			27	490	520	55
62	740			26	480	510	54
61	730			25	480	500	53
60	720			24	470	490	52
59	700			23	460	480	51
58	690			22	460	480	50
57	690			21	450	470	49
56	680			20	440	460	48
55	670			19	440	450	47
54	660	800		18	430	450	46
53	650	790		17	420	440	45
52	650	760		16	420	430	44
51	640	740		15	410	420	44
50	630	720		14	400	410	43
49	620	710	80	13	400	410	42
48	620	700	80	12	390	400	41
47	610	680	80	11	380	390	40
46	600	670	79	10	370	380	39
45	600	660	78	9	360	370	38
44	590	650	76	8	350	360	38
43	590	640	74	7	340	350	37
42	580	630	73	6	330	340	36
41	570	630	71	5	320	330	35
40	570	620	70	4	310	320	34
39	560	610	69	3	300	310	32
38	550	600	67	2	280	290	31
37	550	590	66	1	270	280	30
36	540	580	65	0	250	260	28
35	540	580	64	−1	230	240	27
34	530	570	63	−2	210	220	25
33	520	560	62	−3	200	200	23
32	520	550	61	−4	200	200	20
				and below			

This table is for use only with the test in this book.

* The Writing multiple-choice score is reported on a 20–80 scale. Use the SAT Score Conversion Table for Writing Composite for the total writing scaled score.

SAT Score conversion table for writing composite

Writing Multiple-Choice Raw Score	Essay Raw Score						
	0	1	2	3	4	5	6
−12	200	200	200	210	240	270	300
−11	200	200	200	210	240	270	300
−10	200	200	200	210	240	270	300
−9	200	200	200	210	240	270	300
−8	200	200	200	210	240	270	300
−7	200	200	200	210	240	270	300
−6	200	200	200	210	240	270	300
−5	200	200	200	210	240	270	300
−4	200	200	200	230	270	300	330
−3	200	210	230	250	290	320	350
−2	200	230	250	280	310	340	370
−1	210	240	260	290	320	360	380
0	230	260	280	300	340	370	400
1	240	270	290	320	350	380	410
2	250	280	300	330	360	390	420
3	260	290	310	340	370	400	430
4	270	300	320	350	380	410	440
5	280	310	330	360	390	420	450
6	290	320	340	360	400	430	460
7	290	330	340	370	410	440	470
8	300	330	350	380	410	450	470
9	310	340	360	390	420	450	480
10	320	350	370	390	430	460	490
11	320	360	370	400	440	470	500
12	330	360	380	410	440	470	500
13	340	370	390	420	450	480	510
14	350	380	390	420	460	490	520
15	350	380	400	430	460	500	530
16	360	390	410	440	470	500	530
17	370	400	420	440	480	510	540
18	380	410	420	450	490	520	550
19	380	410	430	460	490	530	560
20	390	420	440	470	500	530	560
21	400	430	450	480	510	540	570
22	410	440	460	480	520	550	580

Writing Multiple-Choice Raw Score	Essay Raw Score						
	0	1	2	3	4	5	6
23	420	450	470	490	530	560	590
24	420	460	470	500	540	570	600
25	430	460	480	510	540	580	610
26	440	470	490	520	550	590	610
27	450	480	500	530	560	590	620
28	460	490	510	540	570	600	630
29	470	500	520	550	580	610	640
30	480	510	530	560	590	620	650
31	490	520	540	560	600	630	660
32	500	530	550	570	610	640	670
33	510	540	550	580	620	650	680
34	510	550	560	590	630	660	690
35	520	560	570	600	640	670	700
36	530	560	580	610	650	680	710
37	540	570	590	620	660	690	720
38	550	580	600	630	670	700	730
39	560	600	610	640	680	710	740
40	580	610	620	650	690	720	750
41	590	620	640	660	700	730	760
42	600	630	650	680	710	740	770
43	610	640	660	690	720	750	780
44	620	660	670	700	740	770	800
45	640	670	690	720	750	780	800
46	650	690	700	730	770	800	800
47	670	700	720	750	780	800	800
48	680	720	730	760	800	800	800
49	680	720	730	760	800	800	800

Chart for self-appraisal based on the practice test you have just taken

The Chart for Self-Appraisal below tells you quickly where your SAT strengths and weaknesses lie. Check or circle the appropriate box in accordance with the number of your correct answers for each area of the Practice Test you have just taken.

	Writing (Multiple-Choice)	Sentence Completions	Reading Comprehension	Math Questions*
EXCELLENT	42–49	16–19	40–48	44–54
GOOD	37–41	13–15	35–39	32–43
FAIR	31–36	9–12	26–34	27–31
POOR	20–30	5–8	17–25	16–26
VERY POOR	0–19	0–4	0–16	0–15

*Sections 2, 6, 8 only.

Note: In our tests, we have chosen to have Section 3 as the experimental section. We have also chosen it to be a math section since we felt that students may need more practice in the math area than in the verbal area. Note that on the actual SAT you will take, the order of the sections can vary and you will not know which one is experimental, so it is wise to answer all sections and not to leave any section out.

SAT-I VERBAL AND MATH SCORE/PERCENTILE CONVERSION TABLE

Critical reading and writing

SAT scaled verbal score	Percentile rank
800	99.7+
790	99.5
740–780	99
700–730	97
670–690	95
640–660	91
610–630	85
580–600	77
550–570	68
510–540	57
480–500	46
440–470	32
410–430	21
380–400	13
340–370	6
300–330	2
230–290	1
200–220	0–0.5

Math

SAT scaled math score	Percentile rank
800	99.5+
770–790	99.5
720–760	99
670–710	97
640–660	94
610–630	89
590–600	84
560–580	77
530–550	68
510–520	59
480–500	48
450–470	37
430–440	26
390–420	16
350–380	8
310–340	2
210–300	0.5
200	0

EXPLANATORY ANSWERS FOR PRACTICE TEST 4

THE SAT SCORING GUIDE
Section 1: Essay

Score of 6	Score of 5	Score of 4
An essay in this category is *outstanding*, demonstrating *clear and consistent mastery*, although it may have a few minor errors. A typical essay	An essay in this category is *effective*, demonstrating *reasonably consistent mastery*, although it will have occasional errors or lapses in quality. A typical essay	An essay in this category is *competent*, demonstrating *adequate mastery*, although it will have lapses in quality. A typical essay
• effectively and insightfully develops a point of view on the issue and demonstrates outstanding critical thinking, using clearly appropriate examples, reasons, and other evidence to support its position	• effectively develops a point of view on the issue and demonstrates strong critical thinking, generally using appropriate examples, reasons, and other evidence to support its position	• develops a point of view on the issue and demonstrates competent critical thinking, using adequate examples, reasons, and other evidence to support its position
• is well organized and clearly focused, demonstrating clear coherence and smooth progression of ideas	• is well organized and focused, demonstrating coherence and progression of ideas	• is generally organized and focused, demonstrating some coherence and progression of ideas
• exhibits skillful use of language, using a varied, accurate, and apt vocabulary	• exhibits facility in the use of language, using appropriate vocabulary	• exhibits adequate but inconsistent facility in the use of language, using generally appropriate vocabulary
• demonstrates meaningful variety in sentence structure	• demonstrates variety in sentence structure	• demonstrates some variety in sentence structure
• is free of most errors in grammar, usage, and mechanics	• is generally free of most errors in grammar, usage, and mechanics	• has some errors in grammar, usage, and mechanics

Score of 3	Score of 2	Score of 1
An essay in this category is *inadequate*, but demonstrates *developing mastery*, and is marked by ONE OR MORE of the following weaknesses:	An essay in this category is *seriously-limited*, demonstrating *little mastery*, and is flawed by ONE OR MORE of the following weaknesses:	An essay in this category is *fundamentally lacking*, demonstrating *very little* or *no mastery*, and is severely flawed by ONE OR MORE of the following weaknesses:
• develops a point of view on the issue, demonstrating some critical thinking, but may do so inconsistently or use inadequate examples, reasons, or other evidence to support its position	• develops a point of view on the issue that is vague or seriously limited, demonstrating weak critical thinking, providing inappropriate or insufficient examples, reasons, or other evidence to support its position	• develops no viable point of view on the issue, or provides little or no evidence to support its position
• is limited in its organization or focus, or may demonstrate some lapses in coherence or progression of ideas	• is poorly organized and/or focused, or demonstrates serious problems with coherence or progression of ideas	• is disorganized or unfocused, resulting in a disjointed or incoherent essay
• displays developing facility in the use of language, but sometimes uses weak vocabulary or inappropriate word choice	• displays very little facility in the use of language, using very limited vocabulary or incorrect word choice	• displays fundamental errors in vocabulary
• lacks variety or demonstrates problems in sentence structure	• demonstrates frequent problems in sentence structure	• demonstrates severe flaws in sentence structure
• contains an accumulation of errors in grammar, usage, and mechanics	• contains errors in grammar, usage, and mechanics so serious that meaning is somewhat obscured	• contains pervasive errors in grammar, usage, or mechanics that persistently interfere with meaning

Essays not written on the essay assignment will receive a score of zero.

EXPLANATORY ANSWERS FOR PRACTICE TEST 4

Section 2: Math

> When a specific Math Strategy is referred to in the solution, study that strategy, which you will find in "19 Math Strategies."

1. Choice B is correct. **(Use Strategy 2: Translate from words to algebra.)**

   The quotient of x and 3

   $$\frac{x}{3}$$

   $\frac{x}{3} - 8\} = 8$ less than the quotient

   and is the required answer.

2. Choice C is correct. **(Use Strategy 2: Translate from words to algebra.)**

   $$7 \text{ of Phil's buckets} - 7 \text{ of Mark's buckets} =$$
   $$7 \times 11 \text{ gallons} - 7 \times 8 \text{ gallons} =$$
   $$77 \text{ gallons} - 56 \text{ gallons} =$$
   $$21 \text{ gallons}$$

3. Choice D is correct. **(Use Strategy 7: Use number examples.)** You can show that

   $$\frac{|x|}{|y|} = \left|\frac{x}{y}\right|$$

   For example: $\frac{|-2|}{|4|} = \left|\frac{-2}{4}\right| = \frac{1}{2}; \frac{|-3|}{|-6|} = \left|\frac{-3}{-6}\right| = \frac{1}{2}$

   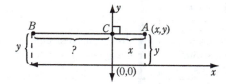

4. Choice D is correct. **(Use Strategy 14: Label unknown quantities.)**

   As shown in the diagram above, the y-coordinates of A and B must be the same because they both lie along the same horizontal line. Since B lies to the left of the y-axis, its x-coordinate must be negative. Since $3AC = BC$, then the x-coordinate of B is $-3x$

   and we already know that the y-coordinate is y. Thus, $(-3x, y)$ is the answer.

   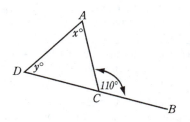

5. Choice D is correct. **(Use Strategy 18: Remember triangle facts.)**

   Since $AC = CD$, we know that

   $$x = y \qquad \boxed{1}$$

   We also know that

   $$m\angle ACB = m\angle D + m\angle A \qquad \boxed{2}$$

   Substituting the given into $\boxed{2}$, we have

   $$110 = y + x \qquad \boxed{3}$$

   Substituting $\boxed{1}$ into $\boxed{3}$, we get

   $$110 = y + y$$
   $$110 = 2y$$

6. Choice E is correct. **(Use Strategy 16: The obvious may be tricky!)**

   Given: $(x + y)^2 = 9$
   So that $x + y = 3 \text{ or } -3$

   From the information given, we cannot determine whether $x + y$ equals 3 or -3.

7. Choice E is correct.

   (Use Strategy 5:

   $$\text{Average} = \frac{\text{sum of values}}{\text{total number of values}}\Big)$$

Let x, y = two unknown numbers.

Thus, $\dfrac{28 + 30 + 32 + x + y}{5} = 34$ ⬚1

Multiplying ⬚1 by 5,

$$28 + 30 + 32 + x + y = 170$$
or $$90 + x + y = 170$$
or $$x + y = 80$$

8. Choice C is correct. **(Use Strategy 2: Translate from words to algebra.)**

Let x = side of one of the eight squares.

Thus, we are given

$$4x = 16$$
$$\text{or } x = 4 \qquad ⬚1$$

From what we are told in the problem, we conclude that

$$AE = MF = LG = 4x \qquad ⬚2$$
and $$AL = BK = CJ = DH = EG = 2x \qquad ⬚3$$

(Use Strategy 3: The whole equals the sum of its parts.)

Thus, using ⬚1, ⬚2, and ⬚3,

$$AE + MF + LG + AL + BK + CJ + DH + EG$$

$$= 4x + 4x + 4x + 2x + 2x + 2x + 2x + 2x$$

$$= 22x = 88$$

9. Choice A is correct. **(Use Strategy 11: Use new definitions carefully.)**

Given: $\textcircled{x} = \dfrac{x^2}{3}$ and $\boxed{x} = \dfrac{9}{x}$

Thus, $\textcircled{x} \times \boxed{x} = \dfrac{x^2}{3} \times \dfrac{9}{x} = 3x$

10. Choice C is correct. **(Use Strategy 17: Use the given information effectively.)**

For I, we have:

Clearly $DB < DA$, so I could not be true.

Clearly D can be the same distance from 2 points (A and B), but not from 3, so II does not apply.

Only Choice C, III only, is now possible.

Choice III is demonstrated below, although it was not necessary for us to examine it.

By definition, all points on the circle are the same distance from the center, so $DA = DB = DC$.

11. Choice A is correct. It can be seen that the dark region in Choice A is common to sets A, B, and C. Thus the diagram in Choice A describes the dark region as the set of elements that belongs to all of the sets A, B, and C.

12. Choice A is correct. **(Use Strategy 17: Use the given information effectively.)** Since the slope of a line is constant, the *ratio* of the *difference* in y-coordinates to the *difference* in x-coordinates must be constant for any two points on the line. For points $(1,3)$ and $(3,5)$, this ratio is

$$\dfrac{5 - 3}{3 - 1} = 1$$

Thus, for points $(6,y)$ and $(3,5)$ we must have

$$\dfrac{y - 5}{6 - 3} = 1$$

Therefore,

$$y - 5 = 3$$

and $y = 8$.

13. Choice D is correct. **(Use Strategy 10: Know how to use units.)**

$$\left(\frac{p \text{ gallons}}{\text{car}}\right) \times (r \text{ cars}) = pr \text{ gallons for each month}$$

$$\frac{q \text{ gallons}}{pr\frac{\text{gallons}}{\text{months}}} = \frac{q}{pr} \text{ months}$$

14. Choice E is correct. **(Use Strategy 11: Use new definitions carefully.)**

By definition, the l-length from -3 to $3 =$
$$3 - (-3) =$$
$$3 + 3 =$$
$$6$$

15. Choice A is correct.

By definition, the l-length from -4 to each of the other points follows:

$$R - (-4) = R + 4 \qquad \boxed{1}$$
$$S - (-4) = S + 4 \qquad \boxed{2}$$
$$T - (-4) = T + 4 \qquad \boxed{3}$$
$$U - (-4) = U + 4 \qquad \boxed{4}$$
$$V - (-4) = V + 4 \qquad \boxed{5}$$

From their position on the number line we know that

$$R < S < T < U < V \qquad \boxed{6}$$

(Use Strategy 6: Know how to manipulate inequalities.)

Adding 4 to each term of $\boxed{6}$, we get

$$R + 4 < S + 4 < T + 4 < U + 4 < V + 4 \qquad \boxed{7}$$

It is obvious from $\boxed{7}$ that $R + 4$ is smallest.

Thus, $\boxed{1}$ above, point R, has the least l-length from -4.

16. Choice D is correct. **(Use Strategy 2: Translate from words to algebra.)**

Let $x, x + 1, x + 2, x + 3, x + 4$ represent the 5 consecutive integers.

Then, $x + x + 1 + x + 2 + x + 3 + x + 4 = w$

$$5x + 10 = w \qquad \boxed{1}$$

The next 5 consecutive positive integers will be

$$x + 5, x + 6, x + 7, x + 8, x + 9$$

Their sum will be

$$x + 5 + x + 6 + x + 7 + x + 8 + x + 9 =$$
$$5x + 35 \qquad \boxed{2}$$

We can write $\boxed{2}$ as

$$5x + 35 = 5x + 10 + 25 \qquad \boxed{3}$$

Substituting $\boxed{1}$ into $\boxed{3}$, we get

$$5x + 10 + 25 = w + 25$$

17. Choice C is correct. **(Use Strategy 2: Translate from words to algebra.)**

We are told that the area of the square is twice the area of the triangle. This translates to:

$$a^2 = 2\left(\frac{1}{2} \times b \times c\right)$$
$$a^2 = bc \qquad \boxed{1}$$

We are given that $bc = 100 \qquad \boxed{2}$

Substituting $\boxed{2}$ into $\boxed{1}$, we get

$$a^2 = 100$$

18. Choice A is correct.

Given that the radius of the circle equals 2, we have

$$\text{Circumference} = 2\pi(\text{radius}) = 2\pi(2)$$
$$= 4\pi \text{ inches} \qquad \boxed{1}$$

We are given that $\overparen{AD} + \overparen{BC} = 3\pi$ inches $\qquad \boxed{2}$

(Use Strategy 3: The whole equals the sum of its parts.)

We know that $\overparen{AD} + \overparen{BC} + \overparen{AC} + \overparen{DB} =$ circumference of the circle. $\qquad \boxed{3}$

Substituting $\boxed{1}$ and $\boxed{2}$ into $\boxed{3}$, we have

$$3\pi \text{ inches} + \overparen{AC} + \overparen{DB} = 4\pi \text{ inches}$$
$$\overparen{AC} + \overparen{DB} = \pi \text{ inches} \qquad \boxed{4}$$

Let's figure out how to relate the length of $\overparen{AC} + \overparen{DB} = \pi$ inches with the angle y. We know that the central angle is measured by its arc.

Now get a proportion:

$$\frac{360°}{2\pi r} = \frac{y°}{\overparen{AC}}$$

Since $r = 2$,

$$\frac{360°}{4\pi} = \frac{y°}{\overset{\frown}{AC}} \qquad \boxed{5}$$

But $\overset{\frown}{AC} + \overset{\frown}{DB} = \pi$ inches, and since $\overset{\frown}{AC} = \overset{\frown}{DB}$,

$$\overset{\frown}{AC} = \frac{1}{2}\pi$$
$$\boxed{6}$$

From $\boxed{5}$, using $\boxed{6}$, we get:

$$\frac{360°}{4\pi} = \frac{y°}{\frac{1}{2}\pi}$$

and we get

$$\frac{180}{4} = y = 45.$$

19. Choice B is correct. **(Use Strategy 2: Translate from words to algebra.)**

Let r = Ross's age now.

19 = Amanda's age now.

Thus, $r - 5$ = Ross's age five years ago. $\qquad \boxed{1}$

$19 - 5 = 14$ = Amanda's age five years ago. $\qquad \boxed{2}$

We are given: Five years ago, Ross was N times as old as Amanda was. $\qquad \boxed{3}$

Substituting $\boxed{1}$ and $\boxed{2}$ into $\boxed{3}$, we have

$$r - 5 = N(14)$$
$$r = 14N + 5$$

20. Choice C is correct.

The volume of the rectangular solid to be immersed is:

$$V = (1\text{ ft})(1\text{ ft})(2\text{ ft}) = 2\text{ cu ft} \qquad \boxed{1}$$

When the solid is immersed, the volume of the displaced water will be:

$$(2\text{ ft})(6\text{ ft})(x\text{ ft}) = 12x\text{ cu ft} \qquad \boxed{2}$$

where x represents the height of the displaced water. $\boxed{1}$ and $\boxed{2}$ must be equal. So

$$2\text{ cu ft} = 12x\text{ cu ft}$$

$$\frac{1}{6}\text{ ft} = x$$

(Use Strategy 10: Know how to use units.)

$$\left(\frac{1}{6}\text{ft}\right)\left(\frac{12\text{ inches}}{\text{foot}}\right) =$$

$\frac{12}{6}$ = 2 inches that the displaced water will rise.

> When a specific Math Strategy is referred to in the solution, study that strategy, which you will find in "19 Math Strategies."

1. Choice C is correct. **(Use Strategy 17: Use the given information effectively.)**

   Given:
   $$x + by = 5 \quad \boxed{1}$$
   $$3x + y = 5 \quad \boxed{2}$$
   $$y = 2 \quad \boxed{3}$$

   We want to find b.

   Substituting $\boxed{3}$ into $\boxed{2}$, we get
   $$3x + 2 = 5$$
   or $\quad x = 1 \quad \boxed{4}$

   Substituting $\boxed{3}$ and $\boxed{4}$ into $\boxed{1}$, we have
   $$1 + 2b = 5$$
   or $\quad\quad 2b = 4$
   or $\quad\quad\; b = 2$

2. Choice B is correct.

   The ratio of boys to girls in the class is $2 : 3$. Choice C is the answer because $9 : 12 = 3 : 4$, which does not equal $2 : 3$.

3. Choice C is correct. **(Use Strategy 10: Know how to use units.)**

   Since 7 days = 1 week, 24 hours = 1 day, and 60 minutes = 1 hour, then

   $$1 \text{ week} = (1 \text{ week})\left(\frac{7 \text{ days}}{\text{week}}\right)\left(\frac{24 \text{ hours}}{\text{day}}\right)\left(\frac{60 \text{ minutes}}{\text{hour}}\right)$$
   $$= (7)(24)(60) \text{ minutes}$$

   Thus,

   $$\frac{24 \text{ minutes}}{1 \text{ week}} = \frac{24 \text{ minutes}}{(7)(24)(60) \text{ minutes}} = \frac{1}{420}$$

4. Choice D is correct. **(Use Strategy 17: Use the given information effectively.)**

   $$2 \times 10^{-5} \times 8 \times 10^2 \times 5 \times 10^2$$
   $$= 2 \times 8 \times 5 \times 10^{-5} \times 10^2 \times 10^2$$
   $$= 8 \times 10^0$$
   $$= 8 \times 1$$
   $$= 8$$

5. Choice C is correct. **(Use Strategy 2: Translate from words to algebra.)**

   Allowance $= \$30$

   Amount spent on candy $= \frac{2}{5} \times \$30 = \$12$

   Amount left after
   Jaxon bought candy $= \$30 - \$12 = \$18$

   Amount spent on ice cream $= \frac{5}{6} \times \$18 = \$15$

   Amount left after buying
   candy and ice cream $= \$18 - \$15$
   $= \$3$

6. Choice A is correct. **(Use Strategy 17: Use the given information effectively.)** $y = -x^2$ $= -4$. $x = 2$ or $x = -2$. Since point B lies on the left side of the y-axis, $x = -2$.

7. Choice A is correct. **(Use Strategy 17: Use the given information effectively.)** It is seen from the graph of $y = f(x)$ that when $x = 0$, $y = 0$. Thus $0 = m(0) + b$ and $b = 0$.

8. Choice C is correct. When the graph intersects the x-axis, $y = 0$. Thus we set $y = 0 = x^4 + x^3$.

   We can write this as

   $$x^3(x + 1) = 0$$

   Thus $x = 0$ and $x = -1$

   The graph therefore intersects the x-axis at two points.

9. **24 (Use Strategy 2: Translate from words to algebra.)**

Given: $\dfrac{5}{8}$ of x is 40

$$\downarrow \quad \downarrow \ \downarrow \ \downarrow \quad \downarrow$$

$$\dfrac{5}{8} \times x = 40 \qquad \boxed{1}$$

(Use Strategy 13: Find unknowns by multiplication.)

Fast Method: To get the value of $\dfrac{3}{8}$ of x, multiply $\boxed{1}$ by $\dfrac{3}{5}$ to get

$$\dfrac{3}{5}\left(\dfrac{5}{8}x\right) = \dfrac{3}{5}(40)$$

$$\dfrac{3}{8}x = \dfrac{3}{\not{5}} \times \not{5} \times 8$$

$$\dfrac{3}{8}x = 24$$

Slow Method: Solve $\boxed{1}$ for x by multiplying $\boxed{1}$ by $\dfrac{8}{5}$:

$$x = 64 \qquad \boxed{2}$$

Now substitute $\boxed{2}$ into the unknown expression:

$$\dfrac{3}{8}x = \dfrac{3}{8}(64)$$

$$= \dfrac{3}{\not{8}} \times \not{8} \times 8$$

$$= 24$$

10. **9 (Use Strategy 2: Translate from words to algebra.)** We are given that the wire is bent to form a circle of radius 3 feet. This means that its length is equal to the circumference of the circle.

$$\text{Thus, Length of wire} = 2\pi r = 2\pi(3) \text{ feet}$$

$$= 6\pi \text{ feet}$$

$$\approx 6(3.14) \text{ feet}$$

$$\text{Length of wire} \approx 18.84 \text{ feet} \qquad \boxed{1}$$

(Use Strategy 3: Know how to find unknown quantities.)

$$\dfrac{\text{Number of pieces}}{\text{2 feet long}} = \dfrac{\text{total length}}{\text{2 feet}} \qquad \boxed{2}$$

Substituting $\boxed{1}$ into $\boxed{2}$, we have

$$\dfrac{\text{Number of pieces}}{\text{2 feet long}} \approx \dfrac{18.84 \text{ feet}}{\text{2 feet}}$$

$$\approx 9.42$$

$$= 9 \text{ complete pieces}$$

11. **7 (Use Strategy 2: Translate from words to algebra.)**

Let b = number of baseballs that Dick bought

t = number of tennis balls that Dick bought

$.70b$ = amount spent on baseballs

$.60t$ = amount spent on tennis balls

Thus, we are told

$$.70b + .60t = 7.00 \qquad \boxed{1}$$

Multiply $\boxed{1}$ by 10:

$$7b + 6t = 70 \qquad \boxed{2}$$

Solve $\boxed{2}$ for t:

$$t = \dfrac{70 - 7b}{6} = \dfrac{7(10 - b)}{6} \qquad \boxed{3}$$

(Use Strategy 17: Use the given information effectively.) From $\boxed{3}$, we see that the maximum value of t occurs at the minimum value of b. Since b and t are numbers of balls, b and t must be nonnegative integers. Thus, the minimum value of b is 0. When $b = 0$, $t = \dfrac{70}{6}$, which is not an integer. For t to be an integer, $\boxed{3}$ tells us that $(10 - b)$ is a multiple of 6. The smallest value of b that makes $(10 - b)$ a multiple of 6 is $b = 4$. Thus, $t = 7$ is the maximum value of t, and 7 is the answer.

12. **2 (Use Strategy 11: Use new definitions carefully.)**

Given:

$$f(x) = 12x + 8 \qquad \boxed{1}$$

$$\text{and } f(x) \div f(0) = 2x \qquad \boxed{2}$$

Calculate $f(0)$:

$$f(0) = 12(0) + 8 = 8 \qquad \boxed{3}$$

Substitute $\boxed{1}$ and $\boxed{3}$ into $\boxed{2}$:

$$\dfrac{12x + 8}{8} = 2x \qquad \boxed{4}$$

Multiply both sides of $\boxed{4}$ by 8:

$$12x + 8 = 16x$$

or $$8 = 4x$$

or $$x = 2$$

13. **8 (Use Strategy 11: Use new definitions carefully.)**

In the given letter columns, only 8 triples have the property that exactly 2 of the letters in the triple are the same. Thus, 8 triples have a value of 1, and all the other triples have a value of 0. Hence, the value of the entire group of letter columns is 8.

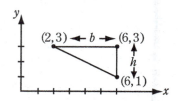

14. **4 (Use Strategy 17: Use the given information effectively.)**

It is clear from the diagram above that the triangle is a right triangle whose area is

$$A = \frac{1}{2}bh \qquad \boxed{1}$$

From the given coordinates, we can also say that

$$b = 6 - 2 = 4 \qquad \boxed{2}$$
$$h = 3 - 1 = 2 \qquad \boxed{3}$$

Substituting $\boxed{2}$ and $\boxed{3}$ into $\boxed{1}$,

$$A = \frac{1}{2}(4)(2)$$
$$A = 4$$

15. **18 (Use Strategy 17: Use the given information effectively.)**

The area of a rectangle is length × width. The number of squares that can be packed into the rectangle

$$= \frac{\text{area of entire rectangle}}{\text{area of each square}}$$

$$= \frac{6 \times 12}{2 \times 2}$$

$$= \frac{72}{4}$$

$$= \frac{\cancel{4} \times 18}{\cancel{4}}$$

$$= 18$$

16. **60** Since we are given the radii of the circles, we have

$$AN = AM = 1 \qquad \boxed{1}$$
$$BM = BP = 2 \qquad \boxed{2}$$
$$CN = CP = 3 \qquad \boxed{3}$$

We want to find

$$(AB)(BC)(AC) \qquad \boxed{4}$$

(Use Strategy 3: The whole equals the sum of its parts.) From the diagram, we see that

$$AB = AM + BM \qquad \boxed{5}$$
$$BC = BP + CP \qquad \boxed{6}$$
$$AC = AN + CN \qquad \boxed{7}$$

Substituting $\boxed{1}$, $\boxed{2}$, $\boxed{3}$ into $\boxed{5}$, $\boxed{6}$, $\boxed{7}$ we have

$$AB = 3$$
$$BC = 5$$
$$AC = 4$$

Thus,

$$(AB)(BC)(AC) = (3)(5)(4)$$
$$= 60$$

17. **9500**

(Use Strategy 5:

$$\mathbf{Average} = \frac{\text{sum of values}}{\text{total number of values}}\Big)$$

We are given:

$$\frac{x + y + z + w}{4} = 8{,}000 \qquad \boxed{1}$$

(Use Strategy 13: Find unknowns by multiplication.) Multiplying $\boxed{1}$ by 4, we get

$$x + y + z + w = 32{,}000 \qquad \boxed{2}$$

We are given that any 3 have an average of 7,500, so using x, y, and z as the 3, we get

$$\frac{x + y + z}{3} = 7{,}500 \qquad \boxed{3}$$

Multiplying $\boxed{3}$ by 3, we get

$$x + y + z = 22{,}500 \qquad \boxed{4}$$

Substituting $\boxed{4}$ into $\boxed{2}$, we get

$$22{,}500 + w = 32{,}000$$

or

$$w = 9{,}500$$

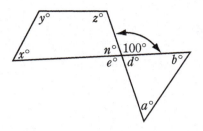

18. 280

(Use Strategy 17: Use the given information effectively.)

From the diagram, $n = d$ (vertical angles). $\boxed{1}$

We know $x + y + z + n = 360$ $\boxed{2}$

Substituting $\boxed{1}$ into $\boxed{2}$, we get

$$x + y + z + d = 360 \qquad \boxed{3}$$

Subtracting d from $\boxed{3}$, we have

$$x + y + z = 360 - d \qquad \boxed{4}$$

We know that $100 + d = 180$ from the diagram.

$$\text{So, } d = 180 - 100 = 80 \qquad \boxed{5}$$

Substituting $\boxed{5}$ into $\boxed{4}$, we get

$$x + y + z = 360 - 80$$
$$x + y + z = 280$$

EXPLANATORY ANSWERS FOR PRACTICE TEST 4
Section 4: Critical reading

> As you read these Explanatory Answers, you are advised to refer to "16 Verbal (Critical Reading) Strategies."

1.   Choice D is correct. See **Sentence Completion Strategy 2**. Examine the first word of each choice. Choice B, pacifism, and Choice E, oblivion, are incorrect choices because a rising tide of pacifism or oblivion in public education does *not* make good sense. Now consider the other choices. Choice A, compromise...inept, and Choice C, ambiguity...average, do *not* make good sense in the sentence. Choice D, mediocrity... dedicated, *does* make good sense.

2.   Choice C is correct. See **Sentence Completion Strategy 2**. First we eliminate Choice A, foretold, Choice B, impossible, and Choice E, glaring. Reason: These choices do not make sense in the sentence up to the word "eclipses." We further eliminate Choice D, true...rational, because it does not make sense for anyone to consider an eclipse rational. Only Choice C, understandable... magical, makes sense.

3.   Choice D is correct. The fact that the girl had become more self-confident indicates that she would be more active in participating in a conversation. If you used **Sentence Completion Strategy 3**—trying to complete the sentence *before* looking at the five choices— you might have come up with any of the following appropriate words:

starting   beginning
launching   originating

The other choices are, therefore, incorrect.

4.   Choice D is correct. See **Sentence Completion Strategy 2**. Let us first examine the first word of each choice. We can eliminate Choice B, confuse,

and Choice E, misconstrue, because it does *not* make sense to say that an authority would be able to "confuse" or "misconstrue" something in a book. So Choices B and E are incorrect.

Let us now consider the remaining choices. Choice A, understand...general, and Choice C, read... useless, do *not* make sense in the sentence. Therefore, these choices are incorrect. Choice D, comprehend...complex, *does* make sense.

5.   Choice B is correct. See **Sentence Completion Strategy 4**. The words "not only" constitute a *support indicator*. The second part of the sentence is, therefore, expected to reinforce the first part of the sentence. Choice B, reject...refused, supplies the two words that provide a sentence that makes sense. Choices A, C, D, and E are incorrect because their word pairs do not produce sentences that make sense.

6.   Choice A is correct. See **Sentence Completion Strategy 3**. If you used this strategy of trying to complete the sentence *before* looking at the five choices, you might have come up with any of the following appropriate words:

persistence   perseverance
steadfastness

These words all mean the same as Choice A, tenacity. Note that the root "ten" in "tenacity" means "to hold." Accordingly, Choices B, C, D, and E are incorrect.

7.   Choice C is correct. See **Sentence Completion Strategy 4**. The adverb "ironically" means "in a manner so that the opposite of what is expected takes place." So we have an *opposition indicator* here. Choice C, weaken, is, of course, the

opposite of strengthen. Accordingly, Choices A, B, D, and E are incorrect.

8. Choice B is correct. See **Sentence Completion Strategy 4**. The words "in spite of" constitute an *opposition indicator*. We can then expect an opposing idea to complete the sentence. The word "baffled" means "puzzled" or "unable to comprehend." Choice B, baffled, gives us the word that brings out the opposition thought we expect in the sentence. Choices A, C, D, and E do not give us a sentence that makes sense.

9. Choice E is correct. See the beginning sentence, which states, "the greatest acrobats on earth," introducing the monkeys, which in line 4 are called "ceboids." The whole passage is about the "ceboid acrobats."

10. Choice C is correct. See lines 1–4 where the agility and dexterity of the Old World and American monkeys are compared. Only American monkeys are described in terms of size or noise, so Choices A and B are incorrect. Choices D and E are not mentioned in the passage.

11. Choice B is correct. See lines 1–3. Note that even if you didn't know the meaning of "deprecate," you could figure that the word imparted a negative connotation since the prefix "de" means "away from" and is negative. Also don't get lured into Choice D just because "Babel" was mentioned.

12. Choice B is correct. See lines 3–4: "…in politics that their influence is most dangerous…"

13. Choice D is correct. The second paragraph states that "the other classes…adopted many of the outward characteristics of the aristocracy."

14. Choice C is correct. The second paragraph implies that the bourgeoisie was "rising to political power" and rivaling the power of the aristocracy.

15. Choice B is correct. The third and fifth paragraphs describe the castles as "strongholds" and "fortified houses."

16. Choice A is correct. This information is given in paragraph 3, where it states that "the Magyar armies" harried central Europe.

17. Choice C is correct. The fourth paragraph relates how "power passed into the hands of warriors invested by the monarchy and the Church with lands."

18. Choice D is correct. Paragraph 2 states, "Noblemen who became bishops or who founded new Orders helped to implant aristocratic principles…deep within…the Church."

19. Choice C is correct. Given the context of the rest of the sentence, it can be seen that Choice C is correct. See also **Reading Comprehension Strategy 5**.

20. Choice B is correct. The last paragraph states that hunting was a rehearsal for war and it made up "for the lack of butcher's meat."

21. Choice C is correct. See paragraph 2: "Even the unarmed peasantry…long remained tenaciously loyal to their lords, held to their allegiance by that combination of love and fear, *amor et timor*…"

22. Choice A is correct. See paragraph 4: "… warriors…undertook…to protect the unarmed peasantry."

23. Choice B is correct. See paragraph 4: "It was recognized in theory that the Church and the monarchy were the principal powers and that they were bound by the nature of their office to ensure peace and security…but…they were too weak, too torn by internal conflicts to fulfill their obligations."

24. Choice D is correct. Given the context of the rest of the sentence, it would appear that because of the word "themselves," "retinue" must refer to humans. It is more likely that it refers to "attendants" than to "family." See also **Reading Comprehension Strategy 5**.

1.   **(A)** Choice A is correct. Choice B is incorrect because "on account" may not be used as a subordinate conjunction. Choice C is incorrect because it gives the meaning that the judge is doing the charging. Choice D is incorrect because the possessive noun ("defendant") modifying the gerund ("charging") must take the form "defendant's." Choice E creates a run-on sentence.

2.   **(A)** Choice A is correct. Choices B, C, and D are incorrect because they change the meaning of the original sentence. Choice E creates a run-on sentence.

3.   **(E)** If we think of writing as a form of communication, then it can be no surprise that the best sentence choice is usually the clearest one. Read the choices, and ask yourself which answer offers the most clarity. In Choice A, the phrase "were that we…" is unnecessary and creates confusion, not clarity. Note also that Choices A and B are incorrect because they give the idea that the plans are trying to avoid the hot sun. Choice D is a run-on sentence, so it is incorrect. Choice E offers the most succinct and clear thought.

4.   **(B)** Choice A is too wordy. Choice B is correct. Choice C is incorrect because it changes the tense of the original sentence—"Whatever (may) be her thoughts" is in the present tense. Choice D does not retain the meaning of the original sentence. Choice E makes no sense.

5.   **(B)** Choices A and E are incorrect because the subject word "use" requires a singular verb ("makes"). Choice B is correct. Choices C and D are awkward.

6.   **(E)** "Irregardless" (Choice A) is incorrect. "Regardless about" (Choice B) is unidiomatic. Choices C and D change the meaning of the original sentence. Moreover, Choice D makes the sentence ungrammatical. Choice E is correct.

7.   **(A)** Choice A is correct. Choices B, C, and E change the meaning of the original sentence. Choice D is too wordy.

8.   **(C)** The infinitive "to effect" means "to bring about"—this is not the meaning intended in the original sentence. Therefore, Choices A, B, and D are incorrect. Choice C is correct. Choice E changes the meaning of the original sentence.

9.   **(B)** In the original sentence, "who" should replace "whom" as the subject of the subordinate clause ("who were police officers"). "I believe" is simply a parenthetical expression. Therefore, Choice A is incorrect and Choice B is correct. Choice C creates a run-on sentence. Choice D improperly changes the sentence from a complex type to a compound type. Choice E does not retain the meaning of the original sentence.

10. **(D)** In Choice A, we have an improper ellipsis: "never have and never will be trusted." An ellipsis is an omission from a sentence of one or more words that would complete or clarify it. Choice B also suffers from an improper ellipsis. Choice C changes the meaning of the original sentence. Choice D includes the missing words that clarify the sentence: "never have been trusted and never will be trusted." Choice E is far too wordy.

11. **(E)** Sequence of tenses in a past contrary-to-fact condition requires the "had waited" form in the "if" clause. Therefore Choices A, B, C, and D are incorrect, and Choice E is correct.

12. **(D)** "…but a security guard, a fireman, and *me*." The preposition *but* is understood before *me*. Since *me* is the object of the preposition *but*, it has an objective form (*me*)—not a nominative form (*I*).

13. **(A)** "Having drunk…the lemonade…" The past participle of *drink* is *drunk*.

14. **(B)** "…to *whoever*…could present her…" The subject of the dependent clause must have a nominative case form (*whoever*)—not an objective case form (*whomever*).

15. **(C)** "…they had brought *not nearly* the number…" Do not use the expression *nowhere near* for *not nearly*.

16. **(E)** All underlined parts are correct.

17. **(A)** "*Because of* his not studying…" Do not begin a sentence with the words *due to. Due* is an adjective. As an adjective, it must have a noun to modify.

18. **(C)** "…to buy the *kind of* car…" Do not use the article *a* or *an* after *kind of, type of, sort of,* etc.

19. **(D)** "…compare their poems *with those of Robert Frost.*" We have an improper ellipsis in the original sentence. The additional words (*those of*) are necessary to complete the meaning of the sentence.

20. **(A)** "I appreciate *your* offering…" Nouns and pronouns that precede gerunds are in the possessive case. We, therefore, say *your offering*—not *you offering.*

21. **(B)** "…the *slower* of the two…" Since we are here comparing two runners, we must use the comparative degree (*slower*)—not the superlative degree (*slowest*).

22. **(D)** "…is usually easier than passing the driving test." This sentence requires parallelism. Remember that a *parallel structure* or a *parallelism* is the repetition of a chosen grammatical form within a sentence. By making each compared item or idea in your sentence follow the same grammatical pattern, you create a parallel construction. The other choices hold no qualities of parallelism. "*Passing* the driving test" should parallel with "*passing* the written test."

23. **(D)** "…each hoping that *he* would win…" A pronoun should be in the same number as the noun or pronoun to which it refers. In the sentence, *he* refers to *each,* which is a singular pronoun.

24. **(B)** "Her answer…was *altogether* incorrect…" *Altogether* means *entirely, wholly. All together* means *as a group.*

25. **(C)** "…they acted as if they never *had met* before…" We must use the past perfect tense (*had met*) to indicate an action taking place before another past action (*acted*).

26. **(A)** "The realtor felt *bad*…" After the copulative verb (*felt*), the word referring to the subject should be a predicate adjective (*bad*)—not an adverb (*badly*). Remember, a copulative verb is a verb that expresses a state of being rather than an action.

27. **(E)** All underlined parts are correct.

28. **(B)** The pronoun *he* has an indefinite antecedent. The noun or phrase that the pronoun replaces is called an *antecedent.* When the antecedent is not clearly identified, it is known as an *indefinite antecedent.* In our sentence, we cannot tell whether *he* refers to the governor or to the attorney. Therefore, we must be specific by using *the governor* or *the attorney* in place of the pronoun (*he*).

29. **(E)** All underlined parts are correct.

30. **(D)** Choice A is incorrect because sentence 1 is needed to open the paragraph in order to establish the fact that safety devices have been proven to save lives. If this information does not precede every other idea in the paragraph, the logical reasons for the laws and for obeying them are not clear. Therefore, sentence 4 should not be placed before sentence 1. Choices B and C are incorrect in that sentence 4 is in an illogical position in the paragraph and should be moved rather than attached to sentence 3 (Choice B) or left in its present position (Choice C). Choice D is correct: The logical position for the idea about laws governing the use of motorcycle helmets is directly following the idea about laws governing the installation of seat belts. (The two ideas are so closely related that they might appropriately be joined in a complex sentence.) Additionally, in the present position of sentence 4, "these safety devices" seem to apply only to "seat belts"

in sentence 2, whereas the clear intent of the paragraph as a whole is that "safety devices" refer to both seat belts and helmets. Choice E is incorrect because the present position of sentence 4 is not logical and creates the inaccurate reference to only one safety device.

31. **(B)** Choice A is incorrect, since omitting "mandating" creates the illogical sense that government interferes with individuals by using safety devices. Government might possibly be said to interfere with individuals by installing seat belts, but it cannot interfere with individuals by using seat belts, an idea that is awkward in any case since "government" does not constitute an entity capable of using a seat belt. Choice B is correct because "mandating" means "issuing an authoritative command or instruction," a sense that agrees with the idea of passing a law. Choice C is incorrect in that "prohibiting" or "forbidding" the use of safety devices results in a meaning that runs counter to the whole sense of the paragraph. Choice D is incorrect in that nonsense would result from placing "mandating" before "individual." The government would then be said to interfere with the issuing of commands making individual comfort and freedom obligatory. Choice E is incorrect in that such a wordy substitute is never preferable to one correct word; moreover, the phrase is inaccurate in that the "directions" (or laws) do not express a preference ("in favor of") but an order.

32. **(A)** Choice A is correct: The insertion of "these riders are" is necessary to correct the existing situation in which the modifier "if thrown in an accident" incorrectly attaches itself to "their heads." Choice B is incorrect not only because the dangling modifier is not corrected but also because a cantaloupe, with its hard rind and juicy interior, is a better figure of speech for a human head than a flexible, partially transparent balloon filled with gas or air. Choice C is incorrect because replacing "their heads" with "they" would create a situation in which "if thrown in an accident" would modify a pronoun which might refer either to motorcyclists or to helmets. The rest of the sentence referring to cantaloupes would make a poor comparison if

applied to the bodies of the motorcyclists and would convey no pertinent meaning if applied to helmets. Choice D is incorrect because "who refuse to wear helmets" is a restrictive clause defining particular motorcyclists and should not be made into a nonrestrictive clause by placing commas around it. Choice E is incorrect in that the dangling modifier would not be corrected and nothing would be gained in sense by creating the awkwardly repetitive sounds of "measure of pleasure."

33. **(E)** Choice A is incorrect: Turning sentence 7 into two sentences with the first ending after "small ways" would leave the second sentence as a dependent clause fragment. Choice B is incorrect because the subject and its verb should not be separated with a comma. Choice C is incorrect: Beginning the sentence with "while" would be a good choice if "because" were removed, but Choice C does not specify this omission, and "because" is not an appropriate conjunction. Choice D is incorrect: While the phrase "in more important ways" could be omitted (even though it adds balance to the sentence in paralleling "in small ways"), the major problem in the sentence would be passed over in making only this deletion. Choice E is correct: The word "because" should be changed to "but." The second idea in the sentence is not "a reason for" or "the result of" the first idea, relationships indicated by "because." The two ideas in the sentence are contrasting (that devices may "limit" but also "greatly increase" comfort and freedom) and should be connected with a conjunction showing this contrast.

34. **(A)** Statistical backup would qualify the author's position and show the dangers more specifically and in a more documented fashion. Choices B, C, D are weak, and Choice E is irrelevant.

35. **(E)** Since the paragraph supports wearing seat belts and helmets, the author must have a strong first introductory statement for why seat belts and helmets are warranted. Sentence 1 serves that purpose and should be kept as the first sentence.

EXPLANATORY ANSWERS FOR PRACTICE TEST 4

Section 6: Math

> When a specific Math Strategy is referred to in the solution, study that strategy, which you will find in "19 Math Strategies."

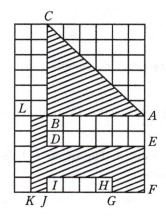

1.   Choice C is correct.

Given: length of side of square = 1. $\boxed{1}$
Using $\boxed{1}$, we get $AB = 6$, $BC = 6$ $\boxed{2}$

We know that

the Area of a triangle $= \frac{1}{2}$(base)(height) $\boxed{3}$

Substituting $\boxed{2}$ into $\boxed{3}$, we get

Area of shaded triangle $ABC = \frac{1}{2}(6)(6)$

$= 18$ $\boxed{4}$

We know that the area of
a square $= (\text{side})^2$ $\boxed{5}$

Substituting $\boxed{1}$ into $\boxed{5}$, we have

Area of each square $= (1)^2 = 1$ $\boxed{6}$

Counting the number of squares in the other shaded figure ($BDEFGHIJKL$), we find 19. $\boxed{7}$

Multiplying $\boxed{6}$ by $\boxed{7}$, we have

Area of $BDEFGHIJKL = 19 \times 1 = 19$ $\boxed{8}$

(Use Strategy 3: The whole equals the sum of its parts.)

We know:

Total Shaded Area = Area of ABC +

Area of $BDEFGHIJKL$ $\boxed{9}$

Substituting $\boxed{4}$ and $\boxed{8}$ into $\boxed{9}$, we get

Total Shaded Area $= 18 + 19$

$= 37$

2.   Choice C is correct. **(Use Strategy 17: Use the given information effectively.)**

Since the triangle is equilateral, all of its sides are equal. Thus,

$$5x - 2 = x$$
$$4x = 2$$
$$x = \frac{1}{2}$$

Perimeter = Sum of 3 sides $= \frac{1}{2} + \frac{1}{2} + \frac{1}{2}$

$$= 1\frac{1}{2}$$

3.   Choice E is correct. **(Use Strategy 10: Know how to use units of time, distance, area.)**

The number of waves that pass through a certain point in t seconds

$$= \frac{w \text{ waves}}{s \text{ seconds}}(t \text{ seconds})$$
$$= \frac{wt}{s} \text{ waves}$$

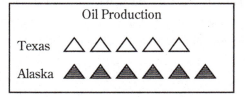

4. Choice C is correct. **(Use Strategy 2: Translate from words to algebra.)**

We are told ▲ = 3△

(Use Strategy 17: Use the given information effectively.)

Texas total = 5
Alaska total = 3(6) = 18

(Use Strategy 3: Know how to find unknown quantities from known quantities.)

$$\frac{\text{Alaska production}}{\text{total production}} = \frac{18}{5+18} =$$

$$\frac{18}{23} = \text{required ratio}$$

5. Choice C is correct. Probability is defined as

$$\frac{\text{number of favorable ways (coins)}}{\text{total number of ways (coins)}} = \frac{F}{N}$$

If the probability of selecting a nickel is $\frac{3}{8}$, then for nickels, $\frac{F}{N} = \frac{3}{8}$. But N [the total number of ways (or coins)] is 24.

So $\frac{F}{N} = \frac{3}{8} = \frac{F}{24}$; $F = 9$ (nickels)

The probability of selecting a dime is $\frac{1}{8}$, so for a dime, $\frac{F}{N} = \frac{1}{8} = \frac{F}{24}$; $F = 3$ (dimes)

Since there are 24 coins and there are 9 nickels and 3 dimes, $24 - 3 - 9 = 12$ quarters. **(Use Strategy 3: Subtract whole from parts.)**

6. Choice C is correct. **(Use Strategy 17: Use the given information effectively.)**

Given: ▢▬   [1]

In order for a given figure to have been formed from [1], it must have the same number of shaded and unshaded squares.

Choice I has 8 unshaded and 6 shaded squares. Thus, it could *not* be formed from [1].

Choice II has 5 unshaded and 6 shaded squares. Thus, it could *not* be formed from [1].

Looking at Choices A through E, we see that the correct choice must be Choice C: III only.

7. Choice D is correct. $f(x + 2) = (x + 2 - 1)^2 + (x + 2 - 2)^2 + (x + 2 - 3)^2 = (x + 1)^2 + x^2 + (x - 1)^2 = x^2 + 2x + 1 + x^2 + x^2 - 2x + 1 = 3x^2 + 2.$

8. Choice D is correct. The procedure, as described, can be summarized in the following table:

Given Container	−	Receiving Container	=	Excess to 50 cm³ Container
25 cm³	−	16 cm³	=	9 cm³
16 cm³	−	9 cm³	=	7 cm³
9 cm³	−	4 cm³	=	5 cm³
4 cm³	−	1 cm³	=	3 cm³
		Total	=	24 cm³

(Use Strategy 2: Remember the definition of percent.)

Thus, $\frac{24 \text{ cm}^3}{50 \text{ cm}^3} \times 100 = 48\%$ of the 50 cm³ container is full.

(Use Strategy 3: The whole equals the sum of its parts.)

So, $100\% - 48\% = 52\%$ of the 50 cm³ container is empty.

9. 10

Given: $ab = 40$ [1]

$\frac{a}{b} = \frac{5}{2}$ [2]

(Use Strategy 13: Find unknowns by multiplication.)

Multiplying [2] by $2b$, we get

$$2b\left(\frac{a}{b}\right) = \left(\frac{5}{2}\right)2b$$

$$2a = 5b$$

$$\frac{2a}{5} = b \qquad [3]$$

Substitute [3] into [1]. We have

$$ab = 40$$

$$a\left(\frac{2a}{5}\right) = 40$$

$$\frac{2a^2}{5} = 40 \qquad [4]$$

Multiplying $\boxed{4}$ by $\frac{5}{2}$, we get

$$\frac{5}{2}\left(\frac{2a^2}{5}\right) = (40)\frac{5}{2}$$

$$a^2 = 100$$

$$\sqrt{a^2} = \sqrt{100}$$

$$a = \pm 10$$

Since we were given that a is positive, we have $a = 10$.

10. 20

(Use Strategy 2: Translate from words to algebra.)

$$
\begin{array}{lll}
\text{Given: Stephanie's earnings} & = \$x & \boxed{1} \\
\text{Stephanie's time} & = 10 \text{ hours} & \boxed{2} \\
\text{Evelyn's earnings} & = \$y & \boxed{3} \\
\text{Evelyn's time} & = 20 \text{ hours} & \boxed{4} \\
x + y = 60 & & \boxed{5}
\end{array}
$$

We know that hourly wage $= \dfrac{\text{total earnings}}{\text{total hours}}$ $\boxed{6}$

Substituting $\boxed{1}$ and $\boxed{2}$ into $\boxed{6}$, we get

Stephanie's hourly wage $= \dfrac{\$x}{10 \text{ hours}}$ $\boxed{7}$

Substituting $\boxed{3}$ and $\boxed{4}$ into $\boxed{6}$, we get

Evelyn's hourly wage $= \dfrac{\$y}{20 \text{ hours}}$ $\boxed{8}$

We are told that they have the same hourly wage. Using $\boxed{7}$ and $\boxed{8}$, we have

$$\frac{\$x}{10 \text{ hours}} = \frac{\$y}{20 \text{ hours}}$$

$$\frac{x}{10} = \frac{y}{20} \qquad \boxed{9}$$

$$\overset{2}{\cancel{20}}\left(\frac{x}{\cancel{10}}\right) = \left(\frac{y}{\cancel{20}}\right)\cancel{20}$$

$$2x = y \qquad \boxed{10}$$

Substituting $\boxed{10}$ into $\boxed{5}$, we get

$$x + 2x = 60$$

$$3x = 60$$

$$x = 20$$

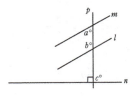

11. 270

$$
\begin{array}{ll}
\text{Given:} \quad m \parallel l & \boxed{1} \\
\qquad\quad p \perp n & \boxed{2}
\end{array}
$$

From $\boxed{1}$ we get that $a + b = 180$, $\qquad \boxed{3}$ because when 2 lines are parallel, the interior angles on the same side of the transversal are supplementary.

From $\boxed{2}$ we get that $c = 90$ $\qquad \boxed{4}$ because perpendicular lines form right angles.

(Use Strategy 13: Find unknowns by addition.)

Add $\boxed{3}$ and $\boxed{4}$. We have

$$
\begin{aligned}
a + b + c &= 180 + 90 \\
&= 270
\end{aligned}
$$

12. 5

We know area of circle $= \pi(\text{radius})^2$ $\qquad \boxed{1}$

$$
\begin{array}{ll}
\text{Given:} \quad \text{radius of larger circle} = r + 3 & \boxed{2} \\
\qquad\qquad \text{radius of small circle} = r & \boxed{3}
\end{array}
$$

Substitute $\boxed{2}$ into $\boxed{1}$. We have

Area of larger circle $= \pi(r + 3)^2$ $\qquad \boxed{4}$

(Use Strategy 4: Remember classic expressions.)

$$(r + 3)^2 = r^2 + 6r + 9 \qquad \boxed{5}$$

Substitute $\boxed{5}$ into $\boxed{4}$. We have

Area of larger circle $= \pi(r^2 + 6r + 9)$ $\boxed{6}$

Substituting $\boxed{3}$ into $\boxed{1}$, we get

Area of small circle $= \pi r^2$ $\qquad \boxed{7}$

(Use Strategy 13: Find unknowns by subtraction.)

Subtract $\boxed{7}$ from $\boxed{6}$. We have

Difference of areas

$$= \pi(r^2 + 6r + 9) - \pi r^2 \qquad \boxed{8}$$

Given: Difference of areas $= 21\pi$ $\qquad \boxed{9}$

Substitute $\boxed{9}$ into $\boxed{8}$. We have

$$21\pi = \pi(r^2 + 6r + 9) - \pi r^2 \qquad \boxed{10}$$

(Use Strategy 13: Find unknowns by division.)

$$\frac{21\pi}{\pi} = \frac{\pi(r^2 + 6r + 9)}{\pi} - \frac{\pi r^2}{\pi}$$

$$21 = r^2 + 6r + 9 - r^2$$

$$21 = 6r + 9$$

$$12 = 6r$$

$$2 = r \qquad \boxed{11}$$

Substitute $\boxed{11}$ into $\boxed{2}$. We get

$$\text{radius of larger circle} = 2 + 3$$

$$= 5$$

13. 2

(Use Strategy 17: Use the given information effectively.)

The most favorable conditions for Team C would be the following:

	FIRST PLACE	SECOND PLACE	THIRD PLACE
	(8 points)	(4 points)	(2 points)
EVENT ③	TEAM C (4 + 8 = 12)	TEAM A (12 + 4 = 16)	TEAM B (12 + 2 = 14)
EVENT ④	TEAM C (12 + 8 = 20)	TEAM B (14 + 4 = 18)	TEAM A (16 + 2 = 18)

Thus, Team C has a total of 4 + 8 + 8 = 20 points after 2 more games. Team A has 12 + 4 + 2 = 18 points. Team B has 12 + 2 + 4 = 18 points. Thus, Team C will have to play at least 2 more games.

14. 2

(Use Strategy 17: Use the given information effectively.)

Since $x = 15$, then

$$m\angle LMN = 90$$

$$m\angle JNK = 75$$

$$m\angle KNM = 15$$

$$m\angle JNM = 90$$

Thus, the figure, with dashed line extensions, follows:

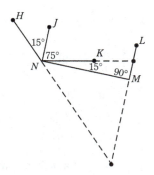

Clearly $\overleftrightarrow{JN} \| \overleftrightarrow{ML}$ and $\overleftrightarrow{JN}$ will not intersect $\overleftrightarrow{ML}$. $\overrightarrow{NK}$ and $\overrightarrow{NH}$ will each intersect $\overleftrightarrow{ML}$ exactly once. Thus, there will be exactly 2 more additional points of intersection.

15. 20

(Use Strategy 2: Translate from words to algebra.)

We are told that

$$a = b + \frac{10}{100}b = \frac{11}{10}b \qquad \boxed{1}$$

$$ac = bd + \frac{32}{100}bd = \frac{33}{25}bd \qquad \boxed{2}$$

In equation $\boxed{2}$, reduce $\frac{32}{100}$ to $\frac{8}{25}$. Then combine:

$$ac = \frac{25}{25}bd + \frac{8}{25}bd = \frac{33}{25}bd$$

(Use Strategy 13: Find unknowns by division.)

We divide $\boxed{2}$ by a

$$c = \frac{33}{25}\left(\frac{b}{a}\right)d \qquad \boxed{3}$$

(Use Strategy 13: Find unknowns by multiplication.)

Multiply $\boxed{1}$ by $\frac{1}{b}$, giving

$$\frac{a}{b} = \frac{11}{10}$$

or $\qquad \dfrac{b}{a} = \dfrac{10}{11} \qquad \boxed{4}$

Substituting $\boxed{4}$ into $\boxed{3}$, we get

$$c = \frac{33}{25}\left(\frac{10}{11}\right)d$$

$$c = \frac{\overset{3}{\cancel{33}}}{25} \times \frac{\overset{2}{\cancel{10}}}{\cancel{11}}d$$

$$c = \frac{6}{5}d$$

or $\qquad c = d + \frac{1}{5}d$

or $\qquad c = d + \frac{20}{100}d$

Thus, c is 20 percent greater than d.

Alternate method:

(Use Strategy 7: Use numerics.) Let $b = 100$, $d = 10$. **(Use Strategy 2: Translate words to algebra.)**

Then $a = \frac{10}{100}(100) + 100 = 110$

$ac = \frac{32}{100}bd + bd = \frac{32}{100}(100)d + 100d$

$110c = 32d + 100d = 132d \qquad \boxed{1}$

$c = \frac{x}{100}d + d = \frac{xd + 100d}{100} = \frac{(x+100)d}{100} \qquad \boxed{2}$

Divide $\boxed{1}$ by 110:

$$c = \frac{132}{110}d \qquad \boxed{3}$$

Compare $\boxed{3}$ with $\boxed{2}$:

$$\frac{132}{110} = \frac{x+100}{100}$$

$$\frac{13{,}200}{110} = x + 100$$

$$120 = x + 100$$

$$20 = x$$

16. $\frac{1}{48}$ or .020 or .021

(Use Strategy 2: Translate from words to algebra.)

Given: $\qquad$ 1 gross = 12 dozen
$\qquad\qquad\qquad$ 1 dozen = 12 (eggs)

Thus,

1 gross of eggs $= (12 \text{ dozen})\left(\dfrac{12 \text{ eggs}}{\text{dozen}}\right)$

$\qquad\qquad\qquad = 144$ eggs

3 eggs, expressed as a fraction of a gross $= \dfrac{3}{144}$

$\qquad\qquad\qquad\qquad\qquad\qquad\qquad\qquad = \dfrac{1}{48}$

17. 5

We are given that

$\qquad$ Volume of 1 brick $= 40$ cubic inches $\qquad \boxed{1}$

Volume of the final pile of bricks $= 8{,}000$ cubic inches $\qquad \boxed{2}$

(Use Strategy 3: The whole equals the sum of its parts.) Logically, we know the number of layers in the final pile of bricks

$= \dfrac{\text{volume of the final pile of bricks}}{\text{volume of each layer of bricks}} \qquad \boxed{3}$

From the diagram in the question, we see that

$\qquad$ 1 layer of bricks $= 40$ bricks $\qquad \boxed{4}$

Thus, by using $\boxed{1}$ and $\boxed{4}$, we know that the volume of each layer of bricks

$\qquad =$ volume of 1 brick

$\qquad\qquad \times$ number of bricks in 1 layer

$\qquad = 40$ cubic inches $\times 40$

$\qquad = 1{,}600$ cubic inches $\qquad \boxed{5}$

Substituting $\boxed{2}$ and $\boxed{5}$ into $\boxed{3}$, the number of layers in the final pile of bricks

$$= \frac{8{,}000 \text{ cubic inches}}{1{,}600 \text{ cubic inches}}$$

(Use Strategy 19: Factor and reduce.)

$$= \frac{8 \times 1{,}000}{16 \times 100}$$

$$= \frac{8 \times 10 \times \cancel{100}}{8 \times 2 \times \cancel{100}}$$

$$= \frac{10}{2} = 5$$

18. 108

(Use Strategy 11: Use new definitions carefully.)

The first few 3-digit numbers are 100, 101, 102, 103, 104, etc.

Clearly, the smallest possible 3-digit number in which no digit is repeated is $x = 102$.

From the definition of y, y must be 210.

$\qquad$ Thus, $y - x = 210 - 102 = 108$

EXPLANATORY ANSWERS FOR PRACTICE TEST 4
Section 7: **Critical Reading**

1. Choice D is correct. See **Sentence Completion Strategy 4**. The words "in addition to" constitute a *support indicator*. We can then expect an additional favorable word to complete the sentence. That word is "dapper" (Choice D), meaning "neatly dressed." Choices A, B, C, and E are incorrect because they do not make good sense in the sentence.

2. Choice D is correct. See **Sentence Completion Strategy 2**. Examine the first word of each choice. We eliminate Choice C, motor, and Choice E, reciprocal, because motor curbs and reciprocal curbs do not make good sense in the opening clause of the sentence. Now we consider Choice A, profitable...drive, which does not make sense in the sentence; Choice B, flexible...produce, which also does *not* make sense in the sentence; and Choice D, import...ship, which *does* make sense in the sentence.

3. Choice A is correct. See **Sentence Completion Strategy 1 and 3**. The UNICEF reports must demonstrate something. If you tried to complete the sentence *before* looking at the five choices, you might have come up with words like "results" or "effects." Therefore, Choice A is correct. The other choices are incorrect because they do not make sense in the sentence.

4. Choice D is correct. See **Sentence Completion Strategy 2**. Examine the first word of each choice. We can eliminate Choice B since the word "advantages" means "benefit" or "gain." Neither of these words fits into the context of the sentence. The first words of Choices A, C, D, and E *do* work in the sentence, so now look at the second words. Within the context, the other choices do not work as well as Choice D. This is a reminder that knowing as many of the vocabulary words provided in this book as possible will benefit you to no end.

5. Choice B is correct. If you used **Sentence Completion Strategy 3**, you might have come up with any of the following words:

   refused   repudiated   shunned

   These words all mean about the same as the correct Choice B, rejected.

6. Choice D is correct. See lines 5–7: "...individual attention...which creates...more efficient learning environment." Note that what is contained in Choice A (flexible standards), Choice B (parent and child), Choice C (travel time), and Choice E (conditions in learning environment) are all mentioned, but an effective learning condition is not based upon them.

7. Choice B is correct. Choice A is addressed in lines 10–12. Choice C is addressed in lines 14–16. Choice D is addressed in lines 13–14 (varied feedback). Choice E is addressed in lines 10–12 (diversity). For Choice B, multicultural ways are not mentioned in the passage, and even though there may be many students, those students may all be of one culture.

8. Choice E is correct. The criterion (a rule for evaluating something) that appears in both passages is the learning experience. See lines 5–7: "There is also the individual attention that the parent or tutor can give the student, which creates a better and more efficient learning environment..." and lines 10–12: "In many studies, it was shown that students benefit...".

9. Choice C is correct. What is missing in homeschooling is the interaction with other students, as stated in lines 10–14. Thus interaction with students on a regular basis would fill the void. Note in Choice B, the "occasional" work may not be adequate. In Choice D, spending one-half time at home and one-half time in school may make it difficult and awkward to coordinate or

relate what is taught or developed at home and what is taught or developed at school.

10. Choice D is correct. See lines 16–17: "The cry for freedom...the birth of the New Man." Choice A is incorrect. Although the author may agree to what the choice says, he does not actually state or imply such. Choice B is incorrect because nowhere in the passage is Choice B stated or implied. Choice C is incorrect. See lines 25–27: "African American literature rejects the despair and cynicism; it is a literature of realistic hope and life affirmation." Choice E is incorrect. See lines 36–37: "...life should not be a sedate waltz or foxtrot..."

11. Choice A is correct. See lines 32–36: "...life should be vivacious, exuberant, wholesomely uninhibited...and man should be loving." Choice B is incorrect because nowhere does the passage indicate that Choice B is true. Choice C is incorrect. Although lines 35–36 state that "life should be passionately lived and man should be loving," these lines do not mean that people should demonstrate their passions in public whenever the urge is there. Choice D is incorrect. Nowhere does the passage recommend Choice D. Choice E is incorrect. Although lines 6–10 state that "In African American literature...there is...the rage of the oppressed," the passage does not state or imply that the descendants of those who have been oppressed should be enraged.

12. Choice D is correct. Let us consider each item. Item I is not true because the passage nowhere expresses the need for *nonviolent* opposition to racism. Item II is true. See lines 42–46: "African American literature in America is... finding deep joy in his humanity." Item III is true. See lines 31–36: "African American literature is a statement...and man should be loving." Accordingly, only Items II and III are true. Therefore, Choice D is correct, and Choices A, B, C, and E are incorrect.

13. Choice B is correct. See lines 23–27: "Like the spirituals...realistic hope and life-affirmation." Choice A is incorrect. See lines 6–15: "In African American literature...the burden of protest." Although an indication of anger is present in the passage, it is not dominant. Moreover, nowhere in the passage is there evidence of vindictiveness. Choice C is incorrect because forgiveness and charity are not referred to in the passage. Choice D is incorrect. See lines 23–30: "Like the spirituals...goodness will prevail." Choice E is incorrect. Although the passage refers to *grief* in line 14 and also *cruelty* in line 38, grief and cruelty do not represent the tone of the passage.

14. Choice E is correct. See lines 20–23: "...for a human world."

15. Choice C is correct. It can be seen from the context of the sentence that the word "iniquity" must mean something bad (the word is preceded by "investigation" and is in contrast to "an investigation...potential godliness," which appears in the same sentence). See also **Reading Comprehension Strategy 5**.

16. Choice A is correct. See lines 71–72: "...as Dr. Skinner argues, that one can extrapolate from pigeons to people..." Choice B is incorrect because, though Skinner agrees that introspection may be of some use (lines 14–18), nowhere does the article indicate that he suggests wide use of the introspective method. Choice C is incorrect since Skinner, so the author says (lines 74–76), "has not satisfactorily rebutted the basic criticism that behaviorism 'is scientistic rather than scientific.'" Choice D is incorrect because lines 81–82 state that "Skinner predicts...impending disaster." Choice E is incorrect because there is nothing in the passage to indicate this statement. Incidentally, this point of view (Choice E) is held by Noam Chomsky of linguistics fame.

17. Choice E is correct. Choice A is incorrect; see lines 83–89: "Two key concepts...not so reassuring." Choice B is incorrect. See lines 11–14: "...an earlier stage of...influence of mentalism." Choice C is incorrect. See lines 60–64: "It is a veritable... to external stimuli." Choice D is incorrect since mentalism evolved before methodological and radical behaviorism. See lines 10–17: "What such people...its possible usefulness." Choice E is correct. The passage, from line 63 to the end, brings out weaknesses in Skinner's presentation.

18. Choice D is correct. Skinner, in lines 26–27, says "…few would contend that behavior is 'endlessly malleable.'" Also, see lines 35–42: "Contingencies of reinforcement…likely to occur." In effect, Skinner is saying that behavior cannot always, by plan or design, be altered or influenced; behavior must depend, to some extent, on the element of chance.

19. Choice D is correct. Skinner is known for his experiments with pigeons. Also, rats have been used frequently by behaviorists in experimentation. See lines 65–73. In addition, see lines 37–38: "In both natural…is crucial." The other choices are not relevant to Darwin or his work.

20. Choice A is correct. From the context in the rest of the sentence where "extrapolate" appears, Choice A fits best. Note that the word "extrapolate" is derived from the Latin "extra" (outside) and "polire" (to polish). See also **Reading Comprehension Strategy 5**.

21. Choice C is correct. Choice A is incorrect because Choice A is true according to lines 14–15. Choice B is incorrect because Choice B is true according to lines 65–70. Choice C is correct because Choice C is *not* true according to lines 68–72. Choice D is incorrect because Choice D is true according to lines 10–18. Choice E is incorrect because Choice E is true according to lines 57–61.

22. Choice B is correct. Choice A is incorrect; see lines 19–22: "…to those who object…Skinner expresses puzzlement." Choice B is correct because Skinner, a radical behaviorist, though believing that environmental influences are highly important in shaping human behavior, nevertheless states in lines 35–38: "Contingencies of reinforcement…[are] crucial." Operant conditioning is, according to behaviorists, a vital aspect of learning. Choice C is incorrect. Although Skinner accepts introspection (lines 16–18) as part of his system, nowhere does he place primary importance on introspection. Choice D is incorrect. Though Skinner may agree with this choice, nowhere in the passage does he state or imply this opinion. Choice E is incorrect.

The word "malleable" means capable of being shaped or formed—from the Latin "malleare," meaning "to hammer." The quote in the stem of the question says, in effect, that few people would say that behavior can always be shaped.

23. Choice A is correct. I is correct; see lines 79–80. II is incorrect; don't be fooled by what is in lines 76–79. It does not refer to *scientistic* areas. III is incorrect; see lines 76–79.

24. Choice D is correct. Given the context of the sentence and the sentences preceding and succeeding it, "veritable" means "true." One may also note the "ver" in "veritable" and may associate that with the word "verify," which means "to prove to be true." This is the association strategy, which can be used to figure out clues to meanings of words. See also **Reading Comprehension Strategy 5**.

EXPLANATORY ANSWERS FOR PRACTICE TEST 4
Section 8: Math

When a specific Math Strategy is referred to in the solution, study that strategy, which you will find in "19 Math Strategies."

1. Choice D is correct.

   Given:

   $$5x = 3 \quad \boxed{1}$$

   (Use Strategy 12: Try not to make tedious calculations.)

   Method 1: Add 3 to both sides of $\boxed{1}$

   $$5x + 3 = 6 \quad \boxed{2}$$

   (Use Strategy 13: Find unknown expressions by multiplication.)

   Square both sides of $\boxed{2}$

   $$(5x + 3)^2 = 36 \quad \boxed{3}$$

   This method involves simpler arithmetic (no fractions) than the next method.

   Method 2: This method is a bit slower. Solve $\boxed{1}$ for x to get

   $$x = \frac{3}{5} \quad \boxed{4}$$

   Using $\boxed{4}$, calculate the unknown expression.

   $$(5x + 3)^2 =$$

   $$\left[5\left(\frac{3}{5}\right) + 3\right]^2 =$$

   $$(3 + 3)^2 =$$

   $$6^2 = 36$$

2. Choice C is correct. **(Use Strategy 2: Translate from words to algebra.)**

   $$\text{Let } 8n = \text{number of boys} \quad \boxed{1}$$

   $$7n = \text{number of girls} \quad \boxed{2}$$

   The ratio of $\dfrac{\text{boys}}{\text{girls}} = \dfrac{8n}{7n} = \dfrac{8}{7}$ and the given condition is satisfied.

(Use Strategy 3: The whole equals the sum of its parts.)

Total number of students = boys plus girls $\boxed{3}$

Substituting $\boxed{1}$ and $\boxed{2}$ into $\boxed{3}$, we get

Total number of students = $8n + 7n = 15n$ $\boxed{4}$

$\boxed{4}$ is a multiple of 15

Choices A, B, D, and E are multiples of 15:

(A) $15 = 15 \times 1$

(B) $45 = 15 \times 3$

(D) $60 = 15 \times 4$

(E) $90 = 15 \times 6$

Only Choice C, 50, is *not* a multiple of 15.

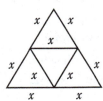

3. Choice A is correct. **(Use Strategy 2: Translate from words to algebra.)**

   Let x = side of smaller triangles

   Thus, $3x$ = perimeter of each smaller triangle

   $6x$ = perimeter of largest triangle

   We are told

   $$3x = 1$$

   $$x = \frac{1}{3} \quad \boxed{1}$$

   (Use Strategy 13: Find unknowns by multiplication.)

   Multiplying $\boxed{1}$ by 6, we get

   $$6x = 2 = \text{perimeter of largest triangle}$$

4.   Choice D is correct. **(Use Strategy 3: The whole equals the sum of its parts.)**

Amount left = Original amount − Amount spent
$$= \$15.25 - \$7.50$$
$$= \$7.75$$

5.   Choice A is correct. **(Use Strategy 17: Use the given information effectively.)**

Given:
$$\frac{4^3 + 4^3 + 4^3 + 4^3}{4^y} = 4$$
$$\frac{4(4^3)}{4^y} = 4$$
$$\frac{4^4}{4^y} = 4$$
$$4^{4-y} = 4^1 \qquad \boxed{1}$$

In $\boxed{1}$ each expression has base 4. Since the expressions are equal, the exponents must also be equal. Thus,
$$4 - y = 1$$
$$-y = -3$$
$$y = 3$$

6.   Choice C is correct. Cross multiply:
$$2(2x^2 + x - 5) = x^3 + 4x^2$$
$$4x^2 + 2x - 10 = x^3 + 4x^2$$

(Use Strategy 1: Cancel quantities to make the problem simpler.)

Cancel $4x^2$ from both sides:
$2x - 10 = x^3$ and so $x^3 - 2x = -10$.

7.   Choice D is correct. **(Use Strategy 2: Translate from words to algebra.)** Perhaps the best way to answer this type of question is to write a description of what occurs:

starting point	100	$t = 0$
after 8 yrs	200	$t = 8$
after 8 × 2 yrs	400	$t = 16$
after 8 × 3 yrs	800	$t = 24$

You can see that this is represented as population $= 100 \times 2^{\frac{t}{8}}$.

8.   Choice D is correct. **(Use Strategy 6: Know how to manipulate inequalities.)** $2x + 5 < 5$

Subtracting 5 from both sides, $2x < 0$.
Dividing both sides by 2, $x < 0$.
Since x must be a positive integer, that is, x is greater than 0, the solution set is the empty set or { }.

9.   Choice B is correct. $(a^b)^b = x^b = y$. $(a^b)^b = a^{b^2} = y$

10.   Choice A is correct. **(Use Strategy 17: Use the given information effectively.)** To find the coordinates of the intersection point, we must first solve the equations $y = x - 1$ and $2x + 5y = 9$. In the equation $2x + 5y = 9$, we substitute $y = x - 1$. We obtain

$$2x + 5(x - 1) = 9$$

Thus

$$2x + 5x - 5 = 9$$

and

$$7x = 14$$
$$x = 2$$

From the first equation, $y = x - 1$, so $y = 2 - 1 = 1$. Thus $x = 2$ and $y = 1$ so the coordinates of the point are (2,1).

11.   Choice B is correct. **(Use Strategy 13: Subtract equations.)** Using $C = md + t$, if the business trip were increased by 5 days, $C' = m(d + 5) + t$. Subtracting equations, $C' - C = m(d + 5) + t - (md + t) = md + 5m + t - md - t = 5m$.

12.   Choice D is correct. **(Use Strategy 6: Know how to manipulate inequalities.)** Since $x - 3 \le 0$,
$x \le 3$. Choice D represents x on the number line.

13.   Choice E is correct. **(Use Strategy 13: Find unknowns by multiplication and subtraction.)** If we multiply the first equation by 2, we get:
$8x - 6y = 18$. Subtract this equation from the second equation in the question:

$$8x + ky = 19$$
$$-[(8x - 6y) = 18]$$
$$\overline{ky + 6y = 1}$$

If $k = -6$, we would have: $-6y + 6y = 0 = 1$, which is not true. Thus if $k = -6$, there will be no solution to the equations.

14. Choice D is correct.

$$\text{Given:} \qquad r = 7a \qquad \boxed{1}$$
$$5w = 7a \qquad \boxed{2}$$
$$\text{From } \boxed{2} \text{ we get } w = \frac{7a}{5} \qquad \boxed{3}$$

(Use Strategy 13: Find unknowns by subtracting.)

Subtract $\boxed{3}$ from $\boxed{1}$. We get

$$r - w = 7a - \frac{7a}{5}$$
$$= \frac{35a}{5} - \frac{7a}{5}$$
$$r - w = \frac{28a}{5}$$

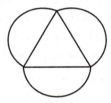

15. Choice C is correct. **(Use Strategy 3: The whole equals the sum of its parts.)**

Total area = area of triangle + 3(area of semicircle) $\boxed{1}$

Given: Radius of each semicircle = 2 $\boxed{2}$

From $\boxed{2}$ we know each diameter = 4

Thus, the triangle has three equal sides of length 4 and is equilateral. $\boxed{3}$

We know: Area of equilateral triangle $= \dfrac{S^2\sqrt{3}}{4}$ $\boxed{4}$

Area of semicircle $= \dfrac{\pi r^2}{2}$ $\boxed{5}$

Substituting $\boxed{4}$ and $\boxed{5}$ into $\boxed{1}$, we get

Total area
$$= \frac{S^2\sqrt{3}}{4} + 3\left(\frac{\pi r^2}{2}\right) \boxed{6}$$

Substituting $\boxed{2}$ and $\boxed{3}$ into $\boxed{6}$, we get

$$\text{Total area} = \frac{4^2\sqrt{3}}{4} + 3\left(\frac{\pi (2)^2}{2}\right)$$
$$= \frac{16\sqrt{3}}{4} + 3\left(\frac{4\pi}{2}\right)$$
$$\text{Total area} = 4\sqrt{3} + 6\pi$$

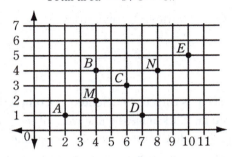

16. Choice E is correct. **(Use Strategy 8: When all choices must be tested, start with E and work backward.)**

In the diagram above, we have plotted each of the points given in the choices. From the diagram, it is clear that

$$MC = CN = NE$$

Thus, since $ME = MC + CN + NE$, then
$$3NE = ME$$

as required, so that point E is the answer.

As you read these Explanatory Answers, you are advised to refer to "16 Verbal (Critical Reading) Strategies."

1. Choice E is correct. See **Sentence Completion Strategy 2**. Examine the first word of each choice. We eliminate Choice B, expedite (meaning "to speed up"), and Choice D, drench (which means "to wet through and through"), because the parked vehicles do not expedite or drench the flow of traffic. Now we consider Choices A, C, and E. The only word pair that makes good sense in the sentence is Choice E, impede...flout. The word "impede" means "to block up or obstruct," and the word "flout" means "scoff at or show contempt for."

2. Choice E is correct. See **Sentence Completion Strategy 2**. Examine the first word of each choice. We eliminate Choice D, recording, because social media is not recording. Now we consider the four remaining word pairs. The only choice that makes sense in the sentence is Choice E, booming...leisure.

3. Choice E is correct. See **Sentence Completion Strategy 2**. Look at the first word of each choice. The first words in Choices B, C, and D do not sound right when inserted in the first blank of the sentence. Thus we can eliminate Choices B, C, and D. Now try both words in the remaining choices, A and E. Choice E is the only one that works.

4. Choice E is correct. See **Sentence Completion Strategy 1**. Try each choice. The *apparent contradiction* of scarcity amidst plenty characterizes even a rich country in a time of inflation.

5. Choice C is correct. See **Sentence Completion Strategy 1**. The word "generate" means "to produce."

6. Choice D is correct. See **Sentence Completion Strategy 1**. Try each choice. The sentence implies that he retained the belief until his death; hence he was *stubborn* or unchanging in his belief.

7. Choice C is correct. Throughout Passage 1, the author is bringing out the fact that violence is widely shown and well received on television. For example: Line 1: "Violence is alive and well on television." Lines 4–5: "...as a result of...the horror of violence." Lines 12–13: "Violence on TV...in recent years." Although Choices A, B, D, and E are discussed or implied in the passage, none of these choices summarizes the content of the passage as a whole. Therefore, these choices are incorrect.

8. Choice D is correct. See lines 29–33: "The simple gunfight...for hundreds to die." Accordingly, Choice A is incorrect. Choices B and C are incorrect because there is no violence shown on the screen in these choices. Choice E is incorrect because the violence of a double murder by a jealous husband hardly compares in intensity with the violence of a bomb exploding in a bus carrying a busload of innocent civilians.

9. Choice E is correct. See lines 29–33: "The simple gunfight of the past...for hundreds to die." Choice A is incorrect because, though the statement may be true, the passage nowhere indicates that TV programs generally are different today from what they were a generation ago. Choice B is incorrect. See lines 37–38: "Many people...the way of the world." Choice C is incorrect. See lines 12–14: "Violence on TV... and more action series," Choice D is incorrect. See lines 38–41: "It is high time...viewing televised violence." No mention is made in the passage that broadcasting stations are doing

any warning or notifying about the dangers of showing violence on TV.

10. Choice C is correct. The cruelties of our prison system are referred to in lines 63–69: "…just as so much of our current violence is socially acceptable…classes of society." The horrors of our prisons were current at the time the author wrote this article, and they are current today. The violence spoken about in Choices A, B, and D were socially acceptable at the time they occurred in the past. The question asks for an illustration of *current* "socially acceptable" violence. Accordingly, Choices A, B, and D are incorrect. Choice E, though it refers to current violence, is *not* socially acceptable. See lines 70–74: "What we have now…familiar 'crime in the streets.'" Therefore, Choice E is incorrect.

11. Choice A is correct. The author's definition of violence is extremely broad—including not only acts of force but also the social infliction of harm as in "exploiting women and children in textile mills and sweatshops" (lines 58–59). Passage 2 refers to acts of violence other than those expressed in Choices B and C. Therefore, these choices are incorrect. One could easily cite illegal conduct on the part of the government or a citizen that is *not* of a violent nature. Therefore, Choice D is incorrect. The FBI could conceivably commit an act of violence. The author would not condone this. See lines 77–79: "But now, too, official violence…numerous sympathizers." Therefore, Choice E is incorrect.

12. Choice A is correct. The author of Passage 2 describes current violence as "acceptable neither to the authorities nor to the victims" [Item I]. Item II and Item III are not indicated anywhere in the passage. Therefore, only Choice A is correct.

13. Choice C is correct. It indicates the only form of violence that is *not* mentioned in Passage 2. The following line references are given to indicate that Choices A, B, D, and E represent forms of violence that *are* mentioned in the passage. Choice A—see lines 48–49: "…the lawlessness… during Reconstruction and after." Choice B—see lines 43–44: "…our almost…against the Indians." Choice D—see lines 44–45: "…and all the others…Mexicans in Texas." Choice E—see lines 46–47: "…the pervasive violence of slavery."

14. Choice D is correct. The author, throughout Passage 2, expresses opposition to any type of violence—whether one engages in violence or tolerates it. Therefore, Choice D is correct because the author would not approve of the violence practiced by football players. Accordingly, Choices A, B, C, and E are incorrect. Although Choice A involves violence, a person who tries to prevent a mugging is obviously opposed to the violence of the mugger.

15. Choice C is correct. In the context of the rest of the sentence in lines 2–3 and line 46, you can see that "pervasiveness" means "seeping through." Note that Choice A is incorrect because in lines 2–3, the word "variety" is used and would be redundant if repeated. This is also true for Choice B, "televised." See also **Reading Comprehension Strategy 5**.

16. Choice E is correct. See lines 17–18, 24, and 31.

17. Choice A is correct. The author's attitude in Passage 2 is that violence as shown historically is "a way of life." Thus if violence were curtailed on television, it would still exist elsewhere.

18. Choice D is correct. Only the author of Passage 1 proposes a direct resolution—lines 38–41. The statement in Choice A is *true*. See lines 70–89. The statement in Choice B is *true*. See lines 29–31 and 43–69. The statement in Choice C is *true*. The author of Passage 1 primarily talks only about televised violence, whereas the author of Passage 2 refers to corporate violence, air pollution, prison violence, and the like. The statement in Choice E is *true*. See lines 38–41 and lines 42–69.

19. Choice C is correct. It can be seen from what precedes in Passage 2 that "polarization" must mean some very great opposing viewpoints. Don't be lured into Choice A, thinking that polarization has to do with electrical current; or Choice B, that polarization has to do with governments, since society was discussed; or Choice D, that polarization has to do with religion, because religious dissent was mentioned; or Choice E, that polarization has to do with climate, because we have a North and South Pole. See also **Reading Comprehension Strategy 5**.

EXPLANATORY ANSWERS FOR PRACTICE TEST 4
Section 10: Writing

1. **(C)** We are concerned here with the apostrophe use with a singular name ending in "s." We are also concerned with improper ellipsis. In Choice A, "James's" is correct but we must either say "to read than *the prose style* of James Joyce" or "to read than James Joyce's." In Choice B, "Jame's" is incorrect—his name is not "Jame." Choice C is correct. Choices D and E are incorrect for the same reason that Choice A is incorrect—improper ellipsis.

2. **(C)** Choice A is incorrect because in a "neither… nor" construction, the number of the verb is determined by the "nor" subject noun ("followers"). Since "followers" is plural, the verb must be plural ("know"). Choices B, D, and E are incorrect for the same reason. Moreover, Choice B is incorrect for another reason: the correlative form is "neither…nor"—not "neither…or." Choice C is correct.

3. **(A)** Choice A is correct. Choice B's passive verb ("was requested") interferes with the flow of the sentence. "It occurred" in Choice C is unnecessary. Choice D is too wordy for what has to be expressed. Choice E changes the meaning of the original sentence—the students did not "insist."

4. **(B)** Choice A is indirect. Choice B is correct. In Choice C, "as a prize" repeats unnecessarily the "Nobel Prize." Choice D is much too awkward. Choice E is incorrect—the scientists did not discover viruses.

5. **(D)** The important thing is not "promptness"; accordingly, Choice A is wrong. Choice B is incorrect because it is not the "loan" that must be returned. In Choice C, "You must understand" is unnecessary. Choice D is correct. Choice E changes the meaning of the original sentence.

6. **(E)** Choice A is incorrect. There has to be a parallel construction; "in addition to a fine scholastic record" has to relate to Bob, such as, "in addition to his having a fine scholastic record…" Choice E does relate to Bob, as it says "as well as a superior student." Choice B would be correct if it were preceded and followed by a dash in order to set the choice off from what goes before and after. Choice C is wrong because one does not "amass a scholastic record." Choice D is a complete sentence within a sentence, thus creating a run-on sentence situation. Choice E is correct.

7. **(E)** In Choice A, the use of the passive verb ("were trounced") reduces the effectiveness of expression. Choice B is indirect. Choice C is incorrect. The word "they" has an antecedent problem: Who won the World Series, the "odds" or the "Mets"? In Choice D, "which is hard to believe" is unnecessary. Choice E is correct.

8. **(E)** In Choice A, "are necessary" is not only not necessary, but the expression makes the sentence ungrammatical with the additional complete predicate ("are necessary"). There are too many "ands" in Choice B. Some grammarians call this an "Andy" sentence. In Choice C, "And other fruit…peaches" is an incomplete sentence—also called a sentence fragment. Choice D also suffers from sentence fragmentation: "Such as pineapples and peaches." Choice E is correct.

9. **(B)** In Choice A, it is unidiomatic to say "instruction to learn." Choice B is correct. Choice C is too wordy. Choice D is not as direct as Choice B. Choice E suffers from lack of parallelism.

10. **(B)** Choice A is incorrect because the words "not only…but also" should be placed immediately before the parallel terms, which are "of the Ways

and Means Committee" and "of the Finance Committee." Choice B is correct. Choice C is too wordy. Choice D is incorrect because it does not place the words "not only…but also" directly before the parallel terms. Choice E is awkward.

11. **(D)** Choices A and B are incorrect because they both contain an unnecessary shift from active to passive voice, resulting in awkwardness. Choice C is too wordy. Choice D is correct. Choice E is a complete sentence, making the original a run-on sentence.

12. **(B)** Choice A is incorrect because "Buckley" and "him" are in apposition with "candidates," the subject of the sentence. Since the subject is nominative, the appositive must also be nominative; hence "he" should be used instead of "him." Choice B is correct. Choice C uses "him" incorrectly for "he." The use of the passive voice ("were made") makes Choice D unnecessarily indirect. Choice E omits "two candidates for the U.S. Senate" which is necessary to the meaning of the sentence.

13. **(E)** Choices A and B are incorrect because they are both misplaced as modifiers—it is not clear who is the student. Choice C is a complete sentence, making the original sentence a run-on sentence. Choice D is incorrect because "being that" is poor English. Choice E is correct.

14. **(C)** Choice A is not correct because the word "who" is incorrectly used; as the object of the preposition, the word "whom" should be used. In Choice B, the second "to" is redundant. Choice C is correct. Choice D uses the word "who" instead of "whom." Choice E does not include a reference to the book, which is in the original sentence.

SAT PRACTICE
TEST 5

ANSWER SHEET FOR PRACTICE TEST 5

Section 1

Begin your essay on this page. If you need more space, continue on the next page. Do not write outside of the essay box.

Continue on the next page if necessary.

Continuation of ESSAY Section 1 from previous page. Write below only if you need more space.

Start with number 1 for each new section. If a section has fewer questions than answer spaces, leave the extra answer spaces blank. Be sure to erase any errors or stray marks completely.

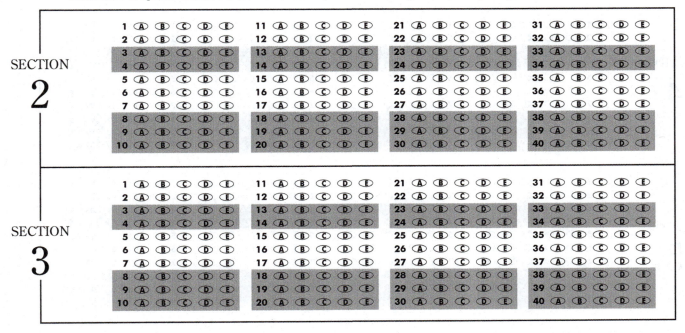

CAUTION Use the answer spaces in the grids below for Section 2 or Section 3 only if you are told to do so in your test book.

Student-Produced Responses ONLY ANSWERS ENTERED IN THE CIRCLES IN EACH GRID WILL BE SCORED. YOU WILL NOT RECEIVE CREDIT FOR ANYTHING WRITTEN IN THE BOXES ABOVE THE CIRCLES.

Start with number 1 for each new section. If a section has fewer questions than answer spaces, leave the extra answer spaces blank. Be sure to erase any errors or stray marks completely.

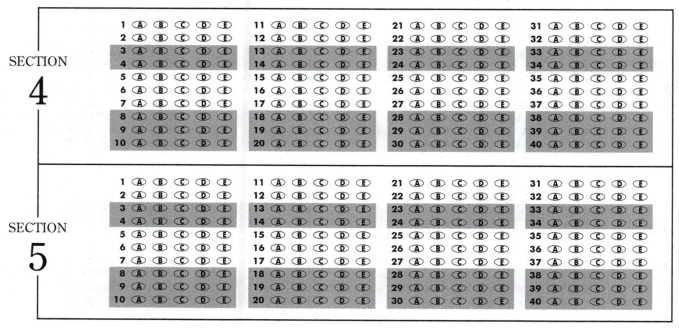

SECTION 4

SECTION 5

CAUTION Use the answer spaces in the grids below for Section 2 or Section 3 only if you are told to do so in your test book.

Student-Produced Responses

ONLY ANSWERS ENTERED IN THE CIRCLES IN EACH GRID WILL BE SCORED. YOU WILL NOT RECEIVE CREDIT FOR ANYTHING WRITTEN IN THE BOXES ABOVE THE CIRCLES.

Start with number 1 for each new section. If a section has fewer questions than answer spaces, leave the extra answer spaces blank. Be sure to erase any errors or stray marks completely.

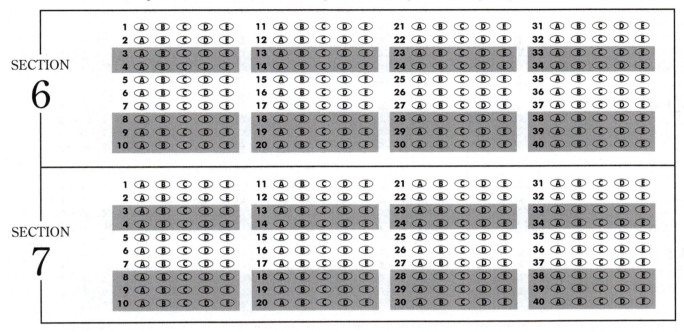

CAUTION Use the answer spaces in the grids below for Section 2 or Section 3 only if you are told to do so in your test book.

Student-Produced Responses

ONLY ANSWERS ENTERED IN THE CIRCLES IN EACH GRID WILL BE SCORED. YOU WILL NOT RECEIVE CREDIT FOR ANYTHING WRITTEN IN THE BOXES ABOVE THE CIRCLES.

Start with number 1 for each new section. If a section has fewer questions than answer spaces, leave the extra answer spaces blank. Be sure to erase any errors or stray marks completely.

SECTION

8

1 Ⓐ Ⓑ Ⓒ Ⓓ Ⓔ	11 Ⓐ Ⓑ Ⓒ Ⓓ Ⓔ	21 Ⓐ Ⓑ Ⓒ Ⓓ Ⓔ	31 Ⓐ Ⓑ Ⓒ Ⓓ Ⓔ
2 Ⓐ Ⓑ Ⓒ Ⓓ Ⓔ	12 Ⓐ Ⓑ Ⓒ Ⓓ Ⓔ	22 Ⓐ Ⓑ Ⓒ Ⓓ Ⓔ	32 Ⓐ Ⓑ Ⓒ Ⓓ Ⓔ
3 Ⓐ Ⓑ Ⓒ Ⓓ Ⓔ	13 Ⓐ Ⓑ Ⓒ Ⓓ Ⓔ	23 Ⓐ Ⓑ Ⓒ Ⓓ Ⓔ	33 Ⓐ Ⓑ Ⓒ Ⓓ Ⓔ
4 Ⓐ Ⓑ Ⓒ Ⓓ Ⓔ	14 Ⓐ Ⓑ Ⓒ Ⓓ Ⓔ	24 Ⓐ Ⓑ Ⓒ Ⓓ Ⓔ	34 Ⓐ Ⓑ Ⓒ Ⓓ Ⓔ
5 Ⓐ Ⓑ Ⓒ Ⓓ Ⓔ	15 Ⓐ Ⓑ Ⓒ Ⓓ Ⓔ	25 Ⓐ Ⓑ Ⓒ Ⓓ Ⓔ	35 Ⓐ Ⓑ Ⓒ Ⓓ Ⓔ
6 Ⓐ Ⓑ Ⓒ Ⓓ Ⓔ	16 Ⓐ Ⓑ Ⓒ Ⓓ Ⓔ	26 Ⓐ Ⓑ Ⓒ Ⓓ Ⓔ	36 Ⓐ Ⓑ Ⓒ Ⓓ Ⓔ
7 Ⓐ Ⓑ Ⓒ Ⓓ Ⓔ	17 Ⓐ Ⓑ Ⓒ Ⓓ Ⓔ	27 Ⓐ Ⓑ Ⓒ Ⓓ Ⓔ	37 Ⓐ Ⓑ Ⓒ Ⓓ Ⓔ
8 Ⓐ Ⓑ Ⓒ Ⓓ Ⓔ	18 Ⓐ Ⓑ Ⓒ Ⓓ Ⓔ	28 Ⓐ Ⓑ Ⓒ Ⓓ Ⓔ	38 Ⓐ Ⓑ Ⓒ Ⓓ Ⓔ
9 Ⓐ Ⓑ Ⓒ Ⓓ Ⓔ	19 Ⓐ Ⓑ Ⓒ Ⓓ Ⓔ	29 Ⓐ Ⓑ Ⓒ Ⓓ Ⓔ	39 Ⓐ Ⓑ Ⓒ Ⓓ Ⓔ
10 Ⓐ Ⓑ Ⓒ Ⓓ Ⓔ	20 Ⓐ Ⓑ Ⓒ Ⓓ Ⓔ	30 Ⓐ Ⓑ Ⓒ Ⓓ Ⓔ	40 Ⓐ Ⓑ Ⓒ Ⓓ Ⓔ

SECTION

9

1 Ⓐ Ⓑ Ⓒ Ⓓ Ⓔ	11 Ⓐ Ⓑ Ⓒ Ⓓ Ⓔ	21 Ⓐ Ⓑ Ⓒ Ⓓ Ⓔ	31 Ⓐ Ⓑ Ⓒ Ⓓ Ⓔ
2 Ⓐ Ⓑ Ⓒ Ⓓ Ⓔ	12 Ⓐ Ⓑ Ⓒ Ⓓ Ⓔ	22 Ⓐ Ⓑ Ⓒ Ⓓ Ⓔ	32 Ⓐ Ⓑ Ⓒ Ⓓ Ⓔ
3 Ⓐ Ⓑ Ⓒ Ⓓ Ⓔ	13 Ⓐ Ⓑ Ⓒ Ⓓ Ⓔ	23 Ⓐ Ⓑ Ⓒ Ⓓ Ⓔ	33 Ⓐ Ⓑ Ⓒ Ⓓ Ⓔ
4 Ⓐ Ⓑ Ⓒ Ⓓ Ⓔ	14 Ⓐ Ⓑ Ⓒ Ⓓ Ⓔ	24 Ⓐ Ⓑ Ⓒ Ⓓ Ⓔ	34 Ⓐ Ⓑ Ⓒ Ⓓ Ⓔ
5 Ⓐ Ⓑ Ⓒ Ⓓ Ⓔ	15 Ⓐ Ⓑ Ⓒ Ⓓ Ⓔ	25 Ⓐ Ⓑ Ⓒ Ⓓ Ⓔ	35 Ⓐ Ⓑ Ⓒ Ⓓ Ⓔ
6 Ⓐ Ⓑ Ⓒ Ⓓ Ⓔ	16 Ⓐ Ⓑ Ⓒ Ⓓ Ⓔ	26 Ⓐ Ⓑ Ⓒ Ⓓ Ⓔ	36 Ⓐ Ⓑ Ⓒ Ⓓ Ⓔ
7 Ⓐ Ⓑ Ⓒ Ⓓ Ⓔ	17 Ⓐ Ⓑ Ⓒ Ⓓ Ⓔ	27 Ⓐ Ⓑ Ⓒ Ⓓ Ⓔ	37 Ⓐ Ⓑ Ⓒ Ⓓ Ⓔ
8 Ⓐ Ⓑ Ⓒ Ⓓ Ⓔ	18 Ⓐ Ⓑ Ⓒ Ⓓ Ⓔ	28 Ⓐ Ⓑ Ⓒ Ⓓ Ⓔ	38 Ⓐ Ⓑ Ⓒ Ⓓ Ⓔ
9 Ⓐ Ⓑ Ⓒ Ⓓ Ⓔ	19 Ⓐ Ⓑ Ⓒ Ⓓ Ⓔ	29 Ⓐ Ⓑ Ⓒ Ⓓ Ⓔ	39 Ⓐ Ⓑ Ⓒ Ⓓ Ⓔ
10 Ⓐ Ⓑ Ⓒ Ⓓ Ⓔ	20 Ⓐ Ⓑ Ⓒ Ⓓ Ⓔ	30 Ⓐ Ⓑ Ⓒ Ⓓ Ⓔ	40 Ⓐ Ⓑ Ⓒ Ⓓ Ⓔ

SECTION

10

1 Ⓐ Ⓑ Ⓒ Ⓓ Ⓔ	11 Ⓐ Ⓑ Ⓒ Ⓓ Ⓔ	21 Ⓐ Ⓑ Ⓒ Ⓓ Ⓔ	31 Ⓐ Ⓑ Ⓒ Ⓓ Ⓔ
2 Ⓐ Ⓑ Ⓒ Ⓓ Ⓔ	12 Ⓐ Ⓑ Ⓒ Ⓓ Ⓔ	22 Ⓐ Ⓑ Ⓒ Ⓓ Ⓔ	32 Ⓐ Ⓑ Ⓒ Ⓓ Ⓔ
3 Ⓐ Ⓑ Ⓒ Ⓓ Ⓔ	13 Ⓐ Ⓑ Ⓒ Ⓓ Ⓔ	23 Ⓐ Ⓑ Ⓒ Ⓓ Ⓔ	33 Ⓐ Ⓑ Ⓒ Ⓓ Ⓔ
4 Ⓐ Ⓑ Ⓒ Ⓓ Ⓔ	14 Ⓐ Ⓑ Ⓒ Ⓓ Ⓔ	24 Ⓐ Ⓑ Ⓒ Ⓓ Ⓔ	34 Ⓐ Ⓑ Ⓒ Ⓓ Ⓔ
5 Ⓐ Ⓑ Ⓒ Ⓓ Ⓔ	15 Ⓐ Ⓑ Ⓒ Ⓓ Ⓔ	25 Ⓐ Ⓑ Ⓒ Ⓓ Ⓔ	35 Ⓐ Ⓑ Ⓒ Ⓓ Ⓔ
6 Ⓐ Ⓑ Ⓒ Ⓓ Ⓔ	16 Ⓐ Ⓑ Ⓒ Ⓓ Ⓔ	26 Ⓐ Ⓑ Ⓒ Ⓓ Ⓔ	36 Ⓐ Ⓑ Ⓒ Ⓓ Ⓔ
7 Ⓐ Ⓑ Ⓒ Ⓓ Ⓔ	17 Ⓐ Ⓑ Ⓒ Ⓓ Ⓔ	27 Ⓐ Ⓑ Ⓒ Ⓓ Ⓔ	37 Ⓐ Ⓑ Ⓒ Ⓓ Ⓔ
8 Ⓐ Ⓑ Ⓒ Ⓓ Ⓔ	18 Ⓐ Ⓑ Ⓒ Ⓓ Ⓔ	28 Ⓐ Ⓑ Ⓒ Ⓓ Ⓔ	38 Ⓐ Ⓑ Ⓒ Ⓓ Ⓔ
9 Ⓐ Ⓑ Ⓒ Ⓓ Ⓔ	19 Ⓐ Ⓑ Ⓒ Ⓓ Ⓔ	29 Ⓐ Ⓑ Ⓒ Ⓓ Ⓔ	39 Ⓐ Ⓑ Ⓒ Ⓓ Ⓔ
10 Ⓐ Ⓑ Ⓒ Ⓓ Ⓔ	20 Ⓐ Ⓑ Ⓒ Ⓓ Ⓔ	30 Ⓐ Ⓑ Ⓒ Ⓓ Ⓔ	40 Ⓐ Ⓑ Ⓒ Ⓓ Ⓔ

Section 1

| **Time:** 25 Minutes—Turn to page 525 of your answer sheet to write your ESSAY. |

The purpose of the essay is to have you show how well you can express and develop your ideas. You should develop your point of view, logically and clearly present your ideas, and use language accurately.

You should write your essay on the lines provided on your answer sheet. You should not write on any other paper. You will have enough space if you write on every line and if you keep your handwriting to a reasonable size. Make sure that your handwriting is legible to other readers.

You will have 25 minutes to write an essay on the assignment below. *Do not write on any other topic. If you do so, you will receive a score of 0.*

Think carefully about the issue presented in the following excerpt and the assignment below.

> One of the main purposes of education is to get students excited about the "process" behind problem solving instead of rushing into an answer and just concentrating on the final result. Often students can extract something from a problem that leads to the answer. Students can relax and think more clearly when they concentrate on the game or the wonderful process, if you will, of thinking.
>
> –Adapted from G. Gruber, "A Superlative Guide to the Hows and Wise," Omni Magazine

Assignment: Do you agree with the above quote? In many cases, is the problem solver concerned just about getting an answer, and not about concentrating on the "process" to get the answer? Do you agree that by not having faith in the process, he or she often does not arrive at the solution? In answering these questions, describe in your own experience, why you agree or disagree and what rewards are lost or gained when you just concentrate on an answer without being aware of or interested in the process in arriving at the answer.DO NOT WRITE YOUR ESSAY IN YOUR TEST BOOK. You will receive credit only for what you write on your answer sheet.

BEGIN WRITING YOUR ESSAY ON PAGE 525 OF THE ANSWER SHEET.

If you finish before time is called, you may check your work on this section only.
Do not turn to any other section in the test.

Section 2

Time: 25 Minutes – Turn to Section 2 (page 527) of your answer sheet to answer the questions in this section. 20 Questions

Directions: For this section, solve each problem and decide which is the best of the choices given. Fill in the corresponding circle on the answer sheet. You may use any available space for scratchwork.

Notes:

1. The use of a calculator is permitted.

2. All numbers used are real numbers.

3. Figures that accompany problems in this test are intended to provide information useful in solving the problems. They are drawn as accurately as possible EXCEPT when it is stated in a specific problem that the figure is not drawn to scale. All figures lie in a plane unless otherwise indicated.

4. Unless otherwise specified, the domain of any function f is assumed to be the set of all real numbers x for which $f(x)$ is a real number.

REFERENCE INFORMATION

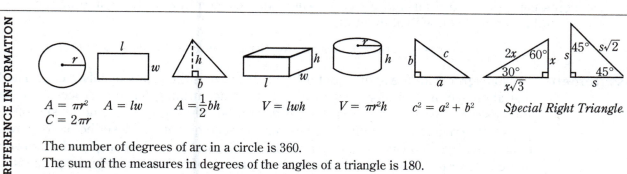

$A = \pi r^2$ $A = lw$ $A = \frac{1}{2}bh$ $V = lwh$ $V = \pi r^2 h$ $c^2 = a^2 + b^2$ *Special Right Triangle.*
$C = 2\pi r$

The number of degrees of arc in a circle is 360.
The sum of the measures in degrees of the angles of a triangle is 180.

$$\begin{array}{r} 5\,9\,\triangle \\ -2\,9\,3 \\ \hline \square\,9\,7 \end{array}$$

1. In the subtraction problem above, what digit is represented by the □?

(A) 0
(B) 1
(C) 2
(D) 3
(E) 4

2. If $\frac{a-b}{b} = \frac{1}{2}$, find $\frac{a}{b}$.

(A) $\frac{9}{2}$

(B) $\frac{7}{2}$

(C) $\frac{5}{2}$

(D) $\frac{1}{2}$

(E) $\frac{3}{2}$

GO ON TO THE NEXT PAGE ➤

Number of pounds of force	Height object is raised
3	6 feet
6	12 feet
9	18 feet

3. In a certain pulley system, the height an object is raised is equal to a constant c times the number of pounds of force exerted. The table above shows some pounds of force and the corresponding height raised. If a particular object is raised 15 feet, how many pounds of force were exerted?

(A) $3\frac{3}{4}$

(B) 7

(C) $7\frac{1}{2}$

(D) 8

(E) 11

P

5. The above line is marked with 12 points. The distance between any 2 adjacent points is 3 units. Find the total number of points that are more than 19 units away from point P.

(A) 2
(B) 3
(C) 4
(D) 5
(E) 6

4. If $\frac{y}{3}$, $\frac{y}{4}$, and $\frac{y}{7}$ represent integers, then y could be

(A) 42
(B) 56
(C) 70
(D) 84
(E) 126

6. Given $(a + 2, a - 2) = [a]$ for all integers a, $(6, 2) =$

(A) [3]
(B) [4]
(C) [5]
(D) [6]
(E) [8]

GO ON TO THE NEXT PAGE ➤

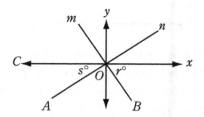

Note: Figure is not drawn to scale.

7. If $mB \perp nA$ in the figure above and COx is a straight line, find the value of $r + s$.

    (A) 180
    (B) 135
    (C) 110
    (D) 90
    (E) The answer cannot be determined from the information given.

9. One out of 4 students at Ridge High School studies German. If there are 2,800 students at the school, how many students do *not* study German?

    (A) 2,500
    (B) 2,100
    (C) 1,800
    (D) 1,000
    (E) 700

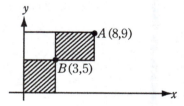

8. Points *A* and *B* have coordinates as shown in the figure above. Find the combined area of the two shaded rectangles.

    (A) 20
    (B) 26
    (C) 32
    (D) 35
    (E) 87

10. The cost of a limousine rental is $y. A group of high school seniors intend to share the cost of their prom ride by paying $40 each. If 6 more friends go, everyone will have to pay only $25 each. What is the value of $y?

    (A) $400
    (B) $600
    (C) $800
    (D) $1,000
    (E) $1,200

GO ON TO THE NEXT PAGE ➤

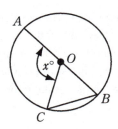

11. If *AB* is a diameter of circle *O* in the figure above, and *CB* = *OB*, then $\frac{x}{6}$ =

(A) 60
(B) 30
(C) 20
(D) 10
(E) 5

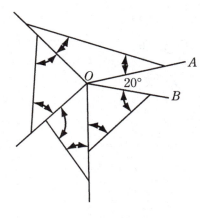

13. If ∠*AOB* = 20° in the figure above and *O* is a common vertex of the four triangles, find the sum of the measures of the marked angles in the triangles.

(A) 380
(B) 560
(C) 740
(D) 760
(E) 920

12. A camping supply store is selling an $80 tent for $64. If a different tent has a list price of $200 and is discounted at $1\frac{1}{2}$ times the percent discount on the $80 tent, what would its selling price be?

(A) $90
(B) $105
(C) $120
(D) $140
(E) $160

14. Some integers in set X are odd.

If the statement above is true, which of the following must also be true?

(A) If an integer is odd, it is in set X.
(B) If an integer is even, it is in set X.
(C) All integers in set X are odd.
(D) All integers in set X are even.
(E) Not all integers in set X are even.

GO ON TO THE NEXT PAGE ➤

15. If $|y + 3| < 3$, then

   (A) $-6 < y < 0$
   (B) $3 < y$
   (C) $0 < y < 3$
   (D) $y = -1$
   (E) $y = -2$

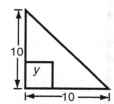

16. In the figure above, the area of the square is equal to $\frac{1}{5}$ the area of the triangle. Find the value of y, the side of the square.

   (A) 2
   (B) 4
   (C) 5
   (D) $2\sqrt{5}$
   (E) $\sqrt{10}$

17. A certain printer can print at the rate of 80 characters per second, and there is an average (arithmetic mean) of 2,400 characters per page. If the printer continued to print at this rate, how many *minutes* would it take to print an *M*-page report?

   (A) $\dfrac{M}{30}$
   (B) $\dfrac{M}{60}$
   (C) $\dfrac{M}{2}$
   (D) $\dfrac{2}{M}$
   (E) $\dfrac{60}{M}$

18. A certain satellite passed over Washington, D.C., at midnight on Friday. If the satellite completes an orbit every 5 hours, when is the next day that it will pass over Washington, D.C., at midnight?

   (A) Monday
   (B) Wednesday
   (C) Friday
   (D) Saturday
   (E) Sunday

GO ON TO THE NEXT PAGE ➤

19. The price of a car is reduced by 30 percent. The resulting price is reduced by 40 percent. The two reductions are equal to one reduction of

    (A) 28%
    (B) 42%
    (C) 50%
    (D) 58%
    (E) 70%

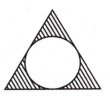

20. In the figure above, the circle is inscribed in the equilateral triangle. If the diameter of the circle is 2, what is the total shaded area?

    (A) $3\sqrt{3} - \pi$

    (B) $3\sqrt{3} - 4\pi$

    (C) $3\sqrt{3} - \frac{3\pi}{2}$

    (D) $6\sqrt{3} - \frac{3\pi}{2}$

    (E) $108 - \pi$

STOP

If you finish before time is called, you may check your work on this section only.
Do not turn to any other section in the test.

Take a 5 minute break

before starting section 3

Section 3

Time: 25 Minutes – Turn to Section 3 (page 527) of your answer sheet to answer the questions in this section. 20 Questions

Directions: For this section, solve each problem and decide which is the best of the choices given. Fill in the corresponding circle on the answer sheet. You may use any available space for scratchwork.

Notes:

1. The use of a calculator is permitted.

2. All numbers used are real numbers.

3. Figures that accompany problems in this test are intended to provide information useful in solving the problems. They are drawn as accurately as possible EXCEPT when it is stated in a specific problem that the figure is not drawn to scale. All figures lie in a plane unless otherwise indicated.

4. Unless otherwise specified, the domain of any function f is assumed to be the set of all real numbers x for which $f(x)$ is a real number.

REFERENCE INFORMATION

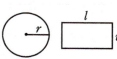   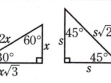

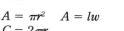

$A = \pi r^2$ $A = lw$ $A = \frac{1}{2}bh$ $V = lwh$ $V = \pi r^2 h$ $c^2 = a^2 + b^2$ *Special Right Triangle.*
$C = 2\pi r$

The number of degrees of arc in a circle is 360.
The sum of the measures in degrees of the angles of a triangle is 180.

---

1. After giving $5 to Greg, David has $25. Greg now has $\frac{1}{5}$ as much as David does. How much did Greg start with?

   (A) $0
   (B) $5
   (C) $7
   (D) $10
   (E) $15

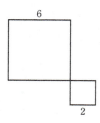

2. The figure above shows two squares with sides as shown. What is the ratio of the perimeter of the larger square to that of the smaller?

   (A) 3 : 2   (D) 6 : 1
   (B) 2 : 1   (E) 9 : 1
   (C) 3 : 1

GO ON TO THE NEXT PAGE ➤

3. A car travels 1,056 feet in 12 seconds. In feet per second, what is the average speed of the car?

(A) 98.0
(B) 78.8
(C) 85.8
(D) 84.0
(E) 88.0

5. $2(w)(x)(-y) - 2(-w)(-x)(y) =$

(A) 0
(B) $-4wxy$
(C) $4wxy$
(D) $-4w^2x^2y^2$
(E) $2w^2x^2y^2$

4. If $2z + 1 + 2 + 2z + 3 + 2z = 3 + 1 + 2$, then $z + 4 =$

(A) 1
(B) 4
(C) 5
(D) 6
(E) 10

6. What is an expression for 5 times the sum of the square of x and the square of y?

(A) $5(x^2 + y^2)$
(B) $5x^2 + y^2$
(C) $5(x + y)^2$
(D) $5x^2 + y$
(E) $5(2x + 2y)$

GO ON TO THE NEXT PAGE ➤

7.   If p and q are positive integers, x and y are negative integers, and $p > q$ and $x > y$, which of the following must be less than zero?

I. $q - p$
II. qy
III. $p + x$

(A) I only
(B) III only
(C) I and II only
(D) II and III only
(E) I, II, and III

9.   If $y = 28j$, where j is any integer, then $\frac{y}{2}$ will always be

(A) even
(B) odd
(C) positive
(D) negative
(E) less than $\frac{y}{3}$

8.   If $a = 1$, $b = -2$ and $c = -2$, find the value of $\frac{b^2c}{(a - c)^2}$.

(A) $-\frac{8}{9}$
(B) $-\frac{2}{3}$
(C) $\frac{8}{9}$
(D) 8
(E) 9

10. If $3a + 4b = 4a - 4b = 21$, find the value of a.

(A) 3
(B) 6
(C) 21
(D) 42
(E) The answer cannot be determined from the information given.

GO ON TO THE NEXT PAGE >

11. If N is a positive integer, which of the following does *not* have to be a divisor of the sum of N, $6N$, and $9N$?

   (A) 1
   (B) 2
   (C) 4
   (D) 9
   (E) 16

13. If $p + pq$ is 4 times $(p - pq)$, which of the following has exactly one value? $(pq \neq 0)$

   (A) p
   (B) q
   (C) pq
   (D) $p + pq$
   (E) $p - pq$

12. If $x = 3a - 18$ and $5y = 3a + 7$, then find $5y - x$.

   (A) -11
   (B) 11
   (C) 18
   (D) 25
   (E) $6a - 11$

14. If $2 + \frac{1}{z} = 0$, then what is the value of $9 + 9z$?

   (A) $-\frac{9}{2}$
   (B) $-\frac{1}{2}$
   (C) 0
   (D) $\frac{9}{2}$
   (E) The answer cannot be determined from the information given.

GO ON TO THE NEXT PAGE ➤

15. How many times does the graph of $y = x^2$ intersect the graph of $y = x$?

   (A) 0
   (B) 1
   (C) 2
   (D) 3
   (E) 4

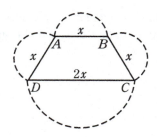

17. The quadrilateral $ABCD$ is a trapezoid with $x = 4$. The diameter of each semicircle is a side of the trapezoid. What is the sum of the lengths of the 4 dotted semicircles?

   (A) 8π
   (B) 10π
   (C) 12π
   (D) 14π
   (E) 20π

16. Let $wx = y$, where $wxy \neq 0$.

   If both x and y are multiplied by 6, then w is

   (A) multiplied by $\frac{1}{36}$

   (B) multiplied by $\frac{1}{6}$

   (C) multiplied by 1

   (D) multiplied by 6

   (E) multiplied by 36

18. $\frac{7x}{144}$ yards and $\frac{5y}{12}$ feet together equal how many inches?

   (A) $\frac{7x}{12} + \frac{5y}{4}$

   (B) $\frac{7x}{12} + 5y$

   (C) $\frac{7x}{4} + 5y$

   (D) $\frac{7x}{4} + 60y$

   (E) $7x + \frac{5}{4}y$

GO ON TO THE NEXT PAGE ➤

19. If $x < 0$ and $y < 0$, which of the following must always be positive?

I. $x \times y$
II. $x + y$
III. $x - y$

(A) I only
(B) I and II only
(C) I and III only
(D) II and III only
(E) I, II, and III

20. Given that $a + 3b = 11$ and a and b are positive integers, what is the largest possible value of a?

(A) 4
(B) 6
(C) 7
(D) 8
(E) 10

STOP

If you finish before time is called, you may check your work on this section only.
Do not turn to any other section in the test.

Section 4

> **Time:** 25 Minutes – Turn to Section 4 (page 528) of your answer sheet to answer the questions in this section. 24 Questions
>
> **Directions:** For each question in this section, select the best answer from among the choices given and fill in the corresponding circle on the answer sheet.

Each sentence below has one or two blanks, each blank indicating that something has been omitted. Beneath the sentence are five words or sets of words labeled A through E. Choose the word or set of words that, when inserted in the sentence, *best* fits the meaning of the sentence as a whole.

Example:

Hoping to _____ the dispute, negotiators proposed a compromise that they felt would be _____ to both labor and management.

(A) enforce...useful

(B) end...divisive

(C) overcome...unattractive

(D) extend...satisfactory

(E) resolve...acceptable

Ⓐ Ⓑ Ⓒ Ⓓ ⬤

---

1. Athens was ruled not by kings and emperors as was common among other _____ at the time, but by a citizenry, which _____ fully in the affairs of the city.

    (A) committees...cooperated
    (B) tribes...engaged
    (C) cities...revolutionized
    (D) populations...applied
    (E) societies...participated

2. Fossils are _____ in rock formations that were once soft and have _____ with the passage of time.

    (A) abolished...corresponded
    (B) interactive...communicated
    (C) preserved...hardened
    (D) created...revived
    (E) discounted...deteriorated

GO ON TO THE NEXT PAGE ➤

3. The social-cultural trends of the 1960s _____ not only the relative affluence of the postwar period but also the coming to maturity of a generation that was a product of that _____.

   (A) dominated...movement
   (B) reflected...prosperity
   (C) accentuated...depression
   (D) cautioned...decade
   (E) accepted...revolution

4. Rotation of crops helps to _____ soil fertility and soil usefulness for a long period of time.

   (A) conserve
   (B) disperse
   (C) employ
   (D) research
   (E) shorten

5. Some illnesses, such as malaria, that have been virtually eliminated in the United States are still _____ in many places abroad.

   (A) discussed
   (B) prevalent
   (C) scarce
   (D) unknown
   (E) hospitalized

6. With lack of _____, almost anyone can develop the disease we call alcoholism, just as any of us can contract pneumonia by _____ exposing ourselves to its causes.

   (A) advice...carefully
   (B) control...foolishly
   (C) opportunity...knowingly
   (D) sympathy...fortunately
   (E) conscience...happily

7. Use of air conditioners and other electrical apparatus had to be _____ that summer because of the _____ of the generating system.

   (A) postulated...reaction
   (B) curtailed...inefficiency
   (C) implemented...residuals
   (D) augmented...responsiveness
   (E) manipulated...intensity

8. The Bavarians consider beer their national beverage, yet at the same time they do not view it as a drink but rather as _____ bread—a staple food.

   (A) fresh
   (B) liquid
   (C) stale
   (D) bitter
   (E) costly

Each passage below is followed by questions on its content. Answer the questions on the basis of what is stated or implied in each passage and in any introductory material that may be provided.

Questions 9–10 are based on the following passage.

Despite the many categories of the historian, there are only two ages of man. The first age, the age from the beginning of recorded time to the present, is the age of the caveman. It is the age of war. It is today. The second age,
5 still only a prospect, is the age of civilized man. The test of civilized man will be represented by his ability to use his inventiveness for his own good by substituting world law for world anarchy. That second age is still within the reach of the individual in our time. It is not a part-time job,
10 however. It calls for total awareness, total commitment.

9. The title below that best expresses the ideas of this passage is:

   (A) The Historian at Work
   (B) The Dangers of All-Out War
   (C) The Power of World Anarchy
   (D) Mankind on the Threshold
   (E) The Decline of Civilization

GO ON TO THE NEXT PAGE ➤

10. The author's attitude toward the possibility of man's reaching an age of civilization is one of

   (A) limited hope
   (B) complete despair
   (C) marked uncertainty
   (D) complacency
   (E) anger

Questions 11–12 are based on the following passage.

Readers in the past seem to have been more patient than the readers of today. There were few diversions, and they had more time to read novels of a length that seems to us now inordinate. It may be that they were not irritated
5 by the digressions and irrelevances that interrupted the narration. But some of the novels that suffer from these defects are among the greatest that have ever been written. It is deplorable that on this account they should be less and less read.

11. The title below that best expresses the ideas of this passage is:

   (A) Defects of Today's Novels
   (B) Novel Reading Then and Now
   (C) The Great Novel
   (D) The Impatient Reader of Novels
   (E) Decline in Education

12. The author implies that

   (A) authors of the past did not use narration to any extent
   (B) great novels are usually long
   (C) digressions and irrelevances are characteristic of modern novels
   (D) readers of the past were more capable
   (E) people today have more pastimes than they formerly had

Questions 13–24 are based on the following passage.

This passage describes the relationship between age and income throughout various periods of American history and the effects this trend will have on the various population groups in the future.

The relationship between age and income is only casually appreciated by recent theories on the purported redistribution of income. It is known, of course, that the average person's income begins to decline after he is fifty-
5 five years of age, and that it declines sharply after sixty-five.

For example, as early as 1957, 58 percent of the spending units headed by persons sixty-five years and older earned less than $2,000. The relationship between old age and low income has often been considered a reflection of socio-
10 logical rather than economic factors—and therefore not to be included in any study of the economy. Actually, the character of the relationship is too integrated to be dissected. However, its significance is mounting with the increase in the number of older persons. The lowest-income groups
15 include a heavy concentration of older persons—in 1957, one-third of all spending units in the $0–$2,000 class were headed by persons sixty-five years and older; in 1948, it was 28 percent.

But in economic planning and social policy, it must be
20 remembered that, with the same income, the sixty-five-or-more spending unit will not spend less or need less than the younger spending unit, even though the pressure to save is greater than that on the young. The functional ethos of our economy dictates that the comparatively unproductive
25 old-age population should consume in accordance with their output rather than their requirements. Most social scientists have accepted these values; they have assumed that the minimum economic needs of the aged should be lower than those of the younger family. But it is precisely at retire-
30 ment that personal requirements and the new demands of leisure call for an even larger income if this period is to be something more enjoyable than a wait for death.

The relationship between age and income is seen most clearly in the unionized blue-collar worker. Except
35 for layoffs, which his seniority minimizes, and wage increments for higher productivity, awarded in many industries, his income range is determined by his occupation. But within that income range, the deciding factor is the man's age. After forty-five, the average worker who loses his
40 job has more difficulty in finding a new one. Despite his seniority, the older worker is likely to be downgraded to a lower-paying job when he can no longer maintain the pace set by younger men. This is especially true of unskilled and semiskilled workers.

45 The early and lower income period of a person's working life, during which he acquires his basic vocational skills, is most pronounced for the skilled, managerial, or professional worker. Then, between the ages of twenty-five and fifty, the average worker receives his peak earnings.
50 Meanwhile, his family expenses rise, and there are children to support and basic household durables to obtain. Although his family's income may rise substantially until he is somewhere between thirty-five and forty-five, per capita consumption may drop at the same time. For the growing,
55 working-class family, limited in income by the very nature of the breadwinner's occupation, the economic consequences of this parallel rise in age, income, and obligations are especially pressing. Many in the low-income classes are just as vulnerable to poverty during middle age, when they
60 have a substantially larger income, as in old age. As family obligations finally do begin declining, so does income. Consequently, most members of these classes never have an adequate income.

GO ON TO THE NEXT PAGE ➤

Thus we see that, for a time, increased age means
65 increased income, and therefore a probable boost in
income-tenth position. Although there are no extensive
data in the matter, it can be confidently asserted that the
higher income-tenths have a much greater representation
of spending units headed by persons aged thirty-five to fifty-
70 five than do the lower income-tenths. This is demonstrably
the case among the richest 5 percent of the consumer
units. The real question is: To what extent does distribution
of income-tenths within a certain age group deviate from
distribution of income-tenths generally? Although informa-
75 tion is not as complete as might be desired, there is more
than enough to make contingent generalizations. Detailed
data exist on income distribution by tenths and by age for
1935–36 and 1948, and on income-size distribution by age
for the postwar years. They disclose sharp income inequali-
80 ties within every age group (although more moderate in
the eighteen-to-twenty-five category)—inequalities that
closely parallel the overall national income pattern. The
implication is clear: A spending unit's income-tenth position
within his age category varies much less, if at all, and is
85 determined primarily by his occupation.

In other words, in America, the legendary land of
economic opportunity where any man can work his way
to the top, there is only slight income mobility outside
the natural age cycle of rising, then falling income. Since
90 most of the sixty-five-and-over age group falls into the
low-income brackets and constitutes the largest segment
of the $0–$2,000 income class, it is of obvious importance
in analyzing future poverty in the United States to examine
the growth trends of this group. The sixty-five-and-over
95 population composed 4.0 percent of the total population in
1900, 5.3 percent in 1930, and 8.4 percent in 1955 and will
reach an estimated 10.8 percent in 2010. Between 1900 and
2010, the total national population is expected to increase
276 percent, but those from ages forty-five through sixty-
100 four are expected to increase 416 percent, and those
sixty-five and over are expected to increase 672 percent.
Between 1990 and 2010, the population aged eighteen to
twenty-five is also expected to grow far more rapidly than
the middle-aged population. With the more rapid expansion
105 of these two low-income groups, the young and the old, in
the years immediately ahead, an increase in the extent of
poverty is probable.

13. According to the passage, most social scientists erroneously assume that

(A) personal expenses increase with the age of the spending unit

(B) the needs of the younger spending unit are greater than those of the aged

(C) the relationship between old age and low income is an economic and not a sociological problem

(D) members of the old-age population should consume in accordance with their requirements

(E) leisure living requires increased income

14. The word "appreciated" in line 2 most nearly means

(A) had artistic interest

(B) increased in value

(C) had curiosity

(D) had gratitude

(E) understood

15. It can be inferred that in the 35–55 age category

(A) income-tenth positions vary greatly

(B) income-tenth positions vary very little

(C) earning potential does not resemble the over-all national income pattern

(D) occupations have little bearing on the incometenth position

(E) there is great mobility between income-tenth positions

16. The author believes which of the following?

I. The aged will continue to increase as a percentage of the total population.

II. Income inequalities decrease with increasing age.

III. Managerial and professional workers have greater income mobility than blue-collar workers.

(A) I only

(B) II only

(C) III only

(D) I and II only

(E) I and III only

17. In the passage the term "functional ethos" in line 23 means

(A) national group

(B) ethnic influence

(C) prevailing ideology

(D) biased opinion

(E) practical ethics

18. The article states that the old-age population

   (A) has increased because of longer life expectancy
   (B) exceeds all but the 18–25 age group in growth rate
   (C) is well represented among the higher incometenths
   (D) is increasing as a percentage of the low income-tenths
   (E) has its greatest numbers among the middle-income group

19. According to the author, aside from the natural age cycle, economic opportunity in America is greatly limited by

   I. occupation
   II. income inequality within every group
   III. class

   (A) I only
   (B) II only
   (C) III only
   (D) I and III only
   (E) I and II only

20. The word "ethos" in line 23 most nearly means

   (A) the character of a group of people
   (B) economic–sociological ramifications
   (C) the productivity of all age groups
   (D) the management of large corporations
   (E) the social scientists who deal with the economy

21. According to the passage, the older, unionized blue-collar workers are

   (A) assured constant salary until retirement
   (B) given preference over new workers because of seniority
   (C) likely to receive downgraded salary
   (D) more susceptible to layoff after 40
   (E) encouraged to move to slower-paced but equalpaying jobs

22. The article states that the average worker finds that

   (A) as family obligations begin escalating, income begins to decline
   (B) he reaches economic stability at middle age because of the parallel rise in age, obligations, and income
   (C) he earns least while he is acquiring vocational skills
   (D) he reaches peak earning power between the ages of 40 and 65
   (E) his wage gains coincide with the decline of family needs

23. It can be inferred that one could most accurately predict a person's income from his or her

   (A) age
   (B) natural age cycle
   (C) occupation
   (D) occupation and age
   (E) seniority position

24. Which lines in the passage illustrate the author's sarcasm?

   (A) lines 19–23
   (B) lines 45–48
   (C) lines 64–66
   (D) lines 86–89
   (E) lines 104–107

STOP

If you finish before time is called, you may check your work on this section only.
Do not turn to any other section in the test.

Take a 1 minute break

before starting section 5

Section 5

Time: 25 Minutes – Turn to Section 5 (page 528) of your answer sheet to answer the questions in this section. 35 Questions
Directions: For each question in this section, select the best answer from among the choices given and fill in the corresponding circle on the answer sheet.

The following sentences test correctness and effectiveness of expression. Part of each sentence or the entire sentence is underlined; beneath each sentence are five ways of phrasing the underlined material. Choice A repeats the original phrasing; the other four choices are different. If you think the original phrasing produces a better sentence than any of the alternatives, select Choice A; if not, select one of the other choices.

In making your selection, follow the requirements of standard written English; that is, pay attention to grammar, choice of words, sentence construction, and punctuation. Your selection should result in the most effective sentence—clear and precise, without awkwardness or ambiguity.

EXAMPLE:

Laura Ingalls Wilder published her first book <u>and she was sixty-five years old then</u>.

(A) and she was sixty-five years old then

(B) when she was sixty-five

(C) at age sixty-five years old

(D) upon the reaching of sixty-five years

(E) at the time when she was sixty-five

1. <u>Joe couldn't wait for his return to his home</u> after being in the army for two years.

   (A) Joe couldn't wait for his return to his home
   (B) There was a strong desire on Joe's part to return home
   (C) Joe was eager to return home
   (D) Joe wanted home badly
   (E) Joe arranged to return home

2. Trash, filth, and muck are clogging the streets of the city, and <u>that's not all, the sidewalks are full of garbage</u>.

   (A) that's not all, the sidewalks are full of garbage
   (B) another thing: garbage is all over the sidewalks
   (C) the garbage cans haven't been emptied for days
   (D) in addition, garbage is lying all over the side-walks
   (E) what's more, the sidewalks have garbage that is lying all over them

GO ON TO THE NEXT PAGE ❯

3. Tired and discouraged by the problems of the day, <u>Myra decided to have a good dinner, and then lie down for an hour, and then go dancing</u>.

   (A) Myra decided to have a good dinner, and then lie down for an hour, and then go dancing
   (B) Myra decided to have a good dinner, lying down for an hour, and then dancing
   (C) Myra decided to have a good dinner, lie down for an hour, and then dancing
   (D) Myra decided to have a good dinner, lay down for an hour, and then dance
   (E) Myra decided to have a good dinner, lie down for an hour, and then go dancing

4. I am not certain <u>in respect to which courses</u> to take.

   (A) in respect to which courses
   (B) about which courses
   (C) which courses
   (D) as to the choice of which courses
   (E) for which courses I am

5. The people of the besieged village had no doubt <u>that the end was drawing near</u>.

   (A) that the end was drawing near
   (B) about the nearness of the end
   (C) it was clear that the end was near
   (D) concerning the end's being near
   (E) that all would die

6. There isn't a single man among us <u>who is skilled in the art of administering first aid</u>.

   (A) who is skilled in the art of administering first aid
   (B) who knows how to administer first aid
   (C) who knows the administration of first aid
   (D) who is a first-aid man
   (E) who administers first aid

7. This is the hole <u>that was squeezed through by the mouse</u>.

   (A) that was squeezed through by the mouse
   (B) that the mouse was seen to squeeze through
   (C) the mouse squeezed through it
   (D) that the mouse squeezed through
   (E) like what the mouse squeezed through

8. <u>She soundly fell asleep</u> after having finished the novel.

   (A) She soundly fell asleep
   (B) She decided to sleep
   (C) She went on to her sleep
   (D) She fell to sleep
   (E) She fell fast asleep

9. This is one restaurant I won't patronize because <u>I was served a fried egg by the waitress that was rotten</u>.

   (A) I was served a fried egg by the waitress that was rotten
   (B) I was served by the waitress a fried egg that was rotten
   (C) a fried egg was served to me by the waitress that was rotten
   (D) the waitress served me a fried egg that was rotten
   (E) a rotten fried egg was served to me by the waitress

10. Watching the familiar story unfold on the screen, he was glad <u>that he read the book with such painstaking attention to detail</u>.

    (A) that he read the book with such painstaking attention to detail
    (B) that he had read the book with such painstaking attention to detail
    (C) that he read the book with such attention to particulars
    (D) that he read the book with such intense effort
    (E) that he paid so much attention to the plot of the book

11. If anyone requested tea instead of coffee, <u>it was a simple matter to serve it to them</u> from the teapot at the rear of the table.

    (A) it was a simple matter to serve it to them
    (B) it was easy to serve them
    (C) it was a simple matter to serve them
    (D) it was a simple matter to serve it to him or to her
    (E) that person could serve himself or herself

GO ON TO THE NEXT PAGE ➤

The following sentences test your ability to recognize grammar and usage errors. Each sentence contains either a single error or no error at all. No sentence contains more than one error. The error, if there is one, is underlined and lettered. If the sentence contains an error, select the one underlined part that must be changed to make the sentence correct. If the sentence is correct, select Choice E. In choosing answers, follow the requirements of standard written English.

EXAMPLE:

The other delegates and him immediately
  A   B   C

accepted the resolution drafted by
                    D

the neutral states. No error.
              E

---

12. Since we first started high school, there has been
   A   B
great competition for grades between him and I
                           C   D
No error.
 E

13. Many people in the suburbs scarcely know about
                  A   B
the transportation problems that city dwellers
                      C
experience every day. No error.
        D   E

14. The subject of the evening editorial was us
                           A
instructors who have refused to cross the picket
          B   C
lines of the striking food service workers.
          D
No error.
 E

15. After the contestants had completed their speeches,
               A
I knew that the prize would go to he whom
                      B   C
the audience had given a standing ovation.
                D
No error.
 E

16. Falsely accused of a triple murder and imprisoned
                 A   B
for 19 years, Ruben (Hurricane) Carter, a former
boxer, was freed when a federal judge declared
         C
him guiltless. No error.
 D   E

17. Your math instructor would have been happy to
                         A
give you a makeup examination if you would have
                         B
gone to him and explained that your parents were
           C
hospitalized. No error.
   D   E

18. The child asking a difficult question was perhaps
      A   B
more shocking to the speaker than to the child's
                   C   D
parents. No error.
     E

19. Now that the pressure of selling the house and
 A   B
packing our belongings is over, we can look forward
                C   D
to moving to our new home in California.
No error.
 E

GO ON TO THE NEXT PAGE ➤

20. My grandmother <u>leads</u> a more active life <u>than</u>
          A   B
    many other retirees <u>who</u> are younger than <u>her</u>.
            C   D
    <u>No error</u>.
     E

21. I appreciate <u>your</u> offering <u>to change</u> my flat tire,
         A   B
    but I would <u>rather</u> have you drive me to my meeting
         C
    <u>so that</u> I will be on time. <u>No error</u>.
     D   E

22. The novelists <u>who</u> readers <u>choose</u> <u>as</u> their
         A   B C
    favorites are not always the <u>most</u> skilled writers.
                D
    <u>No error</u>.
     E

23. The problem of <u>how to deal</u> with all the
           A
    <u>mosquitoes</u> <u>disturb</u> many <u>residents</u> of the Tropics.
      B   C   D
    <u>No error</u>.
     E

24. The <u>family's</u> only son <u>could of</u> <u>gone</u> to college, but
      A   B C
    he decided to join the army after he graduated
    <u>from</u> high school. <u>No error</u>.
     D   E

25. <u>Yesterday</u> at the racetrack, many <u>people</u> were
      A   B
    <u>fearful of</u> betting on the horse <u>who</u> had fallen in the
      C   D
    last race. <u>No error</u>.
         E

26. If someone wants to buy <u>all</u> the antiques <u>that</u> I have
            A   B
    for the rummage sale, <u>then</u> <u>they</u> should make me
            C D
    a reasonable offer. <u>No error</u>.
          E

27. The man <u>who</u> Mexican authorities believe <u>to be</u>
        A   B
    the country's number one drug <u>trafficker</u> <u>has been</u>
                C   D
    <u>arrested</u> in a Pacific resort area. <u>No error</u>.
     D   E

28. <u>While</u> her mother was inside the house <u>talking</u> on
     A   B
    the phone, the child fell <u>off of</u> the <u>unscreened</u>
              C   D
    porch. <u>No error</u>.
       E

29. The racehorse ran <u>swifter</u> in <u>today's</u> race than he
           A   B
    <u>had run</u> in his practice sessions <u>last week</u>. <u>No</u>
                 error.
     C   D   E

GO ON TO THE NEXT PAGE ➤

Directions: The following passage is an early draft of an essay. Some parts of the passage need to be rewritten.

Read the passage and select the best answers for the questions that follow. Some questions are about particular sentences or parts of sentences and ask you to improve sentence structure or word choice. Other questions ask you to consider organization and development. In choosing answers, follow the requirements of standard written English.

Questions 30–35 refer to the following passage.

[1]Lampe-Pigeon is the charming name for a tall kerosene lamp, more than nine and one-half inches in height, created more than 100 years ago for use in the wine caves of France. [2]Its diminutive size makes it suitable for being used on a mantel, as a centerpiece in lieu of candles, or even bracketed as a wall sconce. [3]The brass lamp, which contains within it a glass globe, is still being handmade by the same company, though one is more likely to see it in a French home these days than in a cave. [4]And, of course, it would be a handy source of light in the event of a power failure. [5]Other antique-type lamps have been manufactured and they do not have the elegance or simplicity of the Lampe-Pigeon. [6]Many people prefer more modern lamps especially those of the halogen variety.

30. What should be done with sentence 3?

   (A) It should end after the word company.
   (B) It should remain as it is.
   (C) It should be placed after sentence 4.
   (D) It should follow sentence 1.
   (E) It should introduce the passage.

31. Sentence 1 would be more logical if it read, Lampe-Pigeon is the charming name for

   (A) a tall kerosene lamp, measuring more than nine and one-half inches, created…
   (B) a kerosene lamp, although more than nine and one-half inches tall, created…
   (C) a more than nine-and-one-half-inch-tall kerosene lamp, created…
   (D) a tall, more than nine-and-one-half inch kerosene lamp, created…
   (E) a kerosene lamp, of a height of more than nine and one-half inches, created…

32. The phrase for being used in sentence 2 should be

   (A) changed to for use
   (B) left as it is
   (C) changed to for one to use it
   (D) changed to to being used
   (E) changed to as a piece used on a mantel

33. Sentence 3 would read more smoothly were it to begin

   (A) The glass globed brass lamp…
   (B) The brass lamp with a glass globe…
   (C) The glass globe, found in the brass lamp…
   (D) as it does now
   (E) The brass lamp, inside of which is a glass globe…

34. What should be done with sentence 6?

   (A) It should be left as it is.
   (B) It should be deleted from the paragraph.
   (C) It should be placed before sentence 5.
   (D) It should be placed before sentence 4.
   (E) It should be placed before sentence 3.

35. In sentence 5,

   (A) "manufactured" should be changed to "produced"
   (B) "Lampe-Pigeon" should be changed to "lamp in question"
   (C) "elegance and simplicity" should be changed to "modernization"
   (D) "and" should be changed to "but"
   (E) the sentence should remain as it is

STOP

If you finish before time is called, you may check your work on this section only.
Do not turn to any other section in the test.

Section 6

Time: 25 Minutes – Turn to Section 6 (page 529) of your answer sheet to answer the questions in this section. 18 Questions

Directions: For this section, solve each problem and decide which is the best of the choices given. Fill in the corresponding circle on the answer sheet. You may use any available space for scratchwork.

Notes:

1. The use of a calculator is permitted.

2. All numbers used are real numbers.

3. Figures that accompany problems in this test are intended to provide information useful in solving the problems. They are drawn as accurately as possible EXCEPT when it is stated in a specific problem that the figure is not drawn to scale. All figures lie in a plane unless otherwise indicated.

4. Unless otherwise specified, the domain of any function f is assumed to be the set of all real numbers x for which $f(x)$ is a real number.

REFERENCE INFORMATION

 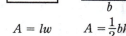 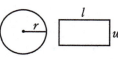 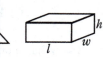

$A = \pi r^2$ $A = lw$ $A = \frac{1}{2}bh$ $V = lwh$ $V = \pi r^2 h$ $c^2 = a^2 + b^2$ *Special Right Triangle.*
$C = 2\pi r$

The number of degrees of arc in a circle is 360.
The sum of the measures in degrees of the angles of a triangle is 180.

1. In the equation $5\sqrt{x} + 14 = 20$, the value of x is

   (A) $\sqrt{\dfrac{6}{5}}$

   (B) $\dfrac{34^2}{25^2}$

   (C) $6 - \sqrt{5}$

   (D) $\dfrac{6}{5}$

   (E) $\dfrac{36}{25}$

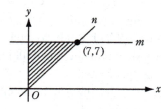

2. In the figure above, m is parallel to the x-axis. All of the following points lie in the shaded area EXCEPT

   (A) (4,3)
   (B) (1,2)
   (C) (5,6)
   (D) (4,5)
   (E) (2,5)

GO ON TO THE NEXT PAGE ❯

3. At Lincoln County High School, 36 students are taking either calculus or physics or both, and 10 students are taking both calculus and physics. If there are 31 students in the calculus class, how many students are in the physics class?

(A) 14
(B) 15
(C) 16
(D) 17
(E) 18

5. Which of the following is always true for real numbers a, b, and c?

I. $\sqrt{a+b} = \sqrt{a} + \sqrt{b}$
II. $a^2 + b^2 = (a + b)^2$
III. $a^b + a^c = a^{(b+c)}$

(A) I only
(B) II only
(C) III only
(D) I, II, and III
(E) neither I, II, or III

4. Mr. Simmons stated that if $a^2 > b^2$ where a and b are real, then it follows that $a > b$. Mr. Simmons's statement would be refuted if $(a,b) =$

(A) (2,3)
(B) (3,2)
(C) (4,−2)
(D) (−4,−2)
(E) (−2,−3)

Question 6 refers to the following:

$$R = \{x : 1 \geq x \geq -1\}$$

$$S = \{x : x \geq 1\}$$

6. The number of elements that is (are) common to both R and S is (are)

(A) 0
(B) 1
(C) 2
(D) 3
(E) infinite

7. Two lines in a plane are represented by $y = x - 1$ and $2x + 5y = 9$. The coordinates of the point at which the lines intersect are

(A) (2,1)
(B) (1,2)
(C) (2,5)
(D) (5,2)
(E) (3,5)

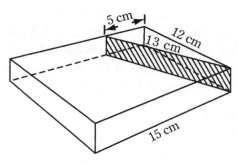

8. The rectangular box above has a rectangular dividing wall inside, as shown. The dividing wall has an area of 39 cm². What is the volume of the trapezoid-shaped box?

(A) 90 cm³
(B) 180 cm³
(C) 360 cm³
(D) 450 cm³
(E) 540 cm³

GO ON TO THE NEXT PAGE ➤

Directions: For Student-Produced Response questions 9–18, use the grids on the bottom of the answer sheet page on which you have answered questions 1-8.

Each of the remaining questions requires you to solve the problem and enter your answer by marking the circles in the special grid, as shown in the examples below. You may use any available space for scratchwork.

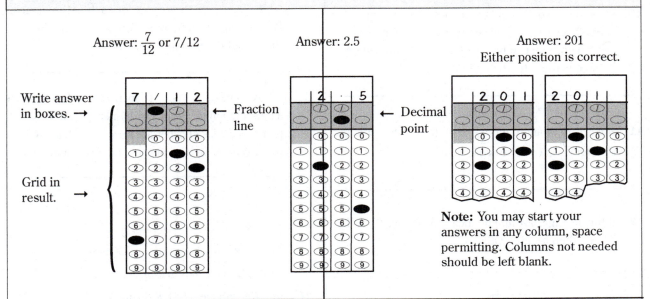

Answer: $\frac{7}{12}$ or 7/12   Answer: 2.5   Answer: 201
Either position is correct.

Write answer in boxes. →   ← Fraction line   ← Decimal point

Grid in result. →

Note: You may start your answers in any column, space permitting. Columns not needed should be left blank.

- Mark no more than one oval in any column.

- Because the answer sheet will be machine-scored, **you will receive credit only if the ovals are filled in correctly.**

- Although not required, it is suggested that you write your answer in the boxes at the top of the columns to help you fill in the ovals accurately.

- Some problems may have more than one correct answer. In such cases, grid only one answer.

- No question has a negative answer.

- **Mixed numbers** such as $2\frac{1}{2}$ must be gridded as 2.5 or 5/2. (If $2\frac{1}{2}$ is gridded, it will be interpreted as $\frac{21}{2}$, not $2\frac{1}{2}$.)

- **Decimal Accuracy:** If you obtain a decimal answer, **enter the most accurate value the grid will accommodate.** For example, if you obtain an answer such as 0.6666..., you should record the result as .666 or .667. **Less accurate values such as .66 or .67 are not acceptable.**

Acceptable ways to grid $\frac{2}{3}$ = .6666...:

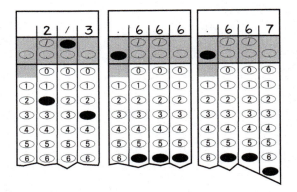

9. $\left(\frac{1}{2} - \frac{1}{3}\right) + \left(\frac{1}{3} - \frac{1}{4}\right) + \left(\frac{1}{4} - \frac{1}{5}\right) +$

    $\left(\frac{1}{5} - \frac{1}{6}\right) + \left(\frac{1}{6} - \frac{1}{7}\right) + \left(\frac{1}{7} - \frac{1}{8}\right) +$

    $\left(\frac{1}{8} - \frac{1}{9}\right)$ is equal to what value?

10. If the first two elements of a number series are 1 and 2, and if each succeeding term is found by multiplying the two terms immediately preceding it, what is the fifth element of the series?

11. If p is $\frac{3}{5}$ of m and if q is $\frac{9}{10}$ of m, then, when $q \neq 0$, the ratio $\frac{p}{q}$ is equal to what value?

12. If the average (arithmetic mean) of 40, 40, 40, and z is 45, then find the value of z.

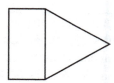

13. In the figure above, the perimeter of the equilateral triangle is 39 and the area of the rectangle is 65. What is the perimeter of the rectangle?

Game	Darrin	Tom
1	69	43
2	59	60
3	72	55
4	70	68
5	78	73
Totals	348	299

14. Darrin and Tom played five games of darts. The table above lists the scores for each of the games. By how many points was Tom behind Darrin at the end of the first four games?

15. A box contains 17 slips of paper. Each is labeled with a different integer from 1 to 17 inclusive. If 5 even-numbered slips of paper are removed, what fraction of the remaining slips of paper are even-numbered?

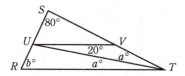

Note: Figure is not drawn to scale.

16. In $\triangle RST$ above, $UV \parallel RT$. Find b.

17. Riley has earned \$440 in 8 days. If she continues to earn at the same daily rate, in how many *more* days will her total earnings be \$990?

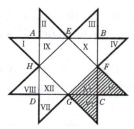

18. The areas of triangles I, II, III, IV, V, VI, VII, VIII, IX, X, XI, XII are the same. If the region outlined by the heavy line has area = 256 and the area of square $ABCD$ is 128, determine the shaded area.

STOP

If you finish before time is called, you may check your work on this section only.
Do not turn to any other section in the test.

Take a 5 minute break
before starting section 7

Section 7

Time: 25 Minutes – Turn to Section 7 (page 529) of your answer sheet to answer the questions in this section. 24 Questions

Directions: For each question in this section, select the best answer from among the choices given and fill in the corresponding circle on the answer sheet.

Each sentence below has one or two blanks, each blank indicating that something has been omitted. Beneath the sentence are five words or sets of words labeled A through E. Choose the word or set of words that, when inserted in the sentence, <u>best</u> fits the meaning of the sentence as a whole.

Example:

Hoping to _____ the dispute, negotiators proposed a compromise that they felt would be _____ to both labor and management.

(A) enforce…useful

(B) end…divisive

(C) overcome…unattractive

(D) extend…satisfactory

(E) resolve…acceptable

Ⓐ Ⓑ Ⓒ Ⓓ ●

1. The Forest Service warned that the spring forest fire season was in full swing and urged that _____ caution be exercised in wooded areas.

   (A) moderate
   (B) scant
   (C) customary
   (D) extreme
   (E) reasonable

2. The Classical Age of Greek art ended with the defeat of Athens by Sparta; the _____ effect of the long war was the weakening and _____ of the Greek spirit.

   (A) cumulative…corrosion
   (B) immediate…storing

   (C) imagined…cooperation
   (D) delayed…rebuilding
   (E) intuitive…cancellation

3. Mia, bored by even the briefest periods of idleness, was _____ switching from one activity to another.

   (A) hesitantly
   (B) lazily
   (C) slowly
   (D) surprisingly
   (E) continually

GO ON TO THE NEXT PAGE ➤

4. The bee _____ the nectar from the different flowers and then _____ the liquid into honey.

   (A) consumes...conforms
   (B) observes...pours
   (C) rejects...solidifies
   (D) crushes...injects
   (E) extracts...converts

5. The plan turned out to be _____ because it would have required more financial backing than was available.

   (A) intractable
   (B) chaotic
   (C) irreversible
   (D) untenable
   (E) superfluous

The two passages below are followed by questions based on their content and on the relationship between the two passages. Answer the questions on the basis of what is <u>stated</u> or <u>implied</u> in the passages and in any introductory material that may be provided.

Questions 6–9 are based on the following passages.

Passage 1

    All the arts contain some preposterous fiction, but the theatre is the most preposterous of all. Imagine asking us to believe that we are in Venice in the sixteenth century, that Mr. Billington is a Moor, and that he is about to
5 stifle the much admired Miss Huckaby with a pillow; and imagine trying to make us believe that people ever talked in blank verse—more than that: that people were ever so marvelously articulate. The theatre is a lily that inexplicably arises from a jungle of weedy falsities. Yet it is
10 precisely from the tension produced by all this absurdity that it is able to create such poetry, power, enchantment, and truth.

Passage 2

    The theater is a venue for the most realistic and direct fiction ever imagined. So many of the contemporary plays make us realize how we are living our lives and perhaps
15 how we should change them. From these "reality shows" we can feel all the poverty, despair, and unfairness in our world, which then affords us the opportunity for change for the better.

6. Which statement best illustrates the author's meaning when he says, "The theatre is a lily that inexplicably arises from a jungle of weedy falsities"?

   (A) The theatre is the "flower" among the arts.
   (B) The theatre helps to raise public taste to a higher level.
   (C) The theatre can create an illusion of truth from improbable situations.
   (D) The theatre has overcome the unsavory reputation of earlier periods.
   (E) In the theatre, real acting talent can be developed from unpromising material.

7. The author's feeling toward contemporary plays is that they

   (A) have no value for the spectator
   (B) can be appreciated by everyone
   (C) elicit the negative aspects of life
   (D) have a long-lasting effect on us
   (E) do not deal with poetry or truth

8. The two passages are similar in that

   (A) both describe specific examples from specific plays
   (B) both are completely objective in their respective arguments
   (C) both authors believe that they depict the accuracy of the particular time
   (D) both authors show the same intensity and passion in their arguments
   (E) both show that something positive can come out of something negative

9. Which of the following is true?

   (A) One author would not disagree with the other's premise.
   (B) The author of Passage 1 despises all characters in 16th-century plays.
   (C) The author of Passage 1 believes that people in the 16th century were very articulate.
   (D) Analogies to objects and places are a literary device used in only one passage.
   (E) The author of Passage 2 believes that the theater compromises reality.

GO ON TO THE NEXT PAGE ➤

Questions 10–15 are based on the following passage.

The following passage deals with adjustment to one's surroundings and the terms and theory associated with such adjustment.

As in the case of so many words used by the biologist and the physiologist, the word acclimatization is hard to define. With increases in knowledge and understanding, meanings of words change. Originally, the term acclimatization was
5   taken to mean only the ability of human beings or animals or plants to accustom themselves to new and strange climatic conditions, primarily altered temperature. A person or a wolf moves to a hot climate and is uncomfortable there, but after a time is better able to withstand the heat. But
10   aside from temperature, there are other aspects of climate. A person or an animal may become adjusted to living at higher altitudes than those it was originally accustomed to. At really high altitudes, such as that which aviators may be exposed to, the low atmospheric pressure becomes a factor
15   of primary importance. In changing to a new environment, a person may, therefore, meet new conditions of temperature or pressure, and in addition may have to contend with different chemical surroundings. On high mountains, the amount of oxygen in the atmosphere may
20   be relatively small; in crowded cities, a person may become exposed to relatively high concentrations of carbon dioxide or even carbon monoxide and in various areas may be exposed to conditions in which the water content of the atmosphere is extremely high or extremely low. Thus in
25   the case of humans, animals, and even plants, the concept of acclimatization includes the phenomena of increased toleration of high or low temperature, of altered pressure, and of changes in the chemical environment.

Let us define acclimatization, therefore, as the process
30   by which an organism or a part of an organism becomes inured to an environment that is normally unsuitable to it or lethal for it. By and large, acclimatization is a relatively slow process. The term should not be taken to include relatively rapid adjustments such as those our sense organs are
35   constantly making. This type of adjustment is commonly referred to by physiologists as "adaptation." Thus our touch sense soon becomes accustomed to the pressure of our clothes and we do not feel them; we soon fail to hear the ticking of a clock; obnoxious odors after a time fail to
40   make much impression on us, and our eyes in strong light rapidly become insensitive.

The fundamental fact about acclimatization is that all animals and plants have some capacity to adjust themselves to changes in their environment. This is one of the most
45   remarkable characteristics of living organisms, a characteristic for which it is extremely difficult to find explanations.

10. According to the reading selection, all animals and plants

(A) have an ability for acclimatization
(B) can adjust to only one change in the environment at a time
(C) are successful in adjusting themselves to changes in their environments
(D) can adjust to natural changes in the environment but not to artificially induced changes
(E) that have once acclimatized themselves to an environmental change can acclimatize themselves more rapidly to subsequent changes

11. It can be inferred from the reading selection that

(A) every change in the environment requires acclimatization by living things
(B) plants and animals are more alike than they are different
(C) biologists and physiologists study essentially the same things
(D) the explanation of acclimatization is specific to each plant and animal
(E) as science develops, the connotation of terms may change

12. According to the reading selection, acclimatization

(A) is similar to adaptation
(B) is more important today than it formerly was
(C) involves positive as well as negative adjustment
(D) may be involved with a part of an organism but not with the whole organism
(E) is more difficult to explain with the more complex present-day environment than formerly

13. By inference from the reading selection, which one of the following would *not* require the process of acclimatization?

(A) an ocean fish placed in a lake
(B) a skin diver making a deep dive
(C) an airplane pilot making a high-altitude flight
(D) a person going from daylight into a darkened room
(E) a person moving from Denver, Colorado, to New Orleans, Louisiana

GO ON TO THE NEXT PAGE ❯

14. The word "inured" in line 31 most likely means

(A) exposed
(B) accustomed
(C) attracted
(D) associated
(E) in love with

15. According to the passage, a major distinction between acclimatization and adaptation is that acclimatization

(A) is more important than adaptation
(B) is relatively slow and adaptation is relatively rapid
(C) applies to adjustments while adaptation does not apply to adjustments
(D) applies to terrestrial animals and adaptation to aquatic animals
(E) is applicable to all animals and plants and adaptation only to higher animals and man

Questions 16–24 are based on the following passage.

The following passage is about the Chinese Empire, the forces that kept the Empire together, its culture, and its philosophy.

First of all, it is important to note that the old China was an empire rather than a state. To the Chinese and their rulers, the word China did not exist and to them it would have been meaningless. They sometimes used a
5 term which we translate "the Middle Kingdom." To them there could be only one legitimate ruler for all civilized mankind. All others were rightly subordinate to him and should acknowledge his suzerainty. From this standpoint, there could not, as in Europe, be diplomatic relations
10 between equal states, each of them sovereign. When, in the nineteenth century, Europeans insisted upon intercourse with China on the basis of equality, the Chinese were at first amused and then scandalized and indignant. Centuries of training had bred in them the conviction that all other
15 rulers should be tributary to the Son of Heaven.

The tie which bound this world-embracing empire together, so the Chinese were taught to believe, was as much cultural as political. As there could be only one legitimate ruler to whom all mankind must be subject, so there
20 could be only one culture that fully deserved to be called civilized. Other cultures might have worth, but ultimately they were more or less barbarous. There could be only one civilization, and that was the civilization of the Middle Kingdom. Beginning with the Han, the ideal of civilization
25 was held to be Confucian. The Confucian interpretation of civilization was adopted and inculcated as the norm. Others

might be tolerated, but if they seriously threatened the Confucian institutions and foundations of society, they were to be curbed and, perhaps, exterminated as a threat to the
30 highest values.

Since the bond of the Empire was cultural and since the Empire should include all civilized mankind, racial distinctions were not so marked as in most other parts of the world. The Chinese did not have so strong a sense of
35 being of different blood from non-Chinese as twentieth-century conceptions of race and nation later led them to develop. They were proud of being "the sons of Han" or "the men of T'ang," but if a people fully adopted Chinese culture, no great distinction was perceived between them
40 and those who earlier had been governed by that culture.

This helps to account for the comparative contentment of Chinese under alien rulers. If, as was usually the case, these invading conquerors adopted the culture of their subjects and governed through the accustomed machinery
45 and by traditional Confucian principles, they were accepted as legitimate Emperors. Few of the non-Chinese dynasties completely made this identification. This probably in part accounts for such restiveness as the Chinese showed under their rule. For instance, so long as they were dominant, the
50 Manchus, while they accepted much of the Chinese culture and prided themselves on being experts in it and posed as its patrons, never completely abandoned their distinctive ancestral ways.

The fact that the tie was cultural rather than racial
55 helps to account for the remarkable homogeneity of the Chinese. Many different ethnic strains have gone to make up the people whom we call the Chinese. Presumably in the Chou and probably, earlier, in the Shang, the bearers of Chinese culture were not a single race. As Chinese culture
60 moved southward, it encountered differing cultures and, almost certainly, divergent stocks. The many invaders from the north and west brought in more variety. In contrast with India, where caste and religion have tended to keep apart the racial strata, in China assimilation made great
65 progress. That assimilation has not been complete. Today the discerning observer can notice differences even among those who are Chinese in language and customs, and in many parts of China Proper there are groups who preserve not only their racial but also their linguistic and cultural iden-
70 tity. Still, nowhere else on the globe is there so numerous a people who are so nearly homogeneous as are the Chinese.

This homogeneity is due not merely to a common cultural tie, but also to the particular kind of culture which constitutes that tie. Something in the Chinese tradition
75 recognized as civilized those who conformed to certain ethical standards and social customs. It was the fitting into Confucian patterns of conduct and of family and community life rather than blood kinship or ancestry which labeled one as civilized and as Chinese.

GO ON TO THE NEXT PAGE >

16. The force that kept the Chinese Empire together was largely

    (A) religious
    (B) military
    (C) economic
    (D) a fear of invasion from the north and west
    (E) the combination of a political and a cultural bond

17. The reason China resisted having diplomatic relations with European nations was that

    (A) for centuries the Chinese had believed that their nation must be supreme among all other countries
    (B) the Chinese saw nothing of value in European culture
    (C) China was afraid of European military power
    (D) such relations were against the teachings of the Son of Heaven
    (E) the danger of disease was ever present when foreigners arrived

18. Confucianism stresses, above all,

    (A) image worship
    (B) recognition of moral values
    (C) division of church and state
    (D) acceptance of foreigners
    (E) separation of social classes

19. Han and T'ang were Chinese

    (A) philosophers
    (B) holidays
    (C) dynasties
    (D) generals
    (E) religions

20. If the unifying force in the Chinese empire had been racial, it is likely that

    (A) China would have never become great
    (B) China would be engaged in constant warfare
    (C) China would have become a highly industrialized nation
    (D) there would have been increasing discontent under foreign rulers
    (E) China would have greatly expanded its influence

21. A problem of contemporary India that does not trouble China is

    (A) overpopulation
    (B) the persistence of the caste system
    (C) a lack of modern industrial development
    (D) a scarcity of universities
    (E) a low standard of living

22. The Manchus encountered some dissatisfaction within the empire because

    (A) of their tyrannical rule
    (B) they retained some of their original cultural practices
    (C) they were of a distinctly foreign race
    (D) of the heavy taxes they levied
    (E) they rejected totally Chinese culture

23. The Chinese are basically a homogeneous people because

    (A) different races were able to assimilate to a great degree
    (B) there has always been only one race in China
    (C) the other races came to look like the Chinese because of geographical factors
    (D) all other races were forcibly kept out of China
    (E) of their antipathy toward intermarriage

24. The word "restiveness" in line 48 means

    (A) authority
    (B) happiness
    (C) impatience
    (D) hyperactivity
    (E) quietude

STOP

If you finish before time is called, you may check your work on this section only.
Do not turn to any other section in the test.

Section 8

Time: 20 Minutes—Turn to Section 8 (page 530) of your answer sheet to answer the questions in this section. 16 Questions
Directions: For this section, solve each problem and decide which is the best of the choices given. Fill in the corresponding circle on the answer sheet. You may use any available space for scratchwork.

Notes:

1. The use of a calculator is permitted.

2. All numbers used are real numbers.

3. Figures that accompany problems in this test are intended to provide information useful in solving the problems. They are drawn as accurately as possible EXCEPT when it is stated in a specific problem that the figure is not drawn to scale. All figures lie in a plane unless otherwise indicated.

4. Unless otherwise specified, the domain of any function f is assumed to be the set of all real numbers x for which $f(x)$ is a real number.

REFERENCE INFORMATION

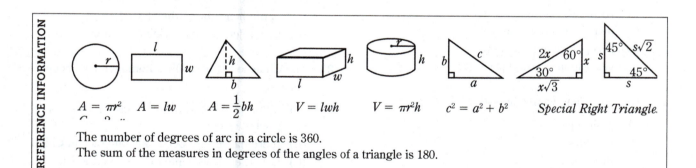

$A = \pi r^2$ $A = lw$ $A = \frac{1}{2}bh$ $V = lwh$ $V = \pi r^2 h$ $c^2 = a^2 + b^2$ *Special Right Triangle.*

The number of degrees of arc in a circle is 360.
The sum of the measures in degrees of the angles of a triangle is 180.

1. James buys a frying pan and two coffee mugs for $27. Aria buys the same-priced frying pan and one of the same-priced coffee mugs for $23. How much does one of those frying pans cost?

   (A) $4
   (B) $7
   (C) $19
   (D) $20
   (E) $21

2. A rectangular floor 8 feet long and 6 feet wide is to be completely covered with tiles. Each tile is a square with a perimeter of 2 feet. What is the least number of such tiles necessary to cover the floor?

   (A) 7
   (B) 12
   (C) 24
   (D) 48
   (E) 192

GO ON TO THE NEXT PAGE ➤

3. If 9 and 12 each divide Q without remainder, which of the following must Q divide without remainder?

(A) 1
(B) 3
(C) 36
(D) 72
(E) The answer cannot be determined from the given information.

5. Given three segments of length x, $11 - x$, and $x - 4$, respectively, which of the following indicates the set of all numbers x such that the 3 segments could be the lengths of the sides of a triangle?

(A) $x > 4$
(B) $x < 11$
(C) $0 < x < 7$
(D) $5 < x < 15$
(E) $5 < x < 7$

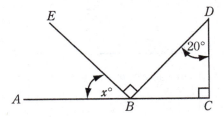

4. In the figure above, $DC \perp AC$, $EB \perp DB$, and AC is a line segment. What is the value of x? (*Note:* Figure is not drawn to scale.)

(A) 15
(B) 20
(C) 30
(D) 80
(E) 160

6. Given three positive integers a, b, and 4, if their average (arithmetic mean) is 6, which of the following could *not* be the value of the product ab?

(A) 13
(B) 14
(C) 40
(D) 48
(E) 49

GO ON TO THE NEXT PAGE ❯

7. If $mn \neq 0$, then $\dfrac{1}{n^2}\left(\dfrac{m^5 n^3}{m^3}\right)^2 =$

(A) mn^4

(B) $m^4 n^2$

(C) $m^4 n^3$

(D) $m^4 n^4$

(E) $m^4 n^5$

Question 9 refers to the figure above, where W, X, Y, and Z are four distinct digits from 0 to 9, inclusive, and $W + X + Y = 5Z$.

9. Under the given conditions, all of the following could be values of Z EXCEPT

(A) 1

(B) 2

(C) 3

(D) 4

(E) 5

8. From a party attended by 3 females and 3 males, 3 people at random enter a previously empty room. What is the probability that there are exactly 2 males in the room?

(A) $\dfrac{1}{4}$

(B) $\dfrac{3}{8}$

(C) $\dfrac{9}{20}$

(D) $\dfrac{2}{3}$

(E) $\dfrac{5}{6}$

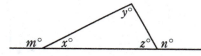

10. In the figure above, $m + n =$

(A) 90

(B) 180

(C) $180 + y$

(D) $90 + x + y + z$

(E) $2(x + y + z)$

GO ON TO THE NEXT PAGE >

11. The volume of a cube is less than 25, and the length of one of its edges is a positive integer. What is the largest possible value for the total area of the six faces?

(A) 1
(B) 6
(C) 24
(D) 54
(E) 150

A B C D E F G

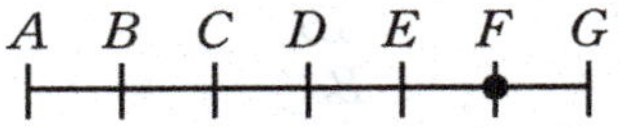

13. AG is divided into six equal segments in the figure above. A circle, not visible, with center F and radius $\frac{1}{5}$ the length of AG, will intersect AG between

(A) F and G
(B) E and F
(C) D and E
(D) C and D
(E) A and B

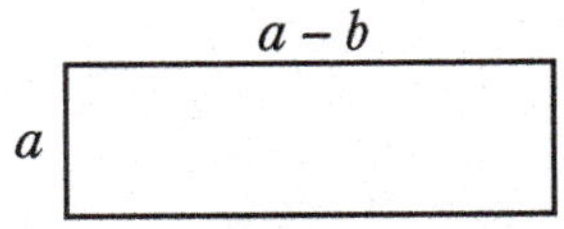

12. The ratio of females to males on a particular flight was $2 : 3$. Females represented five more than $\frac{1}{3}$ of all the people aboard. How many people were on that flight?

(A) 15
(B) 25
(C) 30
(D) 45
(E) 75

$a - b$

a [rectangle]

14. The figure above is a rectangle having width a and length $a - b$. Find its perimeter in terms of a and b.

(A) $a^2 - ab$
(B) $4a - 2b$
(C) $4a - b$
(D) $2a - 2b$
(E) $2a - b$

GO ON TO THE NEXT PAGE ❯

$$AB$$
$$+ \; BA$$
$$\overline{CDC}$$

15. If each of the four letters in the sum above represents a *different* digit, which of the following *cannot* be a value of *A*?

(A) 6
(B) 5
(C) 4
(D) 3
(E) 2

15. If $f(x) = x^2 + x$ and $g(y) = y^2$, then $f[g(-1)] =$

(A) 2
(B) -2
(C) 4
(D) -4
(E) -8

STOP

If you finish before time is called, you may check your work on this section only.
Do not turn to any other section in the test.

Section 9

Time: 20 Minutes – Turn to Section 9 (page 530) of your answer sheet to answer the questions in this section. 19 Questions

Directions: For each question in this section, select the best answer from among the choices given and fill in the corresponding circle on the answer sheet.

Each sentence below has one or two blanks, each blank indicating that something has been omitted. Beneath the sentence are five words or sets of words labeled A through E. Choose the word or set of words that, when inserted in the sentence, <u>best</u> fits the meaning of the sentence as a whole.

Example:

Hoping to _____ the dispute, negotiators proposed a compromise that they felt would be _____ to both labor and management.

(A) enforce...useful

(B) end...divisive

(C) overcome...unattractive

(D) extend...satisfactory

(E) resolve...acceptable   Ⓐ Ⓑ Ⓒ Ⓓ ●

---

1. Joining _____ momentum for reform in intercollegiate sports, university presidents have called for swift steps to correct imbalances between classwork and _____.

   (A) a maximum...studies
   (B) a rational...awards
   (C) an increasing...athletics
   (D) an exceptional...professors
   (E) a futile...contests

2. Thinking nothing can be done, many victims of arthritis ignore or delay _____ countermeasures, thus aggravating the problem.

   (A) tardy
   (B) injurious
   (C) characteristic
   (D) weird
   (E) effective

GO ON TO THE NEXT PAGE ➤

3. A strange and _____ fate seemed to keep him helpless and unhappy, despite occasional interludes of _____.

   (A) malevolent…conflict
   (B) bizarre…disenchantment
   (C) virulent…tension
   (D) ineluctable…serenity
   (E) intriguing…inactivity

4. Samuel Clemens chose the _____ Mark Twain as a result of his knowledge of riverboat piloting.

   (A) protagonist
   (B) pseudonym
   (C) mountebank
   (D) hallucination
   (E) misanthrope

5. For years a vocalist of spirituals, Marian Anderson was finally recognized as _____ singer when the Metropolitan Opera House engaged her.

   (A) a capable
   (B) an unusual
   (C) an attractive
   (D) a cooperative
   (E) a mediocre

6. Leonardo da Vinci _____ the law of gravity two centuries before Newton and also made the first complete _____ charts of the human body.

   (A) examined…colorful
   (B) anticipated…anatomical
   (C) avoided…meaningful
   (D) realized…explanatory
   (E) suspected…mural

The two passages below are followed by questions based on their content and on the relationship between the two passages. Answer the questions on the basis of what is <u>stated</u> or <u>implied</u> in the passages and in any introductory material that may be provided.

Questions 7–19 are based on the following passages.

The following two passages describe two views of the makeup and character of an artist.

Passage 1

The special quality which makes an artist of any worth might be defined, indeed, as an extraordinary capacity for irritation, a pathological sensitiveness to environmental pricks and stings. He differs from the rest of us mainly
5 because he reacts sharply and in an uncommon manner to phenomena which leave the rest of us unmoved, or, at most, merely vaguely annoyed. He is, in brief, a more delicate fellow than we are and hence less fitted to prosper and enjoy himself under the conditions of life that he and we must
10 face alike. Therefore, he takes to artistic endeavor, which is at once a criticism of life and an attempt to escape from life.

So much for the theory of it. The more the facts are studied, the more they bear it out. In those fields of art, at all events, which concern themselves with ideas as well as
15 with sensations, it is almost impossible to find any trace of an artist who was not actively hostile to his environment and thus an indifferent patriot. From Dante to Tolstoy and from Shakespeare to Mark Twain, the story is ever the same. Names suggest themselves instantly: Goethe, Heine,
20 Shelley, Byron, Thackeray, Balzac, Rabelais, Cervantes, Swift, Dostoevsky, Carlyle, Molière, Pope—all bitter critics of their time and nation, most of them piously hated by

the contemporary 100 percenters, some of them actually fugitives from rage and reprisal.

25   Dante put all of the patriotic Italians of his day into Hell and showed them boiling, roasting, and writhing on hooks. Cervantes drew such a devastating picture of the Spain that he lived in that it ruined the Spaniards. Shakespeare made his heroes foreigners and his clowns Englishmen.
30 Goethe was in favor of Napoleon. Rabelais, a citizen of Christendom rather than of France, raised a cackle against it that Christendom is still trying in vain to suppress. Swift, having finished the Irish and then the English, proceeded to finish the whole human race. The exceptions are few and
35 far between, and not many of them will bear examination. So far as I know, the only eminent writer in English history who was also a 100 percent Englishman, absolutely beyond suspicion, was Samuel Johnson. But was Johnson actually an artist? If he was, then a kazoo player is a musician. He
40 employed the materials of one of the arts, to wit, words, but his use of them was mechanical, not artistic. If Johnson were alive today, he would be a United States senator, or a university president. He left such wounds upon English prose that it took a century to recover from them.

Passage 2

45 For the ease and pleasure of treading the old road, accepting the fashions, the education, the religion of society, he takes the cross of making his own and, of course, the self-accusation, the faint heart, the frequent uncertainty and loss of time, which are the nettles and tangling vines in

50 the way of the self-relying and self-directed, and the state of
virtual hostility in which he seems to stand to society, and
especially to educated society. For all this loss and scorn,
what offset? The artist is to find consolation in exercising
the highest functions of human nature. The artist is one
55 who raises himself from private consideration and breathes
and lives on public and illustrious thoughts. The artist is
the world's eye. He is the world's heart. He is to resist the
vulgar prosperity that retrogrades ever to barbarism, by
preserving and communicating heroic sentiments, noble
60 biographies, melodious verse, and the conclusions of
history. Whatsoever oracles the human heart, in all emergencies, in all solemn hours, has uttered as its commentary
on the world of actions—these he shall receive and impart.
And whatsoever new verdict Reason from her inviolable
65 seat pronounces on the passing men and women and
events of today—this he shall hear and promulgate.

These being his functions, it becomes the artist to feel
all confidence in himself and to defer never to the popular
cry. He and he alone knows the world. The world of any
70 moment is the merest appearance. Some great decorum,
some fetish of a government, some ephemeral trade, or
war, or man, is cried up by half mankind and cried down
by the other half, as if all depended on this particular up or
down. The odds are that the whole question is not worth
75 the poorest thought which the scholar has lost in listening
to the controversy. Let her not quit her belief that a popgun
is a popgun, though the ancient and honorable of the earth
affirm it to be the crack of doom. In silence, in steadiness, in
severe abstraction, let him hold by himself; add observation
80 to observation, patient of neglect, patient of reproach, and
bide his own time—happy enough if he can satisfy himself
alone that this day he has seen something truly. Success
treads on every right step. For the instinct is sure that
prompts him to tell his brother what he thinks. The artist
85 then learns that in going down into the secrets of his own
mind he has descended into the secrets of all minds. He
learns that the artist who has mastered any law in his private
thoughts is master to that extent of all translated. The poet,
in utter solitude remembering his spontaneous thoughts
90 and recording them, is found to have recorded that which
men in crowded cities find true for them also. The orator
distrusts at first the fitness of his frank confessions, his want
of knowledge of the persons he addresses, until he finds
that he is the complement of his hearers—that they drink
95 his words because he fulfills for them their own nature; the
deeper he dives into his most private, most secret presentiment,
to his wonder he finds this is the most acceptable, most public,
and universally true. The people delight in it; the better part
of every man feels. This is my music; this is myself.

7. Which of the following quotations is related most
closely to the principal idea of Passage 1?

(A) "All nature is but art unknown to thee, All
chance, direction which thou canst not see."
(B) "When to her share some human errors fall,
Look on her face and you'll forget them all."
(C) "All human things are subject to decay, And,
when fate summons, monarchs must obey."

(D) "A little learning is a dangerous thing, Drink
deep or taste not the Pierian spring."
(E) "Great wits are sure to madness near allied, And
thin partitions do their bounds divide."

8. The author of Passage 1 seems to regard the artist as

(A) the best representative of his time
(B) an unnecessary threat to the social order
(C) one who creates out of discontent
(D) one who truly knows how to enjoy life
(E) one who is touched with genius

9. It can be inferred that the author of Passage 1
believes that United States senators and university
presidents

(A) must be treated with respect because of their
position
(B) are to be held in low esteem
(C) are generally appreciative of the great literary
classics
(D) have native writing ability
(E) have the qualities of the artist

10. All of the following ideas about artists are mentioned
in Passage 1 *except* that
(A) they are irritated by their surroundings
(B) they are escapists from reality
(C) they are lovers of beauty
(D) they are hated by their contemporaries
(E) they are critical of their times

11. Which of the following best describes the author's
attitude toward artists in Passage 1?

(A) sharply critical
(B) sincerely sympathetic
(C) deeply resentful
(D) mildly annoyed
(E) completely delighted

12. It is a frequent criticism of the artist that he lives
by himself, in an "ivory tower," remote from the
problems and business of the world. Which of these
below constitutes the best refutation by the writer of
Passage 2 to the criticism here noted?

(A) The world's concerns being ephemeral, the artist
does well to renounce them and the world.
(B) The artist lives in the past to interpret the present.

GO ON TO THE NEXT PAGE ➤

(C) The artist at his truest is the spokesman of the people.

(D) The artist is not concerned with the world's doings because he is not selfish and therefore not engrossed in matters of importance to himself and his neighbors.

(E) The artist's academic researches of today are the businessman's practical products of tomorrow.

13. The artist's road is rough, according to Passage 2. Which of these is the artist's greatest difficulty?

(A) The artist must renounce religion.

(B) The artist must pioneer new approaches.

(C) The artist must express scorn for and hostility toward society.

(D) The artist is uncertain of his course.

(E) There is a pleasure in the main-traveled roads in education, religion, and all social fashions.

14. When the writer of Passage 2 speaks of the "world's eye" and the "world's heart," he means

(A) the same thing

(B) culture and conscience

(C) culture and wisdom

(D) a scanning of all the world's geography and a deep sympathy for every living thing

(E) mind and love

15. By the phrase "nettles and tangling vines" (line 49), the author is probably referring to

(A) "self-accusation" and "loss of time"

(B) "faint heart" and "self-accusation"

(C) "the slings and arrows of outrageous fortune"

(D) a general term for the difficulties of a scholar's life

(E) "self-accusation" and "uncertainty"

16. The various ideas in Passage 2 are best summarized in which of these groups?

I. truth versus society
the artist and books
the world and the artist

II. the ease of living traditionally
the glory of an artist's life
true knowledge versus trivia

III. the hardships of the scholar
the artist's functions
the artist's justifications for disregarding the world's business

(A) I and III only

(B) I only

(C) III only

(D) I, II, and III

(E) I and II only

17. In line 51, "seems to stand" means

(A) is

(B) ends probably in becoming

(C) gives the false impression of being

(D) is seen to be

(E) the quicksands of time

18. The difference between the description of the artist in Passage 1 as compared with the artist in Passage 2 is that

(A) one is loyal to his fellow men and women, whereas the other is opposed to his or her environment

(B) one is sensitive to his or her environment, whereas the other is apathetic

(C) one has political aspirations; the other does not

(D) one has deep knowledge; the other has superficial knowledge

(E) one could be proficient in a field other than art; the other could create only in his or her present field

19. Which of the following describes statements that refer to the *same* one artist (either the one in Passage 1 *or* the one in Passage 2)?

I. This artist's thoughts are also the spectator's thoughts.
This artist lives modestly and not luxuriously.

II. This artist admires foreigners over his own countrymen.
This artist reacts to many things that most people would be neutral to.

III. This artist is happy to be at his best.
This artist accepts society.

(A) I only

(B) II only

(C) III only

(D) I and III only

(E) I, II, and III

Section 10

Time: 10 Minutes – Turn to Section 10 (page 530) of your answer sheet to answer the questions in this section. 14 Questions
Directions: For each question in this section, select the best answer from among the choices given and fill in the corresponding circle on the answer sheet.

The following sentences test correctness and effectiveness of expression. Part of each sentence or the entire sentence is underlined; beneath each sentence are five ways of phrasing the underlined material. Choice A repeats the original phrasing; the other four choices are different. If you think the original phrasing produces a better sentence than any of the alternatives, select Choice A; if not, select one of the other choices.

In making your selection, follow the requirements of standard written English; that is, pay attention to grammar, choice of words, sentence construction, and punctuation. Your selection should result in the most effective sentence—clear and precise, without awkwardness or ambiguity.

EXAMPLE:

Laura Ingalls Wilder published her first book <u>and she was sixty-five years old then</u>.

(A)   and she was sixty-five years old then

(B)   when she was sixty-five

(C)   at age sixty-five years old

(D)   upon the reaching of sixty-five years

(E)   at the time when she was sixty-five

1.   She bought <u>some bread, butter, cheese and decided</u> not to eat them until the evening.

   (A)   some bread, butter, cheese and decided
   (B)   some bread, butter, cheese and then decided
   (C)   a little bread, butter, cheese and decided
   (D)   some bread, butter, cheese, deciding
   (E)   some bread, butter, and cheese and decided

2.   The things the children liked best were <u>swimming in the river and to watch the horses being groomed by the trainer</u>.

   (A)   swimming in the river and to watch the horses being groomed by the trainer
   (B)   swimming in the river and to watch the trainer grooming the horses
   (C)   that they liked to swim in the river and watch the horses being groomed by the trainer
   (D)   swimming in the river and watching the horses being groomed by the trainer
   (E)   to swim in the river and watching the horses being groomed by the trainer

GO ON TO THE NEXT PAGE ➤

3. If an individual wishes to specialize in electrical engineering, <u>they should take courses in trigonometry and calculus.</u>

   (A) they should take courses in trigonometry and calculus
   (B) trigonometry and calculus is what he should take courses in
   (C) trigonometry and calculus are what they should take courses in
   (D) he or she should take courses in trigonometry and calculus
   (E) take courses in trigonometry and calculus

4. If the dog will not <u>eat its food, put it through</u> the meat grinder once more.

   (A) eat its food, put it through
   (B) eat it's food, put it through
   (C) eat its food, you should put it through
   (D) eat food, put it through
   (E) eat its food, put the food through

5. The bank agreed to lend <u>Garcia the money, which made</u> him very happy.

   (A) Garcia the money, which made
   (B) Garcia the money, a decision which made
   (C) Garcia the money; this made
   (D) Garcia the money, this making
   (E) the money to Garcia and found

6. Miami's daytime attire is <u>less formal than New York.</u>

   (A) less formal than New York
   (B) less formal then that in New York
   (C) less formal than that in New York
   (D) less formal than in New York
   (E) less formal than the daytime attire we see in New York

7. <u>As the fisherman explained that he wanted to hire a guide and row</u> upstream in order to catch game fish.

   (A) As the fisherman explained that he wanted to hire a guide and row
   (B) The reason was as the fisherman explained that he wanted to hire a guide and row
   (C) As the fisherman explained that he wanted to hire a guide and to row
   (D) The fisherman explained that he wanted to hire a guide and row
   (E) The fisherman explaining that he wanted to hire a guide and row

8. The speaker was praised <u>for her organization, choice of subject, and because she was brief.</u>

   (A) for her organization, choice of subject, and because she was brief
   (B) for her organization, her choice of subject and the speech having brevity
   (C) on account of her organization and her choice of subject and the brevity of her speech
   (D) for the organization of her speech, for her choice of subject, and because she was brief
   (E) for her organization, her choice of subject, and her brevity

9. <u>The fact that Charles did not receive a college scholarship</u> disappointed his parents.

   (A) The fact that Charles did not receive a college scholarship
   (B) Because Charles did not receive a college scholarship was the reason he
   (C) Being that Charles did not receive a college scholarship
   (D) Charles not receiving a college scholarship
   (E) Charles did not receive a college scholarship

GO ON TO THE NEXT PAGE ➤

10. The porch of a famous home collapsed during a party last week, <u>which injured 23 people</u>.

(A) which injured 23 people
(B) causing 23 people to be injured
(C) injuring 23 people
(D) damaging 23 people
(E) resulting in 23 people being injured

11. Jack's favorite summer supper includes barbecued chicken, grilled corn on the cob, sliced tomatoes, <u>and he likes green salad</u>.

(A) and he likes green salad
(B) in addition to green salad
(C) adding green salad
(D) including green salad
(E) and green salad

12. I want the <u>best price</u> I can get for my car.

(A) best price
(B) most highest price
(C) price which is the best
(D) most best price
(E) premium price

13. The injured woman was taken to the hospital, <u>where she was treated for facial lacerations and released</u>.

(A) where she was treated for facial lacerations and released
(B) where she was treated and released for facial lacerations
(C) where her facial lacerations were treated and she was released from the hospital
(D) where her treatment was for facial lacerations and she was released from the hospital
(E) where she received facial lacerations treatment and was released

14. The new leader is tough, single-minded, and <u>tries to be independent</u>.

(A) tries to be independent
(B) acting in dependent
(C) independent
(D) an independent person
(E) an independent

STOP

If you finish before time is called, you may check your work on this section only.
Do not turn to any other section in the test.

How did you do on this test?

Step 1.   Go to the Answer Key

Step 2.   Calculate your "raw score."

Step 3.   Get your "scaled score" for the test by referring to the Raw Score/Scaled Score Conversion Tables.

**THERE'S ALWAYS ROOM
FOR IMPROVEMENT!**

ANSWER KEY FOR PRACTICE TEST 5

Math

Section 2

	Correct Answer
1	C
2	E
3	C
4	D
5	D
6	B
7	D
8	D
9	B
10	A
11	C
12	D
13	A
14	E
15	A
16	E
17	C
18	B
19	D
20	A

Number correct

Number incorrect

Section 3

	Correct Answer
1	A
2	C
3	E
4	B
5	B
6	A
7	C
8	A
9	A
10	B
11	D
12	D
13	B
14	D
15	C
16	C
17	B
18	C
19	A
20	D

Number correct

Number incorrect

Section 6

	Correct Answer
1	E
2	A
3	B
4	D
5	E
6	B
7	A
8	D

Number correct

Number incorrect

Student-Produced Response Questions

9	$\frac{7}{18}$ or .388 or .389
10	8
11	$\frac{2}{3}$ or .667 or .666
12	60
13	36
14	44
15	$\frac{1}{4}$ or .25
16	60
17	10
18	48

Number correct

Number incorrect

Section 8

	Correct Answer
1	C
2	E
3	E
4	B
5	E
6	B
7	D
8	C
9	E
10	C
11	C
12	E
13	C
14	B
15	E
16	A

Number correct

Number incorrect

ANSWER KEY FOR PRACTICE TEST 5
Critical reading

Section 4

	Correct Answer
1	E
2	C
3	B
4	A
5	B
6	B
7	B
8	B
9	D
10	A
11	B
12	E
13	B
14	E
15	A
16	E
17	C
18	D
19	D
20	A
21	C
22	C
23	C
24	D

Number correct

Number incorrect

Section 7

	Correct Answer
1	D
2	A
3	E
4	E
5	D
6	C
7	C
8	E
9	D
10	A
11	E
12	A
13	D
14	B
15	B
16	E
17	A
18	B
19	C
20	D
21	B
22	B
23	A
24	C

Number correct

Number incorrect

Section 9

	Correct Answer
1	C
2	E
3	D
4	B
5	A
6	B
7	E
8	C
9	B
10	C
11	B
12	C
13	B
14	C
15	E
16	C
17	C
18	A
19	E

Number correct

Number incorrect

ANSWER KEY FOR PRACTICE TEST 5

Writing

Section 1

_____

Essay score

Section 5

	Correct Answer
1	C
2	D
3	E
4	B
5	A
6	B
7	D
8	E
9	D
10	B
11	D
12	D
13	E
14	A
15	B
16	E
17	B
18	A
19	E
20	D
21	E
22	A
23	C
24	B
25	D
26	D
27	A
28	C
29	A
30	D
31	C
32	A
33	B
34	B
35	D

Number correct

_____

Number incorrect

Section 10

	Correct Answer
1	E
2	D
3	D
4	E
5	B
6	C
7	D
8	E
9	A
10	C
11	E
12	A
13	A
14	C

Number correct

_____

Number incorrect

Scoring the SAT Practice Test

Check your responses with the correct answers on the previous pages. Fill in the blanks below and do the calculations to get your Math, Critical Reading, and Writing raw scores. Use the table to find your Math, Critical Reading, and Writing scaled scores.

Get Your Math Score

How many Math questions did you get **right**?

Section 2: Questions 1–20   _____

Section 6: Questions 1–18 + _____

Section 8: Questions 1–16 + _____

        Total = _____ **(A)**

How many Math questions did you get **wrong**?

Section 2: Questions 1–20   _____

Section 6: Questions 1–18 + _____

Section 8: Questions 1–16 + _____

        Total = _____

      × 0.25 = _____ **(B)**

     A – B = _____

           Math Raw Score

Round Math raw score to the nearest whole number.

_____

Use the Score Conversion Table to find your Math scaled score.

_____

Get Your Critical Reading Score

How many Critical Reading questions did you get **right**?

Section 4: Questions 1–24   _____

Section 7: Questions 1–24 + _____

Section 9: Questions 1–19 + _____

        Total = _____ **(A)**

How many Critical Reading questions did you get **wrong**?

Section 4: Questions 1–24   _____

Section 7: Questions 1–24 + _____

Section 9: Questions 1–19 + _____

        Total = _____

      × 0.25 = _____ **(B)**

     A – B = _____

     Critical Reading Raw Score

Round Critical Reading raw score to the nearest whole number.

_____

Use the Score Conversion Table to find your Critical Reading scaled score.

_____

Get Your Writing Score

How many multiple-choice Writing questions did you get **right**?

Section 5: Questions 1–35 _____

Section 10: Questions 1–14 + _____

Total = _____ **(A)**

How many multiple-choice Writing questions did you get **wrong**?

Section 5: Questions 1–35 _____

Section 10: Questions 1–14 + _____

Total = _____

× 0.25 = _____ **(B)**

A – B = _____

Writing Raw Score

Round Writing raw score to the nearest whole number.

_____

Use the Score Conversion Table to find your Writing multiple-choice scaled score.

_____

Estimate your Essay score using the Essay Scoring Guide.

_____

Use the SAT Score Conversion Table for Writing Composite to find your Writing scaled score. You will need your Writing raw score and your Essay score to use this table.

_____

SAT Score conversion table

Raw Score	Critical Reading Scaled Score	Math Scaled Score	Writing Multiple-Choice Scaled Score*	Raw Score	Critical Reading Scaled Score	Math Scaled Score	Writing Multiple-Choice Scaled Score*
67	800			31	510	550	60
66	800			30	510	540	58
65	790			29	500	530	57
64	770			28	490	520	56
63	750			27	490	520	55
62	740			26	480	510	54
61	730			25	480	500	53
60	720			24	470	490	52
59	700			23	460	480	51
58	690			22	460	480	50
57	690			21	450	470	49
56	680			20	440	460	48
55	670			19	440	450	47
54	660	800		18	430	450	46
53	650	790		17	420	440	45
52	650	760		16	420	430	44
51	640	740		15	410	420	44
50	630	720		14	400	410	43
49	620	710	80	13	400	410	42
48	620	700	80	12	390	400	41
47	610	680	80	11	380	390	40
46	600	670	79	10	370	380	39
45	600	660	78	9	360	370	38
44	590	650	76	8	350	360	38
43	590	640	74	7	340	350	37
42	580	630	73	6	330	340	36
41	570	630	71	5	320	330	35
40	570	620	70	4	310	320	34
39	560	610	69	3	300	310	32
38	550	600	67	2	280	290	31
37	550	590	66	1	270	280	30
36	540	580	65	0	250	260	28
35	540	580	64	−1	230	240	27
34	530	570	63	−2	210	220	25
33	520	560	62	−3	200	200	23
32	520	550	61	−4 and below	200	200	20

This table is for use only with the test in this book.

* The Writing multiple-choice score is reported on a 20–80 scale. Use the SAT Score Conversion Table for Writing Composite for the total writing scaled score.

SAT Score conversion table for writing composite

Writing Multiple-Choice Raw Score	Essay Raw Score						
	0	1	2	3	4	5	6
−12	200	200	200	210	240	270	300
−11	200	200	200	210	240	270	300
−10	200	200	200	210	240	270	300
−9	200	200	200	210	240	270	300
−8	200	200	200	210	240	270	300
−7	200	200	200	210	240	270	300
−6	200	200	200	210	240	270	300
−5	200	200	200	210	240	270	300
−4	200	200	200	230	270	300	330
−3	200	210	230	250	290	320	350
−2	200	230	250	280	310	340	370
−1	210	240	260	290	320	360	380
0	230	260	280	300	340	370	400
1	240	270	290	320	350	380	410
2	250	280	300	330	360	390	420
3	260	290	310	340	370	400	430
4	270	300	320	350	380	410	440
5	280	310	330	360	390	420	450
6	290	320	340	360	400	430	460
7	290	330	340	370	410	440	470
8	300	330	350	380	410	450	470
9	310	340	360	390	420	450	480
10	320	350	370	390	430	460	490
11	320	360	370	400	440	470	500
12	330	360	380	410	440	470	500
13	340	370	390	420	450	480	510
14	350	380	390	420	460	490	520
15	350	380	400	430	460	500	530
16	360	390	410	440	470	500	530
17	370	400	420	440	480	510	540
18	380	410	420	450	490	520	550
19	380	410	430	460	490	530	560
20	390	420	440	470	500	530	560
21	400	430	450	480	510	540	570
22	410	440	460	480	520	550	580

Writing Multiple-Choice Raw Score	Essay Raw Score						
	0	1	2	3	4	5	6
23	420	450	470	490	530	560	590
24	420	460	470	500	540	570	600
25	430	460	480	510	540	580	610
26	440	470	490	520	550	590	610
27	450	480	500	530	560	590	620
28	460	490	510	540	570	600	630
29	470	500	520	550	580	610	640
30	480	510	530	560	590	620	650
31	490	520	540	560	600	630	660
32	500	530	550	570	610	640	670
33	510	540	550	580	620	650	680
34	510	550	560	590	630	660	690
35	520	560	570	600	640	670	700
36	530	560	580	610	650	680	710
37	540	570	590	620	660	690	720
38	550	580	600	630	670	700	730
39	560	600	610	640	680	710	740
40	580	610	620	650	690	720	750
41	590	620	640	660	700	730	760
42	600	630	650	680	710	740	770
43	610	640	660	690	720	750	780
44	620	660	670	700	740	770	800
45	640	670	690	720	750	780	800
46	650	690	700	730	770	800	800
47	670	700	720	750	780	800	800
48	680	720	730	760	800	800	800
49	680	720	730	760	800	800	800

Chart for self-appraisal based on the practice test you have just taken

The Chart for Self-Appraisal below tells you quickly where your SAT strengths and weaknesses lie. Check or circle the appropriate box in accordance with the number of your correct answers for each area of the Practice Test you have just taken.

	Writing (Multiple-Choice)	Sentence Completions	Reading Comprehension	Math Questions*
EXCELLENT	42–49	16–19	40–48	44–54
GOOD	37–41	13–15	35–39	32–43
FAIR	31–36	9–12	26–34	27–31
POOR	20–30	5–8	17–25	16–26
VERY POOR	0–19	0–4	0–16	0–15

*Sections 2, 6, 8 only.

Note: In our tests, we have chosen to have Section 3 as the experimental section. We have also chosen it to be a math section since we felt that students may need more practice in the math area than in the verbal area. Note that on the actual SAT you will take, the order of the sections can vary and you will not know which one is experimental, so it is wise to answer all sections and not to leave any section out.

SAT-I VERBAL AND MATH SCORE/PERCENTILE CONVERSION TABLE

Critical reading and writing

SAT scaled verbal score	Percentile rank
800	99.7+
790	99.5
740–780	99
700–730	97
670–690	95
640–660	91
610–630	85
580–600	77
550–570	68
510–540	57
480–500	46
440–470	32
410–430	21
380–400	13
340–370	6
300–330	2
230–290	1
200–220	0–0.5

Math

SAT scaled math score	Percentile rank
800	99.5+
770–790	99.5
720–760	99
670–710	97
640–660	94
610–630	89
590–600	84
560–580	77
530–550	68
510–520	59
480–500	48
450–470	37
430–440	26
390–420	16
350–380	8
310–340	2
210–300	0.5
200	0

EXPLANATORY ANSWERS FOR PRACTICE TEST 5

THE SAT SCORING GUIDE

Section 1: Essay

Score of 6	Score of 5	Score of 4
An essay in this category is *outstanding*, demonstrating *clear and consistent mastery*, although it may have a few minor errors. A typical essay	An essay in this category is *effective*, demonstrating *reasonably consistent mastery*, although it will have occasional errors or lapses in quality. A typical essay	An essay in this category is *competent*, demonstrating *adequate mastery*, although it will have lapses in quality. A typical essay
• effectively and insightfully develops a point of view on the issue and demonstrates outstanding critical thinking, using clearly appropriate examples, reasons, and other evidence to support its position	• effectively develops a point of view on the issue and demonstrates strong critical thinking, generally using appropriate examples, reasons, and other evidence to support its position	• develops a point of view on the issue and demonstrates competent critical thinking, using adequate examples, reasons, and other evidence to support its position
• is well organized and clearly focused, demonstrating clear coherence and smooth progression of ideas	• is well organized and focused, demonstrating coherence and progression of ideas	• is generally organized and focused, demonstrating some coherence and progression of ideas
• exhibits skillful use of language, using a varied, accurate, and apt vocabulary	• exhibits facility in the use of language, using appropriate vocabulary	• exhibits adequate but inconsistent facility in the use of language, using generally appropriate vocabulary
• demonstrates meaningful variety in sentence structure	• demonstrates variety in sentence structure	• demonstrates some variety in sentence structure
• is free of most errors in grammar, usage, and mechanics	• is generally free of most errors in grammar, usage, and mechanics	• has some errors in grammar, usage, and mechanics

Score of 3	Score of 2	Score of 1
An essay in this category is *inadequate*, but demonstrates *developing mastery*, and is marked by ONE OR MORE of the following weaknesses:	An essay in this category is *seriously-limited*, demonstrating *little mastery*, and is flawed by ONE OR MORE of the following weaknesses:	An essay in this category is *fundamentally lacking*, demonstrating *very little* or *no mastery*, and is severely flawed by ONE OR MORE of the following weaknesses:
• develops a point of view on the issue, demonstrating some critical thinking, but may do so inconsistently or use inadequate examples, reasons, or other evidence to support its position	• develops a point of view on the issue that is vague or seriously limited, demonstrating weak critical thinking, providing inappropriate or insufficient examples, reasons, or other evidence to support its position	• develops no viable point of view on the issue, or provides little or no evidence to support its position
• is limited in its organization or focus, or may demonstrate some lapses in coherence or progression of ideas	• is poorly organized and/or focused, or demonstrates serious problems with coherence or progression of ideas	• is disorganized or unfocused, resulting in a disjointed or incoherent essay
• displays developing facility in the use of language, but sometimes uses weak vocabulary or inappropriate word choice	• displays very little facility in the use of language, using very limited vocabulary or incorrect word choice	• displays fundamental errors in vocabulary
• lacks variety or demonstrates problems in sentence structure	• demonstrates frequent problems in sentence structure	• demonstrates severe flaws in sentence structure
• contains an accumulation of errors in grammar, usage, and mechanics	• contains errors in grammar, usage, and mechanics so serious that meaning is somewhat obscured	• contains pervasive errors in grammar, usage, or mechanics that persistently interfere with meaning

Essays not written on the essay assignment will receive a score of zero.

EXPLANATORY ANSWERS FOR PRACTICE TEST 5

Section 2: Math

> When a specific Math Strategy is referred to in the solution, study that strategy, which you will find in "19 Math Strategies."

1. Choice C is correct.

$$\text{Given:} \quad \begin{array}{r} 5\,9\,\Delta \\ -2\,9\,3 \\ \hline \square\,9\,7 \end{array} \qquad \boxed{1}$$

(Use Strategy 17: Use the given information effectively.)

From $\boxed{1}$ we see that $\Delta - 3 = 7$ $\boxed{2}$

From $\boxed{2}$ we get $\Delta = 10$ $\boxed{3}$

From $\boxed{1}$ and $\boxed{3}$ we get $\Delta = 0$ in $\boxed{1}$ and we had to borrow to get 10. Thus, we have

$$\begin{array}{r} 8 \\ 5\,\cancel{9}\,0 \\ -\,293 \\ \hline \square 97 \end{array} \qquad \boxed{4}$$

Calculating $\boxed{4}$, we get

$$\begin{array}{r} 8 \\ 5\,\cancel{9}\,0 \\ -\,293 \\ \hline 297 \end{array}$$

We see that the digit represented by the $\square$ is 2.

2. Choice E is correct.

$$\text{Given:} \quad \frac{a-b}{b} = \frac{1}{2} \qquad \boxed{1}$$

(Use Strategy 13: Find unknowns by multiplication.)

Multiply $\boxed{1}$ by $2b$. We have

$$2\cancel{b}\left(\frac{a-b}{\cancel{b}}\right) = \left(\frac{1}{\cancel{2}}\right)\cancel{2}b$$

$$2(a-b) = b$$

$$2a - 2b = b$$

$$2a = 3b \qquad \boxed{2}$$

(Use Strategy 13: Find unknowns by division.)

Dividing $\boxed{2}$ by $2b$, we get

$$\frac{2a}{2b} = \frac{3\cancel{b}}{2\cancel{b}}$$

$$\frac{a}{b} = \frac{3}{2}$$

3. Choice C is correct.

Number of pounds of force	Height object is raised
3	6 feet
6	12 feet
9	18 feet

$\boxed{1}$

(Use Strategy 2: Translate from words to algebra.)

We are given that:

$$\text{height raised} = c(\text{force exerted}) \qquad \boxed{2}$$

Substituting the numbers from the first row of $\boxed{1}$ into $\boxed{2}$, we get

$$6 = c(3)$$

$$2 = c \qquad \boxed{3}$$

Given: Height object is raised = 15 feet $\boxed{4}$

Substituting $\boxed{3}$ and $\boxed{4}$ into $\boxed{2}$, we have

$$15 = 2(\text{force exerted})$$

$$7\frac{1}{2} = \text{force exerted}$$

4.   Choice D is correct.

Given: $\dfrac{y}{3}, \dfrac{y}{4}, \dfrac{y}{7}$ are integers. $\boxed{1}$

(Use Strategy 17: Use the given information effectively.)

If all items in $\boxed{1}$ are integers, then 3, 4, and 7 divide y evenly (zero remainder). y must be a common multiple of 3, 4, and 7. Multiplying 3, 4, and 7, we get 84.

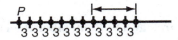

5.   Choice D is correct. **(Use Strategy 11: Use new definitions carefully.)**

We are told that the points are each 3 units apart, as indicated above. We are looking for all those points that are more than 19 units away from point P. By checking the diagram we find 5 such points (marked with arrow in diagram).

6.   Choice B is correct.

Given:

$(a + 2, a - 2) = [a]$ for all integers a. $\boxed{1}$

We need to find $(6,2)$ $\boxed{2}$

(Use Strategy 11: Use new definitions carefully.)

Using $\boxed{1}$ and $\boxed{2}$, we have

$$a + 2 = 6 \quad \text{and} \quad a - 2 = 2$$
$$a = 4 \qquad\qquad a = 4 \quad \boxed{3}$$

Using $\boxed{1}$, $\boxed{2}$, and $\boxed{3}$, we get

$$(6,2) = [4]$$

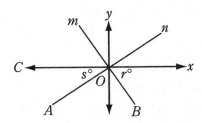

7.   Choice D is correct.

Given: $mB \perp nA$ $\boxed{1}$

From $\boxed{1}$ we know that $\angle AOB$ is a right angle.

Thus $\angle AOB = 90°$ $\boxed{2}$

From the diagram, we see that $\angle COx$ is a straight angle.

Thus $\angle COx = 180°$ $\boxed{3}$

(Use Strategy 3: The whole equals the sum of its parts.)

We know that

$$\angle COA + \angle AOB + \angle BOx = \angle COx \quad \boxed{4}$$

Given: $\angle COA = s°$ $\boxed{5}$

$\angle BOx = r°$ $\boxed{6}$

Substituting $\boxed{2}$, $\boxed{3}$, $\boxed{5}$, and $\boxed{6}$ into $\boxed{4}$, we get

$$s + 90 + r = 180$$
$$s + r = 90$$
$$r + s = 90$$

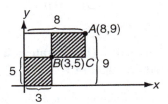

8.   Choice D is correct. **(Use Strategy 17: Use the given information effectively.)**

From the given coordinates, we can find certain distances, as marked above.

Using these distances we find:

$$BC = 8 - 3 = 5 \quad \boxed{1}$$
$$AC = 9 - 5 = 4 \quad \boxed{2}$$

We know that area of a rectangle = length $\times$ width $\boxed{3}$

Using the diagram and $\boxed{3}$, we have

Area of lower rectangle = $5 \times 3 = 15$ $\boxed{4}$

Substituting $\boxed{1}$ and $\boxed{2}$ into $\boxed{3}$, we get

Area of upper rectangle = $5 \times 4 = 20$ $\boxed{5}$

(Use Strategy 13: Find unknowns by addition.)

Adding $\boxed{4}$ and $\boxed{5}$ together, we get

Total area = $15 + 20 = 35$

9. Choice B is correct.

Given: Total number of students = 2,800 $\boxed{1}$

(Use Strategy 2: Translate from words to algebra.)

Number of German students = $\frac{1}{4} \times 2,800$

$$= \frac{2,800}{4}$$

$$= 700 \qquad \boxed{2}$$

(Use Strategy 13: Find unknown by subtraction.)

Subtracting $\boxed{2}$ from $\boxed{1}$, we get

Number of students
not studying German =
$$2,800 - 700 = 2,100$$

10. Choice A is correct. **(Use Strategy 2: Translate from words to algebra.)**

Given: cost of limousine rental = y $\boxed{1}$

Let x = number of students paying $40 $\boxed{2}$

Then $x + 6$ = number of students paying $25 $\boxed{3}$

Using $\boxed{1}$, $\boxed{2}$, and $\boxed{3}$,

We are told that: $x(\$40) = \$y$ $\boxed{4}$

$$(x + 6)(\$25) = \$y \qquad \boxed{5}$$

From $\boxed{4}$ and $\boxed{5}$ we get

$$x(\$40) = (x + 6)(\$25)$$
$$40x = 25x + 150$$
$$15x = 150$$
$$x = 10 \qquad \boxed{6}$$

Substitute $\boxed{6}$ into $\boxed{4}$. We have

$$10(\$40) = \$y$$
$$\$400 = \$y$$

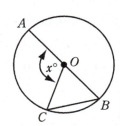

11. Choice C is correct.

Given: AB is a diameter $\boxed{1}$

O is the center of the circle $\boxed{2}$

$CB = OB$ $\boxed{3}$

Using $\boxed{2}$, we know that OB and OC are radii $\boxed{4}$

From $\boxed{4}$ we get that $OB = OC$. $\boxed{5}$

Using $\boxed{3}$ and $\boxed{5}$ together, we have

$$OB = OC = CB \qquad \boxed{6}$$

(Use Strategy 18: Remember the equilateral triangle.)

From $\boxed{6}$, we have $\triangle OBC$ is equilateral $\boxed{7}$

From $\boxed{7}$, we get that $\angle B = \angle C = \angle COB = 60°$ $\boxed{8}$

From $\boxed{1}$, we get $\angle AOB$ is a straight angle. $\boxed{9}$

From $\boxed{9}$, we have $\angle AOB = 180°$ $\boxed{10}$

(Use Strategy 3: The whole equals the sum of its parts.)

From the diagram we see that:

$$\angle AOC + \angle COB = \angle AOB \qquad \boxed{11}$$

Given: $\angle AOC = x°$ $\boxed{12}$

Substituting $\boxed{8}$, $\boxed{10}$, and $\boxed{12}$ into $\boxed{11}$, we get

$$x + 60 = 180$$
$$x = 120 \qquad \boxed{13}$$

(Use Strategy 13: Find unknowns by division.)

Divide $\boxed{13}$ by 6. We have

$$\frac{x}{6} = \frac{120}{6}$$
$$\frac{x}{6} = 20$$

12. Choice D is correct.

Given: Selling price of tent = $64 $\boxed{1}$

Regular price of tent = $80 $\boxed{2}$

(Use Strategy 2: Remember how to find percent discount.)

$$\text{Percent discount} = \frac{\text{amount off}}{\text{original price}} \times 100 \qquad \boxed{3}$$

Subtracting $\boxed{1}$ from $\boxed{2}$, we get

Amount off = \$80 − \$64 = \$16 $\boxed{4}$

Substituting $\boxed{2}$ and $\boxed{4}$ into $\boxed{3}$, we have

$$\text{Percent discount} = \frac{\$16}{\$80} \times 100$$

$$= \frac{\$16 \times 100}{\$80} \qquad \boxed{5}$$

(Use Strategy 19: Factor and reduce.)

$$\text{Percent discount} = \frac{\cancel{\$16} \times \cancel{5} \times 20}{\cancel{\$16} \times \cancel{5}}$$

$$\text{Percent discount} = 20 \qquad \boxed{6}$$

Given: Regular price of different tent = \$200 $\boxed{7}$

New percent discount

$$= 1\frac{1}{2} \times \text{Other tent's percent discount} \qquad \boxed{8}$$

Using $\boxed{6}$ and $\boxed{8}$, we have

$$\text{New percent discount} = 1\frac{1}{2} \times 20 =$$

$$= \frac{3}{2} \times 20$$

$$= 30 \qquad \boxed{9}$$

(Use Strategy 2: Remember how to find percent of a number.)

Percent of a number = percent × number. $\boxed{10}$

Substituting $\boxed{7}$ and $\boxed{9}$ into $\boxed{10}$, we have

$$\text{Amount of discount} = 30\% \times \$200$$

$$= \frac{30}{100} \times \$200$$

$$\text{Amount of discount} = \$60 \qquad \boxed{11}$$

(Use Strategy 13: Find unknowns by subtraction.)

Subtracting $\boxed{11}$ from $\boxed{7}$, we have

Selling price of different tent = \$200 − \$60

$$= \$140$$

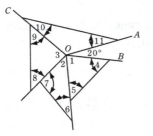

13.   Choice A is correct.

Given: $\angle AOB = 20°$ $\boxed{1}$

(Use Strategy 3: The whole equals the sum of its parts.)

We know that the sum of the angles
of a triangle = 180° $\boxed{2}$

For each of the four triangles, applying $\boxed{2}$ yields:

$$\angle 8 + \angle 9 + \angle 3 = 180 \qquad \boxed{3}$$

$$\angle 6 + \angle 7 + \angle 2 = 180 \qquad \boxed{4}$$

$$\angle 4 + \angle 5 + \angle 1 = 180 \qquad \boxed{5}$$

$$\angle 10 + \angle 11 + \angle COA = 180 \qquad \boxed{6}$$

We know that the sum of all the angles about a
point = 360° $\boxed{7}$

Applying $\boxed{7}$ to point O, we have

$$\angle 1 + \angle 2 + \angle 3 + \angle COA + \angle AOB = 360° \qquad \boxed{8}$$

Substituting $\boxed{1}$ into $\boxed{8}$, we get

$$\angle 1 + \angle 2 + \angle 3 + \angle COA + 20 = 360$$

$$\angle 1 + \angle 2 + \angle 3 + \angle COA = 340 \qquad \boxed{9}$$

(Use Strategy 13: Find unknowns by addition.)

Adding $\boxed{3}$, $\boxed{4}$, $\boxed{5}$, and $\boxed{6}$, we have

$$\angle 4 + \angle 5 + \angle 6 + \angle 7 + \angle 8 + \angle 9 + \angle 10 +$$

$$\angle 11 + \angle 1 + \angle 2 + \angle 3 + \angle COA = 720° \qquad \boxed{10}$$

(Use Strategy 13: Find unknowns by subtraction.)

Subtracting $\boxed{9}$ from $\boxed{10}$, we get

$$\angle 4 + \angle 5 + \angle 6 + \angle 7 + \angle 8 +$$

$$\angle 9 + \angle 10 + \angle 11 = 380° \qquad \boxed{11}$$

Thus, the sum of the marked angles = 380°

14.   Choice E is correct. **(Use Strategy 8: When all choices must be tested, start with choice E.)** If some of the integers in the set are odd, then not all are even. Note the other choices are not correct. For (D), all integers cannot be even since some are odd. For (C), since *some* integers are odd we cannot imply that all integers are

odd. For (B), if an integer is even, it may not be in set X. Similarly for (A) if an integer is odd, it may not be in set X.

15. Choice A is correct. **(Use Strategy 6: Know how to manipulate inequalities.)** Since the absolute value of $y + 3$ must be less than 3, y must be less than 0 but greater than -6.

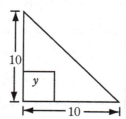

16. Choice E is correct.

We know that area of a triangle =

$$\frac{1}{2} \times \text{base} \times \text{height} \qquad \boxed{1}$$

Using the diagram and substituting into $\boxed{1}$, we get

$$\text{Area of triangle} = \frac{1}{2} \times 10 \times 10$$
$$= 50 \qquad \boxed{2}$$

(Use Strategy 2: Translate from words to algebra.)

We are told:

Area of square $= \frac{1}{5} \times$ area of triangle $\qquad \boxed{3}$

We know that

Area of a square $= (\text{side})^2 \qquad \boxed{4}$

Using the diagram, and substituting into $\boxed{4}$, we get

$$\text{Area of square} = y^2 \qquad \boxed{5}$$

Substituting $\boxed{2}$ and $\boxed{5}$ into $\boxed{3}$, we have

$$y^2 = \frac{1}{5} \times 50$$
$$y^2 = 10 \qquad \boxed{6}$$

Take the square root of both sides of $\boxed{6}$. We get

$$y = \sqrt{10}$$

17. Choice C is correct.

Given: Print rate $= \dfrac{80 \text{ characters}}{\text{second}} \qquad \boxed{1}$

$\dfrac{\text{number of characters}}{\text{page}} = 2,400 \qquad \boxed{2}$

(Use Strategy 13: Find unknowns by division.)

Dividing $\boxed{2}$ by $\boxed{1}$, we have

$$\frac{2,400 \text{ characters}}{\text{page}} \div \frac{80 \text{ characters}}{\text{second}} =$$

$$\frac{2,400 \text{ characters}}{\text{page}} \times \frac{\text{second}}{80 \text{ characters}} =$$

$$\frac{2,400 \text{ seconds}}{80 \text{ pages}}$$

$$= \frac{30 \text{ seconds}}{\text{page}} \qquad \boxed{3}$$

The time for an M-page report will be

$$\frac{30 \text{ seconds}}{\text{page}} \times M \text{ pages} =$$

Time for M-page report $= 30M$ seconds $\qquad \boxed{4}$

(Use Strategy 10: Know how to use units.)

To change time from seconds to minutes, we multiply by

$$\frac{1 \text{ minute}}{60 \text{ seconds}} \qquad \boxed{5}$$

Applying $\boxed{5}$ to $\boxed{4}$, we get

Time for M-page report, in minutes $= 30M$ seconds $\times \dfrac{1 \text{ minute}}{60 \text{ seconds}}$

$$= \frac{30M \text{ minutes}}{60}$$

$$= \frac{M}{2} \text{ minutes}$$

18. Choice B is correct.

Given: On Friday, the satellite passed over Washington, D.C., at midnight $\qquad \boxed{1}$

Complete orbit $= 5$ hours $\qquad \boxed{2}$

(Use Strategy 17: Use the given information effectively.)

Using $\boxed{2}$, we see that five complete

orbits $= 5 \times 5 = 25$ hours $= 1$ day $+ 1$ hour $\qquad \boxed{3}$

From $\boxed{1}$ and $\boxed{2}$ we know that

DAY	TIME PASSING OVER D.C.	
Friday	7:00 P.M., midnight	$\boxed{4}$

Applying $\boxed{3}$ to $\boxed{4}$, and continuing this chart, we have

Saturday	8:00 P.M., 1:00 A.M.	
Sunday	9:00 P.M., 2:00 A.M.	
Monday	10:00 P.M., 3:00 A.M.	
Tuesday	11:00 P.M., 4:00 A.M.	
Wednesday	midnight, 5:00 A.M.	

19. Choice D is correct. **(Use Strategy 2: Know how to find percent of a number.)**

$$\text{Let } x = \text{price of car} \qquad \boxed{1}$$

$$\text{Given: 1st reduction} = 30\% \qquad \boxed{2}$$

$$\text{2nd reduction} = 40\% \qquad \boxed{3}$$

We know that the amount of discount =

$$\text{percent} \times \text{price} \qquad \boxed{4}$$

Using $\boxed{1}$, $\boxed{2}$, and $\boxed{4}$, we get

$$\text{Amount of 1st discount} = 30\% \times x$$

$$= .30x \qquad \boxed{5}$$

(Use Strategy 13: Find unknowns by subtraction.) Subtracting $\boxed{5}$ from $\boxed{1}$, we have

$$\text{Reduced price} = x - .30x$$

$$= .70x \qquad \boxed{6}$$

Using $\boxed{3}$, $\boxed{6}$, and $\boxed{4}$, we get

$$\text{Amount of 2nd discount} = 40\% \times .70x$$

$$= .40 \times .70x$$

$$= .28x \qquad \boxed{7}$$

Subtracting $\boxed{7}$ from $\boxed{6}$, we have

$$\text{Price after 2nd reduction} = .70x - .28x$$

$$= .42x \qquad \boxed{8}$$

(Use Strategy 16: The obvious may be tricky!)

Since $\boxed{8} = .42x$, it is 42% of the original price of x. This is *not* the answer to the question.

Since $\boxed{8}$ is 42% of the original, it is the result of a 58% discount.

The answer is 58%.

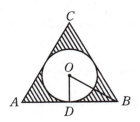

20. Choice A is correct. **(Use Strategy 3: Know how to find unknown quantities from known quantities.)**

The total shaded area = area of triangle ABC − area of the circle.

$$\text{Given: Diameter of circle} = 2 \qquad \boxed{1}$$

The radius, r, of the circle = 1. Thus the area of the circle is $\pi r^2 = \pi(1) = \pi$. $\qquad \boxed{2}$

Now we have to find the area of the equilateral triangle.

(Use Strategy 14: Draw lines to help find the answer.)

Draw radius OD, with D the point of tangency and OB as shown above. $\qquad \boxed{3}$

(Use Strategy 18: Remember the equilateral triangle.)

$$\text{Given: Triangle } ACB \text{ is equilateral} \qquad \boxed{4}$$

From $\boxed{3}$ we get $OD \perp AB$, since radius $\perp$ tangent

at point of tangency. $\qquad \boxed{5}$

From $\boxed{5}$, we get $\angle ODB = 90°$ $\qquad \boxed{6}$

From $\boxed{4}$, we get $\angle ABC = 60°$ $\qquad \boxed{7}$

From the geometry of regular polygons, we know that OB bisects $\angle ABC$. $\boxed{8}$

From $\boxed{7}$ and $\boxed{8}$ we get $\angle DBO = 30°$ $\boxed{9}$

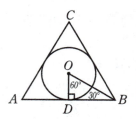

From $\boxed{6}$ and $\boxed{9}$, we have

$\triangle ODB$ is a 30–60–90 triangle

From $\boxed{1}$, we get $OD = 1$ $\boxed{10}$

(Use Strategy 18: Remember the special right triangles.)

Using $\boxed{10}$ and the properties of the 30–60–90 right triangle, we get $OB = 2$, $DB = 1\sqrt{3} = \sqrt{3}$ $\boxed{11}$

We know $AB = 2 \times DB$ $\boxed{12}$

Substituting $\boxed{11}$ into $\boxed{12}$, we have

$$AB = 2\sqrt{3} \qquad \boxed{13}$$

Let CD, the altitude of triangle ABC, be h.

The area of triangle $ABC =$

$$\frac{1}{2}(CD \times AB) = \frac{1}{2}(h \times 2\sqrt{3}) = h\sqrt{3}$$

Now $AD = \sqrt{3}$ and $AC = 2\sqrt{3}$.

By the Pythagorean Theorem,

$$(2\sqrt{3})^2 - (\sqrt{3})^2 = h^2$$

$$(4 \times 3) - 3 = h^2$$

$$9 = h^2$$

$$3 = h$$

So the area of the triangle $= 3\sqrt{3}$ $\boxed{14}$

(Use Strategy 13: Find unknowns by subtraction.)

Subtracting $\boxed{2}$ from $\boxed{14}$, we get

Shaded area $= 3\sqrt{3} - \pi$

EXPLANATORY ANSWERS FOR PRACTICE TEST 5

Section 3: Math

When a specific Math Strategy is referred to in the solution, study that strategy, which you will find in "19 Math Strategies."

1. Choice A is correct. (**Use Strategy 2: Translate from words to algebra.**)

Let x = Amount that Greg had to start.

Then $x + 5$ = Amount that Greg has after receiving

$5 from David. $\boxed{1}$

$25 = Amount David has. $\boxed{2}$

We are told that Greg now has $\frac{1}{5}$ as much as David does.

This translates to:

$$\text{Greg} = \tfrac{1}{5}(\text{David}) \qquad \boxed{3}$$

Substituting $\boxed{1}$ and $\boxed{2}$ into $\boxed{3}$, we get

$$x + 5 = \tfrac{1}{5}(25)$$
$$x + 5 = \tfrac{1}{5} \times 5 \times 5$$
$$x + 5 = 5$$
$$x = 0$$

2. Choice C is correct. (**Use Strategy 17: Use the given information effectively.**)

The ratio of the perimeter of the larger square to that of the smaller is

$$\frac{6+6+6+6}{2+2+2+2} = \frac{24}{8} = \frac{3}{1} \text{ or } 3:1$$

One can arrive at this result directly if one remembers that the ratio of the perimeters of two squares is the same as the ratio of the lengths of the sides of the two squares.

3. Choice E is correct. (**Use Strategy 9: Remember the rate, time, and distance relationship.**) Remember that rate $\times$ time = distance

or $\qquad$ average rate = $\dfrac{\text{total distance}}{\text{total time}}$

or $\qquad$ average rate = $\dfrac{1{,}056 \text{ feet}}{12 \text{ seconds}}$

$$= 88 \text{ feet/second}$$

4. Choice B is correct.

Given: $2z + 1 + 2 + 2z + 3 + 2z = 3 + 1 + 2$

(**Use Strategy 1: Cancel numbers from both sides of an equation.**)

We can immediately cancel the $+1$, $+2$, and $+3$ from each side. We get

$$2z + 2z + 2z = 0$$
$$6z = 0$$
$$z = 0$$

Thus, $z + 4 = 0 + 4 = 4$

5. Choice B is correct.

$$2(w)(x)(-y) - 2(-w)(-x)(y) =$$
$$-2wxy - 2wxy =$$
$$-4wxy$$

6. Choice A is correct. (**Use Strategy 2: Translate from words to algebra.**)

The sum of the square of x and the square of y

$$\underbrace{}_{\displaystyle x^2} \quad + \quad \underbrace{}_{\displaystyle y^2}$$

So, five times that quantity is

$$5(x^2 + y^2)$$

7. Choice C is correct. (**Use Strategy 2: Translate from words to algebra.**) We are given

$$p > 0 \qquad \boxed{1}$$
$$q > 0 \qquad \boxed{2}$$
$$x < 0 \qquad \boxed{3}$$
$$y < 0 \qquad \boxed{4}$$

(**Use Strategy 6: Know how to manipulate inequalities.**)

$$p > q \text{ or } q < p \qquad \boxed{5}$$
$$x > y \text{ or } y < x \qquad \boxed{6}$$

For I: Add $-p$ to both sides of inequality $\boxed{5}$:

$$q - p < 0$$

Thus, I is less than zero.

For II: From inequalities $\boxed{2}$ and $\boxed{4}$, $qy < 0$, and II is less than zero.

For III: The value of p and x depends on specific values of p and x.

(**Use Strategy 7: Use numerics to help decide the answer.**)

EXAMPLE 1

$$p = 3 \text{ and } x = -5$$

Thus, $\qquad p + x < 0$

EXAMPLE 2

$$p = 5 \text{ and } x = -3$$

Thus, $\qquad p + x > 0$

Thus, III is not always less than zero. Choice C is correct.

8. Choice A is correct.

Given: $a = 1, b = -2, c = -2$ $\qquad \boxed{1}$

$$\frac{b^2 c}{(a - c)^2} \qquad \boxed{2}$$

Substitute $\boxed{1}$ into $\boxed{2}$. We get

$$\frac{(-2)^2(-2)}{(1 - (-2))^2} =$$
$$\frac{4(-2)}{(3)^2} =$$
$$\frac{-8}{9}$$

9. Choice A is correct.

Given: $\qquad y = 28j \qquad \boxed{1}$

$\qquad j$ is any integer $\qquad \boxed{2}$

(**Use Strategy 13: Find unknowns by division.**)

Divide $\boxed{1}$ by 2. We have

$$\frac{y}{2} = \frac{28j}{2}$$
$$\frac{y}{2} = 14j \qquad \boxed{3}$$

(**Use Strategy 19: Factor.**)

Factor the 14 in $\boxed{3}$. We get

$$\frac{y}{2} = (2)(7)(j) \qquad \boxed{4}$$

Using $\boxed{2}$ and $\boxed{4}$, we see that $\frac{y}{2}$ is an integer with a factor of 2.

Thus, $\frac{y}{2}$ is even.

10. Choice B is correct.

Given: $3a + 4b = 4a - 4b = 21$ $\qquad \boxed{1}$

From $\boxed{1}$, we get

$$3a + 4b = 21 \qquad \boxed{2}$$
$$4a - 4b = 21 \qquad \boxed{3}$$

(**Use Strategy 13: Find unknowns by addition.**)

Add $\boxed{2}$ and $\boxed{3}$ together. We get

$$3a + \cancel{4b} = 21$$
$$+\; 4a - \cancel{4b} = 21$$
$$\overline{7a \qquad\;\; = 42}$$
$$a \qquad\;\; = 6$$

11. Choice D is correct. (**Use Strategy 2: Translate from words to algebra.**)

$$N + 6N + 9N = 16N$$

Any divisor of 16 or of N will divide $16N$.

(**Use Strategy 8: When all choices must be tested, start with Choice E and work backward.**) Starting with Choice E, we see that 16 divides $16N$ evenly. Choice D, however, does *not* divide $16N$ evenly. Thus we have found the answer.

12. Choice D is correct.

We are given: $x = 3a - 18$ $\boxed{1}$

$$5y = 3a + 7 \quad \boxed{2}$$

We need $5y - x$. $\boxed{3}$

(Use Strategy 13: Find unknown expressions by subtracting equations.) Subtracting $\boxed{1}$ from $\boxed{2}$, we get

$$5y - x = 3a + 7 - (3a - 18)$$
$$= 3a + 7 - 3a + 18$$
$$5y - x = 25$$

13. Choice B is correct. **(Use Strategy 2: Translate from words to algebra.)**

Given:
$$p + pq = 4(p - pq) \quad \boxed{1}$$

(Use Strategy 13: Find unknown expressions by division.) Since $pq \neq 0$, divide $\boxed{1}$ by p.

$$1 + q = 4(1 - q) \quad \boxed{2}$$

or $\quad 1 + q = 4 - 4q$

or $\quad 5q = 3$

or $\quad q = \dfrac{3}{5}$

Thus, q has exactly one value.

Since p cannot be determined from equation $\boxed{1}$, none of the other choices is correct.

14. Choice D is correct. **(Use Strategy 17: Use the given information effectively.)**

Since $2 + \dfrac{1}{z} = 0$, we have

$$\dfrac{1}{z} = -2$$

$$z = -\dfrac{1}{2} \quad \boxed{1}$$

We need $9 + 9z$. $\boxed{2}$

Substituting $\boxed{1}$ into $\boxed{2}$, we get

$$9 + 9\left(-\dfrac{1}{2}\right) = 9 - 4\dfrac{1}{2} = 4\dfrac{1}{2} = \dfrac{9}{2}$$

15. Choice C is correct. **(Use Strategy 17: Use the given information effectively.)** We set $y = x^2 = x$.

$x = 1$ or $x = 0$

Thus they intersect twice.

16. Choice C is correct.

We are given: $wx = y$ $\boxed{1}$

or $w = \dfrac{y}{x}$ $\boxed{2}$

(Use Strategy 2: Translate from words to algebra.) If x and y are multiplied by 6, in $\boxed{1}$, we have

$$w(\cancel{6})(x) = (\cancel{6})(y)$$

$$wx = y$$

$$w = \dfrac{y}{x} \quad \boxed{3}$$

$\boxed{2}$ and $\boxed{3}$ are the same.

Therefore $\dfrac{y}{x} = 1\left(\dfrac{y}{x}\right)$

The answer is now clear.

17. Choice B is correct. **(Use Strategy 3: The whole equals the sum of its parts.)** The path is made up of 4 semicircles, three of diameter 4 and one of diameter 8.

Diameter $(d) = 2 \times$ radius (r) or $r = \dfrac{d}{2}$. Remember circumference is $2\pi r$. Thus,

$$\dfrac{1}{2} \text{ circumference} = \dfrac{1}{2}(2\pi r).$$

Therefore, the length of the path is

$$\dfrac{1}{2}(2\pi)\left(\dfrac{4}{2}\right) + \dfrac{1}{2}(2\pi)\left(\dfrac{4}{2}\right) + \dfrac{1}{2}(2\pi)\left(\dfrac{4}{2}\right) + \dfrac{1}{2}(2\pi)\left(\dfrac{8}{2}\right)$$

$$= 10\pi$$

18. Choice C is correct. **(Use Strategy 10: Know how to use units.)**

$$\dfrac{7x}{144} \text{ yards} = \left(\dfrac{7x}{144} \text{ yards}\right)\left(\dfrac{36 \text{ inches}}{\text{yards}}\right) =$$

(Use Strategy 19: Factor and reduce.)

$$= \dfrac{7x}{\cancel{12} \times 12} \times \cancel{12} \times 3 \text{ inches}$$

$$= \dfrac{7x}{\cancel{3} \times 4} \times \cancel{3} \text{ inches}$$

$$\dfrac{7x}{144} \text{ yards} = \dfrac{7x}{4} \text{ inches} \quad \boxed{1}$$

$$\dfrac{5y}{12} \text{ feet} = \left(\dfrac{5y}{\cancel{12}} \text{feet}\right)\left(\cancel{12}\dfrac{\text{inches}}{\cancel{\text{foot}}}\right) =$$

$$\dfrac{5y}{12} \text{ feet} = 5y \text{ inches} \quad \boxed{2}$$

(Use Strategy 13: Find unknown expressions by addition of equations.) Adding $\boxed{1}$ and $\boxed{2}$, we have

$$\frac{7x}{144}\text{ yards} + \frac{5y}{12}\text{ feet} = \left(\frac{7x}{4} + 5y\right)\text{ inches}$$

19. Choice A is correct.

$$\text{Given: } x < 0 \qquad \boxed{1}$$
$$y < 0 \qquad \boxed{2}$$

(Use Strategy 6: Know how to manipulate inequalities.)

Multiplying $\boxed{1}$ by $\boxed{2}$, we get

$$x \cdot y > 0 \qquad \boxed{3}$$

Thus I is always positive.

Adding $\boxed{1}$ and $\boxed{2}$, we get

$$x + y < 0 \qquad \boxed{4}$$

Thus II is not positive.

(Use Strategy 7: Use numerics to help find the answer.)

$$\text{Let } x = -2, y = -3$$
$$\text{III becomes } x - y = -2 - (-3)$$
$$= -2 + 3$$
$$= 1 \qquad \boxed{5}$$
$$\text{Now let } x = -3, y = -2$$
$$\text{III becomes } x - y = -3 - (-2)$$
$$= -3 + 2$$
$$= -1 \qquad \boxed{6}$$

From $\boxed{5}$ and $\boxed{6}$, we see that III is not always positive.

Using $\boxed{3}$, $\boxed{4}$, and $\boxed{6}$, we find that only Choice A, I only, is correct.

20. Choice D is correct.

$$\text{Given: } a + 3b = 11 \qquad \boxed{1}$$
$$a \text{ and } b \text{ are positive integers} \qquad \boxed{2}$$

(Use Strategy 17: Use the given information effectively.)

From $\boxed{1}$, we get

$$a = 11 - 3b \qquad \boxed{3}$$

From $\boxed{3}$, we see that a will be largest when b is smallest. Using $\boxed{2}$, we get

$$b = 1 \text{ is its smallest value} \qquad \boxed{4}$$

Substituting $\boxed{4}$ into $\boxed{3}$, we have

$$a = 11 - 3(1)$$
$$a = 11 - 3$$
$$a = 8$$

EXPLANATORY ANSWERS FOR PRACTICE TEST 5

Section 4: Critical reading

> As you read these Explanatory Answers, you are advised to refer to "16 Verbal (Critical Reading) Strategies."

1. Choice E is correct. See **Sentence Completion Strategy 2.** Examine the first word of each choice. Choice A, committees, and Choice B, tribes, are incorrect because it is clear that committees and tribes cannot be equated with cities such as Athens. Now consider the other choices. Choice E, societies...participated, is the only choice with a word pair that makes sense in the sentence.

2. Choice C is correct. See **Sentence Completion Strategy 2.** Examine the first word of each choice. Choice A, abolished, and Choice E, discounted, do not make sense because we cannot say that fossils are abolished or discounted in rock formations. Now consider the other choices. Choice C, preserved...hardened, is the only choice with a word pair that makes sense in the sentence.

3. Choice B is correct. See **Sentence Completion Strategy 2.** Examine the first word of each choice. We eliminate Choice A, dominated, and Choice D, cautioned, because the trends do *not* dominate or caution affluence. Now consider the other choices. Choice C, accentuated... depression, and Choice E, accepted...revolution, do *not* make sense in the sentence. Choice B, reflected...prosperity, *does* make sense in the sentence.

4. Choice A is correct. See **Sentence Completion Strategy 1.** The word "conserve" (meaning "to protect from loss") completes the sentence so that it makes good sense. The other choices don't do that.

5. Choice B is correct. See **Sentence Completion Strategy 1.** The word "prevalent" (meaning widely or commonly occurring) completed the sentence so that it makes good sense. The other choices don't do that.

6. Choice B is correct. Since this question has two blanks, let us use **Sentence Completion Strategy 2.** When we use Step 1 of Strategy 2, we find a very unusual situation in this question—the first words in all five choices make sense: "With lack of" *advice* or *control* or *opportunity* or *sympathy* or *conscience,* "anyone can develop the disease of alcoholism..." Accordingly, we must go to Step 2 of Strategy 2 and consider *both* words of each choice. When we do so, we find that only Choice B, control...foolishly, makes good sense in the sentence.

7. Choice B is correct. See **Sentence Completion Strategy 4.** "Because" is a *result indicator.* Since the generating system was not functioning efficiently, the use of electricity had to be *diminished* or *curtailed.*

8. Choice B is correct. See **Sentence Completion Strategy 1.** Something staple, such as bread, is in constant supply and demand. Beer, then, is considered a liquid bread by the Bavarians. Choices A, C, D, and E do not make good sense in the sentence.

9. Choice D is correct. One can see from the gist of the whole passage that the author is warning the reader of the dangers of anarchy and war. See line 4, "It is the age of war," and line 5, which speaks of the need for "the age of civilized man." Thus Choice D would be best.

10. Choice A is correct. See line 10 where the author says that "It calls for total awareness, total commitment," indicating limited hope.

11. Choice B is correct. It can be seen that the author contrasts novel reading in the past with novel reading in the present throughout the passage. Although the author does mention a "defect in today's novels" (Choice A), that is not the main consideration in the passage.

12. Choice E is correct. See lines 2–6: "there were few diversions…not irritated by the digressions and irrelevances…" Do not be lured into Choice B: Although some great novels are long, not all are.

13. Choice B is correct. See lines 26–29: "Most social scientists…have assumed that the minimum economic needs of the aged should be lower than those of the younger family."

14. Choice E is correct. Choice A does not make sense because artistic interest has nothing to do with the relationship between age and income. Choices C and D do not make sense because theories cannot casually have curiosity or gratitude. Of the remaining choices, Choice E, understood, is the only one that makes sense in the sentence. See also **Reading Comprehension Strategy 5.**

15. Choice A is correct. See lines 79–82: "[The data] disclose sharp income inequalities within every age group…"

16. Choice E is correct. For I, see lines 100–101: "…those sixty-five and over are expected to increase 672 percent." For III, see lines 54–58: "For the growing working-class family, limited in income by the very nature of the breadwinner's occupation…"

17. Choice C is correct. See lines 26–29: The sentence after the "functional ethos" sentence refers to "these values." See also **Reading Comprehension Strategy 5.**

18. Choice D is correct. See lines 104–107: "With the more rapid expansion of these two low-income groups, the young and the old…"

19. Choice D is correct. For I, see lines 83–85: "A spending unit's income-tenth position *within his age category* varies much less, if at all, and is determined primarily by his occupation." For III, see lines 54–58: "For the growing, working-class family, limited in income by the very nature of the breadwinner's occupation…"

20. Choice A is correct. Notice that "ethos" sounds a lot like "ethics," which has to do with moral principles, or character. See also **Reading Comprehension Strategy 5 and Vocabulary Strategy 3.**

21. Choice C is correct. See lines 40–43: "Despite his seniority, the older worker is likely to be downgraded to a lower-paying job…"

22. Choice C is correct. See lines 45–48: "The early and lower income period of a person's working life, during which he acquires his basic vocational skills…"

23. Choice C is correct. See lines 83–85: "A spending unit's income-tenth position is…determined primarily by his occupation."

24. Choice D is correct. The phrase "the legendary land of economic opportunity where any man can work his way to the top" (lines 86–88), in contrast to what the author really believes, represents *sarcasm*.

EXPLANATORY ANSWERS FOR PRACTICE TEST 5

Section 5: Writing

1. **(C)** Choice A is awkward and wordy. Choice B is indirect. Choice C is correct. Choice D is unacceptable idiomatically even though the meaning intended is there. Choice E changes the meaning of the original sentence.

2. **(D)** Choice A has incorrect punctuation. A dash (not a comma) is required after "that's not all." In Choice B, the expression "another thing" is too general. Choice C changes the meaning of the original sentence. Choice D is correct. Choice E is too indirectly expressed.

3. **(E)** Choice A suffers from too many "ands" (anditis). Choices B and C are incorrect because they lack parallel construction. In Choice D, the correct form of the infinitive meaning "to rest" is "(to) lie"—not "(to) lay." Choice E is correct.

4. **(B)** Choice A is awkward. Choice B is correct. Choice C is ungrammatical—"courses" cannot act as a direct object after the copulative construction "am not certain." Choice D is too wordy. Choice E does not make sense.

5. **(A)** Choice A is correct. Choice B is too indirectly stated. Choice C is verbose—since the people "had no doubt," there is no need to use the expression "it was clear." Choice D is indirect and awkward. Choice E changes the meaning of the original sentence.

6. **(B)** Choice A is too wordy. Choice B is correct. Choice C is indirectly stated. Choices D and E change the meaning of the original sentence.

7. **(D)** Choice A is indirectly stated. Choice B deviates from the original statement. Choice C makes the sentence a run-on. Choice D is correct. Choice E changes the meaning of the original sentence.

8. **(E)** Choice A is awkward. Choice B has a meaning which differs from that of the original sentence. Choices C and D are unidiomatic. Choice E is correct.

9. **(D)** The clause "that was rotten" is misplaced in Choices A, B, and C. Choice D is correct. Choice E is incorrect because the passive use of the verb is not as effective as the active use, in this context.

10. **(B)** Choice A uses the wrong tense sequence. Since the reading of the book took place before the watching of the picture, the reading should be expressed in the past perfect tense, which shows action prior to the simple past tense. Choice B corrects the error with the use of the past perfect tense, "had read," instead of the past tense, "read." Choices C, D, and E do not correct the mistake, and Choice E also changes the meaning.

11. **(D)** Choice A is wrong because the word "them," being plural, cannot properly take the singular antecedent, "anyone." Choices B and C do not correct this error. Choice D corrects it by substituting "to him or to her" for "to them." Choice E, while correcting the error, changes the meaning of the sentence.

12. **(D)** "...between *him* and *me*." The object of the preposition *between* must be an objective case form (*me*—not *I*).

13. **(E)** All underlined parts are correct.

14. **(A)** "The subject...was *we*..." The predicate nominative form is *we*—not *us*.

15. **(B)** "...the prize would go to him..." The object of the preposition *to* must be an objective case form (*him*—not he).

16. **(E)** All underlined parts are correct.

17. **(B)** "...if you *had gone to him*..." In the "if" clause of a past contrary-to-fact condition, one must use the past perfect subjunctive form *had gone*—not the future perfect subjunctive form *would have gone*.

18. **(A)** "The *child's* asking..." A noun or pronoun that precedes a gerund is in the possessive case. We, therefore, say *child's asking*—not *child asking*.

19. **(E)** All underlined parts are correct.

20. **(D)** "...who are younger than *she*." The nominative case (*she*—not *her*) must be used after the conjunction *than* when the pronoun is the subject of an elliptical clause ("than she is").

21. **(E)** All underlined parts are correct.

22. **(A)** "The novelists *whom* readers choose..." The direct object of the verb (choose) must be the objective case form (*whom*—not *who*).

23. **(C)** "The problem...disturbs..." The subject (*problem*) is singular. Therefore the verb (*disturbs*) must be singular.

24. **(B)** "...son *could have* gone..." The phrase *could of* is always incorrect, as it is a speech-based error from could have. Do not use *of* for *have*.

25. **(D)** "...the horse *which* had fallen..." The pronoun *which* should be used to refer to animals and things; *who* should be used to refer only to people.

26. **(D)** "...then *he or she* should make..." A pronoun must agree with its antecedent (*someone*) in number. Since *someone* is singular, the pronoun must be singular (*he or she*—not *they*).

27. **(A)** "The man *whom* Mexican authorities believe to be..." The subject of an infinitive must be in the objective case. The pronoun "whom" in the objective case—not "who" in the nominative case—is the subject of the verbal infinitive "to be."

28. **(C)** "...the child fell *off* the unscreened porch." The correct preposition is simply "off"—not "off of"—to introduce a noun or pronoun.

29. **(A)** "...ran *more swiftly*..." We must use an adverb—not an adjective—to modify a verb. Therefore, we use the adverbial comparative construction "more swiftly" instead of the comparative adjective "swifter" to modify the verb "ran."

30. **(D)** Choice A is incorrect because ending the sentence after company would destroy the charming contrasting idea which follows. Choice B is incorrect because sentence 3 clearly interrupts the flow of thought between sentences 2 and 4. Choice C is incorrect because sentence 3 relates closely in structure and content to sentence 1, especially in the reference to the caves of France, and should follow sentence 1. Choice D is correct. Choice E is incorrect because the explanation for Lampe-Pigeon which now introduces the passage is the best opening sentence. Sentence 3 clearly needs prior information to explain its references to the lamp and to the caves of France.

31. **(C)** Choices A and D are incorrect because they create a contradictory impression by equating tall with more than nine and one-half inches, even though Choice D is preferable because it is more concise. Choice B is incorrect because it conveys an unwarranted apologetic note for the height of the lamp by using the conjunction although. Choice C is correct because it concisely and clearly describes the height and type of lamp being described. Choice E is incorrect because it is wordy and therefore awkward.

32. **(A)** Choice A is correct because the simple prepositional phrase is preferable to the more awkward gerund form of the incorrect Choice B. Choice C is incorrect because it is too wordy and awkward. Choice D, in addition to being the above-mentioned more awkward gerund form, is incorrect also because of the inappropriate use of the preposition <u>to</u> after the adjective <u>suitable</u>. Choice E is incorrect because it is overly long and also would create an inappropriate repetition with the word <u>centerpiece,</u> which is used in the next phrase.

33. **(B)** Choice A is incorrect because <u>glass globed</u> is an awkward descriptive phrase. Choice B is correct because it is more concise than the repetitive clause <u>which contains within it a glass globe</u>. Choice C is incorrect and completely changes the focus of the sentence from the lamp to the globe. Choice D is incorrect because it is wordy and repetitive. Choice E is incorrect because it is too verbose.

34. **(B)** Sentence 6 contradicts and is not consistent with the paragraph and should be deleted. It would also make no sense to include that sentence in any other part of the paragraph.

35. **(D)** Since the author of the paragraph wants to show the beauty of the Lampe-Pigeon, he would contrast that lamp with the modern lamps and use the word "but" not "and." Therefore, Choice D is correct and Choice E is incorrect. For Choice A, "manufactured" is appropriate and it is not necessary to change the word to "produced." For Choice B, "Lampe-Pigeon" sounds better than "lamp in question." After all, this is not a legal document! For Choice C, "modernization" would contradict the antiquity of the lamp.

EXPLANATORY ANSWERS FOR PRACTICE TEST 5

Section 6: Math

When a specific Math Strategy is referred to in the solution, study that strategy, which you will find in "19 Math Strategies."

1. Choice E is correct. **(Use Strategy 1: Cancel quantities to make the problem simpler.)** Subtract 14 from both sides of the equation:

$$5\sqrt{x} + 14 = 20$$
$$5\sqrt{x} = 6$$

Divide by 5:

$$\sqrt{x} = \frac{6}{5}$$

Square both sides:

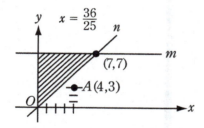

$$x = \frac{36}{25}$$

2. Choice A is correct. **(Use Strategy 17: Use the given information effectively.)** Since n goes through point O, the origin, whose coordinates are $(0,0)$, and through $(7,7)$, all of the points on n have x- and y-coordinates that equal each other. Choice A, $(4,3)$, is 4 units to the right of O but only 3 units up. It is below n and not in the shaded area.

3. Choice B is correct. **(Use Strategy 2: Translate from words to algebra.)** This problem tests the concepts of set union and set intersection. We can solve these types of problems with a diagram.

Thus, draw the diagram:

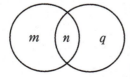

Where

m = number of students taking *only* calculus

q = number of students taking *only* physics

n = number of students taking *both* calculus and physics

Thus,

$m + n$ = number of students in calculus class

$n + q$ = number of students in physics class

$m + n + q$ = number of students taking either calculus or physics or both

We are given that

$$m + n + q = 36 \qquad \boxed{1}$$
$$n = 10 \qquad \boxed{2}$$
$$m + n = 31 \qquad \boxed{3}$$

We want to find

$$n + q \qquad \boxed{4}$$

(Use Strategy 13: Find unknowns by subtracting equations.) Subtract equation $\boxed{2}$ from equation $\boxed{3}$ to get

$$m = 21 \qquad \boxed{5}$$

Now subtract equation $\boxed{5}$ from equation $\boxed{1}$ to get

$$n + q = 15$$

4. Choice D is correct. **(Use Strategy 7: Use numerics to help find the answer.)** In order to show a counterexample to refute Mr. Simmons's argument, we must come up with two numbers a and b such that $a^2 > b^2$ but a is not greater than b. Choice A is incorrect since it is not true that

$a^2 > b^2$ in this case. Choice B is incorrect since it is true that $a^2 > b^2$ and that $a > b$. Choice C is incorrect because $a^2 > b^2$ and $a > b$. Choice D is correct: a^2 is greater than b^2 since $(-4)^2 > (-2)^2$. But it is not true that $a > b$ since -4 is *not* greater than -2. Choice E is incorrect since it is not true that $a^2 > b^2$ in this case.

5. Choice E is correct. **(Use Strategy 7: Use specific numerical examples to prove or disprove your guess.)**

$$\sqrt{2+2} \neq \sqrt{2} + \sqrt{2}$$

$$2^2 + 2^2 \neq (2+2)^2$$

$$2^1 + 2^2 \neq 2^{1+2}$$

Therefore, neither (I) nor (II) nor (III) is generally true.

6. Choice B is correct. The only element common to R and S is $x = 1$.

7. Choice A is correct. To find the coordinates of the intersection point, we must first solve the equations $y = x - 1$ and $2x + 5y = 9$. In the equation $2x + 5y = 9$, we substitute $y = x - 1$. We obtain

$$2x + 5(x - 1) = 9$$

Thus

$$2x + 5x - 5 = 9$$

and

$$7x = 14$$
$$x = 2$$

From the first equation, $y = x - 1$, so $y = 2 - 1 = 1$. Thus $x = 2$ and $y = 1$, so the coordinates of the point are (2,1).

8. Choice D is correct. **(Use Strategy 3: The whole equals the sum of its parts.)**

Volume of rectangular solid

= Volume of triangular box

+ Volume of trapezoid-shaped box $\boxed{1}$

Area of rectangular dividing wall

$$= l \times w$$

$$39 \text{ cm}^2 = 13 \text{ cm} \times w$$

$$3 \text{ cm} = w \qquad \boxed{2}$$

$\boxed{2}$ is the height of the rectangular solid as well.

Volume of rectangular solid $= l \times w \times h$

$$= 15 \text{ cm} \times 12 \text{ cm} \times h \qquad \boxed{3}$$

Substituting $\boxed{2}$ into $\boxed{3}$, we get

Volume of rectangular solid =

15 cm × 12 cm × 3 cm

Volume of rectangular solid = 540 cm^3 $\boxed{4}$

Volume of triangular box

$$= \text{Area of base} \times \text{height}$$

$$= \frac{1}{2} \times 12 \text{ cm} \times 5 \text{ cm} \times 3 \text{ cm} \qquad \boxed{5}$$

Volume of triangular-shaped box = 90 cm^3

Substitute $\boxed{4}$ and $\boxed{5}$ into $\boxed{1}$. We get

540 cm^3 = 90 cm^3 + Volume of trapezoid-shaped box

450 cm^3 = Volume of trapezoid-shaped box

9. $\dfrac{7}{18}$ or .388 or .389

(Use Strategy 1: Simplify by cancelling.)

$$\left(\frac{1}{2} - \frac{1}{3}\right) + \left(\frac{1}{3} - \frac{1}{4}\right) + \left(\frac{1}{4} - \frac{1}{5}\right) +$$

$$\left(\frac{1}{5} - \frac{1}{6}\right) + \left(\frac{1}{6} - \frac{1}{7}\right) + \left(\frac{1}{7} - \frac{1}{8}\right) +$$

$$\left(\frac{1}{8} - \frac{1}{9}\right) =$$

$$\frac{1}{2} + \left(-\frac{1}{3} + \frac{1}{3}\right) + \left(-\frac{1}{4} + \frac{1}{4}\right) +$$

$$\left(-\frac{1}{5} + \frac{1}{5}\right) + \left(-\frac{1}{6} + \frac{1}{6}\right) + \left(-\frac{1}{7} + \frac{1}{7}\right) +$$

$$\left(-\frac{1}{8} + \frac{1}{8}\right) - \frac{1}{9} =$$

$$\frac{1}{2} + 0 + 0 + 0 + 0 + 0 + 0 - \frac{1}{9} =$$

$$\frac{1}{2} - \frac{1}{9} =$$

$$\frac{9}{18} - \frac{2}{18} =$$

$$\frac{7}{18}$$

10. 8

(Use Strategy 11: Use new definitions carefully.) The first five elements of the series, calculated by the definition, are

$$1, 2, 2, 4, 8$$

11. $\frac{2}{3}$ **or .667 or .666**

(Use Strategy 2: Translate from words to algebra.)

$$p = \frac{3}{5}m \qquad \boxed{1}$$

$$q = \frac{9}{10}m \qquad \boxed{2}$$

(Use Strategy 13: Find unknowns by division of equations.)

Thus, $\dfrac{p}{q} = \dfrac{\frac{3}{5}m}{\frac{9}{10}m}$

$$= \dfrac{\frac{3}{5}}{\frac{9}{10}}$$

$$= \frac{3}{5} \times \frac{10}{9} = \frac{\cancel{3}^{1}}{\cancel{5}} \times \frac{\cancel{10}^{2}}{\cancel{9}_{3}}$$

$$\frac{p}{q} = \frac{2}{3}$$

12. 60

(Use Strategy 5:

$$\textbf{Average} = \frac{\textbf{sum of values}}{\textbf{total number of values}})$$

Given: $\dfrac{40 + 40 + 40 + z}{4} = 45$ $\boxed{1}$

Multiplying $\boxed{1}$ by 4,

$$40 + 40 + 40 + z = 180$$
$$120 + z = 180$$
$$z = 60$$

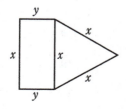

13. 36

(Use Strategy 2: Translate from words to algebra.) When the given diagram has been labeled as above, then we know

$$3x = 39 \qquad \boxed{1}$$
$$xy = 65 \qquad \boxed{2}$$

From $\boxed{1}$, we have

$$x = 13 \qquad \boxed{3}$$

Substituting $\boxed{3}$ into $\boxed{2}$, we have

$$13y = 65$$

$$\text{or} \quad y = 5 \qquad \boxed{4}$$

The perimeter of the rectangle

$$= 2x + 2y$$
$$= 2(13) + 2(5)$$
$$= 36$$

14. 44

(Use Strategy 17: Use the given information effectively.)

Game	Darrin	Tom
1	69	43
2	59	60
3	72	55
4	70	68
5	78	73

We need the scores at the end of the first four games. We have been given the totals for all five games.

(Use Strategy 13: Find unknowns by subtraction.)

Darrin's Total = 348	$\boxed{1}$
Darrin's Game 5 = 78	$\boxed{2}$
Tom's Total = 299	$\boxed{3}$
Tom's Game 5 = 73	$\boxed{4}$

Subtract $\boxed{2}$ from $\boxed{1}$. We get

Darrin's total for 1st four games = 348 − 78

$$= 270 \qquad \boxed{5}$$

Subtract $\boxed{4}$ from $\boxed{3}$. We get

Tom's total for 1st four games = 299 − 73

$$= 226 \qquad \boxed{6}$$

Subtracting $\boxed{6}$ from $\boxed{5}$, we have

Number of points Tom was behind Darrin after the first four games $= 270 - 226$
$$= 44$$

15. $\frac{1}{4}$ **or .25**

(Use Strategy 17: Use the given information effectively.)

The 17 slips, numbered from 1 to 17, consist of $\boxed{1}$

8 even numbers (2, 4, 6,…16) and $\boxed{2}$

9 odd numbers (1, 3, 5,…17). $\boxed{3}$

Subtracting 5 even-numbered slips from $\boxed{2}$ leaves

$$8 - 5 = 3 \text{ even-numbered slips.} \qquad \boxed{4}$$

Adding $\boxed{3}$ and $\boxed{4}$, we have

$$9 + 3 = 12 \text{ slips remaining} \qquad \boxed{5}$$

We need $\dfrac{\text{even-numbered slips}}{\text{total numbered slips}}$ $\boxed{6}$

Substituting $\boxed{4}$ and $\boxed{5}$ into $\boxed{6}$, we have

$$\frac{3}{12} = \frac{1}{4}$$

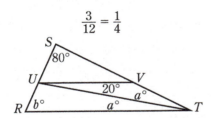

16. 60

Given: $UV \parallel RT$ $\boxed{1}$

From $\boxed{1}$, we get $a = 20$, since alternate interior angles are equal $\boxed{2}$

(Use Strategy 3: The whole equals the sum of its parts.) From the diagram we see that

$$\angle STR = a + a \qquad \boxed{3}$$

Substituting $\boxed{2}$ into $\boxed{3}$, we have

$$\angle STR = 20 + 20 = 40 \qquad \boxed{4}$$

We know that the sum of the angles in a triangle $= 180$, thus

$$\angle R + \angle S + \angle STR = 180 \qquad \boxed{5}$$

We are given, in the diagram, that

$$\angle R = b \qquad \boxed{6}$$
$$\angle S = 80 \qquad \boxed{7}$$

Substituting $\boxed{6}$, $\boxed{7}$, and $\boxed{4}$ into $\boxed{5}$, we get

$$b + 80 + 40 = 180$$
$$b + 120 = 180$$
$$b = 60$$

17. 10

(Use Strategy 2: Translate from words to algebra.)

Given: Riley's earnings $= \$440$ $\boxed{1}$

Riley's time worked $= 8$ days $\boxed{2}$

(Use Strategy 13: Find unknowns by division.)

Dividing $\boxed{1}$ by $\boxed{2}$, we have

$$\text{Riley's daily rate} = \frac{\$440}{8 \text{ days}}$$

$$\text{Riley's daily rate} = \frac{\$110}{2 \text{ days}} \qquad \boxed{3}$$

Given: Total earnings to equal $\$990$ $\boxed{4}$

Subtracting $\boxed{1}$ from $\boxed{4}$, we get

Amount left to be earned $= \$550$ $\boxed{5}$

We know

(daily rate)(days worked) $=$ money earned $\boxed{6}$

Substituting $\boxed{3}$ and $\boxed{5}$ into $\boxed{6}$, we get

$$\left(\frac{\$110}{2 \text{ days}}\right)(\text{days worked}) = \$550 \qquad \boxed{7}$$

Multiplying $\boxed{7}$ by $\dfrac{2 \text{ days}}{\$110}$, we have

$$\frac{2 \text{ days}}{\$110}\left(\frac{\$110}{2 \text{ days}}\right)(\text{days worked}) = (\$550)\frac{\overset{5}{2}}{\$110} \text{ days}$$

$$\text{days worked} = 10 \text{ days}$$

18. 48

Given: Areas of all 12 triangles are the same   1

          Area of outlined region = 256   2

          Area of square $ABCD$ = 128   3

(Use Strategy 3: The whole equals the sum of its parts.)

By looking at the diagram, we observe

Area of 8 triangles (I, II, ..., VIII) = Area of outlined region − area of square $ABCD$.

Substituting 2 and 3 into the above, we get

Area of 8 triangles (I, ..., VIII)

$$= 256 - 128$$

$$= 128 \qquad \boxed{4}$$

Using 1, we get

Area of each of the 12 triangles =

$$\frac{\text{area of 8 triangles}}{8}$$

Substituting 4 into the above, we get

    Area of each of the 12 triangles $= \dfrac{128}{8}$

    Area of each of the 12 triangles = 16   5

(Use Strategy 3: The whole equals the sum of its parts.)

Shaded area = Area ΔV + area ΔVI +
area ΔXI 6

Substituting 1 and 5 into 6, we get

    Shaded area = 16 + 16 + 16 = 48

EXPLANATORY ANSWERS FOR PRACTICE TEST 5

Section 7: Critical reading

As you read these Explanatory Answers, you are advised to refer to "16 Verbal (Critical Reading) Strategies."

1. Choice D is correct. See **Sentence Completion Strategy 1.** The word "extreme" is the most appropriate among the five choices because the forest fire season is in *full swing*. The other choices are, therefore, not appropriate.

2. Choice A is correct. See **Sentence Completion Strategy 2.** Examine the first word of each choice. We eliminate Choice C, imagined, and Choice E, intuitive. Reason: The effect of the long war was *not* imagined or intuitive (meaning knowing by a hidden sense). Now we consider Choice B, immediate…storing, and Choice D, delayed…rebuilding. Neither word pair makes sense in the sentence. Choice A, cumulative… corrosion, *does* make sense in the sentence.

3. Choice E is correct. See **Sentence Completion Strategy 3.** If you had tried to complete the sentence *before* looking at the five choices, you might have come up with any of the following words meaning "continually" or "regularly":

constantly	always
perpetually	persistently
habitually	

   The other choices are, therefore, incorrect.

4. Choice E is correct. See **Sentence Completion Strategy 2.** Examine the first word of each choice. Choice D, crushes, is eliminated because it is not likely that the bee will crush the nectar from different flowers. Now consider each pair of words in the other choices. We find that Choice E, extracts…converts, has the only word pair that makes sense in the sentence.

5. Choice D is correct. See **Sentence Completion Strategies 1 and 4.** The plan turned out to be impractical, unable to be logically supported. Note

the root "ten" *to hold,* so "untenable" means *not holding.* Also note that the word "because" in the sentence is a *result indicator.*

6. Choice C is correct. In lines 8–11, the author is showing that through the "weedy falsities," truth can be created.

7. Choice C is correct. See the last lines, 15–18: "we can feel all the poverty, despair, and unfairness in our world…" For Choice A, there may be value for the spectator: see lines 14–15, "and perhaps how we should change them."

8. Choice E is correct. See lines 8–11, 13–15, and 15–18. This describes how something positive can come out of something negative. In Choice A, although specific references (lines 4 and 5) are made, there are no specific references in Passage 2. In Choice B, there is no indication of both being completely objective, especially in Passage 1 line 2 where the author states that the theater is the "most preposterous of all." Choice C is incorrect in that in Passage 1, the author certainly does not believe in the accuracy of the time (16th century), whereas in Passage 2, the author does believe in the accuracy of the time. Choice D is incorrect in that it appears that the intensity and passion of the author's arguments in Passage 1 is far greater than that of the author's in Passage 2.

9. Choice D is correct. In lines 8 and 9, note the words "lily" (a flower) and "jungle" (a place), which are used as analogies. We do not see such analogies in Passage 2. In Choice A, both authors would disagree, as the author in Passage 1 states that theater is fiction, not reality, and the author in Passage 2 states that the theater is real. In Choice B, see line 5: "the much admired Miss Huckaby." In Choice C, in lines

7–8, the author is sarcastic when he says that "people were ever so marvelously articulate." In Choice E, see lines 13–14: the author believes the contrary, that the theater is quite realistic.

10. Choice A is correct. See lines 42–44: "The fundamental fact.... in their environment." Choices B, D, and E are incorrect because the passage does not indicate that these statements are true. Choice C is incorrect because it is only partially true. The passage does not state that *all* animals and plants are successful in adjusting themselves to changes in their environments.

11. Choice E is correct. See lines 4–7: "Originally, the term acclimatization...altered temperature." Also see lines 9–12: "But aside from temperature... originally accustomed to." Choices A, B, C, and D are incorrect because one *cannot* infer from the passage what any of these choices state.

12. Choice A is correct. Acclimatization and adaptation are both forms of adjustment. Accordingly, these two processes are similar. The difference between the two terms, however, is brought out in lines 32–36: "By and large... as adaptation." Choice D is incorrect because the passage does not indicate what is expressed in Choice D. See lines 29–32: "Let us define acclimatization...lethal for it." Choices B, C, and E are incorrect because the passage does not indicate that any of these choices are true.

13. Choice D is correct. A person going from daylight into a darkened room is an example of adaptation—not acclimatization. See lines 32–36: "By and large...as 'adaptation.'" Choices A, B, C, and E all require the process of acclimatization. Therefore, they are incorrect choices. An ocean fish placed in a lake (Choice A) is a chemical change. Choices B, C, and E are all pressure changes. Acclimatization, by definition, deals with chemical and pressure changes.

14. Choice B is correct. Given the context in the sentence, Choice B is the best. By describing the environment as "normally unsuitable to it or lethal for it" (lines 31–32), the author implies that the organism will survive, and the only way to do that is to grow accustomed to it. See also **Reading Comprehension Strategy 5.**

15. Choice B is correct. See lines 33–36: "The term [acclimatization] should not be taken...as 'adaptation.'" Choices A, D, and E are incorrect because the passage does not indicate that these choices are true. Choice C is partially correct in that acclimatization does apply to adjustments, but the choice is incorrect because adaptation also applies to adjustments. See lines 35–36: "This type of adjustment...as 'adaptation.'"

16. Choice E is correct. See paragraph 2 (beginning): "The tie which bound this world-embracing empire together...was as much cultural as political."

17. Choice A is correct. See paragraph 1 (end): "Centuries of training had bred in them the conviction that all other rulers should be tributary to the Son of Heaven."

18. Choice B is correct. See the last paragraph about the close relationship between "ethical standards" and "Confucian patterns."

19. Choice C is correct. The reader should infer from paragraphs 3 and 4 that Han and T'ang were dynasties—just as there was a Manchu dynasty.

20. Choice D is correct. The passage points out that since more emphasis was placed on being members of the same culture, rather than on being members of the same race, there was a "comparative contentment of Chinese under alien rulers" (paragraph 4: beginning).

21. Choice B is correct. See paragraph 5 (middle): "In contrast with India, where caste and religion have tended to keep apart the racial strata, in China assimilation made great progress."

22. Choice B is correct. Paragraph 4 (end) points out that the Manchus never gave up some of their ancestral ways, and this disturbed segments of the population.

23. Choice A is correct. The passage states that assimilation made great progress in China. (See the answer to question 21.)

24. Choice C is correct. From the context of the sentence and the sentence before and after it, it can be seen that "restiveness" must mean impatience or restlessness. See also **Reading Comprehension Strategy 5.**

EXPLANATORY ANSWERS FOR PRACTICE TEST 5

Section 8: Math

When a specific Math Strategy is referred to in the solution, study that strategy, which you will find in "19 Math Strategies."

1. Choice C is correct. **(Use Strategy 2: Translate from words to algebra.)** The key is to be able to translate English sentences into mathematical equations.

   Let p = price of one frying pan
   m = price of one coffee mug
   We are given:

   $$p + 2m = \$27 \qquad \boxed{1}$$
   $$p + m = \$23 \qquad \boxed{2}$$

   Subtract equation $\boxed{2}$ from equation $\boxed{1}$ to get

   $$m = \$4 \qquad \boxed{3}$$

   Substitute equation $\boxed{3}$ into equation $\boxed{2}$ to get

   $$p + \$4 = \$23$$

   Subtract $4 from both sides of the above equation to get

   $$p = \$19$$

2. Choice E is correct. **(Use Strategy 2: Translate from words to algebra.)**

   Each tile is a square with perimeter = 2 feet

   Each side of the tile is $\frac{1}{4}(2 \text{ feet}) = \frac{1}{2}$ foot $\boxed{1}$

   The area of each tile is (side)^2.

   Using $\boxed{1}$, we get the area of each tile

   $$= \left(\frac{1}{2}\right)^2 \text{ square foot} = \frac{1}{4} \text{ square foot} \qquad \boxed{2}$$

   The area of the floor is $b \times h =$
   $$8 \text{ feet} \times 6 \text{ feet} =$$
   $$48 \text{ square feet} \qquad \boxed{3}$$

   (Use Strategy 17: Use the given information effectively.)

   The number of tiles necessary, at minimum, to cover the floor

   $$= \frac{\text{area of floor}}{\text{area of 1 tile}} \qquad \boxed{4}$$

   Substituting $\boxed{2}$ and $\boxed{3}$ into $\boxed{4}$, we get:

   $$= \frac{48}{\frac{1}{4}} = 48 \times \frac{4}{1}$$
   $$= 192$$

3. Choice E is correct.

   The only restriction is that 9 and 12 must each divide Q without a remainder. $\boxed{1}$

   (Use Strategy 7: Use numerics to help find the answer.)

   Choose specific values for Q that satisfy $\boxed{1}$.

   EXAMPLE 1
   $$Q = 36$$

   Then, Q will divide 36 and 72.

   EXAMPLE 2
   $$Q = 108$$

   Then, Q will divide neither 36 nor 72. Clearly, the answer to this question depends on the specific value of Q.

4. Choice B is correct. Since $DC \perp AC$, $\angle DCB$ is a right angle and has a measure of 90°. **(Use Strategy 3: The whole equals the sum of its parts.)** Since the sum of the angles of a $\triangle$ is 180°, we have

   $$\angle DBC + 90 + 20 = 180$$
   $$\angle DBC = 70 \qquad \boxed{1}$$

Since $EB \perp BD$, $\angle DBE$ is a right angle and has a measure of 90° $\boxed{2}$

(Use Strategy 3: The whole equals the sum of its parts.) The whole straight $\angle ABC$ is equal to the sum of its parts. Thus

$$\angle DBC + \angle DBE + x = 180 \qquad \boxed{3}$$

Substituting $\boxed{1}$ and $\boxed{2}$ into $\boxed{3}$, we have

$$70 + 90 + x = 180$$
$$x = 20$$

5. Choice E is correct. **(Use Strategy 17: Use the given information effectively.)**

Given: x $\boxed{1}$
$11 - x$ $\boxed{2}$
$x - 4$ $\boxed{3}$

as the lengths of the three sides of a triangle.

(Use Strategy 18: Know and use facts about triangles.) We know that the sum of any two sides of a triangle is greater than the third side. $\boxed{4}$

First, we use $\boxed{1} + \boxed{2} > \boxed{3}$. We have

$$x + 11 - x > x - 4$$
$$11 > x - 4$$
$$15 > x \qquad \boxed{5}$$

Next, we use $\boxed{2} + \boxed{3} > \boxed{1}$. We have

$$11 - x + x - 4 > x$$
$$7 > x \qquad \boxed{6}$$

To satisfy $\boxed{6}$ and $\boxed{5}$, we choose $\boxed{6}$.

$$7 > x, \text{ or } x < 7 \text{ satisfies both} \qquad \boxed{7}$$

Finally, we use $\boxed{1} + \boxed{3} > \boxed{2}$. We have

$$x + x - 4 > 11 - x$$
$$2x - 4 > 11 - x$$
$$3x > 15$$
$$x > 5, \text{ or } 5 < x \qquad \boxed{8}$$

(Use Strategy 6: Know how to manipulate inequalities.) Combining $\boxed{7}$ and $\boxed{8}$, we get

$$5 < x < 7$$

6. Choice B is correct.

Given: a, b are integers $\boxed{1}$
Average of $a, b,$ and 4 is 6 $\boxed{2}$

(Use Strategy 5:

$$\textbf{Average} = \frac{\textbf{sum of values}}{\textbf{total number of values}}\Big)$$

Using $\boxed{2}$, we have

$$\frac{a + b + 4}{3} = 6 \qquad \boxed{3}$$

(Use Strategy 13: Find unknowns by multiplication.)

Multiply $\boxed{3}$ by 3. We get

$$3\left(\frac{a + b + 4}{3}\right) = (6)3$$
$$a + b + 4 = 18$$
$$a + b = 14 \qquad \boxed{4}$$

Using $\boxed{1}$ and $\boxed{4}$, the possibilities are:

$a + b$	ab	
$1 + 13$	13	Choice A
$2 + 12$	24	
$3 + 11$	33	
$4 + 10$	40	Choice C
$5 + 9$	45	
$6 + 8$	48	Choice D
$7 + 7$	49	Choice E

Checking all the choices, we find that only Choice B, 14, is not a possible value of ab.

7. Choice D is correct. **(Use Strategy 17: Use the given information effectively.)**

$$\frac{1}{n^2}\left(\frac{m^5 n^3}{m^3}\right)^2 = \frac{1}{n^2}\left[(m^2 n^3)^2\right] = \frac{m^4 n^6}{n^2} = m^4 n^4$$

8. Choice C is correct. Label the females F_1, F_2, and F_3 and the males M_1, M_2, and M_3. The total number of combinations of three people (such as F_1–F_2–M_1 or F_1–M_2–M_3) is 6 combinations taken 3 at a time, or $_6C_3$, which is equal to $\frac{(6 \times 5 \times 4)}{(3 \times 2 \times 1)}$ 20. There are 9 favorable combinations (trios that include exactly two men): M_1–M_2–F_1, M_1–M_2–F_2, M_1–M_2–F_3, M_1–M_3–F_1, M_1–M_3–F_2, M_1–M_3–F_3, M_2–M_3–F_1, M_2–M_3–F_2, and M_2–M_3–F_3. The probability of exactly two males in the room is:

$$\frac{\text{favorable combinations}}{\text{total combinations}} = \frac{9}{20}$$

9. Choice E is correct. **(Use Strategy 8: When all choices must be tested, start with Choice E and work backward.)** In Choice E, if $Z = 5$, then $5Z = 25$. Thus $W + X + Y = 25$. Note that even if you used the highest ("distinct," which means "different") values of W, X, and Y, we would get $7 + 8 + 9 = 24$ as a maximum value. So Choice E could not be a value of Z. Now go to Choice D: If $Z = 4$, then $5Z = 20$, and you would have $W + X + Y = 20$. An example that would work in that equation is $W = 9$, $X = 8$, and $Y = 3$. You can also see that for Choices C, B, and A, $W + X + Y$ could equal 5×3 or 5×2 or 5×1, by easily adjusting the values of W, X, and Y. Don't forget, you can use 0 for any one (but just one) of the variables W, X, or Y.

10. Choice C is correct. **(Use Strategy 3: The whole equals the sum of its parts.)** From the diagram, we see that each straight angle is equal to the sum of two smaller angles. Thus,

$$m = 180 - x \qquad \boxed{1}$$
$$n = 180 - z \qquad \boxed{2}$$

(Use Strategy 13: Find unknown expressions by addition of equations.) Adding $\boxed{1}$ and $\boxed{2}$, we have

$$m + n = 180 + 180 - x - z \qquad \boxed{3}$$

We know that the sum of the angles of a triangle $= 180$

Therefore, $y + x + z = 180$ or

$$y = 180 - x - z \qquad \boxed{4}$$

Substituting $\boxed{4}$ into $\boxed{3}$, we have

$$m + n = 180 + y$$

Accordingly, Choice C is the correct choice.

11. Choice C is correct. **(Use Strategy 2: Translate from words to algebra.)**

We know that the volume of a cube $= e^3$

We are told that $e^3 < 25$

(Use Strategy 17: Use the given information effectively.)

Since e is a positive integer (which was given),

e can be: $1 \rightarrow 1^3 = 1$
$$2 \rightarrow 2^3 = 8$$
$$3 \rightarrow 3^3 = 27$$
etc.

For $e = 2$, the volume is 8, which is < 25

Any larger e will have a volume > 25

Thus, area of one face $= e^2 = 2^2 = 4$

Total area $= 6(4) = 24$

12. Choice E is correct. **(Use Strategy 2: Translate from words to algebra.)**

Let s = number of females

n = number of males

Then $s + n$ = total number of people.

We are given: $\dfrac{s}{n} = \dfrac{2}{3}$ or $s = \dfrac{2}{3}n$ $\qquad \boxed{1}$

and: $s = \dfrac{1}{3}(s + n) + 5$ $\qquad \boxed{2}$

Substituting $\boxed{1}$ into $\boxed{2}$, we have

$$\frac{2}{3}n = \frac{1}{3}\left(\frac{2}{3}n + n\right) + 5$$

$$\frac{2}{3}n = \frac{1}{3}\left(\frac{2}{3}n + \frac{3}{3}n\right) + 5$$

$$\frac{2}{3}n = \frac{1}{3}\left(\frac{5}{3}n\right) + 5$$

$$\frac{2}{3}n = \frac{5}{9}n + 5 \qquad \boxed{3}$$

Multiplying both sides of $\boxed{3}$ by 9, we get

$$9\left(\frac{2}{3}n\right) = 9\left(\frac{5}{9}n + 5\right)$$

$$\frac{18}{3}n = 5n + 45$$

$$6n = 5n + 45$$

$$n = 45$$

$$s = \frac{2}{3}(45) = 30$$

$$s + n = 75$$

$$
\begin{array}{ccccccc}
A & B & C & D & E & F & G \\
\end{array}
$$
$$| \underset{a}{\quad} | \underset{a}{\quad} | \underset{a}{\quad} | \underset{a}{\quad} | \underset{a}{\quad} | \underset{a}{\quad} |$$

13. Choice C is correct.

Given:

AG is divided into 6 equal segments.　　$\boxed{1}$

Radius of circle, centered at $F = \frac{1}{5}AG$　　$\boxed{2}$

(Use Strategy 14: Label unknown quantities.)

Label segments with "a" as shown in above diagram.

Using $\boxed{2}$, radius of circle centered at $F = \frac{1}{5}(AG)$

$$= \frac{1}{5}(6a)$$

$$= 1\frac{1}{5}a$$

This means from the center at F, the left tip of the radius of the circle is $1\frac{1}{5}a$ from point F. Thus the circumference hits the line between D and E.

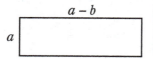

14. Choice B is correct. **(Use Strategy 2: Translate from words to algebra.)**

Perimeter of a rectangle

$$= 2(\text{length}) + 2(\text{width}) \boxed{1}$$

Substituting from the diagram into $\boxed{1}$, we have

$$\text{Perimeter} = 2(a - b) + 2(a)$$
$$= 2a - 2b + 2a$$
$$\text{Perimeter} = 4a - 2b$$

15. Choice E is correct.

$$
\begin{array}{r}
AB \\
+ \ BA \\
\hline
CDC
\end{array}
$$

Given: A, B, C, and D are different digits.　　$\boxed{1}$

(Use Strategy 8: When testing the choices, start with Choice E.)

Let's see if $A = 2$ will work.

We get:

$$
\begin{array}{r}
2B \\
B2 \\
\hline
CDC
\end{array}
$$

Now for the range $B = 1, 2, 3, 4, 5, 6, 7$, the left C won't equal the right C. So we try $B = 8$. (Note we can't use $B = 2$ because A would equal B, which is incorrect.)

We would get:

$$
\begin{array}{r}
28 \\
82 \\
\hline
110
\end{array}
$$

Also, the left C doesn't equal the right C.

The only digit left for B is 9. We then get:

$$
\begin{array}{r}
29 \\
92 \\
\hline
121
\end{array}
$$

But then $D = A$, which is incorrect.

Thus $A = 2$ doesn't work.

16.　　Choice A is correct. $g(-1) = 1$,

$f[g(-1)] = f(1) = 1^2 + 1 = 2.$

> As you read these Explanatory Answers, you are advised to refer to "16 Verbal (Critical Reading) Strategies."

1. Choice C is correct. See **Sentence Completion Strategy 2.** Examine the first word of each choice. Choice E, a futile, does *not* make good sense because we do not refer to momentum as futile. Now consider the other choices. Choice C, an increasing…athletics, is the only choice that makes sense in the sentence.

2. Choice E is correct. See **Sentence Completion Strategy 1.** The word "effective" (meaning "serving the purpose" or "producing a result") makes good sense in the sentence. The other choices don't do that.

3. Choice D is correct. See **Sentence Completion Strategy 4.** The word "despite" is an *opposition indicator*. A strange and inevitable, or *ineluctable* fate seemed to keep him helpless and unhappy, despite occasional periods of calm peacefulness, or *serenity*.

4. Choice B is correct. See **Sentence Completion Strategies 1 and 4.** Try each choice, being aware that "result" is, of course, a *result indicator*. Samuel Clemens chose the pseudonym (pen name) Mark Twain.

5. Choice A is correct. See **Sentence Completion Strategy 1.** The word "capable" means "skilled" or "competent." Clearly, Choice A, a capable, is the only correct choice.

6. Choice B is correct. See **Sentence Completion Strategy 2.** Examine the first word of each choice. We eliminate Choice C, avoided, and Choice D, realized, because it does not make sense to say that Leonardo realized or avoided the Law of Gravity. Now we consider Choice A, examined…colorful, and Choice E, suspected… mural, neither of which makes sense in the sentence. Choice B, anticipated…anatomical, is the only choice that makes sense in the sentence.

7. Choice E is correct. The author is stressing the point that the true artist—the person with rare creative ability and keen perception, or high intelligence—fails to communicate well with those about him—"differs from the rest of us" (line 4). He is likely to be considered a "nut" by many whom he comes in contact with. "Great wits" in the Choice E quotation refers to the true artist. The quotation states, in effect, that there is a thin line between the true artist and the "nut." Choices A, B, C, and D are incorrect because they have little, if anything, to do with the main idea of the passage.

   [Note: Choices C and E were composed by John Dryden (1631–1700), and Choices A, B, and D by Alexander Pope (1688–1744).]

8. Choice C is correct. See lines 8–10. The artist creates because he is "less fitted to prosper and enjoy himself under the conditions of life which he and we must face alike." Choices A and E are incorrect. Although they may be true, they are never mentioned in the passage. Choice B is incorrect because, although the artist may be a threat to the social order, he is by no means an unnecessary one. The author, throughout the passage, is siding with the artist against the social order. Choice D is incorrect. See lines 10–11: "Therefore he takes…attempt to escape from life."

A person who is attempting to escape from life hardly knows how to enjoy life.

9.   Choice B is correct. The author ridicules Samuel Johnson, saying that he is as much a true artist as a kazoo player is a musician. He then says that if Johnson were alive today, he would be a senator or a university president. The author thus implies that these positions do not merit high respect. Choice A is the opposite of Choice B. Therefore, Choice A is incorrect. Choice C is incorrect because, although the statement may be true, the author neither states nor implies that senators and university presidents are generally appreciative of the great literary classics. Choice D is incorrect. The fact that the author lumps Johnson, senators, and university presidents together as nonartistic people indicates that the author believes that senators and university presidents do not have native writing ability. Choice E is incorrect for this reason: The author believes that Johnson lacked the qualities of an artist. Johnson, if alive today, would be a senator or a university president. We may conclude, then, that the author believes that senators and university presidents lack the qualities of an artist.

10. Choice C is correct. Although a love of beauty is a quality we usually associate with artists, that idea about artists is never mentioned in the passage. All of the other characteristics are expressly mentioned in the first two paragraphs of the passage.

11. Choice B is correct. The author's sincere sympathy is shown toward artists in lines 17–24: "From Dante to Tolstoy…actually fugitives from rage and reprisal." There is no evidence in the passage to indicate that the author's attitude toward artists is Choice A, C, D, or E. Therefore, these choices are incorrect.

12. Choice C is correct. See line 69: "He and he alone knows the world."

13. Choice B is correct. See lines 54–61 and 64–66 in Passage 2.

14. Choice C is correct. From the context in Passage 2, we see that "world's eye" and "world's heart" refer to culture and wisdom, respectively. See lines 56–60: "…public and illustrious thoughts… resist the vulgar prosperity…by preserving and communicating…noble biographies…melodious verse…" This is all about *culture* and *wisdom*.

15. Choice E is correct. See the first sentence in Passage 2: "…the self-accusation, the faint heart, the frequent uncertainty and loss of time, which are the nettles and tangling vines…" Here "nettles and tangling vines" refers to "self-accusation" and "uncertainty." Nettles are plants covered with stinging hairs. Tangling vines give the impression of weaving all around in no particular or certain direction. So nettles can be thought of as "self-accusation"—something "stinging." And "tangling vines" can be thought of as "uncertainty." See also **Reading Comprehension Strategy 5**.

16. Choice C is correct. See Passage 2: The most appropriate groups are the hardships of the scholar, the scholar's functions, and the scholar's justifications for disregarding the world's business, as can be seen from the structure and content of the passage.

17. Choice C is correct. So far the tone of the passage is sympathetic toward the difficulties of the artist, so by placing "seems to be" in the context of the "virtual hostility" the artist feels from society, it is clear that the author is contrasting what the artist is and what he is perceived to be. The words "false impression" in Choice C fit best. See also **Reading Comprehension Strategy 5**.

18. Choice A is correct. See lines 91–98 and 54–56 in Passage 2 and lines 13–17 and 25–34 in Passage 1.

19. Choice E is correct. The statements in I can be seen to be associated with the artist in Passage 2 from lines 85–86 and 57–58, respectively. The statements in II can be seen to be associated with the artist in Passage 1 from lines 27–33 and 5, respectively. The statements in III can be seen to be associated with the artist in Passage 2 from lines 53–54 and 45–52, respectively.